A GRAMMAR OF EGYPTIAN ARAMAIC

HANDBUCH DER ORIENTALISTIK
HANDBOOK OF ORIENTAL STUDIES

ERSTE ABTEILUNG
DER NAHE UND MITTLERE OSTEN
THE NEAR AND MIDDLE EAST

HERAUSGEGEBEN VON
H. ALTENMÜLLER · B. HROUDA · B.A. LEVINE · R.S. O'FAHEY
K.R. VEENHOF · C.H.M. VERSTEEGH

ZWEIUNDDREISSIGSTER BAND
A GRAMMAR OF EGYPTIAN ARAMAIC

A GRAMMAR OF
EGYPTIAN ARAMAIC

BY

TAKAMITSU MURAOKA

AND

BEZALEL PORTEN

BRILL

LEIDEN · NEW YORK · KÖLN

1998

This book is printed on acid-free paper.

Library of Congress Cataloging-in-Publication Data

Muraoka, T.
A grammar of Egyptian Aramaic / by Takamitsu Muraoka and Bezalel Porten
      p.   cm. — (Handbuch der Orientalistik. Erste Abteilung, Der Nahe und Mittlere Osten, ISSN 0169-9423 ; 32. Bd.)
      Includes bibliographical references and index.
      ISBN 9004104992 (cloth : alk. paper)
      1. Aramaic language—Egypt—Grammar.   I. Porten, Bezalel. II.
      Title. III. Series.
      PJ5202.M87 1997   97-35502
      492'.2—dc21   CIP

Die Deutsche Bibliothek – CIP-Einheitsaufnahme

Handbuch der Orientalistik / hrsg. von B. Spuler unter Mitarb. von C. van Dijk ... Leiden ; New York ; Köln : Brill.
    Teilw. hrsg. von H. Altenmüller. – Literaturangaben. – Teilw. hrsg. von B. Spuler. – Teilw. mit Parallelt.: Handbook of oriental studies
Abt. 1, Der Nahe und Mittlere Osten = The Near and Middle East / hrsg. von H. Altenmüller ...
    NE: Spuler, Bertold [Hrsg.]; Altenmüller, Hartwig [Hrsg.]; Handbook of oriental studies
Bd. 32. Muraoka, Takamitsu: A grammar of Egyptian Aramaic. – 1997
Muraoka, Takamitsu:
A grammar of Egyptian Aramaic / by Takamitsu Muraoka and Bezalel Porten. – Leiden ; New York ; Köln : Brill, 1997
    (Handbuch der Orientalistik : Abt. 1, Der Nahe und Mittlere Osten ; Bd. 32)
    ISBN 90-04-10499-2

ISSN 0169-9423
ISBN 90 04 10499 2

PRINTED IN THE NETHERLANDS

In fond memory of our esteemed teacher

Prof. E.Y. Kutscher ז"ל

a great scholar

an outstanding Aramaist

CONTENTS

PART II: MORPHOLOGY

SECTION A: THE NOUN, ADJECTIVE AND PARTICLES

PART II: MORPHOLOGY

SECTION B: VERB

PART III: MORPHOSYNTAX

SECTION A: THE PRONOUN

SECTION B: THE NOUN AND THE ADJECTIVE

SECTION C: THE VERB

PART IV: SYNTAX

SECTION A: NOUN PHRASE EXPANDED

SECTION B: VERB PHRASE EXPANDED

SECTION C: OTHER SYNTACTIC ISSUES

APPENDICES

PREFACE

We have the pleasure of presenting herewith a comprehensive grammar of Egyptian Aramaic. Until now Aramaic and Semitic scholarship has had at its disposal P. Leander's classic *Laut- und Formenlehre des Ägyptischen Aramäisch* (1928). Although Leander's grammar is a solid piece of work along the lines of historical grammar, it suffers from one major drawback: it lacks syntax. In this grammar, by contrast, well-nigh half of its space has been allocated to morphosyntax and syntax. Moreover, the past seven decades have witnessed a considerable increase in new Aramaic texts, significant in quantity and quality alike. This is, as far as texts from Egypt are concerned, evident in Porten and Yardeni's *Textbook of Aramaic Documents from Ancient Egypt*, soon to be completed with its fourth and final volume. The present grammar is based on this edition, which incorporates not only many new documents which were unknown to Leander, but also old texts reexamined at their source and reedited. S. Segert's *Altaramäische Grammatik* (1975) deals with Early Aramaic in a much wider context, wider geographically as well as chronologically. We believe, however, that the corpus represented by *Textbook* justifies a grammar dedicated to it. When combined with Degen's Aramaic grammar dealing with the 10th-8th centuries (1978), Dion's (1974) and Tropper's (1993) dealing with Samalian, the present work fills a gap to provide an almost complete picture of Early Aramaic grammar.

This is not a beginners' grammar. We assume that the reader already possesses basic knowledge of Aramaic with some vocabulary acquired from a study of an Aramaic idiom with a reasonably firm tradition of vocalisation, such as Biblical Aramaic, Targumic Aramaic or Classical Syriac. Hence there are no exercises. However, for the benefit of those who are not trained as grammarians or linguists, a simple glossary of technical terms has been appended. We have also translated almost every Aramaic citation, whether single words, phrases or clauses.

Our approach is essentially descriptive and synchronic. However, given the nature of the texts in question it was often felt necessary to draw upon data in earlier or later phases of Aramaic and other cognate Aramaic dialects.

The basic research for the purpose of this grammar was undertaken by Muraoka, who subsequently wrote a draft, which was jointly and fully discussed by both of the undersigned at three intensive meetings. Both of us therefore are jointly responsible for the data and their analysis and interpretation presented in this grammar.

It remains for us to acknowledge our debt of thanks to a number of individuals and organisations: the Dutch Organisation for Scientific Research (NWO) and Research School CNWS of Leiden University, each for a generous grant supporting Porten's visits to Leiden; Prof. S. Kaufman and Dr. E.M. Cook of the Comprehensive Aramaic Lexicon Project for a keyword-in-context concordance of the entire corpus, which has saved us hundreds of hours in locating and collecting words and forms; Prof. Shaul Shaked of the Hebrew University in Jerusalem, who reviewed all the Persian loanwords; Prof. K.-Th. Zauzich of Würzburg and Dr G. Vittmann (*Demotisches Namenbuch*), and Mr Alejandro Botta regarding the Egyptian loanwords; the publisher E.J. Brill, which has agreed to add the volume to its renowned series Handbuch der Orientalistik; Dr F. Dijkema, formerly of Brill, with whom we initially negotiated this project and its inclusion in the series; Mr A. Hoffstädt and Ms P. Radder of Brill's Near East section; and last but not least, Keiko Muraoka, the spouse of one of us, who patiently undertook the tedious task of keying-in Aramaic phrases and sentences anew, and assisting with preparation of Indices.

September, 1997.
Leiden and Jerusalem

Takamitsu Muraoka
Bezalel Porten

INTRODUCTION

Scope of the corpus

The first discovery of an Egyptian Aramaic document by a European was made in 1704—a funerary stela now in the municipal library/museum of Carpentras, France (D20.5). The most recent discovery was of some papyrus fragments and ostraca in 1988 by the German archaeological expedition at Elephantine (D3.16-18, 21; 4.23; 5.33-35, 41; 11; 14). An exhaustive catalogue of all "Egyptian Aramaic texts" is found in an entry by that name in E.M. Meyers, ed., *The Oxford Encyclopaedia of Archaeology in the Near East* (New York, 1997), V, 393-410. The dated documents span the fifth century BCE (515-399 [B1.1; A3.9]), when Aramaic was the *lingua franca* of the Persian Empire. A seal goes back to the time of Assyrian rule (D14.1); a few texts are palaeographically and/or historically dated in the seventh (A1.1; D11.1, 16.1) or sixth century (D14.2), while several point to the fourth century (A3.10, 11; B5.6; C3.27; D1.16, 31, 2.35, 3.47, 8.2) or to the time of Ptolemaic rule (C3.28, 29, 4.9; D1.17, 7.55-57, 8.3-13, 9.15, 10.2, 11.26, 15.5, 21.4-16). The major find site is the Jewish military colony on the island of Elephantine, alongside its sister Aramaean garrison on the mainland at Syene (Aswan). These soldiers came with their familites under the Saites, served their Persian successors, and left us letters, both private and official, legal documents, lists and accounts, a couple of literary pieces (C1.1-2) and an historical text (C2)—all written on papyrus; ephemeral items on ostraca, such as lists and messages sent from the mainland to the island (D7); and a single dedicatory inscription on stone (D17.1). At the same time there existed an Aramaean (and Jewish) centre at Saqqarah and this has yielded some 250 papyrus fragments and a handful of ostraca, published by N. Aimé-Giron in 1931 and 1939 and by J.B. Segal in 1983. All of the Aimé-Giron papyri have been newly collated. Unfortu-nately, the Segal texts were not reproduced 1:1 and lack measure. The excavation director, Harry Smith, made available to us the original negatives, and we published 26 of Segal's texts, legal documents and land registries (B4.7, 5.6, 8.1-4, 6-12; C3.3, 6, 11, 18, 20, 22-24). But since we

were not given access to the originals and were therefore unable
to vouch for the readings in many of the problematic texts, we
decided not to reproduce any of them, except for a few ceramic
pieces (D11.22-25). The primary source of Aramaic material
during the Ptolemaic period was Edfu (D1.17, 7.55; 8.3-6; 9.15,
11.22-25, 21.7-16) and pieces of unknown origin may have come
from there as well (C3.28-29; D7.56-57; 8.7-11). Isolated items,
particularly graffiti, come from numerous sites throughout Egypt,
but for the most part they lack grammatical context. Notable
exceptions are the libation bowls from Tel el-Maskhuta (D15.1-4);
the funerary stelae, probably all from Memphis-Saqqarah
(D20.1-6); the graffito from Giza (D22.1), a couple from Abydos
(D22.25, 27) and the ones from Wadi el-Hudi (D22.46-51); and
the tantalizing but all too fragmentary narrative from Sheikh
Fadl (D23).

Previous studies on the language of the corpus

This grammar presents results of a linguistic analysis of the
corpus of Egyptian Aramaic texts whose historical, geographical
and literary scope has been outlined above and which have been
published in B. Porten - A. Yardeni's *Texbook of Aramaic
Documents from Ancient Egypt* (Jerusalem, 1986-).

A sketch of the Aramaic language of the first batch of the
corpus was attempted by A.E. Cowley and appended to A.H.
Sayce and A.E. Cowley, *Aramaic Papyri Discovered at Assuan*
(London, 1906), pp. 14-23. An outstanding Aramaist of all times,
Th. Nöldeke, devoted a series of important studies to the newly
discovered texts: "Die aramäischen Papyri von Assuan," ZA 20
(1907) 130-50, "Neue jüdische Papyri," ZA 21 (1908) 195-205,
and especially "Untersuchungen zum Achiqar-Roman,"
AbhKWGW 14/4 (1913) 1-63. An attempt at a full-scale grammar
was made by Pontus Leander, but its title indicates that it is
incomplete, lacking syntax: *Laut- und Formenlehre des
Ägyptisch-Aramäischen* (Göteborg, 1928). Leander had co-
authored a grammar of Biblical Aramaic with H. Bauer (Bauer -
Leander 1927), which is, however, complete. The linguistic
method and approach adopted in these two works is identical: an
attempt to describe Biblical and Egyptian Aramaic from the
perspective of a reconstructed historical development of the
language. Given the limited amount of data preserved and their

antiquity, a purely synchronic approach is not capable of adequately describing and evaluating these data. A comparative and historical approach is indispensable, though Bauer and Leander went at times a little too far in this direction.

Having a solid tradition of vocalisation, Biblical Aramaic has always, and justly, been accorded a prominent place in any study of Aramaic of our period. Baumgartner's 1927 study on the Aramaic of Daniel ushered in a new era of Aramaic dialectology, a study which has not been surpassed by Rowley's on the Aramaic of the Old Testament published two years later.

Joüon published in 1934 an article of near-monograph length, offering a host of interesting and original observations on diverse grammatical, lexicographical and philological matters arising from Egyptian Aramaic papyri.

Though never published, Fitzmyer's 1956 Johns Hopkins doctoral dissertation on the syntax of Imperial Aramaic of Egyptian provenience presents a wealth of data and contains not a few illuminating observations.

Kutscher's magisterial survey of 1970 on the achievements in Aramaic linguistics and outstanding desiderata as far as Classical Aramaic is concerned still contains many a valuable and insightful observation based on his first-hand familiarity with the subject matter.

Segert's original intention was apparently to write a grammar which would replace and complete Leander's above-mentioned work, but in the end his grammar (1975) came to cover a much wider ground, as a result of which the treatment of Egyptian Aramaic or Imperial Aramaic suffers slightly from dilution in depth. Degen's thorough—44 pages!—review article (1979) is an essential reading.

Lindenberger's philological commentary on the proverbs of Ahiqar (1983) contains some valuable data, and together with an appendix discussing some important linguistic issues and Aramaic dialectology, represents a valuable contribution to Aramaic linguistics.

Hug's grammar of the Aramaic of the 7th and 6th centuries BCE, designed as a sequel to Degen's grammar of Old Aramaic of the 10th to 8th centuries, deals with a number of texts, notably the Hermopolis papyri, which constitute part of our own corpus.

Last but not least, Folmer's tome on the Aramaic of the Achaemenid period (1995) is a meticulous discussion of select linguistic issues arising from the corpus as delimited by the title of the original Leiden dissertation. Her main thrust is to address the question of linguistic diversity which one might expect to discover in texts so diverse in chronological and geographical spread, scribal tradition and register. Folmer is not the first to speak for such diversity. The difference in grammar between the Ahiqar narrative and the proverbs ascribed to this sage had become accepted by Aramaic linguists. So also was the unique nature of the Aramaic of the Hermopolis papyri universally recognised almost with their initial publication.

In addition to the above-mentioned major studies touching on the Aramaic represented more or less by our corpus there is a considerable number of *Einzeluntersuchungen,* as any casual glance through the pages of Fitzmyer - Kaufman's valuable bibliography makes plain. Our indebtedness to those numerous studies is apparent at innumerable places throughout our present grammar. Mention ought also to be made of lexicographical work such as Baumgartner's contribution on Biblical Aramaic in Koehler - Baumgartner's dictionary (1953), Vogt's excellent dictionary of Biblical Aramaic (1971) and the recent two-volume dictionary of Northwest Semitic inscriptions by Hoftijzer - Jongeling (1995).

Another important issue, highlighted by Kutscher in particular, is that of interaction between Aramaic and contemporary languages, non-Semitic as well as Semitic. Aramaic has proved to be very flexible and pliable in this respect in absorbing a host of elements from languages as diverse as Hebrew, Egyptian, Akkadian, Persian, and some more. Such an absorption took place not only as lexical borrowings, but also affected depth and intricacies of syntax. Aramaic, however, did not remain a mere importer, but also influenced langauges with which it came into contact.

ABBREVIATIONS

1QS: the Community Rule from Qumran Cave 1
1QapGn: the *Genesis Apocryphon* from Qumran Cave 1
A: Afel
AAL: *Afroasiatic Linguistics*
act.: active (voice)
adj.: adjective
AfO: *Archif für Orientforschung*
AION: *Annali dell' Istituto Orientale di Napoli*
AJBI: *Annual of the Japanese Biblical Institute*
AJSL: *American Journal of Semitic Languages and Literatures*
AN: *Abr-Nahrain*
Akk: Akkadian
ap.: apodosis
BA: Biblical Aramaic
BASOR: *Bulletin of the American Schools of Oriental Research*
B.C.E: before the Common Era, = B.C.
BH: Biblical Hebrew
BHK: R. Kittel and P. Kahle, *Biblia Hebraica* (Stuttgart, 1929-37, 1951).
BHS: W. Rudolph and K. Elliger, *Biblia Hebraica Stuttgartensia* (Stuttgart, 1967-77).
Bib: *Biblica*
BN: *Biblische Notizen*
BO: *Bibliotheca Orientalis*
BTA: the Aramaic of the Babylonian Talmud
BZAW: Beihefte zur *Zeitschrift für die alttestamentliche Wissenschaft*
c.: common gender; century
C: Cowley 1923; consonant
ca.: = circa, "approximately"
CD: the Damascus Covenant from the Cairo Genizah and Qumran
cent.: century
cp.: compare
CAD: *The Assyrian Dictionary of the Oriental Institute of the University of Chicago.*
C.E.: the Common Era, = A.D.

conj.: conjunctive (pronoun)
CPA: Christian Palestinian Aramaic
cst.: construct (state)
D: Pael
det.: determinate, determined
disj.: disjunctive (pronoun)
diss.: dissertation
Dn: Daniel
DN: divine name
DS-NELL: *Dutch Studies in Near Eastern Languages and Literatures*
Eth.: Classical Ethiopic
f.: feminine
fem.: feminine
fp: feminine plural
fs: feminine singular
Fschr: Festschrift
G: Grundstam, Peal
GN: geographical name
H: Hafel
HAL: W. Baumgartner, B. Hartmann, E.Y. Kutscher, Ph. Reymond, and J.J. Stamm, *Hebräisches und aramäisches Lexikon zum alten Testament* (Leiden: E.J. Brill, 1967-90).
IA: Imperial Aramaic, Official Aramaic, *Reichsaramäisch*
IEJ: *Israel Exploration Journal*
impf.: imperfect
impv.: imperative
inf.: infinitive
IOS: *Israel Oriental Studies*
JA: Jewish Aramaic
JA: *Journal Asiatique*
JAOS: *Journal of the American Oriental Society*
JJS: *Journal of Jewish Studies*
JNES: *Journal of Near Eastern Studies*
JS: *Journal for Semitics*
JSOT: *Journal for the Study of the Old Testament*
JSS: *Journal of Semitic Studies*
JThSt: *Journal of Theological Studies*
juss.: jussive
K: Kraeling 1969
KAI: Donner, H. and W. Röllig, *Kanaanäische und aramäische Inschriften mit einem Beitrag von O. Rössler*, in 3 volumes.

Bd. I Texte (1971), Bd. II Kommentar (1973), Bd. III Glossare und Indizen, Tafeln (1969). Wiesbaden: O. Harrassowitz.

Lĕš:*Lĕšonénu*

m.: masculine

MA: Middle Aramaic

Mand.: Mandaic

mas.: masculine

mrg: margin (of a document)

mp: masculine plural

ms: masculine singular

MUSJ: *Mélanges de l'Université de Saint Joseph*

N: noun

NC: nominal clause

NESE: *Neue Ephemeris für semitische Epigraphik*

NP: noun phrase

OA: Old Aramaic

OLA: Orientalia Lovaniensia Analecta

OLZ: *Orientalistische Literaturzeitung*

Or. *Orientalia*

OS: *Orientalia Suecana.*

pass.: passive (voice)

et passim: "and often elsewhere"

pc.: prefix conjugation, also called Imperfect including Jussive and Energic

pf.: perfect

ph.: phrase

pl.: plural

PN: personal name

prep.: preposition

prep.ph.: prepositional phrase

prot.: protasis

PS: Proto-Semitic

ptc.: participle

PY: Porten and Yardeni 1986, 1989, 1993

QA: Qumran Aramaic

RA: *Revue assyriologique*

RB: *Revue Biblique*

RdQ: *Revue de Qumran*

RES: *Répertoire d'épigraphie sémitique* (Paris, 1900ff.)

RO: *Roznik Orientalistyczny*

RSO: *Revista degli studi orientali.*

s.: singular

SA: Samaritan Aramaic
sc: suffix conjugation, also called Perfect
sg.: singular
sim.: similarly
SO: *Studia Orientalia*
st.: status (of the noun: absolute, constructus, determinatus)
suf: suffix; suffixed
s.v.: *sub voce*, i.e., under a given lexeme in a dictionary
Syr.: Classical Syriac
pl.: plural
tA: Ettafal
TA: Targumic Aramaic
TAD: Porten, B. and A. Yardeni, *Textbook of Aramaic Documents from Ancient Egypt. Newly Copied, Edited and Translated into Hebrew and English.* vol. 1 (1986), vol. 2 (1989), vol. 3 (1993).
Taj: תאג ... ספר כתר תורה (Jerusalem, 1894-1901)
TBA: the Aramaic of the Babylonian Talmud
tD: Ethpaal
tG: Ethpeel
tH: Ettafal
TJ: Targum Jonathan to the Prophets (ed. A. Sperber)
TO: Targum Onkelos to the Pentateuch (ed. A. Sperber)
UF: *Ugarit Forschungen*
Ugr.: Ugaritic
V: verb; vowel
VC: verbal clause
VP: verb phrase
VT: *Vetus Testamentum*
WO: *Welt des Orients*
YBA: the Yemenite tradition of Babylonian Aramaic
ZA: *Zeitschrift für Assyriologie und vorderasiatische Archäologie*
ZAH: *Zeitschrift für Althebraistik*
ZAW: *Zeitschrift für die alttestamentliche Wissenschaft*
ZDMG: *Zeitschrift der deutschen morgenländischen Gesellschaft*

OTHER SYMBOLS

+ following a reference or references, it means that the listing is not exhaustive.
† following a reference or references, it means that the listing

is complete.
√ root of a lexeme
// parallel to
> X > Y: X changes to X
< X < Y: X developed from Y
<X> consonant grapheme X; with a Hebrew letter for X, a letter
    assumed to be missing and to be supplied
/X/ phoneme X
[X] phone X

MODE OF CITATION FROM *TAD*:

The general style is, for example, A2.4:5, which means
TAD, volume I, document no. 2.4, line 5.

Where a cited phrase, clause or sentence extends over
more than one line, the line number indicates that the first
word of the citation is found in that line, except in cases
where ambiguity could arise.

INDEX OF PASSAGES

The Index of Passages appended to this grammar covers
only the data in the main body of the text, and not those in
footnotes. Despite this imperfection, due to a technical
difficulty which has proved insurmountable, the Index as it is
is hoped to be of use for the user of this volume.

LITERATURE

Alexander, P.S. 1978. Remarks on Aramaic epistolography in the Persian period. *JSS* 23:155-70.

Andersen, F.I. 1966. Moabite syntax. *Or* 35.81-120.

Andersen, F.I. and D.N. Freedman. 1992a. *Aleph* as a vowel letter in Old Aramaic. In *Studies in Hebrew and Aramaic Orthography*, eds D.N. Freedman, A.D. Forbes and F.I. Andersen, 79-90. Winona Lake: Eisenbrauns. Originally published in *To Touch the Text: Biblical and Related Studies in Honor of Joseph A. Fitzmyer*, eds M.P. Horgan and P.J. Kobelski (New York: Crossroad, 1989), 1-14.

_____. 1992b. The spelling of the Aramaic portion of the Tell Fekherye bilingual. In *Studies in Hebrew and Aramaic Orthography*, eds D.N. Freedman, A.D. Forbes and F.I. Andersen, 137-70. Winona Lake: Eisenbrauns. Originally published in *Text and Context: Old Testament and Semitic Studies for F.C. Fensham*, JSOT Suppl. Series 48, ed. W. Claassen (Sheffield: Sheffield Academic Press, 1988), 9-49.

Aristar, A.M.R. 1987. The Semitic jussive and the implications for Aramaic. *Maarav* 4:157-89.

Aro, J. 1964. *Die Vokalisierung des Grundstammes im semitischen Verbum*. Studia Orientalia 31. Helsinki: Societas Orientalis Fennica.

Bar-Asher, M. 1977. מחקרים בסורית של ארץ ישראל. מקורותיה מסורותיה ובעיות נבחרות בדקדוקה [Palestinian Syriac Studies. Source-texts, Traditions and Grammatical Problems]. Ph.D. diss. Jerusalem.

Barth, J. [2]1894. *Die Nominalbildung in den semitischen Sprachen*. Leipzig: J.C. Hinrichs.

_____. 1911. *Sprachwissenschaftliche Untersuchungen zum Semitischen*. II. Leipzig: J.C. Hinrichs..

_____. 1913. *Die Pronominalbildung in den semitischen Sprachen*. Leipzig: J.C. Hinrichs.

Bauer, H. and Leander, P. 1927. *Grammatik des Biblisch-Aramäischen*. Halle: Niemeyer.

Baumgartner, W. 1959. Das Aramäische im Buche Daniel. In id., *Zum Alten Testament und seiner Umwelt* , 68-123. Leiden: E.J. Brill.

With short additions to an article published in *ZAW* 45 (1927) 81-133.

_____. 1953. A Dictionary of the Aramaic Parts of the Old Testament in English and German. In *Lexicon in veteris testamenti libros*, ed. L. Koehler and W. Baumgartner, 1045-1138. Leiden: E.J. Brill.

Ben-Ḥayyim, Z. 1951. הנסתרות בארמית הקדמונית [The feminine plural in Ancient Aramaic.] In *Eretz Israel (Schwabe Volume)* 1:135-39.

_____. 1971. עם העיון בכתובות ספירה [Comments on the inscriptions of Sfire.] *Leš* 35:243-53.

Bennett, S.F. 1984. Objective pronominal suffixes in Aramaic. Ph.diss. Yale.

Bergsträsser, G. 1918. *Hebräische Grammatik. I. Teil: Einleitung, Schrift- und Lautlehre*. Leipzig: J.C. Hinrichs.

Bergman, B.Z. 1968. Hanᶜel in Daniel 2:25 and 6:19. *JNES* 27:69f.

Beyer, K. 1966. Der reichsaramäische Einschlag in der älteren syrischen Literatur. *ZDMG* 116:242-54.

_____. 1984, 1994. *Die aramäischen Texte vom Toten Meer* etc. Ergänzungsband (1994). Göttingen: Vandenhoeck & Ruprecht.

Biran, A. and J. Naveh. 1993. An Aramaic stele fragment from Tel Dan. *IEJ* 43.81-98.

Blass, F. and A. Debrunner, tr. and rev. by R.A. Funk. 1961. *A Greek Grammar of the New Testament and Other Early Christian Literature*. Chicago and London: The University of Chicago Press.

Blau, J. 1970. *On Pseudo-corrections in some Semitic Languages*. Jerusalem: Israel Academy of Sciences and Humanities.

Bloomfield, L. 1933 (1950). *Language*. London: George Allen & Unwin.

Bogaert, M. 1964. Les suffies verbaux non-accusatifs dans le sémitique nord-occidental et particulièrement en hébreu. *Bib* 45:220-47.

Borger, R. 1982. Die Chronologie des Darius-Denkmals am Behistun-Felsen. *Nachrichten der Akademie der Wissenshcaften in Göttingen.1. Philologisch-historische Klasse*. Jahrgang 1982, Nr. 3. Göttingen: Vandenhoeck & Ruprecht.

Bresciani, E. 1960. Papiri aramaici egiziani di epoca persiana presso il Museo Vicico di Padova. *RSO* 35:11-24.

Breuer, M. 1977-82. תורה נביאים כתובים מוגהים על פי הנוסח והמסורה של כתב יד ארם צובה וכתבי יד הקרובים לו, 3 vols. Jerusalem.

Brockelmann, C. 1908. *Grundriss der vergleichenden Grammatik der semitischen Sprachen. I. Laut- und Formenlehre*. Berlin: Reuter und Reichard.

_____. 1913. *Grundriss der vergleichenden Grammatik der semitischen Sprachen. II. Syntax*. Berlin: Reuter und Reichard

_____. 1928². *Lexicon syriacum*. Halle: M. Niemeyer.

Brown, F., S.R. Driver, and Ch.A. Briggs. 1907. *A Hebrew and English Lexicon of the Old Testament* etc. Oxford: Clarendon Press.

Brown, M.L. 1987. "Is it not?" or "Indeed!": *HL* in Northwest Semitic. *Maarav* 4: 210-19.

Cantineau, J. 1930. *Le Nabatéen. I. Notions générales—Écriture, grammaire*. Paris: Ernest Leroux.

_____. 1935. *Grammaire du palmyrénien épigraphique*. Le Caire: L'Institut Français d'Archéologie orientale.

Caquot, A. 1971. Une inscription araméenne d'époque assyrienne. In *Hommages à André Dupont-Sommer*, ed. A. Caquot and M. Philonenko, 9-16. Paris: Maisonneuve.

Carmignac, J. 1966. Un aramaïsme biblique et qumrânien: l'infinitif placé après son complément d'objet. *RdQ*5:503-20.

Cohen, D.R. 1975. Subject and object in Biblical Aramaic: a functional approach based on form-content analysis. *AAL* 2.1.

Cook, E.M. 1986. Word order in the Aramaic of Daniel. *AAL* 9:111-26.

_____. 1990. The orthography of final unstressed long vowels in Old and Imperial Aramaic. *Maarav* 5-6: 53-67.

Cowley, A. 1923. *Aramaic Papyri of the Fifth Century B.C. Edited with Translation and Notes*. Oxford: Clarendon Press.

Cross, F.M. and D.N. Freedman. 1952. *Early Hebrew Orthography. A Study of the Epigraphic Evidence*. New Haven: American Oriental Society.

Curme, G.O. 1931. *A Grammar of the English Language*. vol. 3, *Syntax*. Boston etc.: D.C. Heath and Company.

Dalman, G. ²1905. *Grammatik des jüdisch-palästinischen Aramäisch nach den Idiomen des palästinischen Talmud des Onkelostargum und Prophetentargum und der jerusalemischen Targume*. Leipzig: J.C. Hinrichs.

_____. 1938. *Aramäisch-neuhebräisches Handwörterbuch zu Targum, Talmud und Midrasch*. Göttingen: Vandenhoeck & Ruprecht.

Degen, R. 1967. Zur Schreibung des Kaška-Namens in ägyptischen, ugaritischen und altaramäischen Quellen: Kritische Anmerkungen zu einer Monographie über die Kaškäer. *WO* 4:48-60.

_____. 1969. *Altaramäische Grammatik der Inschriften des 10.-8. Jh. v. Chr.* Wiesbaden: Franz Steiner.

_____. 1972a. Zum Ostrakon CIS II 138. *NESE* 1:23-37.

_____. 1972b. Ein neuer aramäischer Papyrus aus Elephantine: P. Berol. 23000. *NESE* 1:9-22.

_____. 1979. Review of Segert 1975. *Göttingische Gelehrte Anzeigen*. 231:8-51. Göttingen: Vandenhoeck & Ruprecht.

Dempsey, D. 1990. The "epistolary perfect" in Aramaic letters. *BN* 54:7-11.

Denz, A. Strukturanalyse der pronominalen Objektsuffixe im Altsyrischen und klassischen Arabisch. Diss. München. 1962.

Diem, W. 1986. Alienable und inalienable Possession im Semitischen. *ZDMG* 136:227-91.

Dolgopolsky, A. 1994. The Aramaic reflexes of the Semitic glottalized lateral consonant. *RO* 49:5-14.

Donner, H. and W. Röllig. 1969-73. *Kanaanäische und aramäische Inschriften mit einem Beitrag von O. Rössler,* Bd. I Texte (1971), Bd. II Kommentar (1973), Bd. III Glossare und Indizen, Tafeln (1969). Wiesbaden: Otto Harrassowitz.

Dotan, A. 1976. תורה נביאים וכתובים מדויקים היטב על פי הניקוד הטעמים והמסורה של אהרון בן משה בן אשר בכתב יד לינינגרד. Tel Aviv.

Driver, G.R. 1957. *Aramaic Documents of the Fifth Century B.C.* Abridged and revised edition. Oxford: Oxford University Press.

Driver, S.R. ³1913. *Notes on the Hebrew Text and Topography of the Books of Samuel.* Oxford: Clarendon Press.

Drower, E.S. and R. Macuch. 1963. *A Mandaic Dictionary.* Oxford: Oxford University Press.

Dupont-Sommer, A. 1942-44. La tablette cunéiforme araméenne de Warka. *RA* 39:35-62.

Eilers, W. 1935. Das Volk der *karkā* in den Achämenideninschriften. *OLZ* 38:201-13.

_____. 1940. Iranische Beamtennamen in der keilschriftlichen Überlieferung I. *Abhandlungen für die Kunde des Morgenlandes* XXV/5. Leipzig.

Eph'al, I. and J. Naveh. 1989. Hazael's booty inscriptions. *IEJ* 39:192-200.

Encyclopaedia Judaica. 16 vols. Jerusalem, 1971-72.

Epstein, J.N. 1960. דקדוק ארמית בבלית [*A Grammar of Babylonian Aramaic*]. Jerusalem: Magnes.

Fales, F.M. 1986. *Aramaic Epigraphs on Clay Tablets of the Neo-Assyrian Period.* Materiali per il lessico aramaico 1. Roma: Università degli Studi "La Sapienza."

Fassberg, S.E. 1990. *A Grammar of the Palestinian Targum Fragments from the Cairo Genizah* [Harvard Semitic Studies 38]. Atlanta: Scholars Press.

_____. 1991. תוארי הפועל "מיד" ו"על יד על יד" בלשון חז"ל. In סוגיות בלשון חכמים, ed. M. Bar-Asher, 95-97. Jerusalem: The Institute for Advanced Studies, The Hebrew University of Jerusalem.

_____. 1992. Hebraisms in the Aramaic documents from Qumran. In

Studies in Qumran Aramaic [*AN*, Supplement 3], ed. T. Muraoka, 48-69.

Fitzmyer, J.A. 1956. The syntax of Imperial Aramaic based on the documents found in Egypt. Ph.D. diss. Johns Hopkins University.

———. 1962. The Padua Aramaic papyrus letters. *JNES* 21:15-24.

———. 1971. A re-study of an Elephantine Aramaic marriage contract (*AP* 15). In *Near Eastern Studies in Honor of William Foxwell Albright*, ed. H. Goedicke, 137-68. Baltimore /London: The Johns Hopkins Press. Reprinted in Fitzmyer 1979, 243-71.

———. ²1971a. *The Genesis Apocryphon of Qumran Cave I. A Commentary*. Biblica et Orientalia 18a. Rome: Biblical Institute Press.

———. 1979. *A Wandering Aramean. Collected Aramaic Essays*. Missoula: Scholars Press.

———. ²1995. *The Aramaic Inscriptions of Sefire* [Biblical et orientalia 19-a]. Rome: Pontifical Biblical Institute Press.

Fitzmyer, J.A. and D.J. Harrington. 1978. *A Manual of Palestinian Aramaic Texts*. Rome: Biblical Institute Press.

Fitzmyer, J.A. and S.A. Kaufman. 1991. *An Aramaic Bibliography. Part I. Old, Offical, and Biblical Aramaic*. Baltimore and London: The Johns Hopkins University Press.

Folmer, M.L. 1991. Some remarks on the use of the finite verb form in the protasis of conditional sentences in Aramaic texts from the Achaemenid period. In *Studies in Hebrew and Aramaic Syntax Presented to Professor J. Hoftijzer on the Occasion of His Sixty-fifth Birthday*, eds K. Jongeling, H.L. Murre-van den Berg and L. Van Rompay, 56-78. Leiden: E.J. Brill.

———. 1995. *The Aramaic Language in the Achaemenid Period. A Study in Linguistic Variation*. OLA 68. Leuven: Peeters.

———. 1996. Instances of so-called (*k*)*zy-recitativum* in Aramaic texts from the Achaemenid period. *DS-NELL* 2:145-55.

Garbini, G. 1993. *Aramaica*. Studi semitici NS 10. Roma: Università degli Studi «La Sapienza».

Garr, W.R. 1985. *Dialect Geography of Syria-Palestine, 1000-586 B.C.E.* Philadelphia: University of Pennsylvania Press.

———. 1990. On the alternation between construct and *di* phrases in Bibliccal Aramaic. *JSS* 35:213-31.

Gesenius, W. and F. Buhl. ¹⁶1915. *Wilhelm Gesenius' hebräisches und aramäisches Handwörterbuch über das Alte Testament*. Leipzig: F.C.W. Vogel.

Gibson, J.C.L. 1975. *Textbook of Syrian Semitic Inscriptions*. Vol. 2. *Aramaic Inscriptions* etc. Oxford: Clarendon Press.

Gildersleeve, B.L. 1900, 1911. *Syntax of Classical Greek from Homer to Demosthenes*. 2 vols. New York: American Book Company.

Ginsberg, H.L. 1936. Aramaic dialect problems. II. *AJSL* 52:95-103.

_____. 1955. Aramaic proverbs and precepts. In *Ancient Near Eastern Texts Relating to the Old Testament*, third edition (1969) with supplement, ed. J.B. Pritchard, 427-30. Princeton: Princeton University Press.

_____. 1969. Aramaic letters. In *Ancient Near Eastern Texts Relating to the Old Testament*, third edition with supplement, ed. J.B. Pritchard, 491f., 633. Princeton: Princeton University Press.

Gordon, C.H. 1937-39. The Aramaic incantation in cuneiform. *AfO* 12:105-17.

_____. 1940. The cuneiform Aramaic incantation. *Or* 9:29-38.

_____. 1965. *Ugaritic Textbook*. Analecta Orientalia 38. Rome: Pontifical Biblical Institute.

Goshen-Gottstein, M.H. 1949. Afterthought and the syntax of relative clauses. *JBL* 68:35-47.

Greenfield, J.C. 1968. קווים דיאלקטיים בארמית הקדומה [Dialect traists in Early Aramaic]. *Leš* 32:359-68.

_____. 1969. The 'periphrastic imperative' in Aramaic and Hebrew. *IEJ* 19:199-210.

_____. 1974. Standard Literary Aramaic. In *Actes du premier congrès international de linguistique sémitique et chamito-sémitique*, eds A. Caquot and D. Cohen, 280-89. Janua Linguarum, ser. Practica 159. The Hague: Mouton.

_____. 1978. The dialects of early Aramaic. *JNES* 37:93-100.

_____. 1990. לצורת המקור בשטרות הארמיים מואדי מורבעאת ומנחל חבר [The infinitive in the Aramaic documents from the Judaean Desert]. In שי לחיים רבין *Studies on Hebrew and Other Semitic Languages* [Fschr. C. Rabin], eds M. Goshen-Gottstein, S. Morag, and S. Kogut, 77-81. Jerusalem: Academon.

Greenfield, J.C. and J. Naveh. 1975. Hebrew and Aramaic in the Persian period. In *The Cambridge History of Judaism*, Volume One, *Introduction, The Persian Period*, eds W.D. Davies and L. Finkelstein, 115-29. Cambridge: Cambridge University Press.

Greenfield, J.C. and B. Porten. 1982. *The Bisitun Inscription of Darius the Great. Aramaic Version. Text, Translation and Commentary*. London: Lund Humphries.

Grelot, P. 1956. On the root עבץ/עבק in Ancient Aramaic and in Ugaritic. *JSS* 1:202-5.

_____. 1972. *Documents araméens d'Égypte. Introduction, traduction, présentation*. Paris: Cerf.

Gropp, D.M. 1990. The language of Samaria papyri: a preliminary study. *Maarav* 5-6:169-87.

Haneman, G. 1975. על מלת־היחס "בין" במשנה ובמקרא [On the preposition בין in the Mishnah and the Bible]. *Lĕš* 40:33-53.

Harrak, A. 1992. Des noms d'année en araméen. *WO* 23:68-74.

Hayes, J.P. and J. Hoftijzer. 1970. Notae hermopolitanae. *VT* 20:98-106.

Hesterman, K. 1992. "מבני" (= מְבַנֵי)—צורה דקדוקית "חדשה" בארמית של יֵב [(מבני* =) מְבַנֵי)—a 'new' grammatical form in Elephantine Aramaic]. *Lĕš* 57:7-15.

Hetzron, R. 1969. Third person singular prnoun suffixes in Proto-Semitic. *OS* 18:101-27.

Hinz, W. 1975. *Altiranisches Sprachgut der Nebenüberlieferungen.* Wiesbaden: Otto Harrassowitz.

Hoftijzer, J. 1976. In *Aramaic Texts from Deir ʿAlla,* J. Hoftijzer and G. van der Kooij. Leiden: E.J. Brill.

———. 1983. De Hermopolis-papyri. Arameese brieven uit Egypte (5^e eeuw v. Chr.). In *Schrijvend verlden. Documenten uit het Oude Nabije Oosten vertaald en toegelicht,* ed. K.R. Veenhof, 107-19. Leiden: Ex Oriente Lux.

Hoftijzer, J. and Jongeling, K. 1995. *Dictionary of the North-West Semitic Inscriptions with Appendices by R.C. Steiner, A. Mosak Moshavi and B. Porten.* 2 vols. Leiden: E.J. Brill.

Hopkins, S. 1997a. על הצירוף שמה לגברא "שמו של האיש" בארמית [On the construction šmēh l-g̱abrā "the name of the man" in Aramaic]. In *Massorot IX-X-XI. Studies in Language Traditions and Jewish Languages,* ed. M. Bar-Asher, 349-61. Jerusalem.

———. 1997b [= 1997a]. On the construction šmēh l-g̱abrā 'the name of the man' in Aramaic. *JSS* 42.23-32.

Hug, V. 1993. *Altaramäische Grammatik der Texte des 7. und 6. Jh.s v.Chr.* Heidelberg: Orientverlag.

Huehnergard, J. 1987. The feminine plural jussive in Old Aramaic. *ZDMG* 137:266-77.

Jastrow, M. 1886-1903. *A Dictionary of the Targumim, the Talmud Babli and Yerushalmi, and the Midrashic Literature.* London:Trübner/New York: G.P. Putnam.

Jespersen, O. 1909-31. *A Modern English Grammar on Historical Principles,* Parts 1-7. Heidelberg: Carl Winter.

———. 1924. *The Philosophy of Grammar.* G. Allen & Unwin:London/New York: H. & Holt Co.

———. 1933. *Essentials of English Grammar.* London: George Allen & Unwin.

———. 1937. *Analytical Syntax.* Copenhagen: Munksgaard. Quoted from a reprint: 1969.

Joosten, J. 1989. The function of the so-called dativus ethicus in Classical Syriac. *Or* 58: 473-92.

Joüon, P. 1934. Notes grammaticales, lexicographiques et philologiques sur les papyrus araméens d'Égypte. *MUSJ* 18:3-90.

Joüon, P. - T. Muraoka. 1993. *A Grammar of Biblical Hebrew*. 2 vols. Reprint of 1st edition [1991] with corrections. Roma: Editrice Pontificio Istituto Biblico.

Kaddari, M.Z. 1963. Studies in the syntax of Targum Onqelos. *Tarbiz* 32:232-51.

_____. 1969. Construct state and *di-* phrases in Imperial Aramaic. In *Proceedings of the International Conference on Semitic Studies Held in Jerusalem, 19-23 July 1965*, 102-15. Jerusalem: The Israel Academy of Sciences and Humanities.

_____. 1983. The existential verb *HWH* in Imperial Aramaic. In *Arameans, Aramaic and the Aramaic Literary Tradition*, ed. M. Sokoloff, 43-46. Ramat Gan: Bar-Ilan University Press.

Kaufman, S.A. 1974. *The Akkadian Influences on Aramaic.* Assyriologiccal Studies 19. Chicago: The University of Chicago Press.

_____. 1977. Review of S. Segert 1975 in *BO* 34:92-97.

_____. 1977a. An Assyro-Aramaic *egirtu ša šulmu*. In *Essays on the Ancient Near East in Memory of Jacob Joel Finkelstein*, ed. M. de Jong Ellis, 119-27. Memoirs of the Connecticut Academy of Arts and Sciences 19. Hamden, CT: Archon.

_____. 1982. Reflections on the Assyrian-Aramaic bilingual from Tell Fakhariyeh. *Maarav* 3:137-75.

_____. 1983. The history of Aramaic vowel reduction. In *Arameans, Aramaic and the Aramaic Literary Tradition*, ed. M. Sokoloff, 47-55. Ramat Gan: Bar-Ilan University Press.

Khan, G. 1988. *Studies in Semitic Syntax*. Oxford: Oxford University Press.

Kienast, B. 1957. Das Possessivsuffix der 3.m.sg. am pluralischen Nomen des Maskulinum in Südostaramäischen. *Münchener Studien zur Sprachwissenschaft* 10:72-6.

_____. 1987. ᵈÉ-a und der aramäische «status emphaticus». In *Ebla 1975-1985. Dieci anni di studi linguistici e filologici. Atti del convegno internazionale (Napoli, 9-11 ottobre 1985)*, ed. L. Cagni, 37-47. Napoli: Istituto Universitario Orientale, Dipartimento di Studi Asiatici.

Klein, M.L. 1986. *Genizah Manuscripts of Palestinian Targum to the Pentateuch.* 2 vols. Cincinnati: Hebrew Union College Press.

Koopmans, J.J. 1962. *Aramäische Chrestomathie. Ausgewählte Texte (Inschriften, Ostraka und Papyri) bis zum 3. Jahrhundert n. Chr für das Studium der aramäischen Sprache gesammelt.* 2 vols. Leiden: Nederlands Instituut voor het Nabije Oosten.

Kornfeld, W. 1978. *Onomastica aramaica aus Ägypten.* Vienna: Verlag der österreichischen Akademie der Wissenshcaften.

Kottsieper, I. 1988. Anmerkungen zu Pap. Amherst 63. *ZAW* 100:217-44.

_____. 1990. *Die Sprache der Aḥiqarsprüche.* BZAW 194. Berlin/New York: Walter de Gruyter.

_____. 1991. Die Geschichte und die Sprüche des weisen Achiqar. In *Texte aus der Umwelt des Alten Testaments.* 3.2, Weisheitstexte II, ed. O. Kaiser, 320-47. Gütersloh: Gerd Mohn.

Kouwenberg, N.J.C. 1997. *Gemination in the Akkadian Verb.* Studia Semitica Neerlandica 32. Assen: Van Gorcum.

Kraeling, E.G. 1953. *The Brooklyn Museum Aramaic Papyri. New Documents of the Fifth Century B.C. from the Jewish Colony at Elephantine.* New Haven: Yale University Press.

Kroeze, J.H. 1991. Die chaos van die 'genitief' in Bybelse Hebreeus. *JS* 3:129-43.

_____. 1993. Underlying syntactic relations in construct phrases of Biblical Hebrew. *JS* 5: 68-88.

_____. 1997. Semantic relationships in construct phrases of Biblical Hebrew: a functional approach. *ZAH* 10:27-41.

Kutscher, E.Y. 1954. New Aramaic texts [review article on E.G. Kraeling, *The Brooklyn Museum Aramaic Papyri*]. *JAOS* 74:233-48.

_____. 1961a. לשונן של האיגרות העבריות והארמיות של באר כוסבה ובני דורו. מאמר ראשון: האיגרות הארמיות [The Hebrew and Aramaic letters of Bar Koseba and his contemporaries: Part I, Aramaic letters]. *Leš* 25:117-33.

_____. 1961b. לשונן של האיגרות העבריות והארמיות של באר כוסבה ובני דורו. מאמר שני: האיגרות העבריות [The Hebrew and Aramaic letters of Bar Koseba and his contemporaries: Part II, Hebrew letters]. *Leš* 26:7-23.

_____. 1969. Two 'passive' constructions in Aramaic in the light of Persian. In *Proceedings of the International Conference on Semitic Studies Held in Jerusalem, 19-23 July 1965.* Jerusalem: The Israel Academy of Sciences and Humanities.

_____. 1970. Aramaic. In *Linguistics in South West Asia and North Africa* [Current Trends in Linguistics], ed. T.A. Sebeok, vol. 6: 347-412. Paris: Mouton.

_____. 1971. The Hermopolis papyri. *IOS* 1:103-19.

_____. 1972. תולדות הארמית. חלק א' [*A History of Aramaic. Part I*]. Jerusalem: Academon.

_____. 1977. *Hebrew and Aramaic Studies*. Ed. Z. Ben-Ḥayyim, A. Dotan and G. Sarfatti. Jerusalem: Magnes Press.

Lambdin, T.O. The junctural origin of the West Semitic definite article. In *Near Eastern Studies in Honor of William Foxwell Albright*, ed. H. Goedicke, 315-333. Baltimore / London: The Johns Hopkins Press.

Leander, P. 1928. *Laut- und Formenlehre des Ägyptisch-Aramäischen*. Göteborg: Elanders.

Lemaire, A. 1995. Les inscriptions araméennes de Cheikh-Fadl (Égypte). In *Studia Aramaica: New Sources and New Approaches* [*JSS* Supplement 4], eds M.J. Geller, J.C. Greenfield and M.P. Weitzman, 77-132. Oxford: Oxford University Press.

Lerner, Y. 1981. במסמכי יב. /d/ בייצוג ז/ד חילופי הסבר [The *Zayin/Daleth* interchange in the Elephantine documents: an alternate (sic!) explanation]. *Leš* 46:57-64.

_____. 1982. לְמִבְנָא/לְמִבְנָיה/לִבְנָא. *Leš* 47:62-65.

Levy, J. [3]1867-68. *Chaldäisches Wörterbuch über die Targumim und einen grossen Theil des rabbinischen Schriftthums*.

_____. 1876-89. *Neuhebräisches und chaldäisches Wörterbuch über die Talmudim und Midraschim*. Leipzig: Brockhaus.

Lewis, A.S. 1910. *The Old Syriac Gospels or Evangelion da Mepharreshê* etc. London: Williams and Norgate.

Lindenberger, J.M. 1982. The gods of Ahiqar. *UF* 14:105-17.

_____. 1983. *The Aramaic Proverbs of Ahiqar*. Baltimore and London: The Johns Hopkins University Press.

_____. 1985. Ahiqar (Seventh to Sixth Century B.C.). A new translation and introduction. In *The Old Testament Pseudepigrapha*, ed. J.H. Charlesworth, vol. 2, 479-507. London: Darton, Longman & Todd.

_____. 1994. Ed. by K.H. Richards. *Ancient Aramaic and Hebrew Letters*. Writings from the Ancient World, no. 4. Atlanta, GA: Scholars Press.

Lipiński, E. 1975. *Studies in Aramaic Inscriptions and Onomastics. I*. OLA 1. Leuven: Leuven University Press.

_____. 1978. La correspondance des sibilantes dans les textes araméens et les textes cunéiformes néo-assyriens. In *Atti del secondo congresso internazionale di linguistica camito-semitica*, ed. P. Fronzaroli, 201-10. Quaderni di semitistica 5. Florence: Istituto di linguistica e di lingue orientali.

_____. 1990. Araméen d'Empire. In *Le Language dans l'antiquité*, eds

P. Swiggers and A. Wouters [La Pensée linguistique 3], 94-133. Paris/Louvain: Peeters.

_____. 1991. Monosyllabic nominal and verbal roots in Semitic languages. In *Semitic Studies in Honor of Wolf Leslau*, ed. A.S. Kaye, vol. 2, 927-30. Wiesbaden: Otto Harrassowitz.

_____. 1994. *Studies in Aramaic Inscriptions and Onomastics*. II. OLA 57. Leuven: Peeters.

Macuch, R. 1965. *Handbook of Classical and Modern Mandaic*. Berlin: De Gruyter.

_____. 1971. Gesprochenes Aramäisch und aramäische Schriftsprache. In *Christentum am Roten Meer*, eds F. Altheim and R. Stiehl, I, 537-57. Berlin: De Gruyter.

_____. 1990. Some orthographico-phonetic problems of Ancient Aramaic and the living Aramaic pronunciations. *Maarav* 5-6:221-37.

Margain, J. 1994. L'araméen d'empire. In *La Palestine à l'époque perse*, ed. E.-M. Laperrousaz, 225-43. Paris: Cerf.

Masson, G. 1975. Le nom des Cariens dans quelques langues d'antiquité. In *Mélanges linguistiques offerts à Émile Benveniste*. Collections linguistiques 70, 407-18. Leuven: Peeters.

Milik, J.T. 1961. *Les grottes de Murabbaʿât*. Discoveries in the Judaean Desert. II. Oxford: Clarendon Press.

_____. 1967. Les papyrus araméens d'Hermopolis et les cultes syro-phéniciens en Égypte perse. *Bib* 48:546-622.

Millard, A.R. 1976. Assyrian royal names in Biblical Hebrew. *JSS* 21:1-14.

Montgomery, J.A. 1923. Adverbial *kúlla* in Biblical Aramaic and Hebrew. *JAOS* 43:391-95.

Morag, Sh. 1964. Biblical Aramaic in Geonic Babylonia: The various schools. In *Studies in Egyptology and Linguistics in Honour of H.J. Polotsky*, 117-31. Jerusalem: The Israel Exploration Society.

_____. 1988. לשון התלמוד הבבלי. מבוא, תורת ההגה ותצורת־הפועל במסורת חימן. Jerusalem: Ben Zvi Institute.

Morgenstern, M., E. Qimron and D. Sivan. 1996. The hitherto unpublished columns of the Genesis Apocryphon. *AN* 33:55-73.

Moriya, A. Aramaic epistolography: The Hermopolis letters and related material in the Persian period. Ph.D. diss., Hebrew Union College, Cincinnati.

Moscati, S. (ed.) [S. Moscati, A. Spitaler, E. Ullendorff, W. von Soden]. 1964. *An Introduction to the Comparative Grammar of the Semitic Languages. Phonology and Morphology*. Wiesbaden: Otto Harrassowitz.

Muchiki, Y. 1994. Spirantisation in fifth-century B.C. North-west Semitic. *JNES* 53: 125-30.

Müller-Kessler, Ch. 1991. *Grammatik des Christlich-Palästinisch-Aramäischen. Teil 1. Schriftlehre, Lautlehre, Formenlehre.* Hildesheim/Zürich/New York: Georg Olms.

Muraoka, T. 1966. Notes on the syntax of Biblical Aramaic. *JSS* 11:151-67.

_____. 1972. Notes on the Aramaic of the Genesis Apocryphon. *RdQ* 29:7-52.

_____. 1973. Review of *Israel Oriental Studies I* in *JSS* 18:169-72.

_____. 1974. The Aramaic of the Old Targum of Job from Qumran Cave XI. *JJS* 25:425-43.

_____. 1977. The status constructus of the adjective in Biblical Hebrew. *VT* 27:375-80.

_____. 1978. On the so-called *dativus ethicus* in Hebrew. *JThSt* 29:495-98.

_____. 1979. Hebrew philological notes. *AJBI* 5:88-104.

_____. 1983. On the morphosyntax of the infinitive in Targumic Aramaic. In *Arameans, Aramaic and the Aramaic Literary Tradition*, ed. M. Sokoloff, 75-79. Ramat Gan: Bar-Ilan University Press.

_____. 1983-84. The Tell-Fekherye bilingual inscritpion and Early Aramaic. *AN* 22.79-117.

_____. 1985. *Emphatic Words and Structures in Biblical Hebrew.* Jerusalem: The Magnes Press / Leiden:E.J. Brill.

_____. 1987. *Classical Syriac for Hebraists.* Wiesbaden: Otto Harrassowitz.

_____. 1992. The verbal rection in Qumran Aramaic. *AN Supplement* 3: 99-118.

_____. 1993a. Further notes on the Aramaic of the *Genesis Apocryphon.* *RdQ* 16:39-48.

_____. 1993b. *A Greek-English Lexicon of the Septuagint (Twelve Prophets).* Leuven: Peeters.

_____. 1995. Review of Kottsieper 1990. *JSS* 40: 332f.

_____. 1997a. Notes on the Aramaic of the Achiqar proverbs. In *Built on Solid Rock.* [Fschr E.E. Knudsen.], ed. E. Wardini, 206-15. Oslo: Novus forlag.

_____. 1997b. *Classical Syriac. A Basic Grammar.* With a Chrestomathy and a Select Bibliography Compiled by S.P. Brock. Porta Linguarum Orientalium 19. Wiesbaden: Harrassowitz.

_____. 1997c. The alleged final function of the Biblical Hebrew syntagm <w + a volitive verb form>. In *Narrative Syntax and the Hebrew*

Bible. Papers of the Tilburg Conference 1996, ed. E. van Wolde, 229-41. Leiden: E.J. Brill.

_____. 1997d. Review of Tropper (1993). *BO* 54:464-68.

_____. [Forthcoming]. On the Classical Syriac particles for "between."

_____. [Forthcoming]. The tripartite nominal clause in Biblical Hebrew revisited.

Mustafa, A.H. 1982. Die sogenannte Geminatendissimilation im Semitischen. *Hallesche Beiträge zur Orientwissenschaft* 4:13-39.

Naudé, J.A. 1994. The verbless clause with pleonastic pronoun in Biblical Aramaic. *JS* 6:74-93.

Naveh, J. 1970. *The Development of the Aramaic Script*. Jerusalem: The Israel Academy of Sciences and Humanities.

_____. 1971. The palaeography of the Hermopolis papyri. *IOS* 1:120-22.

Nebe, G.W. 1997. Die hebräische Sprache der Naḥal Ḥever Dokumente 5/6Ḥev 44-46, in *The Hebrew of the Dead Sea Scrolls and Ben Sira: Proceedings of a Symposium Held at Leiden University, 11-14 December 1995*, eds. T. Muraoka and J.F. Elwolde, 150-57. Leiden: E.J. Brill.

Nims, C.F. and R.C. Steiner. 1983. A paganized version of Psalm 20:2-6 from the Aramaic text in Demotic script. *JNES* 103:261-74.

Nöldeke, T. 1868a. *Grammatik der neusyrischen Sprache am Urmia-See und in Kurdistan*. Leipzig: O. Weigel.

_____. 1868b. Beiträge zur Kenntniss der aramäischen Dialekte; II Über den christlich-palästinischen Dialect. *ZDMG* 22:443-527.

_____. 1875. *Mandäische Grammatik*. Halle a.d. Saale: Buchhandlung des Waisenhauses.

_____. ²1898. *Kurgefasste syrische Grammatik*. Leipzig: Ch.H. Tauchnitz [1966: repr. with Anhang prepared by A. Schall, Darmstadt: Wissenschaftliche Buchgesellschaft].

_____. 1907. Die aramäischen Papyri von Assuan. *ZA* 20:130-50.

_____. 1910. *Neue Beiträge zur semitischen Sprachwissenschaft*. Strassburg: Trübner.

_____. 1913. Untersuchungen zum Achiqar-Roman. *Abhandlungen der Königlichen Gesellschaft der Wissen-schaften zu Göttingen* 14/4:1-63. Berlin: Weidmann.

Noth, M. 1928. *Die israelitischen Personennamen im Rahmen der gemeinsemitischen Namengebung*. Beiträge zur Wissenschaft vom Alten und Neuen Testament 46. Stuttgart: W. Kohlhammer.

Nyberg, H.S. 1938. Deuteronomium 33.2-3. *ZDMG* 92:320-44.

Opree, J. 1997. De konstituenten-patronen van de verbale zin in de Aramese- en de Babylonische versie van de Behistun-inscriptie. Leiden: Department of Near Eastern Studies, Leiden University.

Pardee, D. 1976. The preposition in Ugaritic. *UF* 8:215-322.

Paul, H. ⁶1960. *Prinzipien der Sprachgeschichte*. Tübingen: Max Niemeyer.

Pennacchietti, F.A. 1968. *Studi sui pronomi determinativi semitici*. Napoli: Istituto Orientale di Napoli.

Perles, F. 1911-12. Zu Sachaus 'Aramäischen Papyrus und Ostraka'. *OLZ* 14:497-503, 15:54-57.

Porten, B. 1968. *Archives from Elephantine. The Life of an Ancient Jewish Military Colony*. Berkeley and Los Angeles: University of California Press.

_____. 1984. The Jews in Egypt. In *The Cambridge History of Judaism*, vol. 1, Introduction; the Persian Period, eds W.D. Davies and L. Finkelstein, 372-446. Cambridge: Cambridge University Press.

_____. 1985. Two Aramaic contracts without dates: new collations (C11,49). *BASOR* 258:41-52.

_____. 1987. Cowley 7 reconsidered. *Or* 56: 89-92.

_____. 1996. [with J.J. Farber, C.J. Martin, G. Vittmann et al.] *The Elephantine Papyri in English. Three Millennia of Cross-cultural Continuity and Change*. Leiden: E.J. Brill.

_____. 1998(?). The revised draft of the letter of Jedaniah to Bagavahya (TAD A4.8 = Cowley 31). In *Boundaries of the Near Eastern Word: A Tribute to Cyrus H. Gordon - Four Score and Eight*, eds M. Lubetski et al. Sheffield: Sheffield Academic Press.

Porten, B. and J.C. Greenfield. 1968. The Aramaic papyri from Hermopolis. *ZAW* 80:216-31.

_____. 1974. Hermopolis Letter 6. *IOS* 4:14-30.

Porten, B. and H.Z. Szubin. 1987. An Aramaic deed of bequest (Kraeling 9). In *Community and Culture. Essays in Jewish Studies in honor of the Ninetieth Anniversary of the Founding of Gratz College: 1895-1985*, ed. N.M. Waldman, 179-92. Philadelphia: Gratz College Seth Press.

_____. 1992. An Aramaic joint venture agreement: a new interpretation of the Bauer-Meissner papyrus. *BASOR* 288: 67-84.

Porten, B., and A. Yardeni. 1986. *Textbook of Aramaic Documents from Ancient Egypt Newly Copied, Edited, and Translated into Hebrew and English*. Vol. 1, Letters: Appendix Aramaic Letters from the Bible. Department of the History of the Jewish People. Texts and Studies for Students. Jerusalem: The Hebrew University.

_____. 1989. *Textbook of Aramaic Documents from Ancient Egypt Newly Copied, Edited, and Translated into Hebrew and English*. Vol. 2, Contracts. Department of the History of the Jewish People. Texts and Studies for Students. Jerusalem: The Hebrew University.

_____. 1993. *Textbook of Aramaic Documents from Ancient Egypt Newly Copied, Edited, and Translated into Hebrew and English.* Vol. 3, Literature, Accounts, Lists. Department of the History of the Jewish People. Texts and Studies for Students. Jerusalem: The Hebrew University.

Qimron, E. 1981. ‏המלֹת **אשר**, ‏ש-, די בראש משפט עיקרי בעברית ובארמית [‏אשר, ‏ש (and ‏די) introducing a main clause]. *Leš* 46:27-38.

_____. 1986. *The Hebrew of the Dead Sea Scrolls.* Harvard Semitic Studies 29. Atlanta: Scholars Press.

_____. 1992. Pronominal suffix ‏כה in Qumran Aramaic. In *Studies in Qumran Aramaic* [*AN*, Supplement 3], ed. T. Muraoka, 119-23.

_____. 1993. ‏ארמית מקראית [*Biblical Aramaic*]. Jerusalem: The Bialik Institute.

Quirk, R., S. Greenbaum, G. Leech and J. Svartvik. 1972. *A Grammar of Contemporary English.* London: Longman.

Reckendorf, H. 1895-98. *Syntaktische Verhältnisse des Arabischen.* Leiden: E.J. Brill.

Rosenthal, F. 1936. *Die Sprache der palmyrenischen Inschriften und ihre Stellung innerhalb des Aramäischen.* Mitteilungen der vorderasiatisch-aegyptischen Gesellschaft 41/1. Leipzig: J.C. Hinrichs.

_____. 1939. *Die aramaistische Forschung seit Th. Nöldeke's Veröffentlichungen.* Leiden: E.J. Brill.

_____. 1961. *A Grammar of Biblical Aramaic.* Wiesbaden: Otto Harrassowitz.

Rowley, H.H. 1929. *The Aramaic of the Old Testament. A Grammatical and Lexical Study of its Relations with other Early Aramaic Dialects.* London: Oxford University Press.

Salonen, E. 1967. *Die Gruß- und Höflichkeitsformeln in babylonisch-assyrischen Briefen.* Studia Orientalia Fennica 38. Helsinki: Societas Orientalis Fennica.

Sarfatti, G.B. 1994. ‏ראשית אימות־הקריאה בכתב השמי המערבי. ניסיון של סיכום [The origin of vowel letters in West-Semitic writing: a tentative recapitulation.]*Leš* 58:13-24.

Schaeder, H.H. 1930. *Iranische Beiträge I*: Schriften der Königsberger Gelehrten Gesellschaft, Geisteswissenschaftliche Klasse, 6. Jahr, Heft 5. Königsberg.

Schulthess, F. 1924. *Grammatik des christlich-palästinischen Aramäisch.* Tübingen: J.C.B. Mohr.

Segal, J.B. 1983. *Aramaic Texts from North Saqqara with some Fragments in Phoenician.* Texts from Excavations, Memoir 6. London: Egyptian Exploration Society.

_____. 1987. Five ostraca re-examined. *Maarav* 4:69-74.

Segert, S. 1975. *Altaramäische Grammatik*. Leipzig: VEB Verlag Enzyklopädie.

_____. 1984. *A Basic Grammar of the Ugaritic Language*. Berkeley/Los Angeles/London: University of California Press.

Silverman, M.H. 1969. Aramean name-types in the Elephantine documents. *JAOS* 89:691-709.

Skaist, A. 1983. The *clasula* [sic!] *salvatoria* in the Elephantine and Neo-Assyrian conveyance document. In *Arameans, Aramaic and the Aramaic Literary Tradition*, ed. M. Sokoloff, 31-41. Ramat-Gan: Bar-Ilan University.

von Soden, W. 1965-81. *Akkadisches Handwörterbuch*. Wiesbaden: Otto Harrassowitz.

_____. ³1995. *Grundriß der akkadischen Grammatik*. Analecta Orientalia 33. Rome: Pontifical Biblical Institute.

Sokoloff, M. 1990. *A Dictionary of Jewish Palestinian Aramaic of the Byzantine Period*. Ramat Gan: Bar Ilan University Press.

Speiser, E.A. 1939. Progress in the study of the Hurrian language. *BASOR* 74:4-7.

Spitaler, A. 1954. Zur Frage der Geminantendissimilation im Semitischen. Zugleich ein Beitrag zur Kenntnis der Orthographie des Reichsaramäischen. *Indogermanische Forschungen* 61:257-66.

Staerk, W. ²1912. *Jüdisch-aramäische Papyri aus Elephantine*. Bonn: A. Marcus und E. Weber.

Steiner, R.C. 1991. *Addenda* to "The case for fricative-laterals in Proto-Semitic." In *Semitic Studies in Honor of Wolf Leslau*, ed. A.S. Kaye, vol. 2, 1499-1514. Wiesbaden: Otto Harrassowitz.

Steiner, R.C. and A.M. Moshavi.1995. A selective glossary of Northwest Semitic texts in Egyptian script. In Hoftijzer - Jongeling 1995:1249-66.

Steiner, R.C. and C.F. Nims. 1985. You can't offer your sacrifice and eat it too: a polemical poem from the Aramaic text in Demotic script. *JNES* 43:89-114.

Swiggers, P. 1982. The Hermopolis papyri III and IV. *AION* 42:135-40.

_____. 1988. Possessives with predicative function in Official Aramaic. In *Fucus. A Semitic/Afrasian Gathering in Remembrance of Albert Ehrman*, ed. Y.L. Arbeitman, Current Issues in Linguistic Theory 58, 449-61. Amsterdam / Philadelphia: John Benjamin.

Szubin, H.Z. and B. Porten. 1988. A life estate of usufruct: a new interpretation of Kraeling 6. *BASOR* 269:29-45.

Tallqvist, K. 1914. *Assyrian Personal Names*. Acta Societatis Scientiarum Fennicae, t. 43.1. Helsinki: Societas Scientiarum

Fennica.

Testen, D. 1985. The signifiance of Aramaic *r* < *n. *JNES* 44:143-46.

Tropper, J. 1993. *Die Inschriften von Zincirli. Neue Edition und vergleichende Grammatik des phönizischen, sam'alischen und aramäischen Textkorpus.* Abhandlungen zur Literatur Alt-Syrien-Palästinas 6. Münster: Ugarit-Verlag.

Tsereteli, K.G. 1991. About the state of nouns in Aramaic. In *Semitic Studies in Honor of Wolf Leslau,* ed. A.S. Kaye, vol. 2, 1571-76. Wiesbaden: Otto Harrassowitz.

Vleeming, S.P. and J.W. Wesselius. 1985. *Studies in Papyrus Amherst 63.* Amsterdam: Juda Palache Instituut.

Vogt, E. 1971. *Lexicon linguae aramaicae veteris testamenti documentis antiquis illustratum.* Rome: Pontifical Biblical Institute Press.

Voigt, R. 1991. Die sog. Schreibfehler im Altaramäischen und ein bislang unerkannter Lautwandel. *SO* 40:236-45.

_____. 1992. Die Lateralreihe /*š ṣ ẓ*/ im Semitischen. *ZDMG* 142:37-52.

Wagenaar, C.G. 1928. *De joodsche kolonie van Jeb-Syene in de 5de Eeuw voor Christus.* Groningen/Den Haag: J.B. Wolters.

Waltke, B.K. and O'Connor, M. 1990. *An Introduction to Biblical Hebrew Syntax.* Winona Lake: Eisenbrauns.

Wesselius, J.W. 1980. Reste einer Kasusflektion in einigen früharamäischen Dialekten. *AION* 40:265-68.

_____. 1984. Review of Greenfield - Porten 1982 in *BO* 41:440-45.

Whitehead, J.D. 1974. Early Aramaic epistolography: The Arsames correspondence. Diss., the University of Chicago.

Widengren, G. 1971. Aramaica et Syriaca. In *Hommages à André Dupont-Sommer,* eds A. Caquot and M. Philonenko, 221-31. Paris: Librairie d'Amérique et d'Orient.

Wilson, R.D. 1912. The Aramaic of Daniel. In *Biblical and Theological Studies by the Members of the Faculty of Princeton Theological Seminary,* 261-306. New York: Scribner.

Wright, W. [3]1896-98. Revised by W. Robertson Smith and M.J. de Goeje. *A Grammar of the Arabic Language.* 2 vols. Cambridge: Cambridge University Press.

Yalon, H. 1964. מבוא לניקוד המשנה [*Introduction to the Vocalization of the Mishna*]. Jerusalem: Bialik Institute.

Yaron, R. 1961. *Introduction to the Law of the Aramaic Papyri.* Oxford: Clarendon.

Zadok, R. [2]1978. *On West Semites in Babylonia.*

_____. 1985. Review of J.B. Segal, 1983. *WO* 16:173-76.

_____. 1988. *The Pre-Hellenistic Israelite Anthroponomy and Prosopography.* OLA 28. Leuven: Peeters, 1988.

Zuckerman, B. A fragment of an unstudied column of 11QtgJob: a
preliminary report. *Newsletter: The Comprehensive Aramaic
Lexicon* 10:1-7.

PART ONE

PHONOLOGY

§ 1. Preliminary remarks.

A study and description of phonetics and phonology of an ancient language attested only in written form is beset with familiar problems and difficulties. Firstly, to what extent does the Aramaic alphabet of twenty-two consonant letters represent the phonetic reality of the language of a given document? Is there one-to-one correspondence, so that the language possessed twenty-two consonants, not more nor less? Secondly, do the letters represent phonemic entities, or are they a mixture of phonemes and allophones? Thirdly, what can one learn about the phonetic character of each consonantal phoneme and/or allophone? Fourthly, vowels and prosody present particularly difficult problems.

In order to deal with these questions, a strictly descriptive approach does not seem to be adequate. Even if one's primary interest is confined to the language as used in a delimited corpus of written texts dating from an equally delimited period of time, one's description would gain extra clarity and perspective by judicious and controlled use of comparative and historical data. The adoption of such an approach may be considered almost mandatory where the text corpus is rather limited in extent.

In addition to comparative and historical data to be found in ancient cognate Semitic languages and diverse dialects of Aramaic, we are also in possession of data available in the form of non-Aramaic names (and occasional loan words) used in our corpus, but known in their original form in the source languages, or Aramaic words borrowed by other languages. When those other languages, like Greek and Akkadian, use vowel graphemes as well, the information to be gained from that source is extremely valuable. Even then, however, there are bound to remain a great deal of uncertainty and more than an element of circular argument, since our knowledge of the phonetics and phonology of those ancient languages is also incomplete. Moreover, no two languages possess an identical phonological system, so that due allowances need to be made for the incongruities between the two systems.

§ 2. Consonants

Our starting point is the familiar 22 consonantal letters: א,
ב, ג, ד, ה, ו, ז, ח, ט, י, כ, ל, מ, נ, ס, ע, פ, צ, ק, ר, ש, ת. There is hardly
room for doubt that they represented a minimum of 22 different
consonantal phonemes. It seems to us that the Aramaic of our
corpus possessed 26 distinct consonantal phonemes at an early
phase of the period covered by it.[1] Four out of the 22 letters of
the alphabet are bivalent: ד = PS /d/ and /ḏ/; ק = PS /q/ and /ḍ/; ש
= PS /š/ and /ś/; ת = PS /t/ and /ṯ/.

These consonantal phonemes, including semi-vocalic or
semi-consonantal /w/ and /y/, may be set out as below, although
one is naturally much in the dark as to the precise phonetic
nature of many such phonemes.[1a]

	plosive	fricative	lateral	latera-lised?	rolled	nasal	frictionless continuant
bilabial	p˙ (פ) b⁺ (ב)					m (מ)	w (ו)
inter-dental		t̲˙ (ת) d̲⁺ (ז)		g̲°̄ (ק)			
dental and al-veolar	t˙ (ת) d⁺ (ד) ṭ° (ט)	s˙ (ס) z⁺ (ז) ṣ° (צ)	l (ל)		ś (ש)	r (ר)	n (נ)
palato-alveolar		š (ש)					
velar	k˙ (כ) g⁺ (ג) q° (ק)						
pharyngal		ḥ˙ (ח) ᶜ⁺ (ע)					
laryngal		ʾ (א) h (ה)					
palatal							y (י)

---

[1] Segert (1975:93) admits only 22, the same number of the letters of the
alphabet.

[1a] The feature of voicing is indicated as ⁺ (voiced), ˙ (unvoiced or voiceless),
and that of "emphatic" as °.

Problems of interpretation arise regarding the following letters:

a) ד and ז(²)

The hypothesised Proto-Semitic voiced interdental /d̠/ or /ð/ is spelled in our corpus mostly with ז as in Old Aramaic. The later spelling with ד is confined to a small number of texts. There is none that uses ד exclusively. Some of them also use both the older and younger spellings side by side, often of the same word(s).(³) Thus once in A2.3 כדי (4) // כזי (7), and זי (2,6,12) and זנה 'this' (13); דכין 'pure' (A4.1:5) // זי (ib. 6) and זא 'this' (ib.2); demonstrative pronouns דכי (B2.8:9), דכא (ib.6) // זנה (ib.7,11) and consistently זי (5x); די (B3.4:12) // זי (passim in B3.4) and זכר 'male' (ib.21); דנה (A5.2:8,9; B3.11:3) // זי *bis* (A5.2:7) and // זנה (B3.11:7*bis*, 8*bis*,10,14,15,16,17); דה (A2.5:7) // זי (passim); ביתא זילך ודי בניך ודי תנתן לה רחמת 'the house is yours or your children's or his to whom you give (it) affectionately' (B3.12:30) // זי (passim in B3.12); דך 'that' (B3.10:10) and דילך 'your' (ib.14) // זילך (ib.11); דילכי (B2.7:7,11, 16) // זילי (ib.8) and זך (ib.9,13) and זי (passim); זכם 'selfsame' B2.9:4 // דכם B3.8:2, written by same scribe in same year (420 BCE); דהב 'gold' (B3.1:9) // זנה, זי (ib. passim) and // זהב passim in the corpus; אחד 'to take' (B3.4:5) // *אחז (e.g. B8.10:3 et passim); דכר 'male' B2.6:17, 20 // זי ib. passim and // זנה ib. Most instructive is one of the above-quoted documents, namely B3.4, which has זין וזבב 'suit or process' (17) // דין ודבב (12, 14). The spelling here with ז is best interpreted as hyper-correction(⁴): Haggai, on the alert for the common misspelling by ד for the correct ז, here inadvertently writing Zayin instead of the correct Dalet. This would indicate that, by 437 BCE when the document was drawn up, the sound in question was considered better represented by ד than by ז.(⁵)

---

² Cf. Folmer 1995: 49-63.

³ It does not seem to us right to ignore counter-evidences altogether, as Beyer (1984:100) does: whilst innovations, if genuine, often provide a valuable glimpse into possible changes taking place in the language, an attempt ought to be made to account for the co-existence of variations.

⁴ So Kutscher (1954:235); "hyper-archaic form" according to Blau (1970:47).

⁵ Beyer (1984:100), followed by Hug (1992:51), holds that as early as in the 9th century BCE the earlier dentals /t̠ d̠ t̠/ had shifted to / t d t̠ /. Strangely, there is no mention made of a reasonable case made by Degen (1969:32-4) to the contrary. Moreover, when one studies the evidence presented by Beyer, one notes that the dates apparently evidencing the changes in question vary significantly from one dental to another, the earliest being that of /t̠/ > /t/

Chronologically speaking, the earliest dated instance of ד for ז is למאחד 'to seize' B4.4:17 (483 BCE). From the first quarter of the 5th century come דרע 'arm' D7.9:4 and דכר 'to remember' D7.40:9. In addition, some examples from the Hermopolis papyri datable to the late 6th or early 5th century have been noted above: e.g. דא 'this' A2.5:7. Apart from these, the remaining examples are mostly, as far as they are datable, somewhat later, from the mid-5th century BCE.

Among our scribes, Haggai (446-400 BCE) stands out with 10 examples of Dalet for Zayin, followed by Nathan (459-446 BCE) (5x) and Mauziah (446-406 BCE) (3x). None of them, however, uses Dalet consistently.

In addition, one must also take note of names containing some of the roots already mentioned above: הדדעזר D14.1 vs. נשכעדרי; זבעדרי, אתעדרי, עדרי; יאזניה vs. יאדניה([6]). In general, proper nouns tend to be rather conservative, but even here absolute dogmatism is to be avoided: cp. עזריה C3.13:11 (411 BCE) vs. עדרי C3.8IIIA:8 (471 BCE). A complicating factor here is that some of these names are borne by Jews, and the question is to what extent their names had been Aramaised.

This orthographic fluctuation gives rise to a couple of questions as regards the phonetic reality lying behind it. On the one hand, it appears almost certain that by the end of the fifth century ד had come to be felt to stand closer to the phonetic value of the consonant in question, although such awareness appears to have existed already about a century earlier. However, it is not to be assumed outright that some significant phonetic or phonemic change had taken place in the course of the fifth century. It is quite possible that the grapheme <z> represented two distinct sounds or phonemes, namely /d̠/ and /z/, a thesis corroborated by the subsequent neat correspondence in Middle Aramaic, namely

---

(e.g., שׁקל > תקל), which generally agrees with what we see in our corpus as well. There is no absolute reason for assuming that phonetically kindred sounds underwent a certain change at the same speed.

[6] This last form also occurs in a variant spelling, ידניה, in one and the same document, A4.2. Silverman (1969:697) would derive the name from the root דין. However, the Alef in the middle of the form is hardly a vowel letter, whereas the syncope of a word-medial Alef is commonplace: a spelling יזניה also occurs. Grelot (1972:390 *r*, and 498) thinks the spellings with a Dalet are Aramaising forms. This presupposes, however, a degree of abstraction and etymologisation on the part of the Aramaic-speaking Elephantine Jews, since the root אזן, unlike in Hebrew, is not used as a verb in Aramaic: the Biblical name יַאֲזַנְיָה must ultimately derive from this root.

/d̲/ = ד and /z/ = ז([7]). Why /d̲/ began to be spelled with ד is puzzlesome. We may suggest tentatively that this had to do with the onset of the spirantization of the plosives, /d/ > /d̲/ after a vowel.([8]) In fact, the majority of the names and actually occurring forms of the verbs and nouns are those in which the grapheme in question does follow a vowel: e.g., כדי (with a so-called "vocal shewa") A2.3:4; most forms of the verb אחד 'to seize.' One may apply the same interpretation to cases of sandhi as well, e.g. מומאה דכי B2.8:9, though not every case of such a ד lends itself to such an explanation: e.g. ... למן די B3.4:12. Should this explanation be found acceptable([9]), it would give us a plausible and rough post quem for the process of spirantisation (see below § 3 j).([10]) The position of Leander (1928:9 i) is that the living language of our period had already undergone the change /d̲/ to /d/([11]), and he ascribes the use of <z> to the conser-vatism of the administrative officialese register of Aramaic, in other words this spelling is historical and etymological, although it is true that the innovative spelling with <d> is first attested in the Hermopolis papyri, private letters. Whilst Leander (ib.) rightly draws our attention to the fact that this <z> occurs mostly with the high-frequency pronouns, and verbs and nouns normally use <d>, the adverb אדין, which occurs 23 times in our corpus, is spelled with <d> without exception.([12]) Note also זהב, which occurs countless times as against דהב (1x; see above), and the noun זכרן 'record' (12x) and the verb זכר (יזכרני C1.1:53) as against דכרו (1x: A4.4:8).([13])

---

[7] For a similar argumentation, see Kottsieper 1990:27.

[8] See also Schaeder 1930:244.

[9] Cf. Muraoka 1983-84:90. For a similar view, see Lerner 1981. Folmer (1995:61f.), instead, attempts to account for the variation in terms of the position of the sounds in question within a word, initial or medial/final. The issue seems to us basically a phonetic/phonemic rather than graphemic one.

[10] Whereas Beyer (1984:127) also rightly holds that the spirantised allophones of /d, t/ could not have coexisted with the phonemes /d̲, t̲/, his dating for the onset of the spirantisation is rather late, 3rd century BCE, which is said to be the date of the disappearance of the latter phonemes from Aramaic. His cross-reference on this point to p. 100, however, is puzzling, for there he states that "das alte t̲ um 800 v. Chr. bereits geschwunden war. Die Dentale t̲ d̲ ṭ wurden also > t d ṭ im 10. oder 9., eher im 9. Jh. v. Chr."

[11] Kottsieper (1990:30) dates the completion of this process to as early as the end of the 7th century BCE.

[12] For a possible explanation, see Kutscher 1972:69.

[13] Thus Kottsieper (1990:30) is not very precise when he says: "Da im

The following words are consistently spelled with ד: אדין 'then' (e.g. B8.1:8); *אדן 'ear' (e.g. C1.1:215); *דבח 'animal sacrifice' A4.8:27; *מדבח 'altar' A4.7:26+; *דחל 'to fear' C1.1:45; *דנח 'to shine' C1.1:138†; מדנח 'east' B3.7:7†; *דרע 'arm' D7.9:4,5†; √ כדב 'to tell lies' B2.3:17+; *עדר 'assistance' C1.1:83+. We would mention here *אחז 'to seize,' which is spelled only once([14]) with ז, but some 26 times with ד.

b) ש

This grapheme also appears to be bivalent, representing two distinct phonemes, conventionally symbolised as /ś/ and /š/, on which latter see below at § *c*.([15]) Unlike in Middle Aramaic([16]), the PS phoneme /ś/ is fairly consistently spelled with ש, and very rarely with ס. Thus בשר 'flesh' C1.1:88; דמשק 'Damascus' A6.9:2; verb נשא 'to carry'; משאן 'shoe' A3.2:2([17]); עשרה 'ten' A6.2:11; שחר 'to destroy' C1.1:173†; שגיא 'much' A6.3:1; שהד 'witness' C1.1:140; שטר 'side' B2.1:5; ישמו 'May they put!' A6.6:1 (< שם 'to put'); שמוח PN C3.15:21,28 //(?) סמוח B4.6:3 (400 BCE); שנאתה 'what he hates' C1.1:132 (< שנאה 'hate'); שערן 'barley' (pl.) A4.10:14; שק 'sackcloth' A4.7:15; שרף 'to burn' A4.7:12. This applies to שפיק 'sufficiently' (A6.10:3,7) as well.([18]) The name of the Assyrian king Sennacherib is spelled in two different ways in the Ahiqar narrative: שנאחריב C1.1:3 and סנאחריב ib.50, whilst the Akkadian form is *Sin-aḫḫe:-eri:ba*.([19]) The only certain exceptions are סכין

Rarm. die Schreibungen mit *d* für /ḏ/ bei weitem überwiegen ..."

[14] B8.10:3.

[15] See Beyer (1984:102f.). An idiosyncratic view of Garbini (1993:43-49) on the evolution of sibilants in Northwest Semitic may be safely left out of account.

[16] Segert's scepticism (1984:91) is unjustified: "Es ist ungewiß, ob das ś sich erhalten hat oder ob es mit dem š zusammenfiel." How would one otherwise account for an etymologically neat orthographic distinction in later Aramaic between ש and ס?

Note that the earlier sibilant phoneme /ś/ distinct from /s/ still lingered on in Palmyrenian (Cantineau 1935:41-43 as against Rosenthal 1936:25f.) as well as in old Syriac inscriptions (Beyer 1966:243 and Muraoka 1997b: *9, n. 23, 10*, n. 48). The situation in Nabataean is more complicated: see Cantineau 1930:42-44.

[17] Cf. Akk. /še:nu/, QA מסאן (1QapGen 22.21), Syr. /suna:/, /msa:na:/, and Heb. סְאוֹן Is 9.4, all meaning 'shoe.'

[18] On the etymology of the word, see *HAL*, s.v., p. 1257, and Beeston (1977:56).

[19] In BH the name is always spelled with Samech: see Millard 1976:8.

'knife' C1.1:84,88 (Heb. שַׂכִּין[²⁰]) and סב 'old' B3.10:17 // שב 'old man' C1.1:17.(²¹) Possibly also סערן 'barley' D7.12:4; מסמרין 'nails' A6.2:16(²²); יסגה 'he shall proceed' C1.1:126 // ישגא D7.4:2. The interpretation of אל תסתכל at C1.1:147 is still disputed.(²³) No satisfactory interpretation has been found of שף at A4.2:10; A6.2:11,19, either. סמש 'sun' B3.6:9 for the usual שמש still remains a puzzle.(²⁴)

c) PS /t̲/.

Unlike in the case of the voiced interdental /d̲/, the PS unvoiced interdental /t̲/ is consistently spelled with ת(²⁵): e.g., תאתא 'ewe' D7.8:2; תוב 'again' B7.1:5; התיב 'he returned' B2.9:7; תור 'bull' A4.1:10; תלת 'three' A6.9:3; תקל 'to weigh' B2.6:24, C1.2:23†.(²⁶) The only certain exception is the ubiquitous monetary unit, שקל, often abbreviated as ש. The influence of the Akkadian šiqlu is suspected.(²⁷) Note four cases of תקל at B1.1:13bis; B3.1:5, B3.3:8, in each document // שקל B1.1:12, B3.1:3, B3.3:5,6,10,16.(²⁸)

---

²⁰ Kottsieper's identification of a root √סכ 'to cut' (1990:36) does not convince.

²¹ סערן D7.12:4 might also be considered if it means 'barley.' Cf. שערן D7.16:5.

²² On the etymology of the noun, see Gesenius - Buhl 1915:465.

²³ See a discussion in Lindenberger (1983:147f.).

²⁴ The simplest etymology, which seems to have remained unnoticed so far, of the verb נדש 'to destroy (?)' A4.5:24 etc. is Arb. /nadasa/ 'to throw down, bring to the ground.' The usually cited Arb. /nataša/ is difficult for a couple of reasons: /t/ for /d/ and its meaning "to pull out, snatch away," though the sibilant is no problem, for Arb. /š/ = Heb./Aram. /š/.

²⁵ A beginning of the development is foreshadowed by an exceptional form אל ירת 'let him not inherit' Sefire I C 24 for the regular ירש.

²⁶ Cf. Folmer 1995: 70-74.

²⁷ So already Schaeder (1930:243), but "historical spelling": Kaufman (1974:29).

Another instance where foreign influence has often been suspected is ישפטון 'they will contest' C1.1:88. See also ונשפט 'and we shall contest(?)' C3.3:5. Fales (1986:65) suspects that the Assyrian word may have sounded [siqlu], which would be in favour of Kaufman's position.

²⁸ Even the Ashur letter of ca. 650 BCE attests to יהתב (11) 'he shall return' alongside אשור 'Assyria' (ib.). There is no need to invoke, as Cowley (1923:205) does, Persian influence to account for the spelling אתור in the Ahiqar document. One may assume a PS /t̲/ in this name: see Degen 1967:55, 58 (n. 49), 60 and also Beyer 1984:100.

In אחי בתי ואנשתה 'my brother Bitia and his ?' A2.1:14, and particularly אחי בתי ואנשתה ובנוהי ' ... and his children' A2.4:3, the context requires 'his wife,' but then it would make a most unusual phonology (אנתתה = אנשתה). Yet one should not be dogmatic, since among the Hermopolis papyri there does not occur any other word or form with ת corresponding to the primitive /t̠/, so that we cannot tell whether this idiom still retained the earlier /t̠/ spelled with ש or not.[29]

Finally, if the reading be certain at שחלין D7.45:8, it could be a form of JA תַּחְלֵי and Syr. /taḥla:/ 'cress.'

Whilst both of the two Proto-Semitic interdentals would eventually become corresponding plosives, it appears that the speed of the change was not the same. Furthermore, it is not likely that the grapheme ש ever represented three phonemes in our period: /š/, /ś/, and /t̠/.

d) ק and ע[30]

The Proto-Semitic voiced emphatic interdental /ḍ/ is represented by these two graphemes.[31] The spelling with ק is decidedly more frequent.[32] The word עק 'tree, timber' in all its forms (עק, עקא, עקי, עקיא, עקהן, עקן, עקא) is always spelled with ק as the second consonant. Also spelled with ק are קן 'sheep' A4.1:10, sg.det.

---

[29] One possible way-out of this enigma may be to postulate a variant lexeme (with a prosthetic א?) *אנשה related to the pl. נשן. See also Swiggers 1982:136. Incidentally, the preservation of /n/ against its near total assimilation in the Hermopolis papyri (see § 3 *a*) indicates the presence of a vowel after the /n/. Hug (1993:51) apparently assumes a historical spelling. Folmer (1995:73) favours Kutscher's view (1971:115f.) that the word is cognate with אנשותא, which in Syriac, for instance, means 'servants, relatives, family.' But that would make the logical sequence of the three terms in our Hermopolis document somewhat unusual.

[30] Cf. Folmer 1995: 63-70.

[31] From this spelling fluctuation and the historical development ק > ע Segert (1975:91) concludes that the consonant in question must have been a postvelar spirant, no interdental. This may be right for this transition period, but it is not clear how the consonant may have sounded earlier when it was consistently spelled with ק. See further Steiner (1991) and Dolgopolsky (1994).

Voigt (1992) argues for a voiced lateral for Egyptian Aramaic as well as for Proto-Semitic. As far as Egyptian Aramaic is concerned, his theory is not supported by the available evidence, which does not display a neat graphic distribution as Voigt would have, and the only instance for such a voiced lateral is עלע 'rib,' which occurs but once in his corpus.

[32] On the question how the phoneme so represented may have sounded in OA, see, for example, Kutscher 1972:16.

קנא, D7.1:4; לעבק 'quickly' B3.11:6 and עבק 'hurry' C1.1:87.[33] Graphic alternation occurs in three words: ארק (22x) 'ground' // ארע (9x); קמר (21x) 'wool' // עמר (10x); לערק (6x) 'to meet, towards' and ערקי impv. fs. 'Meet!' D7.16:2 // לערע (1x). Chronology does not offer a satisfactory explanation: ארק and ארע occur in the same document dated to 464 BCE (B2.2:6,16) just as in BA Jer 10.11; קמר occurs in two documents datable to 420-400 BCE (A3.8:9; B3.8:6,7) and four times in C3.7 (475 BCE), but עמר 4 times in Hermopolis papyri (A2.2:7,9,16; A2.6:10) and at B2.6:7,10 (458 BCE); לערע 1x (C2.1:9), but לערק in the same document (the Bisitun text: C2.1:12+ 5x). עלע (Arb. ḍila') 'rib' occurs only once at C1.1:90. The word מועא 'east' is always (16x) spelled with ע, never with ק. Note also תרחענה 'you will wash it' D7.8:7 and ארחעה 'I will wash it' ib.11.

As in the case of the spelling flunctuations discussed above, this one is also difficult of interpretation. Is the use of ק an archaism? The presence of both in a single document, the Bisitun text, suggests that at least at the time of the writing of the Elephantine copy of the document, say ca. 421BCE, the phonetic development was not complete yet. On the other hand, Jer 10.11 with both אַרְקָא and אַרְעָא shows that the process had begun by the beginning of the 6th century at the latest.[34]

e) PS /z̧/

The Proto-Semitic emphatic interdental /z̧/ is still represented once by צ as in OA[35]: נצר 'he preserved' A1.1:8, but generally by ט as in later Aramaic, e.g. מטאו 'they reached' ib. 4; טללך 'your shadow' C1.2:6; טביא 'gazelle' C1.1:168; יעט 'counsellor' ib.12; עטה 'advice' ib.57; למנטר 'to guard' ib.191.

f) PS /ḡ/

There is no direct evidence whatsoever to be found in our corpus for the existence of a Proto-Semitic /ḡ/, which is sometimes postulated for a word such as בעה 'to seek.'[36]

---

[33] Despite the often-quoted article by Perles (1911-12) and one by Grelot (1956), Nöldeke (1913:12) confesses to his ignorance of the Arabic root ʿbd or ḡbd. Grelot's etymology is based on a supposed Ugaritic word. See also Beyer 1994:42. The idiom appears in its late form לעבע at 1QapGen 20.5,9. Cf. also Vleeming - Wesselius 1985:25f.

[34] Note a cuneiform transliteration a-ra for ארע 'earth' of the 6/5th century BCE, though one should not, on the strength of this evidence, go quite as far as Beyer (1984:101): "ḡ wurde also um 600 v. Chr. > ʿ."

[35] Degen 1969:35f. Perhaps also in Deir Alla: Hoftijzer 1976:284.

[36] Even for an earlier period, i.e. 7-6th centuries BCE, covered by Hug

g) PS /ḥ/ and /ḫ/

The same reservation is in order as regards the possible distinction between /ḥ/ and /ḫ/.[37]

§ 3. Consonantal changes

It appears that some consonants undergo certain changes due to contact with another consonant, whether identical or different, whether in direct and immediate contact or at some remove.

a) *Assimilation and non-assimilation of /n/*[38]

An /n/ followed immediately by another consonant sometimes assimilates regressively to the latter. This is the traditional and probable explanation for there being no graphic trace of such an /n/: e.g., אתנה (= אנתננה) 'I will give it' A2.1:5; נתן (= ננתן) 'we shall give' A4.10:13; חטן (= /ḥiṭṭi:n/ ?) "wheat" B4.1:2 // חנטן C3.28:77 and חנטתא C1.1:129; אתת [= אנתת] 'the wife of' A4.4:5*bis*[39]; יחתון (= ינחתון) 'they will descend' G impf. 3mpl (C1.2:6); הלה (= הן לא) 'if not' A2.2:10; שתא (= שנתא) 'the year' D7.40:2. Leander's position that the assimilation is largely confined to late documents (Leander 1928:14) is no longer tenable. It is attested in B1.1, the Bauer-Meissner papyrus of 515 BCE: אתננהי 'I shall give it' (11), תשא 'you shall carry' (13); אצל probably Afel, 'I shall reclaim' (14). Whilst it may be dialectal, the assimilation of /n/ is quite common in the Hermopolis papyri of the late 6th/early 5th century BCE[40]: אתננה 'I will give it' A2.1:5; נתנהי 'we shall give it' ib.7; מפקן A ptc. mpl. of √ נפק 'to exit'

(1992:50), its existence may be assumed only on the strength of cuneiform transcriptions with <ḫ>. The same applies to a slightly earlier time span, 9-7th cent. BCE: see Beyer 1984:101. However, the papyrus Amherst 63 of the late 2nd cent. BCE from Thebes still retains the distinction: Steiner - Nims 1985:93. E.g., /zġyr/ 'small' but /ʿlm/ 'eternity': for references and other examples, see Steiner - Moshavi 1995. But note that the representation of the PS emphatic interdental, /ḍ/ is not uniform in this text: thus <ʾrq> 'earth' on one hand and <ġn> 'flock' on the other. See also Fales 1986:73f.

[37] *Contra* Hug (1992:49), for instance. However, the papyrus Amherst 63, mentioned in the preceding note, still retains the distinction: Nims - Steiner 1983:263. E.g., /ʾḥ/ 'brother' but /ʾnḥn(h)/ 'we': for references and more examples, see Steiner - Moshavi 1995.

[38] Cf. Folmer 1995:74-94, esp. 76-84.

[39] This and the following case are merely two random examples disproving the theory of Gropp (1990:173-75) that the non-assimilation/dissimilation is typical of Elephantine legal papyri and the Arsames correspondence.

[40] On their dating, see Naveh (1971:122).

A2.5:3; אפקני 'he brought me forth' A2.6.4; למחתה A inf. of √ נחת 'to bring down' A2.5:6; אפיך 'your face' A2.1:2. In fact, the language of the Hermopolis papyri is consistent in this regard([41]), whereas that of the Bauer-Meissner papyrus is mixed, for we also find forms such as אנתן (10), cf. also אלקח (9). On the contrary, the fact that the assimilation of /n/ is also a regular and known feature of Old Aramaic([42]) points rather to the reverse of Leander's view.([43])([44]) That the chronology is only one of several possible factors involved is indisputable in view of מהנחת 'to bring down,' מלקח 'to take,' and the like in the 9th cent. BCE Tel Fekheriyeh bilingual.([45])

The general tendency in our corpus, however, is unquestionably towards writing נ in such cases.([46]) This is true, for instance, with independent personal pronouns of the 2nd person: אנת, אנתי([47]), אנתם (see below § 11). Of more than 100 occurrences of the verb נתן in G impf. and inf. we find only five examples of the assimilated first Nun.([48]) Note also נתנת 'you gave' B4.2:1,

---

[41] On forms such as מדעם A2.3:10 and תדען 'you will know' A2.5:2, see below § 31 a. One could thus take a spelling זבנת 'I bought' as an indication that already at this early stage the Pf. 1s morpheme /-t/ was, as in later Aramaic, preceded by a vowel. Cf. ḥa-al-li-tú 'I entered' (BA עַלֵּת) (line 4, 29) and za-ki-it 'I won' (Syr. zkē:t) (line 10) in the Uruk incantation text.

[42] See Degen (1969:39f. esp. with n. 35). I fail to comprehend Hug (1993:53): "Etymologische Schreibung mit n ist in älteren Texten die Regel und nimmt in HermB [=Hermopolis papyri] etwas ab"

[43] For Kutscher (1971:106), this aspect and the associated one of degemination by means of /n/ (see below § c) prove the western origin of these papyri, for he lists the assimilation of /n/ as one of the traits typical of Western Aramaic. At least in this matter, these private letters might display spellings which are more phonetic than historical and "correct."

[44] Segert (1975:112) "Die assimilierten Formen kommen im Rahmen des RA fast ausnahmslos in den Ostraka vor, ..." I do not see on what basis Segert can say this.

[45] See our discussion in Muraoka (1983-84:91f.). It should not be taken for granted, however, that מלקח necessarily belongs here, for the assimilation of /l/ in this case in Semitic is strictly not of the same order as that of /n/, for it was most likely triggered by a semantic analogy to יתן.

In his characterisation of Old Aramaic Garr (1985:42,44) leaves the Fekheriyan evidence out of account.

[46] An important exception is כעת 'now,' which is considerably more frequent than כענת: 79 vs. 19.

[47] At B3.7:13 the Nun has been added above the line.

[48] A2.1:5, B1.1:11, D1.1:12, D1.17:8,9. For further details on Pe-Nun

4.3:12. Take another high-frequency verb, נפק: 9 cases[49] of assimilation as against some 73 of נ remaining. The same holds for nouns: אנפין 'our presence' A4.2:8,9 and several forms of the noun (as against the consistent spelling without Nun of the noun in the Hermopolis papyri: A2.1:2, A2.2:2, A2.3:2, A2.5:2, A2.6:2 and אפנא 'our presence' C3.28:1,91); אנתתך 'your wife' B2.2:4; מנדת, מנדתא 'rent(?)' A6.13:3; מדינתא (and not *מדיתא as in 1QapGen 22.4 מדיתון) 'the province' A6.1:2; ספינתא (and not *ספיתא) 'the boat' A6.2:3; עזא 'the goat'; שנתא 'the year' C1.2:5 // שתא D7.40:2. Note also the usual spelling מנפי 'Memphis(?)' A3.3:10 + 10x as against מפי A2.2:3. Absolute consistency is not to be expected: thus אנפי ... אפיכי 'my face ... your face' D7.16:12.

There is not a single case of <n> of the preposition מן assimilated to the following consonant[50]: thus מן סון 'from Syene' A2.5:3.[51]

b) *Assimilation of consonants other than /n/*

In OA the verb לקח G 'to take' shows the assimilation of /l/[52] in impf. and inf., though not without an exception such as ילקח for יקח at Sefire I B.35.[53] In our corpus ל is consistently written[54], the only exception being ויקחונה D4.8:1: אלקח B1.1:9; ילקח B3.8:36; ילקחו D7.39:6; תלקחן C1.1:167; למלקח inf. B2.4:11. The impv., however, shows no Lamed: קח D1.14:2, קחי D20.5:3: see § 33 d.[55]

---

verbs in this respect, see below § 33.

[49] A2.5:3, A2.6:4, D3.27:2, D5.6,8, D6.14:1, D7.7:6,8, D7.14:3.

[50] The assimilation is not infrequent in BA: e.g., Dn 4.22 מִטַּל שְׁמַיָּא; Dn 6.5 מִן־טַעַם אֱלָהּ יִשְׂרָאֵל וּמִטַּעַם כּוֹרֶשׁ Ezr 6.14; מִצַּד מַלְכוּתָא.

[51] *Pace* Greenfield (1968:366), a text which is difficult anyway is hardly good evidence for a single exception: B4.1:4 מכל 'food' rather than מן כל = .

[52] Segert's explanation (1975:113) that this is due to the proximity of the points of articulation of /l/ and /q/ is less likely than that of Ungnad (1905:278), who thinks of the analogy of the antonym נתן with יתן, a proposal followed by Brockelmann (1908:176), Bergsträsser (1918:108) and Joüon - Muraoka (1993: § 72 j).

[53] On this exception, possibly twice attested, see a discussion by Degen (1969:40 with n. 38).

[54] Thus Leander (1928:14) suggests a scribal error in יקחונה at D4.8:1, though it is going a little too far to condemn קח impv. at D20.5:3 also as an error for לקח for one would not correct every impv. of the type חת 'Come down!' and טר 'Watch!' See below on Pe-Nun verbs: § 33.

[55] Unlike in OA our idiom does not attest to the assimilation of /l/ of the verb סלק 'to ascend' as in Sefire III 14 יסק, though we do find two cases of

Assimilation seems to be conditioned by the presence of a dental consonant as one of two contiguous sounds: /dt/ - ילתי < ילדתי G pf. 2fs 'you gave birth' B3.6:5,8 (// לידתי [= ילדתי] ib.6); /ld/ - עדבר < על דבר 'on account of' B7.1:3([56]); /td/ - אדני tG([57]) impv. ms < אתדני (√ דני) 'Approach!' C1.1:107. Note also עזנה 'until this (day)' A4.7:20 where ד has been added above the line, i.e. עד זנה.

A possible case of /zd/ > /zz/ is אזהר 'Guard yourself!' C2.1:65, namely < *אזדהר.([58])

That the assimilation of /l/ in יקח etc. does not appear to have any phonetic motivation is another reason to suggest that the assimilation is due to the analogy of יתן etc.([59])

There is evidence for mere graphic simplification with no phonetic implication.([60]) מתכל 'relying' A2.7:2 is a mere short-hand for *מתתכל, unless one postulates spirantisation, thus /*mittkel/ > /mittkel/. Note also אל תתכלי 'Do not rely!' D7.16:4. Likewise זבן = *זבנן 'we sold' B3.12:3 and זבנהי 'we sold it' B3.4:5 = *זבנהי.

c) *Degeminating* /n/([61])

It is a well-known fact that the nasal /n/ is sometimes found in IA where it is not etymologically expected *and* instead of gemination: כנדן 'jars' C3.7Gr2:8 etc.(> Akk. *kandu*); כנכרין 'talents' A4.7:28; [ב]מנציעת 'in the middle of' A4.5:5 // במציעתא C3.28:112([62]); forms of the verb √ עלל 'to enter'([63]) - למנעל G inf.

מנסק with a typically degeminating <n>: see below. According to Degen (1969:41) Spitaler sees here an analogy of נחת. Note a juxtaposition of the two verbs as in לןמנסק ולמנחת 'to go up and down' B3.7:10; למנסק עלא ולמנחת ולמנפק ברא 'to go up and down and go out' ib. 13.

[56] Likewise עד דְּבְרַת דִי Dn 4.14 // עַל דִּבְרַת דִי Dn 2.30. Note also ועשנתך 'and during your years' (< על שנתך) Pap. Amherst 63:6/14.

[57] Rather than Afel (Lindenberger 1983:175). See also Kottsieper (1990:40).

[58] See below, § 29.

[59] See n. 52 above.

[60] *Contra* Segert (1975:114), who thinks that עשת C1.1:68 = *עשתת 'I thought,' even granting that it is a pf., not a ptc., the text is broken just after the Taw. On our view that there most probably intervened a vowel between the last radical of a verb root in the perfect tense and the personal suffix for 1sg., hence no likelihood of assimilation, see below at § 24 *e*.

[61] Other terminologies are also used: e.g. "substitution of nasalization for gemination" (Rosenthal 1961:16); "dissolution of gemination" (Kaufman 1977:92). See further Kutscher (1970:374).

[62] This must be a noun of a rather rare pattern /mVqti:l/, on which see Barth 1894:252, 265. The initial <m> is not a root letter, for the word is

A6.7:7; הנעלת H pf. 3fs. B2.6:6,7,24; יהנעלן H impf. 3mpl. A3.8:12; הנעלו H impv. m.pl. A6.10:7. Here also belongs [ל]מנסק G inf. of סלק 'to ascend' B3.7:10 // למסלק B3.10:15([64]); מנדע 'knowledge' C1.1:53. According to Kottsieper (1990:54-58), the nasal of the word צנפר 'bird' (C1.1:82,186,198) is an infix, not a result of the degeminated /p/.([65])

However, no example such as יִנְדְּעוּן, תִּנְדַּע (< ידע) of BA([66]) occurs in our corpus. On the other hand, the indefinite pronoun for 'something' occurs in two forms: מדעם A2.3:10 + 4x and מנדעם A4.7:14 + 20x (including the declined form מנדעמתא, e.g. A4.7:12). As against the common view which derives the word from ידע 'to know' with a nominal prefix /m-/, Kottsieper (1990:51-54) has made a reasonable case for an alternative etymology of the word, according to which /n/ would be part of the interrogative /man/ 'who?' Then the /n/-less form could only have resulted from the assimilation of /n/ to the following /d/. All the examples of the assimilation of /n/ are to be found in early documents dating from the late 6th or early 5th century BCE: A2.1:10, A2.3:10, A2.5:2 (all Hermopolis papyri); B4.1:3,4.([67])

Whether כרסא 'throne' occurring at B2.2:2 and C1.1:133 attests to a case of degemination by means of /r/ (cf. Heb. כִּסֵּא and Akk. *kussû*) is debatable: see Kaufman (1974:28f.).([68]) דַּרְמֶשֶׂק 'Damascus' in Late Biblical Hebrew (Chronicles) for דַּמֶּשֶׂק is an assured case of such process; cf. also Syr. /darmsuq/.([69])

d) *Phonetic reality of degeminating /n/*
The difficult question to answer is whether these degeminating

---

derived from √ מצע.

[63] The interpretation of יעל C1.1:205 is debated: see Lindenberger (1983:205) and Kottsieper (1990:51).

[64] The forms such as יסק G impf. and למסק inf. may be due to the analogy of יחת and למחת respectively from נחת 'to descend,' its antonym. So also Spitaler apud Degen (1969:41). See n. 55 above.

[65] Note, however, that Arabic, on which Kottsieper's argument rests quite heavily, has ʿuspu:r.

[66] See Bauer - Leander (1927:50, 142), and below § 31 *a*. At D4.25:1 ל[מנדעם the text is too fragmentary for us to determine precisely what the form is.

[67] Note, however, מנדעם A2.5:4 (Hermopolis).

[68] The form כרסא is attested already in Fekheriyan (line 13), as pointed out by Lipiński 1994:63.

[69] Cf. Brockelmann (1908:245, g, z) and Bergsträsser (1918: § 20b).

consonantal graphemes, especially <n>, as well as etymological <n>'s discussed above (§ *a*), carried their usual consonantal value, so [yinten], or as some authorities argued, were a mere orthographic device for indicating the length of the following consonant, so [yitten].([70]) Kottsieper (1990:58), having concluded that this kind of <n> in the dialect of the Vorlage of the proverbs of Ahiqar was clearly audible, goes on to say that, in IA, by contrast, it was nothing but a matter of etymological orthography, lacking any phonetic reality.([71]) Whilst one may agree that in Early IA the etymological /n/ tended([72]) to assimilate, it is patently untrue that the <n> in forms such as הנעלו H impv. mpl. of עלל√ is etymologically conditioned.([73]) Besides, the hypothesis of mere orthographic convention([74]) would not adequately account for the reading tradition as preserved in, for instance, the Tiberian tradition of Biblical Aramaic with the use of shewa as יִנְדְּעוּן. To disregard such evidence seems to us to be tantamount to throwing out the baby with the bathwater.([75]) Tiberian scholars could always

---

[70] So Spitaler (1954), who was harshly criticised by Macuch (1965: XLVII-LIII), though the latter has subsequently reassessed his position in favour of the former (1990:232-37).

[71] As an argument for his position, Kottsieper (ib.) writes: "sie [= IA scribes] oft genug ein etymologisch anzusetzendes /n/ vor Konsonant nicht in der Schrift ausdrückten," without mentioning a single case of the kind. What appears in small print (ib., c) shows that he is somewhat hesitant.

[72] We mentioned already conflicting evidence in the Bauer-Meissner papyrus (late 6th century) - אתהני vs. אנתן, which shows that the picture is not clear-cut. Furthermore, that the antiquity cannot be the sole relevant dimension is proven by a much earlier Aramaic document, the Tel Fekheriyeh bilingual (9th century?), where one finds מהנחת 'bringing down' (line 2). It is not, of course, certain that here also we have to do with a case of degemination, for it may represent a stage prior to the onset of assimilation. This inscription contains three examples of the ל of the verb לקח G preserved. See our discussion in Muraoka (1983-84:91f.).

[73] Unless one postulates, along with Bergman (1968), a secondary root *נעל on the analogy of its antonym, נפק.

[74] So also Folmer 1995: 89f.

[75] He who takes the Tiberian tradition as the starting point for a discussion on Biblical Aramaic would not necessarily have to postulate that the G impv. of ידע would have been בְּדַע, as Beyer (1984:91) would require: "diese Aussprache [= without /n/] wird durch den Imperativ qal I*n* bestätigt, der im gesamten Reichsaramäisch ohne *n* gebildet wird." Likewise, one would have seriously to take into account the possibility of two alternative forms existing side by side as in BA: יִנְתֵּן Dn 2.16 // יִתְנַהּ Dn 4.14, which is in contrast to

have resorted to the Qre/Ktiv device if such <n> had been trans-
mitted to them as silent. On the other hand, to suggest that
"nasalization was always present but often ... not written"
(Kaufman 1974:121, n. 23)[76] is going too far in the other
direction. For at the time when the practice of not writing such
<n> was first introduced, it must have been an attempt to reflect
a certain phonetic reality, i.e. the absence of /n/.[77]

  e) /ʔ/ > /tt/

This type of assimilation[78] happens to be confined to tG
(Ethpeel) of Pe-Alef verbs, as in some later Aramaic dialects[79]:
אתחדו (< אתאחדו) 'they were seized' A4.4:6. Likewise יתסר < יתאסר
'he will be restrained' C1.1:175, if not from √ יסר 'to discipline.'[80]
The evidence available is too scanty to allow us to determine
whether the assimilation was conditioned by the presence or
absence of a full vowel immediately after /ʔ/. In any case, the
only example of tD[81] in our corpus has retained א: יתאלף 'he

---

Beyer's position: "eine einheitliche Aussprache des Reichsaramäischen voraus-
gesetzt" (1984:91). Beyer (1984:90f.,92), however, does admit the existence
of an earlier Babylonian substratum of IA, which did not assimilate /n/.

[76] Approvingly cited by Kottsieper (1990:59, n. 233).

[77] Thus *pace* Degen (1969:40, Anm. 1). That *ḫa-an-du-a-te* on a cuneiform
tablet from Nineveh is represented in Aramaic as הודה does not prove, *pace*
Kottsieper (1990:59f.), that, in the Aramaic idiom represented here, an /n/
was phonetically present before the /d/. On the contrary, one may conclude
that the Aramaic idiom in question was in the habit of assimilating an /n/ in a
phonetic environment such as presented here. To say, as Kottsieper (1990:60,
n. 236) does with respect to another Assyrian/Aramaic contrast, "nichts spricht
dafür, daß der assyrische Schreiber den Namen anders aussprach als der
aramäische" may be dogmatic. On the other hand, a cuneiform representation
such as *manḫalu* 'entrance' for Aram. מנעל, mentioned by Kutscher (1970:374),
probably indicates the phonetic reality of the <n> of the Aramaic word.

[78] Assumed on the basis of later Aramaic traditions, such as Syriac.

[79] On Syriac, see Nöldeke (1898:113) and Widengren (1971:221-23). See
also Morag (1988:169f.) on the Aramaic of the Babylonian Talmud. Dalman
(1927:298) assumes, for Palestinian Jewish Aramaic, the gemination of /t/ as
compensation for the loss of /ʔ/, whilst the Yemenite vocalised Targum Onkelos,
Taj, points the Taw with a dagesh in those examples mentioned by Dalman
when no Alef is written, e.g. Nu 31.30 אִתְּחַד; Dt 23.26 תִּתְּגַר.

[80] See Lindenberger (1983:46f.), and esp. Kottsieper (1990:145).

[81] Kottsieper (1990:42) does not take into account the fact that this verb is
most likely of a different binyan than the two remaining ones mentioned
above.

will be instructed,' /yiṭallap/(?).([82])

f) *Partial assimilation /t/ > /ṭ/*

The adjective עתיק 'old' is also spelled עטיק: B3.10:22, B3.11:15, B3.12:31 (// עתיק ib.29)†, all by same scribe. This looks like a case of partial and optional—note עתיק B3.12:29—assimilation of ת to its emphatic counterpart ט in the vicinity of the emphatic ק.([83])

g) /b/ > /p/

Another interesting variation involves a personal name. An obviously Jewish name מבטחיה, which occurs many a time in our corpus (e.g., B2.3:2), is spelled מפטחיה (e.g., B2.6:3), in fact more often with פ than with ב: 23x vs. 14x. A similar alternation is attested with their shortened forms: מבטח B2.3:36, מפטח B3.6:17. Scribes for whom we possess more than one document write consistently either ב (Attarshuri in B2.3 and B2.4) or פ (Nathan son of Ananiah in B2.6 and B2.7).([84]) Both spellings occur on a roughly comparable chronological span: ב 460 - 400 and פ 485 (or 445) - 400 BCE. It appears that, where the voiced labial, /b/, is not followed by a vowel, it undergoes partial assimilation to the following voiceless consonant, /ṭ/.([85]) Note a similar alternation with respect to the feature of voicing in Modern Hebrew: e.g. הִבְטִיחַ [hiftiaḥ] 'he promised'; הֶסְבֵּר [hezber] 'explanation.' See below, § *j*.

h) *Progressive assimilation*

There is found in our corpus one instance wherein a consonant closing a syllable influences the immediately following consonant: in אזדהרי (< אזתהרי) tD impv. f.sg. 'Take care!' (√ זהר) A2.1:8 where /t/ has become its voiced counterpart /d/ under the influence of the voiced sibilant /z/.([86]) Likewise אזדהרו tD impv.m.pl. A4.1:5.

---

[82] Syr.: /net(ʔ)allaf/. See our reference to Dalman's view cited above in n. 79. The picture in the Aramaic of the Babylonian Talmud is not clear-cut: see Morag (1988:174).

[83] That the word is most likely cognate with Akk. /eteːqu/ and Ugr. /ʕtq/, both 'to pass by,' speaks against Segert (1975:108), who regards עתיק as dissimilated from עטיק.

[84] The only exceptions are C3.15:25 with ב, but with פ at line 138. For the form with ב at B2.8:2, one with פ occurs at ib.14 in the endorsement, which appears to be by a different hand. The name of the scribe of B5.5 has not been preserved.

[85] Cf. also Beyer 1994:278f.

[86] See also below, § *r* on metathesis.

i) *Dissimilation*([87])

The process opposite to what has just been described above seems to occur less frequently. The consonant ק sometimes dissimilates to its non-emphatic counterpart, כ, when it is followed, immediately or otherwise, by another emphatic within the same word.([88]) Three such examples occur in the Proverbs of Ahiqar: כצפה 'his anger' C1.1:85; הכצר כל כציר 'Harvest every harvest!' C1.1:127; כשיטא 'upright' C1.1:158.([89]) The only other examples to be found elsewhere are בכצת 'in part' C3.11:9 // קצתה 'its part' or 'the part' (= קצתא) A2.2:7; כרצי < קרצי 'calumny' D20.5:2. These few examples do not allow us to determine with certainty whether the sequence of the emphatics is a determining factor or not, for derivatives of √ צדק with ק following another emphatic, never show similar dissimilation.([90]) On the other hand, עזכתיה D7.57:7 (for the standard spelling עזקתיה), if it mean 'its seals,' seems to attest to unconditioned dissimilation. Note also קתן C3.11:12 // כתן ib.4, should the former also mean 'flax.'([91])

An example which does not involve emphatics, but two identical sibilants is סמשא B3.6:9 for שמשא, i.e. /šimšaʔ/ or /šamšaʔ/.([92]) Finally, we would note in passing תרין 'two' over against תנין 'second,' and בר 'son' over against בנין 'sons.' The obviously secondary forms with /r/ instead of /n/ seem to have something to do with the (virtual) absence of a vowel before the original /n/ and the word-initial consonant.([93])

---

[87] Cf. Folmer 1995: 94-101.

[88] The same phenomenon is attested already in OA: כיצא 'summer.' See Degen (1969:42).

[89] Cf. a discussion by Kottsieper (1990:42).

[90] The word קטל, though with <q> preceding, does not show dissimilation in our idiom as in OA, e.g., Tel Dan line 6 ואקתל 'and I killed,' though we do find יכמלוך 'may they kill you' in an early 7th century document, not from Egypt, but from Nerab in Southern Syria, and that a different mode of dissimilation compared with אקתל just quoted. Moreover, the original shape of the root is disputed: קתל or קטל. On this last issue, see Kutscher 1972:22 and Garr 1985:72, n. 168. If it were קתל, the Nerab example would present a complex process: assimilation followed by dissimilation!

[91] Folmer (1995:99) assumes that it does, whereas for Hoftijzer - Jongeling (1995:1040) its meaning is unknown.

[92] Cf. Arabic /šams/, for /*sams/, and see Brockelmann (1908:159).

[93] Cf. Brockelmann 1908:230. See also below at p. 75, n. 170.

j) *Spirantisation*

The origin and date of the process whereby the six plosives /b, g, d, k, p, t/ developed each its positional variant, /b̠, g̠, d̠, k̠, p̠, t̠/ immediately following a vowel has been much discussed.([94]) On the basis of the fluctuating transcription of the names of the Persian kings Xerxes and Artaxerxes in a sixth century Akkadian document with <k> and <h̠> Eilers([95]) concluded that the process had already begun by then. Driver (1957:78) considers the spelling variation וכנדסירם A6.14:1 // וחנדסירם ib.6. This personal name of apparently Anatolian origin is thought to be related to Luvian *hant(a)* and Hittite *hanza*.([96]) It occurs in a document dated to the late 5th century BCE. The assumption would be that, in the speech habit of the anonymous scribe concerned, כ was, under certain conditions, pronounced similarly to ח. Note that, in yet another variant spelling of the name, there is no vowel preceding it, yet it is also spelled with Kaph: כנוסרם A6.11:1. It is thus not clear whether these spelling variations represent the phenomenon familiar in Hebrew and Aramaic conditioned by a preceding vowel or not.

There is no telling whether or not the partial assimilation of ב to פ̠, discussed above (§ *g*), was realised as /v/ (or bilabial /b̠/) > /f/.([97])

An early 7th century document from Nerab with יכטלוך 'may they kill you' (Nerab 1.7) shows that the spirantisation had not

---

[94] See Kutscher (1971:374).

[95] Eilers (1935:207, n. 5) and Eilers (1940:70, n. 6). Rosenthal (1961:13) holds that this is "an Aramaic development which, in all likelihood, was under way in the sixth century B.C."

The fact that in 37 cases of Egyptian words or names containing *ḥ* or *h̠* our Aramaic sources use ח, and not כ as in comparable Phoenician transliterations leads Muchiki (1994) to conclude that the spirantisation was not yet operative in Egyptian Aramaic. It is, however, possible that members of the speech community of Egyptian Aramaic perceived the Egyptian *h̠*, if this were phonetically equivalent to a spirantised /k/, as identical with *ḥ*. Besides, Muchiki does not appear to be aware of views of scholars such as Eilers and Kutscher.

[96] On the literature, see Grelot (1972:476). Segert (1975:96,118), possibly relying on Speiser (1939:5), mentions Hurrian as a possible source of this development, which conceivably penetrated Old Aramaic.

[97] Kaufman (1974:119) rejects the Akkadian origin of this development, though he does not mention a study by Eilers (1940) showing Aramaic influence in this respect in Akkadian transliterations. See also above, § 2 *a*, and Kaufman 1974:151f.

yet begun in this period and/or in Southern Syria. On the dissimilation of /q/ to /k/, see above § *i*.

In this connection we ought to bear in mind a point aptly made by Degen (1979:21f.) that positional allophones of the plosives could only begin to function after the interdental phonemes /ḏ, ṯ/ had shifted to /d, t/ respectively.([98])

k) *Possible weakening or elision of gutturals*

The conditional particle is consistently spelled הן (once הין D7.56:7), with the sole exception of אן at A2.1:9, one of the Hermopolis papyri, which also prefers Afel to Hafel; see below § 28. Another possible case of a weakened ה is פתי B2.3:4 for the expected פתיה 'its breadth' // ארכה 'its length' ib., but cf. ארך פתי ... in a generally similar context (B3.12:7f.)([99]); משחת for the expected משחתה 'its measurements' B3.5:12 // תחומוהי 'its boundaries.' Also at the end of a word (a personal name), we note יהישמ B3.6:18 (in the endorsement of a document) for יהישמע elsewhere in the document. Furthermore, the abnormal spellings ידניא A4.4:5, B2.8:2 PN for ידניה A4.3:1+ as well as צפליא PN C3.15:96 for צפליה ib.109 attest to the weakening of the consonantal ה as part of the theophoric name, the Alef having become a mere vowel letter. The same applies to the occasional use of א at the end of a word where the standard orthography has ה, or vice versa: שליטא אנתי 'you are empowered' B3.10:13,14,15 // שליטה אנתי ib.11; זנא 'this' (repeating the preceding זנה at the end of the preceding line) B3.10:16; אל תהשגא לבבא 'Do not lead astray the heart' C1.1:137([100]); תלתא זי 'third' C1.1:187.

An abnormal spelling such as ביתה כלה (= ביתא) 'the entire house' B3.5:20 shows that the st. det. morpheme spelled with Alef no longer carried any consonantal value. Cf. § 18 *f*.

Forms such as אושעיה B2.9:18 // אושע A3.3:14, D1.6 Frag. b+ as variants of הושעיה A3.6:5+ // הושע A4.4:5 probably attest to the weakening of the initial He, thus making the Alef a mere vowel-carrier.([101]) Since the root ישע is foreign to Aramaic, one cannot cite these names as evidence for the coexistence at an

---

[98] See also Muraoka (1983-84:90) and our remark below (§ 31 *a*).

[99] See also B3.8:6 (פתי) and ib.12 (ארך), where, however, just as in B3.12:7f., the words in question are immediately followed by a phrase <אמן + cipher>, which suggests that they may be adjectives rather than the corresponding abstract nouns.

[100] שגיא לבב (= /śaggi/) is an unlikely collocation. Hence תהשגא = תְּהַשְׁגֵּה. Cf. Lindenberger (1983:134).

[101] Cf. Syr. / ʾiḏaʾ/ = JA יְדָא.

early stage of two separate Aramaic causative binyanim Hafel and Afel, but rather they evidence the phonetic change /h/ > /ʔ/ or /h/ > /ø/ already in our period. Because -אושע is no part of the ancient Hebrew onomasticon, this must have resulted from an inner-Aramaic phonetic development.

The name of Eshor's wife, מבטחיה, is spelled twice מפטיה B2.6:3,32. Both occur in Eshor's personal reference (direct speech) to her, alongside the usual spelling in this document, viz. מפטחיה.([102]) Is it possible to speak of hypocoristic or endearing syncope?

The aphaeresis of א in the numeral for 'one' is a universal Aramaic phenomenon attested from Old Aramaic onwards, shared also by Samalian([103]): m. חד, f. חדה. On the other hand, another pan-Aramaic word, אחתה 'sister,' appears in our corpus as אחה A2.2:5 et passim.([103a]) A similar aphaeresis may be considered possible in a personal name חתובסתי A6.13:3,4, an alternative form of אחתבסתי A6.14:1,4.([104]) Finally, we may note יתלי B4.1:2 for אית לי 'I have.'([105])

l) *Apocope of /ʔ/*([106])

The glottal stop at the end of a word-form not followed by any sound is often elided. Thus שגי 'much' A3.5:1 (// שגיא ib.2);

---

[102] On this spelling instead of מבטחיה, see above, § g. The name is misspelled at B2.8:10 as מטחיה.

[103] See Dion (1974:118) and Tropper (1993:184f.). The shift of the stress to the ultima can hardly account for the aphaeresis, since that would leave too many words and forms unaffected by such a development.

[103a] The two forms, /ḥa:ta:/ and /ʔaḥa:/, are probably two distinct lexemes in origin. The one is not derivable from the other. The long internal /a:/ of the first is genuine in view of the Hebrew /ʔa:ḥo:t̲/ < */ʔaḥa:t/. See also § 12 c, n. 23.

[104] See a discussion by Driver ad loc. (1957:76, 79).

[105] Cf. also our observation at § 21 e, n. 216. On יה for אית, see also Porten 1985:50. Is it at all possible to infer from this that the widely accepted development (/ʔalpu/ > /ʔalp/ > /ʔalep/ or /ʔalap/ > /ʔalép/ or /ʔaláp/), namely the shift of penultimate to ultima stress, had already occurred? That is perhaps going a shade too far?

As regards נשיבתן A6.11:2 Ginsberg (1969:633, n. 4) suggested a Baby-lonianism /niše: bi:ti/ 'household members' instead of 'women of household.' The phrase recurs at A6.12:2 (נשי ביתה) and may be restored at A6.11:4 (ditto). It also occurs in נשיביתן D6.8b and נשיבתה D6.8f:2. As it is thus confined to the three related documents, Ginsberg's view is more likely than the assumption of aphaeresis, i.e. נשי > אנשי.

[106] Cf. Folmer 1995: 102-23.

A4.3.10 where an Alef was added later above the line; מוע 'exit'
B2.2:8 // מועה B2.10:6, B3.4:9, B3.10:3 and מועא B2.3:4,6; לממטה
'to reach' C2.1:20,25 // למם[טא ib.41. See also under Lamed-Alef
verbs: § 34. The occasional use of ה instead of א for the st. det.
morpheme, especially in the Hermopolis papyri([107]), shows that,
by our period, the glottal stop, if the morpheme was -*a*ᵓ or -*a:*ᵓ,
had elided. See below § 18 *f.* Likewise the disjunctive personal
pronouns for 'he' and 'she,' הו, הי respectively (§ 11), which are
both spelled in OA as הא.([108]) Note also לה (= לא) 'not' A2.3:4 +
9x and לא אשכב = לאשכב 'I shall not sleep' D23.1 II:15; ביתה 'the
house' B3.13:9. More examples may be found below in § 5 *g.*

   m) *Syncope of* /ᵓ/, which takes two forms.

   (i) V + /ᵓ/ + C > VC.([109])

The glottal stop at the end of a syllable may be elided.
This occurs with Pe-Alef roots. Thus אמר G impf. 1sg. of אמר
(B2.1:12, 471 BCE), never spelled אאמר; לממר G inf. of same
(A4.9:2†, later than 407 BCE) // למאמר C1.1:163, D7.39:10; למחד
G inf. of אחד 'to seize' (B3.13:10, 402 BCE) // למאחד B4.4:17; יתה
'he will come' B3.4:22 (437 BCE) // יאתה C1.1:213+. Likewise
מכלא 'food (?)' C3.14:34, if < מאכלא; מכל < מאכל, same word,
B4.1:4. Of course, it is not absolutely certain that the /ᵓ/ has
been elided also where א is still written: e.g. יאמר A3.10:2. Given
the fairly frequent spelling without א, the odds are that forms
with it are more likely historical or correct spellings. Here also
belongs קן 'sheep' A4.10:10, D7.1:3, i.e. /*qaᵓn/ (= PS /*ḏaᵓn/) >
/*qa:n/. Cf. also מאן 'vessel,' spelled once without Alef, מני נחשא
'bronze vessels' A3.9:5; ברא 'well' A4.5:8*bis* as against its historical spelling באר ib.6 (< /*biᵓr/)([110]); רשא 'the capital' B3.1:6*bis* //
the more common, historical spelling ראשא, e.g. B2.2:1.([111])

---

[107] E.g., כספה (= כספא) 'the silver' A2.2:4. For more details, see § 18 *f.*

[108] In the light of the OA forms, which Kottsieper (1990:46) neglects
altogether, his hypothetical Proto-Aramaic /huwa/ and /hiya/ are unacceptable.
Cf. Degen (1969:54f.), Segert (1975:17), and Dion (1974:58).

[109] Cf. Folmer 1995:106-9.

[110] Cf. Sefire I B 34 בירא.

[111] Though we have only two nouns, presumably of an identical structure,
i.e. /*CᵓC/, which probably shifted to /CᵓiC#/ or /CᵓeC#/, but remained /CᵓC-/,
we could perhaps extrapolate from this and suggest that the same process
applied to all segholate nouns, e.g. /*malk/ > /mlek#/ and /malk-/. [The
symbol # signifies that there is no further inflectional addition to the stem.] It
so happens that the absolute or construct state of a typical Aramaic segholate
noun shows /e/ as its vowel, and the only /CaᵓC/ type is attested in our corpus

n) (ii) C + /ʾ/ + V > CV([112])

An example illustrating this process is בבל 'Babylon' A6.15:1 as against its historical spelling בבאל ib. 5.

The spelling לוסרי (= /losiri/?) 'to Osiris' D20.2 for the expected לאוסרי may indicate that the proclitic preposition had already lost its vowel, though the standard spelling of the divine name may simply be a graphemic accommodation to the Semitic principle of using an Alef to indicate a word-initial vowel.([113])

Although the performance of the scribe of B3.3 leaves something to be desired, he spells a f.s. noun שנאה 'hate' in two different ways: שנא (8) and שאה (9). Both, however, could be scribal errors for שנאה, as occurs several times in the same document, though the first form may attest to a syncope of the glottal stop, /śinʾa:/ > /śina:/, as corroborated by B3.8:40 שנאהי < שנאה הי, namely /śina:hi/ < /śinʾa:hi/.([114]) Note also רפאה 'cure,' f.sg.abs. with the Alef added above the line([115]): the /ʾ/ had probably been syncopated, but added subsequently by way of orthographic correction

The frequent word באיש 'evil,' which is always (7x) spelled with Alef, e.g A6.7:8, is probably a case of historical or etymological spelling.([116])

Since the Hermopolis papyri (A2.1-7; D1.1) typically prefer Afel to Hafel([117]), forms such as ישכח 'he will find' A2.2:15 and תשכח 'you will find' A2.4:10 probably attest to a syncope of /ʾ/ rather than /h/. Likewise יתו (< *יאיתו) 'let them bring' A2.1:7; תושר (< *תאושר) A2.2:7 'she shall dispatch.' In the following cases which occur elsewhere in our corpus, however, it is hardly possible to determine whether it is /ʾ/ or /h/ that is to be assumed to have been syncopated: תשכחון A4.2:10, תשכח B3.1:9,10,17; ישכחן D7.9:6. Our assumption is that, just as in the D stem, the prefix of the impf. and ptc. of the A or H stem was, synchronically speaking,

---

by קן 'sheep,' which does not show the type of orthographic alternation as the other two nouns under discussion.

[112] Cf. Folmer 1995: 109-15. This is a phenomenon well known in Classical Syr.: see Muraoka (1987:12; 1997b:13).

[113] Interestingly the accompanying Egyptian text shows *Wsir*.

[114] See also Folmer 1995:112.

[115] If the glottal stop had already syncopated, Lindenberger's alternative (1983:79), /rᵉpûʾa:h/, becomes unlikely.

[116] ביש is attested in a 5th cent. BCE document from Asia Minor: KAI 258:3.

[117] See below § 28.

vowelless.([118])

A word with Alef as final radical appears to retain the glottal stop not only graphically, but also perhaps phonetically when it is followed by a suffix beginning with a vowel: כרסאא 'the throne' C1.1:133, כרסאה 'his throne' B2.2:2; מומאה 'the oath' B2.2:6; מטאה G ptc.f.sg. 'arriving' A2.4:4, B2.8:5. Interpretation of other Lamed-Alef verb forms is debatable: e.g., מטאני 'he reached me' B2.11:5; אמחאנך 'I will hit you' C1.1:177; תקראון 'they will call' ib.165 // ירפון 'they will heal' ib.154. For details, see § 34. Forms of the noun מרא (/*maːriʔ/) are split: see the following subsection.

o) /ʔ/ > /y/([119])

This is attested, for instance, by the noun מרא 'master'([120]): מרי 'my lord' D7.15:3, D7.21:1; מריה 'its (f.) master' A3.10:2.([121]) מרידהם 'their owners' A4.4:8 can be considered a haplography for מרייהם (= מראיהם A6.10:4+), whilst מרא]יהם on the same line([122]) and חטאיך 'your sins' C1.1:50 could be a historical/etymological spelling. Cf. also שירית 'the remainder of' A4.7:11 // שארת B3.8:26; כיבי > כאבי 'my pain' C1.2:19. This change may be a case of a weak glottal stop assimilating to the following homogenic vowel _i_ or _e_, which implies that the m.pl.cst. morpheme /ay/ had contracted to /eː/.

p) V + /y/ + V > V + /ʔ/ + V

This feature, which occasionally occurs in BA in the Tiberian

---

[118] See also below § 30 e on the binyan -tA.

[119] Cf. Folmer 1995:113f. מקריא 'declaration' B7.2:6 (det.sg.) cited by Folmer (1995:114) is better explained in terms of the merger of original Lamed Alef roots with Lamed Yod roots, as Folmer herself indicates.

[120] Cf. Syr. /maːryaːʔ/ with reference to the God of Israel or Christ.

[121] This form, appearing in a text which was unknown to him as well as to Baumgartner, whom he criticises, undermines Schaeder's (1930:239f.) view that in EA every Alef of this lexeme was etymological and that the st.abs./cst. מרי, מרה, מרא represented a mere secondary formation, _maːreː_. Such a view cannot account for the Yod. The spelling מריה suggests further that מרי 'my master' was probably pronounced _maːryiː_ rather than _maːriː_, and that despite cuneiform evidence mentioned by Tallqvist (1914:135a) and Zadok (1978:64f.), the apocope of the final radical _y_ had not yet become universal. Note also מרי 'my lord' Ashur letter 6 for מרא elsewhere in the letter.

[122] Cowley (1923:129) and Grelot (1972:397) restore מראון A4.4:8 instead. See also Widengren 1971:228-31. There is no compelling reason for seeing the form as singular.

Qere tradition([123]), seems to be unknown in our corpus.([124]) Thus we find, e.g. יהודיא, not יהודאה 'the Jews' A3.8:12([125]); יוניא 'the Ionians' C3.7Jv2:10: cf. below, § 18 *h*. See also a form such as צימין, not צאמין A4.7:15; see § 35 *h*.

q) *Syncope of* /h/

The only certain case is that of sandhi in הן לו 'if not' C1.1:176, i.e. לָא הוּ < לוֹ. We are probably dealing with a scribal error([126]) in ביניהם 'between them' (B3.11:5), for otherwise there would result a most extraordinary case of hiatus. In our corpus we find two synonymous verbs for 'to be able': כהל and יכל. The latter, occurring 25 times, appears to be confined to the imperfect([127]), whilst the former occurs also as participle (twice out of 47 occurrences of the verb: כהל B3.10:17, כהלן B3.4:22). The question is whether a form such as אכל could be interpreted as derived from *אכהל with a syncopated ה. Old Aramaic knows only the כהל type as in יכהל Sefire I B 25. On the other hand, the Tiberian tradition of Biblical Aramaic with its יִכַּל, תִּכַּל demonstrates that the impf. of יכל is just as firmly established.([128]) It is more likely, then, that אכל and the like are derivatives of √ יכל.

r) *Metathesis*

Our idiom attests to a pan-Semitic([129]) phonetic feature whereby /t/ of the prefix of a t-binyan swaps its position with

---

[123] E.g., כַּשְׂדָּיָא. See Bauer - Leander (1927:51).

[124] See also Kaufman 1977:93.

[125] In the Tiberian tradition, this gentilic as well as *לֵוִי 'Levite' are exceptions, preserving the original Yod, even including יְהוּדָאִין Dn 3:12 where the Ktiv is in keeping with the general trend in question.

[126] So Kraeling (1953:253), who also mentions בניהם B2.7:14; B2.10:7, which of course is a different kind of 'error.' See § 8 *a*.

[127] יכל at B2.7:11, B5.1:5, B5.3:2 is most likely impf. 3m.sg. rather than the ptc. m.sg. or pf. 3m.sg.

[128] BA has no example of the יכהל type, though כהל is of rather rare occurrence, attested only four times as a participle: Dn 2.26, Dn 4.15, Dn 5.8,15.

[129] *Pace* Kaufman (1977:92) and Fitzmyer (1995:87) it seems to us too daring to say, on the basis of a sole instance (Sefire I A 29 יתשמע), possibly a mason's slip (so Degen 1969:67), that OA was not subject to this rule. Ben-Ḥayyim (1971:249) sees here a form of Ettafal, causative passive: /yittašmaʿ/. The slight difficulty is that this frequent verb, also in the causative Afel, is not attested in Ettafal elsewehre in Aramaic. Kutscher (1972:33) has other reservations.

the initial radical when the latter is a sibilant([130]): יסתבלון 'are supported' tD impf. 3mpl of √ סבל (C1.1:73)([131]); אשתאר 'remained' B3.12:6, and quite a few similar examples. In אזדהרי 'Take care!' A2.1:8, A2.2:17, הזדהרי D7.9:9, tD impv.f.sg. of √ זהר we also observe partial assimilation of /t/ to /d/ under the influence of the voiced /z/. See also ישתבע 'he will be sated' C1.1:124; תשתאלו 'you will be called to account' A6.8:3; אשתבק 'was abandoned' A6.11:4; אשתדרו 'they intervened' A4.3:4; אשתוין 'we reached an agreement' B2.11:2; אשתכח 'was found' A4.5:13; ישתלח 'will be sent' A6.2:21; ישתמע 'will be listened to' B3.8:42; אשתמר 'Guard!' C1.1:81; תשתנה 'you will change' C1.1:200; תסתכל 'you will be clever' C1.1:147.

s) *Fluctuation between /m/ and /n/*

The change /m/ > /n/, as in עליהם 'on them' A3.8:4 vs. עליהן A2.2:10, is particularly common with pronominal or personal morphemes, namely those of the second and third person plurals at word-final positions: e.g., כם- vs. כן- or כון- 'your' (m.pl.), הם-, הום- vs. הן-, הון- 'their' and שאילתם 'you (m.pl.) were interrogated' B2.9:8 vs. זבנתון 'you bought' A3.10:5. For details and discussion, see §§ 11 *e*, 12 *i*, *k*, 24 *d*. שצו 'they succeeded' A6.7:7 seems to be the only certain case of this change in word-medial position, if the root be √מצא.([132])

t) *Word-final cluster of two identical consonants*

A word-final consonantal cluster consisting of two identical consonants is, as in Hebrew, simplified. Thus *בניי (= בני pl.cst. + י 'my') > בני 'my sons.'([133])

§ 4. Vowels

What information we can retrieve from the written texts of our corpus about the vowels of their language and their behaviour is naturally meagre in the extreme. Our main sources of knowledge

---

[130] On the possibility that we might be dealing here with a residue of an infixed *t*, and not a case of genuine metathesis, see Joüon - Muraoka (1993:74). Segert (1975:110) admits that this is a morphologically conditioned phenomenon.

[131] Whatever the precise phonetic nature of the sound represented by ס may have been, it is clear that it shared a certain phonetic feature with the other sibilants.

[132] See Driver 1957:54.

[133] It is assumed here that the pronoun for 'my' had already lost the original *a* of *ya*, and subsequently C*y* > C*i*. By analogy this process affected a noun whose cst. form ended in a vowel.

are (a) the use of the so-called matres lectionis, namely the use of א, ה, ו, and י, and (b) features of spelling, especially alternative spellings of what may be assumed to be an identical phonetic entity. Furthermore, we may draw upon our knowledge of vocalism in later Aramaic dialects and also take cognate languages into account.([134])

In any discussion of possible use of certain consonant letters to represent vowels, i.e. matres lectionis, it is imperative to distinguish two types of data: a) cases in which these letters are used deliberately to indicate vowels, especially where no such letter was used at an earlier phase of the language or they alternate within the corpus itself with cases where no such letter is used, and b) cases in which those letters appear where vowels can be assumed to occur, and that generally for historical or etymological reasons, but have not been used by design in order to indicate vowels, for they have lost their original consonantal value as a result of some phonetic development or other([135]). The former are matres lectionis by design, the latter by default.

§ 5. Word-final vowels

A word-final vowel is mostly spelled with a vowel letter.([136])

a) *Word-final i vowel*

A word-final *Yod* indicates *i* as in זי passim, the relative pronoun or conjunction; הי 'she' A2.1:6; אחתי 'my sister' A2.1:1, possessive suffix, 1sg., hardly /ʔaḥaːtiya/ or the like; שלחי 'Send!' A2.3:12, impv. f.sg.; הדדנורי 'Hadadnuri' A2.2:19, a personal name.

b) *Word-final Yod = /y/*

A word-final Yod probably indicates a semi-vowel /y/ as in a gentilic such as יהודי 'Jewish' A2.2:3, which most likely ended

---

[134] The classic treatment of the subject is Cross - Freedman (1952). Since then, however, some significant advances have been made, especially as a result of the discovery of new texts such as the famed Tel Fekheriyeh bi-lingual (9th century BCE?), rendering some significant revision of Cross and Freedman's theory necessary. See Freedman - Forbes - Andersen (1992). Sarfatti 1995 is an insightful survey in the light of these recent advances.

[135] The fact that גר 'foreigner' or כן 'upright' is never spelled with a Yod, as pointed out by Kottsieper (1990:78), does not invalidate Lindenberger's suggestion (1983:281) that בית might contain a vowel letter.

[136] In contradistinction to Beyer (1984:88), who holds that unstressed word-final vowels were only graphically represented in order to avoid mis-understandings. Cook (1990) agrees with Beyer that final unstressed long vowels, especially /aː/, were often not graphically represented in OA and IA.

with /-a:y/: likewise ארמי 'Aramaean' B2.1:2, בחתרי 'Bactrian'
D2.12:2, ורכני 'Hyrcanian' B8.3:3, חרזמי 'Khwarezmian' B2.2:2,
יוני 'Greek' C3.7Ar2:21, כספי 'Caspian' B3.4:2, מדי 'Median'
B3.6:17, מצרי 'Egyptian' C3.19:33, ערבי 'Arabian' C1.1:207, פרסי
'Persian' C2.1:19, צידני 'Sidonian' C1.1:207, צעני 'Zoanite' C1.2:25.
Similarly a nisbéh תחתי 'lower' A3.5:8.

Whether or not every word-final *i* vowel was indicated by a
Yod is somewhat debatable. In this regard, contrasting pairs
such as אבוהי B3.6:11 // אבוה ib.12 both 'his father' and לכי
B3.10:2,3 // לך ib.12 'to you' (both referring to a woman) deserve
our attention. See below § 12 *e*. Did the length of the vowel
concerned and/or the position of the stress have anything to do
with this fluctuation? Later Aramaic shows little trace of such a
vowel, though historical spelling usually retains the Yod.

There is no internal clue for determining how the m.pl./du.cst.
ending as in ספרי 'the scribes of' A6.1:1 may have sounded.
Whilst the absolute number of occurrences of the morpheme is
rather small, there is not a single case in which the Yod is wanting. But if the original diphthong had already contracted to /e:/,
the spelling with Yod would be merely traditional/historical, in
which case the letter would be, synchronically speaking, a mater
lectionis by default only. Cf. the preposition אחרי 'after' C1.1:83.
On the other hand, the conjunctive pronoun 'my' with a m.pl./du.
noun as in בני is likely to have ended with /ay/. Cf. § 8 *a*.

c) *Word-final Waw = u*

A word-final *Waw* may indicate *u* as in הו 'he' A2.1:8; שמעו
'Hear!' C1.1:59, impv. m.pl.; אמרו 'they said' A3.5:4, pf. 3m.pl.;
נבו A2.3:1 'Nabu,' a divine name. One may safely assume that,
excepting some proper nouns, every word-final *u* vowel is
represented by a mater lectionis Waw. On the other hand, the
reverse is not always true; in other words, not every word-final
Waw is an indication of an *u* vowel. Thus the ubiquitous Tetra-
grammaton יהו, ending rather with *o*, as is evident from the
alternative spelling יהה: see below § 5 *e*. Likewise בנו 'they built'
A4.7:13, ending with *aw* or *o*; on the contraction of diphthongs,
see below § 6 *e*.

d) *Word-final Waw = o*

A word-final Waw, as just stated, may indicate *o*. This may
be the case with some forms of Lamed-Yod and Lamed-Alef
(on the latter, see § 34 *b*) verbs. So most likely יאתו 'May they
come!' A6.5:3, G juss. 3m.pl. of אתה; כלו 'they detained' A4.2:15,
G 3m.pl. of כלא. See further below at § 34 on Lamed-Yod and

Lamed-Alef verbs.

e) *Word-final He = a, e,* or *o*

A word-final He may stand for *a, e,* or *o.*

For *a*: ספרה זנה (the first word for the standard ספרא) 'this document' A2.3:12; ביתה כלה (for the standard כלא ביתא) 'the whole house' B3.5:20; זנה זנא ביתא 'this house' B3.10:15 (with dittography); נפקה G ptc. f.sg. of נפק 'to exit' C1.1:171; הוה G pf. 3m.sg. of הוה 'to be' C1.1:72([137]); אנה 'I' passim; לה 'not,' often in the Hermopolis papyri instead of the standard לא. The use of He for a word-final *a* is one of the well-recognised hallmarks of the Hermopolis papyri.([138])

As regards an attempt to admit a much more widespread defective spelling of word-final, unstressed long vowels, /aː/ in particular, than the orthography of our corpus seems to suggest([139]), a few observations must be made. (1) The co-existence of defective spellings and occasional plene spellings, such as ן- vs. אנ- 'our' (§ 12 *h*) does not have to mean that the long form, which had never earlier existed, made its appearance out of the blue late in the history of Aramaic, only to be replaced subsequently by the shorter variant as a result of apocope of unstressed word-final vowels. The two forms may have coexisted for quite some time, even if diachronically the one developed from the other. Otherwise one would be compelled to assume that, on account of כה- 'your' (m.s.) in QA, every single ך in OA and IA is a defective spelling for /-ákaː/, whereas not a single case of plene spelling for this morpheme is attested in OA and IA. Likewise, are we to interpret every אנת 'you' (2m.s.) in OA and IA as /ʔántaː/ on the strength of BA Ktiv and QA אנתה, despite the fact that the pronoun is never spelled plene in Early Aramaic? (2) In addition to theoretical considerations on the history of Aramaic phonology and orthography, each individual case must be considered with reference to general orthographic patterns of a given document or scribe and the professional quality of scribes.

For *e*: אריה 'a lion' C1.1:184; אלה 'these' B3.7:14([140]); אתה

---

[137] That the final He is a mere mater lectionis is apparent from its absence in the rest of the Pf. conjugation including a form such as גרכי 'he brought (suit) against you' B2.8:9.

[138] As emphasised by Kutscher (1971:103,105f.). See also § 14 *b*, 18 *f*.

[139] See especially Cook 1990.

[140] That the Heh is a vowel letter is evident from the way in which אלך 'those' is formed, namely by adding <k> or <ky> to a form of the near deixis (§ 14 *c*).

'coming' G ptc. m.sg. A2.5:6; יהוה 'will be,' G impf. 3m.sg. of הוה A3.6:3; למבנה 'to build,' G inf. of בנה A4.7:23. For more examples of this type, see under § 37 *d-k*.

For *o*: rather exceptional is יהה, obviously instead of יהו, the name of the Jewish deity at Elephantine—B2.7:14, B3.3:2, D7.16.3,7, D7.18:3, D7.21:3, D7.35:1†. This is an archaic Hebrew form of the name. See also יההאור 'Jehour' B5.1:2 (495 BCE) // יהואור B2.11:16 (410 BCE).

f) *Word-final Alef = a or e*
A word-final *Alef* may also stand for either *a* or *e*.([141])
For *a*: מטא 'he arrived' B7.2:7; שמיא 'the sky' A1.1:2([142]); לא 'not' passim; ברא 'a daughter' B2.8:9; תנא 'here' D1.11:1.
For *e*: תתמלא B3.1:11, tG impf. 2m.sg. of מלא 'to be full'; most likely אקרא B7.2:7, G impf. 1sg. of קרא 'to call' B7.2:7(*'eqre* rather than *'eqra*: see § 34); ישגא 'he will proceed' D7.4:2.([143])
In most of these cases, however, the final Alef is essentially historical or etymological, no genuine mater lectionis. But the rare spelling of the plene forms of the conjunctive pronouns, נא- 1pl. and הא- 3fs.([144]), non-standard spellings זנא 'this' (§ 14), and תנא 'here' (§ 22 *a*) must be considered cases of Alef as genuine mater lectionis, which probably dates from a period when the originally consonantal word-final Alef had, as a consequence of a phonetic development, become a virtual mater lectionis. In point of fact, some of the cases of נא- and הא- are found in documents dating from as early as the 5th century BCE, which probably indicates that the phonetic process in question was effectively complete by then, but the conservative scribal tradition prevented further spread of this spelling innovation until another phonetic development, namely the apocope of the final vowel, came to preclude such a spelling once and for all.

g) *Multivalence of word-final matres lectionis*
Thus each of the four matres lectionis is multivalent, there

---

[141] See a recent reconsideration by Andersen (1992:79-90) of Cross and Freedman's position regarding Alef as a mater lectionis in Old Aramaic (1952). In conclusion, Andersen agrees with Cross and Freedman, though for different reasons.

אריא at C1.1:183, being parallel to אילא 'gazelle,' is likely to be in the st.det. (generic? - see below § 46 *fb*), whereas אריה ib. 165 is in the st.abs. (/ᵖarye:/ ?).

[142] On the interpretation of the st.emph. morpheme א, see above, § 3 *l*.

[143] On the last verb see below, § 37, n. 197.

[144] See below § 12*g,h*.

being no one-to-one correspondence. This multivalence is compounded by variations and inconsistencies such as למטה 'to reach' C2.1:20,25 // למן[ט]א ib.41; מן עליה לתחתיא 'from "above" to "below"' B3.12:16 // ומן תחתיא לעליא ib.8; מועה שמש 'east' B2.10:6 // מועא שמש B2.3:6 (two different scribes of 416 and 460 BCE respectively); even with a personal name and in same document—אוריה D7.9:1 // אוריא ib.3.([145]) Note also ידניא B2.8:2 for the usual ידניה 'Jedaniah'; ארמיא 'an Aramaean (woman)' ib.3; אלהתה 'the goddess' for the usual אלהתא ib.5; ברא 'daughter' ib.9 for the usual ברה. One can hardly speak of scribal consistency, as is clearly illustrated by the just-quoted scribe of B2.8. However, the Hermopolis papyri are consistent in their spelling לה for the standard לא 'not.'

h) *Word-final long* a *graphically not visible?*

Whether a supposedly long word-final a may occasionally have not been graphically indicated will be discussed later under Pronouns (§ 11 a).

i) *Spelling of unstressed word-final long* a

Kottsieper (1990:80) cites אנחנה 'we' as the sole exception to his rule that an unstressed word-final a: is spelled defectively. However, one should include here זילנא 'our' A6.10:2 (see below § 12 g) and the adverbial כלא 'entirely' (see below § 22 c), the latter of which, according to the Tiberian accents, is mil'el, i.e. stressed penultimately.([146])

j) *Pronouns* הו *and* הי

The forms of the pronouns הו 'he' and הי 'she' indicate that by our period([147]) a word-final, short vowel had been lost. Their earlier forms are generally assumed to have ended with a short a preceded by a glottal stop. Thus the subsequent development was probably: */huʔa/ > /huʔ/ > /hu/ and */hiʔa/ > /hiʔ/ > /hi/.

Since הא in OA([148]) suggests that the Proto-Aramaic 3rd sg. disjunctive pronouns had, like the Hebrew counterparts, a glottal stop as their component and thus differed from Classical Arabic with /huwa/ and /hiya/, the Waw and Yod in our forms are

---

[145] On the fluctuation in spelling of the theophoric element, cf. also Folmer 1995:121.

[146] On the stress position, see Bauer - Leander (1927:88).

[147] By any account, Beyer's view (1984:88) that these vowels must have dropped by the 12th century BCE at the latest seems to be too extreme; see also a critique by Kottsieper (1990:83).

[148] Segert's reading of הו at Sefire III 22 (Segert 1975:166) is now generally rejected.

genuine vowel letters, though they do not necessarily indicate a long *u* and *i* respectively; they may simply be a graphic distinction between the two vowel qualities.

k) *Pleonastic word-final Alef*

There are two examples, both in a single document, of an otiose word-final Alef following another mater lectionis: פרעה נכוא 'Pharaoh Necho ' D23.1 Va:11, XII:7 // פרעה נכו ib. VIII:12; היא 'she' ib. XIII:4.([149])

§ 6. **Word-medial vowels**

a) *Yod = i*

A *Yod* is often written in the middle of a word to indicate what is presumably *i*. Thus איתי 'there is' A5.5:8; מדינתא 'province' A6.1:1; ספינתא 'boat' A3.9:7; עבידתהם 'their work' C1.1:207([150]); many *qatti:l* pattern adjectives such as חכים 'wise' C1.1:35; חסין 'strong' C1.1:89; יקיר 'precious' C1.1:159; עזיז 'strong' C1.1:83; עתיק 'old' B2.7:6; עתירא 'rich' C1.1:206; צדיק 'righteous' C1.1:126; קליל 'light' C1.1:160; קריב 'near' B2.1:9; רחיק 'distant' B2.1:9; רשיען 'evil' C1.1:104; שגיא 'abundant(ly)' C1.1:29; שליט 'em-powered' B2.1:11; שפיר 'beautiful' C1.1:92; passive G - כתיב 'was written' B2.1:10; קטילו 'were killed' A4.7:17; שמיע ptc. 'heard' A3.3:13; hollow-root verbs - מית 'he died' B2.1:8; ישימון 'they will put' C1.1:163; הקימת 'I reestablished' C2.1 III:1. Unusual is הין 'if' D7.56:7 for the standard הן.

b) *Waw = u*

A *Waw* is often written in the middle of a word to indicate what is presumably *u*. Thus אחוכן 'your brother' A2.5:1; בתולה 'virgin' C1.1:134; כתון 'tunic' A3.3:9, A3.8:9([151]); עבור 'grain' A3.10:5*bis*([152]); מלוכתא 'reign' B2.2:1; אגורא 'temple' A4.7:17 et

---

[149] An orthographic practice, known as digraph, typical of Qumran Hebrew and Aramaic documents: e.g., הווא for הוו 'they were' 1QapGen 19.24 and the ubiquitous כיא for כי. Once in BA: Ezr 6.15 שֵׁיצִיא. See Qimron 1986: § 100.51.

[150] The word ימן 'the right-hand side' is consistently so spelled: B2.11:4,6; B3.6:3. Cf. Arb. *yaman* alongside *yami:n*, Heb. יָמֵן, and Eth. *yama:n.* as against JA and Syr. *yammin*.

[151] Also כתונך 'your tunic' A3.3:9. This is probably affiliated to JA כֻּתּנָא (= χιτών) as distinct from כִּתָּנָא 'linen': cf. Arb. *katta:n.* In Syr. *ketta:na:ʾ* contrasts with *kuttina:ʾ*, for the latter of which we find a variant *kytwnʾ* at John 21.7 in the Vetus Syra: see Lewis 1910. This useful orthographic distinction, however, is not observed in כתן 1 זי כתן 'one linen tunic' A3.3:11.

[152] Syr. /ᴋvura:ʾ/; JA עֲבוּר.

passim (< Akk. *ekurru*)([153]); נבוסמסכן 'Nabusumiskun' C1.1:54 et passim([154]); ישבקון 'they will release' A3.1r:6; ימות 'he will die' B2.6:17.

c) *Waw = o*

In חשוך 'darkness' C1.1:173 and ארון 'chest' A2.5:4, however, the Waw most likely indicates *o*.([155])

d) *Frequent defective spellings*

Spellings in which vowels are not graphically represented, are by no means rare, even in the same words and forms as quoted above: מדנתא A5.2:7 (for מדינתא); שלט B4.4:16,17 (for שליט); ברתא 'fortress' B3.4:4 (for בירתא); אחכי 'your brother' A2.1:2 (usually אחוכי). This is so even in the same documents: אנתתכי 'your wifehood' B3.11:7 (supra-linear correction) // אנתותכי ib.10; יהישמע Jehoishma B3.7:2 // יהוישמע ib.8; יהב 'given' G ptc.pass. A6.1:2 // יהיב ib.3; עתק 'old' B2.7:12 // עתיק ib.6; אביגרנא B2.9:14, B2.10:15, B2.11:10, B3.8:31, B6.3:10, אביגרן B3.7:17, B3.9:7, B3.10:20, B3.11:10,14, B3.12:30, B5.5:6,11 // אבגרן B3.6:8,14, B3.13:6, אבגרנא B3.13:7([156]); ארדיכל 'architect' B2.8:2 // ארדכל B2.6:2([157]); כתיבן 'written' B3.11:7 // כתבן ib.11,15; תקם G impf. 3f.s. of קום // יקום ib.7; names—ודרנג Vidranga B2.10:4 // וידרנג ib.2; אחתבסתי Ahatubasti A6.14:1,4 // חתובסתי A6.13:3,4([158]); בגושת B3.4:2 // בגזושת B3.5:3([159]); גשרן 'beams' B3.4:5 // גשורן B3.10:13, B3.11:2, B3.12:13 (B3.4, B3.10-12 by same scribe); שקא 'street' B2.7:14 // שוקא B2.1:14. Observe a variation in an idiomatic phrase: קריב ורחיק B2.1:8 (471 BCE) // קרב ורחק B2.7:10 (446 BCE), though of two different scribes([160]); תחמי 'boundaries of'

---

[153] For the *k/g* correspondence, see Kaufman (1974:139).

[154] See Kornfeld (1978:61).

[155] See Bauer - Leander (1927:188).

[156] If the scribe of B3.6, Haggai, is the same as that of B3.10, Haggai son of Shemaiah, his spelling is not consistent.

[157] Borrowed from Akk. *arad ekalli* 'palace slave.'

[158] Cf. Driver (1957:76, 79).

[159] According to Grelot (1972:507), the *u* is short.

[160] Whilst Kottsieper (1990:74-7) makes a plausible case for the consistent plene spelling of this pattern of adjectives and its derivatives in the Ahiqar proverbs, rejecting the suggestion by Lindenberger (1983:281) to the contrary, one wonders whether a scribe can ever be thoroughly consistent: note "fehlerfreie Schreibung" (Kottsieper 1990:84). For one of the disputed cases at C1.1:89, Porten - Yardeni read אנזערתא for Kottsieper's and Lindenberger's אף זעררתא. Another case of possible defective spelling, זעריהם 'their paucity'

B3.4:7 // תחומי B3.10:8, B3.12:9 (same scribe), תחמוהי 'its boundaries' B3.4:17 // תחמוהי B3.10:16, B3.12:17+ (same scribe);
חטיב 'striped' B3.8:7 // חטב B2.6:7; חצן 'palm-leaf' B2.6:16 // חוצן
B2.9:6, B3.8:17; קבילה 'complaint' A6.15:5,11 // קבלת A6.8:3.
The last pair may be two synonymous, but distinct lexemes.

e) *Contraction of diphthongs and word-medial Yod or Waw*
Whether a given word-medial Yod or Waw represents *e*, *i*
or *o* respectively depends also on one's view regarding the possible
contraction of diphthongs *ay* or *aw* respectively; see below § 8.
Other than that, these two letters do appear to be used to
transliterate *e*, *i* or *o* of foreign names. E.g. חור Hor B1.1:16+;
פטוסירי Petosiri B2.11:4+([161]); הרמונקתוס Hermoniketos C3.29:17
([162]); the name of the 12th Egyptian month Mesore spelled מסורע
C3.7Jr2:26+; חילכיא 'the Cilicians' A6.7:11 // חלכיא A6.5:3,4,5.

f) *Alef or He hardly used as word-medial* mater lectionis
Alef or He is hardly ever used as a word-medial vowel
letter. Rare exceptions are foreign names: e.g. פליקראתס Polykrates
C3.29:16([163]); and possibly יאדניה A4.2:17, which is spelled at
ib.1 without א.([164]) The unique לאם B6.3:8, if genuine, for the
usual לם marking direct speech, would be a more archaic spelling,
if the particle go back to לאמר.

g) *Yod or Waw = historically long* i *or* u
If one leaves out names and foreign words([165]), a Yod or
Waw, where it represents *i* or *u* respectively, seems to be used
where one expects a historically long *i* or *u*, e.g., חכים (= /ḥakki:m/)

C1.1:90 is derived by Kottsieper (1990:77) from */zuʕaːru/, for which he
cites Syr. /zˁoraːʾ/, which however is not of the pattern *quta:lu*, but of *qutta:lu*.
Pace Beyer (1984:414) there is no need whatsoever to see a case of defective
spelling in צידן 'Sidon' C3.12:7+; cf. Syr. *ṣydn*.

[161] See Grelot (1972:486).

[162] Kornfeld (1978:117).

[163] Kornfeld (1978:118).

[164] According to Grelot (1972:390, 498), the spelling with Alef reveals the
etymology of the name: "Que Yah ouïsse !" The form with Dalet, identical
with יַאֲנְיָה (Jer 35.3; Ez 11.1), is said to be Aramaising. See n. 6 above.

[165] אגור 'temple,' for instance, is considered to be an Akkadian loan-word,
ekurru with a short *u*: see Kaufman (1974:48). The first vowel of the Greek
form for 'Cilician,' Κίλιξ, is considered to be short. The phenomenon is
attested already in the Tel Fekheriyeh inscription: גוגל (line 2) = Akk. *gugalu*
'water-master.' We are not convinced by Andersen - Freedman (1992:137-70,
esp. 143, 145, 168f.) that the inscription uses <w> for long /u/ and/or short
/u/ under stress. Cf. חיפתיא 'police' A4.5:9, which is spelled תִּפְתָּיֵא at Dn 3.2,3.

'wise' C1.1:35 and קוֹם 'Stand!' D7.24:5. For this reason, the defective spelling of the m.pl. abs. morpheme /-i:n/, which is the rule, is most striking([166]): e.g. כון 'windows' B3.5:8 // כוין (an exceptional spelling) B2.10:6. Compare also משחין 'anointing' A4.7:20 with the improved spelling משחן A4.8:20; אמרין 'saying' A4.7:22 // אמרן A4.8:22; כנכרין 'talents' A4.7:28 // כנכרן A4.8:27. For further rare exceptions to this rule([167]), see below § 18 b. On the other hand, the plene spelling of a partly restored word צביח C1.1:3 in an expression צבית עזקה 'seal-bearer' is puzzlesome, since the first constituent is generally assumed to be derived from Akk. ṣa:bitu with a short i.([168]) See also the unusual spelling הין 'if' D7.56:6 for the standard הן.

h) *Consonantal Yod or Waw*

Needless to say, not every word-medial Waw or Yod is a vowel letter. Apart from cases of preserved diphthongs, /aw/ or /ay/, such as יומא 'the day' and ביתא 'the house' (see above § 6 e), our decision in this matter is often informed by our knowledge of forms of lexemes and grammar of later dialects with traditions of vocalisation or pronunciation. To give several examples and categories, no vowel letter is likely in: גויא 'inner' C3.19r:1 (= /gawwa:y/?); מין 'water' C1.1:161 (= /mayyi:n/?); כון 'windows' B3.10:13 (= /kawwi:n/?); כות 'thus' A2.3:7 (= /kwa:t/?); שפות 'the lips of' C1.1:151 (= /šipwa:t/?); צימן 'fasting' A4.7:20 (a masculine plural G participle of a hollow root, √צום: /ṣa:ymi:n/?); חיבוני 'they obligated me' B8.6:10 (a D perfect of a hollow root, √חוב: /ḥaybu:ni/?).

§ 7. Vowel length

Notwithstanding what we have stated just above (§ 6 g) it is not likely that vowel length was phonemic in the case of /i/ and /u/. Though there were most likely stable i's and u's which were not subject to the vowel deletion rule as in כתיבן 'written,' Peal passive participle, masculine plural (B3.5:12) and ימותון 'they will die' C1.1:110, we cannot think of any minimal pair where the length of either vowel would have led to semantic opposition of two forms which would otherwise be identical. But as for /a/, such a

---

[166] This orthographic feature is shared by OA, but not by Fekheriyan, which has אלהין as well as אלהן, on which see Muraoka (1983-84:84-87) and Andersen - Freedman (1992:153). See below § 18 b.

[167] *Pace* Lindenberger (1983:281), חסין C1.1:89 is no exception to this rule: the word means 'strong': see also Kottsieper (1990):74.

[168] Kaufman (1974:96) is sceptical about the suggested Akkadian etymology.

phonemic opposition may be assumed: thus /malkat/ 'the queen of' vs. /malka:t/ 'the queens of.' None the less, we shall here follow the widespread convention of transliterating historically long *i* and *u* as /i:/ and /u:/ respectively.

The length of word-final vowels, especially those of inflectional morphemes, is also uncertain. Their occasional plene spelling does not by itself indicate long vowels: e.g. אנחנה 'we' vs. אנחן; הו 'he'; הי 'she'; כה- vs. ך- 'your'; והי- 'his'; כתבתי 'you (f.sg.) wrote.'

§ 8. Contraction of diphthongs

a) *Diphthong* /ay/

The diphthong /ay/ is likely to have been contracted or monophthongised to /e:/ or the like([169]) as is shown by such unorthodox spellings as בניהם for ביניהם B2.7:14, B2.10:7, B3.5:10,11 'between them'([170]); שקפוני רגלן 'they beat me on the legs' B8.4:5([171]) as against עינין 'eyes' C1.1:157 and ידין 'hands' B2.6:8; אדן 'then' B3.6:1 as against the usual אדין B2.8:4+; ין 'wine' (*not* st.cst.) C3.1:2,3,4,5. This feature is most prominent in the Hermopolis papyri: e.g. בת בנת 'Temple of Banit' A2.2:12 // בית בנת ib.1; בבתה 'in his house' A2.2:15; בביתי 'in my house' A2.3:12 (with the middle Yod written above the line by the same scribe); יהתו 'let them bring' A2.5:4 // תהיתן 'you will bring' ib.5, both A of אתה; למתיה 'to bring' A2.4:11 // למיתיה ib., both A inf. of same verb, at A2.4:11; אתה (= איתה) 'I shall bring' A2.1:10; הות 'I was' A2.5:8 (§ 37 *b*) as against הוית A3.5:4. Cf. also זניהם 'their weapons'([172]) A4.8:8 (407 BCE) // זינא 'the weapon' D7.57:9; בתנא 'our house' C3.28:53 // ביתנא ib.48 (3rd cent. BCE); אנפכם 'your face' A5.1:4 (436/35 BCE) // אפיכן A2.5:2. Some nouns, including diminutive *qutayl* nouns, however, are regularly spelled with a Yod: עלים 'lad' A4.3:8+; עלימתה 'his lass' C7.9:6; היכל 'palace' C1.1:9; possibly זעיר 'small' C1.1:145, D7.5:3; the numeral

---

[169] Cf. Folmer 1995: 173-78.

[170] The last two examples, from a Kraeling papyrus (no. 4), were unknown to Leander (1928:16 g), who put down the other two to scribal errors, though holding it possible ("wohl eher") that the process of contraction had already begun.

[171] Something seems to be amiss with the text: parallel to the immediately preceding כתשוני בכפיד 10 בכפרגל 6 'they struck me on the palm of the hand 10 (times and) on the sole of the foot 6 (times),' one misses a preposition with רגלן.

[172] Rather than 'their kinds, types' ?

'two' תרין A6.2:18+, תרתין B6.4:4+; מין 'water' A4.5:7; מצרין 'Egypt' A6.9:2+; שמין 'heaven' A4.3:3+. All these are admittedly cases of word-medial diphthong.([173]) However, note סוסה 'a horse' < /susay/ (?) A6.12:2([174]), C1.1:38.([175])

There is no knowing with certainty how the m.pl./du. cst. ending may have sounded.([176]) However it is always spelled with a Yod as in עלימי 'lads of' C3.27:30; בני 'sons of' B2.9:2+; יומי 'days of' A4.7:13; ידי 'hands of' C1.1:170. The same applies to a m.pl./du. noun with a possessive suffix for 'my' as in אחי 'my brothers' A3.10:1; בני 'my sons' B2.10:9+; ידי 'my hands' C1.1:155(?).([177]) Significant is אנפכם 'your face' A5.1:4 (436/35 BCE), which was evidently pronounced /-pe:-/. Note also אנפא 'our presence' C3.28:1,91= אַפֵּנָא (?)([178]). This document, however, is of a relatively late date, 3rd c. BCE: see also בתנא 'our house' mentioned in the preceding paragraph. More important, however, is the spelling pattern of the pl. tantum חין 'life.' The st.abs., which we may postulate as /ḥayyi:n/, is always spelled with a single Yod (A2.4:5, A2.7:1, A4.7:3, D7.21:2), but the cst. with a double Yod, (ספרא זנה) חיי 'the life of (this document)' B4.7:5, as well as forms with conjunctive pronouns such as חיי 'my life' B2.3:8 and חייך 'your life' B3.6:12. The cst. חיי could, in theory, have been spelled חי, if the diphthong had contracted (/ḥayye:/), although one could explain the actual spelling as a result of scribal inertia, namely it was felt appropriate to add a second Yod as a mere graphic representation of the m.pl.cst. mor-

---

[173] The last three, particularly מין and שמין, might have to be viewed separately, if they ended with /-ayin/ rather than with /-ayn/.

[174] See Driver (1957:73).

[175] So *pace* Leander (1928:97 h "sein Pferd," i.e. < סוס). Note ססה Deir Alla II 15.

Also *pace* Leander (1928:15 c) one reads now מנין 'number, sum' at B4.5:3, which therefore does not contrast with מנן 'minas' A6.2:17. The only sure case of contraction of stressed, word-medial /ay/ that Leander (1928:15 c) was able to cite was העדת H pf. 1sg. of עדי at B2.6:35 // העדית C1.1:50, on which see below, § 37 *i.*

[176] Cf. § 8 *a* and Folmer 1995:182-84.

[177] Cf. עֲבָדַי 'my deeds' Gn 4.8 (Klein 1986: I, 7) for the standard ending /-ay/. This example is not discussed by Fassberg 1990:115.

[178] Grelot (1972:13, n. *o*) offers quite a different interpretation: 'à échéance.' (At C3.28:1 the form is prefixed by ב and at ib.91 by ל.)

Pace Segert (1975:173), לבנן B3.13:11 does not belong here, because it means 'bricks,' not 'to our son' (Degen 1979:26).

pheme.([179]) Note, however, רבי אבי רבי מן חד 'one of the officers of my father' C1.1:33: if it be to be derived from √ רבי, the final Yod could represent /ye:/.([180])

b) *Diphthong /aw/*

The etymological diphthong /aw/ is mostly spelled plene, i.e. with a Waw([181]): במותי 'on my death' B2.3:3; מוזנא 'the balance-scale' B2.6:24. The plene spelling is standard even in the Hermo-polis papyri, regularly with verb forms of the A or H binyan of יש 'to dispatch': הושר A2.5:4 (pf.), תושר (impf. 3f.sg.), מושרתהם A2.5:7 (inf. plus suf.). The only examples of defective spelling are: תשרי A2.3:10 (juss. 2f.sg.); אתרתן for אותרתן 'you had in abundance' A2.1:5 (A pf. 2mpl); ימין 'days' B3.10:17([182]); זנה ימא 'this day' D7.24:3,4; מאנהי for מאנוהי 'its/his vessels' ib.7.

One may conclude that the speed of contraction was greater with /ay/ than with /aw/.([183])

§ 9. Elision of short unstressed vowels

This process may be observed in our consonantal orthography through spelling fluctuations of forms in which one may assume a short vowel to have existed earlier between two identical con-sonants([184]): דשיהם 'their doors' A4.7:10 as against דששיא ib.11 (pl.st.det.) and דששן B3.11:3 (pl. st.abs.); כדא 'the pitcher (?)' A4.2:13 // כדדן pl. D7.57:7; בטלה 'with his protection' C2.1:10,16,26,42 // בטללה C2.1 I:2, III:4. The spellings with a single consonant indicate that the original short vowel between

---

[179] The occasional use of Yod for the standard He in the Lamed-Yod verb ms ptc. may be an analogical extension of the contracted m.pl./du. ending. See below § 37 *i*.

[180] See Kaufman 1977:94.

[181] Cf. Folmer 1995: 184-88.

[182] Except Samalian with ימי 'in the days of' and 'my days', on which see Tropper (1993:296) and Muraoka (1997:467), no Aramaic dialect attests to an alternative lexeme as in Hebrew יָמִים. In view of זנה ימא mentioned next, the complementary distribution in Hebrew —/yo:m/ sg. and /ya:m/ pl.—does not apply here. See also Folmer 1995: 212f. *pace* Beyer 1984: 596.

[183] We have an examaple of the contraction of /ay/ already in the 9th century BCE (Tel Fekheriyeh bilingual, הדד בת ' the house of Hadad,' line 17): see Muraoka 1983-84:87f. Within his overview of the diachronic phonetics of Aramaic, Beyer's position on the contraction of the diphthongs is conservative in the extreme: the earliest possible terminus post quem is the second century BCE (1984:118).

[184] See Kaufman 1983 and Muraoka 1997a: 206f.

the two identical consonants had begun to be elided.

In the following cases, where no abbreviated spelling is attested, it is difficult to say whether the process of elision had already set in or not: לבבי 'my heart' A3.3:2; לבבהם 'their heart' C1.1:98([185]), לבבא 'the heart' C1.1:88,137; שקקן 'sack-cloths' A4.7:15,20; עממא 'the people' C1.1:98,189. In the light of לבבי 'my heart' and לבבהם 'their heart' (sg.) there is no need to take עממא here as late עֲמְמָא, pl.st.det. as in עַמְמַיָּא Dn 3.7 et passim.([186]) בטללה/בטלה also shows that the phenomenon is not confined to plural nouns, unless one should postulate two distinct variants, say טֵל and טְלָל-/טְלָל([187]). Whereas Beyer (1984:128-36) has collected a considerable amount of data showing that short, unstressed, open-syllabic vowels were still maintained in various Aramaic dialects until the first half of the third century CE, the process of elision had manifestly begun in our period([188]), at least where such a vowel occurred between two identical consonants.([189]) A spelling such as מרי 'my lord' D7.21:1 (< מראי*)

---

[185] In the light of this, one should perhaps prefer בידה to בלבה, two alternative restorations suggested by Porten - Yardeni at C1.2:23: the word, לבב, with or without an inflectional ending or a conjunctive pronoun, occurs some 33 times in our corpus, but no instance of לב is to be found.

[186] See Muraoka 1997b:206f.

Kottsieper (1990:118-20), postulating a separate lexeme עֲמַם* "Weltbevölkerung, Gesamtheit der Menschen, Menschheit," arrives at the same conclusion against the majority view as represented by, e.g. Kaufman (1974:127f.) and Segert (1975:185). The often-quoted two cases from the 3rd c. Uruk inscription—mid 2nd c. according to van Dijk apud Beyer 1984:45, private ocmmunication from Prof. E.E. Knudsen—in the cuneiform script, *ra-ba-ra-bi-e* and *ga-ab-ri-e*, let us note, present a morphophonemic environment different from that in view here. In OA, Sefire, for example, the noun לבב is spelled with a double Bet, whereas the noun עם is spelled with a single Mem: עמא, עמהם, עמיא. BA attests to לִבִּי (Dn 7.28) as well as לְבְבֵה or the like, which latter occurs more frequently. To suggest a synonym עממא 'gentile nation' might be too clever, for are the proverbs of Jewish origin?

Wesselius (1984:444) proposes to see a pl.det. ending /e:/ in חרא 'the nobles' C2.1:48 instead of taking it as sg. but used as collective noun. We do have a pl. form in חרי יהודיא 'the nobles of the Jews' A4.7:18, but unlike all the geminate root nouns mentioned above this one never appears spelled with a double Resh.

[187] The second is the form attested in Syriac, meaning 'shade,' and cf. JA טְלָלָא and Eth. /ṣela:lo:t/. Cf. also Beyer 1984:590, s.v. טלל.

[188] See also Kaufman 1983: esp. 89f., 94f., who speaks of gradual reduction.

[189] Kutscher's attempt (1972:139), endorsed by Qimron (1993:25), to seek

presupposes an elision of *i*: /*maːriʔiː/. What vowel has possibly been elided cannot be determined or generalised.([190])

Kutscher (1972:51) is right in seeing a spelling such as שנה instead of the earlier שנת 'year' in Samalian as an indication that the short vocalic case endings in the singular had already ceased to exist, for the change from the latter to the former is only possible after the loss of such vowels. This, however, does not necessarily mean that *all* word-final short vowels had been lost. See below: § 11 *b, d, f*; 12 *e, g, h*; 24 *b*.

§ 10. Sandhi

Assimilation which may take place across a word boundary has been noted above: § 3 *b*. The phenomenon of clisis mediated by clitics, whether proclitics or enclitics, may also be subsumed under this heading. Two contiguous words which form a close grammatical or logical whole may show a degree of phonetic cohesion, given graphic expression by being run together. However, in actual manuscripts, it is not always clear whether two successive words were intentionally spelled together or not. ([191])

a) *First word = preposition*

The first word may be a preposition: עלזנה 'about this' A6.2:6([192]), A6.15:8([193]); עדזנה (ד supralinear) 'until this (day)' A4.7:20; עלדבר 'on account of' A4.3:3, B2.2:6, B2.11:8, B8.4:7; עדבר 'on account of' B7.1:3, D7.33:2; עלדברה 'on account of it' B2.2:5; עלדברהם 'on account of them' B5.6:6; עלידן 'to our hand' B4.4:13; מצעל 'above' B3.4:18, B3.13:5,7,8,9,10,11; מצעלא B2.10:6; מיומא זנה 'from this day' B3.8:4; מגכן 'on account of that' B2.9:7.([194])

---

evidence for such a vowel syncope in מריהם 'their owners' A4.4:8 cannot be sustained in view of מריה 'her [=its] owner' A3.10:2; see above § 3 *o*.

[190] See Nöldeke 1913:11 and Lindenberger 1983:68f. Segert (1975:115) is inclined to view these double consonants as indication of gemination. One wishes to know, however, why the feature is confined to ע"ע roots, and one never meets with an example such as *קבבל 'he received.'

[191] Are זי and לן at C2.1 III:1,4 written as two separate words? How about זילן at C2.1 I:3? Note also זילא 'which are not' C3.7Kr 2:13. In מנכתא (= מן כתא) 'from the aftergrowth' C3.28:80 the Nun appears to be different from its typical final form in the document.

[192] So transcribed by Cowley 1923:89.

[193] Commented on by Driver 1957:83.

[194] Though both Nuns are identical and typical of the word-final shape.
Note also an Aramaism ענפשה 'for himself' (= על נפשה) in a Heb. document from Naḥal Ḥever (134 C.E.): see Nebe 1997:153.

b) *Second word = preposition*

The second word may be a preposition, ל in particular, with a conjunctive pronoun attached to it: כתבלי 'he wrote to me' B2.3:23; כתבתלה 'I wrote for her' B2.4:4; ימאתלה 'I swore to him' B2.3:24; יהבלי ... יהבתהלכי 'he gave (it) to me ... I gave it to you' ib.25. The ubiquitous, disjunctive possessive pronouns זילך, זילי etc. must have had their origin here.([195])

c) *Frequent in construct phrases*

This phenomenon is rather frequent in construct phrases([196]): רב חיל 'troop commander' A4.7:7; רבחילא B5.1:3 // רב חילא B2.10:2+; רבדגלא 'the head of the detachment' B8.5:11; ברביתא 'the prince' A6.7:10; כפיד 'palm of hand' B8.4:5, B8.6:10; כפרגל 'sole of foot' B8.4:5, B8.6:10.

d) *First word = negator*

The first word may be a negative: לעד 'not yet' B3.13:8; ליאתו 'they should not come' D23.1 Va:10; לאיתי 'there is not' D7.29:4, B3.8:29 // לא איתי ib.34; לא אשכב = לאשכב 'I shall not lie' D23.1 II:10.([197]) The last three are also cases of apocope and/or haplography.([198]) לאתהותבנה (= לא תהיתבנה) 'you shall not restore her' D23.1 II:15 represents a mixture of the two types.

e) *Second word = enclitic pronoun*

The second word may be an enclitic pronoun: שנאהי 'it is hatred' B3.8:40 (= שנאה הי ib.34).([199]) See also מהי A2.5:7 = מה הי. Can the difficult מלו A2.3:7([200]) be decomposed into הו + לא + מה 'what is not?' > 'whatever'?([201])

---

[195] See § 13.

[196] Cf. § 48 *b.*

[197] If correctly restored, [ל] of ול(ד)נא חרא D23.1 II:10 may be of the same kind: colloquially put, "No way! That bloke, Hora!" In any event, the demonstrative must be attributive, for otherwise חרא would have no syntactic slot to fit in. Cf. § 14 *a.*

[198] The proclitic spelling of this negative particle is quite common in OA, e.g. Sefire I A 28 ליתחזה 'it will not be seen' and Deir Alla II 9 ליתמלך 'he will not consult,' indicating that the final Alef had lost its consonantal value.

[199] This is a much simpler solution than Kraeling's: "a part.[= participle] with object suff." (Kraeling 1969:220). See § 3 *n.*

[200] Grelot (1972:151) and Gibson (1975:129) insist on reading הלו 'behold.'

[201] The Akkadian etymology /mala/ 'whatever' suggested by Porten - Greenfield (1968:222) leaves the final Waw unaccounted for. Possibly also in Deir Alla with מה: see Hoftijzer 1976:285. For an alternative interpretation, see Zuckerman (1993:5f. with n. 14 and 15).

f) *Sandhi and asyndeton*

There is one case of asyndesis: התבהב literally 'Restore, give!' A6.15:7([202]) // spelled separately at ib.10.

g) *Sandhi assimilation*

Kottsieper (1990:41f.) is probably right in seeing a case of sandhi assimilation in דרך קשתה 'drew his bow' C1.1:190 in contrast to ד]רגת קשתך C1.1:128, namely voiced /g/ > unvoiced /k/ under the influence of /q/.([203])

---

[202] Driver translates simply "Restore!": see his commentary (1957:83).

[203] It has also been suggested to restore נגת from *נגדת. See Lindenberger (1983:118).

PART TWO

MORPHOLOGY

SECTION A

THE NOUN, ADJECTIVE, AND PARTICLES

§ 11. Disjunctive personal([204]) pronouns.

	Singular	Plural
1	אנה	אנחן; אנחנה
2m.	אנת	אנתם
f.	אנת; אנתי	?
3m.	הו ([205])	הם; המו
f.	הי	? ([206])

Examples and discussion:

אנה: A2.1:7; B5.6:9; C1.1:3; D7.17:3+

a) *2ms.* אנת: A6.3:7; B2.1:11; C1.1:34+. Some authorities, e.g. Beyer (1984:123, 423), Cook (1990:63f.), and Kottsieper (1990:89,93), postulate a defective spelling concealing *a:* (cf. BA Ktiv אנתה[[207]]). All these authors note the alternative, plene spelling אנחנה for אנחן. They further seem to think that, because both pronouns were penultimately stressed, as is generally

---

[204] It is understood here and in the following that 'personal' needs to be rather broadly understood when applied to the 'third person,' for their referent can be a thing, condition, idea, etc., nothing particularly personal.

[205] On the prehistory of the 3s, both m. and f., forms, see an instructive discussion by Kottsieper (1990:89-93). See also above at § 5 *j*. The forms הוא and היא in BA are presumably influenced by BH.

[206] Kottsieper (1990:14,89,93f.) reads הני at C1.1:207 (his Ko. xvi,1), which is a mere speculative reading. Such a form does occur in the Ashur letter, line 12. Kottsieper does not mention הא in Deir Alla, on which see Hoftijzer 1976:286.

[207] Qimron's speculation (1993:7) that the Ktiv form represents a variety of IA must also be evaluated in the light of the total absence of such a spelling anywhere in our IA (or OA, for that matter) corpus.

assumed, אנת must have ended with the same vowel as that of אנחנה. However, is it right to assume that a given vowel in identical phonetic environments must behave in identical fashion and change at the same speed? The evidence of orthography needs to be accorded more weight: nowhere in our corpus or in earlier Aramaic texts is the pronoun in question spelled אנתה. Moreover, whereas the pronoun occurs in our corpus some 50 times, sometimes (A6.2, B2.9, 2.11, 3.12, 4.4, C1.1) alongside אנחנה, it is never written אנתה. This general consideration also applies to the problem of interpretation presented by the conjunctive 2ms. pronoun ך: see below § 12 *d*, *g*.

That אנה is always spelled with a He, but אנחן is not consistently so spelled may have to do with the difference in the positon of stress, as still reflected in later Aramaic dialects: אֲנָה (milra) vs. אֲנַחְנָה (mil'el).

b) *2fs.* אנתי: B2.3:9; D7.26:1 + 17x. At B3.7:13 the Nun has been added later above the line. If the original spelling be genuine, it could be phonetic, i.e. /'atti/, the majority spelling— even when it occurs in the same document with אנת (line 8)—being historical.

אנת: B3.7:8; B3.10:14 (// אנתי 13)†. The two documents are by two different hands, separated by a mere 16 years (420 and 404 BCE). As regards the first, B3.7, one must note that the professional standard of the scribe leaves something to be desired, as is evident in a solecism such as אנת יהוישמע ברתי שליט 'you, Jehoishma my daughter, are entitled' B3.7:8. We have also noted above the pronoun אנתי with a hanging Nun added later. We further observe two more cases in the document where a final Yod is wanting: תחומה 'its boundaries' 9 and לך 14 (// the standard לכי 3,16).([208]) The scribe of the second document, B3.10, which concerns the same matter as that of B3.7, does not show himself to be any better than his colleague, who penned B3.7. Besides four additions he made above the line, note the non-standard שליטא for שליטה five times (13,14*bis*,15,21). Furthermore, our scribe uses the shorter form of the pronoun for 'your' (f.sg.) once: לך 12 alongside the standard לכי 2,3*bis*,22. Note also זילך 11 and דילך 14.([209]) To sum up, whilst it is rather unlikely that the shorter form was *the* form applicable to the whole of our corpus, it occurs fairly widely when considered together with other f.sg. morphemes such as a conjunctive pronoun (§ 12 *e*),

---

[208] Cf. Szubin - Porten 1988: 36.

[209] Cf. Porten - Szubin 1987: 183.

and probably is a harbinger of what would later become the standard as a consequence of the apocope of unstressed, word-final vowels.

c) *3fs.* היא D23.1 XIII:4, a most remarkable spelling, if genuine. The Alef, however, is most likely otiose as in נכוא (// נכו) 'Necho' in this document: see § 5 *k* above. Neither this form nor the masculine form is ever spelled with a final Alef, which latter is the rule in OA and BA.

d) *1pl.* אנחנה vs. אנחן. אנחנה: A4.5:10, B2.11:9,11; C1.1:169; D1.32:11+; אנחן: A2.6:9; B3.4:21; D23.1 XI:8+.([210]) The distribution of these two([211]) forms is something of a problem. In terms of frequency, the difference is significant: אנחנה 38 x, אנחן 17 x. Both forms occur in some of the earliest documents of our corpus: אנחנה B4.4:9,11,15 (483 BCE) and אנחן B5.1:2 (495 BCE), and אנחן twice in the Hermopolis papyri (A2.1:8, A2.6:9). Unlike אנת vs. אנתי, one and the same scribe does not mix both the forms except Haggai b. Shemaiah (אנחנה B3.12:12 vs. אנחן B3.4:3+).

Historically speaking, there is no reason to suppose secondary addition of a vowel at the end of the form, so that the long form must be presumed to be the earlier. Later Aramaic dialects support such a supposition.([212]) Hence, the defectively spelled אנחן was likely pronounced with *-na*. See a discussion above (§ [*b*]) on אנתי. The plene spelling was probably triggered, at least partly, by the singular אנה, which is always spelled plene.

e) *2mpl.* אנתם: A4.1:3+. No form with /-n/ is attested.([212a])

f) *3mpl.* המו: B2.4:7, A3.1:15+ (40 x in all); הם: B6.4:8. The shorter form, hapax, is, as a matter of fact, used as a direct object, conjunctive and disjunctive once each: details in § 38 *f*, 5.([213]) The longer form, המו, is the normal form when used as direct object and appears, as such, always detached from the

---

[210] The second, graphically short form is attested in six documents (A2.1, A2.6, B3.4, B3.6, B5.1, D23.1), and thus can no longer be dismissed as "in éinem Dokument auftretende Nebenform ... lediglich eine orthographische Abweichung" (Leander 1928:26). Cf. also Folmer 1995:152-54.

[211] אנחנן given by Segert (1975:166) and said to occur at B5.1:2 (= Cowley 1.2) and B3.6:11 (=Kraeling 5.11) is a ghost form.

[212] See Nöldeke (1875:87), Barth (1913:5f.), Müller-Kessler (1991:67), and Fassberg (1990:113). /ʾanhína/, which Kottsieper (1988:236f.) wants to identify at Pap. Amherst 63:5/2, is unlikely.

[212a] The reading אנתן at D23.1 XI:8 considered by Koopmans (1962: II, 88) is now read אנחן.

[213] The context is broken in אמו כמרן עבדן הם קרבן[D23.1 XI:9.

verb.

For the morphosyntax of the disjunctive pronouns, see § 39.

§ 12. Conjunctive personal pronouns

	Singular	Plural
1	־י	־נא, ־ן
2m.	־ך	־כם, ־כן ,־כון
f.	־ך, ־כי	־כן(²¹⁴)
3m.	־ה, ־הי	־הם, ־הום ,־הן ,־הון
f.	־הא, ־הה, ־ה	?(²¹⁵)

GENERAL REMARKS

a) The above forms are used whenever a pronominal element is made dependent on a noun, a preposition, or a verb, and not used on its own. Only in the case of the first person singular is a separate form ־ני used as an object of a verb directly attached to the latter: e.g. רחמני 'he loved me' C1.1:51, not רחמי.

These pronouns are presumably attached to the construct form in the same way for the sg., du., pl., ms., and fem.(²¹⁶) nouns(²¹⁷): e.g. אלהך 'your god,' אלהיך 'your gods' (pl.)(²¹⁸), ידך 'your hand,' ידיך 'your hands' (du.), ברתך 'your daughter,' בנתך 'your daughters.' At graphic level, namely when vowels are left

---

²¹⁴ Hug (1993:58) lists כם alongside כן, without giving, however, any example for the former.

²¹⁵ Segert (1975:174) mentions ביניהן 'between them' in אגורא זי יהו ושוק מלכא ביניהן 'the temple of YHW and King's Street between them' B3.12:19 as the sole example of the morpheme in question. However, 'them' refers to בית 'house' and אגור 'temple,' neither of which is known to be a feminine noun in Aramaic.

Although the reading להן is secure at C1.1:211, there is no certainty that in this poorly preserved line this is the preposition ל followed by what Kottsieper (1990:95) wishes to take as the 3fpl. conjunctive pronoun.

²¹⁶ Feminine in form, and not necessarily in gender. We are referring to nouns such as f. ארק 'earth,' f. though lacking a typically feminine suffix, מלן 'words' ending in /-in/ a typically masculine pl. ending, m. שמהן 'names,' ending in /-a:n/, a typically fem. pl. morpheme.

²¹⁷ Here we may include prepositions as well: e.g. לה 'to him,' עלוהי 'on him.'

²¹⁸ One does not know whether already in this period there existed a contrast similar to /-a:k/ vs. /-ayk/ as in later Aramaic dialects. For the 1 sg. 'my' one can reasonably postulate an opposition between /i/ (sg.) and /-ay/ (du. and pl.).

out, there is no difference in form among the suffixed pronouns whether singular, plural or dual. The only exception is forms for 'his': אלהה 'his god,' but אלהוהי 'his gods.'([219]) Otherwise, it may be assumed that the same set of suffixal pronouns was added to the noun in its construct form, whether singular or plural.([220]) Neutralisation as in Hebrew sg. סוּסֵנוּ 'our horse' vs. pl. סוּסֵינוּ 'our horses'([221]) is unlikely in our idiom in view of the near-total([222]) absence of erroneous spellings such as *מלכן for מלכין 'our kings.' Equally unlikely is partial neutralisation as evinced by the Qere of the Tiberian vocalisation of BA אֱלָהַיה 'her gods' and אֱלָהַה 'her god.'([223])

   b) It is scarcely to be doubted that, as in all Aramaic dialects for which there is a known tradition of vocalisation, there intervened a vowel of one sort or another between the end of the

---

[219] On the origin of this striking form, see Dion 1974:154f. and Segert 1975:172. Cf. an attractive, new suggestion by Garr 1985:107: "*-ay-hū > (via regressive assimilation) * -aw-hŭ > (dissimilaiton of u-u) [awh̃ĩ]." His analysis of Samalian ביומיה 'in his days' as [biyawmi:h(u/i)] is unlikely in view of עליה 'against him.' See also Tropper (1993:189) with yet another suggestion—*ayhu: > *-ayhi: > -awhi: (a double dissimilation). Aristar (1987:184f.) would posit the dual nominative (casus rectus) -a:- as the base, thus -a:hu > -a:w > -aw, to which a conjunctive pronoun -hu was subsequently added, producing ultimately -awhi (by dissimilation of -hu to -hi). This would, however, create two quite distinct routes within Aramaic when one takes Samalian into account.

[220] Kottsieper (1990:121) holds that with the f.sg. also the base for suffixation was /t/, and not /at/ "ausweislich der späteren Vokalisierungen." But BA */malkṭe:h/ 'his queen' surely goes back to */malkaṭe:h/? How would one otherwise account for the spirantised /ṭ/ and the /-aṭ-/ in /malkaṭho:n/ 'their queen'? And the /a/ of this latter form is hardly a helping vowel.

[221] There is no phonetic difference between the two forms: see Joüon - Muraoka (1993:37, n.3).

[222] The only possible exceptions occur in אפנא 'our presence' C3.28:1,91 and אנפכם 'your face' A5.1:4, though even here, in theory at least, a distinction was possible: sg. /ʔappána:/ vs. du. /ʔappe:na:/ or the like. Although the Hermopolis papyri attest now to several cases of אַ- with assimilated Nun, the reservation voiced by Leander (1928:31g) is still valid. לבנן B3.13:11, which Segert (1975:173), along with Kraeling (1953:261,264), reads as 'our children,' is best interpreted with Porten - Yardeni (1989:98) and Grelot (1972:253) as the pl. of לבנה 'brick.'

[223] For a discussion, see Bauer - Leander (1927:77f.). See also Brockelmann (1908:480). Segert (1975:171) speaks of possible influence of Babylonian Aramaic, which, however, does not provide a full explanation of the phenomenon: see Epstein (1960:122f.).

st.cst. base of the noun in the singular and the conjunctive pronoun
to be suffixed to it, especially where the latter consisted of a
single consonant, which is the case with ך, כי, ה, ן. The precise
nature of such vowel must remain conjectural; see, however, on
the 2fs. form below.

Examples and discussion:([224])

c) *1sg.*: לי 'to me' A2.1:4; אבי 'my father' A6.11:2([225]); אחי
'my brother' A2.3:8; לבבי 'my heart' A2.1:5; אחתי 'my sister'
A2.1:1([226]); [לבח]י 'anger against me' A3.3:10([227]); אחי 'my brothers'
A3.10:1; עלי 'upon me' A2.3:7; בני 'my sons' B3.5:20; חיי 'my life'
B3.6:4.([228])

d) *2ms*: לך 'to you' B4.2:10; אבוך 'your father' C1.1:15; אחוך
'your brother' A3.3:14, D7.30:1([229]) // אחך A2.4:5([230]) and אחיך(!)
D7.57:2; עבדך 'your servant' A2.4:1; ברתך 'your daughter' B2.6:5;

---

[224] Most of the following examples will be those attached to nouns and
prepositions.

[225] Whether the former was mil'el as in BA in the Tiberian tradition, אֲבִי Dn
5.13, is impossible to say. On this BA form, see Bauer - Leander (1927:77).

[226] In view of אחה, and not אחת, as in אח ואחה 'a brother and a sister'
B2.10:11 et passim, the ה in אחתך presumably did not carry a long *a:*. Hence,
אחתי 'my sister' A2.1:1+ must be read /ʔaḥti/ and אחתי 'my sisters' A2.5.1 as
/ʔaḥa:ti/ or something like that. Likewise, the sg.cst. אחת /ʔaḥat/, and not
/ʔaḥa:t/ as Hug (1993:70) postulates.

[227] So must the form be emended in the light of the idiom attested in
A4.2:11; A3.5:4. See also Ashur letter 19: הלבתי מלא אנת 'Are you filled with
anger against me?' This is an Akkadian idiom as in *ma:diš li-ib-ba-ti-ya
ma-li* 'he was very angry with me': CAD, L, p. 164a. So has the text been
emended also by Gibson (1975:144). The point had already been noted by
the editor of the text, Bresciani (1960:21). The possibility of defective spelling
is highly unlikely, since the 1sg. conj. pron. is never so spelled.

[228] The form חיך 'your life' B3.6:12,13 shows that חיי contains the pl.cst.
form of the noun. ידי in מסת כספה זי הוה בידי 'an amount (?) of money that was
in my hand (hands?)' A2.2:4 is ambiguous. But כספה זי הוה בידה 'the silver
that was in his hand' A2.6:6 clinches the matter in favour of the sg., though
not יתו ביד חרוץ 'let them bring through H.' A2.5:5 nor כזי תמטה ידכי 'as much
as you can' A2.6:5, as Hug (1993:56, n.) thinks, for these latter cases involve
a different paradigmatic environment. We fail to see why ידי in כדי מטאה ידי
'as much as I can' A2.4:4 should be considered ambiguous in this regard.

[229] This last instance is wrongly given by Hug (1993:57) as אחך, though
not in his transcription of the text (1993:30).

[230] Cf. אחכי 'your (fs) brother' A2.1:2, also a Hermopolis papyrus. This
non-standard form without a Waw (for אחוכי) occurs also with the 3mpl.
pronoun. See below § *k*.

בנתך 'your daughters' B3.12:26; עבדיך 'your servants' A6.1:1; חייך 'your life' B3.6:12.(²³¹)

The unique, short form אחך is typical of the Hermopolis papyri.(²³²) Also attested is אחכי A2.1:2, A2.2:1, A2.3:1. However, the standard form also occurs: אחוכי A2.7:1,5; אחוכן A2.5:1.(²³³)

e) *2fs*: כי- vs. ־ך. לכי 'to you' A2.2.7; לך A3.4:2, B2.7:9(²³⁴),12,16, B3.6:8, B3.7:14, B3.10:12, B3.11:7,9; בכי 'in you' B3.6:6 // בך ib.; זילכי 'your' B2.3:12 // זיליכי ib.19; זילך B3.10:11, B3.11:4; מנך 'from you' B3.11:10; ברך 'your son' A3.4:1; ברתכי 'your daughter' B3.6:4 // ברתך ib.7; עליכי 'on you' B3.11:15 // עליך ib.12; בניכי 'your sons' B2.7:7 // נכסיך 'your possessions' ib.6; אפיכי 'your face' A2.2:2, A2.6:2 // אפיך A2.1:2, which in turn // אחכי ib., and אפיך A2.3:2 // ברכתכי 'I have blessed you.'

The anomalous short morpheme spelled only with כ is decidedly in the minority. It is, however, frequent enough to speak for its genuineness.(²³⁵) One may hypothesise that the shorter spelling indicates blurring, if not total loss, of the original final *i*: see above at § 5 *b*. It is further possible that such a shortening of the vowel resulted from the change of pitch accent to stress accent. Such a reconstruction would confirm the antiquity of the traditional position of the stress, namely penultimate.(²³⁶) Cf. § 11 *b*.

The short forms are confined to a small number of documents, and they are used side by side with the corresponding, standard forms with Yod, as is apparent from some examples quoted above. Furthermore, the fluctuation between אבוהי and אבוה 'his father' (see below at § *f*) in a document which also attests to a fluctuation between ך- and כי- suggests that the phenomenon is phonetic, and not one of grammatical incongruence or careless syntax.

On the striking form, זיליכי 'yours,' see § 13 below. If genuine,

---

²³¹ On the question whether ך could be a defective spelling for *ka:*, see below, § *g*.

²³² Once also in אבהון 'their father' D1.17:12 .

²³³ No relevant example of אב occurs in the Hermopolis papyri.

²³⁴ Or should one possibly restore [י]לכ?

²³⁵ Thus Cowley's restoration at his 13.12 (= B2.7:12) [י]לכ is misleading and to be rejected: see Porten - Yardeni (1989:35).

²³⁶ Folmer (1995: 167), who cites יהבתה 'you (f.sg.) gave it' B5.5:7 as evidence for the length of the vocalic suffix of the verb, has not taken the position of the stress into account: in this particular form the verb suffix was likely stressed.

the form points to an *i*-type vowel after ל, and also indicates that
the form was stressed on the penultimate syllable.

f) *3ms*: ה- vs. הי-. לה 'to him' A2.3:4; ברה 'his son' A6.14:5;
אבוהי 'his father' B3.6:11 // אבוה ib.12; אחוהי 'his brother' B2.10:21
// אחוה ib.3; ברתה 'his daughter' C3.9:18; כנותה 'his colleagues'
A6.1:1; עלוהי 'about it' A3.10:7 // עלוה D7.15:12; בנוהי 'his sons'
A2.4:3; רגלוהי 'his feet' A4.7:16; אגרוה 'its walls' B3.4:4; תחומה
'its boundaries' B3.7:9 // the standard תחומוהי B2.3:5+; משחתה 'its
measurements' B2.3:4.([237]) A possible case of contraction of the
diphthong /aw/ is מאנהי 'its/his vessels' D7.24:7: see § 6 *e*.

The longer morpheme, הי, occurs where the stem of the
noun ends in an originally long vowel or diphthong *aw*: e.g.,
אבוהי (= /ʾabu:hi/), בנוהי (= /banawhi/). The short spelling of this
morpheme such as אבוה([238]) may be explained in the same way as
that for the 2fs: see above under § *e*.([239])

g) *3fs*: ה- vs. הה- or הא-. לה 'to her' A2.1:5; ידה 'her hand'
B2.6:6; אבוה 'her father' B2.10:7, B3.8:28, C1.1:55; אחוהא 'her
brother' D7.57:4; ברתה 'his daughter' B2.3:3; אחתהה 'her sister'
A2.7:4; בניה 'her children' A2.7:3; נכסיה 'her possessions' B2.6:21;
עליהא 'upon her' D1.17:11.([240])

---

[237] The noun is likely pl. in view of the parallel תחומוהי ib. as well as משחת
[כתיב] משחתה =] B3.5:12, and the pronoun masc. in view of זך משחת ביתא
B2.4:4.

[238] Forms analogous to אגרוה are known to OA, Fekheriyan, and the Deir
Alla dialect: e.g., קדמוה 'before him' Nerab 2.2 (7th c.); אחוה 'his brothers'
Sefire III 17: see Degen (1969:57f.) and Muraoka (1983-84:94). Samalian is
unique in proffering a form such as יומיה 'his days' (casus rectus): see Dion
(1974:151-55) and Tropper (1993:189). Dion's view that the element -*ay*- has
been preserved in Eastern Aramaic dialects (1974:154f.) clashes with the
picture presented by Fekheriyan with וה-.
Pace Garr (1985:107) we prefer Hug's (1993:70) analysis of Tel Halaf
ostracon 4.3 רביה as 'its interest, interest on it,' and not 'his elders.'
Pace Hoftijzer (1976:286) אלוה in Deir Alla I 1 cannot mean 'to her.' Nor
can כפהו ib. IXa 3 mean 'her hands.'
We would not, as Degen (1979:24) does, dismiss as a mere late innovation
a form such as /ya:tibayhi/ in the Uruk incantation text and analogous forms
in Palmyrenian (Rosenthal 1936:47). Nor would we follow Degen (1979:26)
in dismissing the short morpheme as mere scribal error when it occurs four
times (three or four different scribes).

[239] It is probably unwise to build too much on a most striking form, עזכתיה
D7.57:7, should it mean 'its seals,' spelled in the manner of late Aramaic
dialects, עִזְקָתֵיה, with a possible dissmilation of /q/ to /k/ (see above § 3 *i*).

[240] The last text, though broken at this point and // אחתה line 10, is to be

The long spelling in אחתהה, אחוהא, and עליהא attested thrice
only([241]) in a Hermopolis papyrus, a Strasbourg ostracon of the
late 3rd cent. BCE, and a text likewise of the 3rd cent. BCE, is
most remarkable. It is generally([242]) assumed that the original
ha: of this morpheme had lost its vocalic component already in
OA, apparently on the ground of its spelling with a simple ה.
The form in our corpus must represent this morpheme. On the
other hand, a total innovation cropping up after the elapse of
three centuries or so sounds rather unlikely, all the more so in
view of exactly the same phenomenon surfacing four or five
centuries later in Qumran Aramaic as הה-/הא.([243]) Is it possible
that this represents an ancient feature preserved as an undercurrent
in living speech cropping up from time to time? Let it be noted,
however, that Qumran Aramaic attests also to 2ms. כא-/כה-([244]),
no trace of which is to be found anywhere in our corpus, even in
the Hermopolis papyri, nor in earlier Aramaic documents.([245])
The widely assumed underlying common shape of the two
conjunctive pronouns, C*a*, anceps or otherwise, might suggest

---

dated to the third century BCE.

In 1979 Degen could state (1979:26) that אחוהא is the sole instance of the
morpheme in IA, and that in a document of the Hellenistic period. But we
have two more now, one of which is of an early date, attested in a Hermopolis
papyrus.

[241] Kutscher's wording (1971:106), "A further trait that does occur in the
other papyri ...," is misleading. Gibson (1975:143) dismisses the first as a
scribal error. So Hug (1993:57). In fact, many think that the referent of the
pronoun, הריומא, is an Egyptian male, hence 'his sister': so Grelot (1972:472).
The matter, however, is debatable. Cf. also Folmer 1995:237-41.

[242] E.g., Brockelmann (1908:312) and Barth (1913:56). But Bauer - Leander
(1927:79) and Leander (1928:31) suggest an anceps form. The short *a* attested
in BA in its Tiberian tradition, for instance, is probably a linking vowel in
origin, the vowel of the suffix itself having been apocopated.

[243] Spelled הא. We pointed this out in our review (Muraoka 1973:171) of
Kutscher's study (1971).

[244] Discussed in Fassberg (1992:51-54), Qimron (1992:119-23) and Muraoka
(1993:40-42).

[245] As justly emphasised by Fassberg (1992:52), who is inclined to consider
a combination of Qumran Hebrew influence with its ubiquitous כה and internal
Aramaic pressure, i.e. *a:*, a plausible explanation for the long morpheme in
Qumran Aramaic (1992:53). There is, of course, no question of Hebraism in
our form in the Hermopolis letter. Qimron is inclined to the view that the
feature in QA is genuine Aramaic (1992:121f.).

that the two ought to be viewed together([246]), though their later reflexes are not uniform([247]), but these new data which have emerged after the traditional view was formulated seem to call for revision of it.

It is certainly too daring to generalise on the strength of this sole instance that every ה- of the morpheme in question in our corpus is defectively spelled. Statistics must be given some weight: our treatment of אחתהה and אחוהא, assuming of course that they are not scribal errors, must differ from that of ך- for כי- (see above at § *e*) and זילנא for זילך (see below at § *h*).([248])

We would also note that the feature represented by אחתהה, אחוהא (and זילנא) is the reverse of that represented by ך for כי: the former is, so to speak, swimming against the stream, whereas the latter is a harbinger of what was to become more or less universal in subsequent phases of Aramaic.([249])

On the thrice-attested אבוה 'her father,' see our discussion above.

h) *1pl*.: ן- vs. נא-. לן 'to us' A6.1:2; מראן 'our lord' A6.10:2; ביתנא 'our house' C3.28:48; בתנא ib.53; זילנא 'our' A6.10:2, C3.28:108,112; בנתן 'our daughters' B2.9:10; עלין 'on us' A3.9:7; בינין 'between us' B2.1:13,14; נשין ובנין 'our wives and our children' A4.7:15; אפנא 'our presence' C3.28:1,91; החון 'he let us see' A4.7:16 // חוינא *ditto* A4.8:15 (407 BCE).

Here again, as in the case of הה- 'her' discussed above (§ *g*), the long form, though, in contrast with the disjunctive pronoun for "we," far less frequent than the short form, raises the same sort of questions.([250]) Diachronically, *na:* is the primitive form.

---

[246] So still Qimron (1992:121, n. 9).

[247] E.g., BA הָ- vs. ךְ-; but Syr. *a:h* vs. *a:ḥ*. (None of the three cases in BA mentioned by Bauer - Leander [1927:73p], the Codex Leningradensis as printed in Biblia Hebraica Stuttgartensia or Adi edition of A. Dothan or the Aleppo codex as edited by Breuer [1977-82] displays qamatz.) For a useful listing of comparative data, see Fassberg (1990:116). Has the Tiberian tradition of BA possibly preserved something genuinely archaic?

[248] According to Qimron (1992:121), QA has as many as 38 cases of כה-.

[249] Beyer (1984:122-25) not only postulates the general preservation of word-final, unstressed long vowels for IA and earlier, but also holds that their shortening occurred only around 100 BCE. Cook (1990) also maintains that ך in OA and IA is a defective spelling for *ka:*. On the basis of the assumed unstressed, long, word-final *a:* in the papyrus Amherst 63, Kottsieper (1990:88f.) argues equally for the defective spelling of our morpheme. See also above at § 12 *a*.

[250] Cf. Folmer 1995:155-58. For the spelling alternation between נא- as a

The long spelling is first attested in the late 5th cent., and is particularly frequent in C3.28, a 3rd cent. document([251]): A4.8 and A6.10 (both late 5th c.), C3.18 (end 5th c.), C3.28 (3rd c.).([252])

i) *2mpl.*: ‑כם vs. ‑כן or ‑כון. לכם 'to you' A3.10:2, B2.9:12, D7.29:10; מנכם 'from you' A3.10:8; אבוכם 'your father' B2.9:6; ידכם 'your hand' A3.10:2; לכן 'to you' A2.2:13 (preceded by הם‑ 'them'), A2.4:12, A3.3:5; פרסכן 'your salary' A3.3:4; שלמכן 'your well-being' A2.2:17 (in a letter addressed to a woman[[253]]), A2.4:13; מדינתכם 'your province' A6.9:2; לבחכם 'anger (pl.) against you' A4.2:11; עליכם 'to you' A4.3:9 // עליכון D7.56:14; אחריכם 'after you' B2.4:8; תניכם 'your chambers' A4.1:8; אחיכם 'your brothers' B2.9:12, אחיכון 'your brother' (sg.!) D7.56:3; בניכם 'your sons' B2.9:14.

Many examples of the morpheme with final Nun are from the Hermopolis papyri.([254]) Let us further note that these papyri also contain the 3mpl. morpheme with final Nun (see below at § k).([255]) Both morphemes are perhaps best interpreted as precursors of the corresponding forms in later Aramaic dialects.([256])

j) *2fpl.*: ‑כן. אחוכן 'your brother' A2.5:1([257]); שלמכן 'your well-being' ib.9; אפיכן 'your face(s)' ib.2.

One cannot say with absolute certainty how the masculine

---

conjunctive pronoun and אנחנה (never אנחנא), see Folmer 1995:160f. Folmer's explanation applies also to the only case of ‑הא 'her' in אחוהא 'her brother' D7.57:4 (3rd cent. BCE), not discussed by Folmer.

[251] Not "erst in dem jungen Papyrus C81 [= C3.28]" (Degen 1979:26).

[252] BA shows /-ána:/, the last vowel spelled plene with Alef. Bauer - Leander (1927:72,79,81) gives the form as /-á:na:/, though noting /-ána:/ as a variant reading (1927:73r). Rosenthal (1961:26) also records אֱלָהָא Dn 3.17, where Biblia Hebraica (ed. Kittel), on which Rosenthal (1961:1f.) states to have based his grammar, reads the form with a patach, though Biblia Hebraica Stuttgartensia does indicate ad loc. a variant reading with a qamatz.

[253] Hug (1993:56f.) includes this, along with A2.4:13 and A2.1:12, among cases of the masculine ‑כן. Note אל תצפו A2.2:3.

[254] Already Baumgartner (1927:106), without the Hermopolis papyri, had indicated the 5th or 6th cent. BCE for the onset of this development.

[255] Note an inconsistency in למושרתהם 'to dispatch them' A2.2:13 with a Mem, followed by לכן 'to you (m.pl.).

[256] The *-n* forms do not occur in any text dealt with by Hug (1993:56f.) except in the Hermopolis papyri.

[257] Grelot (1972:163) is probably right in interpreting the suffix as fem. pl. and the preceding אחתי as pl. "my sisters.'

כֹּ- and the feminine כֹּ- were possibly distinguished. The analogy of later Aramaic dialects suggests a vocalic difference. The presence of הם- and הן- next to each other (A2.2:13; see n. 52 above), both referring to masculine, cautions us against concluding that the idiom of the Hermopolis papyri may have totally neutralised the distinction between the two genders in the 2nd and 3rd persons in favour of the masculine forms.

k) *3mpl.:* הם-, הום- vs. הן-, הון-. להם 'to them' B8.4:7+; בהם 'in them' C2.1:21, C3.7Kr2:4; עמהם 'with them' B8.9:2+; עמהון 'with them' D7.56:11; אבוהם 'their father' B8.4:14 // אבהון D1.17:12 and תריהון 'the two of them' ib.11; אמהם 'their mother' B2.11:13; להן 'to them' A2.3:8, A4.2:4,14; שלמהן 'their well-being' A2.3:3; קדמתהן 'ahead of them' A2.3:9; לנפשהום 'for themselves' A4.7:13; שמהתהם 'their names' C3.11:12; עליהם 'on them' A3.8:4 // עליהון A4.7:24 // עליהן A2.2:10(?); ביניהן 'between them' B3.12:19,21; בהום 'upon them' A4.7:17; מליהם 'their words' A3.8:13; תליהם 'their weapons' A4.7:8 // זניהום A4.8:8; נכסיהום ובתיהם 'their possessions and their houses' C2.1 III:2.

The morpheme הון- is late, first attested in 3rd cent. documents, D1.17 and D7.56.

The occasional spelling with a Waw, הום and עמהון([258]), provides a vital clue to the vowel of the morpheme, *u* or *o*. The same applies to the occasional כון-.

On the consonant alternation, *m* or *n*, see above at § *i*. No scribal consistency is to be sought in this regard: in one and same document we find להן 'to them' A4.2:4,14 and לבתכם 'anger against them' ib.11; בהן ... מריהם 'in them ... their owners' A4.4:8 and להן ib.9. Nor is there consistency between the final consonant of the conjunctive pronoun for the 2pl. and that of the perfect: אחוכם 'your brother' A3.10:1, ידכם 'your hand' ib.2, לכם 'to you' ib.2 vs. זבנתון ... ויבלתון 'you bought ... and brought' ib.5, נפקתם 'you went out' A3.3:3 vs. פרסכן 'your pay' ib.4 and לכן 'to you' ib.5.

l) *3fp.* There is no assured example of a 3fp suffix. The gender of רגל in the sense of 'foot' cannot be determined on the basis of internal evidence, so that מנחתתהם 'to put them [= רגלהם 'their leg(!)'] down' C1.1:170 cannot be adduced as evidence. The suffix of שלמהן 'their welfare' is probably masculine, for, according to Grelot, only one of the four persons mentioned, Isireshut, is female, thus masculine gender as *genus potior*.([259])

---

[258] *Pace* Joüon (1934:10), hardly an erroneous spelling.

[259] Grelot 1972:475.

m) *Object pronouns attached to the verb*

The conjunctive pronouns suffixed to the verb are basically identical with those suffixed to the noun and the preposition, except for the first person singular: see below § 38. Hence only a handful of examples have been quoted above of pronouns added directly to verbs. Only in one instance we find נ‍א-, a long suffix attached to a verb (חוינא 'he showed us' A4.8:15). For a fuller listing of conjunctive pronouns attached to verbs, see below, § 38.

n) *Disjunctive instead of conjunctive pronoun*

No instance of a disjunctive pronoun notionally dependent on the preceding noun or preposition is found in our corpus, as in Old Aramaic: Tel Dan 10 הם. ארק. 'their land'; Barrakkab II 7 נבשת. הם 'their souls'; Zakkur A 9 הם. מחנות. 'their armies.'

§ 13. Disjunctive possessive pronouns

The use of disjunctive possessive pronouns compounded with זיל(‍[260]) and the appropriate pronominal suffix is very frequent and characteristic of IA. The forms and problems presented by them are identical with those of the preposition ל with the pronominal suffixes. On their morphosyntax, see § 40.

Singular	Plural
1 זילי([261]) A6.8:1	זילנא B2.9:13; זילן
A6.10:2	
2m זילך B3.4:16; דילך B3.10:14 זילכם B2.10:8	
f זיליכי B3.5:4; זיליכי B2.3:19 ?	
דילכי B2.7:11; זילך B3.10:11([262])	
3m זילה B3.11:5 זי לה D23.1 II:11([263]) זילהם B3.5:22	
f זילה D7.8:4 ?	

The striking form זיליכי, which occurs only at B2.3:19, may be accounted for by the emphasis laid on who is to own the property: ארקא זך זיליכי 'that land is *yours*.' The transfer of the

---

[260] On the forms with ד, see above § 2 *a*.

[261] These pronouns are sometimes spelled as two separate components. On this question, see above § 10 *b*.

[262] See above, § 12 *e*.

[263] It could be feminine.

On the graphic separation of the two components, see Dn 2.20 גְּבוּרְתָא דִּי־ לֵהּ הִיא the strength is his' where, however, the pronoun is predicative. The spelling in Vogt (1971:88b) is misleading: בר זי לה C 8.26 (= B2.3:26), איש זי לכם C 20.14 (= B2.9:14) where the gap ought to be closed.

property from Mahseiah to his daughter Mibtahiah is mentioned more than once in the document: lines 3,8,9,10,12f. Though Leander (1928:32) regarded our זיליכי as a possible scribal error, a similar form has now turned up in QA: בטליכי ... בדיליכי 'thanks to you ... on your account' 1QapGen 19.20, where, too, a measure of emphasis is not out of place.([264])

In תאתא זי לך רבתא 'your big sheep' D7.8:2 the pronoun is broken up into its etymological components, but followed by זילה 'its' ib.4, whereas in זילי הוה B2.3:3, the first word is to be understood as זי לי*, for the meaning is apparently "which was mine."([265])

§ 14. Demonstrative pronouns

The pronouns for deixis in our corpus present a remarkably rich variety.([266])

a) For an object physically or mentally near: 'this, these'

Sg.m.: זנה, זנא, דנה([267]), דנא([268])

   f. : זא, דה, זה([269])

Pl.c. : אלה([270])

Examples:

b) *m.s.*: ספרה זנה 'this letter' A2.1:12; כזנה 'like this' A4.7:15;

---

[264] The feature recurs in a much later idiom, CPA, according to some partially pointed examples collected by Bar-Asher (1977:326), though Bar-Asher is mainly interested in the final vowel. *Pace* Beyer (1984:451) this is hardly a suffix attached to a plural noun.

[265] See § 10 *b*.

[266] Cf. Folmer 1995: 198-209.

[267] On the alternation between ז and ד, which also applies to the sg.f. forms, see above § 2 *a*.

[268] This last form only at D23.1 II:10.

[269] The consistent spelling in OA with Alef, including Fekheriyan זאת (on which see Muraoka 1983-84:93f.), suggests its original consonantal character, no mere vowel letter (*pace* Garr [1985:83—"a secondary, syllable-closing *aleph*"). The striking ז in ... ז דמת 'this is the statue of ...' in a ninth cent. BCE inscription from Gozan suggests that already at this early period and in this area the consonant had quiesced in this word-final position. Lipiński's (1994:17) suggestion of a possible Phoenicianism does not materially affect this interpretation.

[270] It is precarious to postulate אל on אלה B3.4:7 where a He has been added below the line, the shorter form being known in OA, Samalian and BA alongside אלן. Our idiom, however, does not know אלן of OA and BA. אלה occurs in our corpus 21 times.

ספרא זנא 'this document' B3.11:15; על דנה 'on this' A5.2:9.

זנה is the standard spelling, whereas דנה occurs only three times (A5.2:8,9; B3.11:3) and זנא five times (B3.11:15[271]; C3.16.4,5[272]; D2.24:2).(273)

f.s.: אגרתא זא 'this letter' A3.3:13; דה only once at A2.5:7.

pl.c.: בתיא אלה 'these houses' B3.7:14; מליא אלה 'these words' A3.9:5.

The spelling with He in דה A2.5:7 is typical of the Hermopolis papyri: see § 5 *e*.

c) For an object physically or mentally removed, 'that, those':

Sg.m.: זך, דך, זנך(274)

f. : דכי, דכא(275), זכי, זך

Pl.c. : אלכי, אלך

The pronouns of this series appear to be composed of those given above under § *a* and the morpheme for the second person *k* or *ky*.(276) Thus it would be more correct to view, for instance, זך as /za:/ + /k/ and זכי as /za:/ + /ki/ rather than as two variant forms, the one shortened from the other, analogous to אנת and

---

[271] In a rather poorly executed document and as a dittography following the standard spelling זנה at the end of the previous line.

[272] In a very poorly preserved text.

[273] ילד בון בי B5.6:4, which Porten - Yardeni (1989:128) tentatively render 'born in this house,' is extremely difficult: the spelling ילד, the form זן, which admittedly does occur in a 5th c. inscription from Tema in the Arabian peninsula and in Samalian (Dion 1974:156) alongside the standard זנה, and the abs.st. בי with the demonstrative.

Cook (1990:64f.) suggests that the original form was /dína/, but unlike most of the forms discussed by him this demonsrative, in our corpus and earlier phases of Aramaic, is always spelled plene with the very few exceptions mentioned above. Then MA דן in QA and דֵן in TA (on the latter, see Fassberg [1990:120]) cannot have resulted from BA זֶנָה by apocope of unstressed word-final vowels as in /ʔanta/ > /ʔant/. It appears that one has to postulate for Early Aramaic two variant demonstratives, one mil'el and the other milra. In order to admit the former alone, the milra BA form would have to be accounted for. Analogy of the feminine form? Then one would, however, have to interpret דנה in QA as mil'el.

[274] דכי in מומאה דכי 'that oath' B2.8:9 listed by Leander (1928:33) as masculine is actually feminine, for מומאה is clearly f. in gender: see מומאה מטאה 'the oath comes' B2.8:4. Hence Leander's observation in the paragraph *q* becomes redundant. Cf. also above § 3 *n*.

[275] Leander (1928:33) is probably right in regarding this unique form as a scribal error for דכי in the same document.

[276] See below § 41 *d*.

אנתי or לך and לכי, both 2fem.sg. forms.([277])

Examples:

d) *m.s.*: ביתא זנך 'that house' B2.3:8, B2.4:6†(same scribe)

ביתא זך 'that house' B2.4:4; זך ספרא 'that document' B2.3:16

דרגא דך 'that stairway' B3.10:10†

f.s.: זך ספינתא 'that boat' A6.2:22

מנתא זכי 'that share' B5.1:4; מן זכי 'from that (time)' A4.7:21([278])

מומאה דכא 'that oath' B2.8:6†

מומאה דכי 'that oath' B2.8:9†

pl.c.: דששיא אלך (m.) 'those doors' A4.7:11; חקלתא אלך(f.) 'those fields' B8.10:4

נכסיא אלכי 'those possessions' B2.8:8; see also A2.7:3, A3.1:3, A5.2:4†

e) It is a fair supposition that the m. זך and the feminine זך contrasted by virtue of vowel differentiation after ז as in BA m. דֵּךְ vs. f. דָּךְ.

f) The disjunctive pronoun for the third person may be used as demonstrative: so יומא הו 'that day' C3.15:123; פלגא הו 'that half' B2.4:12; עדנא הו 'that time' D7.17:3.([279])

g) A special form is זכם or דכם 'selfsame'([280]), always attributively with, and preceding, דגלא 'detachment': דכם דגלא B3.8:2; זכם דגלא B2.4:2, B2.9:4, B5.2:3.([281])

On the morphosyntax and syntax of the demonstrative

---

[277] See above § 12 *e*.

[278] Indiscriminately with the name of a male: [פ][סמש]כחסין זכי 'that [P]samshe[khasi]' A6.3:6. Even if Folmer (1995:199f.) be right in seeing here an appositively, not attributively, used pronoun, its reference to a male remains problematic.

[279] *Pace* Fitzmyer (1956:32f.) we are hardly dealing here with an "emphatic" use: in the first instance, the pronoun is simply anaphoric, referring back to the first line of the document, and in the second the emphasis is not on פלגא, but on the following words as emphasised by the following המו, and in the third we do need a demonstrative pronoun, עדנא being barely sufficient in the context.

[280] The etymology of the word is obscure; cf. Leander (1928:35). *Pace* Segert (1975:193), the mimation is rather unlikely with demonstrative pronouns.

[281] Whether the fact that a phrase containing this pronoun is always prefixed by a preposition is, as Fitzmyer thinks (1956:58), significant or not is difficult to say.

pronouns, see below at §§ 41, 65.

§ 15. Relative pronoun

The so-called relative pronoun, זי/די(²⁸²), is used in ways significantly different from the way in which its Indo-European equivalent is used.(²⁸³) This particle is also used in a rich variety of
other ways. In essence it indicates a relation of dependence
between what precedes it and what follows it, the latter being
dependent on the former. The so-called independent relative clause
lacking an antecedent can be regarded as elliptical. For details,
see below § 42 d.

§ 16. Interrogative words

A limited number of words are used to elicit information on the
identity of persons or objects, their nature, their location, a time
of action, a reason for action, a manner of action, a place of
action, and a quantity of an entity, etc. For example:

מן הו זי יקום קדמוהי 'Who is he that can stand up in front of
him?' C1.1:91

מה חסין הו מן חמר 'What is more robust than an ass?' C1.1:174

הודע ... איך הלכתך 'Make known ... how your conduct is'
C2.1:66

למה הו יחבל מתא עלין 'Why should he damage the land against
us?' C1.1:36

אמת תעבדן 'when you celebrate ...' D7.6:9 (indirect question)

אן 'Where?, Whither?' is used in our corpus only in conjunction
with זי in a generalising statement: אן זי צבית 'wherever you
please (to go) to' B2.6:25,29†.

§ 17. Indefinite pronouns

מדעם/מנדעם(²⁸⁴) is used to refer to an unspecified object, translatable
as 'something, anything.' E.g., אהה לכן מדעם 'I shall bring you
something' A2.1:10; מדעם אל תזבני 'Buy nothing' A2.3:10.
Syntactically different is מנדעם כסנתו יהוה 'Should there be any
decrease' A6.10:8 and מנדעם באיש 'something bad' A6.7:8 (§ 44
a). מנדעמתא זי אשתכחו בה 'the things which were found in it'
C3.7Gr2.23 represents an extension of the original indefinite
use: 'something' > 'the thing' with the st.det. morpheme attached.

---

²⁸² On the alternation between /d/ and /z/, see above § 2 a.

²⁸³ Cf. Joüon - Muraoka (1993: § 158a*).

²⁸⁴ On the etymology and the Nun of the form, see above § 3 c.

Similarly in מזרקיא זי זהבא וכסף ומנדעמתא זי הוה באגורא זך 'the golden and silver basins and the things which were in that temple' A4.7:12. Cf. also A4.5:23, A4.8:11.

איש 'person, one' is also used in an analogous fashion: כל מדעם זי יחיה בה איש 'something whereby one could live' B4.1:3; איש מנדעם באיש לא יעבד 'no one should do anything bad' A6.7:8.([285])

§ 18. The Noun

The noun is declined with respect to number (singular, dual, and plural), and state (absolute, construct, and determined).([285a]) Moreover, each noun is either masculine or feminine in gender([286]), which is, just as the categories of number and state, marked by means of sufformatives.([287])

a) *Declensional endings*

The sufformative exponents of the above-mentioned categories look as follows:([288])

---

[285] For more examples, see Hoftijzer - Jongeling 1995: 119.

[285a] By proposing a three-way opposition of emphaticus, pronominalis and constructus as determinatus on the one hand and indeterminatus (our absolute) on the other, Tsereteli (1991:1572) is confusing morphology and morphosyntax. Judging from later Aramaic dialects with tradition of vocalisation, the status pronominalis and status constructus constitute one morphological category. Morphosyntactically also they are two manifestations of a single category.

[286] Three cases of common gender are עגז 'goat'—m. עגז חד 'one goat' D7.57:5; f. עגזא ואמרת [עגזת] 'the goat [answered] and said' C1.1:165: מחזי 'mirror'—m. ... מחזי 1 זי נחש שוה 'l mirror of bronze worth ...' B2.6:11; f. 1 מחז ... שויה 'l mirror worth ...' B3.3:5: מרבי 'interest'—m. יהוה ראש (the subject: מרבית) 'it will become interest' B4.2:5; f. ... ותהוה מרבית כספך 'and the interest on your silver shall be ...' B4.2:3.

[287] But see the following note.

[288] It is understood of course that, as in every Semitic language, there are masculine nouns which take typically feminine endings in either the sg., du. or pl., and conversely feminine nouns which take typically masculine endings in one of the numbers. Such a discrepancy does not arise in the case of adjectives, and participles which are to a certain extent inflected like adjectives. Therefore, the above scheme may be taken roughly as that of (substantivally used) adjectives. In the following listing, only the typically masculine or feminine *form* is taken into consideration, so that מלי 'the words of," the pl. cst. of a feminine noun, מלה, is listed under the category "m.cst.pl." See below at § 18 *v*.

	Singular	Dual	Plural
m.abs.	ø	‏-ין‏	‏-ן‏ / ‏-ין‏
cst.	ø	‏-י‏	‏-י‏
det.	‏-ה/-א‏	‏-יא‏	‏-יא‏ / (‏-יה‏)
f.abs.	‏-ה, -א / -ת‏	‏-תין‏	‏-ן‏
cst.	‏-ת‏	‏-תי‏	‏-ת‏
det.	‏-תא/-תה‏	?	‏-תא/-תה‏

Examples and discussion:

b) *m.abs.sg.*: אח 'brother' B2.1:8; בר 'son' B3.6:5.

du.: תרין 'two' A6.9:4; ידין 'hands' B2.6:8, B3.8:8; עינין 'eyes' C1.1:212,214; אדנין 'ears' ib.157,215; רגלן 'legs' B8.4:5.([289]) Except the last item (scribal error?), all the remaining lexemes and the masculine du. תרין 'two' are spelled in their du.abs. form with a Yod, which may suggest that the original diphthong was still maintained. Though not genuine duals, here also belong(שפין) מין ' (calm) waters' C1.1:161+([289a]); שמין 'sky' A2.1:1+.([290])

pl.: נונן 'fishes' B7.1:4 // נונין ib.3,6; שנן 'years' B7.1:8 // שנין B6.3:2. The fluctuation between the plene and defective spelling can be observed even within the same documents as in the above quoted נתנין/נתנן.([291]) So also אמרן 'say' A4.7:4 // אמרין ib.22 (change of hand); לקדמן 'formerly' A4.9:8 // לקדמין ib.10; גרבן 'flagons' C3.28:85 // גרבין ib.86,87. See also לקן עתיקין 'old poles(?)' C3.7Fr1:21.([292]) Other examples of the plene spelling are: גברין

---

[289] The f. gender of these lexemes, excepting the numeral, is inferred from cognates.

[289a] It cannot be determined, however, whether or not the Yod was followed by *i* as in Targumic Aramaic מַיִן, and not *מֵיִן.

[290] Kottsieper (1990:113) regards /-maː-/ more likely, as in Arb., than /-may-/. So also for מין (1990:109).

[291] These make Ginsberg's (1936:99ff.) theory on a pl. morpheme /-aːn/ highly unlikely: see on this question, Kaufman 1974:128f. and the literature cited there. Kutscher (1972:67f.) had effectively laid this novel theory to rest for good.

[292] Of course the first word may end with /-aːn/. For its meaning, cf. Syr. *liqaːʾ* 'oar,' the pl. of which ends in *e*. This instance in a document datable to ca. 475 BCE is earlier than B3.4 (437 BCE), which Segert (1975:184) quotes as the earliest attesting to the plene spelling of the m.pl.abs ending of regular nouns other than those f. nouns ending in /-aːʲ/. It is true, however, that the plene spelling of this morpheme is common in later texts such as A4.7 (407 BCE) and C3.28 (3rd cent. BCE) as can be confirmed by a glance at the examples cited above.

'men' A4.10:5+; חמרין 'beads' C3.28:105; ימין 'days' B3.10:17(²⁹³) besides the standard יומן (8x); ירחין 'months' C3.28:97 // ירחן B7.1:8; כנכרין 'talents' A4.7:28 // כנכרן A4.8:27(²⁹⁴); כוין 'windows' B2.10:6 // כון B3.10:13(²⁹⁵); כסין 'cups' C3.13:1,3,13 // כסן B2.6:12, B8.6:6; מסמרין 'nails' A6.2:16†; נכסין 'possessions' A4.7:16, A4.8:5† // נכסן (16x); עבידין 'made' (ptc.) A4.7:20; צימין 'fasting' (ptc.) A4.7:15,20 // צימן A4.8:19; תלתין 'thirty' B3.9:8. Where no alternative plene spelling is attested, one can only resort to comparative/historical or syntactical considerations or look for pl. forms in the det., cst. or with conjunctive pronouns in order to tell whether the ending is that of the m. /-i:n/ or f. /-a:n/.(²⁹⁶) Thus פתיחן in כוין פתיחן B2.10:6, seemingly ambiguous, may be usefully compared with כַּוִּין פְּתִיחָן 'windows are open' Dn 6.11. Or again, מלן 'words' C1.1:29 by itself is ambiguous, whilst its det. form מליא B8.7:3, its cst. form מלי 'the words of' C1.1:1 and a form such as מלוהי 'his words' C1.1:62 all point to the masculine ending /-i:n/. עינין טבן in טבן 'good eyes' C1.1:157 can be feminine if we take יאכמו of אל יאכמו as impersonal: 'Let them not darken (good eyes).'

In so-called *nisbéh* nouns the Yod must be considered conso-nantal: e.g., יהודין 'Jews' B2.9:2+(²⁹⁷); חלכין 'Cilicians' A6.15:2, C3.28:96.

c) *m.cst.sg.*: בר (אבה) 'son of (Abah)' B2.2:16; מלך (אתור) 'the king of (Assyria)' C1.1:10; בית (ענני) 'the house of (Anani)' A4.3:10; בת (בנת) 'the temple of (Banit)' A2.2:12.

There is no instance in our corpus of אב or אח used in the sg.cst. Hence one cannot say whether it differed from its abs. state form. The expected distinct cst. form is *אבו and *אחו respectively. Therefore, a name such as אחוטב 'Ahutab,' if it mean 'a good person's brother,' might contain such a cst. form, but its

---

²⁹³ For a possible contraction of the diphthong, see above § 8 *b*.

²⁹⁴ A4.8 is a revised draft of A4.7. The scribe of the second half of A4.7 appears to be fond of plene spelling. See Porten 1998.

²⁹⁵ There are two variant lexemes for 'window': כוה (so Vogt [1971:81]), the two alternative spellings of whose plural are cited here, and כון as in כונה 1 פתיח 'its only window is open' B3.12:21. Kraeling (1953:313) lists all under כון, Porten - Yardeni (1989:xxviii) under כוה.

²⁹⁶ Leander (1928:91), Segert (1975:186), and Beyer (1984:449) quote חמראן from Cowley's edition (81:16) 'she-asses' or 'pearls' as the unique example of the plene spelling of the f.pl.abs. morpheme, but it is now (C3.28:92) read as חמ כאן 40 'win(e) 40 ka's.'

²⁹⁷ /yhuda:yin/ or the like? Cf. BA Dn 3.12Q יְהוּדָאיִן vs. Dn 3.8 כַּשְׂדָּאיִן.

interpretation is in no way certain.(²⁹⁸) אחיאב B4.4:2, if it mean 'father's brother,' and not 'my brother is father,' is a Hebrew name.

d) *m.cst.du.*: ידי 'hands of' C1.1:170; עיני 'eyes of' ib.172; בתרתי רגליא 'a second time (?)' C2.1:11. On the analogy of Heb. אפים 'face' one might postulate du. (אסרחאדן) אנפי 'the face of (Esarhaddon)' C1.1:14; (מ]ל[ך) אנפי 'the face of a (king)' ib.85.(²⁹⁹)

e) *m.cst.pl.*: ספרי 'scribes of' A6.1:1; מלי 'words of' C1.1:1. There is no graphic distinction whatsoever between this morpheme and that of the m.cst.du. There are reasons to think that the two did not differ phonetically.

f) *m.det.sg.*: אלפא 'the ship' A3.10:3; כתנה 'the tunic' A2.1:4; עמרה 'the wool' A2.2:9; אבנא 'the stone' A4.7:9; עבורה 'the eve' D7.8:15. The use of He instead of the standard Alef is typical of(³⁰⁰) the Hermopolis papyri except the letter no. 7, penned by a scribe different from the one who wrote the other seven letters of the corpus: ספרא 'letter' A2.7:4 // ספרה A2.1:12, A2.2:17, A3.4:5. As can be seen from the above table, this orthographic feature applies to the st. det. morpheme of both genders and all three numbers. In the Tiberian tradition of BA, this morpheme is stressed.

g) *m.det.du.*: רגליא (בתרתי) '(for a second) time' C2.1:11, if it is dual indeed.(³⁰¹)

h) *m.det.pl.*: אלהיא 'the gods' A6.1:1; יומיא 'the days' A4.1:8; מליא 'the words' B8.7:3; ינקיא 'the infants' A2.7:3 // ינקיה A3.4:2.

So-called *nisbéh* nouns, or gentilicia(³⁰²), are problematic.(³⁰³)

---

²⁹⁸ According to Grelot (1972:463) it rather means "Le Frère est bon." Noth (1928:67f.) is firmly of the opinion that Northwest Semitic names with אב or אח as the first component are nominal clauses, and not st. cst. phrases. Zadok (1988:47-49, 53, 59) wavers between a nominal clause and a genitive phrase.

²⁹⁹ BA attests no st.abs. form. The dagesh in the Pe of the forms of the BA noun is said to prove that they are to be viewed as dual: Bauer - Leander (1927:226). The occasional assimilation of the Nun as in אפיך 'your face' A2.1:2 also favours such an interpretation.

³⁰⁰ Though not confined to them: see above § 5 *e* and Folmer 1995:115f.

³⁰¹ Cf. Greenfield - Porten (1982:29).

³⁰² In terms of word-formation, /-k/ and /-kn/ (the latter of Persian origin) are also used to form gentilics: כרתך 'Cretan' B8.3:1 (but see Zadok 1985:174); סונכן 'resident of Syene' B5.2:2; סיכן 'resident of Sais (?)'; כרכיא 'Carians' A6.2:8. See also Masson 1975:410.

³⁰³ Cf. Folmer 1995: 213-17.

Thus our orthography makes no distinction between the sg. (חילא)
יהודיא 'the Jewish (force)' C3.15:1 and the pl. (כזי יהנעלן המו)
יהודיא '(when) the Jews (bring them in)' A3.8:12. So also מצריא
(מרדו) 'the Egyptians (rebelled)' A6.10:1 as against מצריא 'the
Egyptian' D8.4:16; פקידיא [קד]מיא 'the former (officials)' A6.10:7.
What about מה אמר לנכריא '(What am I supposed to say to) the
stranger(s)?' C1.1:139.([304]) Etymologically, *יהודייא˚ < יהודי + יא-)
is expected, somewhat like Dn 2.30 חַיַּי (< חַי). In a case like
this, BA presents a simplified form: יְהוּדָיֵא Ezr 5.1.([305]) תיפתיא
A4.5:9 is generally identified with BA תִּפְתָּיֵא Dn 3.2,3, the
vocalisation of which agrees with what has been suggested
above.([306])

The f.sg.det. תחתיתא 'the Lower (Egypt)' A6.10:11 is regular.
On the difficult עממא C1.1:98,189, see above § 9.([307])

i) Dual as distinct from plural

The existence of dual as distinct from plural is not apparent
from our consonantal texts, but may be assumed on the basis of
later vocalisation traditions such as the Tiberian tradition of BA,
an assumption supported to some extent by the way the numeral
for 'two' is spelled: m. תרין (14x), f. תרתין (5x). Whether it was
pronounced /-ay(i)n/ or, with contraction([308]), it was not /-i:n/,
the m.pl.abs. ending([309]), which is only rarely spelled plene with
a Yod([310]), and which would not apply to the f. form anyway.
One may also note some nouns which presumably had a distinct
dual form: אדנין 'ears' C1.1:157,215†; ידין 'hands' B2.6:8, B3.8:8†;
מאתין 'two hundred' A6.2:13,14,15,16†; עינין 'eyes' C1.1:157,212,
214†, but רגלן 'legs' B8.4:5([311]). But *שפה 'lip' is used in the

---

[304] Is the st.det. generic in force? Then the sg. is more likely: see below §
46 *l*.

[305] See Bauer - Leander (1927:55,204).

[306] Kottsieper (1990:130f.) argues for /a:yya:/. Beyer (1994:41) reminds us
that the later, typically East Aramaic morpheme, /e:/, is amply attested already
in the 7th cent. in Aramaic place names written in the cuneiform.

[307] Cf. Leander (1928:102), Kaufman (1974:127f.), Lindenberger
(1983:285), and Muraoka (1997a:206f.).

[308] See above § 8 *a*.

[309] *Pace* Segert (1975:185), פרסין B3.8:20 is no dual, but the m.pl.abs. of
the gentilic פרסי 'Persian': see Degen 1979:28.

[310] See above § 6 *b*.

[311] Despite the generally accepted interpretation of סכין פמי[ן] 'double-edged
knife' C1.1:84 there is no absolute necessity to take the second word as dual:
cf. Heb. Pr 5.4 חֶרֶב פִּיפִיּוֹת with Pesh. /saypa: daṯre:n pummaw/.

pl.(^{312}): שפות cst. C1.1:151; שפותה 'his lips' ib.132. The addition of the cipher for '2' suggests that כף 'hand, palm' was used in the pl. form, though in 2 כפן '2 ladles' B2.6:16, the word does not mean 'hand, palm,' and thus it cannot be used to prove the disuse of the du. of this particular noun.(^{313})

j) *f.abs.sg.*: מלה באישה 'bad thing' A4.3:6; אחה 'sister' B2.1:8+, a form unique to Egyptian Aramaic(^{314}) for the standard אחת, the Taw of which should not be confused with that which is about to be discussed, for later vocalisation traditions indicate /-a:t/.

One finds occasionally the archaic f.sg.abs. morpheme ה(^{315}): (חדה) אגרת '(one) letter' A3.5:5; A6.15:1+ // אגרה A3.6:3, A4.7:18, 19(^{316}); זפת 'loan' B3.1:3; קבלת 'complaint' A6.8:3(^{317}) // קבילה A6.15:5,11; ושררת (שלם) '(well-being) and strength' A3.3:1, A3.8:1, D1.4:1, D1.12:1; אנתת (לא תהוה לי) '(she shall not be my) wife' B3.8:22, similarly at ib.25.(^{318}) This feature is another trait

---

^{312} On the pl. base expanded with Waw, see below, § *f*.

^{313} מוזנא 'scales' B2.6:24, B3.8:26 can only be singular. Note also BA Dn 5.27 מאזניא (v.l. מֹאזַנְיָא). On the expanded BA form, cf. Bauer - Leander 1927: 234 j, l.

^{314} At least we have no relevant evidence from elsewhere in earlier or contemporary Aramaic dialects. See also above at § 3 *k*.

^{315} In our corpus we find only suffixed forms of the word for 'bow': קשתה 'his bow' C1.1:190; קשתך 'your bow' ib.126,128. Hence it is impossible to say whether its sg.st.abs. was ever קשה or not: on the etymology of the word, see Gesenius - Buhl (1915:733). Cf. also Folmer 1995: 252-57.

Leander (1928:24) explains בי 'house' st.abs. as an analogical development following the loss of the f.sg. morpheme /t/.

There is no ground for assuming, as Garr (1985:93) does, a long *a* as the vowel preceding the f.sg.abs. morpheme spelled ה. As late as Classical Syriac we see remains of this old morpheme preserved as /-at/: Muraoka (1997b: § 47). Otherwise the sg./pl. distinction would have been neutralised.

^{316} The form with He speaks for the naturalisation of what appears to be a loan from Akk. *igirtu*: cf. Kaufman (1974:48). This, incidentally, speaks against Gibson's (1975:128) suggestion that this spelling fluctuation reflects the contemporary, local Demotic substratum in which the fem. ending <t> was still written, though it had ceased to be pronounced in speech.

^{317} Wesselius sees here a functional opposition, but see the following footnote.

קבלת here is hardly in st. cst. with the following מנך 'from you,' for unlike in BH, in which a cst. followed by a prepositional phrase is fairly well attested (Joüon - Muraoka 1993: § 129 *m-o*), this is hardly the case in Aramaic.

^{318} Kutscher's explanation (1954:236) that this is possibly a fossilised archaic accusative as in Arb. following *ka:na* sounds too ad hoc. See also Sefire I B

characterising the language of the Hermopolis papyri([319]), though not confined to it: שפרת 1 תקבת 'one pretty vessel' A2.2:11([320]); חטבת 'striped cloth' A2.4:10; יהבת 'giving,' ptc., A2.2:14; שלחת 'sending,' ptc., A2.3:11; חזית 'seeing,' ptc., ib., A2.7:3; שנטת A2.1:4 (?).([321]) But there is no question of consistency: תקבה A2.1:5; למיתית 'to bring,' A inf. A2.4:11 // למתיה ib.([322])

The form אחרה 'other' in אנתה אחרה 'another wife' B2.6:32 (m. אחרן) is highly irregular, if it is not a scribal error for an innovative אחרנה. There also exists the standard אחרי, e.g. נפקה אחרי 'another outlay' C3.27:29.([323])

The occasional spelling with final Alef is a mere orthographic variant([324]): ארמיא 'an Aramaean (woman)' B2.8:3([325]); ברא 'daughter' ib.9; השקיא 'to give to drink' A4.5:7, H inf.; חנטא 'wheat' C3.28:104; מדינא 'province' A4.2:6 where מדינתא (st. det.) is expected; ספא 'jar (?)' D7.33:2; מן תחתיא לעליא 'from below to above' B3.12:8 // מן עליה לתחתיא 'from above to below' ib.16; on the substantivised adjective, see below, § 48 *b*.

k) *f.abs.du.*: תרתין 'two' A6.9:3+3x.

l) *f.abs.pl.*: מסרסרן 'soaring'(?), ptc. C1.1:162; מלן 'words' ib.29.

m) *f.cst.sg.*: (ארשם) אגרת 'the letter of (Arsham)' A6.15:4; מלכת 'the queen of' A2.1:1; שנת 'the year of' A4.1:2; אתת 'the wife of' A4.4:5*ter*; ברת 'the daughter of' A4.4:6. There is no knowing if this form phonetically differed from its st.abs. form as given above, (*j*).

---

10 מזן בקעת 'from the valley.' For a critical review of the thesis put forward by Wesselius (1980) as to possible case opposition (ה- nom./gen. vs. ת- acc.), see Folmer (1995: 252f.). In any event, this Taw must represent phonetic reality, not a mere historical spelling, a possibility mentioned by Hug (1993:65). Such is unlikely in private letters such as the Hermopolis papyri.

[319] Cf. Kutscher 1971:104,107.

[320] See Porten 1968:267f., n. 7.

[321] On the interpretation of this difficult word, see Gibson (1975:138) and Hoftijzer (1983:115, n.*l*). נפרת B2.8:3, B8.9:5, which Porten - Yardeni (1989:39) translate 'litigation' with some hesitation, does not belong here, because the original Persian word is *nifriti*; Grelot makes a verb of it - "j'avait fait opposition' (1972:190). Cf. also Hoftijzer - Jongeling 1995:744.

[322] This is another exception, missed by Hug (1993:65), beside מטאה 'arriving,' ptc., A2.4:4. As regards the difficult לחנת C1.1:178, we are inclined to analyse it as a case of haplography: ללחנת < לחנת 'for a slave girl' (with a radical Taw). In the light of the alternation תקבה/תקבת cited above, it is not right, *pace* Greenfield (1968:365), to correct למיתית to למיתיתהם.

n) *f.cst.du.:* תרתי 'two' C2.1:11.†(³²⁶).

o) *f.cst.pl.:* שמהת 'the names of' A4.4:4,6. Since there is no graphic distinction between the f.sg.cst. and the f.pl.cst., מנדת בניא A6.13:3,4 is ambiguous of interpretation: 'the rent (or: rents) of the estates.' עזקתה זי סנחאריב 'the seal (or: seals) of Sennacherib' C1.1:3 gets clarified by עזקה (sg.) ib.19. For משחת, cst. of משחה 'measurement,' B2.4:4+ and משחתה 'its measurement(s)' B2.3:4+, reference may profitably be made to משחת (= משחתה) כתיבן 'its measurements are recorded' B3.5:12.(³²⁷) One would postulate /-at/ for the former and /-a:t/ for the latter as in BA, Syriac, and other later dialects.

p) *f.det.sg.:* אגרתא 'the letter' A3.3:9; אלהתא 'the goddess' C3.12:27; אלהתה B2.8:5 // אלהא 'the god' C3.12:26; ספינתא 'the ship' A3.9:7. Graphically one cannot always tell the sg. from the

---

³²³ The latter with Yod is known from BA אׇחֳרִי and Syr. /ʔḥreːtaːʔ/ The phonetic shape of the morpheme is unclear: cf. Brockelmann 1908:412f.

³²⁴ See above, § 5 *g* and Folmer 1995: 118-20.

³²⁵ But cf. below, § 70 *g*.

³²⁶ Comparison with forms occurring in OA, שפתיך 'your lips' Sefire III 14f and שפתה 'his lips' ib.15, makes it plain that the forms in our corpus, שפות C1.1:151 (cst.) and שפותה ('his'), are pl., not du., but *pace* Leander (1928:92k), not "wie im Aram. überhaupt." Incidentally, there is no basis for regarding, with Kottsieper (1990:132), */śafa:t/ as the sg.abs./cst. of the noun, though he is probably right on מנת 'portion' as in מנתכי 'your portion' B5.1:7; cf. Syr. /mna:ta:ʔ/. A similar problem arises for *כנה (?) 'colleague' and פחה 'governor,' both Akk. loanwords. The st.abs. of the former is not attested anywhere in Aramaic, whilst BA knows פֶּחָה. The attested and/or vocalised examples indicate *כְּנָוָת (or such like) and *פַּחֲוָת (or such like) as their respective pl.st.abs. form. Whilst the sg.abs. פֶּחָה seemingly presupposes the analysis of /t/ in Akk. *pi:ḥa:tu*, as a fem. morpheme, synchronically the Taw of מנת is no longer a f. morpheme. BA פֶּחַת cst.sg. and פַּחֲוָתָא det.pl. do not lend support to the view that the underlying base of its sg. form was conceived as having /-a:ta:/ with a long *a:* before the *t*. Beyer (1984:443) lists a whole range of nouns as having a fem. ending *-á:t.* אחה, מנה, קצת, צלו, כנה, פחה, etc., but this does not make any synchronic sense; for Beyer's revised view, see Beyer 1994:285. We take exception to Vogt's proposed vocalisation of כנתה C1.1:99,185 as /kina:teh/ (Vogt 1971:84): /kinteh/ might be suggested instead. Cf. further Kutscher 1961.

The IA use of פחה in the sense of 'governor' must be elliptical for בעל פחה or such like, since the Akk. word means 'responsibility, jurisdiction': on its form and usage, see von Soden (1965-81:862) and Kaufman (1974:82, n.263).

³²⁷ Another reason that הוה B2.3:3 cannot have משחתה (4) as its subject.

pl.(³²⁸), but שנתא A4.1:2 must be sg., 'the year,' for the pl.det. would be שניא in view of its pl.abs. שנין B6.3:2 // שנן B7.1:8.

q) *f.det.pl.*: אגרתא (מטו) 'the letters (arrived)' A4.2:15; חקלתא (אלך) 'those fields' B8.10:4; ארקתא 'the lands' A6.15:6.

r) *Nouns with Yod or Waw as final radical*

There are a fair number of nouns whose basic form ends with Yod or Waw(³²⁹). One needs to distinguish three groups: **1)** *nisbéh* words (see above [*b, h*], **2)** other nouns or adjectives to the root of which a Yod or Waw has been added, and **3)** those whose final Yod or Waw is a root letter, thus derived from Lamed-Yod/Waw roots. Some examples follow.

With Yod:

(1) *m.sg.abs.* יהודי 'Jew' B2.2:3+, תחתי (בי) 'lower (house)' B3.10:12+; *f.sg.abs.* יהודיה B5.5:2, *m.sg.det.* יהודיא (חילא) 'the Jewish (army)' A4.1:10, C3.15:1; *m.pl.abs.* יהודין B.2.9:2; *m.sg.det.* כלביא 'doglike' A4.7:16 // A4.8:15(³³⁰); *f.sg.det.* תחתיתא 'the Lower (Egypt)' A6.10:11; *m.pl.det.* קד[מיא] 'the former' A6.10:8

(2) possibly זערי in זעריהם 'their paucity' C1.1:90(³³¹); כברי 'sulphur' A6.2:17, כבריתא *sg.det.* ib.21; *sg.abs.* קלבי an unknown liquid measure C3.12:3+, pl.abs., קלבין ib.4+

(3) *m.sg.abs.* בלה 'worn out' B3.8:10, *f.sg.abs.*(?) בליה ib.12; *m.sg.det.* בניא 'the building' B2.4:12(³³²); *m.sg.+suf.* גדיכי 'your kid' C1.1:209; *m.pl.abs.* דכין 'pure' A4.1:5; *f.sg.cst.* זוית 'corner' B2.1:5, זויתה 'its (m.sg.) corner' ib.4; *m.sg.abs.* זכי 'innocent' C1.1:46; *f.sg.abs.* (?) חויה 'snake' A2.5:8(³³³); *f.sg.abs.* חליה 'sweet' C1.1:131; *f.sg.abs.* ... שויה (מחזי 1) '(a mirror) worth ...' B3.3:5(³³⁴); *m.sg.det.* טביא 'gazelle' C1.1:168; *sg.+ suf.* כסיכי 'your covering' C1.1:167; *m.pl.abs.* מלין 'full' A4.2:11; מקריא *m.sg.det.* 'the declaration' B7.2:6; *sg.abs.* מרבי 'interest' B4.2:7(³³⁵), מרביתא

---

³²⁸ Hence, *pace* Cowley (1923:97), רקעתא A6.2:20 does not necessarily allow one to vocalise its pl. form as רקען ib.14.

³²⁹ Etymologically such a Waw may or may not be part of the root of the noun. In אנתו 'wifehood' it obviously is not, but rather an abstract noun morpheme.

³³⁰ On this interpretation, see Grelot 1972:410, n. *s*.

³³¹ The form is hardly m.pl., but possibly an abstract fem. noun ending with /-ay/, on which see Brockelmann (1908:412) and Barth (1894:378f.).

³³² /binnu:y/ according to Leander (1928:83).

³³³ Possibly masculine: see § 46 *o*.

³³⁴ Cf. JA מחזיתא; Syr. same.

³³⁵ Cowley (1923:34) and Leander (1928:112d) regard abs.sg. מרבית B4.2:5

sg.det., B3.1:6, 'the interest on your silver' B4.2:3., מרביתה 'its (m.sg.) interest' B3.1:16; *sg.det.* נגיא 'the region' B4.4:3; *f.sg.abs.* נקיה 'lamb' A2.2:8+([336]); *m.sg.abs.* סי 'a kind of iron' C3.7Fv2:14; *m.sg.det.* סניא 'the bramble' C1.1:101; *sg.det.* עביא 'the thickness' A6.2:18†; *m.pl.abs.* עבין 'thick' A6.2:14; *f.sg.abs.* עליה, עליא 'upper' B2.3:5+, *det.* עליתא A6.4:3; *f.sg.abs.* עריה 'naked' or 'cold' C1.1:166†; *m.sg.det.* רביא 'the young man' C1.1:38+, *m.pl.cst.* רבי ib. 33([337]); *m.sg.det.* רעיא D7.1:3, רעיה A2.2:16, *pl.abs.* רען 'shepherds' C1.1:161([338]); sg.cst. שירית 'remainder' A4.7:11, [שארית B8.1:11; *sg.det.* שביא 'captives' C1.2:5([339]); *m.pl.abs.* שפין 'calm' C1.1:161;(?) תלי 'weapon'(?) D7.7:6, *suf.* תליהם A4.7:8.

The m.sg.abs. of these nouns in group **3** is spelled with He, but without Yod: חדה 'happy' A4.7:3, *f.sg.det.* חדיתא A5.1:4([340]); לחה 'evil' C1.1:199, f.sg.abs. לחיה ib.172, *m.sg.det.* לחיא A4.7:7, *f.sg./pl.det.* לחיתא C1.1:134, *sg./pl.suf.* לחיתי ib.139; *m.sg.abs.* סוסה 'horse' C1.1:38, A6.12:2, *pl.abs.* סוסין C2.1:44.([341]) Not much can be made of קנה C3.13:6, קנן ib.15,20, קניא ib.50 because of the extremely fragmentary nature of the document, even if they are all forms of קנה 'rod'; קשה 'rough' C1.1:85, *m.pl.det.* קשיא B2.2:11,

---

a scribal error.

[336] Hug 1993:148 is in favour of the m. gender.

[337] An irregular spelling for /ra:bye:/ or the like? See also תליהם 'their weapon' A4.7:8. If one is to follow Hoftijzer (1976:210, 221, 290), possibly also in גרי 'adversaries of' Deir Alla I 12 and רוי 'saturated with' ib. II 4. The certain data currently available are too scanty for us to come to a firm conclusion on the shape of the m.pl.cst., with or without a conj. pron., of Lamed-Yod nouns. On JA, see Dalman 1905:193, 207f.

[338] In many late dialects we find pl.abs. רען; but cf. 1QapGen 22.1 חד מן רעה 'one of the herdsmen of the flock'(?) with our comment (Muraoka 1972:37).

[339] For the collective force of the sg. שבי, cf. Ashur letter 15, and possibly 1QapGen 22.2.

[340] אריה 'a lion' (sg.abs.) C1.1:165 vs. אריא 'the lion' (sg.det.) C1.1:94 is an exception, probably because the /r/ was primitively not followed by a vowel, whereas in the words mentioned above the second root consonant was followed by one.

[341] The etymology of the word is disputed: see Gesenius - Buhl (1915:538) and Driver (1957:73f.). In spite of the Heb. סוס and *pace* Leander (1928:70, 97*h*) the basic form must have ended with /y/, perhaps /-ay/, hence סוסה = *suse*. This is clear from OA ססיה (Sefire I A 22), Syr. /susya:ʔ/ and JA, on which see Beyer (1984:644f.) and Sokoloff (1990:371). On account of the following חד קליל,סוסה at C1.1:38 cannot mean 'mare,' and 'his horse' (Leander ib.) is most unnatural. The form סוסא in 500 סוסא '500 horses' D22.1:2 (// גמלן 'camels') is most peculiar.

B2.3:8†; *m.sg.abs.* שׁוה 'worth' B2.6:8; *f.sg.abs.* שׁויה B3.3:5,
f.pl.abs. שׁוין B2.6:13. Though not of Lamed-Yod roots, מין 'water'
and שׁמין 'sky,' discussed above ([*b, e*]), belong here. Note also
סרושׁיתא 'punishment' A6.3:6,7†.([342]) The consistent spelling sg.abs.
פתי 'width,' e.g. B3.8:6 (det. פתיא e.g. A6.2:18) indicates a vowel
of different order following /t/ than the one to be postulated in
the analogous position of, e.g., חדה and סוסה. The latter may be
assumed to have been /a/, thus /ay/ > /e:/, whereas for the former
we may note BA פְּתָיֵהּ Dn 3.1, Ezr 6.3([343]), and Syr. /pṯa:ya:ʔ/([344])

   With Waw: **2)** אנתו 'wifehood' B2.8:4, אנתותכי B4.6:5; הימנותה
'his trustworthiness' C1.1:132; מלכותא *sg.det.* 'kingdom' C1.1:79;
מררותא *sg.det.* 'bitterness' C1.1:123; שרחו[ ]א *sg.det.*(?) 'foulness'(?)
C1.1:106; **3)** *sg.det.* בכותא 'crying' C1.1:210; *sg.cst.* דמות 'likeness'
B3.4:21†; מקלו 'burnt offering' A4.10:10([345]); *sg.abs.* עלוה 'burnt
offering' A4.7:28, *sg./pl.det.* עלותא A4.7:25; *sg.abs.* ענוה 'poverty'
C1.1:89; *f.sg.abs.* צבו 'matter, affair' A5.1:3, *sg.cst.* צבות A6.8:2*bis*,
sg.det. צבותא B8.11:3; *sg.abs.* צהוה 'thirst' C1.1:123; שרחא *sg.det.*(?)

---

[342] On the etymology of the word, see Driver (1957:47), and cf. BA לְשָׁרֹשִׁי
Ezr 7.26.

[343] There is no absolute necessity, as does Vogt (1971:141), to emend the
MT to פְּתָיֵהּ in conformity with QA forms like פותי.

[344] Although Syr. also has a synonymous segholate, /puṯya:ʔ/, the pattern
qVta:l seems more likely, as also supported by the spelling of the above-
mentioned זכי, most likely /zakka:y/ as in Syr. and, with a secondary shortening
in JA (Dalman 1905:161). No Aram. dialect shows a segholate of this word.
QA forms, along with עובי 'width,' must be treated separately. Leander (1928:77)
assigns our זכי to the *qatil* pattern, but how would he account for the consistent
spelling with He of all the remaining words in that category such as שׁוה, לחה?
The disputed קמח רמיח A6.9:3 may be seen in this light. The phrase is usually
understood to mean 'flour of inferior quality' (but Grelot 1972:311 - "farine
grise") on the basis of JA רמי 'rejected,' seemingly ptc.pass. of רמה 'to throw';
see Driver (1957:60). But in our corpus and BA the m.sg.abs. of the ptc.pass.
of Lamed-He verbs is regularly spelled with He (see below § 37 *f*). We
would rather suggest רַמִי 'fraudulent, suspect, dubious' instead. Levy (1867-
68:427) mentions Buxtorf, who took רמיא in Trg Pr 10.4, 14.25 in this sense,
but rejects the interpretation ("da letzteres [= רַמָּא] diese Bedeut. im syr.
Sprachgebrauch, wonach das Trg. der Prov., nicht hat"). Brockelmann
(1928:733f.) lists, however, D of the root in the sense of "caluminatus est," a
noun /ramma:ya:ʔ/ 'fraudator, caluminator,' and a few other derivatives of
related meaning. For a totally different interpretation of רמי as meaning 'fine,
excellent,' see Hinz 1975:198.

[345] If it is a loan from Akk. *maqlu:tu*. No declined form is attested.

'dinner'(?) C3.12:7([346]). In the customs account we find a new word, שתות C3.7Gr2:6, apparently meaning 'a sixth,' but it is not followed by any noun but by בגו 'herein.' This may be some unknown elliptical expression, if the form is in the st.cst.([347])

On the morpheme of certain infinitives such as משלמותה 'repaying it' C1.1:131, see below at § 24 *p*.

s) *Loss of original final Taw of nouns with Yod or Waw as last radical*

As regards nouns of roots with a final Waw or Yod such as צבו 'matter' and מחזי 'mirror' (see above § [*r*]), they have lost the original Taw([348]) possibly by analogy with מלת sg.abs. versus מלה sg. abs.([349]).

t) *Derivation of st.det. from st.cst*

The st.det. may be said to be derived or derivable from the st.cst. form by the addition of a morpheme common to every number and gender. Whereas its well-nigh regular graphic representation with Alef points to its original consonantal value([350]), its not infrequent replacement by He in our corpus suggests that

---

[346] The word, apparently related to Syr. /ša:ruṯa'/ of similar meaning, occurs in this document five more times, always spelled in the same way. Other examples in which the postulated Waw or Yod as the third root consonant is not evident includes Zakkur A.5 מחנתה (< √חני) 'his encampment' and מאן (< √אני) 'vessel' C1.1:93+.

[347] Does the ending have anything to do with Late Babylonian fractions such as *sebû* 'one seventh,' *tišû* 'one ninth,' *ešrû* 'one tenth': cf. von Soden (1995:117). רבעת in an Ashur document (Hug 1993:25,71) may be compared: ורבעת לקח מן ... 'and he took a quarter out of ...'

[348] Despite the final ת, מרבי is of mixed gender (m. in B4.2:5, 9; f. in ib.3, B3.1:6.

[349] Similarly Segert (1975:182).

[350] So argued for OA by, e.g., Fitzmyer (1967:147), Degen (1969:25, n. 4) and Andersen - Freedman (1992:83f.). Segert (1975:190) holds that OA scribes wished to distinguish between two similar-sounding endings, namely the st.det. and the f.sg.abs. This, however, attributes our sort of analytical grammar to ancient scribes. Beyer (1984:106) postulates /-há:'/, whereas Segert (ib.) suggests /-há:/ as a second possibility beside /-'á:/.

If our Alef is no mere mater lectionis, it does not appear to be, *pace* Kienast (1987:45), a direct offshoot of the status determinatus morpheme /-a/ identified by him in Akkadian texts as early as the mid-third millennium BCE and borrowed even into Sumerian. Then one could still regard the absence of the determined state in Samalian as indicative of the archaic nature of the idiom.

in our period the morpheme sounded /a:/.([351])

u) *Differences between nouns and adjectives*

Notwithstanding our earlier observation (§ 18, n. 288), adjectives and nouns differ in three important respects.

Firstly, every adjective is declinable in both genders, e.g. m. לחה 'evil' and f. לחיה. It is highly exceptional that a noun should be so declined without any semantic contrast: one such rare example is יום 'day' - pl.cst. יומי A4.7:13 vs. יוֹמָי Ezr 4.15.([352]) In our corpus there occur some examples of the cst. form of the adjective: e.g. עויר עינין 'blind of eyes' C1.1:212; חרש אדנין 'deaf of ears' ib.215.([353])

Secondly, the adjective shows a regular match between its grammatical gender and its form, whereas a masculine noun can take a typically feminine pl. ending, and vice versa.

Thirdly, the adjective is declined only in the sg. and pl., but not du.

v) *Mismatch between form and grammatical gender*

There are **1**) masculine nouns which take the overtly feminine pl. ending, **2**) masculine nouns which take the overtly feminine sg. ending and masculine pl. ending, **3**) masculine nouns which take the overtly feminine sg. and pl. endings, **4**) feminine nouns which are not so marked in the singular([354]), **5**) feminine nouns which take the overtly m.pl. ending, and **6**) feminine nouns which are not marked in the sg. as feminine and take the overtly masculine du. ending. The grammatical gender of a noun can be syntactically recognised in the light of the so-called concord or agreement, i.e. the gender of a verb, adjective, demonstrative pronoun, numeral, or a pronoun to which it relates. Some examples follow.

1) שם 'name' - שמהת pl.cst. A4.4:6([355])

---

[351] Whether the glottal stop of the primitive morpheme preceded or followed the vowel *a:* is debatable. If our assumption of the primacy of the st.cst. be acceptable, the BA Tiberian form of the m.pl.det. such as טָבַיָא with a geminated Yod might speak for a following glottal stop, *-aʾ*, for the gemination may have been introduced in order to retain the preceding short *a*: /*ṭaːbayaːʾ/ > /ṭaːbayyaːʾ/. For an alternative explanation, see Segert (1975:184).

[352] Note also ימן Ashur letter 16. The form יומן B8.7:8+ is best taken as a defective spelling of יומין B3.10:17 rather than = /yawma:n/ as in later Aramaic dialects.

[353] Cf. Muraoka 1977.

[354] For an attempt to determine which semantic categories of Aramaic nouns belong to this group, see Segert (1975:181).

[355] The references given in these listings are where the grammatical gender

2) אמה 'cubit' A6.2:12(³⁵⁶), pl.abs. אמין B3.12:8 // אמן חמשה A6.2:14

3) *פחה 'governor'; sg.cst. פחת A4.7:1; pl.det. פחותא A3.3:4(³⁵⁷)

4) אגר 'wall' B2.1:4,5; (חדה) אלף 'a boat' A3.10:2—pl.cst. אלפי C1.2:7; אם 'mother' D7.6:8; ארק 'land' B2.2:6—pl.det. ארקתא A6.15:6; (חדה) באר 'a well' A4.5:6; חרב 'sword' C1.1:161; חפנא 'handful' B3.3:6 —pl. חפנן A6.9:3(³⁵⁸); כף 'hand' B2.6:28—כפיך pl.suf. C1.1:87; כתן 'tunic' A2.1:4f. (but treated as m. in נתנהי ib.7)(³⁵⁹); מומה/מומא 'oath' B2.3:24(³⁶⁰); מת 'land' C2.1:29; נפש 'soul' C1.1:122(³⁶¹); סס 'moth' C1.1:121

5) אנתה 'woman'—נשיא pl.det. A4.4:4(³⁶²); sg.det. חנטתא 'wheat' C1.1:129—pl.abs. חטן B4.1:2; מלה 'word'—מליא pl.det. B8.7:3, + 3ms מלוהי C1.1:43; pl.abs. פרן 'bran' C1.1:160(³⁶³); *שערה 'barley,' pl.det. שעריא D7.39:3; שנה 'year'—שנין pl.abs. B6.3:2(³⁶⁴) // שנן

---

of the noun in question can be determined on syntactical grounds.

³⁵⁶ Other examples showing the masculine gender of the noun are: אמן תרין A6.2:12, A6.9:4; אמן חמשה A6.2:14; אמן עשרה ותרין A6.2:10, *pace* Hoftijzer - Jongeling (1995:70), who do not make it clear enough that there is a dialectal variation in this respect. No other noun belonging to this group is attested in our corpus.

³⁵⁷ Analogy suggests the existence in IA of כנה st.abs. 'colleague.' פֶּחָה does occur in BA, e.g. Ezr 5.14.

³⁵⁸ Always spelled defectively, but חפנין in JA. The corresponding word is f. in Syr., but m. in JA. See חפן חדה A6.9:4.

³⁵⁹ This could be a highly abnormal use of הי as a fs suffixal pronoun; cf. an equally unusual use of הי in line הי מלבש אנה 'that I am wearing' ib.6.

³⁶⁰ The Alef is a radical, so that the first is an etymological spelling, the second a phonetic: see above, § 3 *n.* Since מומאה B2.8:9 is clearly a st.det. form for מומאא (note the attributive demonstrative pronoun דכי), מומאתא restored by Porten - Yardeni at B7.1:5 is a ghost form and should be replaced by מומאה or the like. See also Folmer 1995:111f.

³⁶¹ On the interpretive implication of the gender of the noun at C1.1:153, see Lindenberger (1983:153).

³⁶² The treatment of נשיא as m. at A4.7:20 is obviously unduly influenced by the form: see below § 76 *cf.*

³⁶³ On the etymology and semantics of the word, see the literature cited in Hoftijzer - Jongeling 1995:934.

³⁶⁴ We assume that the word for a dry measure 'seah' had, though unattested in our corpus, the f.sg.abs. סאה as elsewhere in IA (see Hoftijzer - Jongeling 1995:772) and Syr. abs. /saːʔ/ < /sʔaːʔ/ = Heb. סְאָה, whilst its pl. סאן B3.13:3 ended with /-iːn/ as in סאין in QA and a document from Naḥal Ḥever, and in both clearly feminine (see Beyer 1984:643). For comparative data, see Nöldeke

B1.1:1

6) יד 'hand' A2.4:4—ידין B2.6:8(³⁶⁵); רגל 'time' (of frequency) C2.1:11.

The available evidence does not allow us to know how to classify such a pair as sg.det. חקלא A5.2:2—pl.det. חקלתא B8.10:4+.(³⁶⁶) אבן with אבנא, pl.cst. אבני is perhaps m., if צרף in אבנצרף A4.3:3 be a defectively spelled pass. ptc. meaning 'coloured.'(³⁶⁷) So is צבע 'finger' in the light of צבע חד 'one fingerbreadth' A6.2:20; see also ib.16,18,19. From the evidence available in our corpus we cannot determine the gender of the noun in אנפין 'our face' A4.2:8.(³⁶⁸) The name of a country, מצרין, is treated as f.: במצרין בתחתיתא 'the Lower Egypt' A6.10:11. See below at § 45 d.

w) *Base expanded in plural forms*

Some nouns expand their base before pl. inflectional morphemes are added(³⁶⁹):

[1] with He - *אב 'father'(cf. אבי 'my father' A2.1:13) vs. אבהין 'our fathers' A4.7:13, A4.8:12, אבהיהם 'their fathers' D23.1 XII:5(³⁷⁰); עק 'tree' with two pl. forms—abs. עקין C1.1:88+, det. עקיא A6.2:18, cst. עקי A6.2:10+ vs. עקהן A4.7:11 // A4.8:10(³⁷⁰ᵃ); שם 'name' C1.1:180, שמהם 'their name' B8.2:23 vs. שמהתהם 'their names' A4.6:15

[2] with Waw—*כנה 'colleague' (cf. כנתה 'his colleague' C1.1:185 and Akk. *kina:tu*) but כנותה 'his colleagues' ib.67; מאה

(1910:131), Gesenius - Buhl (1915:533), and Brockelmann (1928:453). In the light of Akk. /sa:ti/, pl. of /su:tu/ (von Soden 1965-81:1064) and Syr. /sa²ṭa:²/ the word must have begun with /sa-/.

³⁶⁵ On the gender of the noun at C1.1:157, see above (*b*).

³⁶⁶ Syr. /ḥaqla:²/ f. (as in Peshsitta Gn 27.27); likewise in JA according to Dalman (1938:158) and Sokoloff (1990:213).

³⁶⁷ See Grelot (1972:392).

³⁶⁸ For BA and related idioms, Vogt (1971:12) indicates m., whilst some later dialects use the word clearly as f.: Syr. Peshitta /²appe: biša:ṭa:²/ in Pr 25.23 and זיוהן דאפוי 'the look of his face' Gn 4.5 of the Palestinian Targum (Klein 1986:7).

³⁶⁹ Such a process is not necessarily confined to bi-consonantal roots: see, e.g., Syr. /²aṭra:/ 'land' vs. /²aṭrawa:ṭa:²/; /nahra:²/ 'river' vs. /nahrawa:ṭa:²/.

³⁷⁰ Thus distinct from later Aramaic dialects with a fem. morpheme, /-ha:n/, and accordingly restored—in line with our (TM) private suggestion—in the Tel Dan inscription, line 3 אבההה. Cf. also Folmer 1995:211f.

³⁷⁰ᵃ For an attempt to establish semantic opposition between the two forms, see Joüon 1934:53f.

'century' A6.2:14, מאותהם 'their centuries' A5.5:7; שׂפה 'lip,' pl.cst.
שׂפות C1.1:151, + suf. 'his,' שׂפותה ib.132([371]). A special form of
root expansion is reduplication reinforced by the addition of the
normal pl. ending([372]): m.pl.abs. רברבן (תרעין) 'enormous (gates)'
A4.8:9.

x) *Suppletion* The phenomenon of suppletion, namely
complementary distribution of two distinct inflectional bases of
one lexeme, is pan-Aramaic with sg. בר 'son' vs. pl. -בנ (e.g. בר
B3.6:5 vs. בנן 'sons' B2.6:33([373]), and ברה 'daughter' B3.4:22 vs.
בנתך 'your daughters' B3.12:26 and בנתן 'our daughters' B2.9:10);
sg. -אנת 'woman' vs. pl. נש- (e.g. אנתה B2.6:32 vs. נשׁיא 'the women'
A4.4:4).

y) *Irregular nouns*
We have mentioned above cases of root expansion (§ *w*)
and root suppletion (§ *x*). It remains to mention here only בי
m.sg.abs. 'house' B5.6:4+, בת/בית cst. A2.2:1+, ביתא det. B2.4:12,
and בתיא pl.det. A4.4:8+. Here the absence of ת in the sg.abs. is
striking. So is the absence of י in the pl., whose peculiarity,
according to later traditions such as BA בָּתֵּי is further compounded
on account of the geminated ת and the first vowel.([374])

z) It is of course impossible to say whether כלא 'totally'
(also ברא, עלא etc.) was, as in BA([375]), stressed penultimately or

---

[371] Comparative Semitics (Heb. שָׂפָה, Arab. *šafatun*, Syr. /sefta:ʔ/) and
historical developments in Aramaic (OA שׂפתיך, שׂפתוה 'his lips') show that the
Waw is a secondary increment. Cowley's reading (1923:186) אחותה has now
been rectified by Porten - Yardeni (1989:244) to אופסתה. Thus the pl. of אחה
'sister' (not אחת) is *אחין, and not אחן as in later Aramaic dialects (see, e.g.
Sokoloff 1990:46) and Syr. ʔaḥwa:ta:ʔ/. אחותה in Cowley 75:8 is now read
אופסתה, C3.21:9, whatever it might mean: see Porten - Yardeni 1993:244.

Pace Garr (1985:96) there is no reason for assuming the gemination of this
infixal *w*: note BA עֲלָוָן 'burnt offerings.' Nor does Mandaic know such a
gemination: see Macuch 1965: §166.

[372] Just as Heb. segholate nouns like מלכים etc., if it represent a broken
plural /malak/ + /-i:m/: see Jouüon - Muraoka 1993: § 96 A*b*.

[373] If read correctly, בריהם 'their sons' D23.1 Va:13 is most striking. Lemaire
(1995: 90) reads with a Pe, 'leurs agneaux.'

Testen (1985) attempts to account for this *r-n* alternation by formulating a
phonetic law which, however, applies to a mere two lexemes.

[374] A spelling *bwtm* alongside *btm* and *bhtm* in Ugaritic leads Gordon
(1965: Glossary, 371f.) to the view that the Hebrew בָּתִּים should be pronounced
/bottîm/.

[375] See Bauer - Leander (1927:205). If these be ancient accusatives, they
are certainly no active part of the language system, but fossilised relics. Cf.

not. On their use, see below § 69 d.

§ 19. Formal patterns of nouns and adjectives

The following is a classified inventory of patterns of nouns and adjectives presented on account of some implications which our knowledge of word-formation patterns may have for grammar. In view of the considerable uncertainty and difficulty in identifying vowels of particular words in their basic form, namely, absolute state, singular, (and masculine in the case of adjectives)(376), no attempt is made to classify lexemes in accordance with the conventional, diachronically and comparatively orientated scheme in terms of qal, qil, qatl, qitl etc. An asterisk signifies that the basic form is not actually attested.

a) *Biconsonantal roots*(377)

Without mater lectionis: אב* 'father' B2.10:7+; אח 'brother' B2.1:8+; אם(!) 'mother' C4.1:1+; אר kind of wood A6.2:10; בי 'house' B4.3:18+; בל* 'mind' C1.1:81; בר 'son' A3.5:9+; גץ 'chalk' D7.23:4; דב(!)* 'bear' C1.1:168; דם* 'blood' C1.1:168+; דם* (pl. tant.) 'price' A4.7:28+; חד 'one' A4.2:3+; חט(!)* 'arrow' C1.1:126+; חי(!) 'alive' A2.5:9+; חל* 'sand' C1.1:125+; חן(!) 'favour' C1.1:132; חר(!)* 'noble' A4.8:18+; טב 'good' A6.13:2+; טל(!)* 'shadow' B3.6:9; טס* 'plate' A6.2:16; יד 'hand' D7.36:1; ים(!)* 'sea' C1.1:207+; כא liquid measure C3.28:2+; כב(!)* 'thorn' C1.1:102+; כד(!)* 'vessel' A4.2:13+; כו* liquid measure D8.9:6+; כל(!)* 'all' A6.5:2+; כס 'cup' B3.8:14+; כף(!) 'ladle' B3.8:24+; לג* liquid measure C3.29:209+; מי* 'water' C1.1:191+; מץ* boat part A6.2:17; מת 'dead' A2.5:9; סב 'old' B3.10:17; סס* 'worm' C1.1:119+; עם(!) 'people' D3.39:2+; עק 'wood' B3.8:19+; פם(!) 'mouth' C1.1:171+; צל(!) 'leather' B3.8:20+; קב a measure B7.1:8+; קל* 'voice' C1.1:91+; קן 'sheep' A4.10:10+; קף 'chest(?)' B3.8:19;

Segert (1975:193). However that may be, it is not right, in any discussion of the function of כלא in BA, to ignore its consistent penultimate stress.

[376] In the case of nouns not formally marked as feminine, the m.sg.cst. form has also been regarded as equivalent for our purpose to the abs. form.

[377] Lexemes of geminate roots are marked with !. An asterisk (*) signifies that the form so marked occurs only with some inflectional increment or conjunctive pronoun.

Lipiński (1991) prefers the term "monosyllabic" to "biconsonantal," for, according to him, middle vowels are also constitutive elements. This argument, however, would equally apply to "triconsonantal" roots. Would he prefer "polysyllabic" to "triconsonantal"?

קף(!)* water animal C1.1:165 ([378]); רב(!) 'great' C1.1:60+; רם 'high' C1.1:142+; רע* 'comrade' C1.1:221+; שב 'old man' C1.1:6+; שק(!)* 'sack' D7.26:1+; שם 'name' C1.1:180+; שש 'marble' B3.8:18; שת 'six' D3.4:9+; תם(!)* 'completion(?)' C1.2:5; תרין 'two' A6.9:4.([379])

With fem. suffix ה- or ת-: אחה 'sister' B3.9:4+; אמה(!)* 'cubit' B6.2:1+; אמה 'maidservant' B3.13:11+; אשה(!) 'fire' C1.1:88+; ברה 'daughter' B3.4:15+; גזה(!)* 'fleece' A2.2:8; חטה(!) 'wheat' D4.4:3+; חמה* 'anger' C1.1:140; כוה(!)* 'window' B3.12:21+; מאה 'hundred' A6.2:15+; מלה(!) 'word' A3.9:6+; מנה 'mina' A6.2:17; מנה* 'portion' A6.1:2+; מסה(!)* 'measure' A2.2:4+; סאה* grain measure B3.13:3+; סכה(!)* 'nail(?)' D7.24:3; עדה 'assembly' B2.6:26+; עטה 'advice' C1.1:57+; עלה(!)* 'income' C3.25:16; עשה* 'measuring rod' B3.5:7+; פרה* 'bran' C1.1:160; קפה* 'basket' D7.12:3+ שבה(!) 'Sabbath' D7.34:7+; שנה 'year' B3.1:7+; שרה* 'meal' C3.12:28+([380]); תאה* 'ewe' D7.8:2.

With mater lectionis: א(י)ש 'person' C1.1:164+; דין 'lawsuit' B2.2:12+; זון 'food' B3.1:10+; חוט 'thread' B2.6:25+; חון* 'palm leaves' B2.9:6; טוב* 'goodness' C2.1:69; טור* 'mountain' C1.1:62+; טיב 'satisfied' A3.3:2+; טין 'mud' C3.7Gr2:25; כיב* 'pain' C1.2:19; לוח 'tablet' D3.26:3+; מות* 'death' B3.5:21+; נון* 'fish' B7.1:6+; פיק 'tray(?)' B3.3:6+; ציר 'hinge' A4.8:9+; רוח 'wind' C1.1:104; שוק 'street' B3.4:8+; שור 'wall' A4.5:5+; שים boat part A6.2:10+.

b) *Triconsonantal roots*

Without mater lectionis([381]): אבן 'stone' A4.8:9+; אבץ 'tin' C3.7Dv3:10; אגן 'basin'(?) D7.57:7; אגר 'wages' C1.1:100+; אדן* 'ear' C1.1:132+; אדר 'threshing floor' B1.1:13; און 'force' C1.1:96; אחד 'bar'(?) C1.1:83; איל* 'deer' C1.1:183; אכר* 'farmer' D8.11:5; אלה 'god' A4.3:2+; אלף 'thousand' A5.1:2+; אמן* 'artisan' A6.10:3+; אמר* 'lamb' C1.1:169+; אמר* 'saying' C1.1:86; אנפין* 'face' (pl. tant.) C1.1:14+; אנש 'person' B3.9:5+; אסי* 'physician' D2.31:3+; אסר* 'bond' B8.4:5+; אסר* 'oath' B5.6:10+; ארב 'ambush' C1.1:83+; ארז 'cedar' A6.2:10+; ארח 'way' B2.10:6+; ארי* 'lion' C1.1:94+; ארך 'length' B2.6:8+; ארע/ק 'earth, ground' B2.3:8+; אשד 'wormwood' D8.3:9 (probably error for אשל); אתן* 'she-ass'

---

[378] See Lindenberger 1983:106.

[379] Diachronically speaking, the form is a dual of the root ת-ר-י < ת-נ-ת.

[380] שרותא = שרתא?

[381] "Mater lectionis" is meant here in its etymological sense. Thus the lexeme יום 'day' is listed here, though in some parts of its inflection the Waw may not represent an etymological value of /w/ any longer.

B7.3:4+; אתר 'place' A6.10:2+; באר 'well' A4.5:6+; בות 'shame'
C1.1:185; בזק 'pebble' C1.1:205; בטן 'belly' C1.1:97+; בכא '?'
D8.3:15; *בכו 'crying'; *בכי 'weeping' D8.11:2; *בלי 'worn-out'
B3.8:10+; בעל 'husband' B2.1:9+; ברק 'lightning' C1.1:85; בשם
'spice' A2.2:12+; בשר 'flesh' C1.1:88; גבה 'high' C1.1:91; *גבר 'man'
C1.1:42+; *גדי 'kid' C1.1:209; *גוי 'inner' C3.19:1+; *גלד 'skin'
A6.16:3+; *גמל 'camel' C1.1:186+; גנב 'thief' C1.1:173+; גנן
'gardener' B3.10:10+; *גרם 'bone' C1.2:6; *גרש 'grits' D7.33:3;
גשר 'beam' A2.2:15+; דבב 'lawsuit' B2.8:10+; *דבח 'sacrifice'
A4.8:27+; דבש 'honey' A4.2:10; דגל 'military detachment'
B2.7:10+; *דגן 'grain' C1.1:129; דהב 'gold' B3.1:9; דין 'judge'
B4.6:14+; *דכי 'pure' A4.1:5; דכר 'male' B2.6:17+; דלע 'gourd'
D7.3:6; דמו 'likeness' B3.4:21; דקק 'fine' D7.7:3; *דרג 'stairway';
*דרע 'arm' D7.9:4+; הדר 'glory' C1.1:92; *הלך 'tribute' A6.11:5;
*ולד 'fetus, child' D7.33:1; זהב 'gold' C1.1:192+; *זוי 'corner'
B2.1:5+; *זין 'weapon' D7.57:9; זית 'olive' B3.8:20+; זכר 'male'
B3.4:21+; *זמן 'time' B8.9:4; זער 'diminution' C1.1:90; זפת 'loan'
B3.1:3+(³⁸²); זרע 'seed' A6.11:2+; זרת 'span' B6.2:6; *חבל 'rope'
A4.2:10; *חבר 'companion' D7.56:2; *חדי 'happy' A4.7:3+; חדת
'new' B3.5:8+; חוב 'debt' B1.1:19+; *חוי 'snake' A2.5:8; חור 'white'
D6.13:1; חטא 'sin' C1.1:128; חטר 'rod' C1.1:176; חיב 'guilty'
B3.8:42+; חיל 'troop; wealth' A4.6:12+; *חלי 'sweet' C1.1:131+;
חלם 'dream' D7.17:1; חלק 'portion' B3.5:11+; *חלר small weight
B6.2:7+; חמד 'delight' C1.1:88; חמם 'hot' D7.17:4; חמס 'violence'
C1.1:140; חמר 'wine' A4.7:21+; חמר 'ass' B1.1:14+; *חמר 'jewel'
B3.8:19; חמר 'heat(?)' C1.1:81; חמש 'five' A6.2:12+; *חנך 'palate'
C1.1:163; חנן part of a ship A6.2:11+; חפן 'handful' A6.9:4+; חצף
'coarse' D7.7:3; חקל 'field' B1.1:19+; חרב 'sword' C1.1:161+; *חרם
'fishing-net' D3.46:4+; חרש 'deaf' C1.1:215; *חתם 'seal' D14.6:1;
*חתן 'son-in-law' A2.6:3; *טבי 'gazelle' C1.1:168; *טלל 'protection'
C1.2:6; טמא 'unclean' D7.44:7+; טעם 'order' A6.2:25+; *טפר
'(toe-)nails' D3.27:5; טרן 'rock' C3.7Dv3:15+; *טרף 'prey' C1.1:81;
יום 'day' A4.1:4+; יין 'wine' C3.1:3+(³⁸³); *ינק 'child' A2.7:3+; ירח
'month' A6.1:3+; *כבל 'fetter' A4.7:16+; כדב 'false thing'
B3.11:16+; *כדב 'liar' C1.1:133+; כהן 'priest' A4.3:1+; *כון
'window' B3.12:21; *כלב 'dog' A4.7:16+; כמר 'priest' A5.4:2+;
*כנד vessel C3.7Gr2:8+; *כנף 'wing' C1.1:107; *כנת 'spelt'
C3.18:10+; *כסו 'garment' C1.1:204(³⁸⁴); *כסי 'cover' C1.1:167;
כסף 'silver' B4.5:3+; כעס 'anger' C1.1:124; כפן 'hunger' C1.1:123;

---

³⁸² Diachronically the Taw is no radical, for the root is זיף.

³⁸³ Spelled ין.

³⁸⁴ Actually spelt כסתך 'your garment' C1.1:204.

כפר 'compensation' A4.2:14; כצף* 'anger' C1.1:85; כרג* type of tax D7.27:8; כרם* 'vineyard' B8.4:6; כשר 'suitable' A6.14:4; כתן 'linen' A3.2:5+; לבב 'heart' C1.1:82+; לבש 'garment' B2.6:7+; לחי* 'bad' C1.1:138+; לחי* 'cheek' C1.1:172+; לחם 'bread' C1.1:181+; לשן 'tongue' C1.1:156+; מאן 'vessel' B3.13:11+; מדד* 'stature' C1.1:95; מהר 'bride-price' B3.8:4+; מות* 'death' B3.5:21; מחא '?' C1.1:178; מלח 'salt' C1.1:159; מלך 'king' C1.1:3+; מרא 'master' A4.7:15+; מרד* 'rebellious' C2.1:8; מרש 'beam' B3.10:14; משח 'oil' A2.2:12+; משך 'skin' A2.4:8+; נבו 'receipt' B4.2:6; נגד* 'ruler(?)' C1.1:10; נהר* 'river' D7.9:14+; נזק 'damage' A4.2:14; נחש 'bronze' B2.6:12+; נטח* 'attacker(?)' C1.1:103; ניח* 'quiet' C1.1:92; נמר 'leopard' C1.1:210+; נסך* 'libation' D7.9:1+; נפא type of lawsuit B2.9:4+; נפש 'soul' C3.9:5; נקי* 'lamb' A2.2:8+; נשן 'woman, lady' B3.4:3+ (pl.); נתר 'natron' C3.7Kv2:4+; סבר 'porter(?)' C3.27:31+; סגד/ר '?' C3.13:45; סגר* 'confinement' D7.10:2; סדר* 'order' D6.3:4; סלק '?' B3.8:18+; סמש* 'sun' B3.6:9; סני* 'thorn bush' C1.1:101+; סני kind of iron C3.7Fv2:14+; ספר 'scribe' C1.1:18+; ספר 'document' B2.1:20+; סתר 'secret' C1.1:111+; עבד 'slave' B2.11:17+; עבי 'thick' A6.2:14; עבי 'thickness' A6.2:18; עדב* 'lot' C1.1:136; עדר/ד 'time, number(?)' C1.1:83; עדן 'set time' A4.7:26+; עדר* 'help' C1.1:126; עזל* 'cloth(?)' A6.2:13+; עין 'eye' C1.1:212+; עלם 'eternity' B2.9:9; עלע* 'rib' C1.1:90; עמל 'labour' A3.6:2; עמר 'wool' B2.6:7+; ענ 'goat' D7.1:10+; ערב 'guarantor' A2.3:9+; ערד* 'wild ass' C1.1:204+; ערי* 'cold' C1.1:166; ערר 'legal claim' C1.1:103; עשך '?' C3.22:5+; עשר* 'ten' B2.3:14+; עשק 'injustice' A5.2:9+; עתר 'wealth' C1.1:206; פגע 'meeting' C1.1:184; פגר* 'corpse' C1.1:63+; פלג 'half' B2.4:11+; פסח* 'passover' D7.6:9+; פסק 'section(?)' D3.27:3; פרי 'produce' D11.7:9+; פרס 'salary' A3.3:3+; פרס small dry measure B1.1:5+; פרש 'horseman' A6.12:2; פשך 'handbreadth' B3.8:8+; פתי 'breadth' B3.8:6+; צבו 'desire' A4.3:6+; צבע 'colour' B2.6:8+; צבע 'finger' A6.2:20+; צות 'order' A4.2:14; צפר* 'morning' D3.47:9; קדל 'neck' C1.1:134; קדש* 'holiness' C1.1:79; קטו* 'cucumber' D7.3:2; קטל 'execution' C1.1:46; קים 'enduring' A3.10:7; קים* 'covenant' B5.6:10; קמח 'flour' A6.9:3+; קמר 'wool' A3.8:9+; קני 'reed' C3.13:6+; קפס 'granary' D1.30:2; קפף 'chest(?)' B3.8:17; קפת* 'basket' D7.7:4; קצת 'part' B4.5:3+; קרב 'battle' C2.1:57; קשי 'hard' C1.1:85+; קשת* 'bow' C1.1:190+; ראש 'head' B4.2:5+; רבע 'fourth' C3.7Gr2:9+; רגל* 'foot' C1.1:170+; רחם* 'friend' C1.1:112+; רחם* (pl. tant.) 'mercy' B5.2:10+; רכב* 'horseman' A6.12:2+; רכל* 'peddlar' A4.3:4+; רכש* 'horse' A3.11:2+; רמן 'pomegranate' B3.8:18+; רעי 'shepherd' D7.1:3; שאן* 'shoe' C1.1:205; שדק 'sharp cutting' C1.1:84; שהד 'witness' B4.1:5+; שטר 'side' B2.1:5; שאר 'remainder' D7.27:6+; שבי

'captivity' C1.2:5; שבע 'seven' B3.7:4+; שוי 'equal' B2.6:8+; שחד
'bribe' A4.2:4; שחל* 'cress' D7.45:8; שיט* 'sailor'; שכר 'intoxicating
drink' A6.9:3+; שלי 'calm' C1.1:130; שלם 'welfare' A3.4:5+; שמי*
(pl. tant.) 'heaven' C1.1:79+; שמש 'sun' B2.2:9+; שנט* 'ripped'
A2.1:4; שנן 'pair' B3.8:20+; שפי* 'flat' C1.1:161; שקל 'shekel'
B2.6:12+; תבל* 'dry land' A6.2:8+; תבן 'straw' C1.1:160; תון*
'chamber' B3.5:6+; תור 'bull' A4.10:10; תלי* 'weapon' A4.7:8+;
תלת 'three' A6.9:3+; תקל 'shekel' B1.1:13+; תרע 'gateway' B2.1:3+.

With fem. suffix ה- or ת-: אחרה 'other' B2.6:32+; אילה*
'doe' C1.1:182; אלהה* 'goddess' B2.8:5+; אנשה* 'wife' A2.4:3+([385]);
אנתה 'woman' B2.6:32+; ברכה* 'blessing' D7.1:1; דבלה* 'cake of
figs' D1.11:2; הלכה* 'going' C2.1:16; זבנה* 'purchase' B3.12:31;
חנטה* 'striped cloth' A2.4:10; חכמה 'wisdom' C1.1:105+; חנטה*
'wheat' C1.1:129; כאיה 'rebuke' C1.1:178; כדבה* 'lie' C1.1:132+;
כתיבה* 'writing' D22.51:2; לבנה* 'brick' B4.3:18+; לחנה 'female
temple servitor' B3.12:2+; מחאה 'blow' C1.1:178; מלאה* 'full
value(?)' B1.1:9; מלכה* 'queen' A2.1:1; מנחה 'meal offering'
A4.10:11+; מראה* 'mistress' A3.7:2+; משחה* 'measurement'
B2.4:4+; נפקה 'expense' C3.27:29+; נקבה 'female' B3.4:21+; סבלה*
'burden' D11.2:4; סמכת 'support(?)' C3.7Jv2:19+; סערה* 'barley'
D7.12:4; עזקה 'ring' C1.1:60+; עלוה 'burnt offering' A4.7:28+;
ענוה 'poverty' C1.1:89; עשרה* 'ten-weight' B3.9:8+; צדקה 'merit'
A4.7:27+; צהוה 'thirst' C1.1:123; צפחא 'griddle' D7.57:8; קבלת
'complaint' A6.8:3; קדמה* bow of a boat(?) A6.2:11; קומה* 'stature'
A6.2:11; קרבה* 'offering' D20.2:1; קריה 'city' B6.3:7+; רחמה 'love'
B3.7:14+; רפאה 'cure'; רקעה piece of cloth A6.2:20+; שנאה 'hatred'
B3.3:8+; שערה* 'barley' B4.1:2+; שפוה* 'lip' C1.1:151+; שארה
'remainder' B3.8:23+; שררת 'strength' A3.3:1.

With mater lectionis: אנוש 'human being' D8.42:24;
אסיר* 'captive' A4.4:5+; ארון 'chest' A2.5:4; אריך* 'long' A4.7:3+;
באיש 'evil' A6.7:8+; בניו 'construction' B2.4:12; בשים 'perfumed'
D3.16:8; הדיר 'splendid' C1.1:206; זלוע 'jug' B2.6:13+; זעיר 'small'
D7.14:11+([386]); חטו(י)ב 'striped' B2.6:7+; חכים 'wise' C1.1:1+; חליף
'replacement(?)' B8.5:12; חמוש '?' C3.7Dr3:17+; חמיר 'leaven'
A4.1:6; חסין 'strong' C1.1:89+; חציף 'impudent' C1.1:143; חשוך
'darkness' C1.1:173; חתיל 'string(?)' A4.2:10; טעון 'load' C1.1:186;
ימין 'right' B3.6:3+; יקיר 'heavy' C1.1:159+; יתיר 'exceeding' A5.3:2+;
כביר 'large' C1.1:136+; כדיב 'liar' C2.1:65; כציר 'harvest' C1.1:127;
כשיט* 'honest' C1.1:158; כתון 'tunic' A3.3:9+; לבוש 'clothing'
B2.8:4+; מהיר 'skilled' C1.1:1; מריר 'bitter' C1.1:89+; נשיף(?) 'pure'

---

[385] On the problematic spelling with Shin instead of Taw, see above at § 2 *c*.

[386] Possibly with a diphthong /ay/.

D8.2:2+; סבול 'support' B5.5:4+; סויר* 'hiding place' C1.1:183; סוסי* 'horse' A6.12:2+([387]); סחיק 'worn-out' A3.8:10; סכין 'knife' C1.1:88+; ספיק* 'sufficient' D6.8:1; סריס 'eunuch' C1.1:61+; עבור 'grain' B2.9:6+; עויל 'child' C1.1:215+; עויר 'blind' C1.1:212+; עזיז 'strong' C1.1:83+; עטיק 'old' B3.11:15; עמוד* 'column' A4.7:9+; עמיר 'fodder' A6.9:4; עתיק 'old' B2.3:16+; עתיר* 'rich' C1.1:206; פקיד 'official' A5.5:2+; פריץ(?) 'licentious' C1.1:179; פתור 'table' D3.22:1; צדיק 'righteous' B7.3:6+; צריף 'refined' B2.1:7+; קלול liquid measure C3.12:4+; קליל 'light' C1.1:38+; קפיר* 'pot' D7.9:12+; קריב 'near' B2.1:9+; רביע 'fourth' B4.2:2+; רחים 'beloved' C1.1:163+; רחיק 'distant' B2.2:15+; רכיך 'soft' C1.1:84+; רשיע* 'wicked' C1.1:107+; שגיא 'abundant' C1.1:90+; שפיק 'sufficient' A6.10:3+; שאול 'netherworld' C1.2:6; שביט 'shawl' B2.6:9+; שליט 'having power' B2.4:6+; שפיע* 'copious' C1.1:74; שפיר 'beautiful' C1.1:95+; שריר 'firm' A4.7:3+; תחום* 'border' B2.2:7+; תמים 'perfect' D1.16:2; תקין(?) 'firm' C2.1:70.

With fem. suffix -ה or ת-: בזיזה* 'spoil' C1.1:104; בסולה '?' C1.1:217; בתולה 'virgin' C1.1:134; גזירה 'decree' D7.35:11; חליפה* 'substitute' A6.2:13; כודנה* 'she-mule' D22.1:2; כתיבה* 'writing' D7.9:4+; לבונה 'incense' A4.8:21+; מלוכה* 'kingship' B2.2:1+; ספינה 'ship' C3.7Jv2:4+; עבידה 'construction' C1.1:127+; ערובה 'eve' D7.8:7; פסילה 'cut stone' A4.7:10+; קבילה 'complaint' A6.15:5+; שניתה* 'slave mark' B8.2:4+.

c) *Stems or compound words with more than three consonants*—אבנצרף 'dye stone' A4.3:3; אוצר 'treasury' B3.7:7; טלפח* 'lentil' B4.3:5+; כברי 'sulphur' A6.2:17+; כוכב* 'star' C1.1:164; כנכר 'talent' A6.2:17+; כרסא 'throne' C1.1:133+; לילי* 'night' C1.1:80; נעבץ* 'stone inlay' B2.6:15+; נשחט 'finely-woven(?)' B2.6:10; עלים 'boy' A4.3:8+([388]); עקרב 'scorpion' C1.1:180; פרזל 'iron' B2.8:4+; פרכס 'box' B2.6:16+; פשרן 'fail' D7.20:2+; צנפר 'bird' C1.1:82+; שארי* 'remainder' B8.1:11+; תולע 'purple' A6.16:3; תותב 'resident' C1.1:160; תימן 'south' C1.1:134; תמני* 'eight' B3.8:16.

With fem. suffix -ה or ת: ארמלה 'widow' A4.7:20+; כרבלה 'hat' A3.2:6; עלימה 'girl' C3.26:37+.([389])

d) *With suffix* -י: אחרי 'other' C3.27:29+; ארמי 'Aramaean' B2.1:2+; בבלי 'Babylonian' B2.2:19; בחתרי 'Bactrian' D2.12:2+; גוי 'inner' C3.19:1; ורכני 'Hyrcanian' B8.3:3; חורי 'white' A6.9:3; ח(י)לכי* 'Cilician' D6.7:2+; חרזמי 'Khwarezmian' B2.2:2+; יהודי

---

[387] See § 18 *r* (1), and n. 341.

[388] The root is ע-ל-מ. The noun is of *qutayl* pattern for diminutives.

[389] The root is ע-ל-מ.

'Jew' B2.2:3+; יוני 'Ionian' C3.7Jr5:25+; כלבי* 'curlike' A4.7:16+;
כספי 'Caspian' B2.7:18+; כרכי* 'Carian' A6.2:3+; כשי* 'Nubian'
D23.1 Va:8; מגושי, מגושי 'Magian' B3.5:24+; מדי 'Median' B3.6:17+;
מצרי 'Egyptian' C3.19:33+; נכרי 'foreign' C1.1:159+; עלי* 'upper'
A6.4:3+; ערבי 'Arabian' C1.1:207+; פרסי 'Persian' C2.1:19+; צידני
'Sidonian' C1.1:207+; צעני 'Zoanite' C1.2:25; קדמי* 'former'
A6.10:1; תחתי 'lower' B3.5:8+.

e) *With suffix* ך-: כרתך 'Cretan' B8.3:1.

f) *With suffix* ן- [= *-a:n*?]: אחרן 'other' B2.4:8+; אלפן 'discipline' C1.1:178; בנין* 'building' B3.4:22; דכרן 'memorandum'
D3.1:1; זכרן 'memorandum' A4.9:1+; חסרן 'loss' A4.3:9+; יתרן
'surplus' C3.11:6; מנין 'number' B4.5:3+; ערבן 'pledge' B3.1:13+;
פלגן 'division' B2.11:17+; פקדן 'deposit' B2.9:7; פשרן 'delay'; קנין
'possession' B2.8:4+; רחמן 'merciful' C1.1:53+; ריקן* 'empty'
C3.7Ar2:18+; שהין* 'desolation' C1.1:104; שלטן* 'power' D7.56:12;
תנין 'second' B3.1:7; תנין 'sea serpent' C1.1:90(?).

g) *With suffix* כן-: סונכן 'Syenian' B5.2:2([390]); סיכן 'Saite'
B8.6:5+.([391])

h) *With suffix* ו [= **u:*]: אנתו 'wifehood' B2.8:4+; הימנו*
'trustworthiness' C1.1:132; מלכו 'kingdom' C1.1:79; מררו* 'bitterness' C1.1:123; שהדו 'witness' D1.17:6; שלמו* 'perfection'
C3.7Kr4:21+; שרחו 'foulness(?)' C1.1:106; שתות 'sixth' C3.7Fv2:2+.

i) *With prefix* א: ארבע 'four' A6.2:16+; אחבר* (only in the pl.
אחברוהי 'his colleagues' D7.56:3); ארמלה 'widow' A4.7:20+.([392])

j) *With prefix* מ: מאכל 'food' B8.1:14+; מבשים 'scented' B3.8:20;
מדבח* 'altar' A4.7:26+; מדנח 'east' B3.7:7; מהימן 'trustworthy'
A2.1:9; מובל* 'burden' C1.1:185+; מוזן* 'scales' B2.6:24+; מומא
'oath' B2.8:9+; מועא 'east' B2.3:4+; מותב 'seat' D23.1 Va:9; מזרק*
'bowl' A4.7:12+; מחזי 'mirror' B2.6:11+; מטלל 'roof' A4.8:10+;
מכל* 'food' D8.8:4; ממלל 'speech' C1.1:84+; מנדע 'intelligence'
C1.1:53; מסגד* 'veneration' B7.3:3; מסמר* 'nail' A6.2:16+; מסתר(?)*
'secret' C1.1:141; מערב 'west' B3.5:7+; מעשר 'tithe' C3.7Kr2:19+;
מקרא 'script' B2.11:4+; מקרי* 'declaration' B7.2:6; מרבי 'interest'
B4.2:7; מרזח* '?' D7.29:3; מרחק 'withdrawal' B2.2:22+; משאן 'shoe'
A3.2:2+; משחק 'worn-out' D7.26:3; משתל* 'basket(?)' D7.57:9.

With fem. suffix ה or ת: מאסרה 'bundle' D7.28:3; מדינה
'province' A6.9:5+; מנטרה* 'watch' A4.5:1; מ(נ)ציעה* 'middle'
C3.28:112; משאלה* 'interrogation' D2.30:2+; מתקלה* 'weight'

---

[390] See § 18 *h*, n. 302.

[391] See § 18 *h*, n. 302.

[392] On the etymology of the word, cf. Gesenius - Buhl 1915: s.v. אַלְמָנָה.

A6.2:21+.

k) *With prefix* -ת: תכונה 'money' B3.8:5+; תרבי 'interest' D7.57:2.

l) *Words of obscure origin*

אברת 'area (?)' B3.5:7+; אגר 'wall' B2.1:4+; *אדנסה '?' C3.5:4; אדיהבן '?' C3.7Ev2:6+; ארכל or אדכל '?' D7.47:9; אדרנג 'guarantor' B3.11:12+; אופתחתו '?' B8.8:3+; איטשרי '?' C3.11:4+; אכדפך or אכרפך '?' C3.7Fr2:20+; אנזעררה '?' C1.1:89; אסוח '?' C3.7Ar3:21+; בינבן '?'; ביכנא '?' A6.2:10; בטק '?' A2.5:6; אתריה '?' D7.47:9; *ארכל '?' A2.5:5; *בק 'jar' D7.44:6; בקל 'legumes' D7.16:6+; גמידה kind of garment B3.8:7; דוגי 'sea-going vessel' C3.7Fr1:23+; דוגית 'fishing boat' C3.8 I:10+; דחן 'millet' B8.3:9+; ר/דחפן '?' A4.5:11; דפני 'harmed' B8.4:4; *דר '(panel) section'(?) A6.2:20; *דשתו '?' B1.1:7; *היכל 'temple' C1.1:17+(392a); הנדו '?' A6.7:6+; *הנפן 'protecting wall' B3.10:9+; ואסה kind of garment A3.8:8; *זלוח 'sprinkler' C3.13:7+; זן 'kind' A6.1:3+; חגב '?' C3.8 IIIB:25; *חוץ 'palm leaf' B3.8:17+; חליך '?' B8.5:12; חמוש '?' C3.7Cr1:10+; *חנה 'gift(?)' D7.9:1+; חפוש 'excess' A6.2:18; *חתחפב '?' B8.5:12; כא liquid measure; לק 'oar(?)' C3.7Fv2:5+; *נחתם 'baker' D8.9:7; סגנן boat part A6.2:10; *סודה '?' C2.1:70; *סחה 'neighbour' A2.1:12; סעבל '?' A6.2:11; *סך 'jar(?) C3.7Kr2:19+; ספא 'jar(?)' D7.33:2+; סרחלך kind of garment A3.8:9+; פכלול '?' D7.7:10; פמטן '?' B1.1:15+; פסלד/רשי '?' C3.7Jv2:3+; פעמי kind of wood C3.7JvI:28+; פעקס '?' A3.8:9; פתף 'ration' A6.9:6+; צלצל 'sailboat(?)' C3.8:18+; *קלבי liquid measure C3.12:3; קלעס part of a boat A6.2:11; קנרתע '?' C3.7Jv2:6; רמי 'of inferior quality' or 'refined' A6.9:3; רעי measure C3.19:6+; ר/דשו '?' A6.2:17+; שוי '?' 'papyrus-reed bed' B2.6:15; שטטן kind of tunic A3.8:8; שטי '?' D1.30:3; שע 'plaster' D7.57:6; שמוש '?' C3.7Fr2:23+; שעחסם '?' C1.2:5; שפתם '?' B8.1:13; תחם 'amphora' D7.57:6; תמסא 'bowl' B2.6:12+; תפסה '?' A3.2:8; תקבח '?' D7.16:9.

m) *Loan-words*(393)

אב(י)נרן 'penalty' B3.6:8+; אבשוך 'presser (?)' A6.7:5; אגרה, 'letter' A3.6:3+; אנור *temple' B3.4:9+; *אדון 'route' A6.9:5; אודיס 'investigative report' A4.10:12; אופכרתה 'reckoning'(?) A6.2:5+; אופסתה '?' C3.18:13+; אופשר 'repairs(?)' A6.2:22+; אזד 'known' A4.5:8+; *אזדכר 'herald' A6.1:7+; אזת 'free' B3.6:4; אימש '?' C2.1:69; אלך 'ship' A2.6:9+; *אנב 'fruit' C1.1:101(394); אספרן 'in

---

392a Not quite of obscure origin, of course, but a very early loan from Akkadian, as shown by the initial /ḫ/: see Kaufman (1974:27).

393 For a classified list of loan-words in our corpus, see Appendix III.

394 On the etymology of the word, see Gesenius - Buhl 1915: 2a.

full' A6.13:4; אפיחי 'necessary' A6.2:9; אפסי '?' A6.2:12; כל(י)ארד 'architect' B2.8:2+; ארדב 'ardab' B4.4:4+; אשל* measure of area C3.21:8+; אשרן 'carpentry work' B3.4:23+; אתרודן 'brazier' A4.5:17; בב 'gate' C1.1:17+; בג 'domain' C3.6:214+; בדיכר* 'artist(?)' A6.12:2; בירה* 'fortress' B2.2:3+; בעל טעם'chancellor' A6.2:23; ברזמדן* kind of priest D17.1:1; גושך* 'hearer' A4.5:9; גמא 'papyrus reed' B2.6:15; גנז* 'treasure' B8.5:2+; גסח 'harsh' A6.7:5+; גרב liquid measure C3.28:85+; גרד 'domestic staff' A6.10:2+; גרד אמגן וספון שפיק 'staff of craftsmen of all kinds with sufficient numbers' A6.10:1+; גשור* 'beam' D13:3; דושון* 'ill-willed' B8.4:2; דושכרת* 'crime' A4.5:3; דרות 'peace' D17.1:5; דרי 'wall' A6.2:20; דרירסי 'southern room' B3.10:13; דש(!)* 'door' B3.10:13+; דשן* 'gift' A6.4:1+; הדאבנו 'accrued increment' A6.13:5; הירא '?' B3.2:3+; הלר* small weight B6.2:7+; המכריגרב 'joint holding(?)' B8.10:5; המרכר* 'accountant' D3.28:2; הנבג 'partner in realty' B3.10:18+; הנגית 'partner in chattel' B3.6:5+; הנדונה 'paint(?)' A6.2:5+; הנדרז 'order' A6.13:3+; הפתחפתא 'guardian of the seventh' B.39:2+; וזיך* 'vessel' C3.28:107+; וספון 'of every kind' A6.10:3+; ופר/דת '?' A2.2:5; ורשבר 'plenipotentiary' A6.5:2+; זו weight B4.3:17+; זיני 'damages' A6.15:8; זרניך 'arsenic' A6.2:17+; חל* 'gun-wale(?)' A6.2:12+; חם 'straw' B2.6:25+; חסי* 'praiseworthy' D2.5:4; חתפי 'offering-table' D20.1:1; טף boat part A6.2:10+; יודן* 'barley-house' A4.5:5; יוזא* 'revolt' A6.11:2+; כנת* 'colleague' C1.1:185+; כסמתו 'diminishment' A6.10:2+; כרץ* 'slander' D20.5:2; כרש measure of weight A3.2:10+; לבה* 'wrath' A3.3:10+; לחן 'temple servitor' B3.3:2+; מגוש* 'magus' C2.1:75; מכס 'tax' C3.11:8+; מלות 'board' C3.7Gr3:25; מלח 'sailor' B2.2:11+; מנדה a tax D6.13:1; מנחה 'excellent one' D20.6; מסכן 'poor' C2.1:68; מקלו 'burnt offering' A4.10:10; מת 'region' B8.1:17+; נגי* 'region(?)' B4.3:3; נגר* 'carpenter' A6.2:9+; נופח* 'boat-man' A6.2:7+; נכס* (pl. tant.) 'property' A4.7:16+; נמעתי 'the Lord of the Two Truths'; נפחר 'total' C2.1:49+; נפרת 'litigation' B8.9:5+; נשי 'people' A6.11:4+(³⁹⁵); נשתון* 'document' A6.1:3; סגן 'prefect' B2.3:13+; סי 'beam(?)' C3.7Gr3:23+; ספיתכן 'whitener(?)' A6.2:9+; סרושי* 'corporal punishment' A6.3:6+; סתתר(י) 'stater' C3.7Dr1:9+; פחה* 'governor' A4.7:1+; פחטמוני 'mooring post(?)' A6.2:12; פינך 'dish' D7.57:8 (πίναξ?); פסחמצנותי 'scribe of the book of God'; פסחדת 'after-gift' B3.11:9+; פד/רעד/ר 'prow(?)' A6.2:12; פק 'plank(?)' C3.7Dv5:1+; פריפת 'main beloved(?)' B3.12:11; פרמכר* 'foreman' A6.2:4+; פרתך 'foremost aide(?)' A5.2:7; פרתר 'openly' C1.1:67; פרתרך 'governor' B2.9:4+; פתגם 'sentence' A6.8:3+; פתיפרס 'investigator'

---

³⁹⁵ An Akkadian loan-word always in the st.cst., נשי בי 'household staff.'

A4.2:3; פתכר 'idol' A6.12:2+; פתכרכר 'sculptor' A6.12:1; פתסחו 'praiseworthy' A6.16:4; צפעה '?' D8.10:1+; קנד/רתעא large sea-going vessel(?); קנד/רתשירי small sea-going vessel(?) C3.7Ev1:14+; קנחנתי 'divine shrine' B3.10:9+; רבי* 'young man' C1.1:41; רסי 'southern' B3.11:3; רסתכה 'market' (?) C3.21:2+; שות* 'rioting(?)' A6.10:4; שושן* 'groom' A3.11:3+; שנטא 'garment' B3.8:11; שף '?' A6.2:19+; תחית 'courtyard' B3.7:5+; תיפתיא 'overseer' A4.5:9; תמואנתי 'divine way' B3.10:9; תמא/תמי '?' B3.5:10+; תמיס 'panelling(?)' A6.2:13+; תמנחא 'the excellent one' D20.5:1; תסהרא 'royal barque' C1.2:1; תקבה 'vessel' A2.1:5+; תקם 'castor oil' A2.2:13+; תרבץ* 'court(yard)' B3.7:4+; תרי 'room' B3.5:3+; תשי 'customs duty' C3.7Kv2:8+.

§ 20. Prepositions.

These are a series of words which take on some meaning only by being prefixed to the following word or conjunctive pronoun. They are unlike nouns, adjectives, verbs etc. which, on their own, mean something. Description of these "meanings" is a lexicographer's task. The prepositions attested in our corpus with their necessarily approximative gloss are: אחר 'after,' e.g. אחר מותכי 'after your death' B3.5:17+; אחרי 'after,' e.g., אחרי מותך 'after your death' B3.6:14; אל 'to,' e.g. אל תשי 'To Tashai' A2.2:18 (no example with a conj. pron., and only in letter addresses); ב 'in,' e.g., במנפי 'in Memphis' B8.2:10; בין 'between'(396); חלף 'in exchange for,' e.g., חלף פלגה 'in exchange for its half' B7.3:8; כ 'as, like,' e.g., כמליא אלה 'like these words' A6.11:3; כות 'according to,' e.g., כותה 'according to it' A6.2:24; ל- 'to; for,' e.g., לאמך 'for your mother' A3.3:10; להן 'other than,' e.g., להן אנתי 'other than you, except for you' B2.3:11; לות 'towards,' possibly in לות פמך 'towards your mouth' C1.1:81, if not ... להן 'but ...'; מן 'from,' e.g., מן יומא זנה 'from this day' B2.6:4; עד 'till,' e.g., עד כען 'until now' A4.3:7; על 'on; against,' e.g., יקום על ידניה 'shall stand up against Jedaniah' B3.9:7(397); עלוי 'upon,' e.g., למבנה עלוי אגרא זך 'to build on that

---

396 Cp. בין עני ותמת 'between Anani and Tamet' B 3.3:11 and בין תמת ובין עני ib.12.

397 In למה הו יחבל מתא עלין C1.1:36 the preposition indicates an effect or consequence to be borne. This is a Northwest Semitic lexical isogloss: on BH, see Joüon - Muraoka (1993: § 133f), on Phoenician, Ahiram 2 נחת תברח על גבל 'may peace flee from Byblos!,' and on Moabite, Mesha 14 אחז נבה על ישראל.

על in תחב על מחנא B3.8:26 seems to mean 'next to, beside,' an unusual sense, though well known to BH, e,g, Gn 24.13 נִצָּב עַל עֵין הַמָּיִם. A scribal error for תחוב, תותב etc. is unlikely in view of the similar expression elsewhere

wall' B2.1:6; עם 'with,' e.g., עם אחוהי 'with his brother' C1.1:49;
קבל 'corresponding to,' חמר קבל חמר 'homer for homer' B1.1:5;
קדם 'before' (locative), e.g., קרבתה קדם אסרחאדן 'I presented him
before Esarhaddon' C1.1:10; קדמת 'before' (temporal), e.g., קדמת
זנה 'prior to this' A4.7:17; תחת 'under,' e.g., תחת חלא 'under the
gun-wale(?)' A6.2:12. It suffices to note a few morphological
features which are characteristic of them.

a) *Use of conjunctive pronouns*

When an element following a preposition is equivalent to a
personal pronoun, the latter is expressed in the form of a
conjunctive pronoun: thus "to" + "she" = ל + הי > "to her" = לה.

b) *Proclitic prepositions*

The prepositions ב, כ, and ל, all monosyllabic just like the
conjunction ו, are proclitic. Their graphic unity with the following
word or words appears to indicate that they also formed a phonetic
unit.

c) *Extra final Yod before conjunctive pronouns*

Some prepositions end with the letter Yod and behave like
masculine plural nouns when they govern a conjunctive pronoun:
אחרי(398), עלוי (מן)(399). A second group lacks such a Yod
when it governs a self-standing word, but behaves like the first
group only when a conjunctive pronoun is added: חלף, על, and
קדם(400): e.g., אחרי מותי 'after my death' B3.5:21 vs. אחריך 'after
you' B2.4:13; מן בלעדי מלת מלך 'except for (or: without ..., namely
without royal intervention) a king's word' B1.1:11 vs. בלעדיהם
'without them' D23.1 XII:3; חלף אחיקר 'instead of Ahiqar' C1.1:62
vs. חלפוהי 'instead of him' A6.4:3; על זנה 'about this' A3.3:4 vs.
עלוהי 'about it' A3.10:7; עלוי אגרא זך 'above that wall' B2.1:6 vs.
עלויה 'on it (= אגרא 'the wall' [a fem. noun])' B2.1:11; קדם אלה
שמיא 'before the god of heaven' A4.3:2 vs. קדמיך 'before you'
A6.5:1. Having regard to other dialects, one may assume that בין
behaved in the manner of the second group only when followed
by a conjunctive pronoun for the plural like ביניהם 'between them'

(B2.6:23). Nor is the sense 'to return to' likely with על + an inanimate object:
see below, § 74 *i*.

[398] The loss of Yod in אחר with a noun as in אחר מותכי may be based on the
analogy of its antonym קדם.

[399] Cf. Syr. /ˤella:way/ and JA, e.g., מֵעֵלָוַי, on the latter of which see Dalman
(1905:229).

[400] No example is found in our corpus of תחת 'under' with a conjunctive
pronoun. Note, however, לתחתיך 'under you' Pap. Amherst 63:12/13, 14.

B3.4:8.([401]) The remainder of the prepositions display no such peculiarity.([402])

d) *Compound prepositions*

Some prepositions come together to form compound prepositions: thus מן אחרי 'after me' C2.1:77; מן בלעדי 'without; except' B1.1:11([403]); לקבל 'according to' A4.3:9, C1.2:24+; בר מן 'except' in a compound conjunction בר מן זי 'unless' B3.3:14([404]); מנעל 'above' B2.10:8+; מן קדם 'from before' in מן קדמיכי B3.11:13†; מן תחת 'from under' B3.3:13; ד ל-[ע] 'until' C1.1:52; עלי ל- 'above' B3.7:6; תחת ל- 'below' B3.7:5.

e) *Prepositions + nouns = pseudo-prepositions*

Another category of compound prepositions are combinations of prepositions and nouns. The degree of cohesion of some such combinations is shown in the way they are written, being run together. E.g., בגו 'inside' B2.1:15+; בטלל 'with the help of' A4.3:5+; ביד 'in the hand of,' i.e. through the agency of; במצעיעת 'in the middle of' A4.5:5,6; בשם 'concerning' B2.3:12+; כפם 'at the instruction of' B3.9:9+; ליד 'under the control of' B8.6:1+; לעיני 'in the presence of' A3.5:7; לערק 'towards' C2.1:15+, לערע ib.9 (see § 2 *d*); עליד 'by the hand of' A6.2:21; על דבר([405]) 'on account of' B2.2:6+; על אנפי 'upon' B2.6:19†; על פם 'according to' B4.4:18+; לעלא מן 'above' C1.1:162; שטר מן 'except' B2.10:13; לאפ(י) 'in the presence of' C3.28:91.

§ 21. Numerals

One may include under this heading, in addition to the traditional class of cardinal and ordinal numerals, some quantifiers such as כל, שגיא, קליל, קצת, but these latter, morphologically speaking, are not essentially different from other ordinary nouns.

a) *Cardinals*

These are often given as ciphers, hence their relative infrequency in spite of the nature of our documents where numbers figure prominently. As is the case in Semitic languages in general,

---

[401] ביני A3.10:2 is to be vocalised בֵּינֵי or בֵּינָי.

[402] Or some of them are not attested with a conjunctive pronoun, e.g. אל, עד.

[403] בעדה B2.6:22 and B3.3:7 is better interpreted as 'in an assembly' (Porten - Yardeni 1989:33,63) rather than 'in his favour' (Segert 1975:229).

[404] The correction of the text at B3.4:21 appears to have been left incomplete: one expects בר מן זי בר זי אפולי 'unless a son of A. ...' for בר מן זי אפולי.

[405] Cf. § 3 *b* above.

the cardinal numerals for "one" to "ten" and any compound numeral which contains a unit numeral such as 12, 23, 234 come in two series, one unmarked and the other marked with the typically feminine sufformative. The marking for the numeral for "two," however, is made by means of an infix: תרתין vs. תרין.

When an object is counted, the marked series is used with a noun whose grammatical gender is masculine and the unmarked series with a feminine noun, with the exception of the numerals for "one" and "two." Thus:

בנן תלת	'three daughters'	בנין תלתה	'three sons'
בנן תרתין	'two daughters'	בנין תרין	'two sons'
ברה חדה	'one daughter'	בר חד	'one son'

	UNMARKED	MARKED
"1"	חד A4.2:3	חדה A4.5:17
"2"	תרין C1.1:67([406])	תרתין C1.1:187; cst. תרתי C2.1:11†
"3"	תלת A6.9:3	תלתה A6.2:10; תלתא C1.1:187†([407])
"4"	ארבע A6.2:16	ארבעה B3.1:4
"5"	?	חמשה B3.5:15
"6"	?	שתה B5.5:3
"7"	שבע B3.7:4	שבעה B3.8:16
"8"	?	תמניה B3.8:16,23†
"9"	?	?
"10"	?	עשרה A6.2:11([408])
"12"	?	עשרה ותרין A6.2:10,11†
"15"	?	עשרה וחמשה A6.2:11†
"20"		עשרן A6.2:16
"25"	?	עשרן וחמשה A6.2:16

---

[406] On the etymological relationship between the cardinal root -תר and ordinal -תנ, cf. Segert (1975:216).

[407] This last form following ד has the force of an ordinal, "third." Leander (1928:115) and Kottsieper (1990:104f.) see here the st.det. of תלת, and the latter further holds that the gender of the numeral must agree with that of the noun in question. But Nöldeke (1898:178) mentions Syr. /yawma:ʔ daṯre:n/ 'the second day' and /da:ra: daṯma:nya:/ 'the eighth generation.' This question calls for further investigation.

[408] The form עשרתא 'the tenner,' which occurs in formulas for indicating a pecuniary amount to be paid as in כסף ר 2 לעשרתא 'silver 2 q(uarters) to the ten' B2.2:15+, is usually taken to refer to the weight of ten shekels, but it is sometimes paralleled by a cipher for a numeral, not a substantive: e.g. in כסף ר 2 ל 10 B2.6:7.

"30"		תלתין B3.9:8([409])
"50"		חמשן A6.2:15
"60"		שתן A6.2:12
"70"		שבען A6.2:11
"80"		תמנין A6.2:10,14†([410])
"90"	?	
"100"		מאה A6.2:14; pl. מאון D5.41:1([411])
"150"		מאה וחמשן A6.2:15†
"180"		מאה ותמנין A6.2:14
"200"		מאתין A6.2:13, cf. BA Ezr 6.17 מָאתַיִן.
"250"		מאתין וחמשן A6.2:14
"275"		מאתין שבען וחמשה A6.2:15
"400"		ארבע מאה A6.2:16†
"425"		ארבע מאה עשרן וחמשה A6.2:16
"1000"		אלף A4.8:27([412])

From the table above one may make the following observations, which are bound to be somewhat tentative on account
of incomplete attestation:

b) *Higher numerals, composite numerals*

"Tens" (= 10 x c)([413]) are the plural of the form for the
corresponding unit as in Semitic in general. This seems to apply
to "20," spelled defectively עשרן, which accords with BA spelled
plene, but vocalised as pl.: Dn 6.2 עֶשְׂרִין If the du. were intended,
one would expect עשׂרין([414]) in our corpus: see above § 18 *i*.

As regards composite numerals, the descending order is

---

[409] Leander (1928:116) and Segert (1975:218) read the difficult form ארבעיא
C3.28:1 as the only instance of the st.det.pl. of a ten, 'the forty' (so Cowley
already). Porten - Yardeni (1993:263): 'fours/fourths'; Grelot (1972:112):
'quart.' Cf. Degen 1979:30.

[410] It is not immediately apparent whether the form is, as in תלתין, spelled
plene or not. For the possibility that the Yod may be consonantal, cp. JA תְּמָנֵן
(Dalman 1905:127), Syr. /tma:nin/ beside <tmnʾyn> (unvocalised) (Nöldeke
1898, 1966:93). תלתין, moreover, invalidates Leander's explanation: "תמנין im
Gegensatz zu allen anderen Zehnern mit einem ruhenden ʾ, vielleicht um die
zwei ן von einander zu trennen' (1928:116). See also (Degen 1979:30) and
Beyer (1984:460).

[411] Though not strictly a numeral, מאותהם 'their centuries' A5.5:7 is consonant
with the partly restored form given here.

[412] אלפי C1.2:7 is more likely 'the ships of' (Porten - Yardeni 1993:54) than
'thousands of' (Leander 1928:116f.; Segert 1975:219).

[413] c stands for an integer from 1 to 9.

[414] Segert erroneously gives עשרין K7.32 (= B3.8:32).

used for the arrangement of their constituents.([415]) For "11" to "99" the conjunction Waw is proclitically added to the following unit numeral (**c**) and preceded by the numeral for 10 x **c**.([416]) Numerals for "101" to "999" consisting of up to three components use Waw only once, with the last numeral. Where a composite numeral ends with one for **c**, the marked or unmarked form is selected in accordance with the grammatical gender of the noun which serves as the head of the numeral.

c) *"Eleven" to "Nineteen"*

As regards "11" to "19" specifically, Mandaic is the only later Aramaic dialect whose numerals for these numbers show structural similarity to our idiom. Alongside the gender-indifferent forms such as /hamisar/, Mandaic also has an alternative system in which the decade precedes, joined by the conjunction to the following cipher for a unit, *and* the gender of the two matches: e.g., m. /asra utrin/ vs. f. /asar utartin/ "twelve."([417]) Accordingly, the "unmarked" column in the above table for "12" and "15" can be reconstructed as עשר ותרתין and עשר וחמש respectively. All other dialects show the basic structure of m. חמשת עשר vs. f. חמש עשרי. BA, which has Dn 4.26 תְּרֵי־עֲשַׂר as the only relevant example, seems to agree with these dialects.

d) *Hundreds*

"100" is מאה A6.2:14 without חד. For "200" the dual form is used: מאתין A6.2:13. Only one example is found for "hundreds" (300 - 900): ארבע מאה '400' A6.2:16. The use of the singular (מאה) and the sequence of the components accord with what we find in many other Aramaic dialects.([418])

---

[415] The restoration ארב]עת עשר יומן 'fourteen days' A4.1:3, first put forward by Sachau (1911:38) and accepted since universally, would go against this rule. We also find it odd that all other numbers of days in this document concerning the celebration of the passover are given by means of ciphers. If the restoration be correct, however, its abnormal syntax may be due to the influence of the biblical prescription concerned: Ex 12.6 ארבעה עשר יום לחדש etc. The mixing of ciphers and numerals is attested elsewhere, e.g. B3.8:6,23,32.

[416] This structure obviously differs from the only certain OA example in Zakkur A 4: עשר מלכן שו[שת] (or: ש]בע[ת) 'sixteen (or: seventeen) kings.'

[417] On the preceding ten, cf. also Nöldeke 1875:188, n. 4, where rare exceptional cases in Syriac and Nabataean are mentioned.

[418] JA (Dalman 1905:127f.), Syriac (Nöldeke 1898:95), Mandaic (Macuch 1965:231), BTA (Epstein 1960:128), and CPA (Müller-Kessler 1991:136). Exceptions are SA (Macuch 1982:314), Palmyrene (Cantineau 1935:126), Nabataean (Cantineau 1930:95), and Galilaean Aramaic (Dalman 1905:127f.). On the latter, see also Fassberg 1991:130. Hebrew influence is suspected.

e) *Thousands*

"1,000" is אלף, without חד: כנכרן אלף 'thousand talents' A4.8:27. Otherwise אלף is almost always shortened([419]) to לף and preceded by a cipher, even one higher than '1,' e.g. 3 פרזל כרשן לף 'iron, 3 thousand karsh' C3.7Fv3:9. There are several examples for "2,000," which is always written as לף 2, e.g. C3.7Gr2:26. This seems to suggest that in contrast to מאתין '200,' the dual of אלף was apparently not in use in our corpus and that the abbreviation stands for אלף, not אלפין.([420]) Most Aramaic dialects place the plural form of אלף in the second position.([421]) This makes our idiom distinct from all later dialects which, including the numeral "2,000," use the plural אלפין for a multiple of "1,000."([422])

f) *Ordinals*

The ordinals are only meagrely attested in our corpus([423]): תנין שנה 'a second year'(?) B3.1:7.([424]) A substitute for an ordinal is the syntagm זי + a marked cardinal as in תלתא זי 'the third (one)' C1.1:187.([425])

In B1.1 we find a unique dating formula: בשנן 'in years' followed by a cipher, e.g., בשנן 7 למלכא דרוש 'in year 7 of King Darius' B1.1:1.([425a]) Similarly at lines 4 and 5. The standard formula is בשנת, st. cst., followed by a cipher as in בשנת 14 דריוהוש 'in year 14 of Darius' A4.5:2.

---

[419] Segert (1975:218) raises the possibility of not just graphic, but phonetic elision here in the manner of חד for *אחד 'one.'

[420] Cf. Muraoka 1995:20f. Delete the penultimate paragraph of the article: the cited example (A6.2:13) had been misinterpreted (personal communication: B. Porten).

[421] Syriac (Nöldeke 1898:94) attests to both sequences. So apparently CPA, though Müller-Kessler (1991:136) does not cite an example of the preceding pl. of אלף.

[422] JA (Dalman 1905:128), Syriac (Nöldeke 1898:94), Mandaic (Macuch 1965:231), BTA (Epstein 1960:128), SA with a distinct dual for "2,000" (Macuch 1982:315), and CPA (1991:136).

[423] The twice-attested קדמי (A6.10:1,8) means 'former, previous.'

[424] On this strange syntax, see below § 66 *a*: this numeral is close in meaning to אחרן, which is also found in front of the head noun. Because of the broken context, one cannot make much of the only other instance of the numeral at C3.13:49.

[425] See above, fn. 204, and Kottsieper (1990:103-5).

[425a] Koopmans (1962: II, 95) mentions an Akkadian parallel *ana 3 šana:ti* 'in the third year' and Germ. *mit 13 Jahren kam er*.

g) *Fractions*

The only forms occurring in our corpus are: פלג in the cst. form as in פלג ביתא 'half of the house' B2.4:11. The conjunction Waw is optionally prefixed to פלג to express a figure such as 7.5: e.g., without Waw—פלג 7 '7 and half B3.3:7 or with Waw—אמן ופלג 8 '8.5 cubits' B3.10:6. *רבע 'quarter' is often abbreviated as ר: e.g., 1 ר '1 quarter' C3.7Gv2:3, but spelled out in 10 משח ספן רבע 'oil, 10 (and) a quarter jars (?)' C3:7Gr2:9, C3.7Kr3.22; also pl. as in 2 רבען '2 quarters' C3.28:29. Note the lack of the conjunction Waw. On שתות 'a sixth,' see above § 18 r.

h) *Multiplicatives*

The only instance occurring in our corpus is חד אלף 'one thousand times' A4.7:3. Cf. BA Dn 3.19 חַד שִׁבְעָה 'seven times.'([426])

§ 22. Other word-classes

Under this non-descript heading are covered words which are traditionally subsumed under groupings such as adverbs, conjunctions, interjections and the like all of which are indeclinable and unchangeable. Here again their semantic description belongs to a dictionary. Hence we present a mere list of them with necessarily approximative translations. For their morphosyntactics, see below.

a) *Adverbs*

Of time: אדין 'then' A6.10:1+, אדן B3.6:1, B6.1:1†; אחר 'thereupon, thereafter' A4.7:6+; אתמל 'yesterday' D7.20:7+; כען 'now' A3.8:3+; כענת 'now' A4.2:2+; כעת 'now' A3.3:11([427]); מחר 'tomorrow'B2.1:6; קדמ(י)ן 'formerly, previously' A4.7:25+.

Of place: בגו 'herein' B5.5:11; תמה 'there' A4.7:6+; תנה 'here' A4.5:4 (only once with an Alef, at D1.11:1).

Of logical relation: אם 'still; assuredly' B2.7:11+; אף 'moreover' D7.7:5; אפו 'then' C1.1:52,140†; אפם 'still; assuredly' B2.3:22+([428]); לכן 'then' A4.2:8; מנכן 'therefore' A3.5:4+.

Of manner: אפריע 'immediately' A6.12:3†; כדנה 'so' A3.1v:7, B3.6:3; כזנה 'so' A4.2:8; כות 'thus' A6.7:8+; כן 'thus' C1.1:145+; כנם 'thus' A6.11:3([429]); כחדה 'together' B1.1:6, B2.11:3†([430]); לעבק

---

[426] Note the striking position of the numeral חד: see § 67 b.

[427] On the patterns of distribution of these three synonyms within the Achaemenid period, see Folmer 1995:661-71.

[428] See below, § 90 b. Is the final /-m/ some sort of adverbial morpheme as that of כנם 'thus' in כנם אמרן 'we said thus' B8.9:3 and הן כנם הו כמליא אלה 'if it is thus like these words' A6.11:3?

[429] See below § b.

'quickly' A3.8:8; שויו 'equally'(?) B1.1:6 ([431]); חוב 'again' B5.1:7.
Of degree: שגיא 'abundantly' C1.1:51.

b) *Status absolutus of the adjective used adverbially*
Beside a possible adverbial morpheme /-m/ mentioned in n. 428,
it can be observed that the st.abs.sg. of the adjective is sometimes
used adverbially: נטר חסין 'he guarded firmly' A6.10:2; שגיא חדית
'I rejoiced abundantly' A3.5:2, see also A6.3:1; with an adj., שגיא
פחסתו 'very praiseworthy' A6.16:4. Here also belong forms which
look like f.sg., but are in fact archaic f.st.abs.([432]) —גנבית עבדן
(/ganna:ba:yat/ ?) 'act thievishly' A4.2:5; רחמת 'affectionately'
B2.4:7 // ברחמה B3.7:14; אמרן לה מצרית 'they call it in Egyptian
...' B3.7:5; ארמית 'in Aramaic' B2.11:4,6.([433]) Slightly different is
the pl. קדמן 'previously' A4.2:8, C1.1:46; קדמן A4.7:25: see below
§ 75.

c) *Adverbial /-à:/ (i.e. accented on the penultimate syllable)*
Despite a careful study by Fitzmyer (1979:205-17)([434]), we
believe that BA כלא (and its equivalent in our corpus occasionally
spelled כלה[[435]]) is a special adverbial form meaning 'in every
respect, altogether.'([436]) For example, מנדע[ם] אחרן זי לקחת כלא
התב הב למספת 'any other thing that you took, restore, give (it)
entirely to M.' A6.15:6. What Fitzmyer totally left out of account
is the fact([437]) that our corpus uses a number of other words
ending with א, to which the context allows one to assign some

---

[430] As against Porten - Yardeni's translation "as one" and כאחד in their
Modern Hebrew version (cf. Grelot: "ensemble") one ought to note that the
gender of the numeral is feminine. This appears to be a common Aramaic
idiom: compare Is 65.25 "the wolf and the lamb shall feed together (Heb.
כְּאֶחָד) with Trg. /kaḥda:/ and Peshitta /ʾakhda:/.

[431] See above § 18 *w* [2] on reduplication as a device of pluralisation.

[432] See Brockelmann (1908: § 225 A *l*, 251 *b* α) and also Beyer (1984:96,444).

[433] אַרְמִית at Dn 2.4 is Hebrew. ארמית in our text is to be vocalised / ... yaṯ/.

[434] A study the substance of which was first published in 1957 in *Bib*
38:170-84 under the title of "The syntax of *kl, klʾ* in the Aramaic texts from
Egypt and in Biblical Aramaic." Fitzmyer was writing against Montgomery
1923.

[435] On the orthographic alternation here, see Folmer 1995:116-18.

[436] See also Degen (1979:22) and also further below § 69 *d*. Vogt (1971:83),
and Beyer (1984:606) tacitly, seem to have accepted Fitzmyer's view. The
position of Segert (1975:193, 222) is mixed.

[437] Recognised, however, by Segert (1975:193). This point also needs to be
borne in mind in assessing the suggestion made by Driver (1957:84) to
interpret חובא 'again' (mentioned below) as a long imperative.

sort of adverbial function. Thus למנפק ברא 'to go out' B3.7:14; הנפקה ברא 'Let it go out' C1.1:93; קרבתא בזע 'he thereupon tore up' C1.1:41, cf. also ib.56,59. The position that these are all essentially st.det. forms becomes especially difficult to maintain when one notes the same א with similar function attached to what is hardly a noun: אמר לי כותא 'he said to me thus' C1.1:20; למנסק עלא 'to go upwards' B3.7:13; תובא לא ישלח 'he will not send again' A6.15:11, cf. also C1.1:44. The following are mere extensions of this usage: כתיב מן עלא 'written above' B2.1:10; עד עלא 'upwards' B2.1:5,11; ספר כתבת לי עלא 'you wrote for me a document on it' B3.9:3; לעלא מן 'above' C1.1:162.([438])

    d) *Conjunctions*

    Coordinating: או 'or' B2.3:26+; -ו 'and'([439]) passim; להן 'but' B2.4:6+;

    Subordinating: אמת 'when' D7.6:9; אן 'if' A2.1:9†; זי 'that' passim; הלה 'if not' A2.2:10†; הן 'if passim, הין D7.56:7([440]); הנלו 'if A4.2:8; כדי 'when' A2.3:4, 2.4:4; כזי 'when' A4.7:4+; כי 'because' C1.1:79+; לו 'if A4.2:8+; לולא 'if ... not' C1.2:4; למה 'lest' C1.1:126; עד 'until' A4.8:26+

    זי or די often combines with a preposition to form a compound conjunction: בזי 'inasmuch as' B8.10:5+; בר מן זי 'unless' B3.3:14; כזי, see above; לקבל זי 'as much as' A4.3:9+; מן זי 'since' A2.5:3+; עד זי 'until' C1.1:64+; על דבר זי 'on account of the fact that'(?) C1.1:201; על זי 'concerning the fact that' A6.8:6; קבל זי 'because' B3.11:7†.

    e) *Interjections*

    The following, sometimes also called presentatives, are used to give expression to the speaker's inner tension or to draw the listener's or reader's attention to the situation in view: ארה 'behold' A2.3:5,8†; הא 'behold' B2.7:13+; הלו 'behold'A2.3:8+; יה 'O!'

---

[438] JA has preserved a number of adverbs, mostly of place, with the same morpheme, though largely fossilised and combined with another preposition or prepositions as in לעילא 'upwards.' The process of fossilisation had already begun in our idiom as shown by לעלא מן quoted above. For details, see Dalman 1905:55, 188, 217f., who also postulates penultimate stress, though without referring to BA כְּלָא.

[439] The particle has a wide range of nuances. For details, see Hoftijzer - Jongeling 1995:294-96. Thus, in addition to the simple, additive "and," note: "or" as in בר וברה לי 'a son or daughter of mine' B3.9:4; "but" as in "if I chastise you, my son, you will not die, but if (והן) I leave (you) to your own heart ..." C1.1:177; apodotic "then" as in "if you do thus ... then it would be considered a merit for you (וצדקה יהוה לך) ..." A4.7:27.

[440] On the plene spelling, see above § 6 *g*.

C1.1:127,129†.

f) *Miscellaneous*

איח 'there is; (with the prep. ל) 'have' A3.1:4+, את A2.3:9,
יתלי 'I have' B4.1:2,[4] (beg. 5th cent.: ית only in conjunction
with -ל), איתי B2.4:3+([441]), לאית 'there is not' D7.2:3 // לאיתי ib.6,
D7.29:4; אל 'not' C1.1:157+([442]); לה/לא 'not' passim([443]); לם marking
direct speech, A4.7:6+, לאם B6.3:8; מלו 'whatever' A2.3:7†; עוד
'more' A4.4:9†.

---

[441] The shorter synonym אית may be an analogical development similar to
the process whereby the prep. על could have developped from *עלי. In other
words, רגליה 'her legs': איתיה 'she is' = רגל 'leg' : אית '(there) is.' In our corpus
no instance of אית with a conjunctive pronoun is to be found. Cf. also Leander
1928:119 *h* and Folmer 1995:218-20.

[442] Still sporadically turning up in MA, for instance, 1QapGen.

[443] See § 5 *e*. The form לה occurs already in a 7th century Tel Halaf tablet,
1.4 (Lipiński 1975:118).

PART TWO

MORPHOLOGY

SECTION B

THE VERB

The following description of the verb will be made in terms of the traditional categories of tense, binyan or pattern, mood, and conjugation class.

§ 23. The following inflectional morphemes are attested, excluding those of Lamed-Yod verbs, which will be examined below separately.([444])

a) **Perfect**		**Imperfect**	**Jussive**	**Energic**
sg. 3m	-	־יּ	־יּ	־יּ־־־נ־/ן־
f	־ת	ת־	ת־	ת־־־נ־
2m	־ת	ת־	ת־	ת־נ־/ן־
f	־תי	ת־־־(׳)ן	ת־־־יּ	ת־־נ־/ן־(?)
1c	־ת	א־	א־	א־נ־/ן־
pl. 3m	־ו	יּ־־־־־(ו)ן	יּ־־־־	יּ־־־־נ־
f	־ן	?	(?)־־ן	?
2m	־תן/תון־/תם־/תמה־	ת־־(ו)ן	ת־־־־ן	ת־נ־
f	־תן	ת־־־־ן	ת־־־־ן	?
1c	־ן	נ־	?	נ־־נ־

Imperative	**Participle**		**Infinitive**
	Binyan G	non-G	
sg.m.	--	-	מ־	Binyan G למ־/ל־
f.	־י	ת־/ה־	מ־־ה	
pl.m.	־ו	־(׳)ן	מ־־ן	
f	?	־ן	מ־־ן	non-G: למ־־ה/ל־־ה

---

[444] We find it more sensible to look at some aspects of the verb morphology across all conjugation classes. This way one could avoid a misleading use of asterisk with *כְּתַבְתֶּם in the paradigm facing p. 50 of Leander 1928, though the asterisk is correct, as the paradigm is one of the regular strong verb, and the particular form in question is not attested.

§ 24. Examples and discussion

a) Perfect. *3ms* שלח 'he sent' A6.15:8; *3fs G pass.* יהבת '(it =
a letter) was given' A6.15:1; *2ms* שלחת A3.5:5; *2fs* שלחתי A2.3:5;
1s שלחת A2.2:17; *3mp* שלחו A6.2:6; *2mp* נפקתם 'you left' A3.3:3,
יהבתם 'you gave' D7.27:11; *G pass.* and *H* הוטבתם ... שאילתם 'you
were interrogated ... satisfied' B2.9:8; יבלתון ... זבנתון 'you bought
... brought' A3.10:5; רחמתן 'you love' B2.10:9; אתרתן (< √יתר)
'you had in abundance' A2.1:5; *2fp* שלחתן 'you sent' A2.5:8, הושרתן
'you sent,' ib.7; *1p* שלחן 'we sent' A4.7:29.

b) *Spelling of the 1sg. and 2sg. suffixes*

Our corpus attests no plene spelling such as Dn 2.41 חֲזַיְתָה
and 5.27 תְּקִילְתָּה in BA. This does not, however, have to mean
that the morpheme in question in our idiom was /-t/ with the loss
of an original final vowel. The Tiberian tradition of BA has
ample examples of the type Dn 5.22 יְדַעְתָּ alongside תְּקֵפְתָּ
ib.4.19.([445]) On the other hand, there is hardly a reason for
questioning the phonetic reality of the vocalic ending of the 2fs
sufformative ־תִי.([446])

The presence of a vowel in the second person singular suffix
makes sense. In Biblical Aramaic as well as Classical Syriac the
transitive-fientive class of the G perfect of Lamed-Yod verbs
has a diphthong following the second radical: BA חֲזַיְתָה 'you
(m.sg.) saw' (with a penultimate accent) and Syr. /ḥzayt/: see
below, § 37 *b*. Now both dialects tend to retain the diphthong *ay*
when it is in a closed, stressed penultimate syllable. The Syr.
form represents a stage following the apocope of unstressed
ultima vowels.([447]) By contrast, in the period of Aramaic which
is our direct concern here, that is to say, not in the Proto-Aramaic
or Proto-Semitic period in which all agree both first and second
persons singular suffixes ended with a vowel, both of the above-
named dialects show a contracted vowel, *e:*, in the first person

---

[445] For further examples, see Bauer - Leander 1927:173. /-ta:/ forms
outnumber /-t/ forms. *Pace* Qimron (1993:38) it does not necessarily follow
that the BA /-ta:/ is a secondary influence of the Lamed-Yod class. See also
Fassberg (1990:165) and id. (1992:52).

[446] There is no need to find, as Segert does (1975:247), exceptional defective
spellings in אמרת, עבדת at D20.5:2, which can best be read as the 3fs. So
Grelot (1972:342) and Gibson (1975:121). Besides, the neutralisation of the
two genders is intrinsically more likely in the plural/dual rather than in the
singular. See below § *k*.

[447] Why the diphthong has contracted in BA in the plural forms (רְמֵינָא 'we
threw'; חֲזֵיתוֹן 'you [m.pl.] saw') is not immediately clear. Perhaps a chain
analogical development: חֲזֵית 'I saw' > חֲזֵינָא > חֲזֵיתוֹן?

singular, thus BA חֲזֵית 'I saw' and Syr. /ḥze:ṯ/.([448]) One may thus conjecture that, when this contrast in vowel preceding the suffix between the 1sg. and 2msg. emerged, the former ended with a consonant, while the latter ended with a vowel.

The lack of examples in our corpus of the plene spelled 2ms suffix is probably part of a more general pattern of Northwest Semitic orthography. By contrast, the *i* vowel is more often than not spelled plene in the second feminine singular of the perfect and the personal pronoun, both disjunctive and conjunctive([449]), when the *a* vowel is not. The plene spelling apparently started with two high vowels, *i* and *u*, whether in the middle of words or at their end, though their phonetic nature of being high vowels is not the direct reason for this. The reason is rather that the plene spelling of the low *a* vowel started only after certain phonetic and morphological changes had taken place, notably the feminine singular morpheme /-at/ > /a:/ (both in nouns and verbs (pf. 3fs)—the first change applicable to both Hebrew and Aramaic, and the latter to Hebrew only—and the quiescing of the glottal stop as part of the determined state morpheme, applicable to Aramaic only.

c) *Vowelless 1sg suffix*

The suggestion made in the immediately preceding paragraph that in our idiom the pf. 1sg. did not end with a vowel, but the ת was preceded by one is corroborated by observing the following examples([450]): מיתת 'I died' B3.1:14 (also מאתת B3.13:8)([451]); עשתת 'I thought' B3.6:3, B3.10:2.([452]) If the personal suffix was not

---

[448] But note בְּנַיְתַהּ 'I built it' Dn 4.27, a diphthong in a penultimate syllable, albeit presumably unstressed! The Syriac form is that of the Eastern tradition: in the west it has changed to /ḥziṯ/.

[449] In these categories the silent Yod is the rule in Syriac.

[450] See § 3 *b* on זבן = * זבנן 'we sold.'
For OA both Dion (1974:182f.) and Garr (1985:123) assume a vocalic ending, *i* or *u*, whether short or long, which would imply no vowel before the last radical in the case of triradical roots. This archaic situation is still reflected in the opposition in Classical Syriac between /kṯavte:h/ 'I wrote it (m.)' (< katabtV) and /kṯavṯe:h/ 'she wrote it' (< katabat).
The valuable transcriptions *na-ša-a-a-tú* 'I lifted' (= נשאת) (lines 1,27,32) and *ḫa-al-li-tú* 'I entered' (= עלת) (lines 4,29) of the Uruk inscription have been correctly normalised by Gordon (1937-39:116) as *naśait* and *ġallit* respectively. See also Dupont-Sommer 1942-44:38f. One cannot have a vowel both before and after the last radical.

[451] See below § 35 *f*. Note also מתת 'I died' Nerab 2.4.

[452] The second last example is mentioned by Kutscher 1972:79 and Margain

preceded by a vowel, the spelling מיח and עשת might have been
more natural. In the last case, assimilation of the second /n/
would only be possible when no vowel intervened between it
and the following suffix. Also the fact that a pf. with a 3ms
object suffix is never spelled with הי, but ה as in קטלתה 'I killed
him' C1.1:49[453] indicates /-t/ rather than /-tV/. But מיתתי 'you
(fs) died' B3.5:17, for which no vowel is likely at the morpheme
boundary, suggests that the second Taw may be merely a more
'correct' or etymological spelling comparable with Modern
Hebrew נתנו (unvocalised) 'we gave' instead of Ez 27.19 נָתַנּוּ.[454]
By contrast, the abbreviated spelling זבן (= /zabbinna:/ ?) 'we
sold' for *זבנן (see below [*f*]) is phonetic.

The vowel preceding the ת of the 1s was most likely *i* or *e*
as in Biblical Aramaic, later Aramaic dialects and in the Uruk
incantation text, on which latter see n. 7.

Furthermore, the spelling differentiation between יהבתה 'I
gave it (ms.sg.)' B2.7:16 and יהבתהי 'you (ms.sg.) gave it (ms.sg.)'
B5.5:7 shows that, already at the time when vowels of the form
of the verb itself may have undergone some changes as a consequence of the addition of the object suffix, the /-t/ of the 1sg.
did not end with a vowel, while that of the 2m.sg. did. The two
forms cited above may have sounded something like /yhabte:h/
(= /yhabt/ + /-e:h/) and /yhabtá:hi:/ respectively. See § 38 *f*, 1.

d) The *2mp* sufformative comes in three varieties, though
two of them, תון- and תן-, probably sounded the same. That the
historically old תם- is attested in one of the oldest documents
(A3.3)[455] in our corpus is no surprise. The allomorph תון- provides
a valuable clue regarding the type of vowel to be postulated
after /t/, though it is impossible to choose between /u/ and /o/.[456]
The fluctuation between /-m/ and /-n/ seems to have started with
the verb[457]: there is no single instance of 2mp אנתם in our corpus,
whilst the conjunctive pronoun attests to both consonants (§ 12
i), though the distribution of the /-n/ form is rather limited.

1994:234.

[453] More examples in § 38.

[454] All this makes Kottsieper's interpretation (1990:148) of הבת as < *הבתת
most unlikely.

[455] But the same document uses a conjunctive pronoun פרסכן -:כן 'your pay'
ib.4.

[456] BA shows both תון- (e.g. Ezr 4.18 שְׁלַחְתּוּן) and תן- (e.g. Dn 2.8 חֲזֵיתוֹן).

[457] Schaeder (1930:251) is of the opinion that the young /-n/ morpheme of
the conjunctive pronouns is due to Akkadian influence.

A3.10 (end 5th / early 4th c.) mentioned above showing two instances of -תן uses only -כם with the noun: אחוכם(1,9), ידכם(2), מנכם(2), לכם(8). Finally, one wonders whether the plene spelling -תון suggests some difference in vowel quality—length and/or stress—in comparison with the pronominal morpheme, which is never spelled plene. The question must be left open.

e) Though examples of the *2fp* morpheme are by no means numerous, it may be assumed to have been distinct from its masculine counterpart, -תם, by dint of vowel contrast as well.

f) Unlike the corresponding conjunctive and disjunctive pronouns, the *1pl* morpheme is never spelled with a vowel letter ה or א at the end([458]). Furthermore, the simplified spelling זבן 'we sold' B3.4:3, B3.12:3 is valuable in showing that there intervened no vowel between the last root letter and the final morpheme: cf. Syr. /qaṭṭeln/. The Nun was probably followed by a vowel of some kind, possibly a long *a* in the light of the suffixed form זבנהי 'we sold it' B3.4:5.([459]) Otherwise the above-quoted זבן would have sounded identical with זבן 'he sold' B3.4:25.([460])

g) The only instance of the Perfect *3fp* to be found in our corpus indicates its identity with the 3mp: מטו אגרתא 'the letters arrived' A4.2:15. In this respect, then, our idiom agrees with that of the Ktiv tradition of BA: e.g. Dn 5.5 נְפַקָו([461]) הוה A4.7:12, while having an apparently fp subject in מנדעמתא 'the objects,' can hardly be viewed as instancing the distinct morpheme in question, for if one postulates /-ay/ (Syr.) or /-aya:/ (TA) as the 3fp morpheme, the form would have to be spelled *הוי or *הויה

---

[458] See § 11 *d* and 12 *h*. In BA, נָא- is the rule.

Garr's (1985:104) [na:], posited by him for the Elephantine texts, is a ghost form: Schaeder (1930:240f.), which Garr quotes, had correctly recognised such a morpheme as only applicable to the personal pronoun, whether conjunctive or disjunctive, and a correction inserted by Kutscher (1977:412), whose 1970 version Garr quotes, has apparently escaped the latter, for Kutscher, just as Fitzmyer (1967:73), which Garr quotes, had wrongly analysed יהבנה B5.1:5 as 'we gave,' when it actually means 'we gave it.' Fitzmyer's (1995:115) correction cries for another correction: the fluctuation between חוין A4.7:16 and חוינא A4.8:15 concers the object suffix, "us"!

[459] See below, § 38 *f*, 1, and also Folmer 1995:160.

[460] As in the Samaria papyri of the 4th century BCE: זבנא SP 4.9.

[461] Cf. a classic discussion by Ben-Ḥayyim (1951), which, however, does not take QA into account: see, e.g., 1QapGen 20.6 שלמא and חבלא 'destroyed' ib. 13.16, which latter text is to be found in a recent publication of new fragments of the document by Qimron. See also Kutscher (1971:376).

respectively.([462]) It is rather a case of the lack of grammatical concord. On the other hand, Proto- or Early Aramaic most likely did possess such a distinct morpheme, though it has not so far turned up.([463])

h) Imperfect([464]): *3ms* ישלח A6.8:3; *3fs* A תושר 'she will send' A2.2:7; *2ms* D תשלם 'you will pay' A6.15:8; *2fs* תשמעין 'you will hear' D7.9:11; תכל תעבדן 'you will be able to do' A2.3:4; תאמרן 'you will say' D7.16:12; תצבין 'you will desire' B2.7:16([465]); *1s* אשלח A3.5:3; *3mp* ישבקון 'they will leave' A3.1:6, יכהלון([466]) 'they will be able' B3.10:21, ישפטון 'they will judge' C1.1:88, יהנעלן 'they will bring in' A3.8:12; *2mp* D תזבנון 'you will sell' B2.10:11, A תשכחון 'you will find' A4.2:10, tG(?) תתפטרן 'you will be released' A3.3:13; *2fp* תכל תהיתן 'you will be able to bring' A2.5:5([467]); *1p* נכתב 'we shall write' B2.11:14, נדחל 'we shall fear' A4.2:7.

i) The *2mp* and *3mp* forms are almost always spelled plene with a Waw.

j) *2fp*

Our idiom appears to have used a suffix similar to BH and Classical Arabic, /-na/ as against mp /-u:/ or /u:n/.([468]) This differs from what is known from Middle Aramaic, in which the 2fp (and the non-attested 3fp) sufformative of the impf. differed from the corresponding masc. one vocalically, namely m. /-u:n/

---

[462] Thus *pace* Segert (1975:248). Whilst Segert (1975:249) may be right in attributing the BA Ktiv tradition to Hebrew influence, that is hardly an explanation for our idiom. Qimron (1993:38) also refers, without adducing any example, to the existence of this distinct morpheme in IA.

[463] For comparative Semitic aspects, see Brockelmann (1908:574f.).

[464] The jussive and energic will be treated later separately.

[465] But this is of a Lamed-Yod root: see below § 37 d.

[466] Kraeling (1969:243) wants to read H יכהילון, which is of course most unlikely. Porten - Yardeni see here an erasure of a Yod.

[467] The wording of the opening address, אל אחתי תרו ותבי, is somewhat ambiguous, for אחתי can be read as either sg. 'my sister' or pl. 'my sisters.' That Tabi is a woman is in no doubt, for she appears elsewhere (A2.6:1) as 'my sister.' See also A2.2:5,7. It is also clear that no other addressee is involved, unlike in A2.3. Cf. Hoftijzer (1983:117, n. b).

[468] Classical Semitic languages have two modes of distinguishing the 2/3 m. and f. endings of the prefix conjugation: 1) vowel contrast /-u:/ vs. /-a:/ with or without /-na/ or /n/, to which Akkadian, Classical Ethiopic, Middle Aramaic such as Syriac belong, and 2) /-u:/ with or without /-na/ vs. /-na/ or /-na:/, to which Hebrew and Classical Arabic belong.

vs. f. /-a:n/. This view of ours is supported by תהיתן, one of the above-quoted examples, which would have to be spelled *תהיתין if the usual assumption, based on MA forms such as Dn 5.17 לֶהֱוְיָן, applied here also. The actually attested form probably indicates /the:te:na/ < /the:tayna/.([469])

One of Ben-Ḥayyim's main arguments against the distinct f.pl. in Early Aramaic in general, including BA, was that, in the latter, such forms largely depended on the vocalisation and the Qre.([470]) In BA, even the Ktiv, which in the perfect uses the masc. form for both genders (see above [g]), has occasionally preserved a distinct 3fp form in the impf.: Dn 4.18 יִשְׁכְּנָן 'they will dwell' and ib. 5.17 לֶהֱוְיָן 'they will be,' but ib. 4.9 יְדוּרָן. Especially להוין cannot be revocalised as masculine, which is לֶהֱוֹן.([471]) Hence, where the subject is f.pl., a form ending with a plain Nun has the chance of being a form phonetically distinct from its masculine counterpart.

Lindenberger (1983:285) believes that in the pc. the 3mp with ן- or ו- doubled for the 3fp. Of the four examples mentioned by him three are not unequivocal: י[הנשגון כדבחה C1.1:133 where the verb could be impersonal([472]); likewise עינין טבן אל יאכמו ib.157 (see above § 18 b); יהשחתון ידי ib.155. This leaves only ילוטון שפות א[נ]שא ib.151.

The gender distinction in the 2nd and 3rd person plural is a general issue, which gives rise to a number of specific questions. Is it right to assume that both persons behaved analogously? Were the pronominal morphemes any different from the inflectional morphemes of the verb in this respect? The same sort of questions applies to the distinction of other categories of the verb inflection such as tense and mood. As regards the disjunctive personal pronouns, the attestation is incomplete (§ 11). We have noted above (§ 12 j) that the picture is not quite clear-cut. In the perfect tense, the evidence for the existence of a distinct 3fp morpheme is meagre, there being in our corpus only one case where the subject is 3fpl (§ [g] above). The picture regarding the Hermopolis papyri is ambiguous, since the same spelling תן- is used for both genders (§ [d, e] above). In the prefix conjugation,

---

[469] On a related issue in the jussive, see below, § k.

[470] Ben-Ḥayyim (1951:135).

[471] Ben-Ḥayyim (1951:136) has no choice but to invoke scribal error.

[472] So Porten - Yardeni (1993:43) "they [shall] perceive his lies"; Grelot (1972:441) "on découvrira son mensonge"; Kottsieper (1990:15) "[er]kennt man sch[ließlich] seinen Betrug."

there is a fair chance that the 3mp predominated, whilst in the 2pl. a distinction seems to have been maintained, as will become clear in the following subparagraph. Thus the overall picture is somewhat mixed.([473])

k) Jussive. This category is mostly identified on morphological or morphosyntactic grounds, especially the conjunction with the prohibitive אל and the absence of the so-called Nun-energicum.([474]) But, just as in BH, the distinction between it and the imperfect (indicative) is not always visible in the consonantal orthography. It is visible only([475]) in the 2fs([476]) and 2/3mp([477]) where the corresponding impf. ends with Nun, which is apocopated in the jussive.([478]) In fact the jussive column in the table above ([a]) gives, except 2fp, only those cases where the jussive is distinct from the indicative in our unvocalised orthography. Thus whether יתעשת and אהחסן, for instance, which both occur in the close proximity of the clearly marked jussive ינתנו 'Let them give' A6.11:3, were phonetically any different from their respective indicative counterpart cannot be determined.

Examples: *1s* ארחעה 'Let me wash it' D7.8:11([479]); *2ms* אל תקטלני 'Do not ' kill me' C1.1:52; *2fs* אל תצפי 'Do not worry' A2.1:7, D1.1:14, אל תמלי לבת(י) 'Do not be angry (at me)'

---

[473] Cf. a good discussion in Kottsieper (1990:138-40), who, however, confines himself to the 3pl. due to the scope of attestation of his corpus. In the light of our discussion above, his assertion that IA did not allow the dominance of the 3mpl. needs to be somewhat nuanced.

[474] See below § *l* and § 37 *b.c. f* (3) respectively.

[475] One important exception is discussed below, namely יאפן vs. *יאפי. As we shall see later, Lamed-Yod verbs tend to make an orthographic distinction in some other categories as well: § 37 *d*.

[476] Thus it is better to restore an indicative תתמלאין or תתמלין at B4.6:13,17.

[477] Though the jussive 3fp is not attested in our corpus, one may postulate the same ending as that of the 2fp.

[478] On problems unique to the Lamed-Yod class, see below § 37 *d*. See further § 35 *e* on the Ayin-Waw/Yod class.

[479] Parallel with another volitive form, שלח "Send" (impv.), and following an indicative, תרחענה 'you wash it' (line 7), as noted already by Kutscher (1972:30, 83). Likewise ויתנהי 'and let him give it' parallel with דבר 'Go' (impv.) D7.29:9, following an indicative, אנתננה 'I shall give it' (line 5). On the alleged final ("so that ... may") force of the pc. attached to the conjunction Waw in Biblical Hebrew, see Muraoka 1997c. We agree with Kutscher that both verb forms indicate the speaker's wish.

A3.3:10(^{480}), אל תקמי 'Do not stand' A2.2:15; אל תתכלי 'Do not rely' D7.16:4; *3mp* ישאלו 'May they seek!' A3.7:1(^{481}), ישמו 'May they place' A6.6:1, A6.16:5; יאכלו 'May they eat!' D7.17:10; *2mp* אל תצפו 'Do not worry' A2.2:3, A2.4:12, D1.1:8, אל תנתנו 'Do not give!' A6.9:6; *2fp* תדען 'you should know' A2.5:2.

Since the jussive with an open ultima syllable is, except that of Lamed-Yod verbs (e.g. תמלי quoted above), likely to be penultimately stressed as in BA(^{482}), the defective spelling of תקמי and ישמו cited above is remarkable.

The context makes it likely that we have a rare example of the 2fp jussive in תדען 'you should know' A2.5:2. This form with the final Nun retained, which in its masculine counterpart in the jussive disappears, reminds one of לאפן 'May they [= women] bake!' in Fekheriyan (line 22). These two cases plus תהיתן discussed earlier (§ [j]) suggest that the analogy of Classical Arabic, in which in the 2/3fp the indicative and the apocopate (= our jussive) are identical in form, /-na/, applied to our idiom as well.(^{483}) Our jussive תדען may have ended with /-aːn/, should the MA tradition with a long *a* apply to our period.(^{484}) However, the Fekheriyan לאפן presents a difficulty for such an interpretation, for should one start from MA, one would expect לאפין /-yaːn/(^{485}). All this leads to the conclusion that the Fekheriyan form—likewise להינקן 'May they suckle!' (20, 21), אל ימלאנה 'May they not fill it!' (22) also from the same bilingual, and similar forms from Sefire —ended with /-na/ as in Arabic. Another consideration which renders /-aːn/ as a 2/3fp jussive morpheme unlikely is that, while the jussive 2/3mp and 2fs are characterised by the loss of /-n/, which we assume to have followed a long vowel, the 3fp jussive

---

^{480} In the light of variations of the same idiom at A3.5:4, A4.2:11, and Ashur ostracon 19f., the conjunctive pronoun Yod may have been inadvertently left out.

^{481} יתוספו C3.11:10 is hardly jussive; possibly an error for אתוספו 'were added' following the relative pronoun, זי. Or possibly a jussive erroneously used for an indicative?

^{482} On this point, see Muraoka (1972:29).

^{483} On the analysis of the Fekheriyan form, see Huehnergard 1987. The verb was, *pace* Huehnergard (1987:275, n. 31), probably of /radiya/ type in Arabic, which in the jussive/apocopate 3fp gives /yardayna/. Since the contraction of /ay/ is known to Fekheriyan as in בת הדד 'the house of Hadad' (line 17), the original /-payn/ could have been spelled without Yod.

^{484} Cf. a historical reconstruction by Bauer - Leander (1927:96f.), for a trenchant criticism of which see Huehnergard (1987:272, n. 24).

in OA, Fekheriyan, and Samalian consistently retains this /-n/.[486]
If our jussive form contained a long *a*, we would expect an
n-less form. We must then postulate that, as in Classical Arabic,
our idiom and others, which maintained a formal distinction
between the so-called long and short imperfects, made no such
distinction in the 2/3fp.[487]

l) In contrast to the jussive, the **Energic** is characterised by
the increment of a Nun at the end of a verb form.[488] This is
only visible, unlike in the jussive, where the indicative form
ends with a consonant[489], though when the verb itself ends with
Nun as in the 2/3pl, only one Nun is written as in תנתנונה 'you
(mp) may give it" B2.10:9.[490] Whilst the attestation is patchy, it
may be safely assumed that the 3fs and 1pl also had an extra
Nun. If one leaves out energic forms with conjunctive pronouns[491]
such as יהתיבנהי 'he will turn it back' C1.1:126, self-standing
energic forms are few and far between. The following list is
exhaustive: הן יאחדן 'if he should seize' C1.1:107; אל תלקחן 'Do
not take' ib.167; D אשלמן 'I shall pay' B4.6:5; הן אשבקן 'if I should
leave' C1.1:177.[492]

m) *Function of the Energic*
Whereas the /-n-/ morpheme has admittedly lost its energic
force, Leander (1928:41) makes an important observation that
each of the four free-standing energics attested in our corpus

---

[485] As Kaufman (1982:150) rightly points out. Cf. Dn 5.17 לֶהֱוְיָן.

[486] OA—אל יהרגן 'May they not kill! (?)' at Sefire I A.24; Fekheriyan—
mentioned above; Samalian—לתגמזרן 'Let them [= her kinswomen] be assembled' at Hadad 31 and פלכתשנה 'Let them pound her' ib.32. See also Tropper
1993:217.

[487] So Degen (1969:65): "Lang- und Kurzimpf. sind ... in der 3. fem.pl.
morphologisch nicht unterschieden." Whether such a situation is Proto-Aramaic
or not is a separate issue. This means, among other things, that, *pace* Ben-
Ḥayyim (1951:135), at least one dialect of Old Aramaic did have a distinct
third fem. impf. form.

[488] For the energic in the language of Deir Alla, see Hoftijzer 1976:297.
On the function of the energic, see below § 53, and on its morphology with
the conjunctive pronoun, see § 38 *b*.

[489] To be accurate, excluding Lamed-Yod verbs.

[490] In BA it would be vocalised תִנְתְּנֻנַּהּ. In the above energic column, -נ- is
what is found between a conjunctive pronoun and the preceding verb stem.

[491] See below § 38 *b*.

[492] There is no compelling reason to take תנתן 'you (fs) may give' B2.3:10,
B3.10:21 as energic: it can be easily a usual "long" imperfect. The absence of

implies an object pronoun. Thus, at least diachronically, the two morphemes, i.e. the Nun of self-standing energic forms and one that bridges an imperfect and an object pronoun suffix, point to a common origin.([493]) On the other hand, which of the two possible energic forms represented by Arabic, I /yaqtulanna/ and II /yaqtulan/, applies to our idiom is difficult to say. BA, even disregarding the vocalisation, is obviously aligned to I, as shown by a case such as Dn 7.16 יְהוֹדְעַנַּנִי 'he made me known,' which, if it were an II energic, would be spelled with a single Nun. A case such as יְחַוֻּנַּנִי 'they will show me' A4.4:9 indicates that our idiom aligns itself with BA in this respect. Though the two idioms do not entirely agree (see below § 37 *f* [3]), one may assume that a form such as אשבקן ended with /-anna/.

n) Imperative: *ms* עבד 'Do!' A6.2:22; זף 'Borrow!' C1.1:129; *fs* עבדי B2.3:27; *mp* עבדו A6.8:3.([494])

o) Participle. G: *ms* שבק 'leaving' A2.4:4; *pass.* שמיע 'heard' A3.3:13; *mp* שלחן 'sending' A6.1:3; משחין 'anointing' A4.7:20([495]); *mp.cst.* רכבי 'riders of' C2.1:44; *fs* נפקה 'leaving' C1.1:171; שלחת 'sending' A6.1:3([496]); *fp.pass.* כתיבן 'written' B3.5:12.

The non-G participle is characterised by the prefix /m-/, whilst the sufformatives are identical with those of the G participle,

---

an expected object should be no serious hindrance: cf. § 74 *o*: "Object ellipsis."

[493] Against Kottsieper (1990:177), who mentions Degen (1969:80) approvingly, though the latter is not addressing the past origins of the morpheme nor is Moscati (1964:136). Furthermore, the fact that this /n/ was presumably followed by a vowel, most likely /a/, as Kottsieper also admits, and the fact that the corresponding Hebrew morpheme was apparently not followed by a vowel, can be better explained by the widely accepted theory which connects the Aramaic form with Energic I of Arabic and the Hebrew form with Energic II, for otherwise one would need to seek for two separate origins of the apparently related morpheme in the two languages. See also Lindenberger (1983:51f.).

[494] Hug (1993:77) gives /-n/ as the ending of the impv. 2fp., but no example can be found for it among his presumably exhaustive list of attested forms. However, in view of the overall symmetry between the impv. and jussive, /-n/ (see above § [k]) is more likely than /-a:/ (*pace* Segert 1975:254).

Kottsieper (1990:137) speculates, on the basis of his interpretation of data in the papyrus Amherst 63, that the G imperative inserted a helping vowel between the first two root consonants or before the first (the latter in the manner of Classical Arabic). There is no hard evidence for such a hypothesis, and at least for the second supposition our scribes did not find it necessary to give such a helping vowel some graphic representation as in Arabic.

[495] On the spelling fluctuation, plene or defective, see § 18 *b*.

which in turn agree with those of the nominal declension, though no det. form of substantival use is attested: *ms* D מהלך 'walking' B8.3:4; *fs* H מהשכחה 'finding' A4.3:9; *mp* H מהחסנן 'holding in hereditary lease' A6.2:3; *fp* D מסרסרן 'soaring(?)' C1.1:162; מסבלן 'supporting' A2.3:5.

p) Infinitive. The infinitive appears either prefixed with /m-/ or without it, but often with a proclitic ל, but no other proclitic: למשלח 'to send' A1.1:7; למשבק 'to leave' C1.1:92; לאמר 'to say' A2.3:6 // למאמר C1.1:163; without Lamed—ממלא 'filling(?)' C1.1:131([497]), מנשא 'raising' ib.170. As a matter of fact, לאמר, which occurs nearly 50 times in our corpus, is the only G infinitive without the prefix Mem([498]), and it introduces, in the manner of BH לֵאמֹר, a quote, without an object pronoun, and often in juridical style. Thus it is noteworthy that the form with Mem is used where it is not such a fossilised formula as in ישימון טב בחנכה למאמר 'they will put something good to say in his palate' C1.1:163; see also A4.9:2 (לממר), D7.39:10. The standard G infinitive in our corpus is therefore למכתב.([499])

The non-G infinitive, however, always ends with ה-([500]), and

---

[496] On the spelling fluctuation, ת- or ה-, see above § 18 *j*.

[497] For an exegesis of this difficult saying, cf. Lindenberger (1983:124f.). Should it form a nominal clause with the adjacent משלמותה 'its repayment,' most likely a D inf. of fem. gender, the former would not be a ptc.

[498] Lerner (1982) attempts to show the notorious BA Ezr 5.3,13 לְבְנֵא as tG impf. or inf.. The most one can say, however, is that the Massoretic vocalisation may reflect a later idiom such as Babylonian Jewish Aramaic. Note, however, a possible parallel with Sefire II B 6 יד לאשלח לאכהל פלא 'and I shall not be able to stretch out (my) hand' on one hand, and לֵשֶׁב, לִיתֵּן and such like in Mishnaic Hebrew on the other. The Ktiv can be safely taken as a Mem-less inf. The syntactic parallel he quotes from BA is less than complete. He further needs to demonstrate that a verb of commanding also allows parataxis.

Another possible example is to be found in לאגר at ולא לאגר חמר B1.1:14, if it is to be translated: "a he-ass is not to be hired." Hoftijzer - Jongeling (1995:11) suggest a G inf. or a noun. Cf. also Folmer 1995:189f.

[499] Whether a G infinitive can take the feminine ה- ending is a moot point in Aramaic grammar. חזיה Sefire I A 13 mentioned by Ben-Ḥayyim (1971:250) and Segert (1975:260) has been also interpreted as a D inf., and BA Ezr 5.9 מִבְנְיָה 'to build' can be repointed as מִבְנְיֵה 'to build it.' ממתתה 'his death' Nerab 2.10 analysed as G inf. + suf. by Hug (1993:85) is a verbal noun rather than an inf. used in one of the familiar and typical syntagms. All instances in our corpus of למבניה ought to be interpreted as having a suffix for 'it,' *pace* Lerner (1982:62).

[500] The only exception with Alef is להשקיא 'to give to drink' A4.5:7. See

forms without Mem are quite frequent: D לזבנה 'to sell' B2.4:6, D7.1:5; לשלמה 'to repay' B2.7:5; H להיתיה 'to bring' A4.5:14; להעדיה 'to remove' B3.11:13; להשקיא 'to give to drink' A4.5:7; A למחתה 'to bring down' A2.5:6. That this final He was perceived as identical with the f.sg. morpheme is shown by its alternation with Taw typical of the idiom of the Hermopolis papyri: למתיה A2.4:11 // למיתית A2.4:11.([501]) Another possible M-infinitive, D or A, is למחוה 'to show' (error for למחויה?) D7.24:16.([502])

No clear pattern emerges as to the distribution of the two alternative non-G infinitive forms.([503]) Whereas the *m*-less type is spread over a fairly long time-range of our corpus (460 to 402), the *m*-type is also of respectable antiquity, attested in the Hermo-polis papyri and Ahiqar proverbs.([504])([505])

When a conjunctive pronoun is added to a non-G infinitive, the latter naturally takes the cst. form, either -ת- or ות-([506]), where one does not know whether the former is a defective spelling of the latter or represents /-at/, though the former interpretation is more likely.([507]) Examples are: D לחצלתני 'to rescue me' A1.1:7;

---

above § 18 *j* end.

[501] See above § 18 *j*. Greenfield (1990:77) wants to emend the latter to למיתית[הם], but the absence of an object in a context like ours is a commonplace in Semitic languages.

[502] On this difficult form, see Folmer 1995:191, n. 17.

[503] Cf. Folmer 1995:191-98.

[504] Once outside of these documents: למכתבה D 'to mark' D7.9:10. Along with Kottsieper (1990:138) we regard הימנותה 'his trustworthiness' C1.1:132 as an ordinary, abstract noun.

[505] See a diachronic and comparative discussion on the Aramaic infinitive in Muraoka (1983-84:98-101) and Muraoka (1997:207f.). Kottsieper (1990:140f.) seeks to fit this distribution pattern into his view on the Southern Syrian origin of Ahiqar's proverbs.

[506] Kottsieper's statement (1990:138)—"Der Infinitiv ... endet im D-Stamm auf -[u:]" - must be assessed in the light of the fact that such infinitives occur in his corpus only a few times and always with a conjunctive pronoun.

[507] Greenfield (1990:78) uses this distinction for a classification of Aramaic dialects, but the picture is a little more complex than what he wants us to believe. Several instances of this kind occurring in the Sefire inscriptions are regularly spelled without Waw, and it is not imperative to read, as Fitzmyer does (1967:88, 113), /-u:t/. A morpho-syntactic consideration is to be brought into this discussion: see Muraoka (1983-84:100) and Muraoka (1983). All the relevant examples in OA are those of the objective genitive, including Sefire III 11, 15 להמתתי 'to kill me.' Despite the meagreness of examples, BA uses the /-at/ form when the following noun is an object: Dn 5.12 אַחֲוָיַת אֲחִידָן

לזבנותה 'to sell it' D7.56:13; D לתרכתכי 'to expel you' B3.7:16(⁵⁰⁸)
// לתרכותה 'to expel her' B2.6:30, B3.8:30; D without a Lamed—
משלמותה 'repaying it' C1.1:131; A למנחתותה 'to put it down' ib.171;
A מנחתותהם 'to put them down' ib.170(⁵⁰⁹); A למושרתהם 'to send
them' A2.2:13(⁵¹⁰): H [ל]החסנותה 'to bestow it' B7.3:7.(⁵¹¹)

In this regard the G infinitive presents nothing unusual: e.g.
למעבדה 'to make him' B3.9:6,7; למזלכי 'to sell you' B3.6:6.

In our corpus we find no trace of the infinitive absolute.(⁵¹¹ᵃ)

§ 25. Binyanim

Our idiom attests to all the major binyanim or patterns familiar
from the classical Aramaic dialects: G or Peal, D or Pael, A/H
or Afel/Hafel, and their respective corresponding *t*-binyan, namely
tG or Ethpeel, tD or Ethpaal, tA/tH or Ettafal with a prefixed
t.(⁵¹²) However, our determination as to which binyan to assign a

---

התנדבות עמָא 'with the people volunteering' Ezr 7.16 (subjective genitive).
From the fact that the idiom of the Hermopolis papyri knows both למיתיה and
למתיה as the causative infinitive of אתה (as noted above) it does not necessarily
follow that a suffixed infinitive in that idiom necessarily ended with /-at/, and
not /-ut/.

⁵⁰⁸ Let us note that this document is rather poorly copied with four interlinear
additions, a couple of erasures and that a vowel letter was twice dropped
(תחומה 2; יהישמע 9).

⁵⁰⁹ On the use of a conjunctive, not disjunctive, pronoun for 'them,' see
below § 38, (6).

⁵¹⁰ As for the absence of Waw before the Taw, note a number of unusual
defective spellings in this letter: אחכי for אחוכי 'your brother' 1; H ptc.act. מנס
for מניס 3; G pass.ptc. יהב for יהיב 8,9,10,16; שפרת for שפירת 'beautiful' 12; בת
cst. of בית 12, בתה 'his house' 15.

⁵¹¹ מנפקה without the preposition as in כסף מנפקה לימא 'silver for taking out
to the sea' C3.7Ev2:6 and a few more times (mostly restorations) in the same
document can easily be an action noun.

⁵¹¹ᵃ It is attested in OA: see Fitzmyer 1995:144f. See also Hug 1993:119
and Muraoka 1983-84:100f.

⁵¹² The label G derives from the German term, *Grundstam*, basic stem, and
D also from German *doppelt*, doubled, i.e. doubled second radical.

Even with the support of נאנח 'to sigh' Deir Alla II 12*bis* and possibly נצבו
'they gathered' ib. I 8 (see Hoftijzer 1976:192, 236), we hesitate recognising
Nifal in the system of our corpus on the strength of the solitary examples
נשחט B2.6:10 and נעצבן ib.15 whose interpretation is highly uncertain.

Lipiński (1994:125f., 149f., 162) rejects the presence of Nifal in the Deir
Alla texts, though his argument for taking the Nun of נאנח as the precursor of
the morpheme as in eastern MA dialects fails to convince us.

For Garr (1985:121) to be able to speak of the Nifal "dying out" in Aramaic,

particular verb to is to some extent(^{513}) dependent on our knowledge
of later Aramaic dialects, particularly those with reading and/or
vocalisation tradition. Even so, it is not always possible to achieve
absolute certainty in this matter. For instance, is למנחתותה 'to set
it down' C1.1:171 a D or A infinitive?(^{514}) See below § 33 c. Do
we have a tG or tD in [מה י]שתמר איש עם אלהן 'how can a man
guard himself against gods?' C1.1:96? See below § 29. Our
idiom uses יבל 'to transport' in G, whereas BA uses it in H and
Syr. in D and A. Also ambiguous is √ גלי 'to reveal': both JA and
Syr., for instance, use it in both G and D. The precise significance
of the binyan of the verb in הי מלבש אנה 'that I am wearing'
A2.1:6, presumably a D ptc., eludes us.

Even if one could establish the binyan of a given verb with
reasonable certainty, there still remain some problems. Firstly,
the function of some of the binyanim is still disputed. Why is
the verb for "to begin," שרי, for instance, used in D?(^{515}) Secondly,
when two verbs with identical sequence of consonants are assigned
to two different binyanim, it is not always obvious what logical
relationship exists between the meanings of the two verbs: e.g.,
קבל 'to complain' in G and 'to receive, accept' in D.(^{516}) In other
words, are they derived from the same root? The question is not
confined to relationships between verbs.

By universal consensus none of the *t*-binyanim was originally
passive in force, though it gradually assumed that function as
well. Early Aramaic possessed morphologically distinct passive
patterns, a situation which is still apparent in our idiom, in the G
perfect and participle in particular: § 29.

For Garr (1985:121) to be able to speak of the Nifal "dying out" in Aramaic,
he must be able to produce more substantial evidence for its presence in Old
Aramaic in the first place.

[513] To say with Segert (1975:258), however, that the absence in our
consontantal text of a symbol such as dagesh makes it impossible for us to
distinguish between G and D is not quite accurate, for when the context
makes it plain that זבן in certain cases means 'he bought,' in some others,
however, 'he sold,' and the participle of the former זבן contrasts with מזבן of
the latter, one can safely infer that the former had a geminated second radical,
unless one has a reason to assume that gemination as a feature of binyan
opposition was non-existent in the period represented by our idiom.

[514] Cf. Syr. D /naḥḥeṭ/ and JA D עבר 'to bring across; cause to pass'
(Sokoloff 1990:394b).

[515] With a recent study on the gemination in the Akkadian verb (Kouwenberg
1997) the time-honoured notion of "intensive" has been resurrected.

[516] The common denominator is some interaction between two parties. קבל

§ 26. Binyan G

From some Ayin-Waw/Yod verbs and Lamed-Yod verbs one may infer that there existed a further subdivision among G verbs differentiated by the stem vowel. Compare מית 'I died' B3.1:14 with קמת 'I rose' B1.1:10 on the one hand, and תמות 'you will die' C1.1:177 with תשים 'you will put' ib.130 on the other. For more details, see below §§ 34, 36 d. Even if one is allowed to extend this distinction to other conjugation classes, one could never be absolutely certain whether G דחל in our idiom, for instance, was of *qatil* type as in later Aramaic dialects, for there obtains some fluctuation in this regard between various dialects.([517]) Similar uncertainty exists also with regard to the stem vowel of the imperfect.

§ 27. Binyan D([518])

On the basis of our knowledge of BA and later Aramaic dialects we may safely assume that the second root letter is geminated.

The verb D זבן 'to sell' (e.g. זבנו 'they sold' A3.8:5) contrasts with its G form such as יזבן 'he will buy' A2.2:16, involving a change of direction. D קרב is factitive in relation to G: G 'to be near, come near' vs. D 'to bring near'—קרבתך 'I brought you near, presented you' C1.1:50. Some examples are: *pf.3ms.* שדר 'he sent' C1.1:101; *3fs* סבלתני 'she supported me' B3.10:17; *3mp* זבנו 'they sold' A3.8:5; *1p* זבן 'we sold' B3.4:3, שלמן 'we paid' A3.8:2; *impv.ms.* זבן 'Sell!' A3.8:5; *impf. 2ms* תשלם 'you will pay' A6.15:8; *3mp* ישלמון 'they will pay' B3.1:15; *energ. 1s* אשלמן 'I shall pay' B4.6:5; *inf.* לשלמה 'to pay' B2.7:5; משלמותה 'repaying it' C1.1:131; לזבנותה 'to sell it' D7.56:13; *ptc. ms* מהלך 'walking' B8.3:4; משלחה 'its sender' C1.1:82.

We include שזב 'to rescue' and שצי 'to succeed'(?)([519]) in this category, though the vocalization tradition in BA indicates that the vowel following the first radical is not that of typical D verbs, *a*, but *e*.

The verb הימן 'to believe, trust,' as in מהימן A2.1:9 (ptc.) is no doubt Hafel in origin, but the fact that it must have been thought of for quite a while as the odd man out is demonstrated

---

D happens to be unattested in our corpus.

[517] See Aro (1964:139-51).

[518] In the following paragraphs on the non-G binyanim our observations will be made on, and largely illustrated by the 'strong verb' classes. Peculiarities of the 'weak verb' classes will be dealt with thereafter.

[519] On the etymology and meaning of the word appearing at A6.7:7, see

by its very form in Syriac, /haymen/, a language from which Hafel has totally disappeared.

§ 28. Binyan H or A

This is a so-called Hafel or Afel binyan, often causative in force vis-à-vis G, e.g. H הרכב 'to mount' (tr.) C1.1:190 vs. G רכב 'to ride' C1.1:38; H הנפק 'to bring (or: take) out' C1.1:83 vs. G נפק 'to exit' A4.7:5.

The binyan is, formally speaking, chiefly characterised by the prefix Alef or He. It is still a moot question whether one is dealing here with a historical development, namely Hafel > Afel as a result of a phonetic change /h/ > /ʔ/ or the two existed side by side from the beginning.([520]) One obvious difference is that, whereas He appears not only at the beginning of a word-form, but also after some additional prefixal morpheme such as personal prefixes of the prefix conjugation or the Mem of the participle or the infinitive preceded by a proclitic Lamed, Alef as a morpheme of this binyan appears only at the beginning of a word-form.([521]) This may justify us in interpreting a form such as ישכה as an A-binyan form with /ʔ/ syncopated: ישכה < יאשכה rather than < יהשכה. Whilst the syncope of a word-internal Alef is fairly common, not just in this particular morphological context (see above § 3

Driver (1957:54) and above at § 3 *u*.

[520] See, for example, a discussion in Bauer - Leander (1927:62,113). Folmer (1995:123-37) is more concerned with the spelling alternation. She opts for the view that this is a case of /h/ > /ʔ/, without, however, offering any argument (Folmer 1995:123, n. 570).

[521] Forms such as יאחרם 'he delivers (for destruction)' (mentioned in n. 80 below) or יאוסף 'he adds' are not to be found in our corpus: see Beyer 1984:148, where Beyer states that the process of Hafel > Afel is documented already in the 8th c. However, some of the examples cited as Afels are still open to doubt: see Degen 1969:19, n. 79 on Sefire III 3 יסכר and Degen 1969:68, n. 54 on ib. 17 יעברנה. On יסכר, Ben-Ḥayyim (1971:252) makes a case for its interpretation as Pael, but in the same line we find יהסכר and יהסכרן. The second problematic form can also be a Pael: cf. עבר יתהון יוסף ואגלי יתהון 'Joseph removed them and exiled them' Targum Neofyti Gn 47.21. For further examples, see Sokoloff 1990:394b. The restored תש[ל]מן Sefire I B 24, if it should mean "you carry out, accomplish," can be, *pace* Fitzmyer (1995:108), only a Pael (so Degen 1969:70, n. 58): the verb in Afel means "to deliver, hand over" in Aramaic.

Voigt (1991:236f.) wants to evaluate the form יסכר more positively, namely as a harbinger of a later development, and being the sole instance of such and appearing in the same line next to the standard form with <h> it can hardly be more than a harbinger, scarcely an index of a distinct dialect, which Voigt

m, n), the syncope of /h/ in that position is, in the period under discussion here, virtually unheard of.([522]) It does not sound good phonology to lay down a rule applicable only to a narrowly defined morphological feature.([523])

In our corpus we find some 45 Afel's, which are decidedly a minority compared with Hafel's.([524]) It needs to be stressed that a significant majority of them, 23 out of 45, is concentrated in the Hermopolis papyri([525]). Reference has been made above to some examples of the pc. with Alef in the 7th cent., and Samalian shows the causative pc. without He, e.g. יקם 'he will raise.'([526]) Chronologically speaking, the Hermopolis papyri are, apart from a lone instance in אצל 'I shall reclaim' B1.1:14 (515 BCE), presumably the oldest among our corpus to attest to Afel, but it is attested throughout the fifth century (and the fourth century): ca. 475 (מנפקה 'taking out' C3.7Ev1:15), 2nd quarter of the 5th c. (איתית 'I brought' A3.3:10), 446 (ינפק 'he will take out' B2.7:12), late 5th c. (תשכחון 'you will find' A4.2:10), 414 (ינפקון 'they will take out' B3.10:21), last decade of the 5th c. (אתבו 'they returned' A4.4:8), 402 (ינפקון 'they will take out' B3.11:15), mid 4th c.(מיתי 'bringing' A3.11:5).([527])

---

wants to have.

[522] The corresponding Hebrew forms such as יַבְדִּיל, מַבְדִּיל vis-à-vis הִבְדִּיל can only be clarified by postulating a syncopated /h/, for Hebrew knows only Hifil, no Afel, and beyond the causative binyan, but also in Hithpael (as in Aramaic to some extent), and notably with the definite article linked to proclitics (לְהַסֵּפֶר* > לַסֵּפֶר). Samalian seems to share this feature with Hebrew: see Dion 1974:121f., 201f.

[523] Dion (1974:121f.) apparently does not think so. Also Tropper (1993:182f., 212) would interpret a Samalian form like קם as evidencing a syncopation of /h/, but the postulated syncope of an intervocalic /h/ is confined in Samalian to this morphological environment, whereas the same dialect attests to the conditional particle הן.
The striking spelling יאחרם in a 7th cent. inscription from the Assyrian sphere of influence considered by Caquot (1971:15) possibly constitutes evidence of a genuine, alternative causative binyan. But יאקפונ<נ>י 'they will surround me' 11QtgJob 30.16, an extremely rare form beside a host of regular Hafel and Afel forms, is to be viewed differently.

[524] But not "ganz selten" (Baumgartner 1959:93); 'very rare' (נדירה מאוד) (Kutscher 1972:87); "neben seltenem Afᶜel" (Tropper 1993:212).

[525] The only papyrus which does not use Afel is A2.7, which however does not use Hafel, either.

[526] For details, see Dion 1974:121 and Tropper 1993:212.

[527] Two possible examples occur in C1.1 [= Proverbs of Ahiqar: 5th c.?]:

The language of the Hermopolis papyri, however, is by no means uniform, for it makes use of Hafel as well: הושרי *impv. fs* 'Dispatch!' A2.2:13 // למושרתהם 'to dispatch them' ib.; *pf. 2fs* התתי 'you brought' A2.1:6; *juss. 3mp* יהתו 'Let them bring!' A2.5:4 // יתו ib.5. Note also *impf 2fp* תהיתן ib.5; *impv.* הושר A2.4:7, A2.5:4 // *pf. 2fs* אושרתי A2.1:4 // *2fp* הושרתן A2.5:7; *impf. 3fs* תושר.

The fluctuation is not confined to these papyri: יהנפק 'he will produce' B2.7:11 // ינפק ib.12, B3.12:29; ינפקון 'they will produce' B3.10:21, B3.11:15 // יהנפק ib.16.([528])

Other notable examples of Afel include: תשכחון 'you will find' A4.2:10; יחזני 'he will show me' A2.2:2; *pf. 3ms* אפקני 'he brought me out' A2.6:4; *1s* איתית 'I brought' A3.3:10 *3mp* אתבו 'they returned' A4.4:8; *2mp* אתרתן 'you had in abundance' A2.1:5; *ptc. ms* מנס 'making leave' A2.2:3; מיתי 'bringing' A3.11:5.

In synchronic terms, the fact that a given verb is spelled in the same tense and by the same scribe indiscriminately with an Alef or a He (e.g., אושרתי 'you (f.sg.) dispatched' A2.1:4 // הושרתן 'you (f.pl.) dispatched' A2.5:7) can best be interpreted as an indication of an ongoing phonetic change, viz. /h/ > /ʔ/ rather than as evidence of a symbiosis of the two causative binyanim, though Afel may have existed as a distinct causative binyan at

---

מנחתותהם 'to put them down' C1.1:170 and its variant למנחתותה 'to put it down' ib.171. Though למחתה A2.5:6 is clearly an A infinitive, these two infinitives in Ahiqar would constitute the only exceptions in this idiom, which otherwise uses Hafel: e.g. תהשכח 'you will find' C1.1:34, אל תהנשק 'Don't kindle' ib.87, לא יהחה 'he will not tell' ib.188. On the other hand, Syr. uses the verb /nḥt/ in D as well. The use of verbs of physical movement such as קרב, עבר in D as well as in H/A is well documented. Kottsieper (1990:148) is of the same view. Another possible A form, אדני C1.1:107, has been interpreted above (§ 3 *b*) as tG. The notorious יניקנה ib.187 we would parse as G impf. derived from √ניק, a root unattested elsewhere: see Lindenberger (1983:66f.). If we admit the partially restored יחזנהי at אל יחזנהי C1.1:86 'Let him not show it,' it would make a rare Afel, whereas Kottsieper's אליח[רר]הי is more unlikely. There remain two instances in the proverbs of Ahiqar that Kottsieper has not taken into account: אלהיא יסגה C1.1:126, where Lindenberger (1983:118) suggests an emendation יסגן, which he takes as a D form (1983:346). The verb occurs in JA (see Levy 1876-89: III 472f.) and Mandaic (Drower - Macuch 1963:317) in G/A, and in Syr. rarely in H. Dalman (1938:282) lists it only as an Afel verb. The other instance is יפקד לך מראך מין 'if your master entrusts you with water' C1.1:191. Kottsieper (1990:226) takes the verb as a G and meaning "to command," for which the analytic structure with ל is problematic, whereas a H form in the sense of 'to deposit' is probably found in הפקדו B2.9:7.

[528] B3.10, B3.11, and B3.12 were written by the same scribe.

an earlier stage of Aamaic.([529]) Such a phonetically orientated interpretation is corroborated by spelling variations of a personal name אושעיה or אושע for הושעיה or הושע, or the conditional particle אן for הן 'if.'([530])

As intimated above, we would then consider a form such as ינפק as a result of the next stage of this phonetic development: first the initial <h> changing to <ʾ> in the suffix conjugation and the impv. where the morpheme in question comes at the beginning of a word-form, thereafter the syncope of <ʾ> in the prefix conjugation, participle, and infinitive. ([531])

The so-called binyan Shafel is attested by a handful of vocables: שזבותי 'they rescued us' A4.3:5; שצית 'they succeeded' A6.7:7; ישזב 'he will rescue' D2.33:2. It is obvious that the pattern forms no integral, productive part of the binyan system of our idiom. Despite its assumed vowel pattern, it can conveniently be subsumed under D.

§ 29. -t binyan

Like other Aramaic dialects, our idiom knows forms with /t/ positioned immediately before the initial consonant of a verb, subject to the rule of metathesis (§ 3 r) applicable where the initial root consonant is a sibilant.

What has not been sufficiently stressed before, to the best of our knowledge, is that the prefixal /t/ is never preceded by /h/, thus producing ʾit-([532]) binyan, and this applies to the perfect as well. The only exception is הזדהרי 'Take heed!' tG impv. fs. D7.9:9 // אזדהרו A4.1:5. The binyan hit- is attested only once in OA in the notoriously difficult התנאבו Barrakab 1.14.([533]) No

---

[529] "... the prefixes h- and ʾ- are not found simultaneously in the various languages" (Moscati 1964:126) is simply not true.

[530] For details, see above at § 3 k.

[531] Whereas Segert's observation (1975:259) that Afel is largely confined to irregular verbs is synchronically true, it is to be doubted that that had been the case right from the beginning. A glance at the examples given above shows that the picture is far from straightforward even among irregular verbs. The conjugational category seems to be playing a more decisive role than the root type. A similar complementary distribution has been noted with respect to the Aramaic Targum of Job from Qumran Cave XI: Muraoka 1974:433f. See also Schaeder 1930:249 and Beyer 1984:467.

[532] We assume the intervening vowel to have been i.

[533] Cf. Degen 1969:67.

example is to be found in Samalian or in Fekheriyan.([534]) Since, however, such a formation *is* amply attested in BA and QA, alongside ʾit- patterns, in forms such as הִתְגְּזֶרֶת (// אֶתְגְּזֶרֶת) and הִתְקְטָלָה, though only in the pf. and the inf., it must be considered a genuine Aramaic feature.([535]) Its limited distribution, however, cannot be overemphasised. Its rare occurrence in idioms earlier than BA must then be an accident of incomplete attestation.

But how could we account for the total absence of hit- pc.'s in Aramaic, including BA, which attests quite a number of pc.'s in one of the -t binyanim, but without He? Unless one postulates syncopation of /h/, the only plausible explanation is that, whereas originally there did exist both hit- and ʾit- pc., the former gave way to the latter under the influence of the perfect and the imperative, and this as a result of a phonetic process, namely word-initial /h/ > /ʾ/, attested also elsewhere (§ 3 *k*). See also our discussion above on the coexistence of Hafel and Afel.

It may reasonably be supposed that our idiom possessed, as later Aramaic dialects, a -t binyan for each of the three basic binyanim, thus -tG, -tD, and -tH. The only -tH (actually -tʾ) examples found in our corpus are pf. אתוסף 'it was added' C3.11:8 and juss. יתוספו ib.10([536]), and אתעדי 'he was removed' A6.6:3.([537])

The identification of a -t form as either -tG or -tD relies on our knowledge of later dialects, the context, or the opposition to non -t form, where attested. Even then the decision is not always certain.

More or less certain examples of **-tG** are([538]): *pf. 3ms* אשתאר 'remained' B3.12:6([539]), אשתבק 'was abandoned' A6.11:2; *3mp*

---

[534] In Fekheriyan there occurs once a *t*-infixed form: אל יגחזר 'let it not be removed' (line 23).

[535] Beyer (1984:463, 466) must be considered extreme and oversimplifying in attributing all Hit- forms in BA and in later Aramaic idioms to a Hebrew influence. The above-quoted הזדהרי is no Hebraism. See also Bauer - Leander (1927:107f.).

[536] Perhaps to be corrected to pf. אתוספו. For Cowley's אתנפק (71.29), read now יהנפק C1.2:22.

[537] This last verb could be a tG form: Syr. knows both tG and tD of it with the same meaning, but note TO Taj Lv 4.31 אתּעֲדָא, ib. 4.35 מתּעֲדָא. In line with later dialects, we are inclined to analyse אשתכח as tG though its non-t binyan is H/Afel.

[538] For examples of the imperative, see above.

[539] So in TO Gen 7.23 *pace* Jastrow 1903:1509.

אשתכחו 'were found' A4.4:6, אתחדו 'were seized' A4.4:6([540]); *1p*
אשתוין 'we acted as equals' B2.11:2; *pc*. *3ms* יתבנה 'will be built'
A4.10:8, יתיהב 'will be given' A3.3:5, יתנגד 'let it be pulled up'
A6.2:4, יתנטר 'will guard himself' C1.1:96, יתנתן 'will be given'
B3.13:4, יתלקח 'will be taken' A2.3:9, יתעבד 'will be made' A4.5:9,
יתקטל 'let him be killed' C1.1:62, יתשים 'let it be placed' A4.5:21
// יתשם A6.7:8, ישתלח 'let it be sent' A6.2:4; *2mp* תתפטרן 'will be
released' A3.3:13; *impv*. *ms* possibly אדני (< *אתדני*) 'Submit
yourself!' C1.1:107([541]), אזהר 'Take heed!' C2.1:65([542]); *fs* הזדהרי
'Take heed!' D7.9:9; *mp* אשתמעו 'Obey!' A6.8:3; *ptc*. *ms* מתחזה
'becoming visible' C1.1:90, מתעבד 'being made' A4.9:11;*mp* משתמען
'obeying' A6.8:1; מתעשתן 'considering' D23.1 XI:8. A highly
peculiar form, אשתמיע 'it was heard' C1.1:70, is best interpreted
as an unusual mixture of a passive ptc. שמיע and the standard tG
אשתמע.([543])

Of -**tD** one may note: *pf*. *3mp* אשתדרו 'intervened' A4.3:4;
אתבצרו 'were diminished' D1.34:4; *impf*. *3ms* יתאלף 'will be
taught' C1.1:175; יתסר (= יתאסר) 'will be restrained(?)' ib. (or an
error for יתיסר 'will be chastised'); ישתבע 'will be satiated' C1.1:124;
3mp יתכנשון 'will come together' C1.2:25 ([544]), יתכסון 'will be
concealed' A4.3:11, יסתבלון 'will be supported' C1.1:73([545]); *impv*.
ms אתנצח 'Be diligent' A6.16:1; אתעשת 'Take thought!' A4.7:23([546]);
ptc. *mp* מתנצחן 'being diligent' A6.10:4.

As -**tH/-tA** forms we mention *pf*. *3ms* אתעדי 'was removed'
A6.6:3([547]), אתוסף 'was added' C3.11:8.

The following cases are debatable as regards their binyan:
impf. *2ms* תתמלא 'you will be fully (paid)' B3.1:11, B4.4:17;
תשתאל 'you will be interrogated' A6.8:3([548]); *2mp* תשתאלון A6.10:9;

---

[540] On the assimilation of a of the root אחד, see § 3 *e*.

[541] On this last example, see above § 3 *b*.

[542] A G pc or A impv. is unlikely in view of the Akkadian version here:
see Greenfield - Porten 1982:47. On the assimilation of /d/, see § 3 *b*.

[543] So already Leander (1928:55). Another argument in support of this
interpretation is that the standard tG אשתמע in our corpus means "to act
obediently," whereas שמיע has definitely to do with physical aural perception.

[544] D in BA, Syr. etc.

[545] The active counterpart is in D: e.g. ptc. מסבל C1.1:48,72.

[546] Vogt (1971:136) postulates tG, apparently based on BA G Dn 6.4 עֲשִׁית,
but TJ has D אתעשׁתוּן at Is 33.11.

[547] Cf. TO Lv 4.31,35 אתעדּא.

[548] Cf. Syr. tD /ʼeštaʼʼal/, but שאילתם 'you were interrogated' B2.9:8, an

impv. ms אשתמר 'Guard yourself!' C1.1:81,85. On Ayin-Waw/Yod verbs, see below § 35 *p*, and on Lamed-Yod verbs, see below § 37 *j, k*.

§ 30. The passive voice

Our idiom makes use of patterns marked specifically as passive in which the grammatical subject indicates the agent or doer of an action. Apart from instances of some -t binyanim mentioned above, we must single out the G passive, which in the perfect and ptc. is clearly visible in most cases because of the plene spelling with Yod: e.g., pf. קטיל 'he was killed' C1.1:71. It is not certain what vowel, if any, followed the first root consonant. Other examples are: *pf. 3ms* עבד 'he was made' A6.4:3; spelled plene, עביד A4.7:15; *3fs* יהבת 'it was given' A6.15:1; טעינת 'it was imposed' B2.3:24(⁵⁴⁹); שאילת 'she was interrogated' B8.10:6; *1s* שאילת A5.2:3; *2mp* שאילתם B2.9:8; *3mp* קטילו 'they were killed' A4.7:17; *ptc ms* גניב 'stolen' A4.3:4; *mp* עבידין 'made' A4.7:20; כתיבן 'written' B2.10:8.

The passive G may be occasionally identified in the prefix conjugation as well. An obvious and incontrovertible case is יובל [= *yubal* or *yubbal*?] 'Let it be delivered!' A2.7:5.(⁵⁵⁰) This same expression, though spelled defectively, occurs at the end of most of the Hermopolis papyri: A2.2:18, A2.3:14, A2.4:14, A2.5:10, A2.6:11. The only other passive G impf. occurs in כביר זי ימנע מנך 'a great (thing) which might be denied you' C1.1:136.(⁵⁵¹)

Equally rarely does one encounter passive forms of a binyan

---

obviously G passive (see below § 30 with a couple of other G pass. forms of the same verb), perhaps speaks for the interpretation of the forms as -tG.

⁵⁴⁹ The text reads: מומא טעינת לה ומאת לה. Cowley (1923:289), Hoftijzer - Jongeling (1995:428), Bauer - Leander (1927:105), and Leander (1928:54) take the verb טעינת as G pass. 1s. So seemingly Grelot (1972:179) with his translation: "je fus astreint à un serment envers lui." But a document closely related to it, B 2.2 (Cowley 6), has an illuminating expression: טענוך לי מומאה למומא 'they imposed upon you the oath to swear to me' B2.2:6. A comparison makes it clear that טעינת is actually 3fs with מומא as the subject: the noun, despite its misleading ending, is a fs abs. form (see above § 14, n. 71).

⁵⁵⁰ Since יבל 'to transport' is, unlike in BA, used in our idiom in G (e.g. בלני 'Take me!' C1.1:52), this is not likely to be a passive Afel, as Fitzmyer (1979:204, n.56) thinks, though we do seem to have a Hafel היבלו at C3.28:56, where, however, the reading is not certain, and the pl. form with a sg. subject is also odd. See also below § 31 *b* on the infinitive of יבל. Cf. also Folmer 1995: 221.

⁵⁵¹ *Pace* Lindenberger (1983:63), there is no possibility of reading יטעננהי

other than G, but they are mostly confined to the participle.([552])
Thus: D *ms* מפרש 'separated, separately' A6.1:3; מערב 'mixed'
B4.4:5; *fs* מכתבה 'marked' D7.9:7; *mp* ממנין 'appointed' A4.5:9,
A6.7:5([553]). In three documents written by Haggai son of Shemaiah
towards the end of the 5th c. we come across a curious phrase,
מבני בי תחתי B3.10:12, B3.11:2, sim. B3.12:13, translated by
Porten - Yardeni (1989:89, 93, 97) as 'built is (the) lower house.'([554])
מבני is perhaps a D([555]) passive ptc., meaning, however, something
slightly different than G pass. ptc. בנה 'built,' namely 'renovated.'
One must then admit a lack of concord in מבני דרגה ותרבצה 'built
is its stairway and courtyard' B3.11:3 with a multiple subject.
An example other than D is a passive H in הפקדו 'they were put
on deposit' B2.9:7, if it is not an impersonally used active H,
3mp.

Finally, there is one possible case of Afel passive perfect:
לעד אשכח אש 'nobody has been found yet' A2.2:12, though לה
אשכחת אש 'I have found nobody' A2.4:11 (similar context) indicates
a possible scribal error.([556])

§ 31. Pe-Yod verbs

C1.1:186 as passive on account of the object suffix.

[552] Cf. מקמיא B7.2:10 (§ 35 *n*).

[553] The possibility of D active is not to be foreclosed.

[554] The crucial word, מבני, is taken by others, however, as a simple noun:
'bâtiment' (Grelot 1972:244), 'construction' (Hoftijzer - Jongeling 1995:591).
The first editor of the texts, Kraeling (1969:241), gives 'construction,' though
his view is that the form is an infinitive. But a singular noun ending with a
Yod would be most unusual; such a fem. noun is also unknown. See also the
following note.

[555] בנה D is well established: see lexica. Note the Syr. D nomen agentis
/mvanna:ya:ʾ/ 'builder, architect.' Cf. a recent study by K. Hesterman (1992),
who also argues for a D passive ptc. with the meaning "newly built, rebuilt,"a
meaning said to be known to Syr. and CPA. But 'to rebuild' is also expressed
in our idiom in G with reference to a damaged Jewish temple in Elephantine
(e.g. A4.7:23,25). It has rather to do with working on some already existing
edifice or remains of it, for otherwise "to rebuild the ancient ruins" (Is 61:4,
where a CPA version uses the verb in D) makes little sense. Note must also
be taken of a G pass. ptc. in similar context: ... בנה בי תחתי 'a lower house
built, new ..' B3.5:8, sim. B3.7:3.

[556] The passive in binyanim other than G and in forms other than the ptc.
as attested in BA need not to be attributed to Hebrew influence: see Bauer -
Leander 1927:94. Such is attested even in QA: e.g. 4QEn 1 xii 27 אחזיאת 'I
was shown': cf. Beyer 1984:152, 467. For an alternative solution to this form

Verbs which show Yod as the first root letter in their G perfect
and participle share certain inflectional features.([557])

a) In **G *pf*.** and ***ptc*.** these verbs are inflected exactly in the
same way as any other triliteral regular verb: e.g. יבלתך 'I brought
you' C1.1:48. However, in the prefix conjugation, the infinitive,
and the imperative, the initial consonant is absent. Examples:
impf*. *3ms ירתנה 'he will inherit from her' B2.6:21; *3fs* תתב 'she
will sit' B2.6:23, B3.8:26([558]); תלד 'she will bear' B2.6:33; *2ms*
תמא 'you will swear' B7.1:6; תזף 'you shall borrow' (juss.) C1.1:130;
אל תצף 'Do not worry!' A2.4:3; תכל 'you will be able' D7.24:4;
2fs תכלן 'you will be able' A2.3:4([559]); (אל) תצפי 'Do not worry!'
(juss.) A2.1:8, A2.3:4, D1.1:14; *1s* אכל 'I shall be able' B2.6:35,
D7.15:13, D23.1 II:8([560]); *3mp* יכלון 'they will be able' B3.10:15;
***juss*.** יבלו 'Let them bring' D7.39:4; *2mp* (אל) תצפו 'Do not worry!'
A2.2:3, D1.1:8; *2fp* תכלן A2.5:5; *1p* נכל B5.1:4; נבל 'we shall
bring' B4.4:9([561]).

It is difficult to tell whether our idiom knew the secondary
gemination as in some later Aramaic dialects([562]) such as BA Dn
7.26 יִתֵּב (so Syr. /nettev/) Dn 3.29 יִכָּל, but Ezr 7.18 יֵיטַב. The
total absence in our corpus of forms such as BA Dn 4.14 יְנִדְּעוּן
does not have to be an indication that such gemination was
foreign to our idiom. Nor do we know whether such gemination

---

difficult in the context, see Hayes - Hoftijzer 1970:103.

[557] The label "Pe-Yod" is conventional; from a diachronic and/or comparative
standpoint it is, of course, more accurate to speak of "Pe-Yod/Waw verbs."
Furthermore, there could be Pe-Yod/Waw verbs which in historical times
were never used in G.

[558] On the problem of the preposition על, which follows the verb, see
above, § 20 *c*, n. 194.

[559] The context makes it more natural to take this form as 2fs spelled
defectively rather than as 2mp: see § 24 *h*.

[560] Our idiom, like BA, uses a synonymous root כהל as well (e.g. אכהל
B3.7:14,15), though the distribution pattern of the two roots differs between
the two idioms.

[561] There is no compelling reason to regard this and other impf. forms of
יבל as Afels, whereas בלני 'Take me!' C1.1:52 is assuredly a G. Hug (1993:83)
takes אבל in a broken context (.. אבל חי .. "ich werde lebendig gebracht
werden" D1.1:4) as G passive impf.

[562] The question is not addressed by Müller-Kessler (1991:202f.) with
respect to CPA, for which she postulates /yi:tab/ etc. as against Schulthess
(1924:75), who gives /yetteḇ/ etc.

was confined, as in BA (and Syriac[563]), to these three verbs or not.([564])

b) G *inf.*: למובל 'to carry' A3.10:4, B4.4:13, D5.15:1; למומא 'to swear' B2.2:6, B8.9:4; למנק 'to suck' C1.1:168; למותב 'to sit' D23.1 Va:9. The use of Waw in these forms is noteworthy. It is most plausibly taken as indicating *maqtal* as the pattern of the G infinitive in contrast to *miqtal* in later Aramaic dialects([565]), which would have led to *mi:bal < miwbal,* which one expects would be spelled either מיבל or מבל.

The form מונק suggests that for the G infinitive the Pe-Waw type pushed out the Pe-Yod type, for by universal agreement the root concerned is of Pe-Yod type. One may further infer that this applied to the pc. of our idiom, suggesting that no such form as יינק([566]) existed in it

---

[563] For יכל, except in the ptc., Syr. uses Afel /ʾeškaḥ/.

[564] While Leander (1928:59) reconstructs /tizzíf/ for תזף, TO Dt 15.6 has תֵּזִּיף. Similarly Babylonian Talmudic Aramaic נְזִיף (Morag [1988:201], TO Gn 17.19 תֵּלִיד. Though this has not, to our best knowledge, been recognised before, this secondary gemination appears to be confined to verbs whose second radical is one of the six plosives: the so-called Begad-kefath. (This is true of Syriac and JA.) As we cannot identify any phonetic feature of these six sounds which could possibly trigger such gemination, we would tentatively suggest that it is a secondary development arising from the logico-semantic affinity between the prefix conjugation and the imperative, and such a development is likely to have coincided with the onset of spirantisation of the very same six consonants, which would have led to a form such as /yeḏaʕ/ instead of the "desired" /yeḏaʕ/ parallel to /daʕ/. Should this argument be found acceptable, it would provide another indication for the *post quem*, the earliest possible date, of the spirantisation, for a form such as Impf. ידע for ידע could only develop after the hypothesised secondary gemination of the *d*. Further, נבל 'we shall bring' B4.4:9 could, *pace* Beyer's (1984:592) /nabéil/, belong here. In the Aramaic of the Babylonian Talmud in the Yemenite tradition, the verb ידע belongs to both categories: לֵידַע, לֵידְעוּ and נִידַּע (Morag: 1988:201), though the former may be due to an influence of Mishnaic Hebrew. Should our hypothesis prove right, לִינְשְׁבֻן Sefire III 6 should be vocalised as /la:yišibu:n/, not /la:yiššibu:n/ (Fitzmyer 1995: 148). Garr (1985:131) seems simply to project the situation in later Aramaic dialects into the OA period, but without offering any argument for it.

[565] *Pace* Garr 1985:128f.
Segert's (1975:275f.) suggestion that the gemination is due to a desire to keep the sc. יְתֵב from the pc. *יֵתֵב, which would otherwise have resulted as a result of the vowel deletion rule, is unlikely in view of TO forms such as תֵּלִיד, which occur side by side with יְתֵב and יִדַּע.

[566] Comparable to Fekheriyan תישב (line 15), which is, *pace* Muraoka

c) **G** *impv.*: *ms* הב 'Give!' A3.8:5; זף 'Borrow!' C1.1:129; תב 'Dwell!' B2.4:6; *fs* הבי A3.4:4, B2.3:19; *mp* הבו A3.10:3, A4.3:9; בלוה 'Bring it (f.)' D7.9:3. One may assume that, as in BA, the accent fell on the stem as in the jussive, unless a conjunctive pronoun is added as in הבה 'Give it (f.)!' A3.4:3[567] and הבהי B2.7:16, D7.5:7 'Give (fs) it (m.)!' B2.7:16. But in בלני 'Carry me!' C1.1:52 one may postulate a penultimate stress, /bálni/.

d) In the causative binyan **Hafel** or **Afel** we can, as in other Aramaic idioms, recognise two subgroups: the one showing Waw in the slot for the first radical, and the other showing Yod instead.[568]

With **Waw**: *pf.* *2ms* הוטבת 'you satisfied' B2.2:11+[569]; הושרת 'you dispatched' A3.9:4; הוקרת 'you honoured' C1.1:112; *2fs* הושרתי A3.7:3; אושרתי A2.1:4; *2mp* הוטבתם B2.9:8; הושרתם 'you dispatched' D7.47:8; אתרתן (< אותרתן) 'you had in abundance' A2.1:5; *2fp* הושרתן A2.5:7; *1p* הודען 'we made known' A4.7:29; *pc.* *3fs* תושר 'she will send' A2.2:7; *2ms* אל תוכל 'Do not entrust!' D7.6:4; *1s* אושר D7.16:1; *3mp* יהוספון 'they will add' A6.2:18; *2mp* תהוספון A6.10:9; תהושרו (juss.) D7.44:4; *impv.* *ms* הודע 'Make known!' C2:1:66; הושר 'Dispatch!' A2.4:7, A2.5:4; הוקר 'Make heavy!' C1.1:82; *fs* הושרי A2.2:13, D7.2:1; *mp* הושרו A6.12:3, D7.7:1; *inf.* הוספה 'to add' A6.2:17[570]; *ptc.* *mp* מהוס[פן] A6.10:5.

With **Yod**: *pf.* *3ms* הילל 'he lamented' C1.1:41; *3mp* היבלו 'they carried' C3.28:56.[571] An important verb which belongs to this group is אתי 'to come,' which in G is conjugated as Pe-Alef verb (see below § 32): *pf.* *3ms* היתי 'he brought' A6.12:1; *impf.* *3ms* יהיתה A6.2:13; *juss.* *3mp* יתו D1.1:6[572]; *inf.* להיתיה A4.5:14; *ptc.* *ms* מהיתה C3.16:2. See further under Lamed-Yod verbs (§ 37).

e) The binyan Ettafal seems to be attested in pf. 3ms אתוסף 'it was added' C3.11:8.

(1983-84:88), G, not H/A. Cf. למינק 'to suck' in JA: Sokoloff 1990:242b.

[567] Unless the form is a defective spelling for הבהה. It is not to be equated with Heb. הָבָה, an extended imperative.

[568] The question of possible contraction in these positions has been dealt with above (§ 8). See אתרתן A2.1:5 quoted above.

[569] In OA this is a genuine Pe-Yod verb: Barrakab I 12 היטבתה 'I made it better.'

[570] On the syntax of this infinitive, see below § 56 h.

[571] On the problematic nature of this form, note ייבל in Deir Alla I 11, on which see Hoftijzer:1976:205f., 293.

[572] Possibly a G.

f) Apart from the unattested passive H binyan, Pe-Yod verbs can be assumed to be conjugated like the regular verb in all the remaining binyanim. The only attested cases are: **D** *ptc. ms* מיצב 'validated' B3.10:22([573]); **tG** *impf. 3ms* יתיהב 'it will be given' A3.3:5.

g) See also under Pe-Alef verbs (§ 32 *b*).

§ 32. Pe-Alef verbs

Verbs whose initial root consonant is Alef display certain irregularities in the binyanim G, tG, and H/A as a result of the syncope of the glottal stop and the possible consequential gemination of /t/ in the case of tG.([574])

a) In the binyan **G** the said syncope is observable in the following examples of phonetic spelling: *impf. 1s* אמר for אאמר 'I shall say' B2.1:12, B2.3:20, B3.1:11, B3.7:15, B4.1:2; *3ms* יתה for יאתה 'he will come' B3.4:22; *juss. 2mp.* תחדו 'you shall seize' A6.16:3; *inf.* למחד 'to seize' B3.13:10 // למאחד B4.4:17; למר 'to say' A4.9:2† // למאמר C1.1:163, D7.39:10([575]). For a non-standard form lacking the prefix Mem, לאמר C3.13:56+, see above § 23 *p*.

The syncope, however, is exception, not the rule. Thus יאבד 'it will get lost' D7.5:10, D7.16:3; יאמר 'he will say' C1.1:193; למאזל 'to go' D7.1:9; למאכל C3.13:9 and tens of others. In all those cases one may assume historical or etymological spelling.([576])

b) The only Pe-Alef verb in our corpus that appears in the causative binyan is simultaneously a Lamed-Yod verb, namely אתי 'to come,' and it is conjugated like a Pe-Yod verb. See above at § 31 *d* and below at § 37. Since BA, in which the same verb is conjugated in analogous fashion, conjugates other Pe-Alef verbs in the manner of Pe-Yod verbs (e.g. Dn 2.24 תְּהוֹבֵד 'you will destroy'), one may postulate the same for our idiom.

c) The only -**tG** examples found in our corpus are: אתחדו (< אתאחדו) 'they were seized' A4.4:6; *juss. 2ms* אל תתאשד 'Do not

---

[573] Possibly passive: cf. Kutscher (1954:237).

[574] See above § 3 *e, m*.

[575] See above § 23 *p*.

[576] Müller-Kessler (1991:203) is slightly inaccurate and is going a shade too far when she says: "Die Flexion der Verba Iᵖ im Imperfekt Peal ... und Afel ... unterscheidet sich seit dem RA graphisch nicht mehr von der der Verba Iy." The infinitive needs to be mentioned. Spellings such as יאכול 'he can' in CPA do not occur in our idiom.

get upset!' A3.3:7; ***impf.*** *3ms* יתסר (if from √אסר, and not √יסר [577])
'he will be restrained' C1.1:175.

d) No irregularity may be assumed in the remaining
conjugations, which, however, are attested only by -**tD** *impf.*
3ms יתאלף 'he will be taught' C1.1:175.

e) The **G** ***impv.*** shows no sign of the aphaeresis of the
initial Alef as in later Aram. dialects(578): thus *ms* אזל 'Go!' A3.8:8,
C2.1:19; אמר 'Say!' C1.1:58; אתה 'Come!' D7.8:6; *fs* אתי C1.1:166;
אזלי D7.1:5; אמרי D7.18:3; *mp* אזלו C2.1:53; אמרו A5.5:12.

§ 33. Pe-Nun verbs

a) The main thing that calls for our attention in verbs whose
initial radical is Nun is the question of its assimilation in G and
A/H, on the general phonetic aspect of which see above § 3 *a*.
Under this group we subsume also סלק 'to ascend' and לקח 'to
take,' although no instance of analogously assimilated cases of
these verbs is to be found in our corpus, the sole exception being
ויקחונה 'and they will take it' D4.8:1.(579) Since this phonetic
question, which is relevant only to G impf., inf., and H/A as a
whole, but not to Ayin-Waw/Yod roots, has been dealt with
above fairly extensively, we shall content ourselves here with
giving some examples illustrating various inflectional categories.

b) Without Nun written - **G** ***impf.*** *3mp* יחתון 'they will descend'
C1.2:6; יתנן 'they will give' D1.17:8,9; *1p* נתן 'we shall give'
A4.10:13; *2ms* תשא 'you will carry' B1.1:13; - **H/A** *pf.* *3ms* אפק
'he brought out' D7.7:6, אפקני 'he brought me out' A2.5:6; ***impf.***
3ms יהפק 'he will take out' D7.14:3; *1s* אצל 'I shall reclaim'
B1.1:14; *ptc. mp* מפקן A2.5:3; *inf.* למחתה 'to bring down' A2.5:6.

c) With Nun written - **G** ***impf.*** *3ms* ילקח 'he will take'
B6.4:1, D23.1 Va:4; ינסח 'he will tear out' C1.1:156,210(580); אל
ינפי 'Let him not sift!' D7.5:4 (juss.); ינתן 'he will give' A3.8:8,
ינתנהי 'May he give it!' D7.29:9; ינשא 'he will bear' C1.1:185; *3fs*
תנפק 'it will go out' C1.1:172; *2ms* תנפק B3.12:22; תלקחן C1.1:167
(energ.); *2fs* תנתן B3.10:21; *1s* אנתננה 'I will give it' D7.29:5, אנתן
B1.1:10 // אתננהי ib.11; אנתנהם 'I shall give them' D23.1 II:15;

---

577 Cf. above § 3 *e*.

578 Cf. Müller-Kessler 1991:186.

579 The former occurs only three times (למנסק B3.7:10,13; למסלק B3.10:15,
both inf.), but the latter is much more frequent.

580 Our interpretation of the form as G is based on יסחו Nerab 1.9 and BA
Ezr 6.11 יתנסח.

אלקח 'I will take' B1.1:9, D7.16:4; אנשא 'I shall carry' D23.1 Vb:
6; *3mp* ינתנו A6.11:3 (juss.); ינתנון D7.56:12; ילקחו D7.39:6 (juss.);
ינדשו 'Let them demolish!' A4.7:8 (juss.); תנתנון 'you will give'
D2.21:4; תנתנו A6.9:6 (juss.); *inf.* למנסק (< *למסק*) 'to ascend'
B3.7:10,13 // למסלק B3.10:15(see § 2 *b*); למנחת 'to descend'
B3.7:10+; למנטר 'to watch' C1.1:191; למנסך 'to pour libtation'
C3.13:7; למנפק 'to go out' B3.7:14, B3.11:3; (ל)מנשא 'to raise'
B3.8:19+; למנתן. 'to give' A3.10:4+; - **H/A** *pf.* *2ms* הנפקת 'you
brought out' B7.2:5; *3mp* הנפקו A4.7:16; *impf.* *3ms* יהנפק A6.13:3+;
ינפק B2.7:12; יהנצל 'he will reclaim' B3.5:30; *3fs* תהנפק B2.6:28+;
תהנצל B8.4:14+; 1s אהנצל B2.3:18, B3.7:15; אנצל B3.3:13; יהנשג
'he will overtake/perceive' C1.1:199; אל תהנשק 'Do not kindle it'
C1.1:87 (juss.); *3mp* יהנפקון B2.3:15; ינפקון B3.10:21+; *impv. ms*
הנחת 'Bring down!' A3.8:13, D1.13:5; *fs* הנפקי B2.3:27; *inf.* למנחתותה
'to put it down' C1.1:171; מנחתותם 'to put them down' ib.170(581);
ptc. מנפקה C3.7Ev1:15, sim. C3.7Ev2:6.

d) All attested **G** *imperatives* have no initial Nun: *ms* חת
'Descend!' A3.8:8; טר 'Watch!' C1.1:82; שא 'Raise!' C1.1:169;
mp טרו A6.10:6. See also קח 'Take!' D1.14:2; קחי D20.5:3. Though
we do not know for certain whether every Pe-Nun G imperative
suffered aphaeresis or not, the chances are that it did.(582) The
fact that this is so even in the Ahiqar proverbs, the language of
which generally retains the initial Nun, indicates that its aphaeresis
is a time-honoured phenomenon.

§ 34. Lamed-Alef verbs

a) The tendency for verbs whose third radical is Alef to
converge with those whose third radical is Yod is a well-known
general Aramaic phenomenon.(583) This transition was most likely
triggered by the apocope of word-final glottal stop. This feature,
which in later Aram. dialects would effectively lead to the
disappearance of these verbs as a distinct conjugation group, is
clearly visible in our idiom.

b) The following orthographic contrasts demonstrate this
development: **G** *pf.* *3ms* מטא 'arrived' B7.2:7, *3fs* מטה B3.1:6 //
מטאת D7.8:3, and *3mp*(584) מטו A4.2:15; *inf.* [למנ]שא 'upon arrival'
C2.1:41 // לממטה ib.20,25; *impf.* *3fs* תמטא A3.8:7, D23.1 II:7 //

---

581 Both of these can be D infinitives: see above § 25.

582 Some later dialects do retain the initial *n* in some verbs: see, e.g.,
Nöldeke 1898:111, Morag 1988:185f., and Müller-Kessler 1991:197.

583 Cf. Folmer 1995: 222-36.

584 The pl. subject is actually a feminine noun. See above § 23 g.

תמטה A2.6:5. מטה and מטו (and some others to be mentioned shortly) are the most telling examples. The other two pairs, however, could be only orthographic variations.([585])

Furthermore, that the root-final Alef has ceased to exist as consonant even where it did not end a word-form is proven by its graphic absence in the following cases([586]): **G** *pf 3fs* מטתני 'it reached me' A2.1:4; *3mp* כלו 'they detained' A4.2:15; כלוהי 'they detained him' ib.13; *1s* כליתך 'I restrained you' B2.1:7; *ptc. act. mp* כלין 'detaining' A4.2:14([587]); מלין 'are full' ib.11; **G** *pass. pf.* כלי '(was) withheld' A3.3:6.([588])

A complete merger with Lamed-Yod verbs is indicated by מקריא 'the declaration' B7.2:6; **G** *juss. 2ms* תמלי 'You shall be full' A3.3:10([589]); a hybrid spelling in **G** *pf. 2fs* נשאית 'I carried' C1.1:159([590]); a phonetic spelling מלתי 'you were full' A2.3:6; **G** *impf. 3fs* תמטנך 'it will reach you' A3.9:2; *3mp* ירפון 'they will heal' C1.1:154([591]); **G** *pf. 1s* שנית 'I hated' B3.8:21 // שנאת B3.3:7; שניתך 'I hated you' ib.25.

In the light of this marked([592]) drift it is a reasonable assumption that a spelling with Alef in cases as the following was not meant to indicate any phonetic shape which would be different if spelled in conformity with Lamed-Yod verbs: **G** *pc.* אכלא C1.2:18; אכלא 'I shall restrain' B2.1:6 alongside the above-quoted כליתך B2.1:7,13; תמא 'you shall swear' B8.9:3 (simultaneously Pe-Yod and the Waw supralinear); *juss.* יכלאו אל 'let them [not] withhold' D7.10:3; **G** *pf.* מטא B7.2:7 and אקרא ib.7 next to *pf. 1s* קרית 'I declared' ib.10 and מקריא 'the declaration'

---

[585] As rightly pointed out by Folmer (1995:232-35).

[586] Already in Samalian—Hadad 13 קרני 'he used to call me"—as pointed out by Schaeder 1930:233, and see Tropper 1993:75.

[587] Some authorities, e.g. Leander (1928:64) and Segert (1975:295) take the form as pf. 1pl., which is unlikely in view of the following להן: cf. below § 38 *f* (7).

[588] If this were a passive ptc., one would expect *כלה: see § 37 *f*.

[589] On the spelling with a Yod, see below § 37 *d*.

[590] On this conflated form, see an illuminating explanation by Schaeder 1930:234.

[591] An alternative interpretation would derive the form from a Lamed-Yod verb רפה 'to be loose': see Lindenberger (1983:154).

[592] Baumgartner's (1959:101) "zum Teil" is definitely an understatement, which appears to be largely based on the numerical preponderance of cases with an etymological Alef, but not on any analysis of how the forms in question are spelled, whether with or without Alef.

ib.6; תשנא 'she will hate' B3.8:24 // the above quoted שׂנית 'I hated'
ib.21 and שׂניתך 'I hated you' ib.25.

We are inclined to see a mere historical or etymological
spelling in cases like שׂנאת 'I hated' B2.6:23,27 in view of שׂנית
with the same meaning at B3.8:21; *pf. 3fs* מטאת 'it arrived' A3.5:2,
D7.8:3([593]) in view of מטת with the same meaning at B3.1:6 (cf.
also מטתני 'it reached me' A2.1:4); יכלאנך 'he will restrain you'
B2.1:6 and אמחאנך 'will hit you' C1.1:177 in view of תמטנך 'it (f.)
will reach you' A3.9:2 and יْ[מ]חנך B1.1:9 'he will harm you'; **G**
inf. למומא 'to swear' B2.2:6, B8.9:4. See also יקראון 'they will
call' C1.1:165; ימא 'he swore' B7.3:2; ימאת 'I swore' B2.3:24;
same spelling, but *2ms* B2.2:4; *2fs* ימאתי B2.8:5. We should
interpret מ[ט]אוני 'they reached me' D7.54:6 in the light of כלוהי
'they detained him' A4.2:13, namely, the Alef as an etymological,
silent letter. See also מטאני 'he reached me' B2.11:5 and מטאך 'he
reached you' ib.3.

c) The absence of Alef of Lamed-Alef verbs even at the
graphic level and the merger of this conjugation class with Lamed-
Yod verbs is attested over the entire time-span represented by
our corpus.

d) The only instance of which one knows for certain that
the third radical Alef remains consonantal is **G** *ptc fs* מטאה A2.4:4,
B2.8:5, which is hardly /maːtaː/, but rather /maːt(i)ʾaː/.([594]) In
any case, it had not become מטיה. Another instance of a lingering
Lamed-Alef verb is the impv. שא 'Carry!' C1.1:169, not *שי as a
standard Lamed-Yod verb: cf. BA Ezr 5.15 שֵׂא.([595]) ימטאן 'they
will arrive' D23.1 XII:4 is another possible archaic form, though
it could be a historical spelling with /aw/ contracted to /oː/.

The data presented above, then, seem to point to a virtually
systematic convergence of the Lamed-Alef class with the Lamed-
Yod class, and it is hence reasonable to conclude that ימלא, for
instance, was pronounced *yimle* rather than **yimla*([596]), and a

---

[593] This is the correct reading at D7.8:3, not מטיה (Baumgartner 1959:102),
which found its way into the critical apparatus of his BHS edition of the book
of Daniel at Dn 4.21.

[594] The second example, which is parallel with ימאתי, a pf., may be an error
for מטאת, unless a historic present (§ 65 d).

[595] For other attestations of this verb, see under Pe-Nun verbs (§ 33). From
the attested forms it cannot be determined whether its imperfect (ינשא, ישׂא,
תנשא) and infinitive (מנשא) also conformed to the Lamed-Yod pattern or not.
Note for BA a Lamed-Alef form in Ezr 4.19 מִתְנַשְּׂאָה.

[596] So in BA, e.g. Dn 5.17 אֶקְרָא 'I shall read.'

spelling such as תממה is a truer reflection of the contemporary phonetic reality rather than תמטא, which ought to be regarded as a historical or etymological spelling.([597])

§ 35. Ayin-Waw/Yod verbs

a) As is common in Semitic linguistics, we are concerned with verb roots with Waw or Yod as their middle consonant([598]), which in the G functions in fact as a vowel, except in the participle. One can distinguish three subgroups each with its characteristic vowel which is best seen in the prefix conjugation.

b) G *impf*: *u*-type—*3ms* יקום 'he will rise' A3.8:6; ימות 'he will die' B2.6:17; *3fs* תמות B3.7:18; תקם B3.3:9; *2ms* תקום A3.8:7,13, C1.1:85; תמות C1.1:177; *2fs juss.* אל תקמי A2.2:15; *1s* אקם B1.1:10; אמות B3.5:18; אחוב 'I shall be obliged' B3.5:14+; אתוב 'I shall return' B7.1:5; *3mp* ימותון C1.1:110; ילוטון 'they will curse' ib.151; *juss.* יקמו 'let them stand' D1.34:5; *1p* נקום B3.4:20; נחוב B3.6:14.

c) *i*-type: *3ms* ישימנך 'he will put you' A4.7:2; *2ms* אל תשים 'Do not put' C1.1:130; *1s* אשים; *3mp* ישימון C1.1:163; *juss.* ישמו A6.6:1, A6.16:5.([599])

d) *a*-type: *3ms* יהך 'he will go' B3.11:15([600]); *3fs* תהך B2.6:25+; *2ms* תהך C1.1:86+; *1s* אהך B2.3:22; *3mp* יהכון 'they will go' B3.1:19, D8.1:1 // יהכן B3.4:23.

e) Two *jussives* mentioned above, תקמי and ישמו, are spelled with no mater lectionis in the middle. These are to be contrasted with two others which are spelled plene, though the context leads one to expect the jussive: אל תקום C1.1:85+ and אל תשים ib.130. In addition, there is one unusual defective spelling in אקם, though the context is mildly volitive. Leaving the last-mentioned case aside, both of the two sets of forms are surprising: the middle vowel of the first two is in an open *and* presumably stressed syllable, which makes one expect the use of a mater lectionis, whereas in the last two a mater lectionis appears in a syllable which is closed and presumably unstressed. If we are to hazard an explanation, despite the limited amount of evidence, the surprising plene spelling may have to do with the occasional

---

[597] See also Schaeder 1930:233-35.

[598] The roots √חיי and √הוי, however, are dealt as Lamed-Yod verbs, since their middle consonant is consonantal throughout their conjugation.

[599] Here belongs also ניקנה C1.1:187, if correctly interpreted: see above n. 527.

[600] Cf. BA Ezr 7.13 יְהָךְ.

failure of the author (or redactor) of the Proverbs of Ahiqar to keep the indicative and jussive apart([601]), whereas the defective spelling may indicate either a short *u* or a vowel other than *u*, say, a variety of *o* as in BH תָּקָם, in other words, the nature of the vowel in question may not have been determined by the factors mentioned above leading one to expect a long *u*, but rather analogically determined by the jussive form without a vocalic ending such as 2ms whose second vowel was presumably unstressed and short, and even coloured towards *o*.([602]) See also below (§ *g*) on the imperative.

f) The **G** *perfect* comes in two varieties characterised by *a* (?) and *i* as their respective stem vowel.

a-type: *3ms* קם 'he rose' D23.1 V:8; *1s* קמת 'I arose' B1.1:10; שמת 'I put' C2.1:49; *3p* שמו C3.8IIIB:30([603]); *1p* קמן B3.6:13.

i-type: *3ms* טיב 'was good' A3.3:2, B2.6:15, B2.8:5+([604]); מית 'he died' B2.1:8([605]); *3fs*(?) טיבת C1.1:67; *2fs* מיתתי B3.5:17; *1s*

---

[601] Both examples are from the proverbs.

[602] Note an orthographic opposition in Fekheriyan: לשם 'Let him place!' (line 11) vs. ישים 'he will place' (line 12).

Cf. /ye:qom/ reconstructed by Müller-Kessler (1991:215) for CPA with the predominantly penultimate accent, partly on the basis of SA /ye:qom/, also with penultimate accent. Judging from "Formenbelege" provided by Müller-Kessler (1991:215f.) the use of the diacritical point with the letter Waw is not unequivocal.

[603] Possibly an imperative.

[604] In some cases the context does not make it clear whether one is dealing with a pf. or a ptc. This is true, for instance, at A3.3:2 "From the day that you went (אזלת) on the way, my heart has not been satisfied (לבבי לא טיב)." But in other cases the form occurs in conjunction with another pf., which makes its interpretation as pf. somewhat secure as at B2.6:15 "it came (על) into me and my heart was satisfied therein" (טיב לבבי בגו). Likewise B2.8:5, B2.9:9 (note הוטבתם, ib.8), B3.4:6, B3.8:5, B3.12:6,14,26, B5.5:7, although in all these cases the translation with the present tense is satisfactory. However, as far as the form is concerned, טיבה at C1.1:67 "it [= his advice?] was found acceptable to his colleagues" clinches the matter, though it does not occur with לבב as the subject as in all the cases of טיב. As regards the translation value, the pf. of our verb can clearly be translated as a past tense. Whether the form טיב is a pf. or ptc. seems to be a separate issue. The whole question must have to do with a peculiarity of stative verbs; note the remarkable variation at B2.6:5 טב לבבך בגו, where one is likely dealing with a variant pf. defectively spelled for טיב.

[605] The parallel כליתך 'I restrained you' makes it unlikely that מית here is a participle or an adjective.

מיתת B3.1:14, D1.12:6; מאתת (!) B3.13:8.

g) G impv.: *ms* קום 'Arise' D7.24:5; שם 'Put!' A6.3:7, A6.5:3([606]); *fs* קומי D7.1:5; *mp* קמו A4.3:6; זולו 'Sell!' A4.3:8; לשו 'Knead!' D7.6.7.† The defective spelling of שם, לשו, and קמו is striking. In the light of our discussion above (§ *e*), the middle Waw of קום, קומי, and זולו might be an unusual plene spelling for a short *u* or *o*.

h) G ptc.: *act. ms* מית 'dying' A2.5:8([607]); *fs* חיבה 'obligated' B6.4:8([608]); *mp* קימן 'standing' B3.4:4, צימן 'fasting' A4.7:15 // צימין ib.20; *pass. ms* שים 'put' A4.3:10; *fs* שימה C1.1:79; *fp* שימן B8.5:2. The act. ms form such as *שים is graphically indistinguishable from its pass. counterpart, but most likely was phonetically distinct: act. /śa:yim/ vs. pass. /śi:m/ or such like.

i) G inf.: למשם 'to put' D7.2:7; למהך 'to go' A3.1:5; למזלכי 'to sell you' B3.6:6.

j) G pass. pf.: *3ms* שים 'was put' A6.2:22,23,25+; *1s* שימת D7.10:2.

k) H/A pf.: *3ms* התיב 'he returned' B2.9:7; הקים 'he established' C1.1:12; הקם D23.1 Va:8; הקימני 'he established me' C1.1:109; *2ms* הקימת ib.44; *1s* הקימת ib.23, C2.1III:1; *3p* אתבו A4.4:8.

l) H/A impf.: *3ms* יהתיבנהי 'he will return it' C1.1:126; *2ms* +*3ms* לאתהיתבנה (for לאתהתיבנה) 'you shall not bring him back' D23.1 II:15; *1s* אקמנך 'I will have you stand' D7.24:6.

m) H impv.: *ms* התב 'Return!' A6.15:7,10; הקימני 'Establish me!' C1.1:109. Let us note the defective spelling of the impv. התב as against the plene התיב pf. (see above, [*k*]) and our discussion above, *e*).

n) H ptc.: מהתיב 'return' D2.29:2; possibly a substantivised H ptc. in מקמיא אלה 'these supporters' (act.) or 'officials' (pass.)(?) B7.2:10.([609])

---

[606] Unlikely a ptc.

[607] In הות מית 'I was on the point of death.' The form is more likely a ptc. than an adj. 'dead,' for which מת is used in contrast to חי 'alive' ib.9. The word-order also agrees with that of the periphrastic construction הוה + ptc. so typical of the idiom of the Hermopolis papyri: see below § 55 *g*.

The scarcity of documentation prevents us from determining whether an alternative form with a medial Alef as in BA קאם; was possible in our idiom. See Bauer - Leander 1927:145, Morag 1988:215f., Fassberg 1990:185, and Müller-Kessler 1991:213.

[608] Or a verbal adjective, חַיָּבָה.

[609] Cf. a discussion of this difficult word in Porten 1987:90.

o) **D** *pf*.: *3pm* חיבותי 'they obligated me' B8.6:10. By the analogy of later dialects one may assume that the binyan D transforms this class of verbs into a regular triconsonantal class by using Yod as the middle root consonant.

p) For **tG** we have only two examples: *impf*. *3ms* יתשׂים A4.5:21, C1.1:175; יתשׂם A6.7:8.([610]) Here we face then a situation somewhat analogous to that in BA with יִתְּזִין 'it will feed itself' Dn 4.9 on the one hand and יִתְּשָׂם 'it will be put' Ezr 4.21 on the other.([611]) However, the second vowel of יתשׂם could be other than *a*. If our יתשׂם is not a defective spelling for יתשׂים([612]), one would have to consider it as a good parallel to BA יִתְּשָׂם, which Bauer-Leander (1927:146) explain as an analogical development from the pf. G שָׂם, tG *הִתְּשָׂם.([613])

Kottsieper (1990:152-55) devotes an extensive discussion to a most difficult form יתרום occurring at C1.1:138. The general sense of the verb is indicated by the context as something like "he exalts himself." The difficulty is the Waw, for which a Yod is expected.([614]) Here a different kind of analogy may be at work: יִתְּרֹם < ירום([615]). Then יתשׂים might be susceptible to a similar explanation: namely, < שׂים. It is indeed more attractive to construct a comprehensive theory to account for all three varieties of the

---

[610] For אתשׂם ..., read now שׂרתית (PN) D9.15:3.

[611] Among various Aramaic dialects, YBA (Morag 1988:219) and GA (Dalman 1905:317; Fassberg 1990:185f.) share this isogloss with BA, whereas Syr. (Nöldeke 1898:120-22) and CPA (Müller-Kessler 1991:217) are consistent with the *i* pattern. Cf. also Deir Alla II 9 ליתעץ 'he will not consult,' on which see a discussion by Hoftijzer 1976:228.

Segert's alternative explanation of the doubling of ת as a device to ensure its correct pronunciation in direct contact with the following sibilant (1975:289) is rendered somewhat unlikely in view of the fact that in a language like Syriac and BTA, which has far more examples than BA, the doubling is not conditioned by the nature of the following consonant.

[612] אתהמו 'they got confused' Nerab 2.6 is equally ambiguous in view of a defective spelling such as לתהנג for *לתהניס 'you will not remove' ib.8. Hug (1993:85) analyses אתהמו as 'Ithpaᶜel'(sic!), for which one naturally expects אתהממו.

[613] For a rather different and somewhat complicated theory on the development of these forms, see Beyer (1984:488).

[614] An alternative approach is, as in Leander (1928:61), to postulate /yitrawwam/, which is, however, unparalleled elsewhere in Aramaic.

[615] In view of BA Dn 5.20 רֻם we may have here a pattern similar to מִית / ימות. Beyer (1984:695) emends the form to יתרוממ on the ground that no D or tD can be formed from רים, but really?

pc.: יִתְּשָׂם as analogy of the יְהָךְ type pc., if not = יתשׂים. The traditional gemination of the Taw can, with Brockelmann (1908:616), be explained as a tendency to bring biradicals into conformity with the dominant triradical type rather than as a substitution of Ettafal for Ethpeel([616]), for which there is no real rationale. The prevalence of Ettfîl pattern as in Syriac could be due to the fact that the verb שׂם is the most commonly used one in a -**t** binyan, as is the case in our own limited corpus as well.

q) One example of **tD** may be identified in יתקים 'it will be confirmed' D1.17:6.

§ 36. Ayin-Ayin verbs

Verbs whose second and third radical are identical are very meagrely attested in our corpus.([617])

a) In the binyan **G** the identical radical appears graphically only once, though it may be assumed that, as in later Aramaic, it was geminated except when it ended a word-form as in, e.g the pf. 3ms, impf. 3s. Where an inflectional prefix followed by a vowel, thus in G and H, is added as in the impf. and inf., an extra /n/ sometimes intervenes between the prefix and the first radical, suggesting that, again as in later Aramaic, in those inflectional categories the initial radical was geminated or subsequently degeminated.([618]) Examples are: **pf**. *3ms* על 'he entered' B2.6:5+; *1s* עלת B7.2:8; *3mp* עלו A4.4:8+; **impf**. *3ms* ינעל Let it enter' C1.1:205 (juss.)([619]); אל יקל 'Let it not be light!' C1.1:141 (juss.); *2ms* תנעל B3.12:22; אל תמר 'Do not be bitter!' C1.1:148; + *suf* תגזנה 'you shall shear it' D7.8:8; *1s* אעל D7.15:13, D7.24:2. ירוק C1.1:133 is possibly an error for ירקון 'they will spit'; **imp**. *ms* על 'Enter!' D7.20:2, +*suf*. *3fs* גזה 'Shear it!' D7.8:6; **inf**. למנעל 'to enter' A6.7:7; למגז 'to shear' D7.8:3; **ptc**. possibly חמם 'feverish' D7.17:4, if not an adjective spelled defectively for חמים /ḥammi:m/.

If restored correctly, [ת]חיי 'Live' C1.1:55, which the context indicates as juss. 2ms, appears to have been regarded as a Lamed-Yod verb: see below § 37 *e*. Likewise יחיה 'he will live' B4.1:3.([620])

---

[616] So Nöldeke 1898:120.

[617] The only exception is √עלל, which occurs quite frequently.

[618] On the degeminating nasal, see above § 3 *c*.

[619] Possibly < √נעל, according to Lindenberger (1983:205) and Kottsieper (1990:51). See above, § 33 *c*.

[620] With which cp. Syr. /neḥḥe:ʾ/.

b) What we have said above on the degeminating nasal applies to the binyan **H/A** as well: *pf*. *3ms* הנעל 'he brought in' D23.1 Vb:9; *3fs* הנעלת B2.6:6+; *1s+suf.* החיתך 'I let you live' C1.1:51, where the root חיי is treated as an Ayin-Ayin root[621], so *impf*. *3ms+suf.* יהחיני 'May he allow me to live!' C1.1:54 (juss.); *3mp* יהנעלן 'they will introduce' A3.8:12; *impv*. *mp* הנעלו A4.1:8 (partly restored), A6.10:7[622]. Most unusual is הגשש 'he spied out' C1.1:139 for the expected הגש.[623] Likewise הילל 'he mourned' C1.1:41 for הֵיֵל (§ 31 *d*).

c) The conjugation in the binyanim **D** and **-tD** is that of the regular triconsonantal root: **D** *pf*. *3ms* מלל 'he spoke' B8.8:4; + *3m* or *3f. suf.* כללה 'he completed it' D23.1 XIII:2; *2m/1s* צררת 'tied' D7.27:4; *impf*. *3ms* ימלל B8.8:9; *2ms juss.* אל תרגג 'Do not covet!' C1.1:136; **-tD** *impf*. *3fs* תתחלל 'will split' C1.1:104.[624]

§ 37. Lamed-Yod verbs

This is a group which comprises a substantial number of verbs. The main problem arises in relation to the third radical. The table below gives the inflectional morphemes of this class of verbs.[625]

In view of the near-total convergence of the original Lamed-Alef class with the Lamed-Yod class (§ 32), in our general structural analysis we shall treat the two classes as one, though for a systematic listing of the attested Lamed-Alef verb forms the reader is referred to § 32.

---

[621] Cf. Dalman 1905:353.

[622] It stands to reason that in forms with a secondary degeminating Nun the last radical should not be doubled, so that one is struck by a form such as BA Dn 5.15 הֻעַלּוּ 'they were brought in.'

[623] For this abnormal retention of the third radical not followed by a vowel, cf. BA תַּמְלֵל Dn 4.9, and a noun in our idiom from the same root, מטלל 'roof' A4.7:11, A4.8:10, though we do not know how it was vocalised. See also Morag (1988:233ff.) for examples in YBA of the retention of the third radical.

[624] Lindenberger (1983:171) mentions the possibility of Itpa:lal of √ חול.

[625] The so-called stative G pf. appears to be inflected like non-G verbs, on which, see below at § *b*.

Perfect G   non-G Imperfect Jussive Energic(626)

	Perfect G	non-G	Imperfect	Jussive	Energic(626)
sg 3m	-ה/-א	-י	י---ה	י ---י	י---נ-
f	-ת	-ית	ת---ה	ת ---י	ת---נ-
2m	-ת	-ית	ת---ה	ת ---י	ת---נ-
f	-תי(627)	תי(628)	ת---ין	ת ---י	ת---נ-
1	-ת-/-ית	-ת-/-ית-	א---ה	?	א---נ-
pl 3m	-ו	-יו	י---ון	י ---ו	י---נו
f	?	?	?	?	?
2m			ת---ון	ת ---ו	ת---נ-ת
f			ת---ן	?	?
1	-ני	-ני	?	?	נ---נ-

Imperative Participle act. pass. G non-G pass. Infinitive

	Imperative	Participle act.	pass. G	non-G pass.	Infinitive
sm	-ה/-י	-ה/-י	-ה ...(מ)	-י	**G:** למ---ה
f	-י	-ית(629)	-יה	?	**non-G:**
pm	-ו	-ין/-י	-י	?	לה/מ---יה/א
f	?	?	?	?	or: לה/מ---ית

a) Examples: **G** *pf*: *3ms* הוה 'there was' A6.11:4+; רבא 'he has grown up' C1.1:18; בדא 'he fabricated (false stories)(?)' ib.30; צבי 'desired/desires' A3.10:3; *3fs* הות 'she was' B2.2:7+; צבית 'she desired/desires' B2.6:25,29, B3.7:15(630); *2ms* בנית 'you built' B2.4:12; צבית 'you desire(d)' B2.11:7+; *2fs* מלתי 'you were full' A2.3:6; צבתי 'you desire(d)' D7.17:8; *1s* חזית 'I saw' A2.1:5; הות 'I was' A2.5:8 // הוית A6.3:2+; חדית 'I rejoiced' A3.5:2; צבית 'I desire(d)' B6.4:7; אתית 'I came' B3.8:3; *3mp* בנו 'they built' B3.11:4(631); ענו 'they answered' C1.1:169; הוו 'they were' A4.7:10+; אבו 'they desired' D7.56:5; *1p* הוין 'we were' A4.7:15+; חזין 'we saw' ib.17.

b) צבי 'he desires' and צבית 'she desires' as against הוה 'there was' and הות 'she was' among the forms listed above and those

---

626 Attested only attached to conjunctive pronouns.

627 A larger corpus would no doubt have produced יתי-.

628 A larger corpus would no doubt have produced יתי-.

629 A larger corpus would no doubt have produced יה-.

630 Rather than 1sg. (Fitzmyer 1956:83); Hebrew examples mentioned by Fitzmyer as parallels to the alleged נפש intensifying the subject of a finite verb are different in nature.

631 בנהו 'they built' B3.10:9 must have resulted by taking בנה as the basic form and adding a Waw as the grapheme for the 3mpl morpheme, if it be not a mere scribal error for בנוה.

listed under Lamed-Alef verbs (§ 32) clearly establish that our idiom, like later Aramaic dialects, distinguished two G patterns in the pf.:

Syr. /ḥdi/ 'he rejoiced' vs. /bna:/ 'he built' (BA בְּעָא 'he sought'), Syr. /ḥedyaṯ/ 'she rejoiced' vs. /bna:ṯ/ 'she built' (BA מְחָת 'she hit'). Thus we would read הוה /hwa:/ 'he was'; צבי /ṣbi:/ 'he desires'; הות /hwa:t/ 'she was'; צבית /ṣibyaṯ/ 'she desires.'

One may safely assume that the same bipartite system prevailed also in the rest of the G pf. conjugation.([632]) Thus 2ms בנית 'you built' and צבית likely differed in the vowel between the second radical and the suffix, /ay/ and /i:/ respectively as in Syr. /bnayt/ vs. /ḥdit/; 1s /e:/ and /i:/ respectively as in Syr. /bne:ṯ/ vs. /ḥdiṯ/; 3mp /aw/ or /o:/ and /i:w/ as in Syr. /bnaw/ vs. /ḥdiw/. Therefore we would read the above-mentioned forms in question as: 2ms בנית /bnayt(a)/ vs. צבית /ṣbi:t(a)/; 1s חזית /ḥze:t/ 'I saw,' הות /hwe:t/ 'I was' vs. חדית /ḥdi:t/, צבית /ṣbi:t/([633]); 3mp בנו /bnaw/ 'they built,' ענו /ʿnaw/ 'they answered'; 1p חזין /ḥzayn(a:)/.

For the second person the non-contracted /-ay-/ in the case of the transitive or fientive verb is more likely, as it has been preserved in BA in the Tiberian tradition and Syriac, though TA attests to contraction (Dalman 1905:338).

We cannot tell whether our idiom made some distinction, as Syriac does, between the 2ms and 1s. Perhaps the /t/ was followed by a vowel as is mostly the case in BA, though there is no graphic trace of it: Dn 2.43 חֲזַיְתָ 'you saw,' ib. 41 חֲזַיְתָה.([634])

Since we see no reason why the vowel following the second radical should differ between the 2fs and 1s, we take צבתי 'you (f.) desired' D7.17:8 as a defective spelling for צביתי /ṣbi:ti:/: note שגא for the standard שגיא in the same document (line 4) and perhaps also חמם for חמים /ḥammi:m/ (line 4). מלתי 'you (fs.) were full' A2.3:6 is also probably a defective spelling for מליתי ([635])

---

[632] See also Folmer 1995:177-80. Note the contrast in the Uruk incantation text between na-šá-a-a-tu (= /našayt(u)/ 'I took' line 1 and za-ki-it (= /zaki:t/) 'I was triumphant' line 10.

[633] So BA Dn 7.19 צבית.

[634] For more examples, see Bauer - Leander 1927:161.

[635] So Beyer (1984:623): /malí:ti:/. Though Brockelmann (1928:388a) gives both /mla:/ and /mli/ for the intransitive, stative, none of the references mentioned by him seems unambiguously to attest to the latter. JA does not seem to attest to the latter: see, e.g., Sokoloff (1990:309b), though all the examples cited are transitive in meaning. The form ma-li-e, which Folmer (1995:225, n. 226) cites from the Uruk incantation text as supporting her interpretation of our verb as stative, is a participle or a verbal adjective,

rather than a contraction of /ay/, though the contraction of the diphthong in question is a feature highly typical of the language of the Hermopolis papyri (§ 8 *a*).

c) It is impossible to say how the 3mpl ending of the transitive-fientive type sounded: *u, aw* or *o*.[636]

Though no example of the stative type is attested[637], we may assume that, as in later Aramaic dialects, the conjugation of the G stative pattern ran parallel with that of the derived binyanim. One could then postulate צביו /ṣbi:w/ on the analogy of actually attested forms such as D שנציו 'they succeeded' and H היתיו 'they brought': see below § *h, i*.

d) In the *pc.* of all binyanim, as in OA[638], the jussive of this group of verbs shows a graphically, and perhaps phonetically, distinct form not only in the 2fs and 2/3mp, but also in the 3m/fs and 2ms, whereby the jussive ends with Yod, and the indicative with He.[639]

Examples: *3ms* יהוה 'he will be' A3.6:3+ // *juss.* יהוי 'he may be' A2.2:14+; אל ינפי 'Let him not sift' D7.5:4; *3fs* תהוה B4.2:3 // *juss.* תהוי C1.1:84; תאתה 'she will come' D7.6:3; *2ms* תהוה C2.1:64 / *juss.* אל תחלי 'Do not be sweet' C1.1:148; *2fs* תצבין 'you will desire' B2.7:16; תחזין 'you will see' D7.16:12; *1s* אהוה B3.8:25[640];

/maːli/ or /mali/.

[636] *Pace* Bauer - Leander (1927:126) it is by no means certain that the verb גר- in גרכי B2.8:9 is mp, evidencing /-oː/ < /-aw/; it depends on our syntactic consideration of the sentence ... גרכי בר לי ובראׁ לי. See below on the agreement: § 76 *cg*. Note further ḫa-za-ú-ni-ʾ 'they saw me' in the cuneiform Uruk text (line 7) with the diphthong intact. On *u* as a 3mp suffix, see Morag 1988:253f., Müller-Kessler 1991:237, and Macuch 1965:334.

[637] צבו A4.3:6 is, *pace* Leander (1928:64), a noun meaning 'matter, thing.'

[638] See Degen (1969:76). See also Wilson 1912:285f.

[639] Whether a similar distinction was maintained in the 1st person, both numbers, or not is not known. Nor do we know what the corresponding jussive form was in the 2/3fp.

Occasional failure to observe this distinction in IA has long been known: e.g. Lindenberger (1983:282). Kottsieper (1990:158-63) claims that the idiom of the Ahiqar proverbs is perfectly consistent, which fails to convince us. See Muraoka 1995:332f. and also a critique by Folmer (1995:505).

[640] אחזא listed by Segert (1975:299) as occurring at C1.1:204 as a rare case of Alef instead of He as the final mater lectionis of sufformative forms of the impf. of Lamed-Yod verbs is now read אחזה. At A6.16:2 we should perhaps restore תחדֿ[ה] instead of תחד[י] D 'you gladden, please.' However, we do find אל ישׂגא 'let him not proceed' D7.4:2 // יסגה C1.1:126, if these be forms of the same verb and it be not an originally Lamed-Alef verb.

3mp יהוון A4.5:7+ // *juss.* יאתו 'May they come!' A6.5:3; dit. יתו
A2.1:7 ליאתו 'they should not come' D23.1 Va:10; *2mp* תאתון
A3.3:5 // *juss.* אל תשתו 'Do not drink!' A4.1:6; *2fp* תהיתן 'you shall
bring' A2.5:5.

It may be assumed that the jussive ending with Yod, except
that of the 2fs, sounded *i*([641]), whether long or short, whereas the
ending spelled with He sounded *e* of one kind or another.([642]) In
any case, the Yod cannot represent a diphthong, as is clear from
spellings such as אל יחזנהי 'Do not show it!' C1.1:86 and יחזיני 'he
will let me live' ib.54; יחוני 'May he show me!' A2.1:2.([643]) Though
the monophthongisation is confined to suffixed verb forms, its
phonetic conditioning is not apparent: the presumed position of
stress, for instance, varies.

Examples of forms with final ה instead of the expected י for
the jussive are: לבבך אל יחדה 'Let not your heart rejoice!' C1.1:90;
אל יהוה 'Let it not be ..' ib.81; אנל [תאתה 'Do not let it come!'
ib.81.

e) G *impv*: *ms* בני 'Build!' B2.4:5([644]); הוי 'Be!' A3.3:7; חזי
'See!'; אתה 'Come!' D7.8:6, D7.20:2,9,([645]); *fs* הוי A2.2:14; בני
'Build!' B2.3:19; בעי 'Seek!' D7.5:8; אתי 'Come!' C1.1:166([646]);
mp הוו A4.3:2; בעו 'Seek!' A6.10:7.([647])

The question as to a possible phonetic opposition between
ms הוי and *fs* הוי is a difficult one. In JA (Dalman 1905:339) the
opposition is expressed as /e:/ or /i:/ vs. /a/ (< /ay/), whereas

---

[641] In JA the pc. 2fs ends in /-an/ (< /-ayn/), and Galilean Aramaic spells
the ending as יין (Dalman 1905:339). Similarly Syriac shows /-e:n/ (also <
/-ayn/). For the complexity of comparing the inflection of this class of verbs
in Aramaic with that in Arabic, see Bauer - Leander 1927:151f.

[642] On the interpretation of this graphic distinction and the question of
vowel length, see Aristar 1987.

[643] Thus it is not quite right to speak, as Lindenberger (1983:297) does, of
"the consistent spelling of the jussive with -y," even in OA (see Degen
1969:39, 79).

[644] This cannot be D (Pael) in view of a G inf. למבנה ib.14.

[645] This is the only G verb spelled with a final He, an indication that the
ending probably sounded differently from that of forms spelled with a Yod.
Cf. the impv. ms. of this verb ending /-a:/ in Syr., TBA, Mand., and JA. This
is a Lamed-Waw verb in Ugr. and Eth. See also Beyer 1994:299.

[646] Note fs אתיי at GA Gn 30.2 (Klein 1986: I 45) and Mand. (Macuch
1965:336).

[647] שתיו 'Drink!' (impv. m.pl.) at Deir Alla I 12, which is hardly a Hebrew
form, is a valuable example of an old Aramaic form of this stative type verb.

Syr. contrasts m. /i:/ with f. /a:y/.([648])

f) G *ptc*.: *act. ms* אתה 'coming' A2.5:6([649]); *fs* מטאה 'reaching' B2.8:5([649a]); חזית 'looking' A2.3:11, A2.7:3; *mp* אתין A4.3:5; כלין 'detaining' A4.2:14; מלין 'are full' ib.11; שתין 'drinking' A4.7:21; בען 'seeking' A2.6:9; צבין 'desiring' D7.56:7; *pass. ms* בנה 'built' A4.5:6+([649b]); *fs* בניה 'built' A4.5:6+([650]); *mp* בנין A4.7:10. One of the above-quoted forms, בען, if genuine, is interesting in indicating a possible contraction of the generally hypothesised /-ay-/.([651]) Note, however, that it is found in a Hermopolis papyrus: see above § 8 *a*.

חזית is in line with one of the prominent characteristics of the Hermopolis papyri in which the archaic f.sg.abs. ending <t> is mostly used instead of <h>: see above, § 18 *j*.

g) G *inf*.: למבנה 'to build' A4.7:23; למרשה 'to bring suit' B2.11:8; למחזה 'to see' C1.1:63,92; למאתה 'to come' D7.20:4, D7.56:6,8; +*suf.* למבניה 'to build it' A4.7:23.

h) D *pf*.: *3ms* מני 'he appointed' C1.1:37; +*suf.* חוינא 'he let us gloat' A4.8:15; *1s* רבית 'I raised, brought up' C1.1:25; נקת 'I cleansed' B1.1:11; *3mp* שנציו 'they succeeded' A6.7:7; *1p* שרין 'we began' D7.9:11.

As in BA and later Aram. dialects, one may assume /-i/ as the ending of the pf. 3ms, and /-iw/ as that of the 3mp.([652]) See שנציו, מני quoted above and החוין, H pf. 1pl mentioned below under § *i*.

---

[648] Similarly GA: see Dalman 1905:339 and Fasssberg 1990:189-91. See also YBA שְׁדִאי 'Throw!' alongside בְּעִי 'Seek!' (Morag 1988:257). The verb אתה is slightly irregular with the impv. ms. ending /-a:/ in Syr. and JA, but note fs אתָיִי (see above, n. 646).

[649] צבי 'desirous' A3.10:3 may be a variant spelling of צבה: see מיתי 'bringing' A3.11:5. See Degen 1972b:16.

[649a] See above at § 34 *d*.

[649b] *Pace TAD* B בנה at ספר אגרא זי בנה is not a passive participle, but rather a pf., for אגר is a feminine noun (§ 18 *v*, 4) and 'built' would have to be בניה. Translate: 'document of the wall which he built.'

[650] Hug (1993:86) parses רעיה A2.2:16 as pass.ptc.ms.det. "der Begehrte." His translation of the entire document (1993:37) has "das Gewünschte an Wolle" for עמר רעיה, which is syntactically impossible.

[651] On this question, see Morag (1964:128f.), Morag (1988:259), and Folmer 1995: 180f.

[652] This allows us to interpret נרה 'to institute (suit),' despite JPA and Syr., both of which know the verb as D, as G in the light of נרו 'they instituted (suit)' B3.4:18; cf. also נרוך (not נריוך) ib. and נרכי (not נריכי) B2.8:9.

נקת is probably a defective spelling for the standard נקית /naqqi:t/, if not a scribal error, but note העדת alongside העדית, and התתי (see below at § [*i*]).

D *pc.*: *2ms* תכסה 'you will cover' C1.1:84,87; *juss.* אל תגלי 'Do not reveal' ib.141; *1s* אקשה 'I shall dispute' C1.1:140([653]); *energ.* *1s+suf* אכסכי 'I shall cover you' ib.166; *2mp* תחדון 'you will gladden me' A6.14:4; *3mp* ילחון 'they will make bad' C1.1:172([654]); possibly *impv. ms+suf.* חוני 'Show me!' D7.14:8 (for the expected חוני, or pl. חוני); *inf.* למחוה (= לממחויה?) 'to show, tell' D7.24:16.([655])

On a possible D pass. ptc., מבני B3.10:12+, see above § 29.

i) H or **A** *pf.*: *3ms* היתי 'he brought' A6.12:1, החוה 'he showed' B8.3:5([656]); החוין 'he made us see' A4.7:16, A6.2:7; *2fs* התתי 'you brought' A2.1:6; *1s* איתית 'I brought' A3.3:10 // היתת D7.9:13; העדית 'I removed' C1.1:50 // העדת B2.6:35; החיתך 'I allowed you to live' C1.1:51([657]); *3mp* היתיו 'they brought' A6.15:4; העדיו 'they removed' C3.8IIIA:3; *1p* החוין 'we showed' B8.12:5.([658])

The fluctuation between 1s העדית and העדת on the one hand and between איתית and היתת on the other may be interpreted in the same fashion as we did above with respect to G *2ms* צבית /ṣbi:t/ as against 2fs צבתי /ṣbi:ti:/ and מלחי /mli:ti:/, namely defective spelling for the standard תי-. An /-e:t/ is rather unlikely.([659]) The same applies to 2fs התתי for היתיתי /he:ti:ti:/ 'you brought.' החיתך 'I allowed you to live,' being of a geminate root at the same time,

---

[653] D rather than A: cf. Dalman (1938:393) and Sokoloff (1990:508).

[654] Factitive, and unlikely Afel: see above § 27.

[655] Possibly an Afel.

[656] A striking form for the expected החוי, though the reading of the final He is not absolutely certain; it may be Yod.

[657] The verb is simultaneously an Ayin-Ayin verb.

[658] JA distinguishes between אחזינא 'he showed us' and אחזינא 'we showed' (Dalman 1905:406f., 410f.). Likewise Syr. /galyan/ vs. /gallin/ (Nöldeke 1898:119,139). Leander (1928:66) presents a completely reverse picture.

[659] The only Aramaic dialect known to me that consistently shows *e* in this position is YBA (in 2ms and 1p): see Morag 1988:263, 267, 272f., 279, 282. Degen (1979:38), noting that the scribe of B2.6 wavers between a defective and a plene spelling, would plead for /-i:t/ as in, Syr., for instance. However, the second example, היתת, was not known to Degen: the scribe of this document (D7.9) dated to the first quarter of the 5th cent. BCE has the only example in our corpus of an impf. 2fs spelled plene, תשמעין (line 11). His fluctuation between קפירא and קפרא must be left out of consideration so long as we are not sure of its form, namely whether it is /-pi:-/ or /-pay-/.

may be analysed as /haḥḥi:ta:k/.([660])

Though no example of the 3fs occurs in the corpus, the analogy of later dialects suggests that it ended with /yat/.([661])

For the pf. of the non-G binyanim, then, we tentatively suggest the following reconstruction:

	Sg	Pl
3m	-i:	-i:w([662])
f	-yat	?
2m	-i:t(a:?)	?
f	-i:ti:	?
1c	-i:t	-i:n(a:?)

Pc.: *3ms* יהחוה 'he will tell' C1.1:188; יהיתה 'he will bring' D3.31:1; +*suf* יחזני 'he shall show me' A2.3:2; *2ms* יהחלה 'he will make sweet' C1.1:123; *juss.* *2ms* אל תהעדי 'Do not remove' C1.1:146; אל תהשגא 'Do not mislead!' C1.1:137; *1s* אתה (< *אאתה) 'I shall bring' A2.1:10; *3mp* יהיתון['] 'they will bring' A3.9:3; *juss.* *3mp* יתו 'Let them bring!' A2.4:12, D1.1:6(?)([663]); dit. יתו A2.5:4, יהיתו A6.12:3; יתונה 'they will bring him' A2.6:10; יהעדו 'Let them remove!' A4.7:6; *2fp* תהיתן 'you will bring' A2.5:5.([664])

As in all Aramaic dialects, the 2/3mp form in a non-G binyan lacks <y> in the pc. in contrast to the sc. This applies to the impv.: see below.

We note that the language of the Hermopolis papyri is characterised by an almost general contraction of the initial diphthong of the causative אתי: see § 8 *a*.

Impv.: *fs*+*suf* אתיה 'Bring him!' A2.3:10; *mp*+*suf* החווהי 'Tell him!' A6.11:5; היתיו 'Bring!' (or: 'they brought') D7.48:4.([665])

---

[660] Beyer analyses the form as /ʾahyi:táka:/, but cf. Peshitta Gn 47.25 /ʾaḥḥita:n/.

[661] Cf. Folmer 1995: 179f.

[662] As applied to tD and tH, this sufformative is probably on the analogy of the corresponding form of D and H.

[663] It appears that there has developed an orthographic opposition whereby the G pc. of אתה is spelled with the radical Alef, whether etymological or not, while the H/A pc. of the same verb is spelled without such. In the light of this we should probably parse יתו as an Afel form in a broken context at D1.1:6.

[664] On the interpretation of this striking form, see above, § 23 *j*.

[665] The final vowel of the verb itself varies from dialect to dialect: /-aw/, e.g. in Syr., but /-u/ in Mand., TBA, and Sam.

Inf.: למתיה 'to bring' A2.4:11 // למיתיה ib.([666]); להיתיה A4.5:14; להעדיה 'to remove' B3.11:13; להשקיא 'to give drink' A4.5:7.

Ptc.: *act. ms* מיתי 'bringing' A3.11:5. Cf. our remark on צבי at § *g* above.

j) **tG**: *pf. 1p* אשתוין 'we have agreed to act as equals' B2.11:2([667]); *impf. 3ms* יתבנה 'it will be built' A4.7:27; *3fs*(?) תתרוה 'it will be sated' C1.1:124; *impv. ms* אדני 'Turn yourself!' C1.1:107([668]); *ptc. ms* מתחזה 'being seen' C1.1:90.

k) **tD**: *pc. 2ms* תשתנה 'you will change' C1.1:200; *3mp* יתכסון 'they will be hidden' A4.3:11.

l) For the sake of convenience we present here a paradigm of the attested forms of a highly irregular and frequent verb אתה: G 'to come,' H/A 'to bring':

	Pf.		**Impf.**		**Juss.**	
	G	**H/A**	**G**	**H/A**	**G**	**H/A**
3ms	אתה	היתי	יתה, יאתה	יהיתה		
f			תאתה			
2ms	אתית		תאתה			
f		התתי				
1s	אתית, איתית	היתת	אתה			
3mp	אתו	היתיו	‎(+suf):יאתו, יתו, יהתו, יתונה, יהיתון, יאתון	יהתו, יתו, יהיתו		
f						
2mp			תאתון			
f			תהיתן			
1p						

	Impv.		**Ptc.**		**Inf.**	
	G	**H/A**	**G**	**H/A**	**G**	**H/A**
ms	אתה	אתה	מהיתה	מיתי, מהיתה, למאתה	למיתית, למתיה, להיתיה	
f	אתי	‎אתיה(+suf)				
mp	אתיו	היתיו	אתין	מהיתין		
f						

§ 38. The verb with suffixal object pronouns

A pronominal complement of a verb other than a participle is

---

[666] On this fluctuation, see above § 23 *p*.

[667] Cf. Hoftijzer - Jongeling 1995: 1117. On a slightly different interpretation of the verb, see Szubin - Porten 1992:76f.

[668] Unlikely Afel: see above § 3 *b*.

normally added synthetically to the end of the verb. The shape of such a conjunctive pronoun is largely identical with that also synthetically attached to a noun or a preposition except in the first person singular for which a verb requires ‑נִי as against ‑י with a noun and a preposition.([669]) Furthermore, the third person plural pronoun takes a disjunctive form in keeping with other Aramaic dialects.([670]) We shall first give examples, followed by

---

[669] A distinction mentioned by Bauer - Leander (1927:122), ‑נָא with verbs vs. ‑(י)נָא; with nouns/prepositions, is highly artificial and most unlikely. There is no trace of the latter in the Codex Leningradensis, though Rosenthal (1961:26) still mentions Dn 3.17 אֱלָהַנָא (not so in Codex L.).

Contra Kraeling (1969:219), who discusses שנאהי B3.8:37 (his reading for the correct שנאה), הי as a suf. for 3fs. with a pf. is unheard of.

[670] The conjunctive shape as in some JA dialects and Samaritan Aramaic is best regarded as a secondary, analogical development. On this matter, see a brief observation by Kutscher (1968:412). The antiquity of this peculiar morphosyntactic feature is in no doubt, though still in the 8th cent. BCE we find the morpheme conjunctively attached as in Sefire III 2 תהסכרהם 'you shall surrender them,' ib. 6 'you shall talk them into submission and send them back.' While in the first and last one may see הם as a disjunctive form, that is impossible with the second (so also Gibson 1975:52), which ought to be divided as תרקה הם. Likewise in the Ashur letter (mid 7th cent. BCE): שאלהמן 'ask them' line 12 and <אכלתהמ>כה 'it consumed them' line 17, though the scribe is far from being consistent in the matter of word-spacing as evidenced by, for instance, קרא המו 'invite them' immediately before the first example. Since there is no conceivable reason for "them" to be treated differently from the rest, this ancient feature itself must be a secondary development which occurred when the third person singular masculine pronominal morpheme had begun to take different shapes depending on whether it was conjunctive (now /‑h/) or disjunctive (still /hu/), leaving the 3rd pl. morphemes unique in that the conjunctive and disjunctive shapes remained identical. The vocalisation of a form such as TO Gn 14.15 רְדָפִינּוּן 'they pursued them' betrays the secondary nature of the amalgamation, for the Aramaic phonology leads one to expect *רְדָפִינּוּן or such like, what one actually finds in YBA (Morag 1988:291), an idiom which is idiosyncratic in some other ways as well, e.g. קַטְלוּהִי 'they killed him,' hardly ever ‑וּהִי (Morag 1988:293; a rare exception in אַמְטְיוּהִי, ib.328), though it is not apparent whether the alternative pattern such as שְׁקָלוּהִ 'they carried him' goes back to *שְׁקָלוּהִי or *שְׁקָלוּהוּ. For more examples, see Dalman (1905:362ff.) and his comments (1905:361). To the best of our knowledge, such a disjunctive pronoun is invariably found immediately after the verb, which is easily understandable according to our reconstruction. Hence, contrary to the current view, הי in הי מלבש אנה 'that I am wearing' A2.1:6 appears to be *sui generis*, apart from the fact that its use with a participle is also anormal: see below § *f*, 7. This question obviously has implications for the dating of the loss of word-final vowels. Cf. also

some comments.

a) Pf. *3ms+3fs*: הנפקה H 'it let it go out' C1.1:93; *3ms+2ms*
מטאך G 'it reached you' A2.4:6, גרך G 'he instituted (suit) against
you' B3.2:8, חבלך D 'he damaged you' C1.1:44; *3ms+2fs* גרכי G
'he instituted (suit) against you' B2.8:9; *3ms+1s* נכתני G 'it bit
me' A2.5:8, רחמני G 'he loved me' C1.1:51, סעדני G 'he supported
me' C2.1:10, הנצלני H 'he reclaimed from me' B8.6:5, אפקני A 'he
took me out' A2.6:4; *3ms+1p* החוין H 'he let us gloat' A4.7:16,
A6.2:7 // D חוינא A4.8:15; *3ms+2mp* רשכם G 'he brought (suit)
against you' B2.10:12; *3fs+2fs* מטחכי G 'it reached you' B5.1:4;
3fs+1s מטתני G 'it reached me' A2.1:4, סבלתני D 'she supported
me' B3.10:17; *2fs+3ms* יהבתהי G 'you gave it' B5.5:7; *1s+3ms*
קטלתה G 'I killed him' C1.1:49, קרבתה D 'I presented him' ib.10,
הנצלתה H 'I reclaimed him' B3.3:14; *1s+2ms* גריתך G 'I instituted
(suit) against you' B5.2:3, יבלתך G 'I transported you' C1.1:48,
קטלתך G 'I killed you' ib.51, שבקתך G 'I abandoned you' ib.111,
ברכתך D 'I blessed you' A2.4:1, קרבתך D 'I presented you' C1.1:50,
שלמתך D 'I paid you' B3.1:7, החיתך H 'I saved your life' C1.1:51,
הצפנתך H 'I hid you' ib.49; *1s+2fs* שבקתכי G 'I released you'
B3.6:4, ברכתכי D 'I blessed you' A2.1:2, A2.2:2, A2.6:1, D1.1:1;
1s+2mp רשיתכם G 'I brought (suit) against you' B2.10:12;
3mp+3ms אסרוהי 'they imprisoned him' B8.5:8, כלוהי G 'they
detained him' A4.2:13, נדשוהי 'they demolished it' A4.7:9 // A4.8:8,
שבקוהי G 'they released him'; *3mp +3fs* בנוה (wrongly spelled
בנהו) 'they built it' B3.10:8([670a]); *3mp+2ms* טעונך G 'they imposed
on you' B2.2:6, גרוך G 'they instituted (suit) against you' B3.4:18;
3mp+1s יבלוני G 'they transported me' B8.1:17, כתשוני G 'they
struck me' B8.4:5, עבדוני 'they did me' ib.4, שקפוני G 'they hit me'
ib.5, חיבוני D 'they obligated me' B8.6:10, הנצלוני H 'they reclaimed

---

Bauer - Leander (1927:124) for their reconstruction of the development under
discussion here. In OA, e.g. the Sefire inscriptions, the synthetic structure
still prevails: see examples in Degen (1969:80).

Moreover, OA attests הם 'their' spelled separately from the immediately
preceding noun: Barrakab 2.7 נבשת הם 'their souls' and Zakkur A 9 מחנות הם
'their encampments.' A recently published 9th cent. inscription from Tel Dan
may also contain a similar syntagm: ארק הם 'their land' (line 10): Biran -
Naveh 1993:94.

Hug (1993:59) gives הם as an object suffix, which is, however, misleading,
since it occurs in his corpus only as attached to an infinitive. See below our
discussion at § *e, f,* 6.

Ugaritic and Moabite also spell *hm* as a separate unit: see Segert 1984:48
and Andersen 1966:97.

from me' B8.2:15([671]); *1p+3ms* זבנהי D 'we sold it' B3.4:5([672]);
1p+3fs יהבנה G 'we gave it' B5.1:5; *1p+2ms* גרינך G 'we instituted
(suit) against you' B3.4:14, רשינך G 'we brought (suit) against
you' B2.11:9; *1p+2mp* רשינכם G 'we brought (suit) against you'
B2.9:4; *1p+2fp* ברכנכן D 'we blessed you' A2.5:1.

b) Impf. with energic Nun([673]): *3ms+3ms* יטעמנהי G 'he will
taste it' or D 'he will feed him' C1.1:208, יטענני G 'he will load
him' ib.186([674]), יכבשנהי G 'he will press him' B3.9:5, ינטרנהי G 'he
will watch it' C1.1:208, יסבלנהי G 'he will carry it' ib.185, יתקלנהי
G 'he will weigh it' C1.2:23, וי]חתלנהי 'he will hang him' ib.3, יחזננהי
A 'he will show it' C1.1:86([675]), יהתיבנהי H 'he will make it return'
C1.1:126; *3ms+3fs* ירתנה G 'he will inherit (from) her' B2.6:21,
B3.8:35; *3ms+2ms* יפלחנך G 'he will serve you' B3.6:11([676]), ישימנך
G 'May he put you!' A4.7:2, יחונך 'May he show you!' D7.15:12([676a]);
3ms+2fs יגרנך G 'he will institute (suit) against you' B3.5:16,
ירשנכי G 'he will bring (suit) against you' B2.7:9; *3fs+2ms* תשנאנך
G 'she will hate you' B2.4:8; *2ms+3fs* תזרענה G 'you will sow it'
B1.1:4([677]), תרחענה תגזנה G 'you shall wash it, you shall shear it'
D7.8:7f.; *2fs+3ms* תנתננה 'you may give it' B2.7:8([678]); *1s+3ms*
אתננהי G 'I shall give it' B1.1:11, D7.29:5, אנתננה 'I shall give it' G

[670a] See n. 631.

[671] Possibly an imperative: there is not enough context.

[672] On the simplified spelling, see above § 3 *b*.
Thus, *contra* Segert (1975:309), our corpus attests to conj. pronouns attached
to the perfect of verbs other than Lamed-Yod verbs. Two more examples are
mentioned above.

[673] On the morphosyntactic significance of the distinction between forms
with energic Nun and without it, see below § *c*. See further our discussion
above at § 23 *l*.

[674] Possibly an error for יטענונהי 'they will ...' or a defective spelling for the
latter? *Pace* Lindenberger (1983:63) an internal passive is unlikely. Does
Kottsieper (1990:19; 1991:335) assume a resumptive pronoun with his "... er
eine Kamelslast trägt"?

[675] On the intrepretation of the form as Afel, see above § 28, n. 84.

[676] An error for נפלחנך.

[676a] An uncertain reading: it could also be read יחון, יחוך, יהוו.

[677] The referent of the suffix, חקל 'field,' is a feminine noun in JA and
CPA. Brockelmann (1928:252) ought to have marked its Syr. counterpart as
f.: see the Peshitta at Gn 27.27.

[678] Possibly without an energic Nun. But see Degen (1979:32), who aptly
cites Dn 4.14 וּלְמַן דִּי יִצְבֵּא יִתְּנִנַּהּ 'and he gives it to whomever he pleases' with a
context similar to that in which our form occurs.

B4.6:5, אשלמנהי D 'I shall pay it' B4.2:3,5,10; *1s+3fs* אתננה G 'I shall give it' A2.1:5'; *1s+2ms* אגרנך G 'I shall institute (suit) against you' B2.2:12, אמחאנך G 'I shall hit you' C1.1:177, אסבלנך D 'I shall support you' C1.1:203, אקמנך A 'I shall raise you' D7.24:6; *1s+2fs* אגרנכי G 'I shall institute (suit) against you' B2.8:7, אכסנכי D 'I shall cover you' C1.1:166, ארשנכי G 'I shall bring (suit) against you' B3.5:13 אמטאנך 'I shall reach you' D7.1:11; *1s+2mp* אגרנכם G 'I shall institute (suit) against you' B2.10:1; *3mp+3ms* יתנה A 'they will bring him' A2.6:10(+3fs? [= "ship"])([679]); *3mp + 3s* יקחונה 'they will take him/her/it' D4.8:1([680]); *3mp+2fs* יגרונכי G 'they will institute (suit) against you' B5.1:6; *3mp+2mp* ירשונכם 'they will bring (suit) against you' B2.9:13; *3mp+1s* ישאלונני 'they will interrogate me' D2.25:2; יחוונני 'they will show me' A4.4:9; *2mp+3ms* תנתנונה G 'you will give it' B2.10:9; *1p+3ms* אל נקטלנהי G 'Let us not kill him' C1.1:61; *1p+2ms* נסבלנך D 'we shall suport you' B3.6:13, נשוזבנך 'we shall rescue you' A3.1:8.

c) Impf. without energic Nun: *3ms+3ms* ינתנהי 'May he give it' G D7.29:9; *3ms+3fs* יערכה 'Let him prepare it' D7.9:2; *3ms+2mp* ירשכם for ירשנכם G 'he will bring (suit) against you' B2.10:15; *3ms+1s* יזכרני G 'May he remember me!' C1.1:53, יחוני D 'May he show me!' A2.1:2, A2.6:2, יהחיני H 'May he save my life!' C1.1:54, יחוני A 'May he show me!' A2.2:2, A2.3:2, A2.4:2, A2.5:2; *2ms+3ms* הן תהצפנהי 'if you conceal it' C2.1:72([681]); *2ms+1s* אל תקטלני G 'Do not kill me!' C1.1:52, תקרבני D 'you shall present me' ib.54; *1s+3s* ארחעה G 'Let me wash it!' D7.8:11; *3mp+3ms* יגרוהי G 'May they sue him!' A3.4:4; *3mp + 3fs* יכתבוה D 'Let them mark her!' D7.9:4; *3mp+2ms* אל [י]ב[ל]עוך G 'May they not swallow you up!' C1.1:148; *1p+3ms* נתנהי 'we shall give it' A2.1:7; *1p+2fs* נגרכי 'we institute (suit) against you' B5.1:4.([682])

The examples quoted above of the *1s* suffix—יחוני, יזכרני, תקרבני, יחוני, יהחיני—have all been translated as if they were jussives. In the context of their occurrences, however, there is no compelling reason to suggest such an interpretation([683]), and, as a matter of fact, all the examples of יחוני and יחוני are part of a standing

---

[679] See Porten - Greenfield 1974:23f.

[680] The gender of the suffix is not to be determined due to the lack of the context.

[681] The reading of the end of the verb is far from certain.

[682] Most likely an error for נגרנכי: see יגרונכי two lines below.

[683] This applies also to a partly restored [ויז]בנהי, if not an error for יזבננהי 'he will buy/sell it' A3.10:7.

formula *and* occur inside a clause introduced by ז'.([684]) But, if these are not jussives, how could one account for this anomaly? A possible explanation is that the energic Nun of the expected form such as *זכרנני*, no example of which is attested in our corpus, was perceived as typical of the verb forms which have an /n/ as part of their morpheme, namely 2/3 pl. and 2fs, and was hence dropped as such from the remaining verb forms which do not carry such a morpheme when another /n/ of the suffix immediately follows. Such a development and interpretation may have been precipitated to some degree by the appearance of the new 2/3 fp morpheme characterised by /-a:n/, for a form such as *זכרנני* 'he will remember me' and *זכרנני* 'they (f) will remember me' could have also phonetically differed from each other but little. Another possible explanation is that our idiom represents the halfway house between OA, in which the energic morpheme is confined to the 3ms suffix([685]), and BA, in which the use of the energic morpheme is universal.([686])

   d) Imperative: *ms+3ms* הבהי 'Give it!' D7.5:7([687]); עבדהי G 'Do it!' C1.1:87; שלחהי 'Send it!' D7.4:7([688]); *ms+3fs* גזה G 'Shear it!' D7.8:6; *ms+1s* בלי G 'Bring me!' C1.1:52, הקימני H 'Establish me!' ib.109; *fs+3ms* החסני H 'Hold it as heir!' B2.3:26; אתיה A 'Bring it!' A2.3:10; הבי G 'Give it!' B2.7:16, D7.5:7; שאלהי 'Ask him!' D7.1:14([689]); *fs+3fs* הבה G 'Give it!' A3.4:3 // הביה D7.9:2; *mp+3ms* החווהי H 'Notify him!' A6.11:5; הושרוהי 'Dispatch it' D7.9:13; *mp+3fs* בלוה G 'Bring it!' D7.9:3; *mp+1s* חוני 'Show me!' D7.14:8.

---

[684] We shall suggest below (§ 53 *b*) a possibility of viewing these verb forms as jussives all the same.

[685] The attestation for the 3fs is incomplete, but there are a number of exmaples of the 1s *n* and 2ms *k*, without the extra *n*. See Degen 1969:80.

[686] E.g. יְשַׁמְשׁוּנַּה, יְשֵׁיזְבִנָּךְ, יְדַחֲלִנַּנִי. The three examples of the 1s, however, are not incontrovertible: יסבן Sefire I B 28, usually emended to יסבני, can be emended to יסבנני, תעשקני ib. III 20 is preceded by ל, which may be restored as אל, making the verb a jussive form, and ויענני 'and he answered me' Zakkur A 11 may be equal to Heb. וַיַּעֲנֵנִי with an apocopated (= jussive) form. This still leaves אחצלך 'I shall rescue you' Zakkur A 14.

[687] The gender of the pronoun in הבה 'Give it!' A3.7:4 escapes us.

[688] The subject is not perfectly certain, possibly a woman, in which case the form of the suffix would be normal, since the imperative itself would end with a vowel.

[689] The subject is, despite the spelling of the verb itself, most likely a woman, in which case the form of the suffix would be normal.

e) Infinitive: +*3ms* למזבנה G 'to buy with it' A3.10:5([690]),
למבניה G 'to build it' A4.7:23, ל]החסנותה[H 'to bestow it' B7.3:7;
לזבנותה 'to sell it' D D7.56:13; + *3fs* למזרעה G 'to sow it' B1.1:3,
לתרכותה D 'to evict her' B2.6:30, B3.8:30, משלמותה 'to repay it'
C1.1:131, למנחתותה D or A 'to put it down' ib.171; + *2fs* למשנתכי
G 'to brand you' B3.6:7, לתרכתכי D 'to evict you' B3.7:16; +*1s*
לחצלתני D 'to rescue me' A1.1:7; + *3mp* מנחתותהם D or A 'to put
them down' C1.1:170, למושרתהם A 'to dispatch them' A2.2:13.

f) Observations

1) As noted above in § 12 *f*, the 3ms conjunctive pronoun
has two allomorphs: ה- and הי-. The general assumption is that
the latter follows a historically long vowel or a diphthong. This
theory certainly works with forms such as אסרוהי 'they imprisoned
him' B8.5:8, החווהי 'Notify him!' A6.11:5, and יגרוהי 'Let them
institute (suit) against him!' A3.4:4. From this one can conclude
that יהבתיה 'you gave it' B5.5:7 is a defective spelling for יהבתיהי([691]),
החסנהי 'Hold it as heir!' B2.3:26 for החסניהי([692]), and הבהי 'Give it!'
B2.7:16 for הביהי, all fem. sg. verb forms.([693]) Likewise the spelling
זבנהי 'we sold it' B3.4:5 allows us to postulate that the pf. 1p
ended with a long vowel.([694]) On the other hand, the pf. 1s does
not seem to have ended with a vowel, as may be concluded from
forms like קטלתה 'I killed him' C1.1:49 and הנצלתה 'I reclaimed
from him' B3.3:14, for otherwise the forms would have been
spelled קטלתהי and הנצלתהי respectively.

2) The reason why אתיה (= /ʔe:taye:h/?) 'Bring him!' impv.
fs+3ms at A2.3:10 does not end with הי-([695]) appears to be that
the impv. itself ends with a consonant, or a semi-vowel, /ʔe:tay-/

---

[690] The syntax is strange; the translation given above is the meaning required
by the context. The direct object המו in זבנתון המו עבור 'you bought grain with
them' ib.5 is equally puzzling.

[691] *Pace* Beyer (1984:475) the verb is of the 2fs, not 2ms.

[692] Segert (1975:310) apparently analyses the form as masculine.

[693] Segert's (1975:310) הביהי is a misprint.

[694] Cf. the occasional plene spelling of the conjunctive 1p morpheme with
nouns and prepositions as in ביתנא 'our house' C3.28:48. See further § 12 *h*.
אגרא זי הנפנא זי בנה מצריא 'the protecting wall that the Egyptians built'
B3.10:9 is probably an error for בנה ..., the conj. pron. referring to אגרא 'wall,'
a f. noun or possibly הנפנא, should the latter also be fem. At B3.11:4 one
reads הנפנא זי בנו מצריא. In any case, to read the first half of בנה as monophthongised and defectively spelled /bno:/ is rather unlikely.

[695] But Beyer (1984:497), consistent with his theory mentioned below,
interprets the form as /ʔaytáyhi:/.

or such like: cf. JA אחיי Megillah 73a(44).([696]) From this we may further conclude that only the diphthong *aw* demanded the conjunctive pronoun הי.

3) The most knotty question is concerned with the 3ms pronoun הי- attached to a verb form, mostly a pc. form, and twice an impv., but never a form of the pf. or any other category of verb inflection.([697]) The general assumption is that such an allomorph follows a long vowel or diphthong. There are, however, too many cases which do not appear to meet such a condition. Examples are יכבשנהי 'he will press him' B3.9:5 or אתננהי 'I shall give it' B1.1:11. For more examples, see above under (b). The difficulty is that no diachronic or comparative consideration points to an originally long vowel or a diphthong ending such verb forms, which are generally considered to have been similar to those of the first energic mood in Classical Arabic ending with /-nna/, e.g. /yaqtulanna/.([698]) A diphthong is out of the question. If it were a long vowel([699]), the only plausible candidate is /a:/.([700]) Such a long *a* could have developed, if it carried stress.([701]) Even

---

[696] Quoted by Sokoloff (1990:81). See also some examples in Dalman 1905:348, and his comments (1905:339). In YBA one finds אִיתִי (Morag 1988:280) and BTA הָאִי (Epstein 1960:97).

[697] Cf. Folmer 1995: 241-52 and Muraoka 1997a: 208-13.

[698] Kottsieper (1990:177), for a reason which appears to us unlikely, denies that any vowel preceded the /n/. Though Beyer (1984:473) breaks down the energic into the jussive /yaqtul/ + /-anna/ or /-nn/, we would suggest, if we are to take the Arabic scheme as our starting point, the energic morpheme is best considered as I /-nna/ or II /n/, both added to the subjunctive, /yaqtula/. In such a case, the /a/ preceding the /n/ would be, *pace* Kottsieper (1990:177), no helping vowel.

Furthermore, Kottsieper makes no distinction between the <n> of the 1sg. suffix <-ny> and our "energic" <n>, which is totally unjustified in view of the fact that no Semitic language adds the latter to the suffix conjugation.

A complementary distribution which Garr (1985:111) postulates and considers Proto-Semitic, namely the *h*-form with verb forms other than the perfect and originally ending in a consonant and the *n*-form with those originally ending in a vowel, is obviously invalid with verb forms having an etymologically long vowel as in f.sg., m.pl.

[699] So Bennett (1984:52-92, esp. 85-89), who generally follows Kutscher (1971:118) in this matter, without specifying, however, what vowel, if any, he considers precedes the suffix הי-.

[700] Leander (1928:51f.) gives no argument for his /-ó:hi:/. Kottsieper (1990:178) indicates a short /a/.

[701] Possibly it did not have to be long.

so, some([702]) problematic cases remain: ‏ה-‏ appears instead of ‏-יהי‏ in ‏יתונה‏ 'they will bring him' A2.6:10, ‏תנתננה‏ 'you (mp) may give it' B2.10:9, ‏תנתננה‏ 'you (fs) may give it' B2.7:8, and perhaps ‏אנתננה‏ 'I shall give it' B4.6:5. One possible interpretation of these rare, Yodh-less forms is to see in ‏ה-‏ a defective spelling for ‏-יהי‏. One finds at least one comparable case in our corpus: ‏יגרנך‏ 'he will institute suit against you (fs)' B3.5:15 (// ‏יגרנכי‏ ib.14). One notes, however, that all of these forms([703]), except the last, happen to show, in their impf. form, the syllabic structure -R₃V$n(a)$. It is just possible that the Aramaic energic of these forms, unlike their Arabic counterpart, retained a long vowel after R₃, thus preventing the shift of the stress to the vowel following the final /n/ and keeping the vowel short.([704]) Finally, ‏נתנהי‏ (= /nittna:hi/?) 'we will give it' A2.1:7 and ‏ינתנהי‏ 'Let him give it!' D7.29:9, if not a scribal error for *‏נתננה‏ and *‏ינתננהי‏ respectively, are probably based on the analogy of the energic forms, for, if we are to start with the Classical Arabic model, the jussive ‏נתן‏ and ‏ינתן‏ would have no vowel ending([705]). The above consideration applies to the impv. ‏עבדהי‏ 'Do it!' C1.1:87([706]) (and possibly ‏שלחהי‏ 'Send it!' D7.4:7). This contrasts with ‏הבה‏ 'Give it (= ‏בית‏) A3.8:6.

An explanation proposed by Beyer (1984:424, 473, 476-79), and accepted by Hug (1993:87), is arbitrary.([707]) According to them, Aramaic, though presumably not every dialect, uses both Energic I and II. Energic I possesses a linking vowel, but Energic II does not. The two can be distinguished only before suffixes([708]):

---

[702] These are exceptions, the norm being ‏-יה‏. Hence Bennet's (1984:82) "occasionally" is misleading, whereas Beyer's (1984:473) "die allein übliche Form" is the other extreme.

[703] ‏אנתננה‏ 'I shall give it' B4.6:5 does not fit this categorization.

[704] Cf. an attempt by Bauer - Leander (1927:123f.) to account for a plene spelling such as Dn 5.6 ‏יְבַהֲלוּנֵּהּ‏ for the expected ‏יְבַהֲלֻנֵּהּ‏, as at ib. 4.16.

[705] Cf. Bauer - Leander 1927:125.

[706] The restoration of a Yod at the end is generally accepted. /ʾabidhî/ of Lindenberger (1983:85) is difficult to accept. A TA form such as ‏סַבְהִי‏ 'Take it!' 2Kg 4.19 (Dalman 1927:375) must be evaluated in the light of the fact that with the pc. the pattern as in ‏יִפְרְקִנֵּיהּ‏ is the rule in that idiom.

[707] Hug (1993:87), for instance, lists ‏אתננהי‏ 'I give it' and ‏תזרענה‏ 'you sow it,' both from one text (B1.1), as instancing the impf. with the 3ms suffix—the former an example of Energicus II with no linking vowel and the latter of Energicus I with such a vowel—though the latter, we believe, refers to a feminine noun.

[708] So Beyer (1984:473), but this manifestly cannot be true in purely

schematically, Energic I ישׁימנה /--minneh/ as against Energic II
ישׁימנהי /--mínhi:/. As long as some functional or morphosyntactic
opposition is not established between the two energic moods,
the argument is obviously circular. Nor can some of the actual
data we have in our corpus, as we have seen above, be fitted into
such a neat pattern. See, for example, a contrasting pair of
imperatives mentioned at the end of the preceding paragraph.([709])
Moreover, Beyer would need another rule to account for the
same morpheme הי- in forms such as אסרוהי 'they imprisoned
him' B8.5:8; בְּנָהִי 'he built it' Ezr 5.11; אבוהי 'his father' B3.6:11;
הבהי /habíhi/ 'Give it!' B2.7:16 (impv. fs + 3ms).

   4) Those pc. forms quoted above with a personal suffix
/-n/ as having an energic Nun are, in fact, ambiguous. One cannot
say confidently whether תנתנונה B2.10:9 has the last Nun geminated
or not.

   5) Examples of the 3pl pronouns as a direct complement
of a verb are: אחד המו 'he seized them' A6.7:7; לא איתית המו 'I did
not bring them' A3.3:10; נפלג המו 'we shall divide them' B2.11:13;
אהנצל הם 'I shall reclaim them' B6.4:8. See further below at § 74
h. False anaology of the syntactic rule under consideration seems
to offer the best solution for the following two striking cases of
הי, once disjunctive and the other time conjunctive: כתנה זי התתי
לי סון הי מלבש אנה 'the garment which you brought for me (to)
Syene, *that* I am wearing' A2.1:6 where the emphatic compound
sentence accounts for the resumptive object pronoun, and רחם
אנה להי שׂגיא 'I love her much' D23.1 II:8, 13. In both cases one
expects לה.([710]) The sole instance in our entire corpus of a 3pl
conjunctive object pronoun directly added to the verb occurs in
this same document אנתנהם 'I shall give them' ib.15 for the expected
אנתן המו.([711]) It is noteworthy that these two unusual forms should

---

consonantal texts, and Beyer's (1984:477) reconstruction as exemplified in
the following examples is patently arbitrary: ירתנה /yaretánha:/ "er beerbt sie"
vs. יתננה /yettenennáha:/ "er gibt sie." Hug (1993:87) justly narrows the
differentiability to the 3ms.

[709] Beyer (1984:479) resorts to emending the "offending" form הבה to הבהי.

[710] Ours is close to the last of Lemaire's (1995:85) three alternative
explanations, which he, however, regards the least plausible.

[711] Although Degen (1979:50), apparently accepted by Hug (1993:20f.),
has convincingly disposed of the only alleged suffixed object הם- in the
Ashur letter (line 17), which in his scheme belongs to the IA period, by
proposing a haplography, <ו>אכלתהם 'it consumed them,' this latest example
cannot be so easily done away with. It seems that one simply has to accept
the form as a lingering feature attested, albeit admittedly only weakly, right

be attested in a document with idiosyncratic grammar.([711a])

6) The third person plural conjunctive object pronouns attached to the infinitive as in למושרתהם 'to dispatch them' and מנחתותהם 'to put them down'([712]) clearly illustrate that, in this respect, the infinitive in our idiom is morphosyntacticaly a separate category from the finite verb. That these pronouns were perceived as "objects" is shown by the form נ-י, and not -י, in לחצלתני 'to rescue me' A1.1:7([713]), a case of verbal inflection.([714]) It is noteworthy, however, that הם- is otherwise, with one exception only (§ 11 ƒ), a conjunctive *possessive* pronoun and the finite verb always uses המו. Thus the form הם- here, attached to the infinitives, represents a conflation of two inflections, nominal and verbal.([715]) See also above § *e* and § 23 *p*.

7) Where a pronoun is attached to a participle, the latter is

---

from the OA period (Sefire) through the Ashur letter and the Hermopolis papyri, and down to the Ahiqar proverbs. We would then not need to invoke the alleged nominal character of the infinitive (so Degen 1979:50) in order to account for למושרתהם 'to send them' and מנחתותהם 'to put them down' (mentioned in the following subparagraph), for there is little doubt that a pronominal suffix attached to the infinitive was perceived as objectival.

[711a] *Pace* Bauer - Leander (1927:337 *i*, 340 *s*) and Vogt (1971:162b) we would interpret להם at Ezr 5.10 שְׁמָהָתְהֹם שְׁאֵלְנָא לְהֹם 'we asked them their names' as indirect object, not a second direct object. Cohen (1975:10f.) has his own reason for objecting to this common interpretation. For him the preposition Lamed is added because the persons being asked are more important in precipitating the asking than their names, an argument which is rather subjective.

[712] On the fluctuation in spelling between -ת- and -ות-, see above § 23 *p*.

[713] Segert (1975:307) and Gibson (1975:113) read לחצלתי, but Hug (1993:16) has להצלנין.

[714] OA appears to prefer the nominal inflection: Sefire III 11 להמתתי 'to kill me' // להמתת ברי 'to kill my son.' Cp. also חזבתהם ולאבדת אשמהם 'to strike them and to destroy their name' Sefire II B.7 with our למושרתהם and מנחתותהם. Note an interesting difference between TA and GA in this respect: Dalman 1927:377-80. On Syr., see Muraoka 1987:55.

[715] As against Folmer (1995: 428), who writes "... only the infinitive *continued* [emphasis ours] to be complemented exclusively by the obj. pron. sf., at least as late as the end of the 5th century," the situation in our corpus represents a different *system* or *structure*, for OA, more specifically the language of the Sefire inscriptions, does not, like in our corpus, present a complementary distribution, but attest to a single pronominal morpheme for the third person plural, whether conjunctive or disjunctive, viz. הם. In the Zakkur inscription (8th cent.), however, there appears to be a beginning of a similar complementary distribution: line 9 הם ומחנות. הֹמו 'they ... and their encampments.'

invariably substantivised.([716]) Thus משלחה D 'one who sends it'
C1.1:82([717]); נטחוהי G 'his attackers' ib.103; א[ח]דדתה 'his title-
holder(?)' B3.8:29; שאני, an error for שנאי, G 'my enemies' ib.110.
In contrast, where a personal pronoun constitutes a direct
complement of a participle, it is mediated by the preposition
Lamed as in כלין להן 'they detain them' A4.2:14: see further on
this subject at § 74 *j*.([718])

8) The conjunctive object pronouns used with verbs show
no allomorph ending with /n/ for the 2mp, but only with /m/,
thus unlike those attached to nouns and prepositions (§ 12 *i*).
Nor does one find any example of הן or הון for 'them (m.)' as
direct object. Whether any significance is to be attached to this
or it is due to imperfect attestation is difficult to say.([719]) The
only -*n* form attested is feminine: ברכנכן 'we blessed you' A2.5:1.

---

[716] Lindenberger's remarks on this subject (1983:76) are confused; unlike
Bauer - Leander (1927:117), he and Leander (1928:50) fail to distinguish
between the purely verbal and the substantival use of participles. Those Aramaic
dialects he mentions as attesting the act. ptc. with a pron. suff. use such a ptc.
substantivally under those conditions.

[717] With Lindenberger (1983:76) we reject Bauer - Leander's analysis
(1927:117) of the form as D ptc.pass., "das Ausgesandte davon."

[718] It is thus impossible to interpret, as Kraeling (1969:220) does, שאהי as
G ptc. + 3fs (object): C1.1:103, which he adduces as supporting evidence, is
irrelevant, as shown above.

[719] In B2.10 the /-m/ morpheme alternates once with /-n/ in רחמתן 'you
liked' B2.10:9, though it is a subject morpheme.

PART THREE

MORPHOSYNTAX

SECTION A

THE PRONOUN

§ 39. Personal pronouns

a) Whether conjunctive or disjunctive, a personal pronoun in the first or second person, refers to the speaker(s) or the person(s) spoken to respectively. Thus הי מלבש אנה '*that* I am wearing' A2.1:6; לכן אנחנה יצפן 'about *you* we worry' ib.8; אנת שם טעם 'you, issue an order!' A6.3:7. The reference may be "personalised" and applied to a non-human living object, animal or plant: "The [bramb]le dispatched to [the] pomegranate, saying, ' ... How goodly is the ab[un]dance of your thorns (כביך) ...?"'C1.1:101; "The lambs ... said to him [= the bear], 'Carry (away) what you (לך) will from us (מנן)" ib.169.

b) A pronoun in the third person, by contrast, may refer not only to a person or persons spoken of, but also to an inanimate object or objects, often with no implication of personalisation. For example, "my son ... he (הו) will succeed me" C1.1:18; חכים הו 'he is wise' ib.28; ברתה 'his daughter' B2.3:3; הי אנתתי 'she is my wife' B2.6:4, but משחתה 'its measurements [= of the property]' B2.3:3f. Such a pronoun must agree in gender and number with the noun to which it refers: זילך הי [= ארקא] 'it [= ארקא] is yours' B3.10:11. The 3ms הו may even refer back to a whole notion or thought as in חטא מן אלהן הו 'it is a punishment from gods' C1.1:128. In such a case it is difficult to identify a single noun or noun phrase to which the pronoun refers: "Give him as much as (לקבל זי) you can. It is not a loss for you (לא חסרן הו לכם)" A4.3:9; ... הן כנם הו עליכי הו 'if it is so according to these words' A6.11:3; כמליא אלה 'it is your responsibility' D7.5:10, and perhaps שכר הו לה 'it/he is hired for him' D7.20:3. A variation on such use of הו is equivalent to "i.e., namely" in an explanatory gloss: כרש חד הו 1 שקלן תלתה תשרי הו 3 'one karsh, that is, 1, three shekels, that is 3' B3.12:5;

אפף 'Tishri, i.e. Epiph' B3.8:1([720]); תחית הו תרבצא 'the _ḥyt_, i.e. the courtyard' B3.10:15.

c) הו also has the grammatical function of extraposing or focusing on the immediately preceding clause constituent: אנה הו אחיקר '*I* am Ahiqar' C1.1:46; צנפר הי מלה 'a word is a *bird*' ib.82.

In הן כנם הו כמליא אלה 'if it is thus (i.e.) as these words' A6.11:3, there is no noun or noun phrase which can be regarded a referent of the pronoun. Such a pronoun may appear as the last of a three-member nominal clause as in זי יהנפק כדב הו 'what he produces is fraudulent' B3.11:16. For more on this syntax, see below at § 77 *ca*.

d) The third person plural disjunctive pronoun הם or המו is, in addition to the uses described above, used as a direct object of a verb form other than the infinitive and the participle, whereas the rest of the pronouns are synthetically attached to the verb as conjunctive pronouns: אהנצל הם 'I shall reclaim them' B6.4:8; לא איתית המו 'I did not bring them' A3.3:10. The use of הי in כתנה זי התתי לי סון הי מלבש אנה 'the garment which you brought for me (to) Syene—*that* I am wearing' A2.1:6 is exceptional.([721]) The pronoun הי, however, is not of the same kind as הם or המו, for the participle מלבש cannot take a conjunctive pronoun as its object. See above § 37 *f* (5) and below § 74 *h*.

e) The finite verb, namely a verb form other than the infinitive and participle, has a built-in marker([722]) of the categories of person, number, and gender.([723]) Yet we often find a disjunctive personal pronoun used next to, and preceding([724]), such a finite verb. In our corpus it almost always appears immediately before the verb.([725]) It is most common in the first and second persons,

---

[720] We would rather assume a scribal error of הוה for הו at B3.1:5 instead of a difficult הוה as ptc.act. (so Joüon 1934:39). On a peculiar use of הו in the sense of "idem, ditto" in a list of names (C3.15:6,26,27,28), see Joüon 1934:66-67.

[721] For similar syntax, cf. לשלח הואה 'to expel him' 1QS 7.16 and להמית הואה 'to kill him' CD 9.1 in Qumran Hebrew (Qimron 1986:76).

[722] Driver's view (1957:78) that a pronoun is required because the [written] form of the verb does not distinguish the 1st and 2nd persons is most unlikely.

[723] The imperative lacks the first and third persons.

[724] Except in cases discussed under (iv) below.

[725] In a seeming exception such as לא אכהל אנה מחסיה בר וברה לי ... דין 'I shall not be able—I, Mahseiah, son or daughter of mine ...—to למרשה עליך bring suits against you' B2.11:7 we may note that the long multiple subject introduced by אנה is, in fact, in apposition to the subject latent in אכהל. So

which seems to suggest that the use essentially belongs to lively, colloquial speech.([726]) Such a use seems to be motivated by a variety of factors.([727]) It is highly frequent with imperatives.

i) *Contrast or opposition*

E.g., ואנה קוניה לא אכהל '(the property is yours), so *I*, Konaiah, shall not be able to ...' B2.1:11; אנחנה מנטרתן לא שבקן '(unlike the rebels) *we* did not desert our posts' A4.5:1; הו עבידתך '*he* shall do your work' C1.1:21; אנת לקבל זי אנה עבדת לך כן אף עבד לי 'you, just as I did for you, so, then, do for me' ib.51, where the unusual position of אנת reinforces the notion of contrast([728]); "should I die before having repaid the loan, it is my children who shall repay it (בני המו ישלמון)" B3.1:15; עבידתא זי אנת בניא זי עבדת 'the work which *you* will have undertaken' B2.4:10; אנת בנית 'the rebuilding which *you* will have executed' ib.12([729]); אסחור הו ירתנה 'it is Eshor that will inherit from her' B2.6:21.([730]) See also B2.4:10 (המו), 13 (המו); B3.3:11 (הי), 12 (הו). Cf. הו טבתא יבעה '*he* will seek the good' C1.1:24; 'למה הו יחבל מתא עלין 'why should *he* harm the land on us?' ib.36 and הו חבלך '*he* (of all persons) harmed you' ib.44: this recurring הו, once referring to Ahikar and then to Nadin, must be a deliberate stylistic device for highlighting a contrast between the behaviour of Nadin and that of Ahiqar.

ii) *Assertiveness*([731])

A pronoun of the first (and rarely second)([732]) person is often used as an expression of the speaker's ego, personal

---

also הן רשינך דינא עלא אנחנה מחסיה ובני 'if we bring suit against you about it—we, Mahseiah or my children' ib.9. This is a partly grammatical, partly stylistic feature common to Biblical Hebrew as exemplified in Gn 6.18 וּבָאתָ אֶל הַתֵּבָה אַתָּה וּבָנֶיךָ 'and you go into the ark, you and your sons': see Joüon - Muraoka 1993:§ 146 c.

[726] Cf. Muraoka 1985:58. See כזי אנה הוית אתה 'whilst I was coming' A6.3:2.

[727] Bauer - Leander (1927: § 72 a), followed by Fitzmyer (1956:28f.) to a certain extent, unjustly hold that such pronouns are mostly pleonastic.

[728] See also הן משלמת לא יצפה לי אנתי מה תאמרן 'if M. doesn't care for me, you, what would *you* say?' D7.16:11.

[729] These last two examples are concerned with a possible future extension and refurbishing to be undertaken by a new owner.

[730] This is actually a variant of the above-mentioned extraposing הו § c, a cleft sentence.

[731] Cf. Muraoka 1985:47-66.

[732] That אנה predominates in this and the following category ("self-centredness") is easy to understand in terms of human psychology.

involvement or self-consciousness. This may occur in emotionally
charged situations such as *an expression of displeasure*—אנה
חדית [א]לן 'I was not pleased' A6.16:4; *promise or commitment*—אנה
אנתן יפלחנך (= נפלחנך) ;B2.3:21, B2.4:14 'I shall give you' אנתן לכי
'we shall serve you' B3.6:11; regularly in *penalty clauses*, often
reinforced by addition of the party's name—אנתן ... אנה פיא 'I Peu
... shall give' B2.8:9; *authoritative statement*—אנה אשים להם טעם
'I shall issue an order for them' A6.3:6; *boasting royal style* - זנה
אנה עבדת 'this I [= Darius] did' C2.1 III:3([733]), sim. C2.1:35;
accusation as if an accusing finger is pointed at the person—הו
קבל 'he complained' A4.2:3*bis*; "you dispatched (אנת הושרת) what
I did not want" A6.16:3; והו החסן 'and he took hereditary possession
(and did not return [them])' B2.9:7; אנת [על]ת 'you brok[e in]'
B7.2:4; אנה נכתני חויה 'I was bitten by a snake (and you couldn't
care less)' A2.5:8; often in *legal contracts* where the demarcation
between the parties involved is important and a measure of
solemnity or pomp is not entirely out of place—אנה אתית עליך 'I
came to you' B2.1:3, likewise B2.6:3, B3.3:3, B3.8:3, B3.13:2,
B6.1:3; אנה קבלת עליך 'I complained against you' B2.2:5, sim.
A6.14:1; אנה יהבת לכי ... בי 1 'I gave you ... a house' B2.3:3; אנה
יהבתה לכי בחיי ובמותי 'I gave it to you in my lifetime and at my
death' ib.8; אנה יהבתה לכי אנתי החסנה 'I gave it to you, you hold it
as heiress!' ib.25; זי אנה יהבת למבטחיה 'which I gave Mibtahiah'
B2.4:3, sim. A6.11:5; אנחן זבן ויהבן לך 'we sold and gave you'
B3.4:3; [אנ[ת קב]לת] 'you complained' B7.2:4([734]); the *legal
parlance* coupled with self-consciousness is manifest when אנה
is followed by the speaker's name as in אנה מחסיה ... לא אהנצל מנכי
'I Mahseiah will not be able to reclaim from you' B2.3:18; כען
אנה עני אנה מחסיה אמרת לך 'Now I Mahseiah said to you' B2.4:5; אנה
אשלם ... 'I Anani ... shall pay' B3.13:3, sim. B3.7:3, 12, 14f.; אנה
מלכיה אקרא לך 'I Malchiah shall call upon you' B7.2:7. Many
contracts or legal documents whose first finite verb is in the first
person use אנה or אנחנה; apart from the examples mentioned
above, see also B2.1:11 (with name), B2.6:3, B2.7:2, B2.8:9
(with name), B2.9:4, B2.10:12 (with name), B2.11:2, B3.3:3,
B3.5:2, 4-6,11-12, 13 (with name),18, B3.6:3, B3.8:3, B3.10:2,
B3.11:9 (with name),16 (with name), B3.12:3 (with name),24,
B3.13:2, B5.1:2, B5.2:3 (plausible restoration), B5.5:2, B6.1:3;
but not אנת as in יהבת לי 'you gave me' B3.1:3, also B2.2:4,
B3.2:3, B4.2:1, B4.4:3, B5.6:2.

---

[733] Akk. *aga: ana:ku e:tepuš*, and cf. Joüon - Muraoka 1993: § 146 *a* (4).

[734] See also B3.3:3,14; B3.4:15; B3.6:3,14; B4.4:15.

In an Ahiqar proverb some beast approaches a wild ass in a patronising tone, saying אנ[ה] [א]אסבלנך 'I shall support you' C1.1:203, an offer which the humble beast rejects out of a sense of self-respect: אנה רכביך לא אחזה 'I shall not see your riding' ib.204.

iii) *Self-centredness*

אנה יהבת לך 'je t'ai donnée moi-même' A3.10:4(735); זבנת לי אנה כתן 1 'I bought for me myself 1 tunic' A3.3:11.(736)

iv) *Coordinate subjects*

A personal pronoun often heads a series of coordinate subjects linked with the following subjects by an associative conjunction Waw or Waw of accompaniment, 'together with'(737): לא אכל אנה ובני וזרע זילי וגבר אחרן ירשנכי דין ודבב 'I shall not be able—I or my children, or descendants who are mine, or another person—to bring against you suit or process' B2.7:8; לא אכהל אנה אוריה ובר וברה לי ... יכבשנהי 'I shall not be able, I, Uriah, or son or daughter of mine ... to press him' B3.9:4(738); ... ימאת לי אנת ואנתתך וברך 'you swore for me ... you, your wife and your son' B2.2:4. All these pronouns follow the verb, and they are to be considered an integral part of the following series of multiple subjects.(739)

v) *Authoritarian*

The 2nd person pronoun is sometimes used in a command issued to an inferior: 'You, do (אנת עבד) according to ...' A6.2:22; אנת שם טעם 'You, issue an order!' A6.3:7, sim. A6.5:3; אנתם הבו 'You, give!' A6.9:2; אנתם [א]תנצחו 'You, be diligent!' A6.10:5, sim. A6.14:2, A6.16:1; אנתם החווהי 'You, notify him!' A6.11:5.(740) See also אנתם הנדרז עבדו 'You, issue instruction!' A6.13:4; אנת חזי 'You, regard!' A6.15:3. Here one may include אנת אשתמר לך 'You, watch yourself!' C1.1:85. The vocative אנת יה ברי 'You, O

---

735 Grelot 1972:504.

736 אנה is likely reinforcing the preceding conjunctive pronoun, for a disjunctive pronoun which is to be construed with a finite verb, as remarked above (e), regularly precedes the latter. Cf. the use of הי mentioned above, also under (e), and see below, (vi)

737 On a similar phenomenon in BH, see Jouön - Muraoka 1993:§ 146 c.

738 Note the 3ms form of the main verb in both cases. See below at § 76 cc, cg.

739 ... אזלת אנה וצחא בר פחה אמרן לפיסן [A3.6:2 can be interpreted in this fashion: '] I went, I and Ṣeha son of Paha. We said to Pisina ...' instead of 'I went. I and Ṣ. ... said to P.' (Cowley 1923:139, Porten - Yardeni 1986:38, and Grelot 1972:129).

740 Also contrasting to אנה ... יהבת ... אנה.

my son' introduces a proverb, followed by an imperative הכצר 'Harvest!' C1.1:127 and זף 'Borrow!' ib.129.

The pronoun of this type is understandably optional. Thus many other Ahiqar proverbs couched in the imperative do not use such a pronoun, e.g. אשתמר לך 'Watch yourself!' C1.1:81; אשתמעו לה ועבדו כן 'Obey him and act thus!' A6.8:3; הבו 'Give!' A6.9:4, 5([741]); טרו 'Guard!' A6.10:6; ... ועבדו ... וסטרו ... בעו והנעלו 'Seek and bring (them) in ... and mark them ... and make over ...!' A6.10:7; הב לה 'Give him!' A6.12:1; הושרו 'Dispatch!' ib.3; התב הב 'Restore, give!' A6.15:7,10. It will be seen that in many letters the two structures freely alternate.

    vi) Somewhat akin to the usage described above under (iv) is the disjunctive pronoun matching and resuming a preceding conjunctive pronoun, which is then expanded by the addition of other coordinate nouns. Examples are: אפקני אנה וברי 'he brought me forth, me and my son' A2.6:4; לא אכהל אגרנכי דין ודבב אנתי ובר וברה לכי 'I shall not be able to institute against you suit or process—(against) you or son or daughter of yours' B2.8:7, sim. B2.3:12; זך ביתא ... זילכם הו אנת ידניה ומחסיה ... וזי בניך אחריכם 'that house ... is yours—you, Jedaniah and Mahseiah ... and of your children after you(r death)' B2.10:8, which is most instructive on account of the last phrase beginning with וזי, demonstrating that the writer, despite the preceding subject form אנת, is still thinking in terms of possession and ownership. It is further to be noted([742]) that the string beginning with the disjunctive pronoun does not always immediately follow the conjunctive pronoun([743]), which may be taken to mean that the thought expressed by the string was perceived as a self-contained thought unit.([744])

    vii) Semantically related to the usage described above under (i) and (ii), but formally related to (vi) above is the use of the disjunctive personal pronoun which, without any other co-ordinated noun phrase, follows a matching conjunctive pronoun. Examples: ... ביתי אנה דרגמן 'my house, I Dargamana, is ...' B2.2:8,

---

[741] But the directive began with אנתם הבו (line 2).

[742] As also noted by Fitzmyer (1954:30).

[743] Exceptions are the first example quoted above and ירש[ו]נ[כ]ם אנת ידניה ומחסיה 'they will bri[ng suit or process] against you, Jedaniah and Mahseiah' B2.9:11.

[744] On a more general plane we might say that, in the consciousness of native users of our idiom the speaker, the person spoken to and the person spoken of were conceptualised by means of the disjunctive, not conjuctive, personal pronouns irrespective of the mode of their syntactic actualisation.

where the issue is the ownership of a piece of land, and the writer must have attached some importance to the second אנה, which has been added subsequently above the line; בשמי אנה ידניה 'in my name, I Jedaniah' B2.10:12; מטאך בחלק אנת ידניה 'came to you as a portion, you, Jedaniah' B2.11:3; מטאני בחלק אנה מחסיה 'came to me as a portion, I, Mahseiah' ib.5; ביתך אנת ענני 'your house, you, Anani' B3.12:17; חלקי אחרנא אנה עני 'my other portion, that of mine, Anani' B3.5:19(745); חלקא זילי אנה עניה 'the portion of mine, I, Ananiah' B3.5:9. It is significant that the great majority of examples discussed here as well as under (ii) and (vi) occur in legal or administrative documents. This is most likely part of the conventional legalese in which the identity of the parties involved is most important and this can be more effectively expressed by means of conspicuous, free-standing forms rather than through morphemes unobtrusively tacked on to verbs, nouns or prepositions.

viii) In one instance a disjunctive pronoun resumes the earlier introduced multiple subjects: אנה מנחם ועניה רחיקן אנחנה 'I M. and A., we are withdrawn from you' B2.9:9.

f) In one rare instance the second person is possibly neutralised to become a form used in making universally applicable statements like the colloquial English *you*: "it is not in your hands (בידיך) to lift your foot to put it down' C1.1:171, which in an alternative version reads: "it is not in the hands of the indivi[dual](אנ[ש]א בידי) to lift their feet and put them down apart fr[om (the) *god*]s" ib.170. But then many a proverb is addressed to an unspecified *you*.

g) A possible solecism may be found in ביד יונתן ואנה C3.28:90, which may be rendered in a matching style as: "in the hand of Jonathan and I" as in "like you and we" for "like you and us."

h) The noun נפש 'soul; life' with an appropriate conjunctive pronoun is used as an equivalent of our reflexive pronoun series, *myself, yourself, himself* etc., but not as subject *I myself* etc.(745a): e.g., לקח עבד לנפשה 'took, appropriated (it) to himself' A6.15:6. The use of such a combination as an equivalent of a disjunctive

---

745 The context, which speaks of the situation after the death of the speaker, Ananiah, militates against Fitzmyer's (1956:257, n.8) interpretation, according to which אנה עני ought to head the following multiple subjects.

745a Thus נפשי צביח B3.7:15 does not mean "I myself desire," but rather "my soul desires." In שלין לנפשך אל תשים 'Do not give rest to your soul' C1.1:130 נפשך is not a reflexive pronoun. The reading and interpretation are uncertain in חקלא ותחצד נפשוך ... B1.1:7.

possessive pronoun (§ 40) seems to be a stylistic feature favoured by some scribes: בזרע נפשך 'with your own seed' B1.1:4; בחמר נפשך 'with your own donkey' ib.13—נפש occurring twice more in this 19-line document;]נ[פקת נפשה 'his own [out]lay' C3.19:7; בכפי נפשה 'with his own hands' B2.7:17.

§ 40. Disjunctive possessive pronouns

Highly typical of our idiom is the abundance of free-standing possessive pronouns composed of-דיל/-זיל- and a conjunctive personal pronoun. -זיל in its turn is of course a combination of the ubiquitous connective זי and the preposition ל of ownership or belonging. This syntactic feature is part of a development[746] whereby a synthetically bonded phrase of nouns or their equivalents is dissolved, each constituent thus becoming a phonetically and morphologically independent unit and the old syntactic relationship of subordination now being marked by a special lexical unit placed in between. Thus

בנת מלכא 'the daughters of the king' > בנתא זי מלכא
בנתה 'his daughters'   >   בנתא זילה

a) Both syntagms are attested already in the Bisitun inscription: e.g,]מלכותא[זי לן 'our kingship' C2.1 III:1 ([747]);]ביתא[זי לן 'our house' ib.4([748]); חילא זי מדי 'the troop of Media' C2.1:39.([749]) The total absence of the second syntagm in BA is all the more striking([750]) in view of its high frequency in our idiom and in view of the abundance therein of Babylonian and Old Persian

---

[746] The Akkadian influence on this development is widely accepted. See Kaufman 1974:130-32. Its Akkadian background has been vividly demonstrated by Fekheriyan: see Muraoka 1983-84:101-3. It ought to be pointed out further that the -זיל + a conjunctive pronoun seems to be an inner-Aramaic development mirroring the Akkadian syntagm *attu* 'belonging to' + suf., and that all the instances known so far from a period earlier than the IA are of predicative type as in עבדן המו זלי 'the slaves are mine' Ashur letter 13, and in the only BA example חָכְמְתָא וּגְבוּרְתָא דִּי לֵהּ־הִיא 'power and might are of his' Dn 2.20. For further examples (only two more), see Segert 1975:328.

[747] Akk. NUMUN-*i-ni*, thus synthetic construction.

[748] Akk. É *at-tu-nu* 'domus nostra.'

[749] Akk. *ú-qu šá* KUR *ma-da-a-a.*

[750] Dn 2.20 חָכְמְתָא וּגְבוּרְתָא דִּי לֵהּ־הִיא 'wisdom and strength are his' is syntactically different.

loanwords..

b) The preceding noun or noun head can be in the status absolutus or determinatus.

st.abs.: e.g., עלים זילי 'a servant of mine' A6.11:1; בר זילה 'a son of his' B2.3:26; מלה זילך 'a matter of yours' A3.6:4; עלימן זילי 'servants of mine' A6.9:4; עבדן זילי 'slaves of mine' A6.7:2.

st.det.: e.g. עלימא זילי 'my servant' A6.3:1, A6.4:2; בבא זילך 'your gate' B3.11:4; גרדא ונכסיא זילנא 'our domestic staff and properties' A6.10:1; ובניה עבדיא זילה 'and her sons, his slaves' B8.7:4. Cf. תשוסרי זילן 'our Tetosiri' D7.9:3.

c) Statistically, זילי is the most frequent with 42 occurrences, followed by זילך 21x (דילך 1x), זילכי 5x (דילכי 3x), זיליכי 1x, זילה 12x, זילן 9x, זילנא 3x, זילכם 5x, and זילהם 1x.([751])

d) Including some cases restored with more or less certainty our corpus attests to a total of 129 disjunctive possessive pronouns used attributively, of which 36 (28 %) occur in the 16 Arsames letters of an average nine lines per letter, which is significant: see below. Moreover, this group of letters never uses these pronouns substantivally or predicatively.

e) The same forms may be used substantivally, i.e. without a noun head: e.g. דילכי הו עד עלם 'it is yours for ever' B2.7:16; מובלא זי לא זיל[ה] 'a load which is not his' C1.1:185; הו [י]לקח זילה 'he will take his' ib.107; וביתי זילהם 'and my house is theirs' B3.5:22; תרעא זך לא זילך הו 'that gateway is not yours' B2.1:12.([752])

f) Just like the disjunctive personal pronouns (see above at § 39 *b*), so the 3rd person disjunctive possessive pronoun may refer to an inanimate object: e.g. אגר ביתא זילה 'the wall of its house' B3.11:5; תרעא זילה 'its gateway' B3.12:21.([753])

g) On the syntax of the disjunctive possessive pronouns, see below § 59.

h) It is difficult to establish *functional opposition*([754]) between the two structures: synthetic ביתי and analytic בית זילי or ביתא זילי

---

[751] Restored forms are included.

[752] On the use of disjunctive possessive pronouns as predicates of nominal clauses, see a brief discussion by Swiggers 1988.

[753] Thus *pace* Folmer (1995:261), who states "The pron. sf. attached to *zyl-* always refers to a living being as the 'possessor'," though her statement applies to the majority of cases, as can be easily seen from the statistics given above under *c*.

[754] Whitehead (1974:224) takes the view that lexical preference may be involved. Folmer (1995:310-12) also takes a similar approach.

Whilst it is not certain that ביתי is necessarily definite, i.e. "the house of mine, the house which belongs to me," and synonymous with ביתא זילי, it is the flexible, analytic structure that removes such ambiguity. The analytic structure is therefore well suited where the noun head needs to be presented as indefinite: אנה ובני וזרע זילי וגבר אחרן 'I, or my children, or any relation of mine or another person' B2.7:8, where the indefinite גבר אחרן is to be noted.

The analytic structure seems to be preferred where personal involvement is evident: "... we with our wives and our children (נשין ובנין) were dressed in sackcloth ... and fasting; our wives (נשיא זילן) have been made like widows ..." A4.7:15-20, where a sense of humiliation and hurt comes through. ארקא זילי 'my land' B2.2:5 occurs where the ownership of the land is in dispute.([755]) Examples in the Arsames correspondence can also be regarded as indicative of the satrap's assertiveness and power of possession: e.g., ביתא זילי 'my estate' A6.11:6; עלימא [זילי 'my servant' A6.12:1. The analytic phrase may be considered appropriate in the first mention of a debt in a loan contract: כספא זילך 'your silver' B3.13:8, but not in subsequent references (כספך ib.9,10,11). In the following case the word-order variation reinforces a contrast: אנת [על]ת [בביתי] כחסן וכתשת לאנתתי ונכסן כחסן הנפקת מן ביתי 'yo[u brok]e [into my house] by force and struck my wife and took out goods from my house' B7.2:4-5 // [לא] עלת ולאנתתא כחסן בביתך לא כתשת ונכסן מן ביתך כחסן לא לקחת זילך 'I did [not] break into your house by force and I did not strike the wife of yours and I did not take goods from your house by force' ib.8f. Analogous to the boasting, royal "I" ([*e*, ii] above) are זילי and זילן in the Bisitun inscription([756]): [ביתא] זי לן [C2.1 III:4 // בזרען זילן] 'of our seed' C2.1 I:3([757]) חילא זילי 'my force' C2.1:16.([758])

---

[755] Cf. "ma part à moi" B3.5:9 (Grelot 1972:222), and also חלקא זילי "ma propre part" A3.10:2 (Grelot 1972:504). On the latter example Folmer (1995:292) notes that it varies with חלקי ib.3. Perhaps the author of the document had emphasied his claim enough in the preceding line. The example at B3.5:9 is also matched by חלקי אחרנא 'my other portion' ib.19. See further B2.1:4, B2.3:3, B2.4:3, B3.12:4,13, B8.4:4, C1.1:48.

[756] They may be spelled as two separate words; see above § 40 *a*.

[757] At C2.1 III:1 we would rather restore מלכותא מן זרעא] זי לן 'the kingship was taken from our line' in the light of *LUGAL-u-tú šá la-pa-ni NUMUN-i-ni šu-ú iš-šu-ú.*

[758] Note the Akk. (line 52): *ú-qu at-tu-u-a,* and similarly line 28 (= C2.1 III:4 ביתא] זי לן cited above) *É at-tu-nu.* The Akkadian disjunctive pronoun is emphatic: see von Soden 1995: § 44 *f.*

The statistical fact that the analytic syntagm is largely confined to the first and second persons (see § c above) is consonant with the notions of personal involvement and concern.

A clustering of disjunctive possessive pronouns is observable in some documents: 9x in A6.10 (13-line document, and all first person pronouns, זילי or זילנא) with מראיהם 'their lords' (twice and third person!) where the threatened diminution or desired expansion of the satrap's properties is the principal concern; 7x in B2.1 (20-line).

The analytic structure is preferred with a loan-word which is not yet completely naturalised: תרי רבתא זילי 'my large room' B3.10:4, B3.11:6, B3.12:13; הנגית והנבג ואדרנג זילן 'partner-in-chattel, or partner-in-land or guarantor of ours' B3.12:27. See also B3.10:18, though אדרנג appears to have become naturalised enough to take a conj. pron. at times: e.g., אדרנגי B3.13:9 (by a scribe different than that of B3.11 and B3.12, though all penned in the same year, 402 BCE).

§ 41. Demonstrative pronouns

a) The basic function of demonstrative pronouns is actually to point to a person or object (deictic), or mentally to refer back to what has been mentioned (anaphoric, like the Engl. "the said") or to what is about to be mentioned (cataphoric).([759]) They may be used either substantivally, i.e. on their own, or adjectivally, i.e. together with a noun head.

Deictic: ספרה זנה 'this letter (i.e., which I am writing now and which you will receive and read)' A2.1:12; ספרא זנה 'this document (i.e., which is being drawn up herewith)' B3.11:7. Though our corpus accidentally lacks an example of the use of demonstrative pronouns actually pointing to a person or an object at some distance from the speaker (such as אלך,זך,זנך), they must have occurred in actual speech situations.

זנה may refer to a point in time near to the moment of speaking as in יומא זנה 'this day, today' B3.11:8; שנתא זא 'this year' A4.1:2. Likewise it may refer to a place near to the scene of speaking: בזנה 'here (i.e. where I am)' A6.3:2.

Anaphoric: the pronouns זנה and זך (and their inflected forms) are often used in contracts and official letters to refer to an initially mentioned entity: e.g., זנה ביתא 'this house (i.e. about which this document is concerned)' B3.11:7; אלה מליא 'these

---

[759] On the morphology of the demonstrative pronouns occurring in our corpus, see above § 14.

words (i.e. the above-quoted)' A6.11:3; אגרא זך 'that wall (i.e. which I have just said you gave me)' B2.1:4,5; פלגא הו 'that half (just specified)' B2.4:12; זך אבד 'that one (i.e. just named) perished' A6.11:2; כזנה '(a thing) like this (i.e. as has just been described)' A4.7:15; על דנה 'on this (i.e. on the matter that has been elaborated above in this letter) A5.2:9; מן זכי 'from that (earlier mentioned time)' A4.7:21. See also זי מסכן יעבד זך חזי 'that which a poor man does, that take note of!' C2.1:68.

Cataphoric: דנה תחומוהי 'this is its boundaries (= its boundaries are as follows)' B3.11:3. Here also belongs כן 'thus' as used in כזי כן שמיע לן לאמר 'when we have heard thus ...' A3.3:13; כן שמיע לי כזי ... 'I have heard thus, (namely) that ...' A6.10:3; ... כן ידיע יהוי לך 'Thus [= the following] ought to be known to you ...' ib.8.

b) A demonstrative noun may be added to a personal name as in נתן זך 'that Nathan' B8.10:2; פרימא זך 'that Pariyama' A6.7:7; וידרנג זך לחיא 'that wicked Vidranga' A4.7:6; אחיקר זך 'that Ahiqar' C1.1:35; אחיקר זנה 'this A.' C1.1:62,63; מנכי זנה 'this Mannuki' B8.7:6, B8.10:7. Such a pronoun always follows a name except in דנא חרא 'this Ḥora' D23.1 II:10. In this last example and at A4.7:6 one hears a tone of contempt, though the demonstrative by itself does not seem to indicate such an emotion.([760])

c) An essential distinction between the זנה series and the זך series is illustrated in a bequest of apartment, B3.5, in which Ananiah begins by declaring that he had given his wife Tamet part of his residence, to which he first refers in a global and detached manner as "that house" (ביתא זך) (line 5), and then he proceeds to give details of the measurements and boundaries of the segment to be bequeathed to her, which is referred to as "this portion of the house" (זנה חלק ביתא) (line 11), and subsequently two more global references are made to ביתא זך (line 14). Likewise ביתא זך B3.4:7 - ביתא זנה ib.13,17.([761]) Similarly, אלך נכסיא 'those goods' B2.9:8 vs. אלה נכסיא 'these goods' (line 15). A document recording the bequest of a house to a daughter is referred to as ספרא זנה 'this document' B2.3:18,22,28, whilst a forged document (ib.16) or a related document of an earlier date mentioned in passing (ib.25,27) is called ספרא זך.

d) It has been suggested that the demonstratives ending with כ-, namely אלכי, זכי, דכי, are used where one addresses a

[760] Cf. Joüon - Muraoka 1993: § 143 *d*.

[761] Still ביתא זך at ib.12, though the demonstrative has been added later.

woman.([762]) From our enlarged corpus it transpires that this is only partially true: true at B2.8:6 (emending דכא to דכי),8,9, B5.1:4,6, A2.7:3, but untrue at A4.7:21, A5.2:4, A6.3:7,8([763]), A6.4:3,4, A6.8:2.([764]) It is quite possible that such a distinction applied at a certain period or in a certain dialect, but it does not apply to our corpus taken as a whole nor is there any neat pattern of distribution to be recognised. It also needs to be noted that זך is often used when one addresses a woman, e.g. B2.3:13,16,24,25,27(*bis*), B2.7:9,13,15.([765])

   e) זנה may be used as a general deictic indifferent with respect to the gender and number of the referent: זנה משחת ביתא 'this is (= these are) the measurements of the house' B3.10:5*bis*, sim. B3.12:6,15; זנה תחומי ביתא 'this is (= these are) the boundaries of the house' ib.8, sim. ib.16; זנה שמהת נשיא 'this is (= these are) the names of the women' A4.4:4; זנה שמהת חילא יהודיא 'this is (= these are) the names of the Jewish troop' C3.15:1. Cf. Dutch: *Dit zijn goede boeken* 'These are good books.'

   f) The substantival use of the demonstrative pronoun is exemplified by זך אבד 'that one (i.e. just named) perished' A6.11:2; כזנה '(a thing) like this' A4.7:15; על דנה 'on this' A5.2:9; מן זכי 'from that' A4.7:21.

§ 42. Relative pronoun([766])

In this paragraph we shall only deal with clauses introduced by זי or די which can function as fully fledged clauses without it, and independent די/זי clauses which lack their antecedent. This would obviously exclude a clause fragment introduced by די/זי, followed by a prepositional phrase, and expanding a preceding noun head as exemplified by אגורא זי ביב בירתא 'the temple in

---

[762] Leander 1928:34. See also Kutscher 1971:114f., where Kutscher unjustly makes an ignoramus of Leander. Moreover, in view of an improved reading אלכי דיני [מדינתא] 'those judges of [the province]' A5.2:4 one can no longer say, as Kutscher does, that the above-mentioned suggestion applies to all Elephantine materials without an exception: A5.2 = Cowley 16. Nor is it necessary to see, as Leander did (Leander 1928:33), a scribal error in מן זכי A4.7:21 // מ[ן] זך ע[ד]נא 'from that time' A4.8:20.

[763] Driver (1957:47) apparently takes זכי as directly qualifying סרוש[י]ן six words earlier, which would, however, leave the following יתעבד subjectless.

[764] At A3.1v:3 the text is poorly preserved.

[765] Cf. also Folmer 1995:201-3.

[766] On some unique features of the relative pronoun and the relative clause in Semitic languages, see Joüon - Muraoka 1993:§ 158 *a**.

Elephantine the fortress' A4.7:7. This type of construction is treated in § 68 c.

a) The fact that the clause following a relative pronoun often lacks explicit reference back to its antecedent suggests that the relative pronoun itself is functioning as an integral part of the relative clause, not as a mere marker of dependence relationship between the antecedent and the clause following the relative pronoun.([767]) Thus כתנה זי אושרתי לי 'the tunic which you dispatched to me' A2.1:4; כספה זי הוה בידי 'the silver that was in my hand' A2.2:4; בר ביתאלשזב זי אתה 'the son of Bethelshezib who is coming' A2.5:6, in which "he is coming" would normally require הו.

b) Where the antecedent corresponds to an element in the relative clause other than its subject or direct object, one normally finds a conjunctive pronoun pointing back to the antecedent. Thus אלה נכסיא זי רשין עליהם 'these goods about which we brought (suit)' B2.9:15; גבר זי תזבנון לה ביתא זך 'a man to whom you will sell that house' B2.10:11; זך ביתא זי תחומחי כתיבן מנעל 'that house the boundaries of which are recorded above' ib.8; ביתה זי... אגרתה קימן 'the house ... whose walls are (still) standing' B3.4:4. By contrast, ומנדעמתא זי הוה באגורא זך 'and the things which were in that temple' A4.7:12 (subject); מטאתני כתנה זי אושרת לי 'the tunic which you sent me has reached me' A2.1:4 (object). This distinction between the two syntagmata with respect to the use or non-use of a resumptive pronoun is illustrated in ביתא זנה זי אנחן זבן ויהבן לך ורחקן מנה 'this house which we sold and gave you and withdrew from (it) B3.4:13: in the first two clauses the antecedent is the direct object of a verb, while in the last it is attached to a preposition. Exceptional with a resumptive pronoun is אגרא זי הנפנא זי בנהו מצריא 'the protecting (?) wall that the Egyptians built' B3.10:8.([768])

Where the antecedent is a noun in the st.abs. that signifies a point in time and serves together with the following זי as a conjunction of time, the following relative clause contains no pronominal reference to the antecedent: מן יום זי אזלת 'from the day that you went' A3.3:2; מן יום זי נפקתם 'from the day that you

---

[767] As against Degen (1979:42), who writes: "... das Relativpronomen זי bzw. דֿ weder als 'Subjekt' noch als 'Objekt' verwendet wird, es ist lediglich der 'Exponent der Verbindung des Relativsatzes mit dem Worte [...], dessen Attribut er bildet' (so Nöldeke § 341)." Nöldeke goes on to say, though not quoted by Degen, "während ein auf jenes Wort zurückweisendes Personalpronomen (resp. Pronominalsuffix) in seiner regelrechten grammatischen Verbindung innerhalb des Relativsatzes steht."

[768] Emend בנהו to בנה. See p. 148, n. 251.

left' ib.3; ... עד יום זי 'until the day that ...' B4.2:3; ביום זי תרחענה תגזנה 'on the day you wash it you should shear it' D7.8:6. With these examples contrasts ירחא זי לא אנתן לך בה מרבית 'the month in which I do not give you interest' ib.4, with ירחא in st.det., which suggests that יום in the former group of examples may be in the st.cst.: see also below at § 61 h.([769])

c) The noun antecedent of the relative pronoun, זי, can be in either the st.abs. or det. If the former, the relative clause is restrictive in the manner of the adjective *white* in *a white house* as against its non-restrictive use as in *white snow*: e.g. איתי באר חדה זי בניה בג[ו]ן ב[י]רחא 'there is a well which is built inside the fortress' A4.5:6; ... גבר זי לא ידע מה 'a person who does not know what ..' C1.1:113; ... גבר זי יקרב 'a person who offers ..' A4.7:28; בעי אש זי יזבן ביתא [ר]בא 'Look for a person who might buy the [bi]g house!' A3.8:6. If the antecedent is in the st.det., however, the relative clause can be either restrictive or non-restrictive: *restrictive*—ירחא זי לא אנתן בה מרבית 'the month in which I do not give you interest' B4.2:4, namely as distinct from the month in which I shall pay the interest; *non-restrictive*—במנתא זכי זי יהבן לכי 'in (regard to) that share, which we have given you' B5.1:6; [ס]פרא חכימא יעט אתור כלה זי הקים לברה 'the wise scribe, the counsellor of the entire Assyria, who established his son' C1.1:12; עם וידרנג זי פרתרך תנה הוה 'with Vidranga, who was Chief here' A4.5:4. There does not appear to exist any syntagmatic, formal distinction corresponding to such a semantic opposition between *restrictive* and *non-restrictive*.

d) *Independent relative clause*

Clauses beginning with זי and without an antecedent, and filling the slot of a noun in a larger construction are fairly common.

Functioning as *subject* of the main clause: ולא איתי זי [מ]ריר מן ענ[ו]ה 'and there is nothing that is more [bi]tter than poverty' C1.1:89, sim. ib.159,160; זנה זי בפרתו עבדת 'this is what I did in P.' C2.1:29, sim. ib.50; *impersonal*—חזו ... וזי צבי יעבד לה 'Regard ... and that which he wants to do to it' A3.10:2; זי תעבדון לה לא יתכסן מן עננ' 'what you do for him will not be hidden from A.'

---

[769] This seems to be confirmed by a 9th c. BCE inscription found at Samos: בשנת עדה מראן נהר ... 'in the year when our lord crossed (the) river': see Eph'al - Naveh 1989:193. See also Kutscher 1972:39f. On a comparable feature in BH, see Joüon - Muraoka 1993: § 129 q.

Harrak (1992:68f.) argues convincingly that the expression at the Samos inscription and similar ones elsewhere are not part of an annalistic dating formula, but the syntagm had become fossilised as a compound conjunction. Our analysis would then be only valid from diachronic perspective.

A4.3:10; שא לך זי ת[נ]שא מנן 'Take with you whatever you will
[t]ake from us!' C1.1:169; *personal*—מן הו זי יקום קדמוהי להן זי אל
עמה 'Who is he who would stand up in front of him but one with
whom El is?' C1.1:91([770]); מן זי יהבו בבבאל (= מֶן, not מֶן) שטר 'apart
from (those) whom they gave in Babylon' A6.15:5; עם זי רם מנך
... 'with one who is more exalted than you ...' C1.1:142; עם זי
חצי[ף] ועזיז מנך 'with one who is more impu[dent] and mightier
than you are' ib.143; זי ירשכי דין ודבב 'Whoever shall bring against
you suit or process' B3.10:19. We would interpret זי יכלא מנהם as
'whoever of them restrains (him)'([771]) B2.1:10 rather than
"Whoever shall restrain (one) of them."([772])

In לא שלמתך בכספך ומרביתה זי כתיב בספרא זנה 'I did not repay
you your silver together with its interest, which is written in this
document' B3.1:7 we would rather see an independent relative
clause than postulate a case of disagreement between כתיב and
the preceding multiple antecedent, which can hardly be the
grammatical direct object of the verb.([773]) In other words, the זי
clause refers to the provision of the agreement: one may translate
"as is written ..."([774]).

זנה זי is once used instead of זי or זי מה: לקבל זנה זי המרכריא מה זי
אמרן 'according to that which the accountants say' A6.2:23. Cf.
לקבל זי אנה עבדת לך 'according to what I did for you' C1.1:52;
עבד לקבל זי אנת עשת 'Do according to what you think' ib.68.

e) When an originally interrogative pronoun מן is used as an
indefinite, personal antecedent followed by זי (§ 42), the
interrogative may take a preposition which strictly belongs to a
pronoun which should appear resumptively within the relative
clause itself. Thus in אנת ... שליט בביתא זך ובניך מן אחריך ולמן די
צבית למנתן 'you ... have right to that house, and your children
after you and one to whom you desire to give (it)' B3.4:11 the
concluding relative clause is equivalent to מן זי צבית למנתן לה lit.

---

[770] הו here is the extraposer, not the usual 3ms personal pronoun: see below
§ 79 *a*.

[771] So Grelot 1972:172: "Cellui d'entre eux qui (l')empêcherait ..."

[772] So Porten - Yardeni 1989:18. Cowley (1923:14) mentions both
possibilities. The preposition מן then would be equivalent to what Arab
grammarians call "*min* of explication (*baya:ni*)," on which see Wright
1898:II.137f.

[773] Cf., however, נכסיא [א]לה וכספא זי כתיבן בספרא זנה 'these goods and the
silver, which are mentioned in this document' B6.4:7.

[774] So Cowley 1923:30. An error for כזי?

'one who you desire to give (it) to him'.([775]) The same interpretation ought to be applied to the following cases, in which the preposition -ל would normally be required with the indirect object of the verb concerned, לא נכהל נגרה לבר לך וברה ולמן זי צבית למנתן :גרה 'we shall not be able to institute (suit) against son of yours or daughter or (anyone) to whom you desire to give (it)' B3.4:13, sim. ib.15.

f) In the following cases, in contrast to the structure discussed above [e], the preposition preceding זי מן 'one who, he who' is to be construed with the verb which stands outside of the relative clause: למן זי רחמתי תנתנן 'To whomever you love you may give (it)' B2.3:9; הבי למן זי רחמתי 'Give (it) to whomever you love!' ib.19; sim. B2.11:7. Possibly also the following difficult text: ישתלח על מן זי הוה 'Let word be sent to whoever is (there)!' A6.2:5.

g) A rare example of *asyndetic relative clause*, i.e. lacking זי, is found in איש שפיר מדדה ולבבה טב כקרנ|י|ה חסינה 'a man whose stature is beautiful and whose heart is good is like a strong city' C1.1:95.([776]) On the other hand, 1 שוי 1 זי גמא בה נעבצן זי אבן 4 '1 papyrus-reed bed on which are 4 stone inlays(?)' B2.6:15 is part of a list, with the following בה rather loosely hanging on to what precedes. It is thus hardly a well-formed asyndetic relative clause.

h) According to Kutscher (1972:115) there is at least one possible example of the so-called "non-restrictive relative clause"([777]) in אנחנה ... הוין ... צימין ומצלין ליהו מרא שמיא זי החוין בוידרנג זך ... 'we were ... fasting and praying to YHW the lord of

---

[775] Cf. § 60 *f*, and note לא נכהל נרשה לבניך ובנתך וזי תנתן לה 'we shall not be able to bring (suit) against your sons and daughters or one to whom you give it' B3.12:26. The two structures are mixed in בניך שליטן אחריך ולמן זי רחמת תנתן או זי תזבן לה 'your children have right (to it) after you and one to whom you give (it) affectionately or one to whom you sell (it)' B3.12:23.

[776] The parallelism with לבבה indicates the ה of מדדה as conj. pron. Hence שפיר is not in the st. cst., an interpretation contradicted also by the word-order of לבבה טב.

[777] A relative clause which is not meant to give more precise information on the antecedent. E.g., "He had four sons, who became lawyers" (non-restrictive: he had no more sons and all became lawyers) as against "He had four sons who became lawyers" (restrictive: he had more sons), examples given by Jespersen (1933:358).
The other examples mentioned by Kutscher, all of the type ברכתכי לפתח זי יחוני אפיך בשלם A2.1:2, and part of the standard greeting formula of the Hermopolis papyri, do not belong here: see our interpretation of them in § 53 *b*.

heavens, who let us gloat over that Vidranga ...' A4.7:15.([778])

i) On the generalising relative clause with an interrogative as antecedent, see below at § 43.

§ 43. Interrogative pronouns

An interrogative pronoun may be used with the immediately following די/ז׳ as an antecedent of indefinite reference, 'one who, whoever,' 'that which, whatever': e.g. למן די צבית למנתן 'one to whom you wish to give (it)' B3.4:12 et passim([779]); למן זי רחמתי תנתן 'to whomever you care for you may give (it)' B2.3:9 et passim; ישתלח על מן זי הוה 'Let word be sent to whomever is (there)' A6.2:5; מה זי תעבדון 'whatever you might be doing' A4.3:8; מה זי הושרת 'what you dispatched' D7.16:9; למה כזי תאתה בזנה מה זי לקחת זיני תשלם 'lest, on coming here, you should have to pay damages for whatever you took' A6.15:7.

§ 44. Indefinite pronouns([780])

a) The character of the indefinite pronoun מנדעם/מדעם as a noun rather than a pronoun is revealed by the fact that it is sometimes expanded by the addition of an adjective: מנדעם באיש 'something bad' A6.7:8, D20.5:2; מנדעם[ם] אחרן 'anything else' A6.15:6; מנדעם קשה 'something difficult' C1.1:85.

b) מנדעם, in conjunction with a noun, may behave like a quantifier: followed by a noun—מנדעם כסנתו לא הוה מן ביתא זיל׳ 'my household did not suffer anything of a loss, no loss' A6.10:2([781]), sim. ib.6; מנדעם מחבל 'some damage' A4.5:2 (מנדעם erased). On מנ[נד]ת[ן]א מנדעם 'any r[en]t whatsoever' A6.14:2, see below § 67 *e*.

c) מנדעם may be further reinforced by כל and the following זי clause: כל מדעם זי יחיה בה איש 'anything on which a man may live' B4.1:3; כל מנדעם זי חמיר 'anything that is fermented' A4.1:6.

d) Our indefinite pronoun may be used entirely on its own:

---

[778] One is tempted, however, to take the particle as introducing direct speech, which would make an imperative of החוין. But there is no certain example in our corpus of such a use of the particle: see below at § 85 *a*.

[779] On the preposition Lamed, see above § 42 *e*.

[780] On the morphology, see above §17. The term "indefinite pronoun" is conventional. Words so termed are essentially nouns used mostly in the sg.abs., have no particularised referents, and are translatable in English with words such as *somebody, something, anything, nothing* etc.

[781] Rather than "nothing became a loss" (Driver 1957:64).

איש מנדעם ... לא חבל 'Don't buy anything!' A2.3:10; מדעם אל תזבני 'one did not damage ... anything' A4.7:14; אתה לכן מדעם 'I shall bring you something' A2.1:10; מדעם לה מפקן לן 'they bring nothing out for us' A2.5:2. Even in the pl.det.: מנדעמתא זי אשתכחו בה 'the things which have been found therein' C3.7Gr2:23([782]); see also A4.7:12, A4.8:11, A4.5:23†.

e) When used negatively, whether on its own or expanded by another element, מנדעם/מדעם precedes the verb: see three examples above under (d) and איש מנדעם באיש לא יעבד 'nobody should do anything bad' A6.7:8. So also A6.10:2,6, A6.13:2, A6.14:2. But in the following case the pronoun precedes in a positive clause: מנדעם כסנתו יהוה 'there will occur some decrease' A6.10:8.

f) אש/איש is often used in the singular in the sense of 'person,' thus gender-neutral: אש זי יזבן ביתא 'a person, someone who might buy the house' A3.8:6. This word can also be expanded by the addition of: *adjective*—איש זעיר 'a small person' C1.1:162; איש אחרן 'another person' B2.3:11; *possessive pronoun*—איש זילכי 'a person of yours' B2.3:12; איש לי 'a person of mine, someone from my circle' B2.10:10([783]); *relative clause*—ולאיש זי תנתן לה־ 'against someone to whom you may give (it)' B3.12:28; *numeral*—איש חד 'a certain man' C2.1:52.

The negation does not seem to affect the position of the word within a clause([784]): שמהתהם לא ידע איש 'nobody knows their names' C1.1:164; לעד אשכח אש למושרתהם לכן 'I have not yet found anyone to send them to you' A2.2:12 (אשכח, an error for אשכחת), also A2.4:11. In the following cases, איש מנדעם appears to be a fossilised, cohesive unit: איש מנדעם באיש לא יעבד 'nobody should do anything evil' A6.7:8; איש מנדעם באגורא זך לא חבל 'nobody caused any damage to that temple' A4.7:14. See also כרצי איש לא אמרת 'she did not say the slander of anybody' D20.5:2, which clearly shows the generalising character of איש, thus the personal counterpart of מנדעם.

g) אנש, though less common than איש, is close to the latter in

---

[782] This example indicates that, despite the sg. הוה in מנדעמתא זי הוה באגורא זך 'the things which were in that temple' A4.7:12 the word concerned must be taken as pl.

[783] These pronouns are never synthetically attached to איש, thus never אישי, for example; note ובנין ובנתן ואיש זילן 'and our sons and our daughters and a person of ours' B2.9:13.

[784] Leander 1928:37 is misleading in suggesting that לא איש occurs without any word intervening.

usage: cf. "I, or son or daughter of mine, or man of mine, or another individual (ואיש לי ואנש אחרן) do not have right to brand him" B3.9:5; "I shall not be able—I, Mahseiah, son or daughter of mine, brother or sister of mine, or an individual who is mine (ואנש זילי)—to bring suit ..." B2.11:8.

The only example in which אנש occurs on its own with a negative agrees with what we have observed above (§ *e*) concerning מנדעם: ואנש לא שליט למשנחה 'nobody has a right to brand him' B3.9:8.

h) איש/אש, as pointed out above (§ *f*, n. 783), never takes a conjunctive pronoun, which also applies to אנש and מדעם/מנדעם. The first two are, moreover, used always in the singular, whereas מנדעם occurs in the plural, e.g. זהבא וכסף ומנדעמתא זי הוה באגורא זך 'the gold and silver and the things which were in that temple' A4.7:12, sim. A4.8:11, A4.5:23, C3.7Gr2:23. While איש/אש is always used in the st.abs., the remaining two are also attested in the st.emph. as in the just quoted example of מנדעמתא. אנשא is confined to Ahiqar proverbs. Though their context is mostly unclear and the reading not completely assured, the emphatic state seems to be generic, and the collocation with עממא at C1.1:98 and the pl. pronoun at ib.170 לא בידי אנ]ש[א מנשא רגלהם 'it is not in man's power to raise his (lit. their) leg' seem to point to the implicitly plural force of the word.

i) גבר, apart from its use as appellative "man, male," is also used in a way similar to the impersonal איש: "I or my children, or descendants of mine, or another person (וגבר אחרן)" B2.7:8; "... against son or daughter of yours, brother or sister, woman or man of yours, or a person (... איש לכם או גבר זי) to whom you sell that house ..." B2.10:11. Although we lack cases where the persons involved are all women, גבר in these cases, like איש, had become a gender-inclusive term, as can be gathered from a case such as גבר אחרן אמי ואבי אח ואחה ואיש אחרן 'another person, (whether) my mother or my father, a brother or sister or another man' B3.5:19.

גבר in the singular, on its own, and with a negative, is not used in the sense of "nobody."([785])

j) Like Heb. דָּבָר, the Aram. מִלָּה is empty of its original meaning in a case like מה צבו ומלה זי צחא חור יבעה ... כזי מלה באישה לא ישכחון 'whatever wish and thing Seha (and) Hor shall seek ... so that they shall not find any bad thing' A4.3:6.

---

[785] As against Leander 1928:37 [ב]לב גבר לא 'a man of no sense' C1.1:82 obviously does not belong here.

PART THREE

MORPHOSYNTAX

SECTION B

THE NOUN AND THE ADJECTIVE

§ 45. Gender

a) The noun distinguishes two genders, namely masculine and feminine. This is primarily a grammatical category, since, at least at synchronic level, the gender of the majority of nouns cannot be explained in terms of the sex distinction in the natural world. Thus one fails to see why אלף 'boat,' for instance, should be a feminine noun.

b) Only rarely does one observe a morphological opposition corresponding to that in the natural world:

	MALE	FEMALE
child	בר[786]	ברה
child of same parents	אח	אחה
person having control	מרא	מראה*[787]
servitor of god	לחן	לחנה
god	אלה	אלהה*[788]

There are also cases of lexical opposition:

parent	אב	אם
spouse	בעל	אנתה
servant	עבד	אמה
donkey	חמר	אתן*[789]

---

[786] At B3.7:3 the word (ברי 'my child') refers to a woman.

[787] E.g.,אל מראתי 'to my mistress' A3.7:1.

[788] E.g., אלהתא 'the goddess' B8.12:7.

[789] E.g., אתנא 'the she-ass' B7.3:4.

c) The principal significance of gender as a grammatical category lies in the fact that it determines the choice of one of two morphologically distinct forms which by themselves have nothing whatsoever to do with sex distinction. Such choice must be made with respect to 1) the adjective whose logical subject a given noun is, 2) the demonstrative pronoun which expands the noun attributively or refers to it, 3) the numeral added to the noun to indicate how many units of the entity denoted by the noun are being talked about, 4) the verb whose subject the noun constitutes, and 5) the pronoun, whether disjunctive or conjunctive, referring to the sex-neutral entity. This feature is traditionally termed congruence, concord or agreement.([790]) To illustrate:

1) Adjective—ספר חכים 'wise scribe' C1.1:35
2) Demonstrative pronoun—מומאה דכי 'that oath' B2.8:9
3) Numeral—אמן חמשה 'five cubits' A6.2:14; אלף חדה 'one boat' A3.10:2; תרתין מלן 'two things' C1.1:187
4) Verb—מטאה ידי 'my hand reaches' (fs.ptc.) A2.4:4
5) Pronoun—צנפר הי מלה 'a bird is a word' C1.1:82; עליה 'concerning it' (referring to ארקא 'the land') B2.3:24; החסנהי 'Take possession of it' (ref. to ספרא 'the document') B2.3:26.

d) The name of a land or country is treated as feminine: אחיקר אבוה זי אתור כלה 'Ahiqar the father of the whole of Assyria' C1.1:55([791]); על עטאתה ומלוהי הות אתור כלא 'on his counsel and his words Assyria was entirely (dependent)' C1.1:43, and perhaps במצרין בתחתיתא 'Lower Egypt' A6.10:11.

e) A general notion under discussion, but not named by a specific lexeme and referred to by a generic pronoun, "it," is also treated as feminine: שנאה הי 'it is hatred' B3.8:34, similarly ib.40. But the f. form here may be conditioned by the same gender of the predicate שנאה; cf. מערב שמש לה הו בבא זילך 'to the west of it it is your gate' B3.11:4.([792])

f) Where an adjective is used as a primary([793]), its gender is determined by the natural sex of the referent when it is animate, thus masculine אל תהרכב חטך לצדיק 'Do not mount your arrow at

---

[790] See further below § 76 on this question.

[791] An example mentioned by Degen (1979:42). אבוהי = אבוה is unlikely here: our copy of Ahiqar does not have such a case (§ 12 f).

[792] Cf. Grelot 1972:248: "à l'occident par rapport à elle, c'est ta porte.'

[793] To use Jespersen's terminology: see Jespersen 1937:109f. This is also known as substantivisation of adjectives.

a righteous person' C1.1:126. The masculine gender may be used generically: קרית] רשיען ביום רוח תתחלל '[a city of] wicked people will be split on a day of wind' C1.1:104.

However, where the referent is inanimate, a matter, state of affairs in particular, the feminine form occurs: הן נפקה טבה מן פם ... 'if something good comes out from the mouth of ...' C1.1:171; הן לחיה תנפק מן] פמהם 'if something bad comes out from their mouth' ib.172; יעבד לחיתא 'does the bad' ib.134; מן בי]תי נפקת לחיתי 'my misfortune came out from my house[hold]' ib.139. The feminine form seems to indicate a concrete instance or manifestation of a given generic property, which latter is indicated by a masculine form(⁷⁹⁴): contrast זי בעו באיש לאגורא זך 'who sought evil to that temple' A4.7:17 with זא באישתא עביד לן 'this evil was done to us' ib. Thus ובאישת]א] לא עבד לך C1.1:50 should be interpreted in the sense that the king did not cause him the harm which could have befallen him rather than that he did not do Ahiqar any harm at all.

Masculine—אל תרגג לכביר זי ימנע מנך 'Do not covet something great which is denied you' C1.1:136; ישימון טב בחנכה למאמר 'they will put something good in his palate to say' ib.163; cf. כזנה 'as follows' B2.11:4,6; על זנה 'concerning this matter' A3.3:4; לקבל זנה זי אנחנה אמרן 'according to that which we are saying' A4.5:10.

§ 46. State

a) A noun is used in the *absolute* state when it refers to an entity which is contextually indeterminate. E.g. למשלח חיל 'to send a force' A1.1:7; לא הות ארק לדרגמן 'it was not a land of Dargamana' B2.2:7; איתי ארק בי 1 זילי מערב לביתא זילך 'there is a land (with) 1 house of mine to the west of your house' B2.4:3.

b) The use of the absolute state is the rule with cardinal numerals: e.g. הן יהוה באתר חד יתיר מן יום חד 'if he be in one place more than one day' A6.9:6; איתי לי אלף חדה 'I have one boat' A3.10:2; אמן חמשה פשכן תלתה 'five cubits (and) three handbreadths' A6.2:14; כרשן מאה 'hundred karsh' A6.2:17; מסמרי נחש ופרזל מאתין 'two hundred bronze and iron nails' ib.12.

c) The numeral for "one" may be used in the manner of the English indefinite article: שור חד בנו] 'they buil[t] a wall' A4.5:5. The cipher for "one" may be used in the same way with the same meaning: see § 67 *b*.

d) כל in the sense of "every, each" is very often followed by a singular noun in the st.abs.: אנה רחיק מן כל דין ודבב 'I am

---

⁷⁹⁴ Cp. the category of unit noun, always of feminine gender, in Arabic.

withdrawn from every suit or process' B2.8:11; בכל עדן 'all the time' A3.6:1 et passim.([795]) Note also the unspecific plural in כל לבשן זי קמר וכתן 'all garments of wool and linen' B3.8:13.

e) Repetition of a noun in the st.abs. has *distributive* force, usually prefixed by a preposition either once or twice: זן זן]ו[רח כירח 'each kind, [mo]nth by month' A6.1:3; יום ליום 'day by day' A6.9:3([796]); לגבר לגבר ... הבו 'Give ... each person' A6.9:4; אשלמנהי לך ירח בירח לגבר 1 שערן 'I shall repay it to you month by month' B4.2:5; יהוה רבה עלי ירח לירח 'it will be adding interest on me from month to month' ib.9; "these are the names of (soldiers of) the Jewish force who gave silver to YHW the God, each person two shekels (יהב ... לגבר)לגבר" C3.15:1, which last case shows that the preposition ל in the above-quoted B4.4:7 does not have to be the marker of an indirect object, which holds also for A6.9:4, again quoted above: הבו פתף לגברן חלכין ... לגבר ליומא קמח חפן חדה 'Give Cilician persons rations ... each person one handful of flour per day.' Cf. also מן פקיד על פקיד ... מן מדינה עד מדינה 'each officer in turn ... from province to province' A6.9:5.

In the following cases, גבר and איש are used distributively without being repeated: גבר חלקה נהחסן 'we shall take hereditary possession, (each) person (of) his portion' B2.11:14 and הוית מסבל לך כאיש עם אחוהי 'I was supporting you as a man in relation with his brother' C1.1:48.

f) A predicative adjective appears in the st.abs.: חדה ושריר הוי 'Be happy and strong' A4.7:3, but with a mixture of the states in חיא חדה ושרירא מראי יהוי 'May my lord be living, happy and strong' A5.3:2.

fa) A classifying noun predicate also favours the st.abs.([796a]): contrast וידרנג זי פרתרך תנה הוה 'Vidranga, who was Chief here' A4.5:4, A4.7:5 and לוידרנג פרתרכא זי תנה הוה 'to V. the Chief, who was here' A4.8:5 (with פ as title); נפין ברה זי רבחיל הוה 'Naphaina his son, who was troop commander' A4.7:7; אבוך]ז[י מלך הוה]קדמי[ך 'your father, wh[o] was king [before you]' C1.1:15. Note also אנה אמר לכם עטתא]זי[לי]ו[עטה טבה הי 'I will tell you the counsel [of mine] and it is good counsel' C1.1:57.

---

[795] See § 69 *a* above.

[796] Cp. ליומא 'per day' A6.9:3,5.

[796a] To say with Tsereteli (1991:1573) "A noun can have a predicative meaning only in the indefinite state (status absolutus)" is oversimplifying. There is no lack of counter-examples: e.g., הי אנתתי ואנה בעלה 'she is my wife and I am her husband' B3.3:3; לא אחי הו חרוץ 'Isn't H. my brother?' A2.3:8.

fb) What one may call "generic" belongs here(⁷⁹⁷), a use quite common in the proverbs of Ahiqar: אל תכסה מלת מלך 'Do not conceal the word of a king!' C1.1:84; מלך כרחמן 'a king is a merciful one' ib.91(⁷⁹⁸); שפיר מלך למחזה כשמש 'Beautiful is a king to look at like Shamash' ib.92(⁷⁹⁹); אל תהרכב חטך לצדיק 'Do not mount your arrow at a righteous (person)!' ib.126(⁸⁰⁰); מה חסין הו מן חמר נער 'What is stronger than a braying ass?' ib.174; אל תהחשך ברך מן חטר 'Do not spare your son from a rod!' ib.176; עזיז ארב פם מן ארב מלחם 'Mightier is ambush of mouth than ambush of battle' ib.83. But when such a noun is qualified by a relative pronoun, it appears in the st.det.: .. ברא זי יתאלף 'the son who will be disciplined ..' ib.175.

g) Occasionally one finds a st.abs. form for the expected st.det. form: ביח אם דילכי 'the house is moreover yours' B2.7:11(⁸⁰¹); אגורא זי יהה אלה 'the temple of YHW the God' ib.14.(⁸⁰²) In the standing expressions מערב שמש 'west' B2.2:9+, מועה/א שמש 'east' B2.3:6+, and מדנח שמש 'dit.' B3.7:7 the st.abs. is striking, as they refer to the unique entity. So are the single-word names of the points of the compass: מן מועא למערב 'from east to west' B2.3:4+, and מן עליה לתחתיא 'from above to below' B3.12:16+.(⁸⁰³) This is possibly an archaism preserved from a period when the st.det. was less commonly used. In מערב שמשא A4.1:7 the meaning is different: 'the sunset.'

ga) Some odd examples of the st.abs. for the expected det. are: למדינא 'of (the) province' A4.2:6, בקריה 'in (the) town'

---

⁷⁹⁷ See below, § *j*. Cf. Joüon 1934:8. For a general discussion of "generic," see Jespersen 1924:203f.

⁷⁹⁸ With a so-called Kaph veritatis, nowadays called "asseverative" or "emphatic" (§ 87 *f*).

⁷⁹⁹ Porten - Yardeni's "the king" is apparently because they believe that this proverb is a sequel to the preceding line with "a king," though there is no compelling reason to think so. In the proverbs of Ahiqar the word מלך always occurs in the st.abs., while in the narrative section its st.abs. occurs only once (see above, § *fa*) and otherwise only in the phrase מלך אתור 'the king of Assyria.'

⁸⁰⁰ Cp. the use of the st. det. of the adjective רשיעא and עתירא mentioned below, § *l*.

⁸⁰¹ A haplography for ... ביתא אם? Cf. ביתא זילך אם (with the same sense) B3.4:16,19.

⁸⁰² These may be mere scribal errors; this document contains a couple of more errors: ספ (= ספרא) 12; בב (= דבב) 10.

⁸⁰³ Cf. Fitzmyer 1956:106f.

B1.1:3.([804])

h) A feminine singular adjective ending with a Taw appears to be used adverbially. The usage may be legacy from an earlier period when the fem. sg. status absolutus was adverbially used.([805]) Examples are: גנבית עבדן (= גְּנֵבִית?) 'behave thievishly' A4.2:5; למנתן רחמת לאחרנן 'to give to others affectionately' B2.4:6([806]), sim. B3.12:23,26 (// בכסף 'for silver'),31; אמרן לה מצרית ו 'they call it in Egyptian [...]' B3.7:5, cf. B3.10:4; ארמית כזנה 'in Aramaic as follows' B2.11:4,6.([807]) נסח 'harshly' A6.8:3, A6.10:9 and המונית 'in concert' A4.5:4, A4.7:5 are considered Persian loanwords.([808])

i) A noun in the *determinate* state is frequently used with *anaphoric* force whereby an entity introduced for the first time with a noun in the abs. state is subsequently referred to in the det. state: כסף צריף ... כספא זי כתיב מן עלא 'pure silver ... the silver that is mentioned above' B2.1:7; לחן זי יהו 'a servitor of YHW' in the opening of a contract introducing the parties B3.11:1, but later לחנא זי יהו ib.17, sim. B3.12:1,33; "there is a well ... (which) does not lack water (מין) to give the garrison drink so that whenever they would be garrisoned (?) (there) they would drink the water (מיא) in [th]at well" A4.5:6. The same interpretation might apply to קרבא 'the battle' in מרדיא אתכנשו אזלו לערקה זי דדרש זלמעבד קרב ... אחר עבדו קרבא 'the rebels assembl[ed they went towards Dadarshu] to do battle. Then they did the battle ...' C2.1:11([809]) and sim. ib.22,43,47, but we also find עבדו קרב in a similar context, e.g. ib.15. See also הנדרזא עבדו 'Issue the instruction' A6.14:3 where the author is referring to an instruction that the recipient of the letter had been directed, in an earlier letter, to

---

[804] See Fitzmyer 1956:108. בעל טעם 'Chancellor' A6.2:23 probably does not belong here: it is either the predicate of a nominal clause (so *TAD* A 96) or apposition (Grelot 1972:293), which in this case amounts to the same thing. Alternatively, it is a fossilised, indeclinable title as in Ezr 4.8 בְּעֵל טְעֵם // סָפְרָא. In הוקר לבב 'harden (your) heart' C1.1:82 one rather expects לבבך in view of the parallel פמך 'your mouth.'

[805] For a comparable phenomenon in Classical Syriac, see Muraoka 1987:41.

[806] Cowley 1923:27 'as a gift'; Grelot 1972:182 'à titre gratuit.'

[807] Cf. Dn 2.4 וַיְדַבְּרוּ הַכַּשְׂדִּים לַמֶּלֶךְ אֲרָמִית, where the last word may not be part of the introduction in Hebrew to the following Aramaic section, but a secondary gloss in Aramaic. Likewise in Ezr 4.7 מְתֻרְגָּם אֲרָמִית.

[808] On the former, see Driver 1957:50, and on the latter, Schaeder 1930:255f. See Appendix III.

[809] Greenfield - Porten 1982:29 attempt to relate the distinction to one in the Akkadian text.

issue (A6.13:3,4 where the st.abs. הנדרז occurs), and שור חד בנו
בןמצעת בירת יב 'they built a wall in the centre of the fortress of
Elephantine' A4.5:5 as against וכען שורא זך בנה (= בֶּנֶה) במצעיעת
ביראֿ 'now that wall (stands) built ...' ib.6.

j) The use of the st. det. is the rule with a noun phrase
expanded by a demonstrative pronoun: יומא זנה 'this day' B3.3:4;
ביתא זך 'that house' B3.5:14; בתיא אלה 'these houses' B3.7:14;
חקליא אלך 'those fields' B8.10:4. Hence the pronoun in כזמרן אלך
תריהם D2.30:3 is probably not attributive 'those [pr]iests,' but the
phrase is to be translated: '[pr]iests, those two of them.'

k) The st. det. is also used when the noun in question refers
to an entity which is thought of as determined or definite from
the general context: e.g. קדם דריוהוש מלכא ובני ביתא 'before Darius
the king and the members of the (= his) household' A4.7:2; נפין
אחרן חילא עם מצריא דבר 'Naphaina led the Egyptians (= the
priests of Khnub [5]?) with the army (= his army, which was
under his command: רבחיל הזה [7]) as reinforcements(?)' ib.8.
See also ברא לם יהוה לי 'he shall be the son to me,' not 'I shall
have a son' C1.1:2.([810]) מומאה in מטאה מומאה אדין 'then the oath
came' B2.8:4 must be considered equivalent to מומאה דכי ib.9.([811])

l) A variation on the use just described appears to be the
use of the st.det. as reference to a specific, but representative
member of a class.([812]) This seems to be rather frequent in Ahiqar's
proverbs: e.g. עתירא יאמר אל 'Let the rich not say ..' C1.1:206; הן
יאחדן רשיעא 'if a wicked man seizes' ib.107; דגנא וחנטתא 'grain and
wheat' ib.129; חמרא ישתה זי 'whoever drinks wine' ib.188([813]); אל

---

[810] Cf. Grelot 1972:433, n. *b*, Degen 1979:46, and Kottsieper 1991:324, n.
2b. In the lacuna at the end of the line there probably was a mention of
Nadin.

[811] Grelot (1972:190) renders: "alors le serment t'incombait.' Cp. the use of
the demonstrative pronoun in colloquial English as in *Then, totally out of the
blue, there comes along* **this** *chap, wearing a funny hat. It took me a while to
figure out who he was.* At B2.2:6, however, we have a case of the usual,
anaphoric use of the st. det.: טענוך לי מומאה למומא ביהו 'they imposed upon you
the oath to me to swear by YHW,' where reference is being made to the oath
which Mahseiah had sworn (line 4). מומאה here is in the st.det.: see above at §
18 *v* (4), n. 157.

[812] See Joüon 1934:8. This is thus to be compared with the "generic" use of
the st.abs.: § *fb* above.

[813] One may think of the wine served on a specific occasion. Such an
example may be: שוקא זי בינין ובין בית פפטעוניﬨ מלחא 'the street which is
between us and the house of Peftuauneit the boatman [who has not been
mentioned before]' B2.1:12.

חזף ז[פתא יקירתא 'Do not borrow the heavy loan' ib.130; יעבד
נמרא פנע[לחיתא 'does the bad' ib.134; often with animal names—נמרא פנע[
דבא אזל על לענזא 'the leopard meets (or: met) the goat' ib.166; אריא
אמרן[יא יהוה מסמה לאילא 'the bear went to the lambs' ib.168;
'the lion would lie in wait for the stag' ib.183; חמרא רכב לאתנא
'the ass mounted the jenny' ib.186. On the striking form ברא in
ברא לם יהוה לי C1.1:2, see above, § *j*.

m) The use of the st.det., however, does not appear to be
regulated by rigid rules: cases which appear to fall under either
of the above-mentioned two categories—[*k*] and [*l*]—are at times
contradicted by those in the st.abs. in similar or related contexts.
Thus מה חסין הו מן חמר נער 'What is stronger than a braying ass?'
C1.1:174([814]); נשאית חלא וטענת מלח 'I carried sand and loaded salt'
ib.159; אל תהשגא[חיל ואל תהשגא לבבא '[Do not multiply] wealth
and do not mislead mind' ib.137 where חילא has been corrected
to חיל; תרען זי אבן // עמודיא זי אבנא 'the stone columns' A4.7:9 //
'stone gates' ib.10([815]); כפן יהחלה מררותא 'hunger will sweeten
bitterness' C1.1:123; אל תלנ[וט יומא עד תחזון לי[לה 'Do not curse
day until you see night' ib.80 (not לליא). In וידרנג זי פרתרך תנה
וידרנג פרתרכא זי תנה הוה 'Vidranga, who was Chief here' A4.7:5 //
הוה 'Vidranga the Chief, who was here' A4.8:5 the use of the
st.abs. in the first version might be due to its being predicate.([816])
    In באשה שרפו // באשא שרפו 'they burned with fire' A4.8:11 //
A4.7:12; מזרקיא זי זהבא וכסף 'the gold and silver basins' A4.7:12
// מזרקיא זי זהבא וזי כספא A4.8:11 the scribe of A4.8 is, as in some
other details, trying to correct some infelicities in the first draft
of the official document.([816a])

    n) In the following cases([817]) it is not apparent why the
st.det. has been chosen: לירחא 'per month' B4.2:3, usually לירח
ib.4; הנגית והנבגא 'partner-in-chattel or partner-in-land' B5.5:9 הנגית
הן רשינך דינא B3.6:5+; 'should we bring suit against you' והנבג //
B2.11:9 // ירשינך דין 'he will bring suit against you' B3.12:27.
    In מ[ננד]ת[א] מנדעם לא מהיתה לי 'he is not bringing me the
(due) re[nt](?) at all' A6.14:2 מנדעם is not to be taken as an
adjective but as an adverbial quantifier.([818])

---

[814] Because of the modifier נער?

[815] An example mentioned by Joüon (1934:8).

[816] So also נפין ברה זי רבחיל הוה בסן בירתא 'Naphaina his son, who was troop
commander in Syene the fortress' A4.7:7.

[816a] See Porten (1998?).

[817] See Fitzmyer 1956:110.

[818] See above, § 44 *b* and below, § 67 *e*.

o) Orthographic irregularities or inconsistencies on the one hand([819]) and the uncertainty as to the basic form, i.e. sg.abs., on the other, lead to occasional difficulty in the interpretation of what appears to be a form in the st.abs. or st.det. In ביתה כלה 'the entire house' B3.5:20 ביתה is clearly an irregular spelling for ביתא.([820]) In הן יהב לכי נקיה 'if you are given a lamb' A2.2:8 the context leads one to expect an indeterminate form. However, should one start from BA with Dn 7.9 כַּעֲמַר נְקֵא 'like the wool of a lamb,' נקיה would rather be det. for נְקֵא. Syr. has /neqyaːʾ/, which is f.det. The gender of the BA word is not to be determined. If נקיה be a fem. form, whether abs. or det., it cannot strictly be the subject of יהב, a m.s. passive participle, but the syntax would be comparable to that of the BH syntax as represented in וַיַּגֵּד לְרִבְקָה אֶת־דִּבְרֵי עֵשָׂו Gn 27.42 and the like.([821]) In חויה נכתני 'a (or: the) snake bit me' A2.5:8 the verb can be interpreted as either m. (נְכָתַנִי?) or f. (נְכָתַתְנִי?), depending on the gender of the subject, חויה. The noun occurs in OA once at Sefire I A 31: חוה, which is most likely s.abs. If חויה is to be related to חוה, the latter could not end in /aː/([822]), for otherwise the Yod of our form would remain inexplicable. Cf. also Syr. /ḥewyaːʾ/, m.det.([823]). In TO we find חִוְיִי([824]), which points to /ḥiwway/ as the original st.abs. form.([825]) All this suggests that the noun is most likely in the st.det.; perhaps the author is referring to a snake known to the recipient of the letter (a pet snake?). Finally, the obscure word שנטא in שנטא 1 זי כתן חדת '1 new linen shirt (?)' B3.8:11 appears to be a Coptic word: the final Alef is then a mere vowel letter.([826])

p) The absence of the st. det. ending with not yet completely naturalised loan-words is understandable: תפמת אנתתה פריפת זי

---

[819] We would, however, not to go as far as Joüon (1934:8) in admitting cases of defectively (but not erroneously) spelled st.det. without the usual Aleph (or rarely He): see § 5 e.

[820] All four cases of a word-final He considered by Lindenberger (1983:284) as possibly emphatic are doubtful; rightly rejected by Kottsieper 1990:47.

[821] Cf. Joüon - Muraoka 1993: § 128 b and below at § 76 bb.

[822] So Degen 1969:26 and Fitzmyer 1967:48 (/ḥiwwaː/).

[823] The noun is masculine: Nöldeke 1898: § 79 A.

[824] The gemination of the Waw is based on the Taj. It could of course be secondary, introduced to preserve a short, unstressed vowel in the first, open syllable. Hug 1993:145 reconstructs /ḥewęː/.

[825] Hence the OA form might be reconstructed as /ḥiwwęː/ with the contraction of the diphthong.

[826] See below Appendix III, List of Egyptian loan-words.

משלם תמי 'T. his wife, (the) main beloved (?) of M.' B3.12:11; זי תמי
חנום אלהא 'the way of Khnum the god' B3.4:8.([827])

q) The state of a construct phrase as a whole is signalled by
the last noun, nomen rectum. Thus שוק מלכא B3.4:8+ is not
about a specific king, but rather about a specific street, 'the
king's street' or 'the royal parade.' Likewise אבני מלכא 'the royal
weights' ib.6+; ספרי אוצרא 'the treasury scribes' B4.4:12; ספר
זבנתא 'the sale document' B3.12:31. Compare also עטה טבה 'good
counsel' C1.1:57 with ספרא חכימא ובעל עטתא טבתא 'the wise scribe
and the master of good counsel' C1.1:42.

§ 47. Number

a) Our idiom knows three numbers: singular, plural, and
dual. Adjectives([828]), pronouns, and verbs, however, do not seem
to possess the category of dual.

b) Judging from necessarily incomplete evidence available
in spelling variations([829]), the use of the dual appears to be highly
restricted, confined to a small number of nouns denoting objects
which go in pairs, all parts of body such as ידין 'hands' (B2.6:8),
עינין 'eyes' (C1.1:212), אדנין 'ears' (C1.1:215), and the numerals
תרתין/תרין 'two' (A6.9:3,4) and מאתין 'two hundred' (A6.2:13).

c) Apart from obvious cases where the plural is used to
refer to an object which numbers two or more, the use of נשן to
refer to a single woman remains enigmatic: e.g. נשן מבטחיה
B2.3:2.([830]) That the form is a plural is evident from the spelling
with <y> in נשין תפמת 'lady(?) Tapamet' B3.12:1. But it was not
obviously perceived as genuine plural, as indicated by the cipher
"1" in גבר 1 נשן 1 '1 man, 1 woman' B3.3:3. It was not a title such
as "Mrs" or "Miss," for once it is used without being followed
by a name: נשן זי יב בירתא 'a lady of Elephantine the fortress'
B3.1:2. Joüon (1934:51f.) argued that it is not a term of mere
politeness, but denotes a woman of some juridical standing, thus
a kind of plural of dignity or majesty. That it does not indicate
by itself a high position in society, however, is evident from its

---

[827] See Folmer 1995:306f. with n. 187. תמא זי חנום אלהא in תמא B3.5:10 is a
variant spelling of תמי.

[828] Grelot (1972:235) proposes a dual adjective פרסין in שן זי צל פרסין 'a
pair of Persian leather shoes' B3.8:20, quoting Aristophanes, *Lys.* 229 τὼ
περσικά.

[829] See § 18 *d, g, k, n* and § 21 *a*.

[830] Porten - Yardeni 1989:25 "lady Mibtahiah"; Grelot 1972:178 "Dame
M."

application to a handmaiden at B3.6:2.([831])

d) There does not seem to exist a sound basis for postulating a special case of the plural of majesty for the word אלה 'god' or Jewish revision of originally pagan texts, proverbs of Ahiqar in particular([832]), as has been argued by Joüon (1934:25-29).([833])

e) Some nouns are regularly used in the plural, so-called *pluralia tantum*: ברחמן 'with affection' B3.5:12+; דמיא 'the price' B3.4:7 and דמוהי 'its price' B3.2:7+; נכסין 'goods, possessions' A4.8:5+, though its synonym קנין is used in the sg.; תחומוהי 'its boudaries' B3.12:22+; משחתה 'its measurements' B2.3:4+([834]); אנפן 'face' C1.1:14+.

f) There are nouns which, though singular in form, refer to an entity consisting of multiple units, so-called *collective nouns*. One such example is גרדא 'domestic staff'([835]): גרדא ונכסיא זילנא 'our domestic staff and goods' A6.10:1+. Such a collective noun is subsequently referred to by means of a plural pronominal morpheme: e.g. מה זי לקחת נכסון מן גרדא התב הב להם 'what you took (in) goods from the domestic staff, restore, give to *them*' A6.15:9. Precisely for this reason, we, *pace* Driver (1957:83), would prefer to interpret מנה in נכסן לקח מנה 'he took goods from ?' A6.15:9 as /minnah/ 'from her,' i.e. 'from my ladyship' rather than /minne:h/ = גרדא מן. See also חילא יהודיא 'these are the names of the Jewish troop' C3.15:1; חילא זילי למרודן]יא ק]טלו 'my troops killed the rebels' C2.1:16; חנ]יל[א זך מרדיא 'that rebel army' or 'that army the rebels' ib.19.

The word אנשא is somewhat problematic. Let us first note that it occurs, including partially restored cases, 9 times (C1.1:98, 103,125,151,164,170,171,172,184) in the proverbs of Ahiqar, and always in the st.det., whilst elsewhere it occurs another four times, and then always in the st.abs. In the proverbs אנשא does not appear to refer to a specific individual or group of specific individuals, but rather to 'men, people in general.' In one such case, it seems to be in contrast to איש, which is, in our corpus,

---

[831] See also below at § 76 *cf.*

Cowley's (1923:24) tentative 'spinster' has now been disproved by B3.6:2 where the word is applied to a mother, though a slave.

[832] We are referring to אלהן at C1.1:79,96,128,135,163,172.

[833] See Lindenberger 1982. See also on agreement/disagreement at § 76 *ch*, n. 18.

[834] Not sg.: see § 18 *o*.

[835] See Driver 1957:63.

used as an indefinite pronoun, 'someone, anyone,'([836]) and it never occurs in the st.det. or in the plural: שמהתהם לא ידע איש הא כן אנשא 'no one knows their names. Behold thus no one knows people' C1.1:164. Cf. לא בידי אנ]ש[א מנשא רגלהם 'it is not in the hands of people to raise *their* leg' C1.1:170. By contrast, the indefinite אנש appears always next to a singular noun in the st.abs.: בר וברה לי אח ואחה לי ואנש זילי 'son or daughter of mine, brother or sister of mine or an individual of mine' B2.11:8; לבר וברה לך ולאנש זילך 'against son or daughter of yours or someone of yours' ib.9. In B3.9 it appears alongside איש: אנה ובר וברה לי ואיש לי ואנש אחרן 'I, or son or daughter of mine, or man of mine, or another individual' B3.9:5, which follows אנה אוריה ובר וברה לי אח ואחה לי ואיש לי 'I Uriah, or son or daughter of mine, brother or sister of mine, or man of mine' ib.4, and cf. אנש לא שליט 'no one has right' ib.8, where איש would be just as good.([837]) Let us also note that the indefinite אנש is treated as singular, agreeing with אחרן and שליט.

§ 48. Adjective

a) Adjectives normally constitute a secondary word-class in relation to nouns, to which they are subordinate as either α) attributives or β) predicates([838]): α) מאן טב 'good vessel' C1.1:93; ספרא חכימא 'the wise scribe' ib.42; ליומן אחרנן שגיאן 'after many more days' ib.49; מיא קשיא 'the rough waters' B2.2:11; מלה באישה 'bad word' A4.3:6; עטתא טבתא 'the good counsel' C1.1:42; עינין טבן 'good eyes' ib.157; β) הן עליך כות טב 'if it be thus good on you [= if this be acceptable to you]' A6.7:8; איש שפיר מדדה ולבבה טב 'a man whose stature is beautiful and whose heart is good' C1.1:95; אנה צדיק בהם 'I am entitled to them' B5.6:8.

b) Attributive adjectives may be substantivised, namely their head nouns may be understood. In some cases the elided noun is reasonably obvious, and the adjective shows agreement with it with respect to gender, number, and state: קריב ורחיק 'near and far (person איש) B2.1:9 et passim; אל תהרכב חטך לצדיק 'Do not mount your arrow against a righteous (man איש) C1.1:126; הן יאחדן רשיעא בכנפי לבשך 'if the wicked (man גברא) takes hold of the

---

[836] Cf. §§ 17 and 44.

[837] Cf. גבר אחרן אמי ואבי אח ואחה ואיש אחרן לא ישלט 'another person, my mother or my father, brother or sister, or another person shall have no right' B3.5:19, where we find איש אחרן substituting אנש אחרן and גבר in use as a synonym of איש or אנש. See Porten - Szubin 1987:58.

[838] Adjectives are secondaries in Jespersen's (1924:96) ranks of word-classes.

corners of your garment' C1.1:107; שזבך מן קטל זכי 'he saved you from the murder of an innocent (one)' C1.1:46([839]); בעליתא ותחתיתא 'in the Upper and Lower (Egypt מצרין)' A6.7:6([840]).

c) However, there are cases of virtual lexicalisation where the speaker or writer was probably not conscious of any elided noun: ... וכל גברין זי בעו באיש לאגורא זך 'and all persons who sought evil for that temple' A4.7:16([841]); זא באישתא 'this evil (deed)' ib.17([842]); ... הן נפקה טבה מן פם 'if (something) good comes out from the mouth of ...' C1.1:171; הן לחיה תנפק מ[ן] פמהם 'if (something) bad comes out from their mouth' ib.172; יעבד לחיתא 'does the bad (thing)' ib.134; [מן בי]חתי נפקת לחיתי 'my misfortune originated in my household' ib.139; אל תרגג לכביר זי ימנע מנך 'Do not covet a large (thing) which is denied you' ib.136. All these examples refer to things, rather than persons. But gentilicia, also frequently substantivised and, by definition, refer to persons: ארמי זי סון 'an Aramaean of Syene' B2.1:2; ארמין זי סון 'Aramaeans of Syene' B2.11:2 and many others.

d) Adjectives (and adverbs) have no morpheme for the comparative and superlative degrees, though the term mentioned as a yardstick is preceded by the preposition מן: e.g. מה חסין הו מן חמר נער 'what is stronger than a braying ass?' C1.1:174; לצדיק מנך 'at one more righteous than you' ib.128; יתיר מן זי כען 'more than now' A4.7:3([843]); ... מן גבר זי ... צדקה יהוה לך 'it will be counted as a merit for you .. more than for any person who ..' A4.7:27.

e) Adjectives in turn may be further qualified by adverbs, which are thus tertiaries: אנה חמם שגיא 'I am very hot' D7.17:4; עטה טבה הי]שגי[א 'it is very good counsel' C1.1:57.

An adjective, probably in the st. cst., may be followed by a noun specifying in what respect the property indicated by the adjective applies: e.g., עויר עינין 'blind of eyes' C1.1:212. See § 48 i.

f) Adjectives may function as tertiaries, namely as adverbials: for details, see above at § 22 b.

---

[839] Cf. Joüon 1934:84.

[840] Cf. במצרין בתחתיתא 'in Lower Egypt' A6.10:11.

[841] Cf. כזי איש מנדעם באיש לא יעבד 'so that nobody would do anything evil' A6.7:8.

[842] On the distinction of gender here, see § 45 f.

[843] On the use of זי here, note an analogous structure in Syriac: Muraoka 1997b: § 100.

MORPHOSYNTAX

SECTION C

THE VERB

§ 49. Binyanim

a) It makes some sense to examine the function of binyanim in terms of the opposition between the unmarked, basic binyan, G or Peal, and the marked, "derived" ones, namely D or Pael, H/A or Hafel/Afel, and the *t*-prefixed one of each of the three, namely tG or Ithpeel, tD or Ithpaal, tH/A or Ittaphal.([844]) Such an approach is justified even for verbs which may never have been used in G. Partly due to the limited scope of our corpus, many verbs are attested only in one binyan. In addition, the unvowelled writing system of our texts does not always allow us to assign a given form of a verb to one of the six patterns with certainty, for which task we often draw on analogy of cognate dialects. It is particularly difficult to tell a tG from a tD except in Ayin-Waw/Yod verbs.([845])

Another general observation to be made is that we sometimes come across verb forms which are assuredly to be assigned to different binyanim with different meanings, but a semantic link between them escapes us, so that they are virtually two or more distinct lexemes. An example of this is the root מנ‬י√: G impv. מנו 'Count!' A4.1:3 // D pf. מנ‬י 'he appointed' C1.1:37. So also שדר√: D pf. 3ms שדר 'he sent' C1.1:101 // tD(?) pf. 3mp אשתדרו 'they

---

[844] The internal passive patterns are considered here as subcategories of three of the six patterns, to wit Peil = passive of Peal, Pual = passive of Pael, Hofal = passive of Hafel.

[845] Thus it is not clear on what ground a concordance produced by the Comprehensive Aramaic Lexicon project distinguishes between tG and tD of נצ‬ל√. Again, Joüon (1934:54f.) argues strongly that שאל in the frequent collocation שאל שלם is not Peal, but Afel, though it is strange that not a single instance of Hafel is to be found in our corpus.

intervened, interceded' A4.3:4.

b) There are a large number of non-G verbs the precise function of whose binyan is hardly definable. Examples are: D √ברך(846)—ברכנכן 'we blessed you' A2.5:1; D √חבל(847)—הו חבלך 'he harmed you' C1.1:44; √חוי(848)—יחוני אפיכי 'May he show me your face' A2.6:2; D √מלל(849)—לא מלל 'he did not speak' B8.8:8; D √שלם—אהוה משלם 'I shall be paying' B4.2:7(850); H √שכח—השכחו 'they found' A4.3:4

c) The semantic connection between some non-G verbs to their G counterpart is quite obvious, though we are not able to put our finger on the precise nature of the connection: e.g. G בנה 'to build' // D מבני בי תחתי 'Renovated, a lower house' B3.10:12; G כתב 'to write' // D עלימתה מכתבה על שמה 'his lass (is) marked under his name' D7.9:6; G לבש 'to wear' // D הי מלבש אנה 'I am wearing it' A2.1:6; G(?) עשתת לכי 'I took thought of you' B3.6:3 // tG (or tD) יתעשת לי 'Let him take thought of me!' A6.11:3; G שלח 'to send' // D משלחה 'one who sends it away' or 'sent away' (pass.f.ptc.)(851); G of √יבל—בלני 'Bring me!' C1.1:52 // H היבלו 'they brought' C3.28:56.

d) Amongst the non-G binyanim it is sometimes difficult to draw a line between two of them. Hardly any semantic opposition can be established between D and H of: √חוי—D חונא בוידרנג 'he let us gloat over Vidranga' A4.8:15 // החוין בוידרנג 'ditto' A4.7:16; √קרב—D קרבתך קדם סנחאריב 'I presented you before Sennacherib' C1.1:50 // H יהקרב קדמיך '(whom) he will present before you' A6.3:7.(852)

e) Where a verb in G indicates a state or quality, its D-transform denotes that its subject confers such a quality on its

---

846 The identification as D depends on our knowledge of cognate dialects. This verb is used in G only as a passive participle as in Heb.: ברך אנת 'you are blessed' A3.3:2.

847 The identification as D depends on our knowledge of cognate dialects.

848 The identification as D depends on our knowledge of cognate dialects.

849 The identification as D depends on our knowledge of cognate dialects.

850 Originally perhaps factitive.

851 Cf. a similar nuance of BH D שִׁלַּח as against G שָׁלַח.

852 A telling example to show how thin the line is between the two binyanim is יקרבון 'they will offer' A4.7:25 where the scribe has erased a ה between the י and the ק, and an alternative version of the same document has נקרב 'we shall offer' A4.8:25, and a related document has יקרבון A4.9:9. All the three documents are dated to 407 BCE.

grammatical object or brings the latter into such a state. Such a D is *factitive* in that sense. Examples are: G אזל קרב אריא 'a lion went (and) came near' C1.1:94 // D קרבתך קדם סנחאריב 'I brought you near to Sennacherib' C1.1:50; G אחוב 'I shall be obligated' B3.5:14 // D חיבוני 'they obligated me' B8.6:10; D חכם לברה 'instructed his son' C1.1:1; מיצב D pass.ptc.(?) 'validated' B3.10:22[853]; G עם מן אצדק 'with whom shall I be found innocent (צדיק)?' B3.10:22 // D מן אפו צדקני 'who then would find me innocent?, who would then acquit me?' C1.1:140. In one case, a D verb indicates a change of direction of movement: G ביתן זי זבן בכסף 'our house, which we bought with silver' B3.12:3 // D ביתא זבן ויהבן לך 'the house which we sold and gave to you' ib.6.

In אנה מהלך 'I walk' C1.1:40 we apparently have a D verb, though the root was most likely not in use in G, for which a related root הוך is in use: e.g. יהכן 'they will go' B3.1:19, exactly as in BA.

f) Most H or A verbs are *causative* in function in relation to their G forms. Thus G זי אתה 'who is coming' A2.5:6 // H לא מהיתין 'they are not bringing' A6.13:2; G למסלק ומנחת 'to ascend and descend' B3.10:15 // A אתה למחתה 'coming to bring down' A2.5:6; G ינפק 'he will come out' D7.10:7 // H יהנפק 'he will bring out' A6.13:3; G נשק באשה 'catching fire' C1.1:221 // H אל תהנשק 'Do not allow (it) to kindle' ib.87; G עלו באגורא 'they broke into the temple' A4.7:9 // H כל זי הנעלת 'all that she brought in' B2.6:24; G יקום עני 'Anani will stand up' B3.3:7 // H הקימני 'Establish me!' C1.1:109; G רכבי סוסין 'those who mount horses' C2.1:44 // H הרכבת חטך 'you mounted (= aimed) your arrow' C1.1:128; G אתוב 'I shall turn back' B7.1:5 // H התב כלא 'Return everything!' A6.15:7; G אל תחלי 'Do not be sweet!' C1.1:143 // H כפן יהחלה מררותא 'hunger will sweeten bitterness' ib.123.

Some obviously H verbs are not attested in G: e.g. [יה]גנון—√גנן 'they will protect' A4.5:23; הגשש ביתי—√גשש 'he spied out my house' C1.1:139; החוין—√חוי 'he showed us' A6.2:7[854]; החסני—√חסן 'Take it in hereditary possession!' B2.3:26[855]; הושרי—√ישר 'Dispatch!' D7.26:5.

g) To distinguish between three different **t**-binyanim, es-

---

[853] Cf. BA Dn 7.19 לְיַצָּבָא D inf., denominative of יַצִּיב.

[854] The root is also attested in D (see above [*d*]). למהחוה is likely an error for למחויה (a D or A infinitive) at שלחת לה למחוה 'I sent to him to explain' D7.24:16.

[855] On the semantic link between this verb and the adjective חסין 'strong,' cp. Heb. חָזָק and הֶחֱזִיק.

pecially between tG and tD, can be problematic. For a reasonably certain classification, see above, § 29.

With the likely exception of H השכח 'to find' vs. tG אשתכח 'was found,' a morphological relationship between a t-form and the corresponding non-t form appears to correspond to a semantic one: thus G vs. tG, D vs. tD, and H vs. tH. In the majority of cases, a t-form is a *passive* counterpart of the underlying non-t form. This applies to the tG of אחד 'to seize,' בנה 'to build,' גבה 'to collect,' יהב 'to give,' לקח 'to take,' נגד 'to draw up,' נתן 'to give,' עבד 'to do, make,' קטל 'to kill,' שים 'to put,' שבק 'to abandon,' שלח 'to send.' In some other G verbs, their t-form denotes an *inchoative* or *ingressive* aspect, namely some new state sets in or the subject takes on a certain property or character: e.g., אתכנש 'to come together' (C2.1:11+), אתמלא 'to become full' (B3.1:11+), אשתאר 'to remain' (B3.12:6), אשתוי 'to become equal, to reach an agreement' (B2.11:2), אשתמע 'to become obedient' (B3.8:42+), and perhaps אתחזי 'to become visible' (C1.1:90). אתנטר 'to guard oneself' (C1.1:96) and possibly אזדהר 'to watch out' (A4.1:5) are rare *reflexive* t-forms. אתאשד in אל תתאשד 'Do not get distraught!'(?) A3.3:7 is obscure.([856])

The same holds for the following tD verbs: אתאלף 'to be taught' (C1.1:175)([857]), אתכסי 'to be concealed (< to be covered)' (A4.3:11) אסתבל 'to be supported' (C1.1:73). The difficult אשתדר (A4.3:4) has been mentioned above at § a.

אתוסף 'to be added' C3.11:8 and אתעדי 'was removed' A6.6:3 appear to be a passive transform of their respective Afel form.

§ 50. Tenses

a) Our basic assumption is that the distinction between the perfect and the imperfect, the latter excluding the jussive and the energic, is essentially that of tense: the former indicates an action already undertaken or a state which once prevailed, thus preterital, and the latter an action yet to be undertaken or a state which will, may or should prevail, thus roughly future.([858])

---

[856] For a semantic development from אשד 'to pour (out),' cf. συγχέω 'to throw into confusion; to disturb composure or temper of': see Muraoka 1993b:220. Fitzmyer's (1962:20) "Do not dissipate" is unlikely. The related Syr. root always takes an inanimate entity as its object. Gibson's (1975:146) "Do not be troubled" is an improvement.

[857] The active D-form does not occur in our corpus.

[858] The question regarding the conditional clause will be looked at separately: § 84. The use of the suffix conjugation in a hypothetical protasis means that,

b) Our idiom shares a universal Semitic feature whereby, unlike in many modern Indo-European languages, the preterite tense of the principal verb does not automatically cause a change in the tense of a verb in a subordinate clause as in: *He said she was being obstinate* < *He said, "She is being obstinate*." Thus ימאת לה כזי זילי הי 'I swore to him that it *was* mine' B2.3:24.([859])

§ 51. Perfect or suffix conjugation

a) Our idiom is not sensitive to a distinction which is essential and meaningful to English, for instance, between "he did" (the simple past), "he has done" (the present perfect), "he had done" (the past perfect), and "he will have done" (the future perfect). Excepting a sparingly used syntagm illustrated by שמיע לן 'we have heard' (§ 54 *c*), one sc. form עבד does duty for all four. It is often difficult, even when the text is reasonably well preserved, to make a confident decision as to which is meant. Thus מטתני כתנה זי אושרתי לי ואשכחתה שנטת כלה (A2.1:4) may be rendered in either of the first three ways, not just 'the tunic which you sent me has reached me and I have found it completely frayed(?)' as translated in *TAD* A.([860]) Examples are: *simple past*—זי רבחיל הוה 'who was commander' A4.7:7; אתו לבירת יב 'they came to the fortress of Elephantine' ib.8; *past perfect*—אבהין בנו אגורא זך 'our forefathers had built that temple' ib.13; כל נכסין זי קנה אבדו 'all possessions which he had acquired perished' ib.16; *future perfect* —כזי הוין עבדן 'as we shall have been doing' B3.6:12([861]); והן מאתת ולעד שלמת ויהבת לך כספא זילך 'should I die, and (by then) I have not yet paid and given you your silver' B3.13:8; עבידתא זי אנת עבדת 'the work which you will have undertaken' B2.4:10; בניא זי אנת בנית 'the rebuilding which you will have executed' ib.12.

b) *Performative perfect*([862])

Uttering a verb in the perfect tense may be like performing it or acting it out. This is very frequent in stereotyped greeting formulas such as: שלם ושררת שגיא הושרת לך 'I (hereby) send you

---

in the speaker's *perception*, the action in question has already taken place or the state in question has already become a reality.

[859] Thus, if כזי introduce an indirect speech in כזי לא הוה B2.2:7, the clause would need to be translated 'it had (never) been': see § 85 *a*.

[860] Cf. also קבלת B2.2:5—"I lodged a complaint" (Cowley 1923:16), "I complained" (*TAD* B, p. 21), "ik .. een klacht heb ingediend"(Wagenaar 1928:51), but "j'avais porté plainte" (Joüon 1934:23 and Grelot 1972:175).

[861] See on the periphrastic construction, see § 55 *g*.

[862] Kutscher (1971:111) speaks of "Koincidenzfall."

abundant welfare and strength' A6.3:1+; also לשלמכן שלחת ספרה זנה '(out of my concern) for your welfare I (hereby) send this letter' A2.1:12+.([863])

Here may belong also a common greeting formula such as ברכתכי לפתח 'I hereby bless you to Ptah" A2.1:2 et passim. Otherwise the writer would conceivably be reassuring the recipient that a prayer had been said for him or her.([864])

The performative perfect is less certain in deeds and contracts, for these latter are essentially written records of past agreements: אנה יהבת לכי בחיי ובמותי בי 1 ארק 'I have given you, during my lifetime and upon my death, 1 house (with) land' B2.3:3; יהבתה לכי ורחקת מנה 'I have given it to you and withdrawn from it' B2.7:7.([964a])

c) *Verbs of mental attitude* are sometimes in the perfect, referring to the state of mind or attitude without specific time reference: e.g., למן זי צבית למנתן 'whoever you desire to give (it) to' B3.4:15+([865]); נפשי צבית 'my soul desires' B3.7:15; שנית לאנתי 'I hate my wife' B3.8:21; שנאת לאסחור בעלי 'I hate Eshor my husband' B2.6:23; למן זי רחמתי תנתנן 'you may give (it) to whomever you love' B2.3:9, sim.ib.19, B2.10:9. Cf. also טיב לבבן 'our heart is satisfied' B3.4:6+, where 'was satisfied' is not to be precluded.

d) *Gnomic perfect*

Occasionally we find the perfect used in the manner of the gnomic aorist in Classical Greek in proverbial sayings of timeless validity([866]): e.g. מאן טב כסי[] מלה בלבבה והו ז[י]תביר הנפקה ברא 'a good vessel cover[s] a word in its midst, but one whi[ch] is broken lets it go out' C1.1:93. But not every perfect in proverbs is to be so interpreted: [ברי]הוה לי שהד חמס ומן אפו צדקני 'my son became for me a malicious witness, and who would then acquit me?' C1.1:140 where the pf. is akin to its use in conditional sentences([867]), and is parallel to the impf.: [מן בי]חי נפקת לחיתי ועם

---

[863] Some of these examples come under what Classical philology calls epistolary aorist: Gildersleeve 1900:127f. Cf. Dempsey 1990:7-11.

[864] So Hug 1993:116 and Porten 1996:90, n. 6.

[964a] Fitzmyer's "contractural" perfect: Fitzmyer 1956:176f.

[865] Cp. למן זי רחמתי תנתננה 'to whomever you love, you may give it' B2.7:8 with למן זי תצבין הבה 'to whomever you desire, give it!' ib.16.

[866] So also Fitzmyer 1956:172, 177f., who, however, goes too far in assuming that all these perfects are atemporal. Thus in a fablelike saying such as נמרא פגע לענזא 'the leopard met a goat' C1.1:166 the usual preterital meaning ought to be recognised. Cf. Blass - Debrunner - Funk 1961: § 333.

[867] Thus *pace* Lindenberger (1983:138). Cf. a similar use of the perfect,

מן אצדק '[from] my hou[se] went out my misfortune, and with whom shall I be acquitted?' ib.139.

e) Our idiom does not use the perfect with optative force to indicate a wish.([868]) Hence Lindenberger's "May the dogs tear his guts out from between his legs etc." for כלביא הנפקו כבלא מן רגלוהי ... A4.7:16 is unlikely.([869])

f) On the use of the perfect tense in conditional sentences, see below, § 84 *b, c, d,* and *i.*

§ 52. Imperfect or prefix conjugation

a) Among the verb forms characterised by the addition of inflectional prefixes supplemented by suffixes one may distinguish three different categories: the so-called "long imperfect," jussive (also called short or apocopated imperfect), and energic. This section will deal with the first, and the remaining two in the following section. Here the term "imperfect" is to be understood in the sense of long imperfect.

b) The imperfect may indicate a state which will prevail in the future or an event which will take place in the future: e.g. יתיהב לכן 'it will be given to you' A3.3:5; כזי יהנעלן המו יהודיא 'when the Jews bring them' A3.8:12. No impf. has been identified which indicates an action in the past, whether punctiliar or durative/iterative/habitual. The latter function is marked by the periphrastic construction, הוה + ptc.act.: see § 55 *g.*

c) An extension of the use described above can be identified in an apodosis of a conditional statement, indicating a logical consequence that would ensue if the condition is met: הן לו לא [תכהל תהנצלנה[י] 'If not, you will not be able to rescue him' C1.1:176;

---

also in a question, in Syriac: Mk 16.3 *man de:n ᶜaggel lan ke:fa:* τίς ἀποκυλίσει ἡμῖν τὸν λίθον;, and see Nöldeke 1898: § 259 "O dass doch einer den Stein abwälzte." Or simply preterital: " .. et qui donc m'a justifié?" (Grelot 1972:442). Kottsieper's (1990:9) restoration *[y]ṣdqny* has little to commend it.

[868] As in Classical Arabic and some other cognates: see Brockelmann 1913: § 16 b (pp. 29f.). This phenomenon in Classical Syriac is confined to a particular syntax, namely <hwa: + adj. or ptc.>: Muraoka 1997: § 87.

[869] Lindenberger 1994:67. The text is difficult enough. To כבלא corresponds כבלוהי, a pl., in the revised version of the document (A4.8:15). The noun mostly denotes "fetters" as an instrument of incarceration or torturing, not a piece of ornamental accessory: see Ps 105.18 עִנּוּ בַכֶּבֶל רַגְלוֹ 'they tormented his foot (!: Ktiv רגליו) with a fetter' and papMur 43:5 אני נתן ת כבלים ברגלכם (again sg.!, though possibly defective for רגליכם) 'I shall put fetters on your foot.'

הן אמחאנך ברי לא תמות '(even) if I struck you, my son, you will not die' ib.177; "if there be any decrease in the domestic staff ..,
you will be strictly called to account (תשתאלון) and a harsh word will be directed (יתעבד) at you" A6.10:8. See also § 84 on the conditional clause.

d) The imperfect may be used in *generic* statements on what might or could happen, but not referring to a specific or particularised event. The imperfect so used, however, does not refer to an event in the past. It stands to reason that such an imperfect often occurs in generalising relative clauses or protases of conditional clauses. Examples are: כל גשר זי ישכח יזבן 'every beam that he might come across, let him buy (it)!' A2.2:15; כל זי תצבה שלח לי 'whatever you desire, send (word) to me (about it)!' A2.4:7; כזי תמטה ידכי 'as much as lies in your power' A2.6:5; "I am doing for him as much as you might be able to do (כדי תכלן (תעבדן"A2.3:4; ... בעי אש זי יזבן ביתא [ר]בא 'Seek out a man who might buy the large house ..' A3.8:6; בכספא זי יקום עלוהי 'for the silver [= price] that might be put on it (when sold)' ib.([870]); חלקא ... זילי זי יאמר לכם 'my portion on which .. might say to you ..' A3.10:2; זי יגרנכי דין ובב 'whoever shall institute against you suit or (pro)cess' B2.7:10; זי תזבנון לה או זי ברחמן תנתנו לה 'to whom you might sell or to whom you might give in affection' B2.10:14, and many more examples in contracts([871]); לא נסבלנך כזי יסבל בר לאבוהי 'we shall not support you as a son would support his father' B3.6:13. Note the contrast between the impf. and ptc. in מה זי תעבדון לחור ... עבדן [אנ]תם 'whatever you might be doing to Ḥor ... you are doing ...' A4.3:8. In the light of this a scribal error may be suspected in ישתלח על מן זי הוה 'Let word be sent to whomever might be (there)' A6.2:5, הוה erroneously for יהוה (haplography) rather than הוה as a ptc.

e) Also typical of the legalese is the use of the imperfect (α) indicating a stipulation or agreement which is deemed binding and to remain in force in accordance with the terms of agreement([872]), and (β) in decrees and administrative orders. Thus תזרענה ... ותפלג ... נפלג ... ותחצד ... ואלקח ... 'you shall sow it .. and

---

[870] Rather than the present perfect as in "the silver that is fixed upon it" (Porten - Yardeni 1986:42).

[871] Note the alternation between the pf. רחמתי and impf. תצבין mentioned above (n. 865).

[872] See also a criticism by Degen (1979:37) against Segert (1975:300), who wants to see in examples cited here and such like a sign of a neutralisation between the indicative and jussive.

you shall divide .. we shall divide .. and you shall harvest .. and I shall take ..' B1.1:4; מחר או יום אחרן לא אכהל אכלאנך 'tomorrow or the next day I shall not be able to restrain you' B2.1:6; "If tomorrow or the next day I bring against you suit or process ... I shall give (אנתן) you silver .." B2.4:13 (not: 'I may have to ..') and tens of similar examples in contracts. That we are not dealing with a merely possible consequence is clear from the use of a nominal clause in similar context such as "If tomorrow or the next day you build up that plot (and) then my daughter hate you and go out from you, she does not have right (לא שליטה הי) to take it and give it to others" B2.4:9. The penalty is a certainty, not an option. An example of an authoritative decree is יתשם טעם כזי איש מנדעם באיש לא יעבד לפירמא 'May an order be issued that nobody shall do anything bad against PN' A6.7:8; see also A6.13:1.

f) כזי with an impf. may indicate a purpose (*final*): כן עב[דו] כזי לי תחדון 'Do thus so that you will gladden me!' A6.14:3; כן תחד[ה] ... עבד כזי לאלהיא 'Do thus so that you will gladden the gods ..' A6.16:2; גרדא ... חסין טרו כן כזי מ[נ]דעם כסנתו לא יהוה 'Guard .. domestic staff .. strictly in such a way that there will not be a[n]y decrease ..' A6.10:5; אנתם קמו קבלהם כן כזי מלה באישה לא ישכחון לכם 'You, stand by them .. so that they shall not find a bad thing about you' A4.3:6; התב הב להם כן כזי מספת קבילה תובא לא ישלח ע]ליך ['Restore, give to them so that Masapata will not send a complaint again against you' A6.15:10. Once without Kaf—זף דגנא וחנטתא זי תאכל ותשבע ותנתן לבניך עמך 'Borrow grain and wheat that you may eat, and be sated, and give to your sons with you' C1.1:129.

g) The use of an imperfect to complement a verb such as יכל and כהל as in לא נכל נגרכי 'we shall not be able to institute (suit) against you' B5.1:4 and לא אכהל אכלאנך 'I shall not be able to restrain you' B2.1:6 is extensively discussed elsewhere: § 73 *a*.

h) *Miscellaneous*

In one case the impf. appears to be equivalent to the present tense, simply stating a fact prevailing at the moment of speaking: נדחל 'we are afraid' A4.2:7. In another case an impf. is used parallel to a ptc.: דבקה לביתא זילי // B2.1:5 תדבק לשטר ביתי ib.4, where, however, the former is probably a case of apodictic impf., 'it shall adjoin the side of my house' as against 'it (in fact) adjoins my house.'

Volitive force may be identified in ברא זי יתאלף ויתסר... 'the son who is willing to be taught and disciplined ..' C1.1:175, and possibly in יהוספון 'Let them add' A6.2:18.([873])

§ 53. Jussive and Energic([874])

a) Morphologically speaking, the jussive, also called apoco-pated, is a variety of the prefix conjugation characterised by a shorter suffixal morpheme. Even though this morphological difference is not always discernible in our unvocalised texts, one can say that our idiom might still have a jussive form distinct from an indicative one. For instance, the 3ms of a verb other than Lamed-Yod such as יזבן from זבן G 'to buy,' D 'to sell,' may mean 'Let him buy/sell!' as well as 'he will buy/sell.'([875]) ישאל in אלה שמ[י]א] ישאל בכל עדן A4.8:2 (sim. A4.7:2) must be seen, at least functionally, as jussive in view of אלהיא ישאלו שלמך בכל עדן 'May the gods seek after your welfare at all times' A4.4:1, sim. A3.10:1, A3.5:1. Likewise at שלחי על תבי ותושר לכי עמר 'Send (word) to Tabi and let her dispatch wool to you!' A2.2:6.

The use of an imperative אתעשת in הן על מראן טב אתעשת ... 'if it please our lord, give thought ...' A4.7:23 renders it likely that we have a volitive/jussive in an analogously worded expression such as הן על מראי לם כות טב אגרת מן מראי תשתלח 'if it indeed thus please my lord, may a letter be sent from my lord' A6.13:2.

b) The primary function of the jussive is to indicate the speaker's wish or will: I or we will or wish that I or we, you, he, she, it or they do, or do not do a certain thing, or be or not be something or somewhere. In practice, the second person is confined to the expression of a negative wish or will, whilst its positive counterpart is indicated by means of the imperative, which in turn is never negated by means of לא איתי or אל, לא. Examples are: תקם יתו לן 'Let them bring us castor oil!' A2.1:7, sim. A2.5:4,5; ינתנו לי 'Let them give (it) to me' A6.11:3; כן ידיע יהוי לך 'Thus let it be known to you' A6.10:8. A jussive is also found in a standard greeting formula: ברכתכי לפתח זי יחוני אפיך בשלם 'I said to Ptah a blessing for you: "May he show me your face in peace!"' A2.1:2; with a synonymous verb חזה at A2.2:2, A2.3:2, A2.4:2. Since the use of the jussive in a final clause, a clause indicating a purpose, is not known elsewhere, the presence

---

[873] But Grelot (1972:292): "On ajoutera."

[874] Cf. Folmer 1995: 496-521.

[875] The jussive is, as far as our idiom is concerned, formally distinct from the indicative in non-Lamed-Yod verbs in the following categories: 2fs, 2/3mpl, whilst in Lamed-Yod verbs the distinction is visible also in the 2ms, 3s. See § 23 *k* and § 37 *d*.

of זי is somewhat problematic. The above translation assumes a syntactic break between the two clauses connected by it.([876])

c) The jussive frequently occurs with the prohibitive אל: e.g. אל תגלי 'Do not reveal!' C1.1:141; עינין טבן אל יאכמו 'Let them not darken good eyes' ib.157([877]); אל תצפי לן 'Do not worry about us!' A2.1:7, sim. A2.2:3, A2.3:4; אל תקטלני 'Do not kill me!' C1.1:52.

d) A jussive verb does not always occupy the initial slot: אלהיא כל ישאלו שלמכי בכל עדן 'May all gods seek after your welfare at all times!' A3.7:1, sim. A3.5:1, A3.7:1, A3.10:1, and possibly A3.9:1 with ישאלו restored; חיא חדה ושרירא מראי יהוי 'May my lord be living, happy, and strong' A5.3:2; אלהיא שלם ישמו לך 'May the gods grant you peace!' A6.16:5.

e) One of the jussives mentioned above, חיא חדה ושרירא מראי יהוי A5.3:2, is paralleled by an imperative חדה ושריר הוי A4.7:3, exemplifying a complementary distribution of the affirmative jussive in the third person and the imperative in the second person. Likewise ... הוי יהבת ... ויהוי זבן 'Do give ... and do let him buy ...' A2.2:14.

f) There are indications in our corpus, particularly in the Ahiqar literature, both the introductory framework story and the proverbs, that the useful functional opposition between the two forms of the prefix conjugation, the indicative and the jussive, was not consistently observed. Thus the grammatically correct jussive אל תקטלני 'Do not kill me!' C1.1:52 is unexpectedly paralleled by an energic אל נקטלנהי 'Let us not kill him!' ib.61

---

[876] Though the text is fragmentary, we probably have a similar case in כל ... אן[?]ן זי יהוי תמה 'every ... let him/it be there ...' D23.1 III-IV:9 and זי ליאתו ... עמהם 'Would that they do not come with them ...!' D23.1 Va:10.

A similar use of די occurs in Aramaic letters of Bar Kochba, e.g. די תשלחון ... ל' 'you are to send to me ...' (Fitzmyer - Harrington 1978: # 56.4). Beyer (1984:551) thinks that the particle introduces the body of a letter. Hence his explanatory "(Hiermit wird euch mitgeteilt), daß ..." Milik (1961:158), followed by Kutscher (1961a:122; 1961b:11), took it as well as its Hebrew equivalent ש as equivalent of ὅτι *recitativum*, which introduces direct speech. Milik, however, makes no distinction between such די or ש introducing a clause with a pc. form and one without. Note the use of *que* followed by the subjunctive in Milik's (1961:156) translation of שידע יהי לך 'Qu'il soit connu de toi ...' The author(s) of these late Aramaic letters has no distinctly jussive form. Cf. Qimron 1981, where, in addition to the usage in the Aramaic letters of Bar Kochba, he mentions a few instances in Nabataean. On an analogous usage of אשר and -ש in Qumran Hebrew, see Qimron 1986:77f.

[877] Or possibly "Let good eyes not become dark!"; cf. § 24 *j*.

(for the expected verb form without an energic Nun).([878])
Indicatives or energics where one expects jussives are evident in
the following cases of Lamed-Yod verbs: ... אל יהוה ... אל תאתה [א]ל
'Do not let it come .. let it not be ..' C1.1:81; .. אל תכסה 'Do not
conceal ..' ib.84 in contrast to a jussive .. תהוי 'Let it be ..' ib. and
an energic אל יחזנהי 'Let him not show it!' ib.86; אל תהנשק .. ותכסה
..'Do not kindle ... (and do not) cover ..' ib.87; אל יחדה 'Let him
not rejoice!' ib.90. In לא יפגעני 'it will not harm me' C1.1:212 one
expects אל תקטלני ... יזכרני ועטתי יבעה ... תקרבני. Also in לא יפגענני
עלוהי ויהחיני ... אל תדחל לם [ת]חיי 'Do not kill me .. he will
remember me and seek my counsel .. you will present me to him
and he will let me live .. Do not be afraid. [You will] live ..'
C1.1:52 the indicative appears to be better suited not only in
יבעה, but also in יזכרני (all jussives).([879]) A similar blurring is also
attested in שלם מראן אלה שמיא ישאל שגיא בכל עדן ולרחמן ישימנך קדם
דריוהוש מלכא 'May the god of heaven seek after the welfare of
our lord at all times and grant you favour before King Darius'
A4.7:1 where one expects a jussive ישמך.([880]) Cp. ידיע יהוי לך
'You ought to know' A6.10:8 with יד[י]ע יהוה לך A6.8:3.([881]) A
likely scribal error is תנתנו 'you give' B2.10:14 (for תנתנון, and //
תזבנון 'you sell').

g) The free-standing *energic* is but rarely attested in our
corpus: once in a declarative clause—אשלמן 'I shall pay' B4.6:5
(// אנתננה 'I shall give it'); once with a prohibitive אל—אל תלקחן
'Do not take!' C1.1:167; twice in a protasis—הן יאחדן רשיעא 'if
the wicked seize' ib.107; הן אשבקן 'if I leave' ib.177 (// אמחאנך הן).†

It is not apparent whether there existed any functional
opposition between the indicative and the energic.([882]) Whatever

---

[878] Our assumption here is that the jussive or voluntative of the prefix
conjugation was in many cases formally distinct from the indicative use of it.
One of the formal manifestations of such a distinction is that a personal
object suffix was directly attached to the former, whereas the latter had an
intervening Nun, the so-called energic Nun. See above § 24 *l, m.*

[879] The "ungrammatical" forms such as אל תשים 'Do not place!' C1.1:130
(instead of תשם); אל תל[ו]ט 'Do not curse!' ib.80 (instead of תלט); אל תקום 'Do
not rise!' ib.85 (instead of תקם) are also to be evaluated in the light of the
"loose grammar" of this document.

[880] That ישאל is a jussive is certain from ישאלו, and not ישאלון, in a similar
greeting formula such as אלהיא ישאלו שלמך בכל עדן 'May the gods seek after
your welfare at all times' A4.4:1.

[881] Whitehead 1974:51.

[882] Leander 1928:40 calls אשלמן "Affekt-aorist," namely indicating an

the original functional load of the energic may have been([883]), its use is, in our idiom, morphosyntactically conditioned. Most of the forms take an explicit pronominal suffix, and those which do not can be said to have one implicitly.([884]) In one case only this is not the case: ... הן יאחדן רשיעא בכנפי לבשך 'if the wicked seize the corners of your garment ...' C1.1:107.

§ 54. Passive voice

The passive voice is a transform of the active, whereby the direct object of a clause in the active voice is made the grammatical subject: e.g. כזנה עביד 'such was done' A4.7:15, cf. כן עבדו 'so they did' ib.27; כל קטילו 'they were all killed' ib.17, cf. קטלו למרדיא 'they killed the rebels' C2.1:13.

a) The passive ptc. indicates the result of an action: נשיא זילן כארמלה עבידין 'our wives have been treated like widows' rather than 'are being treated' A4.7:20. Cf. איך ביתא עביד 'How is the house faring?' A3.3:6; איך זי עביד אנת 'how you are' C2.1:66.([885]) Thus the emphasis is on state rather than on process or action. Hence איתי באר חדה זי בניה בגו בן[י]רתא means 'there is a well which has been built inside the fortress' A4.5:6, not 'under construction.' The same holds true of non-G pass. participles: e.g. ממנין הוו 'had been appointed' A6.7:5. In contrast, the external passive ptc., namely one of a t-binyan, indicates an action: e.g. לקבל זי לקדמין הוה מתעבד 'in accordance with what used to be done formerly' A4.9:10.

A benedictory formula בריך + PN is no real exception: בריך אבה 'Blessed be Abah' D20.3:1. Similarly D20.2:1, D20.4:1, D20.5:1.

b) In a passive transform only the direct object can become

---

intention, but such can be also indicated by the indicative. Cf. also Folmer 1995:518.

[883] Of the uses of the energic, best illustrated in Classical Arabic in free-standing forms, which are mentioned by Brockelmann 1913:159, only its use in prohibitions is illustrated by one of our examples cited above. See also Degen 1969:80f. Segert (1975:392), who believes to be able to identify the original character of the energic in some of the above-named examples, does not, however, say what that original character was.

[884] Leander 1928: 41.

[885] Cf. Peshitta at Mt 4.24 *w-qarrev(w) le:h kulhon ʾayle:n d-viš biš ʿvidin b-ḵurha:ne:ʾ mšaḥlfe:ʾ* 'they brought to him all those who were in rather bad shape with all manners of illness' with the Gk ... πάντας τοὺς κακῶς ἔχοντας .. Moreover, this עביד at C2.1:66, *pace* Greenfield - Porten (1982:31), must

the subject, not like in English, which allows both *I was given
this book* and *this book was given to me*; so in בנא לם זי מן מראי
יהיב לי 'the domain which was given to me by my lord' A6.13:1
for the active ... מרא יהב לי. An English sentence such as *I was
given* cannot be literally transformed into Aramaic. Compare
אנתי שביקה לאלהא 'you have been released to the god (so that you
are no longer in bondage)' B3.6:10 with שבקתכי 'I released you,'
where the accent is on my action.[886] For this reason, מלבש אנה
A2.1:6 cannot be translated "I am made to wear," namely a H
passive participle.[887]

c) The syntagm [passive ptc. + ל] to express a state resulting
from an action, similarly to the Engl. perfect, present or past,
with a pronoun or noun attached to the preposition indicating
the actor, occurs in our idiom rather infrequently[888]: כן שמיע לן
'thus we have/had heard' A3.3:13; כן שמיע לי 'thus I have heard'
A6.10:3.[889] It is doubtful that it is this syntagm that occurs in a
case such as ידיע יהוי לך 'you ought to know' A6.10:8.[890]

d) It is only rarely that a passive verb is accompanied by an
indication of the subject, actor: ... הן אזד יתעבד מן דינא 'if it be
made known by the judges, ..' A4.5:8; מן מראי יהיב לי 'was given
to me by my lord' A6.13:1. The same preposition, מן, in cases
like אגרה מנך ישתלח עליהום 'May a letter be sent from you to
them!' A4.7:24 and מנך יתשם טעם 'Let an order be issued from
you!' A6.7:8 seems still to retain the literal sense of origin,
"from place x." This use seems to be characteristic of
officialese.[891]

The preposition Lamed in a benedictory formula <בריך +
PN + ל-DN> is best interpreted as indicating an indirect object
of verbs of saying: ברכה תמא ברת בכרנף לוסרי 'Blessed be Tuma

---

be distinguished from the same form at ib.17, if the latter be not a scribal
error.

[886] Thus the often-occurring אחזיאה 'I was shown' in the Qumran Aramaic
Enoch fragments (e.g. 4QEn 1 xii 27) is unusual. Cp. Ex 25.40 אַתָּה מָרְאֶה 'you
are shown' with TO אַתְּ מִתְחֲזֵי (tA) and Pesh. *mḥawweːˀ (ˀ)naːˀ laːḵ*.

[887] *Pace* Moriya 1994:130.

[888] See Kutscher 1969, who characterised this syntagm as typical of Eastern
IA. More Syr. examples may be found in Muraoka 1987: § 69. Cf. further
Folmer 1995: 376-80.

[889] The literal rendering is not, *pace* Grelot (1972:314), "il a été entendu
par moi," in other words, the preposition is not the exponent of agent, but that
of possessor or owner.

[890] *Pace* Whitehead 1974:51, and see also Folmer 1955: 391-93.

daughter of Bokrinf to Osiris' D20.2.([892]) Compare בריך אבה ...
קדם אוסרי ... 'Blessed be Abah ... before Osiris for Aba ...' D20.3:1;
קדם אוסרי ברך בלהבה לאסרי 'Blessed be B. to Osiris' D22.13;
בריכה הוי 'Be blessed before Osiris' D20.5:3.

Alternatively, the preposition ל may be that of possession
or ownership. "Be PN (a) blessed of DN," though the use of קדם
as an alternative preposition as in בריך ... קדם and the Lamed in
the active transform ברכתך לפתח cannot be easily reconciled with
such an interpretation.

e) The passive עביד, if the text be in order, is puzzling in
אחר דדרש מנדעם ל[א עביד 'then Dadarshu did n[ot] do any[thing]'
C2.1:17.

§ 55. Participle

a) One of the functions of the participle as a tense form is
to indicate actual present, namely an action indicated by it is
currently in progress at the moment of speaking: אנחן בען אלף
'we are (currently) looking for a boat' A2.6:9; ... לה שבק אנה לה 1
עבד אנה לה 'I am not leaving him alone .. I am taking care of him'
A2.4:4; עליכי מתכל אנה 'it is on you that I am relying' A2.7:2; לא
משתמען לי 'they do not obey me' A6.8:1; לכן אנחן יצפן 'we are
worrying about *you*' A2.1:8.

aa) A variation of actual present is the use of a participle
indicating an action which has been going on up to the moment
of speaking as in מן ירח תמוז ... ועד זנה יומא ... אנחנה שקקן לבשן
וצימין ... 'since the month of Tammuz ... up to this day ... we have
been wearing sackcloth and fasting ...' A4.7:19. Typologically
analogous to this structure is חנום הו עלין מן זי חנניה במצרין עד כען
'Khnum has been against us since Hananiah has been in Egypt
until this day' A4.3:7.

b) A ptc. may follow a noun, qualifying the latter: אשה יקדה
הי 'it is a burning fire' C1.1:87; מה חסין הו מן חמר נער 'What is
stronger than a braying ass?' ib.174; *passive*—כוין פתיחן 'open
windows' B2.10:6. Cf. § 71.

c) A ptc. may be completely substantivised: רכבי סוסין 'cavalry
men' C2.1:44; קטיליא 'the killed' ib.49; שהד 'witness' C1.1:140+;
שנאי 'my enemies' ib.110; D מכדב 'liar' ib.134; H מהחסן 'hereditary
property-holder' B7.2:2+; יעט 'counsellor' C1.1:12.

d) Occasionally a ptc. is used as a historic present, namely

---

[891] On our view about Kutscher's (1969:148-51) *passivum majestatis* in IA,
see below at § 80 *b*.

as a preterital tense: אדין מומאה מטאה עליכי וימאתי לי 'then the oath comes upon you and you swore to me' B2.8:4 (// pf. ימאתי)([893]). Though in the standard opening formula in contracts the verb form spelled אמר is ambiguous—pf. 3ms or ptc. ms—we find two unambiguous cases of the pf.: '.. ... אמרת יהוחן ברת משלך 'Jehohen daughter of Meshullach said' B3.1:2; אדין ביב אמרת מפט[חיה] 'then, in Elephantine, Mipta[hiah] said' B5.5:1. In the light of this last instance one may be tempted to interpret אמר as pf., but such an interpretation is impossible in אדין [ביב בי]רתא אמר אנה ענני 'then I Anani say in Elephantine the fortress' B3.7:1. In כען עבדך ידניה וכנותה כן אמרן A4.7:4 the verb אמרן, in combination with כן, is most likely a participle: note especially כן אמרין A4.7:22 with a mater lectionis. The morphological ambiguity of the above-quoted אמר in B3.7:1 is highlighted by its similarity to מטאה (ptc.) at B2.8:4 on the one hand and its stylistic and syntactic aspect in the light of אמרת, also quoted above from B3.1:2 and B5.5:1, on the other. In any event, it is important to stress that the adverb אדין in our corpus occurs in the past context, which is morphologically clear in אדין ... לא שנציו 'then .. did not succeed' A6.7:6. The only certain exception is אדין תאכל 'then you will eat' C1.1:127.

e) Once an impf. occurs side by side with a ptc., both in a conditional clause [הן נפקה טבה מן פם א[נשא] והן לחיה תנפק מן] פמהם 'if good goes out from the mouth of a m[an ..] and if evil goes out fr[om] their mouth' C1.1:171. However, in the following pair, there is a functional opposition: זבני עמר כזי תמטה ידכי 'Buy wool as much as you possibly can' A2.6:5; כדי מטאה ידי 'as much as I am (actually) able' A2.4:4 (ptc.).

f) The participle may be used to qualify the predicate: e.g., מבני בי תחתי אחד גשורן '(there is) is a lower house renovated, having beams' B3.10:12, sim. B3.5:8; דש חד בה אחד ופתח 'there is one door in it, shutting and opening' ib.13; הוה עלי ... ירבה כסף חלרן 8 'it will accrue against me .., it being silver, 8 hallurs' B3.1:4. Haggai, who penned B3.10, varies the wording slightly in B3.12: ביתה זנה ... יהבתה לך ברחמן מבני בי תחתי אחד גשורן וכון בה דש חד בה אחד ופתח 3 'this house ... I gave it to you in affection B3.12:11. In these two cases what begins with מבני describes the nature of the property in question indicated by the object suffix, and syntactically it constitutes an object complement (§ 74 *k*).

---

[892] On this use of the preposition, see Pardee 1976:221-23 and Muraoka 1979:92-94. Cf. Porten 1996:90, n. 6.

[893] Grelot (1972:190) uses two different tenses in his translation: "t'incombait

What further follows the passive participle specifies the nature of the renovation undertaken. Another scribe, Mauziah, who wrote B3.8, also varies the wording in a different way: בנה בי תחתי חדת אחד גשורן וכון. He uses two words, בנה .. חדת instead of one (מבני). It is best to take this clause also as an object complement somewhat loosely dependent on .. ביתה זך זי אנה עניה יהבת לכי 'this house which I Ananiah gave to you ..' B3.8:5. Otherwise there would emerge a new clause beginning with בי תחתי 'a lower house' in the st. abs. as the subject when one naturally expects ביתא in the st. det. with anaphoric force. In the first two cases and B3.12:11 the participles themselves are further modified, which makes them distinct from the cases mentioned under (b) above.

g) *Periphrastic tense*[894]

Our idiom shares a typically Aramaic feature in which a participle is combined with a form of the verb הוה. Excepting a few examples to be dealt with later, the participle immediately follows a form of הוה. Coodinate verbs may dispense with הוה.[895] The latter can be a perfect, imperative or imperfect. In most cases the syntagm seems to indicate iteration or habit, or an ongoing process, especially with the perfect of הוה: e.g. כזי הוו עבדן ... כזי 'as we shall have been doing' B3.6:12; הוין עבדן 'as ... used to do' A6.10:7; הות מית 'I was dying' A2.5:8 (// הן מת אנה 'if I am dead' ib.9); כזי אנה הוית אתה 'as I was coming' A6.3:2; לקבל זי לקדמין הוה מתעבד 'in accordance with what used to be done' A4.9:10; הוה מהחסן 'was holding as heir' A6.11:2; הוה חשל 'was paying (?)' ib.6; הוית מסבל לך 'I used to look after you' C1.1:48, sim. ib.72; כל כסף ומרבי זי אהוה משלם לך 'all silver and interest that I shall be paying you' B4.2:7.

With the imperative of הוה the picture changes slightly. Whilst in והוי יהבת עבר לוחפרע 'and keep giving grain to Wahpre!' A2.2:14 and [י]רח כירח הוו שלחן '[י] 'Keep sending [mon]th by month!' A6.1:3[896] the syntagm may be assigned the above-mentioned, durative or iterative function, in most cases it seems to indicate a sense of urgency and insistence[897]: שלם יקיה הוי שלחת לה 'Do send greetings (from) Yekia to her!' A2.3:11; הוי שלח שלם ינקא 'Do send greetings of the child!' D7.6:10; והוי לקח שערן ... ויהב בנשרן ושבק ... 'and do

---

... tu m'as fait serment." This reminds us of אז with an imperfect (but not apocopated form!) in BH as in Ex 15.1 אָז יָשִׁיר מֹשֶׁה 'then Moses sings [= sang].'

[894] Cf. Greenfield 1969 and Kaddari 1983.

[895] See § 81 d.

[896] הוו may be a pf. 3mp.

[897] Moriya (1994:285), following Fitzmyer (1971:224), speaks of "conative"

take barley ... and give (it in exchange) for beams and leave ...!'
A2.4:9. In the last-quoted example we have a series of coordinate
participles where they relate to one domain of activity, whereas
we note a shift of the verb form (from or to the imperative)
when the second verb belongs to a different domain of activity
as in הוי חזית על תשי A2.3:11 (sim. A2.7:2) 'Keep an eye on
Tashai' followed by ושלחי 'and send word!' ib.12 and הושרי לי תקם
5 חפנן 'Dispatch to me 5 handfuls of castor oil' followed by ויהוי
זבן גשרן ושבק בבתה 'and let him keep buying beams and leaving
(them) in his house' A2.2:14 (with a jussive). This periphrastic
imperative appears to be a favourite syntactic feature of the
writer of the Hermopolis letters.([898])

With the impf.: אהוה משלם 'I shall be repaying (by instalments)'
B4.2:7; "your (unpaid) silver and its interest will be increasing
upon me (from) month to month (יהוה רבה עלי ירח ירח לירח) until the
day that I repay it to you" ib.9; אריא יהוה מסמה לאילא 'a lion will
be lying in wait for a stag' C1.1:183. The subtle difference between
this periphrastic tense and the plain tense is matched by a difference
in preposition: אשלמנהי לך ירח בירח מן פרסי 'I shall repay it to you
month in month (out) from my salary' B4.2:5, which is to be
contrasted with ib.9 quoted above: the payment of the capital
along with the interest falls due monthly, whereas the interest on
arrears keeps growing from month to month. For an example
with a jussive (A2.2:14), see above.

The participle precedes the auxiliary הוה, when it is an internal
passive.([899]) The syntagm has nothing to do with iteration, habit
or such like, but indicates a state which prevailed or will prevail
([900]): מדבחא ... זי ביב בירתא בנה (= בנה) הוה מן קדמן 'the altar which,

---

force, but we fail to see that the syntagm indicates "more purposive intention
or volition."

[898] It escapes me how one could, with Hug (1993:118), contrast the above-
quoted הוי חזית as "handlungsorientiert: imperfektiv" with שלחי as "ergebnis-
orientiert: perfektiv."

[899] So also Greenfield 1969:204f. He further notes (1969:205-7) that this
rule does not apply to BA and QA. Classical Syriac has developed a different
kind of complementary distribution of the two sequences: see Muraoka 1997a:
§ 86-87. What Greenfield (1969:201) quotes as the only OA example, Sefire
III 6 הוי חלפה, 'be his successor,' does not belong here, as his own translation
suggests, for it is a substantivally used participle, and besides a pronominal
object of a participle is mediated by the preposition Lamed.
   That at A4.7:10 the auxiliary precedes a passive ptc., and that with a few
intervening words indicates a non-periphrastic syntagm: הוה תרען זי אבן 5 בנין
פסילה זי אבן 'there were five stone gates, built of hewn stones.' The interpretation

in Elephantine the fortress, was built from (a long) time ago'
A4.9:3, cf. A4.10:9; ... אבשוכן ממנין הוו 'they held appointment as
pressers (?) ...' A6.7:5; ידיע יהוי לך 'Let it be known to you!'
A6.10:8; מן קדם אוסרי בריכה הוי 'Be blessed before Osiris!' D20.5:3
הוי פלחה נמעתי // 'Do serve the Lord of the Two Truths' ib.4. See
also שליט יהוי 'Let him have the right ..' A6.4:4: this shows that
שליט is not fully verbal. That a stative verb such as כהל displays
this syntagm is easy to comprehend: לא כהל הוית 'I was impotent'
B3.10:17. This syntagm shares with the nominal clause expanded
by הוה following the predicate the feature that both describe a
state, not an action (§ 77 bk). In שקקן לבשן הוין וצימין ומצלין ליהו
A4.7:15 (sim. A4.8:14) we are to take the verb לבש as stative,
"to be wearing, dressed" and not as fientive, "to put on, wear":
'we were wearing sackcloth and fasting and praying to YHW.'(⁹⁰¹)
See also חדה ושריר הוי 'Be happy and strong!' A4.7:3 // A4.8:3
where חדה is, parallel to שריר, most likely adjectival (חֲדֵה?) rather
than a fientive active participle, 'rejoicing' (חָדֵה). An exception is
הוית מלא לבתך 'I was full of anger at you' A3.5:4. When the
external passive ptc. is used, the sequence is reversed, the ptc.
following הוה and emphasising repetition and iteration of action:
לקבל זי לקדמין הוה מתעבד 'in accordance with what used to be
done till (some) time ago' A4.9:10.

One of the examples just quoted above, A4.7:15, however,
contains three participles sharing one auxiliary: לבשן הוין וצימין
ומצלין. Since the last two are fientive verbs, this is elliptic for
לבשן הוין והוין צימין והוין מצלין. The clause is introduced by וכזי כונה
עביד 'when this had been done (to us).' The meaning cannot be
that when all this destruction had taken place, they were *already*
out there, fasting and praying etc., but rather the moment this
happened, they were out there doing this and that. The periphrastic
structure here is thus akin to the inchoative use of the Greek
imperfect. On a similar nuance of the corresponding structure in
BH, see Joüon - Muraoka 1993: § 121 g.

In only one case we find the syntagm [הוה + pc.]: וכל מן זי
הוה יָא[ת]ה עליך הוית אשלח שלמך 'I would send (to enquire about)

─────────

pluperfect force."

⁹⁰¹ Cp. Peshitta Mk 1.6 lviš (h)wa:ʾ lvuša:ʾ d-saʿra:ʾ d-g̱amle:ʾ (Gk. ἦν ...
ἐνδεδυμένος ..) 'was dressed with a robe of camel-hair' with Lk 16.19 la:veš
(h)wa:ʾ buṣa:ʾ (Gk. ἐνεδιδύσκετο πορφύραν) 'he used to dress in purple.'
Thus the possibility of defective spelling for לביש is not to be excluded.

your welfare [with whomeve]r would be co[m]ing to you' A3.5:3.

§ 56. Infinitive

a) The infinitive is a verb form which is always used in syntactical subordination to another verb or a noun. In our idiom, it is only rarely used as the subject of a nominal clause: see below at (**i**).([902])

b) On the use of the infinitive to complement verbs such as יכל, כהל, צבי, אבה as in לא אכהל למפלח בבב היכלא 'I shall not be able to serve in the gate of the palace' C1.1:17 and צבית למנתן 'you desire to give' B3.4:14, see below at § 73 *c*. Here belong אל תפשר למאתה 'Don't fail to come!' D7.20:4; לא שבקן לן למבניה 'they do not allow us to build it' A4.7:23, sim. A4.8:23; לא אכהל אכלאנך למבנה ... 'I shall not be able to restrain you from building ..' B2.1:6, sim. ib.9; טענוך לי מומאה למומא 'they imposed on you the oath to swear for me' B2.2:6([903]); לא שנציו למנעל בבירתא 'they did not succeed in entering the fortress' A6.7:7. Here also belongs שלחת לה למפרש לי מלתא 'I sent to him (asking) to explain the matter to me' D7.24:15. Likewise שלחת לה למחוה טעמא להושע 'I sent to him (asking) to show the order to Hosea' D7.24:16.

c) Another use of the infinitive is final, indicating the purpose of an action: "they assembled, went towards Dadarshu to do battle (למעבד קרב)" C2.1:15.

d) Unlike in Hebrew, the subject of an infinitive is not indicated by a conjunctive pronoun attached to it nor by a noun within the infinitive phrase. In many cases, as in examples dealt with above under (*b*) and (*c*), the subject of the infinitive is identical with that of the finite verb to which the infinitive is syntactically subordinate. This is obviously not the case in the following examples: יהבת לי תרע ביתא זילך למבנה אגר 1 תמה 'you gave me the gateway of your house (for me) to build a wall there' B2.1:3; ... טענוך לי מומאה למומא ביהו 'they imposed upon you the oath to swear for me by YHW' B2.2:6; [א]תית ביתך למנתן לי לברתך 'I came to your house (to ask you) to give me your daughter' B2.6:3, sim. B3.3:3; הן יפקד לך מראך מין למנטר 'if your master deposits with you water in order (for you) to keep (it)' C1.1:191; תאתא זי לך רבתא מטאת למגז 'your big sheep arrived (for you) to shear (it) [= to be sheared]' D7.8:2; שלחת לה למפרש לי

---

[902] Cp. Gn 2.18 לֹא טוֹב הֱיוֹת הָאָדָם לְבַדּוֹ 'it is not good for a man to be alone' with TO לָא תָקֵן דִּיהֵי אָדָם בִּלְחוֹדוֹהִי and Pesh. *la:ʾ šappir d-nehwe:ʾ ʾa:da:m balḥoḏaw*.

[903] The inf. can also be said to indicate a purpose.

מלחא 'I sent to him (asking) to explain the matter to me' D7.24:15.
In all these cases, though the subject of the infinitive differs
from that of the main verb, the former is signalled in one way or
another in the preceding part of the clause. In אתעשת על אגורא זך
למבנה 'Give thought to that temple to have (it re)built' A4.7:23,
though the rebuilding would be executed by the local Jewish
community, there is a sense in which one could say that it was
to be built by the Persian authorities. No explicit subject is to be
found in the context in ומין לא חסרה להשקיא חילא 'and it [= the
well] does not lack water to give to the troops' A4.5:7.

e) Some infinitives *modify a noun*: כפן למנשא משח 'ladles for
carrying oil' B3.8:19; בבה למנפק 'its gate for exit' B3.11:3; מלח
למשם בקמח 'salt to be put into flour' D7.2:7. Perhaps belong here
לה אשכחת אש למיתית לכן 'I haven't found anyone to bring (it) to
you' A2.4:11; זבנת חטבת ... למתיה לכן 'I bought striped cloth .. to
bring to you' ib.10; מין למנטר 'water to be watched over' C1.1:191.
In לעד אשכח אש למושרתהם לכן 'nobody has been found yet to send
them to you' A2.2:12, when compared with the earlier quoted
A2.4:11, not only the verb of the infinitive is different, but the
latter also has a conj. pron., and the infinitive appears to be more
closely bound with the main verb than in the other examples,
being more final in function: to paraphrase, "I have searched for
a carrier in order to send them to you, but so far no carrier has
been found." אש is the logical subject of למיתית (A2.4:11), but
not of למושרתהם.

f) Some infinitives modify a verb or an adjective, and explain
the preceding main word (*epexegetical*): שפיר מלך למחזה כשמש 'a
king is beautiful to look at like sun (or: Shamash)' C1.1:92; מלחי
לבתי לאמר ... 'you were (so) full of anger at me (as) to say ..'
A2.3:6. The ubiquitous, fossilised לאמר introducing a direct speech
may be so interpreted([904]): אמר ... לאמר ... 'he said .. saying ..'
B2.1:1 et passim. The following, though not linked to אמר as the
main verb, are variations on this usage: שלחת לאמר ... 'I have sent
(word), saying ..' A5.2:8; תשמעין לאמר ... 'you will hear say, ..'
D7.9:11; כזי כן שמיע לן לאמר ... 'when we had thus heard said ..'
A3.3:13; אל תפשר למאתה מחר 'do not fail to come tomorrow'
D7.20:4.

See also ביתא זנך לא שליט אנת לזבנה 'you have no right to sell
that house' B2.4:6([905]) and ... צדיק א[נ]ה ל[החסנותה 'I am entitled to

---

[904] Or possibly final: so Fitzmyer 1956:212.

[905] We are inclined to see a defective spelling in [... למא[ן]חד] [ש[לט] 'is
entitled to take possession of ..' B4.3:19 and אנת שלט למאחד 'you are entitled

bestow it ..' B7.3:6.

g) The temporal function of the infinitive, confined to the expression למטמה 'upon arriving (in such and such a place),' may be an Akkadianism: e.g. למטמה מדי בכנדור 'upon arriving (in) Media at Kundur' C2.1:25([906]); למטמה מרד]י[א אתכנשו 'upon (his) arrival the rebels rallied' ib.20; למטמן[טא ברחא 'upon arriving in Rakha' ib.41.

h) הוספה A6.2:17 in the midst of a lengthy catalogue is disputed.([907]) It does not occur in a well-formed clause.

i) Rare examples of the infinitive as the subject of a nominal clause are מחר לי למאזל]ל[ביתי 'tomorrow I have to go [to] my house' D7.1:9; כי לא ... כי לא בידי אנ]ש[א מנשא רגלהם ומנחתותהם בידיך מנשא רגלך למנחתותה 'for it is not in the hands of men to lift their foot and put them down ... for it is not in your hands to lift your foot to put it down' C1.1:170.

§ 57. Imperative

The imperative expresses a wish or command directed to the person(s) spoken to: e.g., זבן 'Sell!' A3.8:5; זף דגנא 'Borrow the grain!' C1.1:129; דין עבדי עמה 'Make suit with him!' B2.3:27. The term "imperative" should not mislead us: it could be used in addressing one's senior or superior: זבני עמר 'Buy wool' A2.6:5 (addressing one's mother).

In an official petition, the writer begins with a standard הן על מראי/ן טב, then takes recourse to an indirect mode of speech, viz. the jussive: e.g., ... הן על מראי לם כות טב אגרת מן מראי תשתלח 'if it thus please my lord, let a letter be sent from my lord ...' A6.13:2; sim. A6.7:8. The indirect and impersonal nature of such a request is evident in ... הן על מראי טב ישתלח 'if it please my lord, let (word) be sent ...' A6.3:5 where ישתלח lacks its grammatical subject. In A4.7 and A4.8 the petitioner first uses the imperative, with which he indicates the desired general attitude and stance on the part of the authorities, and subsequently spells out, by using the standard jussive, specific actions which he wishes to be taken: "if it please our lord, give thought (אתעשת) to

---

to ..' B4.4:17. This leaves לא ישלט בביתה כלה 'he shall have no right to the entire house' B3.5:20 as the only case of שלט as a verb.

[906] The Akk. here (57), for example, has *a-na ka-šá-di*.

[907] *TAD* A 101—impv. "Add," but (ל)הוסיף, i.e. inf. in the Heb. translation (p. 100); Grelot (1972:292)—"Additif:"; Joüon (1934:75)—"en addition" (accepted by Fitzmyer 1956:215); Leander (1928: 60j) and Cowley (1923:96) —long impv.

that temple to have (it re)built ... Regard (חזי) your obligees and friends who are here in Egypt. Let a letter be sent (ישתלח) ..." (A4.7:23f.). See also A4.8:22.

PART FOUR

SYNTAX

SECTION A

NOUN PHRASE EXPANDED

The following paragraphs (§§ 58-71) will describe various ways in which a noun, standing as the focal point of a phrase, may be expanded. Such an expanded noun phrase is endocentric in that it belongs to the same form class as the noun which is the head or nucleus of the phrase.

§ 58. Noun with a conjunctive pronoun

a) The noun נפש 'soul' is sometimes combined with an appropriate conjunctive pronoun to stress the identity of the person indicated by it[908]: e.g., חמרא ... עבד לנפשה 'he made the wine ... his own' A6.15:5, sim. B7.2:6; זרע נפשך 'your own seed' B1.1:4, sim. ib.13; בחמר נפשך 'with your own he-ass' ib.13 נ[ב]פקת נפשה 'his personal out[lay]' C3.19:7 vs. נפקת מדינתא 'the outlay of the province' ib.14. See also above at § 39 *h*.

b) On the opposition between the synthetic syntagm such as ביתי 'my house' and the analytic one such as בית(א) זילי or בית לי, see § 40 *h* and § 46.

c) A noun with a conjunctive pronoun is at times definitely more determinate than other related syntagmata. Thus גבר אחרן אמי ואבי אח ואחה ואיש אחרן לא ישלט בביתה כלה 'Another person—my mother or my father, brother or sister, or another man—shall not have right to the whole house' B3.5:19 where "my father" and "my mother" are unique, which is not the case with other people mentioned. It stands to reason therefore that one often meets בר לי, איש לי and the like, but never אב לי or אם לי.

d) A noun may be expanded by both a conjunctive pronoun

---

[908] So called reflexive.

and a demonstrative pronoun: דמי עבדי אלך 'the value of those slaves of mine' B8.7:1.

§ 59. Noun with a disjunctive possessive pronoun

a) A disjunctive possessive pronoun expanding a noun head or a noun phrase always and typically follows the latter as in בר זילה 'a son of his' B2.3:26; ביתא זילי 'my estate' A6.10:2.

b) A preceding noun phrase may consist of a construct chain or its analytical equivalent as in תרע ביתא זילך 'the gate of your house' B2.1:3, hardly 'your house-gate'; אגר ביתא זילה 'the wall of its house' B3.11:5. In all these cases the hierarchy appears to be $[N_1 + (N_2 + N_3)]$.

c) A preceding noun phrase may consist of a noun followed by an adjective as in עלים אחרן זילי 'another servant of mine' A6.11:5; נכסיא אחרנן זילי 'other goods of mine' A6.10:8([909]); עבד כרתך זילי 'a תרי Cretan slave of mine' B8.3:1; רבתא זילי 'my large room' B3.10:4, B3.11:6; וזיכא רבא זילנא 'our large vessel' C3.28:108. Exceptional are תאתא זי לך רבתא 'your big sheep' D7.8:2 and עמרא זילה קדמא 'its early wool' (?) ib.4.

d) A noun phrase may consist of a noun head followed by a demonstrative pronoun: אגרא זך זילך 'that wall of yours' B2.1:6; אגרא זך זילה 'that wall of his' ib.10. ארקא זך זיליכי B2.3:19 has also been interpreted by some authorities in a similar fashion.([910]) Joüon's argument is that a phrase such as ביתא זילך, which in theory could mean "the house is yours," means in practice "your house," for the former would be expressed as ביתא זילך הו or ביתך. But since the publication of Joüon's study a new text has been brought to light with the very sequence in question, which cannot mean anything but "the house is yours": ביתא זילך B3.12:30.([911]) Thus the above-quoted text of B2.3:19 should be rendered: 'that land is yours,' though this leads to a case of object deletion, for the phrase is followed by בני והבי .. 'Build

---

[909] On the incongruence (אחרניא for אחרנן), see below § 76 *d*.

[910] Joüon 1934:20f. and Grelot 1972:179 ("pour (le) donner à d'autres ce terrain qui t'appartient").

[911] Cowley (1923:25) sees a nominal clause in B2.3:19 (= Cowley 8.19) on the ground that there is a space before ארקא, though the space is not that large. See further below, § 77 *bn* and § 90 *b*.

ארקא זך בני B2.4:5, which can only mean 'Build that land up!,' does not support Joüon's interpretation of the phrase under consideration at B2.3:19, because the context is different and there is unmistakable emphasis in the latter on the ownership of the plot of the land.

(up) and give ..' Cf. B2.4:5.

e) A noun followed by a disjunctive possessive pronoun may be further followed by a phrase indicating a location introduced by זי as in בין בניא זילי זי בעליתא ותחתיתא 'in my domains which are in the Upper and Lower (Egypt)' A6.7:5; ביתא זילי זי במדינתכם 'my estate which is in your province(s)' A6.9:2. Comparing this syntagm and that discussed above in § d one might say that a demonstrative pronoun possesses a greater degree of cohesion with a head noun than a locative expression. A phrase such as ביתא זי במדינתא זילן would most likely mean 'the estate in our province' rather than 'our estate in the province.'

f) That this syntagm is well suited to bring out contrast seems to be indicated by the following example: "Yo[u brok]e [into my house] by force and struck my wife (וכתשת לאנתתי) ..." {and the person denying the charge speaking} "I did [not] break into your house by force and I did not strike the wife of yours (ולאנתתא זילך לא כתשת) ..." B7.2:4-9.

g) Some ambiguity may arise where a disjunctive possessive pronoun is preceded by two or more coordinate terms: מן גרדא או מן נכסיא אחרנן זילי 'in the domestic staff or other goods that are mine' A6.10:8 where זילי likely qualifies both of the preceding terms, cf. גרדא ונכסיא זילנא 'the domestic staff and goods that are ours' ib.1.

§ 60. Noun with the preposition Lamed of ownership or affiliation

a) The syntagm [Noun + ל + Conjunctive Pronoun or Noun] is often used as a substitute for a synthetic construct chain, mostly where the first noun is indefinite([912]), and is largely confined

---

[912] Cf. § 58 c.

This construction does not appear to be widely known among Semitists. Even Barth (1911:50) explicitly denies its existence. The following Syriac examples have come to our notice: Hos 2.1 *bnayya:ˀ lala:ha:ˀ ḥayya:ˀ* בְּנֵי אֵל חָי; Gn 41.16 *ˀala:ha:ˀ neˁne:ˀ šla:ma:ˀ lferˁon* אֱלֹהִים יַעֲנֶה שְׁלוֹם פַּרְעֹה; Is 40.3 *pannaw ˀurḥa:ˀ lma:rya:ˀ waṭroṣ bafqaˁṭa:ˀ švile:ˀ lala:han*; ib. 62.10 *pannaw ˀurḥa:ˀ lˁamma:ˀ* פַּנּוּ דֶּרֶךְ הָעָם; Gn 45.8 *ˀava:ˀ lferˁon* אָב לְפַרְעֹה πατέρα Φαραω; Ezr 4.14 *ṣaˁra:ˀ lmalka:ˀ* עֶרְוַת מַלְכָּא; 1Sm 16.18 *bra:ˀ lišay* בֶּן לְיִשַׁי; 1Kg 18.22 *nviya:ˀ lala:ha:ˀ* נָבִיא לִיהוה. Brockelmann (1913: §160) does not quote any example from Aramaic or Syriac, though he duly notes the syntagm in Hebrew, in which it is fairly widespread (Joüon - Muraoka 1991: 130 *a-c*).

This use of the preposition Lamed is most likely affiliated with its use in the nominal clause expressing possession as in חֶרֶב לַיהוה וּלְגִדְעוֹן (Peshitta: *ḥarba:ˀ lma:rya:ˀ walg̱edˁon*) 'the Lord and Gideon have a sword.'

to legal documents.([913]) The noun following such a ל indicates the owner, possessor, authority above or relative of what is indicated by the first noun. The distribution of this syntagm is thus semantically conditioned: the second term indicates an animate entity. In other words, not every construct phrase can be transformed into this analytic form. Such a force of the Lamed is illustrated in לך יהוה וזי בניך אחריך 'he shall be yours and of your sons after you' B2.11:9 and בני ואנתה ואיש לי 'my children, and a woman or a man related to me' B2.10:10; וביתא ביתכי אפם ולבניכי אחריכי 'and the house is your house likewise and your children's after you' B2.3:15. Further examples are בר לה 'a son of his' B2.1:9; ארק לדרגמן 'land belonging to Dargamana' B2.2:7; ארדיכל לסון בירתא 'a builder of Syene the fortress' B2.8:2.([914]) Here belongs most likely the ubiquitous לדגל as in משלם בר זכור ארמי זי סון לדגל וריזת 'Meshullam son of Zaccur, an Aramaean of Syene of the detachment of Varyazata' B3.3:2. This standing expression with לדגל is never replaced by any other mode of expansion of noun phrases.

b) Instructive is a study of the variety of titles given to "a servitor of YHW":([914a])

with ל	לחן ליה	B3.4:25
	לחן ליהו	B3.2:2, B3.4:3, B3.10:2, B3.12:10([915])
with זי	לחן זי יהה	B3.3:2
	לחן זי יהו	B3.5:2, B3.7:2, B3.11:1, B3.12:1
	לחנא זי יהו	B3.10:23, B3.11:17, B3.12:33
	לחנה זי יהו	(f.s.) B3.12:2

Some of the above examples show that the syntagm [Noun + ל] is synonymous with that mediated by זי, as is also evident in בר וברה לכי ואיש זילכי 'a son and daughter of yours and a man of yours' B2.3:12 where there is no perceptible functional opposition between the two structures. Likewise בר לן is equal to בר זילן, as shown by בר לן וברה אח ואחה לן הנגית והנבג ואדרנג זילן 'a son of ours and a daughter, a brother and a sister of ours, partner-in-chattel and partner-in-land and guarantor of ours' B3.12:27; בנין ובנתן ואחין ואיש זילן 'our sons and our daughters and our brothers and a

---

[913] So Kutscher (1972:102-4), though this does not by itself mean that it is an archaic feature. The only example in a non-legal document is פקיד למדינא 'an official of the province' A4.2:6 (למדינא, an error for למדינתא?).

[914] In this last example, Syene can perhaps be considered to be a personal entity, on the analogy of לחן ליהו, an architect in the service of Syene.

[914a] See also Porten 1996:205, n. 5.

[915] This is a reworked version of לחן זי יהו at line 1.

person of ours' B2.9:10 // בניכם ואחיכם ואיש לכם 'your sons and your brothers and a person of yours' ib.11. See also B2.11:8,9.([916])

c) The synonymity of the syntagm [Noun + Conj. pron.] and [Noun + ל Noun] is evident in: ביתא ביתכי אפם ולבניכי אחריכי 'the house is your house likewise and of your children after you' B2.3:15.

d) Another type of synonymity is between the two syntagmata mentioned above under [b], two noun phrases joined by either ל or זי, as represented in לחן זי יהו B3.12:1, which becomes לחן ליהו in its rewritten version, line 10. See also בר לי וברה לי הנגית זילי והנבג ואדרנג זילי 'son of mine or daughter of mine or partner-in-chattel of mine or parter-in-land of mine' B3.10:18.

e) Though outnumbered in our corpus by the attributive use, the predicative one may represent the earlier stage of this use of Lamed and the disjunctive possessive זיל.([916a])

f) The syntagm [זי + ל + Noun] does not occur. Thus ביתא זילך וזי בניך מן אחריך 'the house is yours indeed and of your children after you' B3.4:16, and not וזי לבניך; similarly B2.10:8, B3.5:4. In other words, there is a morphosyntactically conditioned complementary distribution: [-זיל + conj. pron.] as against [זי + noun phrase].([917]) This is remarkable, since, where no זי is used, both בר לי 'a son of mine' and לחן ליהו 'a servitor of Yaho's' are attested, as we have seen above.

g) A variation on the pattern just mentioned ([f]) is represented by the opposition in דילכי הו ולבניכי מן אחריכי 'it is yours and your sons after you' B2.7:7 and לא הות ארק לדרגמן זילי הא אנה 'it was not land of Dargamana, of me, yes, me' B2.2:7.

h) The Lamed in למן at ביתא זילך אם וזי בניך מן אחריך ולמן זי למן צבית למנתן B3.4:16 is not of the kind under discussion here as becomes clear when one compares it with אנת ... שליט בביתא זך

---

[916] That the Lamed in a phrase like לחן ליהו (likewise in פקיד למדינא 'an official of the province' A4.2:6) resembles the dativus commodi, a servitor serving, for the good of, YHW is immaterial, for such an analysis cannot be made to apply to בר לן which is to בר זילן, what לחן ליהו is to לחן זי יהו.

[916a] For a similar line of thinking, see Pennacchietti (1968:56).

[917] Thus the often-mentioned resemblance between LBH (MH in particular) and Aramaic in this respect is significantly incomplete, for in the former the preposition Lamed must be present whether the second member is a noun or pronoun: הַכֶּרֶם שֶׁלִּי 'my vineyard' and הַכֶּרֶם שֶׁלַּמֶּלֶךְ 'the king's vineyard.' The two Aramaic syntagmata, though both being analytic in character, must have had different origins. On the MH form, see Yalon 1964:26f. and Kutscher 1956:10f.

ובניך מן אחריך ולמן די צביה למנתן B3.4:11 'you ... have right to that house and (so do) your children after you and one to whom you desire to give (it)': מן די לה = למן די.([918])

i) Where more than one NP is to be qualified by a syntagm [ל + conj. pron. with identical referent] there are attested a number of alternative patterns with respect to the position of the syntagm and its repetition or otherwise:

בר לי וברה לי הנגית זילי והנבג ואדרנג זילי

'son of mine or daughter of mine, partner-in-chattel who is mine or partner-in-land or guarantor who is mine' B3.10:18([919])

ובשם בנן ואנתה ואיש לי

'and in the name of children or woman or man of mine' B2.10:12([920])

בר לי וברה אנתה ואיש

'son of mine or daughter, woman or man' B2.10:13.

§ 61. Noun in the status constructus

a) In בר בטני C1.1:139 the syntactic relationship between the three constituents is (בטני + בר)י, not בר + בטני 'the son of my belly,' but 'my own son'([921]): cf. BH פְּרִי בִטְנֶךְ and see below at § *d*.

b) The close semantic cohesion([922]) of the two constituent nouns of a construct phrase is sometimes reflected in their being spelled together: e.g. אבנצרף 'dyer's stone' A4.3:3.([923]) For more examples, see § 10 *c*.

c) The logico-semantic relationships between a nomen regens, which is the noun head, and a following, nomen rectum, displays a remarkably rich variety of relationships.([924]) The former,

---

[918] See on the relative clause, § 42 *e*, and cf. Goshen-Gottstein 1949.

[919] See also בר וברה לכם אח ואחה אנתה ואיש לכם 'son or daughter of yours, brother or sister, woman or man of yours' B2.10:10.

[920] See also בר וברה ואנתה ואיש לכם 'son or daughter or woman or man of yours' B2.10:14.

[921] Also Lindenberger (1985:504) and Kottsieper (1990:16) "mein eigener Sohn."

[922] As noted by Whitehead (1974:219), we find לם breaking up a genitive phrase in גרדא לם זי מראתי 'the domestic staff of my lady' A6.15:8.

[923] The letter Nun here has the shape of a medial Nun, on which see Naveh 1970:27f.

[924] More than one classification system is known. How to "back-transform" a given construct phrase could result in more than one clause: thus Kroeze

in the status constructus, is defined and delimited by the latter in a variety of ways. Such relationships may be classified in terms of underlying syntactic relationships. Morphologically N_1 may be linked with N_2[925] (**a**) by the way of construct chain, (**b**) synthetically by N_2 taking the form of a conjunctive pronoun, and (**c**) analytically by means of ד/זי. Where not every one of these three modes of linkage is attested in our corpus, it is not always possible to determine whether it is due to incomplete attestation or not. Moreover, the assignment of a given phrase to one or other of the logico-semantic categories is not always certain. One may thus compare the title מלך אתור 'the king of Assyria' C1.1:4 with מלך באתור ib.5 in a description of his succession. Again, a slave in the ancient world is a possession of his master. So an example such as עבדיה זי מבטחיה 'the slaves of Mibtahiah' B2.11:3, which has been placed below under (ii) *relational* could arguably be classified under (i) *possessive*. But when officers in the Persian administration address their superior with מראן 'our lord,' calling themselves עבדיך, such a "possessive" interpretation is patently inappropriate, whereas the "relational" one can cover both.[926]

i) *possessive*[927]: N_2 possesses or owns N_1. Such a possession can be inalienable as is the case with body parts, "my eyes." E.g. **a)** ביד רכליא 'in the hand of the merchants' A4.3:4; בצות מלכא 'by the voice of the king' A4.2:14; שמהת נשיא 'the names of the women' A4.4:4; בזרע נפשך 'with your own seed' B1.1:4; אגורא יהו אלהא 'the temple of YHW the god' B3.4:9; אגורי אלהי מצרין 'the temples of the gods of Egypt' A4.7:14; אוצר מלכא 'the treasury of the king' B3.7:7+; בית מלכא 'the house of the king' B3.13:6+; דיני מלכא 'the judges of the king' B5.1:3; אנפי אסרחאדן 'the face of Esarhaddon' C1.1:14; חיל אתור 'the army of Assyria' ib.55; עלעי תנין 'the ribs of a dragon' ib.90; לבב כנתה 'the heart of his colleague' ib.99; חן גבר 'the grace of a man' ib.132; שם אבוהי 'the name of his father' ib.138; עיני אלהן 'the eyes of gods' ib.172; חרב חילך 'the

---

(1993:77) back-transforms אלהי השמים to "the God who created heaven," but it could equally be transformed into "the God who dwells in heaven." See also Kroeze 1991 and Kroeze 1997. Cf. Folmer 1995:262-325; Joüon - Muraoka 1993: § 129 *d-h*; Waltke-O'Connor 1990: 143-54; Curme 1931:77-88; Quirk, Greenbaum, Leech & Svartvik 1972:193.

[925] N_1 and N_2 stand for the referent symbolised by the first noun, nomen regens, and the second noun, nomen rectum, respectively.

[926] It is an intriguing sociological question how עלימא at זילי סריסא עלימא זילי 'the eunuch, the lad (?) of mine' C1.1:63 is to be interpreted in this light.

[927] Possession understood in a rather broad sense, including claim and

sword of your troop' ib.4; אלפי מלכא 'the boats of the king' ib.7;
בתי אלהיא 'the houses of the gods' C3.5:11; כסף גבריא 'the silver
of the men' C3.7Cr2:12+. **b**) חקלי 'my field' B1.1:3; חלקי 'my
portion' ib.11; כתונה 'his garment' C1.1:41; קלה 'his voice' ib.91;
דמה 'his blood' ib.184; הדרה 'his glory' ib.92; חרבי 'my sword'
ib.110; חטך 'your arrow' ib.126; בתין 'our houses' B4.3:8; נכסי 'my
property' A6.3:5; עיני 'my eyes' C1.1:105; גלדי 'my hide' ib.167;
שפותה 'his lips' ib.132; קדלה 'his neck' ib.134; חנכה 'his palate'
ib.163; בשרה 'his flesh' ib.184; דרעה 'her arm' D7.9:4,5; רגלהם
'their leg' C1.1:170; פמהם 'their mouth' ib.172; ידכם 'your hand'
A4.3:9; גרמיך 'your bones' C1.2:6; שמך 'your name' A4.7:26; אנפכם
'your face' A5.1:4; לבבן 'our heart' B2.9:8; בלך 'your mind' C1.1:81;
אדניהם ... פמך 'their ears ... your mouth' C1.1:81; נפשך 'your soul'
ib.130; הימנותה ושנאתה 'his loyalty and his hateful characteristic'
ib.132; עדבך 'your lot' ib.136; שמהתהם 'their names' ib.164; כסיכי
'your cover' ib.167; עתרי 'my riches' ib.206; נכסיהום ובתיהם 'their
goods and houses' C2.1 III:2; כספך 'your silver' B3.1:11.   **c**) יודנא
אוצרא זי מלכא 'the barley-house (?) of the king' A4.5:5; זי מלכא
'the treasury of the king' B3.4:9; אגורא זי יהו 'the temple of YHW'
A4.7:6+; מדבחא זי יהו 'the altar of YHW' ib.26; תמי זי חנום 'the
way of Khnum' B3.4:8; ביתא זילי 'my estate' A6.10:2; חלקא זילי
'the portion of mine' B3.5:9; פלגא דילך 'the half of yours' B3.10:14;
ביתא זילי 'the residence of mine' C1.1:48; זילי 'the army of
mine' C2.1:16; חילא זי מדי 'the army of Media' C2.1:39; ספינה 1 זי
גלפרס '1 ship of Glaphyros' C3.7Ev1:11; with a proleptic
pronoun—ביתה זי אפולי 'the house of A.' B3.4:4; פגרה זי אחיקר 'the
corpse of Ahiqar' C1.1:63; תסהרא זי מלכא 'the barque of the
king' C1.2:1.

ii) *relational*: someone is N₁ in relation to N₂. E.g. **a**) מרא
מלכן 'the lord of kings' A1.1:1; עדר בר פסי 'Eder son of Pasai'
A2.1:11; רב חילא 'the troop commander' A4.3:3+; סגן נגריא 'chief
of the carpenters' A6.2:9; פחת יהוד 'the governor of Judah' A4.7:1;
מלך מצרין 'the king of Egypt' ib.13; דיני מדנתא 'the judges of the
province' A5.2:7; ספרי מדינתא 'the scribes of the province' A6.1:1;
עבד נבו אלהא 'servant of Nabu the god' B8.4:7; מלך אתור 'the king
of Asssyria' C1.1:4+; יעט אתור כלה 'the counsellor for the whole
of Assyria' ib.12; רבי אבי 'the young men of my father' ib.33; בר
פנוש 'the son of Punesh' C1.2:2; ברת מחסה 'the daughter of Mahsah'
B2.3:36.   **b**) עבדך 'your servant' A1.1:1; מריהם 'their owners'
A4.4:8; כנותה 'his colleagues' A4.7:1, B8.4:2; בעלה 'her husband'
B2.6:4+(⁹²⁸); אנתתי 'my wife' B3.3:7+; אבוהי 'his father' B3.6:14;

---

inalienable possession such as parts of the body.

ברך 'your son' ib.([929]); ברי 'my son' C1.1:127; אמה 'his mother'
B3.7:3; אחתך 'your sister' B3.8:3; מראך 'your master' C1.1:191.
c) כהניא זי יהו 'the priests of YHW' A4.3:1; לחן זי יהו 'a servitor of
Yaho' B3.12:1, sim. ib.2; גנן זי חנום 'a gardener of Khnum' B3.10:10,
B3.11:6; המרכריא זי גנזא 'the treasury accoutants' A6.2:4; פקידא
זילי 'the official of mine' A6.13:3; אנתתא זילך 'the wife of yours'
B7.2:9 // אנתתי 'my wife' ib.5; גרדא לם זי מראתי 'the domestic staff
of my lady' A6.15:8; איש זילן 'a person of ours' B2.9:10; בר וברה
זי יזניה 'son or daughter of Jezaniah' B2.10:13; עבד כרתך זילי 'a
Cretan slave of mine' B8.3:1; סריס זילי 'a eunuch of mine' C1.1:61;
with a proleptic pronoun—עבדיה זי מבטחיה 'the slaves of Mibtahiah'
B2.11:3; אבוהי זי אסרחאדן 'the father of Esarhaddon' C1.1:47; אבוה
זי אתור 'the father of Assyria' ib.55;   אחוהי זי ענני 'the brother of
Anani' A4.7:18;

   iii) *appositive*: N₁ is known under the name or symbol of,
or expressible as N₂. E.g. a) מדינת נא 'the province of Memphis'
A4.2:6, C3.14:35; בירח תמוז 'in the month of Tammuz' A4.7:4; מן
שנת 24 עד שנת 31 'from the year 24 to the year 31' A5.2:6; דמי כסף
כנכרין 1 לף 'the value of silver, 1 thousand talents' A4.7:28; דגל
וריזת 'the detachment of Varyazata' B2.2:4; ירח תחות 'the month of
Thoth' B3.13:1; ירח פאפי 'the month of Phaophi' B4.4:1, sim.
B4.5:1,5, B5.1:1, C3.7Gr2:14; במת נביה 'in the land of *Nbyh*'
B8.1:17; מאת נביעקב 'the century of Nabuakab' C3.13:54; יום שבה
'the Sabbath day' D7.35:7([930]); ביום 6 לפאפי 'on the 6th day of

---

[928] Fitzmyer (1971:150), who makes an interesting observation that in
Elephantine marriage contracts a man's relationship to his bride is formally
and explicitly recorded, whereas her consent to the relationship is not, wonders
whether the translation "her husband" is strong enough. Both "husband" and
"wife" are terms of relationship. The examples under discussion here may be
better placed under that of possession: "her owner" and "my woman," though
the Hebrew איש would present a problem.

[929] Although a case like ברך may be assigned to (iv) *origin* (so Curme
1931:78), our classification is supported by an utterance such as לך יהוה וזי
בניך אחריך 'he shall be yours and of your sons after you' B2.11:12, on which
see our discussion above. Compare also [וצ]בית עזקתה זי שנחאריב '[and the
bear]er of the seal of Sennacherib' C1.1:3 with צב[י]ת עזקה יהוה לך 'he will be
bea[rer] of a seal for you' ib.19. On the other hand, the preposition Lamed
can indicate possession or ownership as in מתא לי הות 'the land became mine'
C2.1:29. But then we are not saying that a "relative" construct or genitive
phrase necessarily presupposes the preposition Lamed: see, for instance, "A
Margian—king over them (עליהם) they made" C2.1:30.

[930] Our analysis does not take the history or etymology of the phrase into
account: the abbreviated form שבה 'the Sabbath' D7.16:2 shows that the word

Paophi' A4.2:15(⁹³¹). **c)** if not a scribal error—אמתך זי שמה תמת 'Tamet by name, who is your handmaiden' B3.3:3. Here the syntagm **b** is highly unlikely.

iv) *origin*: N₁ originates in or from N₂. E.g. **a)** אגרת ארשם 'the letter of Arsames' A6.15:4; עבור ארקתא 'the grain of the lands' ib.6; מלת מלך 'a king's word' B1.1:12, C1.1:84,88; מלי מנוכי 'the words of Mannuki' B8.7:2; מלי אחיקר 'the words of Ahiqar' C1.1:1; חמר צידן 'wine of Sidon' C3.12:7. **b)** מלי 'my words' C1.1:4; אמריך 'your sayings' ib.86; כדבתה 'his lies' ib.133; מליהם 'their words' B8.12:1; עטתה 'his counsel' C1.1:28, sim. ib.53; כדבת שפותא 'the lies of his lips' ib.132. **c)** מליא זי מלכא 'the words of the king' C1.2:3.

v) *locational and temporal*(⁹³²): N₁ is localised in N₂. E.g. **a)** אלה שמיא 'the god of heaven' A4.3:2(⁹³³); מרא שמיא 'the lord of heaven' A4.7:15; אלהי מצרין 'the gods of Egypt' C1.2:19,25; בירת יב 'the fortress of Elephantine' A4.5:5 // יב בירתא ib.; שכן יב ברתא 'a dweller of E. the fortress' B3.12:2; ספרי אוצרא 'the scribes of the treasury' B4.4:12. **c)** ארמי זי סון 'an Aramaean of Syene' B2.1:2; יהודין זי יב בירתא 'Jews of Elephantine the fortress' B2.9:2(⁹³⁴); מלח זי מיא קשיא 'a boatman of the rough waters' B2.2:11; רב חילא זי סון 'the troop commander of Syene' B2.10:4, B3.9:2,3; נשן זי יב בירתא 'a lady of ...' B3.1:2; (דגל) וידרן זי מנפי '(the detachment of) Vidarna of Memphis' C3.8 III B:36.(⁹³⁵)

One may assign here חמר זי שנת 11 'wine of year 11' C3.7Gr3:3, and the like.

The syntagm **b** is highly unlikely.

vi) *condition*: N₂ finds itself in a condition denoted by N₁. E.g. **a)** שלם מראי 'the welfare of my lord' A3.1v:1; שלם טביא 'the welfare of the gazelle' C1.1:168; כיבי אלהיהם 'the pains of their gods' C1.2:19. **b)** שלמך 'your welfare' A4.4:1.

vii) *membership*: N₁ consists of N₂'s. E.g. **a)** גרד אמגן 'domestic staff of craftsmen' A6.10:6; נפחר קטיליא 'the total of the killed'

---

was used as the name of the seventh day of the week.

⁹³¹ That the יום here is in the st. cst. is to be inferred by the analogy of שנת: see also Fitzmyer 1971:145.

⁹³² Folmer's (1995:318) statement that the first term is always indeterminate is contradicted by one of her own examples, our fourth under (**c**).

⁹³³ See Lipiński 1994:200f.

⁹³⁴ Cf. יהודי זי בבירת יב 'a Jew in the fortress of E.' B2.2:3. See § 68 *c, d*.

⁹³⁵ The notion of "locational" is more explicit in another syntagm exemplified in יהודי זי בבירת יב 'a Jew who is in the fortress of Elephantine' B2.2:3 and the

C2.1:49. **c)** דגלן זי מצריא 'detachments of the Egyptians' A4.5:1.

viii) *material*([936]): N₁ is made of or from N₂. E.g. **a)** מסמרי נחש ופרזל 'bronze and iron nails' A6.2:12; לבשי קמר וכתן מאני נחש ופרזל 'woolen and linen garments, bronze and iron utensils' B2.9:5; בית נחשא 'the bronze house' C1.1:121; משח זית 'olive oil' B3.8:20; מאן נחש ופרזל 'bronze and iron vessel' following בי זי לבנן 'brick house' B3.13:11; 1 לבש משך '1 leather garment' A2.4:8. **c)** עמודיא זי אבנא 'the stone pillars' A4.7:9; תרען זי אבן 'stone gates' ib.; פסילה זי אבן 'hewn stone, stone slab' ib.10; מזרקיא זי זהבא וכסף 'the gold and silver basins' ib.12; 1 לבש זי עמר '1 woolen garment' B2.6:7, also B3.8:6,7,11,13,14,18,19,20; בי זי לבנן 'brick house' B3.1:9, B3.13:11, B4.3:18; כסין זי נחש 'cups of bronze' C3.13:1,3 immediately followed by כס כסף 'silver cup' ib.4, same at ib.13,14; 1 כתן זי כתן '1 linen tunic' A3.3:11.

The syntagm **b** is rather unlikely in this category. Note לבשי זי קמר 'my woolen garment' B8.2:16.

ix) *time-span*: N₁ is a period of time during which a person referred to by N₂ is active. E.g. **a)** יומי מלך מצרין 'the period of the king of Egypt' A4.7:13. **b)** יומיך 'your days' C1.1:86; C2.1:72.

x) *partitive*: N₁ is part of N₂. E.g. **a)** חרי יהודיא 'the nobles of the Jews' A4.7:19; תרע ביתא זילך 'the gateway of your house' B2.1:3; שטר ביתי 'the side of my house' ib.5; זוית ביתי 'the corner of my house' ib.; ראש מלכותא 'the beginning of the reign' B2.2:1; פלג ביתא 'half of the house' B2.4:11; פלג מנתא 'half of the portion' B5.1:3; אנפי ארעא כלה 'the face of the whole earth' B2.6:19; אגר תרי רבתא 'the wall of the large room' B3.10:11; אגר ביתא 'the wall of the house' B3.11:5; מן קצת כספא 'from part of the silver' B4.6:4; בכפיד ... בכפרגל 'on the plam of the hand ... on the sole of the foot' B8.6:10; בב היכלא 'the gate of the palace' C1.1:17,23; תרע היכלא 'the palace gate' ib.44; כנפי לבשך 'the corners of your garment' ib.107; מנת משחא 'portion of the oil' C3.7Ar2:4+. **b)** תרעיה 'its gates' C1.1:104; פלגה 'half of it' B7.3:6,8; **c)** תרע זי תחית 'the gateway of the _ḥyt_' B3.10:15; תרעא זילה 'its gate' B3.12:21; with prolepsis—תונה זי ביתא 'its chamber, of the house' B3.5:3; קצתה זי כסף ש 1 'its part, of the silver 1 sh(ekel)' A2.2:7.

xi) *topical*: N₁ is about N₂. E.g. **a)** ספר חוב חקל 'land lease document' B1.1:19; ספר אגרא ... 'document of the wall ...' B2.1:20; ספר מרחק 'document of withdrawal' B2.2:22+; ספר בי זי 'document of house' B2.3:35, B3.4:25, B3.5:25+; ספר פלגנן 'document of our division' B2.11:14, sim. ib.17; ספר אנתו 'document of wifehood' B3.8:45; ספר זבנתא 'the document of sale/purchase' B3.12:31;

---

like: see § 68 *c, d.*

ספר עבור 'document of grain' B3.13:15; ספר מומה 'document of oath' B7.4; ספר אסרן 'document of obligation' B8.10:1; דין שנאה 'law of hatred' B3.8:39, B6.4:2,6; חשבון עבורא 'the account of grain' C3.28:79. **b**) מלוהי 'particulars concerning it' B3.10:16. The syntagm **c** is rather unlikely.

xii) *subjective*: N₁ is performed by N₂. E.g. **a**) מוע שמש '(place where) the sun comes out' B2.2:8, sim. מערב שמש '(place where) the sun sets' ib.9; מדנח שמש 'east' B3.7:7; ממלל מלך 'the speech of a king' C1.1:84. **b**) עבידתך 'your service' C1.1:21; עבידתהם 'their work' ib.207; בחיי ובמותי 'in my lifetime and upon my death' B2.3:3; בחייך ועד מותך 'in your lifetime and even unto your death' B3.6:12; חטאיך 'your sins' ib.50; חמתי 'my wrath' ib.140; הלכתך 'your conduct' C2.1:66.

xiii) *objective*: N₂ is affected by N₁. E.g. **a**) ארב פם ... ארב מלחם 'ambush of mouth ... ambush of battle' C1.1:83; דרכי ארקא 'treaders of the earth' ib.92; מפתח פם 'the opening of the mouth' ib.114, sim. 162; רכבי סוסין 'those mounted on horses' C2.1:44; עבד משח ... 'maker of the oil ...' C3.11:4. **b**) יסגה בעדרה 'proceeds to his help' C1.1:126. **c**) לערקה זי דדרש 'to meet Dadarshu' C2.1:15 et passim.

xiv) *contents*([937]): N₁ consists of N₂. E.g. **a**) זפת כסף שקלן 4 'a loan of silver, 4 shekels' B3.1:3([938]); **c**) אביגרנא זי כסף כרשן עשרה 'the penalty of silver, ten karsh' B2.9:14, B2.10:15([939]); תכונה זי כסף 'cash in silver' B3.8:5.

xv) *purpose*: N₁ is for the purpose or in the service of N₂. E.g. **a**) שניתת מקרא 'naming incision' B2.11:4,6; בית קנחנתי 'the house of the shrine' B3.10:9; אגר דרגא 'the wall of the stairway' B3.10:10; מהר אחתך 'mohar for your sister' B3.8:4; אתר עבורא 'the place of grain (= grain depot?) D7.56:6. **b**) דרגה ותרבצה ...בבה 'its stairway and its courtyard ... its gate' B3.11:3.

---

[936] Cf. Folmer 1995:312-17.

[937] Akin to vii) *membership*. This category is further affiliated to that of apposition, (iii) above, as shown by two phrases, mentioned by Folmer (1995:317), analogous to the second example quoted here: אבגרן כסף כרשן 10 'a penalty of silver 10 karsh' B3.7:17 and כסף אבגרן כרש חד 1 'silver, a penalty of one karsh, 1' B3.13:6.

[938] According to Joüon (1934:40f.) זפת is in the st.abs., though I fail to follow his logic: "זפת est à l'accusatif, et donc à l'état indéterminé et non à l'état construit" (ib., p. 40).

[939] Parallel to an apposition: אביגרנא כסף צריף כרשן עשרה B2.11:10, sim. B3.8:31; אבגרן כסף כרשן 50 B3.6:8,14, sim. B3.7:17, B3.9:7, B5.5:6. The first example suggests that אבגרן in the second cannot be in the st. cst. Cf. also

xvi) *species*[940]: N_2 is a species of N_1. E.g. **a)** אבן שש 'alabaster stone' B3.8:18.[941]

xvii) *classificatory*: N_1 is to be classified under the label of N_2. E.g. **a)** כסף יון 'Greek silver' B3.12:5; כתן אישׁתרי 'ʾytšry flax' C3.11:4 (?); זרע קטין 'cucumber seed' D7.3:2; זרע דלען 'pumpkin seed' ib.6; אלפי עבורא 'grain boats' D7.2:4

xviii) *qualitative*: N_1 is characterised by N_2. E.g. **a)** יום רוח 'a day of wind, a windy day' C1.1:104; שׁהד חמס 'malicious witness' ib.140; בחרב חילך 'with your mighty sword' C1.2:4. It is to be doubted that the syntagm **b** could occur in this category.

xix) *miscellaneous*. Here are gathered those examples in which we are not able to formulate a logcial relationship between the two terms. A considerable number of them is comprised by those in which N_1 is בעל. Only the syntagm **a)** is attested, and the other two are highly unlikely. In some cases בעל denotes a person who is possessed of what is denoted by N_2 or who is a member of a social or communal body denoted by N_2. E.g., בעל עטתא טבתא 'the master of good counsel' C1.1:42; בעל אגר 'a master of wages (= employer)' ib.100; בעל טבתכם 'your friend' D7.1:3; בעלי טבתך 'your friends' A4.7:23[942]; בעל פתורא 'members of the table' C3.27:22; בעל דגל 'a member of a detachment' B2.1:9; בעל דגל ובעל קריה 'a member of a detachment and a member of a town' B2.7:10; בעלי יב[943] 'the citizens of Elephantine' A4.7:22.

Other examples are more difficult to classify. Some indicate weights and measures, and others have to do with values. These are, however, meanings of the first terms, and the *logical relationship between the two terms* remains obscure. Thus אבני מלכא 'the royal weights' ib.7; אבני פתח 'the stone(-weight)s of Ptah' B4.2:2; מתקלת מלכא 'the royal measures' B2.11:11, B3.9:8; תחומי ארקא זך 'the boundaries of that land' B2.2:7; משׁחת ביתא זך 'the measurements of that house' B3.5:5; בריום '(1) day old' D7.37:2; ברת שנן 100 '100 years-old female' B3.5:17; מרבית כספך 'the interest

---

[5] דמוהי כסף שׁקלן 'its price [5] shekels' B3.2:7.

[940] This term is used by Folmer (1995:317f.) in a broader sense.

[941] At A4.7:11 the scribe initially wrote עקהי ארז 'cedar trees, subsequently converting the first word to עקהן and adding זי above the line, a reading which agrees with the revised version at A4.8:10.

[942] A calque of an Akkadian idiom, *be:l ṭa:bti,* immediately followed by an Aramaic gloss, רחמיך.

[943] A Northwest Semitic lexical isogloss: see Porten 1996:143, n. 71.

[943a] Cf. Grelot (1972:417): "le sanctuaire de YahoΔ notre Dieu," perhaps in opposition to the above-quoted designation, "the temples of the gods of

on your silver' B4.2:3; סתר ארזא 'the concealment of the cedar'
C1.1:111; מכס פטאסי 'the tax of Peteisi' C3.11:8; יתרן כספא 'the
surplus of the silver' ib.6; כסף שנאה 'silver of hatred' B2.6:23+;
דין ספרא זנה 'the law of this document' B2.6:31; דמי נכסיא 'the
value of the goods' B3.3:6; דמי ביתן 'the price of our house'
B3.12:5; דמי נוניך 'the value of your fish' B7.1:5; דמי נתרא 'the
value of the natron' C3.7Kv2:4+; דמי כסף 'silver value' B2.7:6,
B3.8:15,23, which, however, does not mean "value of silver,"
but value of some commodity expressed in that of silver. Here
we find a few cases of the syntagm **b**): משחתה 'its measurements'
B2.3:4; דמוהי 'its value' B2.7:3; תחומוהי 'its boundaries' B2.10:8+;
מרביתה 'its interest, i.e. interest accruing from a loan'
B3.1:4,8,15,16; B4.2:8,9 (origin?).

d) In a concatenation of two or more successive cst. nouns
in which each constituent is subordinate to what precedes, their
immediate constituent hierarchy can vary:

[N₁ + [N₂ + N₃]]—יומי מלך מצרין 'the days of the king of
Egypt' A4.7:13; אגורי אלהי מצרין 'the temples of the gods of Egypt'
ib.14; בית מראן 'the house of our lord' A4.10:13 // אגורי אלהין
מצריא ' ... of the Egyptians' A4.8:13; ספר חוב חקל 'land lease
document' B1.1:19; גרדא זי מראתי 'the domestic staff of my lady'
A6.15:8.

[[N₁ + N₂] +N₃]—רב חילא זי סון 'the troop commander of
Syene' A5.2:7; אגורא זי יהו אלהא זילן 'our temple of YHW the
god' A4.10:8.([943a])

Ambiguity arises where N₃ is transformed into a conjunctive
pronoun: e.g. ספר אנתתכי B3.11:7,9, בר בטני C1.1:139, and בעל
טבתכם D7.1:3, which are best analysed as [[N₁ + N₂] + N₃], 'your
document of wifehood,' 'my own child'([944]), and 'your friend'
respectively, whereas דמי ביתן 'the price of our house' B3.12:5 is
obviously of the type [N₁ + [N₂ + N₃]]. So are כנפי לבושך 'the
corners of your garment' C1.1:107, שם אבוהי 'the name of his
father' ib.138, מפתח פמה 'the opening of his mouth' ib.162, and
כיבי אלהיהם 'the pains of their gods' C1.2:19.

e) On the other hand, where N₂ is in the form of a conjunctive
pronoun, the analytical structure is unambiguous: לבשי זי קמר
'my woolen garment' B8.2:16. We doubt indeed whether our
idiom would allow here, like הַר קָדְשִׁי 'my holy mountain' in BH,
*לבש קמרי.

f) Where a sequence [N₁ + N₂ + N₃ (= conj. pron.)] is
further followed by a demonstrative pronoun, there could arise a

---

Egypt(ians)."

syntactic ambiguity as in דמי עבדי אלך 'that value of my slaves'
or 'the value of those slaves of mine' B8.7:1, though the latter is
more likely.

g) Where the second component consists of more than one
coordinate term, namely [N$_1$ + [N$_2$ + "and" + N$_3$]], the syntagm
may be shorthand for [[N$_1$ + N$_2$] "and" [N$_1$ + N$_3$]]: e.g. מאן נחש
ופרזל B3.13:11 means 'bronze utensil(s) and iron utensils' rather
than utensils of alloy. Similar consideration applies where the
analytic syntagm is used as in מזרקיא זי זהבא וכסף 'the gold and
silver basins' A4.7:12 // מזרקיא זי זהבא וזי כספא A4.8:11. See also
מסמרי נחש ופרזל 'bronze and iron nails' A6.2:12; בעל דגל וקריה
'member of a detachment or town' B2.1:9, cp. בעל דגל ובעל קריה
B2.7:10; לבשי קמר וכתן מאני נחש ופרזל מאני עק וחוצן 'woolen and
linen garments, bronze and iron utensils, wooden and palm-leaf
utensils' B2.9:5.

h) A clause may occupy the slot of a nomen rectum: e.g. עד
יום זי אשלמנהי ל[ך] 'until the day that I pay it to y[ou]' B4.2:3,10,
with which compare וירחא זי לא אנתן לך בה מרבית 'and the month
in which I do not give you interest' B4.2:4, where one should
note the st. det. of ירחא and the anaphoric בה.([945]) Likewise ביום זי
תרחענה תגזנה 'on the day that you wash it, you should shear it'
D7.8:6; בעדן זי זא באישתא עביד לן 'at the time when this evil was
done to us' A4.7:17; מן יום זי אזלת 'since the day that you went'
A3.3:2; מן יום זי נפקתם 'since the day that you left' ib.3; תבעה אתר
זי אנת תהשכח] ... 'you shall seek a (or: the place) where you will
find [...' C1.1:34.([946])

i) In the light of some Aramaic dialects and particularly
Hebrew, our idiom presumably also knew the use of the adjective
in the status constructus.([947]) E.g. חכים ממלל 'wise/skilful with
respect to speech' C1.1:114; עויר עינין 'blind with respect to eyes'
ib.212; חרש אדנין 'deaf with respect to ears' ib.215. Instead of ימין
סב 'old of days' B3.10:17 one expects: סב ימין.([948])

---

[944] As against 'adopted child.'

[945] On a comparable syntactic phenomenon in Hebrew, see Joüon - Muraoka
1993: § 129 *p,q*.

[946] The last example is mentioned by Degen (1979:43).
All the examples collected by Fitzmyer (1962:18) should be similarly
interpreted, not (*pace* Fitzmyer) as st. abs. For an analysis similar to ours, see
also Lambdin 1971:318, n. 7. See also above at § 42 *b* end.

[947] See Muraoka 1977 on Biblical Hebrew, and Muraoka 1987:50f. on
Syriac.

[948] Cf. Dn 7.9 סב. עַתִּיק יוֹמִין, *pace* Kraeling (1969:242), cannot be a participle,

j) An unusually long construct chain is exemplified by עבד
משח זרע כתן איטשרי 'maker of oil of seed of *ᵓytšry* flax' C3.11:4:
$$[N_1 + [N_2 + [N_3 + [N_4 + N_5]]]].$$
Not only is the hierachy "multi-storeyed," but it represents diverse
kinds of logico-semantic relationship. $[N_1 + ... N_5]]]]$ is objective,
$[N_2 + ... N_5]]]$ is that of material, $[N_3 + ... N_5]]$ is species(?),
whilst the last cst. phrase, $[N_4 + N_5]$ is classificatory.

§ 62. Noun + זי + Noun: periphrasis

The question of possible opposition between various patterns
joining a noun head and its modifier whether this latter be another
noun or a possessive pronoun has already been examined under
several headings: noun in the status constructus + noun (§ 61),
noun + demonstrative pronoun (§ 65), noun + ל with a noun or a
conjunctive pronoun (§ 60), noun + a disjunctive possessive
pronoun, i.e. -זיל (§ 59). Here we shall focus on possible opposition
between the two patterns, namely [noun in the st.cst. + noun]
and [noun זי noun]. Despite some past attempts to establish
functional oppositions between the analytic structure with זי and
the synthetic one([949]), it does not seem to us always possible to
establish clear *functional* opposition between the two
structures.([950]) There seem to be factors other than functional

---

for which סיב is expected.

[949] This analytical structure has been studied in Muraoka 1966:153-55,
where, with special reference to BA, some features of opposition between
this structure and the synthetic one have been identified; in Kaddari 1969
where the analytical structure has been discussed with reference to IA with
the focus on the determinate or indeterminate nature of the nomen rectum;
and in Garr 1990 where an attempt is made to demonstrate that the feature of
prominence or importance is characteristic of the analytical structure, though
sufficient consideration is not given to the question which of the two nouns is
accorded prominence. Folmer (1995:311) is sympathetic to Garr's position.

Degen 1969:89: "Die Umschreibung des Genitivs mit *zy* wird nötig,
wenn das Regens determiniert ist," where he must have meant that with such
a *zy* the determination of the regens becomes unambiguous, for surely כרסא
in כרסא אבי 'the throne of my father,' for instance, must be considered
determinate.

[950] A meticulous analysis by Folmer (1995:301-3) of the syntagm in which
the first term is בית does not appear to have resulted in a clear-cut demarcation
between the two syntagmata.

Folmer (1995:288) draws attention to an intriguing pair of the two contrasting
syntagmata: אגורי אלהי מצרין 'the temples of the gods of Egypt' A4.7:14 as
against אגורא זי יהו אלהא 'the temple of YHW the god' ib.24 (with a few more
analogous examples in this document and its revision, A4.8). Folmer thinks

opposition involved. At least one thing is certain: the analytic structure is not an innovation of IA, for the Tell Fekheriyeh bilingual has as many as five examples of it(⁹⁵¹), which at the same time confirms the long-suspected Akkadian influence of the feature, though in the bilingual the Assyrian version uses *ša* only in one out of the five cases. Hardly any functional opposition is evident between אגור יהו אלהא 'the temple of YHW the god' B3.4:9 and אגורא זי יהו B3.12:18, both in very similar context and penned by the same scribe, Haggai son of Shemaiah. Likewise אוצר מלכא 'the royal treasury' B3.11:4 vs. אוצרא זי מלכא B3.4:9, both by Haggai; פתכר סוסה עם רכבה 'a statue of a horse with its rider' A6.12:2 preceded by פתכרן זי פרש 'statues of a horseman.'(⁹⁵²)

If it is found difficult to establish clear functional oppositions between the two syntagmata, synthetic and analytical, there appear to be some semantic constraints on the choice of either of the two. According to Folmer (1995:311) "inalienable possession is expressed more frequently by the construct noun phrase." Thus no instance of the analytical syntagm is found in which the first term denotes part of body.

a) There are certain collocations which occur only in the synthetic structure(⁹⁵³): e.g. אבני מלכא 'the royal weights' B2.2:14 +31x; אבני פתח 'the stone weights of Ptaḥ' B4.2:2; שוק מלכא 'the street of the king' B3.4:8+6x, perhaps almost a name "King

---

that the synthetic syntagm serves a purpose of showing that the phrase is about heathen gods. But how does this square with the fact, also stressed by Folmer, that בית, in combination with a divine name, pagan or otherwise, never enters the analytical syntagm?

⁹⁵¹ Muraoka 1983-84:101-3. Thus we must now nuance the position expressed by Kaddari (1969:103) that the later a document, the more frequent the analytic structure becomes. Nor is the relatively sparing—so according to Whitehead—use of the analytical syntagm in the Arsames correspondence, *pace* Whitehead (1974:266), indicative of "an early stage in the development of the language." The issue is not only one of chronology. See also Folmer (1995:259-325, esp. 284), who shows, inter alia, that the analytic syntagm with kinship terms as N₁ is especially frequent in texts of eastern origin.

⁹⁵² The last pair is mentioned by Folmer, though she does not draw the same conclusion as we.

Whitehead (1974:219) correctly states that עב]דן זי עחחפי 'servants of A.' A6.3:2 and עבדי עחחפי ib.7 are not free variants, for the latter refers back to the former.

⁹⁵³ In the course of his discussion of three distinct syntagmata used in English to express the "genitive," Jespersen (1909-31: 7.318) mentions fixed phrases as a category where the genitive dominates, citing, among others,

Street" or "Royal Parade"; מועא\מה שמש 'east' B2.3:6+11x; מערב
שמש 'west' B2.7:15+10x; רבחיל 'troop commander' A4.7:7+10x([954]);
ביַ[ת followed by a divine name, foreign or otherwise([955]) as in בֵ]ית
יהו ביב 'the temple of YHW in Elephantine' A3.3:1, בית נבו 'the
temple of Nabu' A2.3:1+. Here belong most likely those
collocations with בעל as in בעל עטתא טבתא 'the master of good
counsel' C1.1:42; בעל אגר 'a master of wages (= employer)' ib.100;
בעל טבחכם 'your friend' D7.1:3; בעלי פתורא 'members of the table'
C3.27:22; בעלי יב 'the citizens of Elephantine' A4.7:22; בעל דגל
'member of a detachment' B2.1:9. So also בר in indicating age:
בר יום '(1) day old' D7.37:2; ברת שנן 100 '100 years-old female'
B3.5:17.

b) Limited distribution is observable in some of the logico-
semantic categories mentioned above (§ 48), though for certain
categories we have not sufficient data to allow us to make confident
assertions. Thus ספר 'document,' as in ספר אנתו 'document of
wifehood' B3.8:45, is always (27x) followed directly by another
noun indicating the subject matter of the document (§ 48 xi). It
is also doubtful that the analytical structure has ever been used
to indicate apposition (§ 48 iii).

c) The analytical structure is a handy substitute when the N₁
is an indeclinable proper noun as in (דגל) זי מנפי וידרן זי מנפי '(the
detachment of) Vidarna of Memphis' C3.8IIIB:36; המרכריא זי גנזא
'the treasury accountants' A6.2:4.([956])

d) A phrase of four concatenated construct nouns such as
mentioned above in § 61 *j* is extremely rare. Not only that, in a
case like בית מדבחא זי אלה שמיא 'the altar of the God of Heaven'
A4.9:3 the analytical structure has the advantage of unambiguously formalising the hierachical structure obtaining between
the four nouns, i.e. $[[N_1 + N_2] + [N_3 + N_4]]$, and a concatenaiton
of the four nouns as בית מדבח אלה שמיא is rather unlikely. Similarly
in BA: e.g. Ezr 7.12,21 ספר דתא די־אלה שמיא 'the scribe of the law
of God of Heaven.'([957])

e) In lists as found particularly in marriage contracts, an
adjective comes at the end of an analytical noun phrase. This is

---

"the king's English" as distinct from "the English of the king."

[954] The degree of cohesion is also indicated by the fact that the collocaiton
is sometimes spelled without any space in-between. See above § 10 *c*.

[955] As pointed out by Folmer (1995:287).

[956] Whitehead (1974:216) points out that, in the Arsames correspondence,
the analytical structure is almost exclusively confined to cases where N₁ is a
Persian loan word. See § 40 end.

evident in פרכס 1 זי חצן חדת '1 new palm-leaf box(?)' B2.6:11 where the adjective חדת cannot modify the plural חצן. See also ... כסן זי נחש 2 ,זי נחש 1 ,תמסא 1 זי נחש שויה '1 bronze bowl worth ...' B2.6:1, ... שוין 'bronze cups, 2, worth ...' B2.6:12, and לבוש 1] בלה 'one worn garment' where בלה is opposed to חדת 'new' and לבש 1 זי עמר חדת B2.6:7 must mean '1 new woolen garment,' and not '1 garment of new wool.'

f) When N_1 takes a cardinal numeral, especially 'one,' and is further qualified by a following noun phrase, the analytical syntagm is definitely preferred: e.g. מחזי 1 זי נחש '1 bronze mirror' B2.6:11 // כסן זי נחש 2 'bronze cups, 2' ib.12; פרכס 1 זי חצן חדת '1 new palm-leaf box(?)' ib.16; לבש 1 זי עמר '1 woolen garment' B3.3:4. The length of the N_2 phrase virtually precludes the use of the synthetic structure in לבש 1 זי עמר חדת חטב צבע ידין '1 new woolen garment, striped with dye doubly-well' B2.6:7. Note also לבש אחרן זי עמר נשחט 'another garment of finely-woven(?) wool' B2.6:10 where אחרן functions like a quantifier.([958])

g) As will be shown in § 65 b, a demonstrative pronoun may follow a construct phrase [$N_1 + N_2$], even when the pronoun modifies N_1. In the following case, however, such a syntax would have resulted in a rather awkward phrase, which may have been the reason for the choice of the analytical structure: דגלא (or: זנה זי מאתה זי ביתאלתקם (חילא 'this detachment (or: troop) of the century of Betheltakum' B4.4:10.

h) In the following case the use of the analytical structure is dictated by the fact that the N_1 consists of two coordinate nouns: בר וברה זי יזניה בר אוריה 'son or daughter of Jezaniah son of Uriah' B2.10:13. Otherwise a wholesale rewriting would have been necessary.

i) Where N_1 is meant as indeterminate, the analytical structure makes that explicit([959]): e.g. דגלן זי מצריא 'detachments of the Egyptians' A4.5:1; תרען זי אבן 'stone gates' A4.7:9; פסילה זי אבן 'stone slab' ib.10; טסן זי נחש 'bronze plates' A6.2:16 // מסמרי נחש

---

[957] Cf. our discussion in Muraoka 1966:153f.

[958] The obscure, last word might be construed with לבש.

[959] A generalising statement such as "determination [of N_1] was demanded by the relative construction itself" (Garr 1985:174) is simply false. Nor is it necessary to consider with Tsereteli (1991:1575) the possibility of N_1 being in the st. cst.: the use of the st. cst. and that of the analytical syntagm are mutually exclusive. By the same token a noun with a possessive suffix is not necessarily determinate: Ex 2.21 צִפֹּרָה בִתּוֹ where Zipporah was one of Reuel's seven daughters, and this is the first mention of her in the story. See Joüon -

ופרזל 'bronze and iron nails' ib.12; בי זי לבנן 'brick house' B3.1:9+;
ארדכל זי 'boatman of the rough waters' B2.2:11; מלח זי מיא קשיא
מלכא 'royal builder' B2.6:2; ארמי זי סון 'Aramaean of Syene' B2.7:2+;
בר זי אפולי 'son of A.'s' B3.4:21 // ברה לה 'daughter of his' ib.22;
לחן זי יהו אלהא 'servitor of YHW the God' B3.7:2 // לחן ליהו
B3.10:2(960); גנן זי חנום אלהא 'gardener of Khnum the god' B3.10:10,
B3.11:6; תרע זי תחית 'gateway of the ḥyt' B3.10:15.

  j) Kaddari (1969:103) has justly underlined the factor of
genre as relevant and important to our question: the analytical
structure is more than three times as frequent in the narrative
framework of Ahiqar as in the proverbs. In a document similar
in nature to the narrative framework of Ahiqar, the tale of Ḥor
son of Punesh, C1.2, we find only two instances of the analytical
structure but six of the synthetic.(961) Private letters such as the
Hermopolis papyri (A2.1-7)(962) and the Padua letters (A3.3-4)
are remarkably and virtually free from the periphrastic structure.
Another set of documents similar in nature, D7.1-57, contains
only two analytical phrases: שעריא זי חנם 'the barley of Khnum'
D7.39:3 and אחוהא זי תם 'the brother of Tam' D7.57:4. By contrast,
documents composed in the officialese of IA are replete with
analytical זי phrases. Hence one may conclude that the analytical
structure first pervaded official documents and annalistic accounts
in which the influence of the language of the political masters,
Akkadian, can be safely assumed, whereas literary documents
and private papers remained long immune to such an innovation.

  k) This survey shows that the analytical structure by means
of זי has opened up new possibilities to express ideas and logical
relationships which would otherwise have been outright impossible to express or which could have been at best expressed in
rather clumsy manners or circumlocutions. This applies to a
disjunctive possessive pronoun, without which a highly personal
touch as in תתוסרי זילן 'Tetosiri of ours' D7.9:3 would have been

---

[960] On the contrast to the structure with -ל, see § 60.

[961] תסהרא זי מלכא 'the barque of the king' (1), מליא זי מלכא 'the words of the
king' (3) vs. חרב חילך 'the sword of your troops' (4), אלפי מלכא 'the boats of
the king' (7), כיבי אלהיהם 'the pains of their gods' (19), אלהי מצרין 'the gods of
Egypt' (19,25), בני מראיהם 'the sons of their masters' (24). The name בר פונש
has not been counted.

[962] The sole exception is חתנה זי נבשה 'the son-in-law of Nabusha' A2.6:3.

impossible, for a proper noun never takes a disjunctive pronoun.

§ 63. Prolepsis

This is a typically Aramaic([963]) phenomenon in which a noun syntactically dependent on the following noun receives in advance a conjunctive pronoun in the third person agreeing with the latter in gender and number, and the two nouns are further linked by means of זי: e.g. אבוה זי אתור כלה 'the father of the entire Assyria' C1.1:55; אבוהי זי אסרחאדן זנה מלכא 'the father of Esarhaddon this king' ib.47([964]); אמהם זי עלימיא אלה 'the mother of these lads' B2.11:13; אחוהא זי תם 'the brother of Tam' D7.57:4; צירידהם זי דששיא אלך 'the hinges of those doors' A4.7:10; אחוהו זי ענני 'the brother of Anani' ib.18. Given the high incidence of the feature, it is unwarranted to speculate whether the ה in, for instance, פגרה זי אחיקר זנה 'the corpse of this Ahiqar' C1.1:63, is a graphic variant of א for the st. det. Likewise עבדיה זי מבטחיה אמן 'the slaves of Mibtahiah our mother' B2.11:3. Other examples may be found at A2.6:3 (probably[965]), A6.4:2, A6.11:3,4, A2.6:18, A2.11:3, A3.11:6, A3.12:4, A4.4:6,10, C1.1:3.

N_2 always refers to a person, mostly a personal name, thus determinate, with the sole exception of צירידהם זי דששיא אלך 'the hinges of those doors' A4.7:10.

That the second term in this syntagm is always determined is rightly stressed by Folmer (1995:303).([966])

---

[963] See Kaufman 1974:132—"to be ascribed at least partially to Babylonian influence." Kutscher (1972:106-9) is in no doubt. Even under the assumption that the Aramaic version of the Bisitun inscription is a translation of the Akkadian—see, hoewever, below at § 78 *ch*, n. 97a—the translator did not work slavishly, for these two standing phrases coined apparently under the Akkadian influence, namely במ(ל)ל זי 'under the protection of' and לערקה זי 'to meet,' have their Akkadian model without a proleptic pronoun: e.g. *ina GIS.MI ša ú-ra-mi-iz-da* (line 50) and *ana [tar]-ṣi ͫda-da-[ar-šú]* (line 49). The idiom is thus no longer a slavish Akkadianism. See von Soden 1995: § 138 *j-k*. Diem (1986:238f.) plausibly seeks the origin of this type of prolepsis in apposition. For a wider, comparative-Semitic perspective, see Barth 1911, Pennacchietti 1968, Diem 1986, and Hopkins 1997a and idem, 1997b.

[964] Or: "the father of this E. the king.'

[965] The ambiguity arising from the practice of writing ה instead of א in most of the Hermopolis letters (§ 16 *f*) is resolved by Folmer (1995:277) by observing that "kinship terms in other texts never have the emphatic state form morpheme when they are the first term of a *zy*- phrase."

[966] In the case of Classical Syriac, which shows perhaps the richest variety of proleptic constructions and the most extensive use of them this condition

In the Bisitun inscrption (C2.1) one often finds זי ל(ל)בט
'with the protection of'([967]) and זי ק/לערע 'in order to face' used in
a similar fashion, and both are virtually prepositional in force:
[זד]בטלה זי אהורמ['with the protection of Ahurama[zda]' C2.1:10
and אזלו לערקה זי דדרש למעבד קרב 'they went towards Dadarshu
to do battle' ib.15.([968]) One recalls a similar feature in Syr.: e.g.,
ʿamme:h d-malka: 'with the king.'([969])

If an authentic reading, תחומוהי ביתא 'the boundaries of the
house' B3.12:17 is extraordinary, whilst in the first version of
the text we read תחומי ביתא ib.9.

This syntactic feature is attested from a very early period of
our corpus: Hermopolis papyrus A2.6 (end 6th/early 5th c.),
Ahiqar (6th c.), B4.4 (483), B2.6 (449).([970])

Prolepsis in our idiom has not been extended to other syntactic
structures, for instance, a prepositional phrase, an object of the
verb, as is highly common in Classical Syriac.([971])

---

applies to all types of prolepsis: Muraoka 1987: § 88, 109; Muraoka 1997b: §
112.

[967] Folmer (1995:309) mentions an example without prolepsis: בטלל אלה
שמיא 'with the protection of the God of Heaven' A4.3:5.
Folmer (1995:312), who states "... the proleptic pron. sf. [= pronominal
suffix] is found especially in combination with nouns which refer to slaves
and real-estate property, and only rarely in combination with other nouns,"
would have to exclude a large number of examples in the Bisitun inscription
with these two phrases. Reference to slaves as the first term we find only
once (B2.11:3). Her more general conclusions must be judged in the light of
all the data and their evaluation. A glance at our examples above contradicts
Diem's (1986:238) position that in Early Aramaic this syntagm is typical of
inalienable relationship.

[968] Cf. the standard rendering in TO of BH , e.g. Gn 46.29, also an infinitive.

[969] See Nöldeke 1898: § 222.

[970] In contrast to Rowley (102), who writes that it is "mostly found in the
later texts."

[971] See Muraoka 1995: § 109, Muraoka 1997b: 112. Nor does our idiom
attest to yet another proleptic syntagm, bayte:h l-malka:, known to some
Semitic languages, both classical and modern. On this last syntagm, see
Hopkins 1997a and idem, 1997b, who, like Barth (1911:50) with respect to
Classical Ethiopic and in view of structural similarities with some cognates,
explains this syntagm as analogical development of a similar syntagm for the
expression of the direct object of a verb, i.e. qatle:h l-malka:, both examples
taken from Classical Syriac. For Aramaic, however, this would lead to a
rather lopsided structure, for to the latter there would correspond two syntagms,
namely the standard and better known bayte:h d-malka: and the extremely
rare bayte:h l-malka:. Significantly Hopkins's as well as Barth's scheme lack

§ 64. Noun with a relative clause

a) A noun phrase may be expanded by a clause introduced by the relative pronoun זי or די. For a discussion of the relative clause, see above, § 42 *a-b*.

b) An extremely rare case of an asyndetic relative clause, namely with no relative pronoun, appears to be found in איש שפיר מדדה ולבבה טב כקרן[י]ה חסינה 'A man whose stature is beautiful and whose heart is good is like a strong city' C1.1:95; גבר לא לב[ב] 'a man with no sense whatsoever' C1.1:82 with a categorical negative: cf. BH אֶרֶץ לֹא אִישׁ 'a land without anybody' Job 38.26.([972])

§ 65. Noun with a demonstrative pronoun

a) A demonstrative pronoun used as a constituent of a noun phrase may either precede or follow its noun head, though in the great majority of cases it follows.([973]) Some examples of preceding demonstratives are: זנה ספרא 'this document' B2.7:12; זנה יומא 'this day' A4.7:20; זנה ביתא 'this house' B2.7:7, B3.10:15 (extraposition in both)([974]); זא באישתא 'this evil' A4.7:10; בוא שנתא 'in this year' B8.10:3, C1.2:5; באלה מליא 'with these words' B8.7:3; זך ביתא 'that house' B2.7:15; בוך עדנא 'at that time' C1.1:70; אלך נכסיא 'those possessions' B2.9:8, אלה נכסיא 'these possessions' ib.15.

The choice of the sequence with a preceding demonstrative does not appear to be a matter of individual style([975]) nor is there any historical development to be observed. To establish some meaningful opposition between the two sequences is not easy.([976])

---

a sixth syntagm of "possession," namely *bay l-malka:* (§ 60), which Hopkins merely mentions en passant (Hopkins 1997a:353 = idem, 1997b:27). The syntagm in question seems to us to be an extension of this latter, the distinction between the two being in the determinedness feature of the first term. Incidentally, to three Syriac examples reportedly noticed by G. Goldenberg we may add John 2.3 *emme:h lišoᶜ* ἡ μήτηρ τοῦ Ἰησοῦ.

[972] Cf. further Joüon - Muraoka 1993:§ 160 *o, oa*.

[973] Cf. Folmer 1995: 325-40.

[974] On the extraposition or casus pendens construction, see below § 79.

[975] Is it of any significance that the sequence occurs three times in B2.7 (lines 7,12,15) written by Nathan son of Ananiah and four times in three different documents penned by Mauziah son of Nathan (B2.9:8,15, B2.10:8, B3.5:11) ? Another scribe, Haggai, however, is not strictly consistent: compare B3.10:15 and B3.11:7 with B3.12:22.

[976] Degen (1979:42) has not demonstrated his assertion: "Nur betont stehen sie [= Demonstrativpronomina] voran."

In part of the Elephantine contracts the demonstrative pronoun precedes its noun head at the end of a logical sequence, rounding off an inclusio: thus "this house (ביתא זנה) whose measurements and boundaries are written in this document ..." B3.10:11 vs. "This {this} house (זנה זנא ביתא) whose boundaries and measurements are written in this document" ib.15; אלך נכסיא 'these properties' B2.9:8 rounding off a statement which started with איתי[ן] נכסיא 'there are the(se) goods' ib. 5. Likewise at B2.9:15, B2.10:8 and B3.11:7. However, we are confronted with a pair such as זנה ספרא at line 16: זנה ספרא זי אנה עני כתבת לכי הו יצב '*this* document that I Anani have written is the valid one' B3.11:16 and ספרא זנה זי אנה עבדת לכי הו מיצב 'this document which I made for you, that is the validated one' B3.10:22. Both statements constitute an inclusio, display the identical syntactic feature, that of cleft-sentence with extraposing הו, were penned by the same scribe, separated by a mere two years, and are concerned with the same piece of property. In the former, the marked sequence, it may be possible to recognise a touch of emphasis. One may also say that the ante-position of the demonstrative is suited to an emotionally charged document such as A4.7: זא באישתא 'this wickedness' (line 17) and עדזנה יומא 'until this very day' (line 20, and in a second copy of same document, A4.8:19).([977]) Contrast may be a conditioning factor in "That document (זך ספרא) which they shall produce against you will be false ... while this document (ספרא זנה) is in your hand" B2.3:18; "no new or old document except this document (זנה ספרא)" B2.7:12. The emphasis that may attach to the sequence in question is also reflected in the fact that the phrase constitutes a casus pendens and is resumed later by a pronoun: זנה ביתא יהבתה לכי 'this house, I gave it to you' B2.7:7, following אנה יהבת לכי לביתא זנה ib.5.([978]) Likewise ib.15 זך ביתא. It must be admitted, however, that in some cases, as

---

[977] Cf. also מ[ן] זך ע[ד]נא ועד ז[נה יומא 'from that time until this day' ib.20. One may also note that the above-quoted sentence with זנה ביתא at B3.10:15, though essentially similar to the sentence with the reverse sequence at ib.11, is rather more personal in tone with the heiress named personally as "Jehoishma my daughter at my death in affection because she supported me when I was old of days."

[978] This syntax, however, does not automatically lead to the ante-position of the pronoun, as can be seen in ביתא זנה זי ... יהבת לך ... B3.10:11, though in this case the considerable distance between the initial phrase and the verb, some ten words, may have occasioned the addition of the resumptive pronoun to the verb.

mentioned above, no satisfactory explanation suggests itself.([979])
In זנה חלק ביתא 'this part of the house' B3.5:11 the demonstrative
modifies the immediately following, first noun of a construct
chain, where ambiguity could arise, were the pronoun at the end
of the phrase.([980]) Generally speaking, it stands to reason that
there should be some measure of opposition between the two
contrasting sequences in view of the fact that, in our corpus, a
noun modifier, with the exception of כל, regularly follows it.([981])

b) A phrase consisting of a noun and a demonstrative may
be further expanded with the addition of an adjective as in וידרנג
זך לחיא 'that wicked Vidranga' A4.7:6; וידרנג זך כלביא 'that curlike
V.' ib.16 // A4.8:15([982]), but with a demonstrative in the last slot
in וידרנג לחיא זך A4.9:6. This last ought to be compared with
כמריא זי חנוב אלך 'those priests of Khnub' A4.5:8. Since a demonstrative may precede its noun head (see above [a]) and an adjective
can be substantivised to make לחיא, for instance, mean 'the wicked
one,' the immediate constituent analysis of these three-member
phrases can be performed in more than one way: e.g.

[[וידרנג] זך [כלביא]] or [[וידרנג זך] [כלביא]]
[[וידרנג] [לחיא זך]] or [[וידרנג זך] [לחיא]].

But in פמון זך אבוהי A6.11:4 the last constituent is more likely in
apposition, hence [[פמון זך] [אבוהי]] 'that Pamun, his father.' Hence
one would see an appositional phrase also in [פמון] שמה אבוהי זך
'Pamun by name, his father, that one' A6.11:3.([983])

c) זנה חלק ביתא 'this portion of the house' B3.5:11 represents
a three-member string with the structure [a+[b+c]] where (a) =
זנה.

d) In two cases a phrase consisting of a noun head and a
demonstrative is further expanded by a disjunctive possessive
pronoun occupying the last slot of the whole string: אגרא זך זילך
'that wall of yours' B2.1:6; אגרא זך זילה 'that wall of his' ib.10.
They contrast with נכסין אלך 'those possessions of yours' B2.7:6,

---

[979] For more inexplicable cases, see Folmer 1995:336-38.

[980] But note the unambiguous כמריא זי חנוב אלך 'those priests of Khnub'
A4.5:8.

[981] אסרחאדן זנה מלכא C1.1:47 is ambiguous, though there does not seem to
be any strong reason to read as Grelot does (1972:449: "A., ce roi-ci"). A
demonstrative pronoun with a name always follows the latter: see above § 41
b.

[982] On this interpretation of כלביא, see Grelot 1972:410, n. *s*.

[983] Alternatively, פמון שמה אבוהי may be in casus pendens, resumed by זך as
the subject of the following אבד.

which shows a syntagm [noun + conj. pron. + dem.]. The reason
why a conjunctive pronoun is not used in the first two cases
appears to be the importance attached to the question as to whose
wall it is: cf. § 41 *h*.

e) Unlike in כמריא זי חנוב אלך 'those priests of Khnub' A4.5:8
the syntactic relationship is that of [a + [b +c]] in מנדת בניא אלך
'the rent (?) of those domains' A6.13:3; תלי שנתא זא 'wine strainer
of this year' C3.28:113; משחת ביתא זך 'the measurements of that
house' B2.4:4; תחו[מ]ן ביתא [ז]ך 'the boun[da]ries of [th]at house'
B3.7:5; דין ספרא זנה 'the law of this document' B2.6:31, B3.8:32;
חיי ספרא זנה 'the life of this document' B4.7:5.

f) A noun qualified by a demonstrative pronoun regularly
takes the st.det. form: יומא זנה 'this day' A4.7:20 et passim. Hence
מומאה דכי in מומאה 'that oath' B2.8:9 and מומאה דכא 'that oath'
must be a st.det. form.

g) On the expansion of a noun by a demonstrative pronoun
as well as by a conjunctive pronoun, see above at § 58*d*.

§ 66. Noun with an adjective

a) An adjective may attributively follow a noun phrase and
expand it: e.g. אתר אחרן 'another location' A6.10:2; נכ[ס]ן אחרנן
'other properties' ib.3; ביתא [ר]בא 'the large house' A3.8:6; פקידיא
[ק]דמ[יא] 'the former officials' A6.10:7. A very rare exception to
this rule may be a case of apposition: thus כאחרנן גרד בדיכרן זילי
'like others, a staff of artists(?) of mine' A6.12:2, though in some
Aramaic dialects this very word, אחרן, displays a peculiar syntax,
for example, preceding its noun head.([984]) Another possible,
equally difficult exception is גסה פתגם (A6.8:3, A6.10:9), if the
first word be an adjective, giving the entire phrase a meaning of
'harsh word' or 'bad business.'([985]) A rare example of a preceding,
attributive adjective is, if the reading be correct, אחרן נכסן 'other
goods' B2.9:6.([986])

b) An attributive adjective to be construed with a noun in a

---

[984] Nöldeke 1868:508; idem 1868a: 269, n. 1; Schulthess 1924: § 158,1.
See also Driver 1957:72.

[985] A take-off from Persian: *gasta patigāma*. Cf. Driver 1957:50. See
Appendix III.

[986] Later in the document we find ואחרן summing up a list: "... and the rest."
Thus נכסן here could be the object of the following לקח, which, however,
would have לאחר breaking up an oratio recta. The disagreement in number
(אחרן נכסן instead of אחרנן נכסן) is not unique in the case of the pseudo-quantifier
אחרן: see § 67 *g*.

construct chain follows the last noun of the chain. This constraint could lead to syntactic ambiguity, which at בעל עטתא טבתא 'the master of good counsel' C1.1:42 has been resolved on account of the difference in gender of the two nouns in question, and, in the case of עקי ארז ואר חדתן 'new cedar and ʾr trees' A6.2:10, by virtue of the plural number of the adjective.

In לבש אחרן זי עמר 'another woolen garment' B2.6:10, however, the position of אחרן may be due to the fact that it is a pseudo-quantifier: see § 67 g.([987])

c) By contrast, the analytical syntagm [NP$_1$ + זי + NP$_2$] allows an adjective to be positioned immediately after either of the two NPs. In the case of the syntagm [NP$_1$ + Adj. + זי + NP$_2$], which NP is modified by the adjective is in no doubt: שביט 1 חדת זי אמן ב 7 4 וזרת '1 new shawl(?) of cubits 7 by 4 and a span' B6.2:5; חסה[.]מן 1 חדתה זי קמר '1 new woolen ??' B6.2:6.

However, it has been shown in § 62 e that an analytic noun phrase of the type NP$_1$ + זי + NP$_2$ can be followed by an adjective qualifying and agreeing with NP$_1$: e.g., גמידה 1 זי קמר חדת '1 new woolen garment' B3.8:7; לבש 1 זי קמר חדת '1 new woolen garment' B3.8:6; שנפא 1 זי כתן חדת '1 new linen robe(?)' B3.8:11.([988]) Cf. also לא איתי לי בר וברה אחרנן אח ואחה ואנתה ואיש אחרן שליט בארקא זך 'I have no other son or daughter, brother or sister, or woman or other man, (he who) has right to that land' B2.3:10.

d) Syntagm [[Noun + Conj. pron.] + Adj.]: e.g. חלקי אחרנא 'my other part' B3.5:19.

e) An attributive adjective normally agrees with its noun head in gender, number, and state, as can be seen in the first four examples cited above under [a]. See also עטה טבה 'good advice' C1.1:57; עטתא טבתא 'the good advice' ib.42. Therefore one would translate יהו אלהא שכן יב בירתא 'YHW the god, dweller of Elephantine the fortress' B3.12:2, not "the god who dwells .." On the phenomenon of disagreement, see § 66 d. No adjective

---

[987] The difficult word following עמר does not affect our statement: on the crux, see Cowley 1923:48.

[988] On the last example, cf. above at § 46 o.
In the following cases, however, the position of the constituent following the NP$_2$ may have been determined by the fact that that constituent consists of more than one word, for otherwise the whole phrase would have looked somewhat cumbersome: מחזי 1 זי נחש שוה כסף שקל 1 ר 2 תמסא 1 זי נחש שוה כסף כסן זי נחש 2 שקל 1 ר 2 כסן זי נחש 2 שוין כסף שקלן 2 זלוע 1 זי נחש שוה כסף ר 2 '1 bronze mirror worth (in) silver 1 shekel 2 q(uarters), 1 bronze bowl worth (in) silver 1 shekel 2 q(uarters), 2 bronze cups worth (in) silver 2 shekels, 1 bronze jug worth (in) silver 2 q(uarters)' B2.6:11-13.

possesses a distinct dual form, for which the plural form doubles: thus עינין טבן 'good eyes' C1.1:157.

§ 67. Noun with a numeral

a) Cardinal numerals, whether spelled out or written as ciphers consisting of straight or curved strokes, and construed with a noun head, mostly follow the latter, and agree with it in gender whereby an unmarked form is used with a feminine noun, and a marked one with a masculine noun (§ 21 a). Where a unit of measurement such as length and weight is also mentioned, the numeral agrees with the noun for such a unit. For example, ביום חדה בכף חד 'on one day, in one stroke' B2.6:28, sim. B3.8:28; חפן תלת 'three handfuls' A6.9:3; לינ[ו]מן אחרנן תלתה 'in three more days' C1.1:39; כסף חלרן 8 לירח חד 'silver, 8 hallurs for one month' B3.1:5([989]); כסף כרשן תרין 'silver, two karsh' B3.8:6; אורך אמן בעשתא שבע '(its) le[ngth] cubits by the measuring rod, seven' B3.7:4.

b) The numeral for "one" also follows the noun even when oneness is emphasised as in אגרת חדה '(not) even a single letter' A3.5:5, sim. אגרה חדה A4.7:19; כל 2 כפם חד 'all two as one mouth, i.e. both unanimously' B3.12:33; כונה 1 'its only window' B3.12:21. See also B2.6:28, B3.8:28.([990]) For this reason alone one would not interpret חדה מנה A4.2:12 as "one portion"([991]), but rather "happy about it."

A cipher for "one" is used as the indefinite article: חלם 1 'a dream' D7.17:1; ספר מרחק 1 'a document of withdrawl' B2.3:23.([992]) It is also used on its own without a noun: לה שבק אנה לה 1 'I am not leaving him alone' A2.4:4; חזי 1 על ינקיא ... אל תוכל המו על אחרנן 'Look after the kids alone ... Don't entrust them to others' D7.6:2 where the numeral is not even spelled out.

c) The following are the only exceptions in which a numeral precedes: תרתין מלן 'two things' C1.1:187; בתרתי רגליא 'for a second time (?)' C2.1:11.([993]) חד אלף 'one thousand times' A4.7:3 is *sui*

---

[989] An Arabic numeral is represented in the actual text by means of the appropriate cipher, in this case eight vertical strokes: II III III.

[990] Classical Syriac thus differs: see Muraoka 1987:48.

[991] So Cowley 1923:135 and Grelot 1972:390. For "portion" we expect מנת: see above, § 18 n, n. 326, and cf. Leander 1928:77.

[992] In אגרה חדה 'one letter' A4.7:29 some contrast may be intended with the preceding כלא מליא 'all the matters.'

[993] חד זיון A4.2:3 is rather difficult: the use of a numeral with a personal

generis where חַד forms part of an idiomatic multiplicative, just as in Dn 3.19 חַד שִׁבְעָה 'seven times as much.': § 21 *h*.

d) The noun is usually in the status absolutus, which makes the above-quoted, problematic expression בתרתי רגליא stand out, where the use of the construct form of the numeral is equally striking. תרתי רגליא cannot mean 'two times.' At כל תרין נופתיא זי כרכיא A6.2:8 the numeral forms a cohesive phrase with כל, "all (told) two, the boat-holders of the Carians.'([994]) See also, if correctly restored: וקפירא [1] רבא 'and the [1] large pot' D7.9:15. The st. det. is used when the noun takes a demonstrative pronoun: see below [*f*].

e) Where the unit (weight, currency etc.) of a counted object is mentioned, the order is: Noun - unit - numeral or cipher. E.g., כסף חלרן 2 זרניך כרשן מאה 'arsenic one hundred karsh' A6.2:17; לכסף ש 1 לירחא 'silver, 2 hallurs to silver, 1 sh(ekel) per month' B4.2:2; משח זית חפנן 4 'olive oil, 4 handfuls' B3.8:20; חמר זי שנת כנדן 8 ופלג 11 'wine of year 11, 8 and 1/2 jars' C3.7Fv2:4.([995]) This sequence of constituents probably owes its origin to the administrative or commercial register of the language where various objects are quantified in lists or in tabular form and where those objects would naturally be mentioned first. See, for instance, an inventory of chattels a woman brought with her on marriage: כפן למנשא משח זי [חסף] 2 זי עק 2 זי אבן 1 כל 5 'Ladles for carrying oil: 2 [pottery], 2 wooden, 1 stone, a total of 5' B3.8:19. The unusual lack of agreement in number in פיק זי סלק 2 '2 trays(?) of *slq*' B3.8:18 is also understandable in this light. Note also the quantifiers שפיק and שגיא in גרד אמגן וספון שפיק בעו 'Seek domestic staff of craftsmen of all kinds in sufficient numbers' A6.10:6; שנן שגיא 'many years' A6.14:4([996]); שלם ושררת שגיא 'abundant welfare and strength' A6.16:1 et passim, and especially שלם מראן אלה שמיא ישאל שגיא בכל עדן 'May the God of Heaven seek after the welfare of our lord abundantly at all times' A4.7:1. The syntactic relationship between a cardinal numeral and an ac-

name, if זיוך is one, and the position of the numeral are both highly irregular. Cf. Grelot 1972:388, n. *e*.

[994] Instead of 'all (told) two boat-holders of the C.' by Porten - Yardeni (1986:99). Their Modern Hebrew translation ... כל שני בעלי הספינה של (סך ה) also reads a little awkward, whereas Grelot (1972:288) offers "tous les deux nautoniers des forts."

[995] On fractions, see § 21 *d*.

[996] Note also a similar lack of concord shown by Syr. *qallil* and *saggi*: see Muraoka 1987:49.

companying noun is somewhat different from that between a
noun and a demonstrative or an adjective. In that sense the usual
position of numerals after nouns is not of the same nature as that
for adjectives or demonstratives. These cardinal numerals can be
better thought of as a kind of adverbial: 'to the amount of.' The
above listing then might be better translated as 'tray(?) of *slq*, 2.'
Consider a striking break between תקם and 5 חפנן in תקם יתו לי
5 חפנן 'Let them bring me castor oil, 5 handfuls!' A2.4:12.([997])
This way we could better understand the striking st.det. מנדתא in
מ[נד]תא[ן מנדעם לא מהיתה לי A6.14:2 which can best be translated:
'is not bringing me the (agreed) rent ... at all' rather than 'not ..
any rent.' We would add also that a noun phrase giving a weight,
measure, monetary value and the like is not therefore to be
considered an appositional phrase, unless one redefines
apposition.([998])

זעיר in זעיר מלח 'a little salt' D7.2:2 precedes the noun head
like מנדעם in מנדעם כסנתו 'some loss' A6.10:2 (§ 44 *b*), probably
because both are quantifiers.

f) When a demonstrative pronoun is added to a syntagm
consisting of a noun and a cardinal numeral, the pronoun occupies
the second slot as in גבריא אלך תרין 'those two men' C1.1:56 and
5 חלכיא אלך 'those 5 Cilicians' A6.15:5. The cohesion between
the noun and the demonstrative appears to be greater than that
between the noun and the numeral. See above, § 65 *d*, and note
the st.det. of the noun head.

g) However, the cohesion between a noun and a cardinal
numeral or cipher is greater than that between a noun and an attributive adjective as is shown by the end position of the adjective:
שפרת 1 תקבת '1 pretty vessel' A2.2:11; סוסה חד קליל 'a swift horse'
C1.1:38([999]); זי גמא 1 חדת .[.]ת '1 new basket(?) of papyrus reed'
B3.8:17; כתן 1 בליה '1 worn linen' ib.12, sim. B6.2:5; לבש 1 מעדר
חדת '1 new, fringed(?) garment' B3.8:8; בי חד מבני 'one renovated
house' B3.11:2. However, אחרן in the sense of 'more, additional,'
being itself a sort of quantifier, does not fully accord with this
rule([1000]): גברן 2 אחרן '2 other men' C1.1:37, but לי[ו]מן אחרן תלתה
'in another three d[a]ys' ib.39. Cf. also ליומן אחרן שגיאן 'after

---

[997] So Grelot 1972:158 rather than Porten - Yardeni (1986:16): "5 handfuls
of castor oil."

[998] *Pace*, for instance, Fitzmyer 1956:128-31.

[999] Not "a swift horse of his" (Cowley 1923:230). See above § 18 *r*, n. 341,
and cf. Driver 1957:73 with n. 2 there.

[1000] Cf. a similar situation in Classical Syriac: Muraoka 1987:47,49.

many more days' C1.1:49. In accounts, however, one finds the
sequence [noun + adjective + numeral] as in 1 לק עתיק 'old oar
(?), 1' C3.7Gr2.:2,12 and 30 ספן ריקן 'empty jars (?), 30' C3.7Cr2:2
// ספינה 1 רבה 'one large ship' C3.7Dr3:11. See our discussion
above at § *e*. Another exception, 5 תרען רברבן 'five enormous
gates' A4.8:9 may be due to some emphasis on רברבן.

h) Where a syntagm [Noun + cardinal numeral] is further
expanded by the addition of a זי phrase, two word-orders are
attested:

[Noun + Numeral + זי + Noun], e.g., לבש 1 זי קמר חדת '1
garment of wool, new' B3.8:6; גמידה 1 זי קמר חדת '1 woolen
garment(?), new' ib.7; פק 1 זי סלק '1 tray(?) of *slq*' B2.6:16; מחזי
נחש זי 1 '1 bronze mirror' ib.11

[Noun + זי + Noun + Numeral] — ר/דמן זי סלק 1—1 *d/rmn* of
slq' B3.8:18; פיק זי סלק 2 'tray(?) of *slq*, 2' ib.; קף זי עק 1 'wooden
chest(?), 1' ib.19 // קפף 1 זי חוצן '1 palm-leaf chest(?) ib.17; תרען
זי אבן 5 'gates of stone, 5' A4.7:9

i) Of the very few([1001]) ordinal numerals attested in our corpus,
תנין in מטא תנין שנה 'a second year came round' B3.1:7 is problematic:
the verb is masculine with the fem. subject, and the numeral is
masculine and is found before the noun. At A6.10:1,8 קדמי means
'former, previous.' An alternative for an ordinal is attested in זי
תלתא רחימה לשמש 'the third is dear to Shamash' C1.1:187.([1002])

§ 68. Noun with a prepositional phrase

a) A phrase consisting of a preposition followed by a
conjunctive pronoun, a noun or a noun phrase may be used as an
adjectival to qualify the preceding noun head: e.g., [חדה] ותרתין
מן נשי כנותה '[one] or two of the wives of his colleagues' B3.8:38;
קפף 1 זי חוצן תחת לבשיה '1 palm-leaf chest (?) for her garments'
ib.17; קף זי עק 1 תחת חמריה '1 wooden chest (?) for her jewels'
ib.19; בניך מן מבטחיה 'your children from Mibtahiah' B2.4:7; בניך
עמך 'your children with you' C1.1:129; ויעבד פתכר סוסה עם רכבה
'and let him make a statue of a horse with its rider (on it)'
A6.12:2; ארמי זי סון לדגל וריזת 'an Aramaean of Syene of the
detachment of Varyazata' B2.1:2.

b) That אחריכי in a recurring phrase בניכי אחריכי 'your children
after you' is an adverbial rather than an adjectival is shown by
comparing an instance such as ירשנכי דין ודבב ירשה לבניכי אחריכי
ויקבל עליכי ... ועל בניכי אחריכי 'bring against you suit or process,

---

[1001] See § 21 *f*.

[1002] A phenomenon known in Syriac, for instance: Nöldeke 1898: § 239.

or bring (suit) against you ... bring (suit) against your children
after you and complain against you... and against your children
after you' B3.10:18 with ואנתי יהוישמע אם שליטא ובניכי שליטן אחריכי
'and you Jehoishma certainly have right and your children have
right after you' ib.20. In the latter clause the breaking up of the
phrase by the intervening שליטן is significant. The total absence
of a prepositional phrase expanding a noun head but separated
from the latter such as *בר מטאני לך 'a son of yours came to me,'
for the expected בר לך מטאני compels us to regard אחריכי as an
adverbial to be construed with שליטן: 'your children (shall) have
right after you.' Similarly אנת עני שליט בה מן יומא זנה ועד עלמן ובניך
שליטן אחריך 'you Anani have right to it from this day and for ever
and your children (shall) have right after you' B3.12:22; ביתא זנך
לא שליט אנת ... להן בניך ... המו שליטן בה אחריכם 'you have no right
(to sell ...) this house ... but your children ..., they have right to it
after you' B2.4:6. See also B2.3:9,15, 2.10:9,16, B3.5:5,
B3.11:9.([1003]) That the breaking up is not a question of individual
style is clear, since more than one scribe displays the same
feature. The same interpretation can be applied to בניך מן אחריך
B2.7:7, B3.4:12,16,19. But choice is difficult in אגרת מן מראי
תשתלח ... A6.13:2 between 'Let a letter be sent from my lord ...'
(Porten - Yardeni 1986:122; sim. at A4.7:24) and 'une lettre de
Monseigneur soit envoyée ...' (Grelot 1972:320[[1004]]), whilst the
matter is less problematic in בבל לם אגרת מן ארשם יהבת 'In Babylon
a letter from Arsames was given' A6.15:1.

   c) A prepositional phrase which shows where a certain object
is located is very often introduced by זי: כהניא זי ביב בירתא 'the
priests who are in Elephantine the fortress' A4.7:1; בין בגיא זילי זי
בעליתא ותחתיתא 'in my domains which are in the Upper and Lower
(Egypt)' A6.7:5; חילא זי לידה 'the troop which is at his command'
A6.8:1; זויתה זי לעליה 'its corner which is above' B2.1:4; קצת כספא
ונכסיא זי על ספר אנתותכי 'part of the silver and the goods which are
(listed) on the document of your wifehood' B4.6:4; חרא זי עמ[ה]
'the nobles who (were) with [him]' C2.1:48. Similarly A4.7:5,7,
A6.8:2, A6.9:1,2, B2.1:5. See also עמרה זי על מכי 'the wool
which is owed by Maki' A2.2:9.

   That the use of such a זי is optional seems to be indicated by
the following pair: אמר עני בר עזריה לחן זי יהו אלהא ביב ברתא
ליהוישמע 'Anani b. Azariah a servitor of YHW the God in

_____

[1003] Cf. in Hebrew 2Sm 7.12 "when you lie down with your ancestors, I will
raise up your offspring after you (וַהֲקִימֹתִי אֶת־זַרְעֲךָ אַחֲרֶיךָ)."

[1004] But '*qu'une lettre* leur soit envoyée par toi' at A4.7:24 (1972:411).

Elephantine the fortress said to Jehoishma ...' B3.11:1 // אמר
B3.3:1 (by two ענניה בר עזריה לחן זי יהה אלהא זי ביב בירתא למשלם ...
different scribes).

d) However, there do remain some cases difficult of interpretation. For instance, does the local phrase ביב בירתא in ימאת לי
ביהו אלהא ביב בירתא 'you swore for me by YHW the God in
Elephantine the fortress' B2.2:4 specify where the swearing took
place or does it localise the god of the Elephantine Jews? The
notion of such a localised deity is evident in לחנה זי יהו אלהא שכן
יב ברתא 'a (female) servitor of YHW the god, dweller of Elephantine
the fortress' B3.12:2.([1005]) The same syntactic ambigui-ty persists
in אמר מיכא ... לע.ני ... לחן ליהו ביב 'Mica ... said to Anani ... a
servitor of YHW in Elephantine' B3.2:2. An example such as ביב
בירתא אמר מנחם ... 'in Elephantine the fortress said Menahem ...'
B2.9:1 seems to favour the adverbial, and not attributive,
interpretation; likewise B2.10:1, B2.11:1, B3.8:1, B3.9:1.([1006])

We face a different kind of difficulty over the construction
in the shape of [V + N_1 (= subject) + זי + N_2 + זי + Prep.ph.] as
to whether the syntagm [זי + Prep.ph.] qualifies N_1 or N_2: e.g. אמר
ענניה ... לחן זי יהה אלהא זי ביב בירתא B3.3:1. Is it God or Ananiah
that is in Elephantine? Further, compare with this the following
sentence: אמר ענני ... לחן זי יהו אלהא ביב ברתא B3.11:1. Is the
closing prepositional phrase adjectival or adverbial? There seem
to be some indications that the prep.ph. headed by זי in these
cases is more likely a juxtaposed co-modifier of N_1 together
with the preceding phrase [זי + N_2]. In יודנא זי מלכא זי ביב בירתא
'the barley-house (?) of the king in E. the fortress' A4.5:5 the
general context makes it more likely that the phrase is about the
location of the installation rather than that of the king. At a deep
level, this example is syntactically analogous to ביתא זילי זי במדינתכם
'my estate in your province' A6.9:2. אגורא זי יהו אלהא זי ביב בירתא
'the temple of ...' A4.7:6 is abbreviated to אגורא זי ביב בירתא ib.7.
Note also על אגורא זי יהו אלהא למבניה ביב בירתא 'on the temple ...
in order to build it in E. ...' ib.24. The following cases may also
be viewed in a similar way: בית מדבחא זי אלה שמיא זי ביב בירתא
'the altar-house of the god of heaven which is in Elephantine ...'

[1005] The fem. gender of לחנה precludes the possibility of construing שכן with
the former.

[1006] Cf. our remarks below at § 78 *cp.*

At אבהין בנו אגורא זך ביב בירתא 'our forefathers had built that temple in
Elephantine the fortress' A4.7:13 we would rather see an adverbial phrase of
place in view of אגורא זי יהו אלהא זי ביב בירתא 'the temple of YHW the god
which is in Elephantine the fortress' ib.6.

A4.9:3; כמריא זי חנוב אלהא זי ביב בירתא 'the priests of Khnub the god who are in E. ...' A4.7:5; ביתה זי אפולי בר מסדי זי ביב ברתא 'the house of A. the son of M., which is in E. ...' B3.4:4, in which last case one may also note that, where a person's provenience or ethnic origin is indicated, זי is not followed by a preposition of place, e.g. אמרת יהוחן ... נשן זי יב בירתא למשלם בר זכור יהודי זי יב בירתא 'Jehohen ..., a lady of Elephantine ... said to Meshullam ..., a Jew of E. ...' B3.1:2; ... ארמי זי סון ... משלם יהב לי 'M. ... an Aramaean of Syene gave me' B2.7:3.([1007]) Nevertheless, even in אלהא זי ביב בירתא, which seems to be easy of interpretation in view of ... שכן B3.12:2, the ambiguity remains because of A4.7:6 vs. ib. 7, and A4.7:24.

e) Typologically akin is the pattern represented by ויהודיא אנחנה ונשן ובנין ויהודיא כל זי תנה // A4.8:26 כלא זי תנה ... 'we and our wives and our sons and the Jews, all (of them) who are here' A4.7:26.

§ 69. Noun with כל

This paragraph will deal with all aspects of the multifaceted use of כל, including cases where the word is not to be directly construed with a noun phrase.

a) *Bare* כל. Where כל indicates that the whole of the object or every single member of the class indicated by the noun concerned is affected, it normally precedes the latter: + a *sg. abs.* noun—כל כסף 'all silver' B4.2:6, כל גשר 'every beam' A2.2:15, כל ערבן 'every security' B3.1:9, בכל עדן 'at all times' A3.6:1; + a *sg.det.* noun—כל כספא 'all the silver' B2.6:13; + a *sg. noun with a conj. pron.*—כל כספך 'all your silver' B4.2:7; + a *pl. abs. noun*—כל נכסין ... כל גברן 'all goods ... all persons' A4.7:16, כל לבשן 'all garments' B3.8:13; + a *pl. det. noun*—כל ספינתא 'all the ships' C3.7Dr1:11, כל אסריא 'all the bonds' B5.6:10; + a *pl. noun with a conj. pron.*—לכל עבדיך 'for all your slaves' C1.1:178; + a *det. cst. phrase*—כל בעלי יב 'all the burghers of Elephantine' A4.7:22; + זי—כל זי איתי לה—זי 'all that he has' B2.6:19, כל זי תצבה 'whatever you desire' A2.4:7. Note also כל מדעם זי יחיה בה איש 'anything on which one may live' B4.1:3 and וכל מנדעם זי חמיר 'and everything that is leavened' A4.1:6.([1008])

[1007] Cf. מחסיה בר ידניה יהודי בבירת יב 'M. son of Y., Jew in the fortress of Elephantine' B2.2:2.

[1008] Another example of a relative clause with no explicit subject might be [פ]רסכן זי כלי כלה 'your sala[ry], which was withheld (in) its entirety' A3.3:6, if כלי be taken as a passive ptc. rather than a G passive pf.: see § 34 *b*.

b) כל often precedes a cipher in order to give a total after two or more items have been enumerated, often followed by an appositional phrase: אמר מנחם ועניה כל 2 בני משלם 'Menahem and Ananiah, all (told) 2, sons of Meshullam ... said' B2.9:1, לגברן זילי עלימן תלתה כל חד אמן תרין חלכין 'to two Cilician persons (and) one artisan, all (told) three, servants of mine' A6.9:4, זי [חסף]2 זי עק 2 זי אבן 1 כל 5 'pottery, 2, wooden, 2, of stone, 1, all (told) 5' B3.8:19 et passim.

A variant on this pattern is given by one in which כל is followed by a noun and a cipher as in כל גברן 5 'all (told) 5 persons' A4.10:5, sim. A6.3:5, A6.7:5, A6.15:2, C4.4:10.

c) כל may immediately follow a determinate noun phrase *with a matching conjunctive pronoun*: יעט אתור כלה 'the counsellor of the entire Assyria' C1.1:12; אבוה זי אתור כלה 'the father of the entire Assyria' ib.55([1009]); [ביתא =] ביתה כלה 'the whole house' B3.5:20; ארעא כלה 'the whole earth' B2.6:19.([1010]) Once כל follows a disjunctive personal pronoun: אנת כלך 'you entirely' C1.1:102. This last example shows that כלה in the remaining examples cannot be dismissed as a variant spelling of כלא.

כלה or כלך here can be taken either as being in apposition to the preceding noun phrase or as quantifier, on which latter see below at § *d, e*.

Twice we find כל with a conjunctive pronoun attached and referring to the noun in question, but at a remove from its head: ואשכחתה שנטת כלה 'and I found it (= כתנה 'the tunic') all of it frayed(?)' A2.1:4; [פ]רסכן זי כלי כלה 'your sala[ry], which was withheld (in) its entirety' A3.3:6.([1011])

d) כלא([1012])

It is noteworthy that the scribe of A4.8, a revised version of A4.7, writes כלא in a parallel passage: כלא קטילו A4.8:16 (// A4.7:16 quoted below), and also most likely at A4.8:13 אגורי [מגרו א]כל[ו] מצריא [אלה]י[ן] (// A4.7:14 also quoted below). There are three more instances where the scribe of A4.8 substitutes כלא for כל of A4.7: עבדיך ידניה וכנותה A4.8:22 // ויהודיא כלא בעלי יב ויהודיא כל בעלי יב 'your servants Jedaniah and his colleagues and

---

[1009] Porten - Yardeni 1993:32 wrongly כלא.

[1010] Cf. also סחתה כלה 'all the neighbourhood (?)' A2.1:12.

[1011] Gibson's translation "(the clerks will pay you) in its entirety your salary, which has been withheld" (Gibson 1975:145f.) is unlikely: כלה would be too far removed from what he would restore before ופ]רסכן and with a relative clause intervening.

[1012] See above, § 22 *c*.

the Jews, all (of them) citizens of Yeb' A4.7:22([1013]); ויהודיא כלא
אנחנה ונשן ובנין ויהודיא כל זי תנה // A4.8:26 זי תנה ...   'we and our
wives and our sons and the Jews, all (of them) who are here'
A4.7:26; כל גברין ... קטילו // A4.8:16 כלא קטילו A4.7:26;
were all killed' A4.7:16.([1014]) Another example of quantifier כל
corresponding to כלא is אלהיא כל ישאלו שלמכי A3.7:1 vs. שלם אחי
אלהיא כ[ל]א[ישאלו 'May the gods seek all (of them) the well-being
of my brothers' A3.10:1, sim. A3.5:1, A3.9:1.

כלא is thus found after a noun phrase or phrases, referring
back to it or to them: e.g. ומנדע[ם] אחרן זי לקחת כלא התב הב
למספת '... and anything else which you took, give all of it back to
Masapata' A6.15:6; ... שלם אמך וינקיא כלא 'your mother and the
children are all well' A3.3:12.

In only one case we find כלא preceding and anticipating a
following noun phrase: ... כלא מליא באגרה חדה שלחן 'we communicated all the matters in one letter' A4.7:29 where the preposed
כלא may be indicative of some emphasis and contrast with חדה.

We see that the grammatical function of the noun phrase(s)
to which such a כלא refers back within the sentence varies:
subject—אלהיא כ[ל]א[A3.10:1 quoted above; *object*—מנדע[ם]
אחרן... כלא A6.15:6 also quoted above; *nomen rectum*—only in
the phrase אתור כלא 'the whole of Assyria' as at C1.1:43, and
plausibly restored at ib.56,61. The same phrase, however, is also
written אתור כלה (see above, § *c*), though they are not likely
mere phonetic variants, but rather genuine morphological
variants.([1015])

e) *Adverbial* כל

The word כל is occasionally used adverbially in the sense of
'in its [or: their] entirety' with a neighbouring noun phrase: אלהיא
כל ישאלו שלמכי 'May the gods unanimously seek after your welfare'
A3.7:1; ואגורי אלהי מצרין כל מגרו 'and they demolished the temples
of the gods of Egypt altogether' A4.7:14; וכל גברין זי ... כל קטילו

[1013] It is immaterial whether כל refers to the entire preceding phrase or, as
Grelot (1972:411) renders with his "tous les Juifs citoyens d'Élephantine,"
only to "the Jews." But "all say thus" of Ginsberg (1955:492) cannot be right.
The same ambiguity exists with the next set of examples, A4.7:26 // A4.8:25,
in which case, logically speaking, the relative clause can be made to apply to
all the groups of individuals mentioned before, though it is not clear whether
that was intended or not.

[1014] On the variations between the two versions of the petition in question,
see Porten 1998.

[1015] Fitzmyer's (1956:81f.) argument that כלה = כלא in these instances does
not convince.

'and all people that ... were killed altogether' ib.16 where the adverbial nature of כל is clearer because of its distance from the noun phrase to which it refers back as well as from its repetition.

f) יתיר is once used as a quantifier preceding a noun in a way analogous to זעיר (§ 67 *e* end): יתיר פתף פתף 'extra ration' A6.9:6.

§ 70. Noun in apposition([1016])

Two noun phrases may be simply placed next to each other without any formal indication of linkage between them. The very lack of such a formal indication points to the presence of subordination, the second term supplying further information on the identity of the first.([1017]) The logical relationship between the two is that of equation.

a) In the great majority of cases one term is a name, whilst the other describes a person or place so named, often a kinship term or title. E.g. אבי פסמי ... עבדך נבושה ... אמי ממה 'my father Psami ... your servant Nabusha ... my mother Mama' A2.1:13; ברי שלמם ... אחוך אושע 'my son Shelomam ... your brother Osea' A3.3:1; בקריה כרב 'in (the) town (of) Korobis' B1.1:3; ליב בירתא 'to Syene the fortress' A4.6:11.

b) A name can be the first term: e.g. נבושזב בר פטחנם 'Nabushezib son of Peṭekhnum' A2.1:15; אל אבי פסמי מן מכבנת בר פסמי 'To my father Psami from Makkibanit son of Psami' A2.4:14; רמי אנת הודו ... תבלא ברת משלם קולא אחתה 'Rami wife of Hodo ... Tabla, daughter of Meshullam (and) Kavla her sister' A4.4:5; חגי אחוהי 'Haggai his brother' A4.4:7. This is the rule in יב בירתא 'Elephantine the fortress' A4.5:3 et passim, סון בירתא 'Syene the fortress' B3.9:1 et passim and other fortresses, and with divine names as in יהו אלהא 'YHW the God' A4.7:6 et passim; חנוב אלהא 'Khnub the god' A4.5:3([1018]); להנאלת אלהתא 'to H. the goddess' D15.2; קדם שמש אלהא 'before Shamash the god' D22.47:4.

With the above-mentioned יב בירתא and such like contrasts בקריה כרב 'in town Korobis' B1.1:3 not only with respect to the word-order, but also on account of the absolute state form of קריה. In view of this, it is not absolutely certain that ירח in ירח

[1016] Cf. Hug 1993:95-97.

[1017] We have seen above that the same logical relationship can be expressed by means of formal subordination, namely the construct phrase or its periphrastic, analytic substitute with זי: § 61 (iii).

[1018] So must one read at A4.7:5, though אלהא is written above to the right of חנוב.

תחות 'the month of Thoth' B3.13:1, ירח מחר 'the month of Meḥir' B1.1:1, and ירח פאפי 'the month of Phaophi' B4.4:1, sim. B4.5:1,5, B5.1:1, C3.7Gr2:14 is in the st. cst., as we interpreted above (§ 48 c [iii]) and as in Heb. Ex 13.4 בְּחֹדֶשׁ הָאָבִיב (TO בְּירחא דאביבא), Neh 1.1 בְּחֹדֶשׁ כִּסְלֵו.([1019]) The picture regarding "year" is no less ambiguous: as against 15 שנת לפחנס 28 יום 'the 28ᵗʰ day of Paḥons, year 15 ...' B2.1:1 we have 8 בשנן 'in year 8 (literally: 'in years 8')' B1.1:5, a case of pseudo-apposition as in בקריה כרב in the same document (see § 21 f, n. 222a).

c) The title regularly follows, possibly excepting פרעה נכוא 'Pharaoh Necho' D23.1 Va:11, ib. XII:7, פרעה נכו D23.1 VIII:12, and מלכא אמורטי[ס ...] מלכא נפעורת 'the king Amyrtae[us ...] the king Nepherites' A3.9:3 to be contrasted with דריוהוש מל[כא] 'Darius the king' A4.5:2. A degree of fluidity is observable with regard to kinship terms—שנאת לתמת אנתתי 'I hate Tamet my wife' B3.3:7 vs. שנאת לבעלי ענני 'I hate my husband Anani' ib.9; שנית לאנתתי יהוישמע 'I hate my wife Jehoishma' B3.8:21 vs. ליהוישמע אנתתה 'J. his wife' ib.38; לאסחור בעלי B2.6:23 vs. [לאנ]תתי מפטחיה ib.27.([1020])

d) A disjunctive personal pronoun occupies the first position: e.g. אנת ידניה ומחסיה ... הוטבתם 'You, Jedaniah and Mahseiah ... satisfied ...' B2.9:8; ... אנה מנחם וענניה רחיקן 'I, Menahem, and Ananiah are withdrawing ...' ib.9; אמר אנה ענני בר עזריה 'I, Anani, son of Azariah, say' B3.7:2.

e) In some cases the first term is not a free-standing word form, but a bound form suffixed to another word: לא אכהל אגרנכי דין ודבב אנתי ובר וברה לכי 'I shall not be able to institute against *you* suit or process, (against) you or son or daughter of yours' B2.8:7; לא יכהלון ירש[ו]נ[כ]ם אנת ידניה ומחסיה 'they shall not be able to bring (suit) against [yo]u, you, Jedaniah and Mahseiah' B2.9:11; ביתך אנת ענני בר חגי '*your* house, you Anani son of Haggai' B3.12:17; יהבת לכי תמת 'I gave to *you*, Tamet' B3.5:6. In all these cases except the last the second term is introduced by a disjunctive personal pronoun, which is further expanded, and there is an element of emphasis on the pronoun. To interpret the

---

[1019] Cf. the Hebrew Ezr 8.31 מִנְּהַר אֲהֲוָא 'from the river A.'

[1020] Stylistically speaking, the scribe of B2.6 and B3.3, Nathan, displays a chiastic variation in this regard: a - b // b - a (B3.3:7 // B3.3:9; B2.6:23 // B2.6:27). However, another scribe, Mauziah, varies the sequence for some unknown reason, displaying a different pattern: b - a // a - b (B3.8:21 // B3.8:38 [= B3.8:40]). The shift from b - a to a - b at B3.8:38 defies an explanation.

second term as vocative is unlikely in view of חלקי אחרנא אנה עננּי 'my other portion, I Anani' B3.5:19.([1021])

Such an appositional disjunctive pronoun may be separated from the suffix to which it refers: זנה חלקא זי מטאך בחלק אנת ידניה 'this is the portion which has come to *you* as (your) portion, you, Jedaniah' B2.11:3. Similarly at ib.5: מטאני בחלק אנה מחסיה 'it has come to *me* (as my) portion, I Mahseiah.'

In אל תצפי לן לי ולמכבנת 'Do not worry about us, about me and about Makkibanit' A2.1:7 the same syntagm is used for both terms.

f) A title like מראן 'our lord,' especially in the opening address of an official letter, has not yet quite fossilised as Syr. /ma:r(y)/ routinely prefixed to a saint's or ecclesiastical dignitary's name.([1022]) Though מראן in אל מראן בגוהי פחת יהוד 'To our lord, Bagavahya, governor of Judah' A4.7:1 is indeed followed by the indication of the recipient's office, the writers call themselves עבדיך 'your servants,' which is clearly in contrast to 'our lord.' Cf. also נשן יהוישמע שמה אחתך 'Lady (?) Jehoishma by name, your sister' B3.8:3.([1023])

g) The basic syntagm of apposition constituted by two juxtaposed terms is expanded by either term or both receiving accretions, where some ambiguity may arise. In מחסיה בר ידניה יהודי מהחסן ביב בירתא לדגל הומדת 'Mahseiah son of Jedaniah, a Jew, hereditary property-holder in Elephantine the fortress of the detachment of Haumadata' B2.3:1 it is not immediately apparent whether "a Jew ..." refers to Mahseiah or Jedaniah. Similarly שמו ב[ר] כנופי סגן נגריא 'Shamou so[n] of Konufi, chief of the carpenters' A6.2:8. That the initial element of accretion does not necessarily refer to the first term is shown by מבטחיה ברת מחסיה בר ידניא ארמיא זי סון 'Mibtahiah daughter of Mahseiah son of Jedaniah, Aramaean of Syene' B2.8:2 where "son of Jedaniah" can only refer to Mahseiah, and it is further unclear who is to be considered Aramaean of Syene. This syntactic ambiguity is compounded by a possible orthographic inconsistency in ארמיא (for the standard ארמיה)([1024]), where ארמיא most

---

[1021] On a similar use of the disjunctive pronoun in BH as in Gn 27.34 בָּרֲכֵנִי גַם־אָנִי 'Bless me, I also!,' see Muraoka 1985:61-66 and Joüon - Muraoka 1993: § 146 c.

[1022] Cf. Fr. *monsieur* and *madame*.

[1023] On the difficult plural נשן, see below: § 76 cf.

[1024] See above, § 18 j.

likely is in apposition to מבטחיה.([1025])

The status of Jedaniah in the famous letter of petition, A4.7 and A4.8, is partly affected by this syntactic ambiguity: עבדיך ידניה וכנותה כהניא 'your servants Jedaniah and his colleagues the priests' A4.7:1. But if Jedaniah in another letter, A4.3, be the same person, as he seems to be, then Jedaniah was probably not a priest, for there we read: אל מראי ידניה אוריה וכהניא זי יהו אלהא 'to my lords, Jedaniah, Uriah, and the priests of YHW the God' A4.3:1. Nonetheless, *TAD* A restores the opening line of the parallel letter A4.8 as [... עבדיך ידני]ה כהנ]א וכנותה כהניא ...]. Similar ambiguity exists in דמידת וכנותה דיניא 'Damidata and his colleagues the judges' B2.2:6.([1026])

h) Semantically, neither of the two terms in apposition needs to be a name: אמר לכנותה גבריא אלך תרין 'he said to his colleagues, those two men' C1.1:56. Here belongs perhaps also מה זי לקחת נכסן] [מן גרדא ... 'what you took, good[s], from the domestic staff ...' A6.15:9([1027]); אחיקר זך שבא ספר חכים 'that Ahiqar, the elderly man, a wise scribe' C1.1:35, where the st. abs. of the noun in apposition should not cause any particular difficulty.

i) In כאיש גנב 'like a thief' C1.1:173 we probably have a feature similar to BH אִישׁ כֹּהֵן (Lv 21.9) and the like where the head noun appears otiose([1028]), provided גנב is not a ptc., but a noun, גַּנָּב.([1029])

j) The frequent use of שם provided with a conjunctive pronoun and immediately following a proper noun as in עבדין זילי במצרין פרמא שמה 1 אמון שמה 1 ... 'slaves of mine in Egypt, a certain Pariyama, 1, a certain Ammuwana, 1 ...' A6.7:2; בתגר שמה 'at a certain (place by the name of) Tigra' C2.1:12; מלי אחיקר שמה ספר חכים 'the words of a certain Ahiqar, a wise scribe' C1.1:1 can also be analysed as appositional. It occurs mostly on the first

---

[1025] Another consideration in support of this interpretation is that in the standard formula at the beginning of a legal document we regularly find the st.abs. of a gentilic: thus contrast דרגמן בר חרשין חרזמי 'Dargamana son of Khvarshaina, a Khwarezmian' B2.2:2 where the man is first introduced, with דרגמן בר חרשין חרזמיא B2.3:23 where the st.emph. has anaphoric force.

[1026] Cf. a discussion in Porten 1968:48, n.77.

[1027] The reading [נכסן is not assured: Driver 1957:35 hesitantly read כחסן 'forcibly.'

[1028] See Joüon - Muraoka 1993: § 131 *b*.

[1029] The scribe had originally written זי between the two words.

[1029a] The origin of this usage, certainly not native, is debated: Persian, or Babylonian. See Kutscher 1954:241, id., 1969:133 and Lipiński 1990:104.

mention of the entity concerned.([1029a]) An exception is פטוסירי
שמה 'Petosiri by name' B2.11:7, already mentioned at ib. 4 with
the same wording.

§ 71. Attributive participle

Only rarely a participle may follow a noun phrase to modify it:
בנה בי תחתי חדת *אחד* גשורן וכון 'Built, a lower house, new, having
beams and windows' B3.5:8; פרסי יתב בפרס 'a Persian resident in
Persia' C2.1:36; .. איש מצלח עקן בחשוכא ולא חזה 'a man who chops
wood in the dark without seeing ...' C1.1:132. In the light of
אלהא in the st.det., שכן at ברתא שכן יב אלהא שכן יהו זי לחנה 'a (female)
servitor of YHW the god residing in Elephantine the fortress'
B3.12:2 is probably substantivised and in the st.cst., 'dweller in
..' It appears to be more idiomatic to embed an attributive participle
in a זי clause as in מנתא לם זי יהבה במדינתא 'the share which is
given in the province' A6.1:2; ... חרוץ בר ביתאלשזב זי אתה למחתה
'H. son of B., who is coming to bring down ...' A2.5:5. Cf. § 55
b.

PART FOUR

SYNTAX

SECTION B

VERB PHRASE EXPANDED

§ 72. Verb expansion

Apart from the subject, a whole variety of elements may be added to a verb in order further to qualify or modify the kind of state or action denoted by it. Such qualifiers or modifiers may be classified into 1) verbs and other parts of speech, 2) clauses and individual words or word-phrases, 3) more or less essential qualifiers and non-essential qualifiers, and 4) qualifiers with a formal marking of subordination to the leading verb and qualifiers lacking such marking (asyndesis). Two other important parameters are 5) whether the head verb is a finite verb or not, and if the latter, whether it is an infinitive or a participle, and 6) whether a qualifier is a conjunctive pronoun or not.

§ 73. Asyndesis

a) The verb יכל or its synonym כהל 'can, to be able' is more often than not followed, without any conjunction intervening to mark a logical connection, by another finite verb which is semantically the main one. With one exception, all examples show a syntagm [כהל/יכל (impf.) +impf.], wherein the two verbs agree, not only in tense, but also in gender, number and person: e.g. לא אכהל אכלאנך 'I shall not be able to restrain you' B2.1:6; לא אכל אעל 'I shall not be able to enter' D7.15:13; לא יכהלון ירשון 'they will not be able to institute (suit)' B2.9:11; [לא תכהל תהנצלנה[י] 'you will not be able to rescue him' C1.1:176. More examples may be found at B2.1:11, B2.2:12, B2.3:15, B2.6:31, B2.8:7, B2.9:11*bis*, B2.10:10, B3.1:11,12,18, B3.3:13, B3.4:12, B3.10:21, B3.11:15, B5.1:4. The principal verb may not immediately follow the lead verb: e.g. ... לא יכהל בר וברה ... יכלא למחסה 'a son or daughter will not be able to restrain Mahsah ...' B2.1:8; לא אכהל אנה עני אהנצל 'I Anani will not be able to reclaim'

B3.7:14; also B2.7:8,11, B2.8:7, B3.4:17, B3.5:12,13, B3.8:41, B3.10:18, B3.11:12, B3.12:27. A long insertion has led to a shift in some grammatical categories of the second verb in לא אכהל אנה אוריה ובר ... יכבשנהי עבד ... 'I Uriah or son ... he shall not be able to press him (into) slave(ry)' B3.9:4, and likewise לא אכהל אנה ובר וברה לי ... נקום ... 'I or son or daughter of mine ... we shall not be able to get up ...' B3.9:6; לא אכל אשבקנה 'I cannot leave her' D23.1 II:8. See also B2.9:10f, B5.1:5f. The one exception mentioned above is ולא כהלן פצלן 'and we were not able to cleanse (it)' B3.4:22, which departs from the standard syntagm by its use of the perfect, which is apparently a function of the opening conditional particle הן.([1030]) The use of the pf. in the second verb is a most remarkable deviation, which can only be accounted for as a mechanical imitation of the standard pattern, where, however, the tense of the lead verb is determined by the general context and that of the second verb, the imperfect, is an indication of syntactical subordination. The following case with the conjunction joining the two verbs is only an apparent exception: לא יכהל עניה ולא יעבד דין ... 'Ananiah will not be able not to do the law of ...' B3.8:37, where the inability not to do something can apparently be expressed only in this way, and not לא יכהל לא יעבד. Similarly in ... לא תכהל יהוישמע ולא תעבד דין 'Jehoishma will not be able not to do the law of ...' ib.39.

Though the majority of the examples under consideration have לא with the lead verb, the negator is not an integral part of the syntagm, as is shown by the following examples: כדי תכלן תעבדן לה 'as you can do for him' A2.3:4; הן תכלן תהיתן 'if you can bring' A2.5:5; הן תכל תהך D7.45:2; הן תכל תעבד/ר 'if you can go' D7.45:2; הן תכל תעבד/ר 'if you can go across/do' D7.24:4.

The following are examples of extension of this syntagm: זי צבי יעבד 'what he wants to do' A3.10:3([1031]); אנצל אהנצל המו 'I desire to reclaim them' B3.8:41, B6.4:7.([1032]) יתעשת לי ינתנו לי אהחסן 'Let one take thought of me. Let them give (it) to me. Let

---

[1030] Though a supralinear correction has יתה, an impf., 'he will come.' But the clause beginning with the conjunction Waw could be understood as a circumstantial clause.

On the corresponding Syr. verb *ʾeškaḥ* used asyndetically with another finite verb, see Nöldeke 1966: § 337B.

[1031] There is no need to take יעבד as a G passive, as Degen (1972b:16) does, when our idiom leads us to expect יתעבד.

[1032] Perhaps possibly in a loose fashion: נפשי צביה אהנצל 'my soul desires to reclaim' B3.7:15, if not 'my soul desires: I shall reclaim.'

me hold-(it)-as-heir'([1033]) A6.11:3 is highly problematic: (a) the change from the 3ms to 3mp, (b) a third verb asyndetically following, and that with yet another change from 3pl to 1s, though the third can be considered logically (and perhaps syntactically also) dependent on the second, and (c) the impersonal use of the 3ms of יתעשה. The above-given translation is in line with the understanding by Whitehead (1974:83)([1034]) of this structure. At A4.7:23, also in a petition to a higher authority, the same verb is used, but in the imperative and expanded by a subordinate infinitive: אתעשת על אגורא זך למבנה 'Give thought to that temple with a view to having (it re)built' A4.7:23. Hence the first two verbs at A6.11:3 are possibly in a relationship of subordinate asyndesis with a new feature of the formal discord between them.([1035]) The final difficulty, namely the 3ms of יתעשה, may be resolved textually by postulating either a scribal error for אתעשת (impv.), perhaps a dittography caused by the preceding אבי 'my father' or an accidental omission of מראי 'my lord' or such like.([1036])

We note that this syntactic feature, particularly with the verb כהל/יכל, is a favourite one in the Elephantine legalese, though by no means confined to it.([1037])

b) A slightly different kind of asyndesis is a syntagm in which the second verb indicates what happend or will happen after the action indicated by the leading verb, or followed or will follow logically. This is common in a stereotypic phrase לקח עבד לנפשה 'he took and made his own' A6.5:16, B7.2:6, and with the following verbs as the leading one: שלח, אתה, אזל (all three

---

[1033] The translation is that of Porten - Yardeni 1986:118.

[1034] "The staccato effect of these orders/requests issued in short asyndetic clauses ...,' though his translation is prosaic: "Please consider giving (it) to me so that I might have it."

[1035] A similar discord is also discernible in the above-quoted A4.7:23, for the subject of the leading imperative is not identical with that of the following infinitive.

[1036] Whitehead (1974:83) adduces ישלח A6.3:5 for his impersonal interpretation, but the actual reading is ישתלח (so his own reading:Whitehead 1974:44), which is a perfectly normal impersonal use of the passive: see below § 80 a.

[1037] An asyndetic syntagm also with כהל as leading verb is known from OA, but with a significant difference, namely repetition of the negator with the second verb—also noted by Degen (1969:123): לאכהל לאשלח יד[ן] 'I shall not be able to put out [a hand]' Sefire II B 5. See Degen 1969:127. It is thus not just that the auxiliary is "followed by a verbal form of the same conjugation & person" (Hoftijzer - Jongeling 1995:489).

verbs of physical movement[1038]), בזע, התב, כתב, אתכנש. Examples
are: אזל קטל א[ז]ל 'Go (and) kill!' C2.1:31(1039); א[ז]ל עבד קרב עם מרג[ו]ן
'[w]ent (and) did battle with the Marg[i]ans' ib.32(1040); אזל אריא
'a lion went (and) approached [= went near]' C1.1:94; אזלת קרב
אזלי קומי עמה ;I went (and) found Ahiqar' C1.1:76' השכחת לאחיקר
'Go, stand with him' D7.1:5; ואהך אגרס 'and I shall go (and)
grind' D7.10:7; שלחן הודען 'we sent (a letter and) informed' A4.7:29;
נשתונא כתיב יהיב לן 'a rescript (?) was written (and) given to us'
A6.1:3; ... אתכנשו אזלו 'they assembled, went ..' C2.1:15+(1041);
לקח עבד לנפשה 'he took (and) made his own' A6.15:6, B7.2:6;
התב הב למספת יעבד על ביתא זילי 'Restore, give [= Give back] to
Masapata. Let him make (them) over to my estate' A6.15:7; התב
הב להם 'Restore, give to them ...' ib.10; אתה על 'Come, enter'
D7.20:2. Here the leading verb is semantically more independent
than כהל/יכל, צבי, and the like, and yet it is fairly closely tied to
the following verb.

This syntagm is exploited with impressive effect in the
manner of the proverbial *veni, vidi, vici* to highlight the speed of
a military expedition consisting of several actions occurring one
after another at A4.7:8f. דבר .. אתו .. עלו ב- .. נדשוהי .. ועמודיא
תברו .. 'led (the troops) .. came .. broke into .. demolished it ..
and smashed the columns ..' This contrasts with a series of
juxtaposed verb phrases all neatly joined with the conjunction
Waw in the immediately following lines, which give details of
different types of vandalism perpetrated on the marauders' arrival:
they' תרען .. נדשו ודשיהם .. באשה שרפו ומזרקיא .. לקחו ולנפשהום עבדו
demolished .. gateways and their doors .. they burned with fire
and they took the basins .. and made their own' A4.7:9-13. The
syndetic structure with a litany of heinous misdeeds perhaps
gives an expression to the intensity of outrage felt by the local
YHW worshippers and their sense of attachment to the symbol
of their piety: "that scoundrel (לחיא) and his soldiers demolished

---

1038 Similarly in OA: ... יאתה יקם דם 'he should come (and) avenge the
blood of ...' Sefire III 11,12 // תאתה ותקם דמי 'you should come and avenge my
blood.' It would be too uncharitable to the stone mason to suggest, as Fitzmyer
(1995:153) does, same error twice in such a proximity. Whether the second
verb indicates a purpose of the first (so Garr 1995:202f.) is largely a subjective
consideration.

1039 The Akk. reads: *a-lik-ma du-[ú]-ku.*

1040 In the Akk. version the two verbs are separated by *itti uqu* 'with the
troops.'

1041 In Akk. the two verbs are idiomatically joined by the enclitic /-ma/:
ip-ḫu-ru-nim-ma .. it-tal-ku.

this, *and* they demolished that, *and* they did this *and* that."

The asyndesis of this kind is not grammatically obligatory, as is shown in כזי ארשם נפק ואזל על מלכא 'when Arsham left and went to the king' A4.7:4.([1042]) The position of אזל in the second slot has not caused this deviation from the majority rule, as demonstrated by the standing phrase אתכנשו אזלו mentioned above. Contrast also לקח עבד לנפשה A6.15:6 quoted above with לקחו ולנפשהום עבדו A4.7:12f., though in the latter case the syndetic structure may have been purposefully chosen, as argued in the preceding paragraph and as also shown by the fronted position of לנפשהום.

That two asyndetically juxtaposed verbs can be separated is exemplified by לקחת לנפשך עבדת 'you took (and) made (them) your own' B7.2:6, with which contrast לקח עבד לנפשה 'he took (it and) made his own' A6.15:6; קרבתא בזע כתונה הילל 'he thereupon tore his garment, lamented' C1.1:41.

In some of the cases cited above the first verb is semantically subordinate to the following one to some extent, which, however, does not have to be the rule, and this has not to do with the formal discongruence between the two verbs: we have two almost independent verbs in הושרו יהיתו עלי אפריע 'Dispatch (them), let them bring (them) to me at once' A6.12:3. The lack of such dependence is manifest in a series of asyndetically juxtaposed verbs widely separated from one another as in "Naphaina led (דבר) the Egyptians ... They came (אתו) to the fortress ..., broke into (עלו) that temple, demolished it (נדשוהי) leading verb... they smashed (תברו) them" A4.7:8f.

In חסין טרו[י זיל]א ונכסי[א]תנצחו גרדא 'You, be diligent in strictly guarding my domestic staff and goods!' A6.10:5 the second verb explicates how the diligence denoted by the first is to be manifested; sim. אנתם אתנצחו] והנדרזא עבדו // מתנצחן ... נטרן ib.4 // 'You, be diligent and issue instruction to [m]y לפקידאן זי]לי official!' A6.14:2.

c) Verbs such as אתעשת, אבה, צבי, כהל/יכל([1043]) and others discussed above can also be expanded by means of an infinitive. Examples are: לא אכהל למפלח בבב היכלא—כהל 'I shall not be able to serve in the gate of the palace' C1.1:17; לא אכהל ... למרשה 'I shall not be able to bring (suit)' B2.11:7; צבית למנתן—צבי 'you

---

[1042] Cf. Dn 3.26 פֻּ֫קוּ וֶֽאֱ֫תוֹ 'Come out!,' and see Muraoka 1966:160.

[1043] For a comparison of the two verbs as regards whether they take an infinitive or a finite verb, see Folmer 1995: 371-76, and on their distribution patterns in the Achaemenid period, see Folmer 1995: 634-40.

desire to give' B3.4:12,14,15,16; לא צבין למאתה 'they do not desire to come' D7.56:7; לא אבו למאתה—אבי 'they did not wish to come' ib. 5; פשר—אל תפשר למאתה 'Do not fail to come' D7.20:4; אתעשת על אגורא זך למבנה—עשת 'Take thought of this temple to (re)build it' A4.7:23; אכלאנך למבנה ... כלא—'I shall restrain you from building ...' B2.1:6, ... למחסה למבנה ... יכלא 'he will restrain Mahsah from building ...' B2.1:9; אמר—זי יאמר לכם ארמנתידת למטען בה 'what Armantidata will tell you to load on it' A3.10:2; שבק—לא שבקן לן למבניה 'they do not allow us to build it' A4.7:23; שנצי—לא שנציו למנעל 'they did not succeed in breaking into' A6.7:7; שלח—שלחת לה למפרש לי מלתא אף שלחת לה למחוה טעמא להושע 'I sent to him (asking) to explain the matter to me and I also sent to him (asking) to show the order to Hosea' D7.24:15(1044); שליט—שליט יהוי למנשא דשנא זכי 'Let him be allowed to carry on that grant' A6.4:4, ... אנת שליט למבנה 'you have right to build ...' B2.1:11, sim. ib.14, שליטן למלקח 'have right to take' B3.1:8(1045); צדיק—צדיק א[נ]ה ל[ה]חסנותה פסמי 'I am entitled to bestow it on Psami' B7.3:6.

It is precarious to postulate another syntagm consisting of זי + צבה phrase on the basis of one broken text: הן צבה אנת ברי זי תהוה[ ] 'if you desire, my son, to be [ ]' C1.1:149.

There are two possible examples of a participle complementing its main verb: שרין יהבן פרס 'we have begun to give (out) allotment' D7.9:11; ולא כהלן פצלן 'and we were not able to cleanse (it)' B3.4:22. In both cases, however, the second verb may be a perfect.(1046)

§ 74. Expansion by noun phrases or pronouns

a) *A noun phrase or a pronoun*, including their equivalents such as a demonstrative pronoun, a substantivised adjective and a numeral, can also expand a verb. A number of distinct parameters

---

1044 On the morphologically difficult למחוה, see above § 37 *h*.

1045 In the following case we observe a transition to an epexegetic infinitive: לא שליט בך למשנתכי ולמזלכי 'not having control over you to brand you and to sell you' B3.6:6, where the infinitives explain how the control can manifest itself. Cf. 1QapGen 20.13 בכול מלכי ארעא אנתה שליט למעבד בכולהון דין 'you have (enough) power over all the kings of the earth to mete out justice to all of them.'

1046 On the second case, see an alternative interpretation discussed above, § *b*. The corresponding Syriac verbs D *šarri* 'to begin' and *meškaḥ* 'to be able' are both attested with the participle: see Muraoka 1987: § 97 and Muraoka 1997b: § 98 *d*. For examples of Jewish Aramaic שרי + ptc., see Sokoloff 1990:567a.

are involved in such a verb complementation: (1) the morphological category of the verb—participle or non-participle; (2) the morphological category of the complement—noun phrase or conjunctive pronoun; (3) whether complementation occurs necessarily mediated by a preposition or not; different meanings of a verb may require different complementation patterns.([1047]) In fact, there are other potentially relevant parameters: (4) the semantic aspect, i.e. whether a given complement refers to an animate or inanimate entity; (5) the aspect of determination, i.e. whether the entity denoted by a given nominal complement can be regarded as determinate or not; (6) multiple complements; (7) verbs of physical movement; (8) the position of the complement in relation to the verb, and (9) the infinitive.

b) *Direct government,* namely no preposition occurs with the complement. E.g. with a definite object—בזע כתונה 'he tore his garment' C1.1:41; כתב חגי ספרא זנא 'Haggai wrote this document' B3.6:15; שלחת ספרה זנה 'I have sent this letter' A2.1:12, A2.2:17; with an indefinite object—לקחת מני ערבן 'you took from me a security' B3.1:13; with a participle—הוי לקח שערן 'Do take barley' A2.4:9.

c) *Indirect government,* i.e. mediated by a preposition. Here one needs to make a distinction between all sorts of non-essential adverbial complements and more or less essential complements, which latter are traditionally called objects, whether direct or indirect. For instance, in שלח לי ביד עקבה 'Send (word) to me through Akbah!' A2.4:6, the notion of agency is less essential than that of what is sent and to whom it is sent. Here we are concerned about essential complements. Which preposition serves as a marker of indirect government of a given verb is essentially a semantic and lexicographical question.([1048]) Let a few examples suffice: ברכתכי לפתח 'I blessed you to Ptah' A2.1:2, A2.2:2, A2.5:1, A2.6:1([1049]); קדם אסרי בריכה הוי D20.5:3 'Blessed be before Osiris'; החוין בוידרנג 'he allowed us to gloat over Vidranga' A4.7:16; גרין לבר 'we instituted (suit) against a son' B3.4:14; דבקה לביתא זילי 'adjoins my house' B2.1:4.

d) The preposition ל marking indirect government is unique in having two distinct roles, both of which are illustrated in למנתן לי לברתך מפטיה 'to give me your daughter Mipta(h)iah' B2.6:3.

[1047] For some general remarks on this subject, see Muraoka 1992:99-104.

[1048] Thus שלח, for instance, can be mediated through either ל or על: שלחי לי 'Send (word) to me!' A2.2:8,9,10,16 // שלחי על תבי 'Send (word) to Tabi!' ib.6.

[1049] On this idiom, see Pardee 1976:221-23 and Muraoka 1979:92-94.

The ל of לי indicates the recipient as indirect or datival object, whereas the ל prefixed to ברתך indicates direct or accusatival object, but the addition of ל for direct object is optional, and is usually lacking as in אנתן לך כספא 'I shall give you the silver' B2.1:13.([1050]) Other examples of ל marking a direct object are: למנתן לי לתמת 'I אנה יהבת לכי לביתא 'to give me Tamet' B3.3:3; אנה יהבת לכי לביתא זנה 'I gave you the house' B2.7:2; אנה יהבת לכי לביתא זנה 'I gave you this house' ib.5 // יהבת לך בתיא אלה 'I gave you these houses' B3.7:14; שאלת מנך לנשן יהוישמע 'I asked you for Lady Jehoishma' B3.8:3; מלכא שאל לגבריא 'the king questioned the men' C1.1:77 // חלכיא גברן 5 שאל מן [נה]תחור 'he asked for Cilicians, 5 persons, from [Nakh]thor' A6.15:3; כתשת לאנתתי 'you struck my wife' B7.2:5, לאנתתא זילך לא כתשת גרדא 'your wife I did not strike' B7.2:9([1051]) // לם זי מראתי כתש 'he struck the domestic staff of my lady' A6.15:8; קטלו למרדיא 'they killed the rebels' C2.1:13 // קטלת המו זי 'you/I killed them' C1.2:4([1052]); השכחת לאחיקר 'I found Ahiqar' C1.1:76; הוש]ר לי חמרא רכב לאתנא 'the ass mounted the jenny' ib.186; [... חילא זילי למר]ד[יא 'Dispatch [to me] ... my tunic' D7.14:1; לכתוני ... חילא זי ל]י ק]טלו 'my troops killed the rebels' C2.1:16; ק]טלו [למרד]יא 'my troops killed the rebels' ib.33; אנה קטלת לגומת 'I killed Gaumata' ib.74; לא שבו לנתן 'they did not capture Nathan' D7.10:6. One notes (1) that the entity referred to by the direct object marked by ל is either animate or inanimate([1053]), (2) that a direct object so marked may either precede or follow the verb([1054]), and

---

[1050] Cf. also Folmer 1995: 340-71. There seems to be a dialectal contrast between the preposition Lamed as exponent of direct object and the particle ית, ית, ות in same function: the former is typical of our idiom and later Eastern Aramaic dialects, the latter of OA including Samalian (once in BA יתהון) and later Western dialects. On the whole question, see Kutscher 1961a:129-33. The author of the Hermopolis papyri does without any of these particles even where he could have used them, e.g. A2.1:2,12, A2.2:17.

[1051] This pair demonstrates that the position of the object, whether before or after the verb, is not a determining factor for the use or non-use of the preposition.

[1052] This ל in the Bisitun inscription corresponds to /ana/ in the Akkadian version, a preposition which is followed by a *dative* conjunctive suffix (von Soden 1965-81:47b), though von Soden (op. cit., 13 and1995: § 114 *e*) regards this as an Aramaism.

[1053] Cf. Bauer - Leander 1927:340f.

[1054] Folmer (1995: 363) finds it significant that in 11 out of 16 certain instances of the absence of the preposition in her corpus the object precedes the verb.

(3) that, though such an object is mostly([1055]) determinate, one comes across a case such as [ה]זה גבר טב לגבר לח[ן יח[כזי 'when a good man sees an evi[l] man' C1.1:99; ם[ר] זי יהשפל לאיש 'one who humbles an exalted man' ib. 150.

Another instance of optional marking of an indirect object involves a G verb קבל 'to lodge a complaint': the word for a person with whom a complaint is lodged may be preceded by קדם 'before,' ל or zero as in לא אכל אקבל עליך קדם סגן ודין 'I shall not be able to complain about you before a prefect or a judge' B3.1:12; יקבל עליכי לסגן ומרא 'he will complain against you to a prefect or a lord' B3.10:19, sim. B3.11:12; יקבל עליכי סגן ודין 'he will complain against you (to) a prefect or a judge' B2.3:13; קבלת עליך דין ומרא 'I complained about you (to) a judge or a lord' B3.2:5.([1056])

Infrequent attestation renders it difficult at times to say whether the preposition ל is obligatory for the introduction of direct object or not. For instance, as against חכם לברה 'he taught his son' C1.1:1 we have only two more instances of the verb, in both of which the complement is a conjunctive pronoun: חכמה 'he taught him' ib.10; חכמתה 'I taught him' ib.9. Likewise אנת תתרך לאמה תמת 'you expel her mother Tamet' B3.3:14, for the verb in question occurs only in its infinitival form with a suffix three more times: לתרכותה 'to expel her' B2.6:30, B3.8:30 and לתרכתכי 'to expel you' B3.7:16. If החוין להם B8.12:5 means 'we showed to them'—להם, and not המו—then the ל in החוין לשמשלך וכנותה 'we showed (it) to Shumshillech and his colleagues' A6.2:8 would be the exponent of an indirect object. Also ambiguous is חמרא רכב לאתנא 'An ass mounted a jenny' C1.1:186, most likely a direct object. See also נמרא פגע לענזא 'a leopard met a goat' C1.1:166.([1057])

e) In the majority of cases a conj. pron. synthetically attached to a verb is a direct (accusatival) object. This is true of such high frequency verbs as יהב and נתן, both meaning 'give': e.g. לא אנחן יהבנה לכי 'we did not give it to you' B5.1:5; למן זי תצבין הבהי 'Give it to whomever you desire!' B2.7:16; למן זי רחמתן תנתנונה 'you may give it to whomever you like' B2.10:9.([1058]) There are,

---

[1055] Thus *contra* Kutscher (1972:101 "רק לפני שם מיודע").

[1056] It is now scarcely warranted to insert קדם, as Joüon (1934:38) proposed. Cf. also 1QapGen 20.14 קבלתך על פרעו 'I complained to you about Pharaoh.'

[1057] Perhaps a different meaning of the verb requires a different preposition: זי פגע בך 'who touches you' C1.1:102.

[1058] In contrast to Hebrew, in which a verb such as נתן often takes a d100tival

however, examples in which such a pronoun represents in fact an indirect object. Such a decision can be made when a noun phrase as a complement of such a verb is consistently marked by ל or some other preposition.([1059])

Thus, a G verb כלא 'to detain, restrain' occurs 4 times with a conj. pron.: כליתך 'I restrained you' B2.1:7,13; כלוהי 'they detained him' A4.2:13; אכלאנך 'I restrain you' B2.1:6. On the other hand, we meet יכלא למחסה או לבר לה 'to restrain Mahsah or a son of his' B2.1:9. In a case like this we can only state that a conjunctive pronoun has the same value as a ל + a noun, without being able to say whether such a ל is an exponent of an indirect object or an optional exponent of a direct object. The same holds for another G verb גרה 'to institute suit.' Our corpus has 24 cases of it with a conj. pron. of person such as לא אכהל אגרנכי דין ודבב 'I shall not be able to institute against you suit or process' B2.8:7 and five cases in which a finite form of the verb is followed by a syntagm [ל + a noun]: e.g. הן גרוך וגרו לבר וברה לך 'if they instituted (suit) against you and instituted (suit) against son or daughter of yours' B3.4:18. Consider a kindred legal term, G רשה 'to bring suit.' Of its 40 occurrences, 24 are with a conjunctive pronoun referring to a person as in רשיתכם ורשכם בר לי 'I brought (suit) against you and a son of mine brought (suit) against you' B2.10:12. A noun complement, whether determinate or indeterminate, however, is always prefixed with ל: e.g. לא יכהלון ירש[ו]נ[כ]ם ... ולא יכהלון ירשון לבניכם ... 'they will not be able to bring (suit) against you ... and they will not bring (suit) against your sons ...' B2.9:11; לא נכהל נרשה לבר וברה לכם 'we shall not be able to bring (suit) against son or daughter of yours' B2.10:10.([1060]) But we do not find a single case of ל + conj.pron.([1061]) In the light of this it is rather likely that the object is direct. In other words, ל is non-obligatory.([1062])

On the other hand, if a verb consistenly takes a pronominal

---

conjunctive pronoun: see Bogaert 1964 and Joüon-Muraoka 1993:§ 125 *b*, *ba*.

[1059] Cf. Folmer 1995: 351f.

[1060] But על also occurs once: למרשה עליך ועל בניך 'to bring suit against you and against your sons' B2.11:8.

[1061] A participle must be treated as a separate category: אנת רשה לי 'you bring suit against me' B7.3:5.

[1062] Thus "+ acc. obj." of Hoftijzer - Jongeling (1995:1086f., s.v.) is misleading unless it is clearly stated that every pronoun synthetically attached to a verb is accusative.

complement mediated by a preposition, especially ל, it is safe to regard such a complement as indirect object. This is true of verbs such as נתן, יצף, יהב, אמר e.g. הו אמר לי 'he said to me' A4.3:9([1063]); כסף ונכסן יהבו לה 'they gave him silver and goods' A4.5:4; תזבן לה בכסף 'you sell (it) to him for silver' B3.12:24. Likewise with G יצף: אל תצפו לן לי ולמכבנת 'Do not worry about us, about me and about Makkibanit' A2.1:7, אל תצפו לה 'Do not worry about him' A2.2:3, אל תצפו לי 'Do not worry about me' A2.4:12, sim. A2.3:4, A2.4.12. In אל תצף לחרוץ 'Do not worry about Ḥarudj' A2.4:3 one is therefore allowed to interpret the חרוץ as indirect object. There is no example of this verb with a conjunctive pronoun.

The D verb סבל 'to support, maintain somebody (materially, financially)' also involves indirect government, and the object appears to be direct. As a participle it occurs three times, each time with ל + a conjunctive pronoun (e.g. מסבלן לה 'are supporting him' A2.3:5), and as a non-participial form it occurs four times with a conj. pron. of person (e.g. נסבלנך 'we shall support you' B3.6:13) and with ל + a noun phrase of person 4 times (e.g. נסבל לזכור ברך 'we shall support Zakkur your son' B3.6:12). In לא נסבלנך כזי יסבל בר לאבוהי ולזכור ברך 'we shall not support you, as a son would support his father, and Zakkur your son' B3.6:13 we have two syntagmata, namely a non-participial verb + a conj. pron. as well as with ל + a noun phrase, juxtaposed in one sentence.([1064])

The G verb שנא, though not of frequent occurrence in our corpus (8, including one reasonable restoration), appears to attest to indirect government: הן ... תשנא לבעלה 'if she ... hate her husband' B3.8:24, שנאת לבעלי 'I hate my husband' B3.3:9, שנית לאנתתי 'I hate my wife' B3.8:21, sim. B2.6:23, B3.3:7([1065]). It is, however, another question whether these objects are direct or indirect: if the use of ל was obligatory with a complement of this verb in our idiom, it would then be an indirect object. Or is the preposition here an exponent of direct object as in לברתך

[1063] We have not found an example such as 1QapGen 19.19 יבעון למקטלני ולכי למשבק 'they will seek to kill me, but you to spare,' where, reflecting וְאוֹתָךְ in the Hebrew text fronted for contrast's sake (Gn 12.12), the preposition ל has been put to effective use.

[1064] Cf. a similar use of את in BH as in Dt 11.6 וַתִּבְלָעֵם וְאֶת בָּתֵּיהֶם וְאֶת אָהֳלֵיהֶם 'and she swallowed them up as well as their houses and their tents' (Joüon - Muraoka 1993: § 125 f).

[1065] Two remaining occurrences of the verb in the corpus are those of a conjunctive pronoun.

discussed above (§ *ec*)?

f) A preposition of indirect object can be other than ל.

הן תהנצל מנך— מן 'if she shall reclaim from you' B2.4:10 and הן הנצלתה מנך 'if I should reclaim him from you' B3.3:14 and לא א[כל] אצל חקלי מנך 'I shall not be able to reclaim from you my field' B1.1:14.([1066]) With these compare, הנצלני כסף כרשן 20 'he reclaimed from me silver, 20 karsh' B8.6:5. The first three examples also show the optional nature of the synthetic complementation, and the second example at B3.3:14 possibly indicates also that, in the case of double objects, one direct and the other indirect, the direct object has the priority over the indirect for synthetic complementation, as perhaps corroborated by the sequence of the two pronominal objects analytically expressed in הושרי המו לי 'Dispatch them to me' D7.9:16. Note יהבתה לך 'I gave it to you' B2.7:16+; שלחהי לי 'Send it to me' D7.4:7.

ירתנה בנכסיה וקנינה— ב 'he will inherit her [= from her] her goods and her property' B2.6:21([1067]); לא שלמתך בכספך 'I did not repay you your silver' B3.1:7,11 // שלמו לך ib.15, ישלמון לך כספא כספא ib.16.([1068])

g) *Double objects*

Some verbs take two objects, direct and indirect. One is usually mediated by a preposition: תושר לכי עמר 'Let her dispatch to you wool' A2.2:7; הן יהב לכי רעיה עמר 'if Reia give you wool' A2.2:16; זבנת משח זית ליקה 'I have bought olive oil for Jake' A2.2:11; נפלג המו עלין 'we shall divide them to ourselves' B2.11:13.([1069]) However, זבן in the sense of "to spend money (to obtain) something" takes two objects, neither of which requires a preposition, a phenomenon strange in our eyes: זבנתון המו עבור 'you bought grain with them' A3.10:5. In the light of this we

---

[1066] The context of הנצלוני B8.2:15 is too fragmentary.

[1067] Thus the restoration in *TAD B*, ירתנה] בתכו[נ]ן[ת]ה ונכסיה וקנינה 'he will inherit from her her [mo]n[ey] and her goods and her property' B3.8:35 is reasonable. Kraeling's text (1969:206) contains a printing error; cf. his commentary (1969:219). The verb occurs no more in our corpus.

[1068] The first example perhaps means "I did not settle the matter with you by means of your silver that I owe you." As with ירת ב-, the preposition is basically instrumental.
Pace Cowley (1923:116), the ב- in חבל לא באגורא מנדעם איש A4.7:14 must be local in view of יחבל מחא עלין 'he will damage our land' C1.1:36: 'nobody caused any damage in that temple.'

[1069] On the striking על, cf. 2Ch 23.18 בֵּית יהוה ... חָלַק עַל.

must take the suffix in למזבנה עבור 'to buy grain with it' ib. 9 as direct object. See also ארעא אזרע מלח 'I shall sow the land (with) salt' D23.1 Va:13.([1070]) The same can be said of some causative verbs: יחוני אפיך 'May he show me your face' A2.1:2, sim. A2.6:2; יחזני אפיכן 'May he let me see your face' A2.5:2, sim. A2.2:2, A2.3:2, A2.4:2; החזין ספינתא 'he showed us the boat' A6.2:7. Examples of חזה([1071]) with a noun of a person to whom something is to be shown are: למחזה טעמא להושע 'to show the order to Hosea' D7.24:16; הַחֲזי לערבי ימא 'show an Arab the sea' C1.1:207; החזין לשמשלך 'we showed (it) to Shumshillech' A6.2:8. The second example with an indeterminate noun indicates that the object is most likely indirect, an interpretation possibly corroborated by החזין להם B8.12:5 if it means 'we showed to them' rather than 'we showed them (to someone)' where the text is unfortunately not well preserved. Likewise צדיק א[נ]ה ל[ה]החסנותה פמסי 'I [am] entitled [to]bestow it on Pamisi' B7.3:6. The suffix in אכסנכי משכי 'I will cover you with my skin' C1.1:166 must also be the exponent of a direct object.([1072]) Examples with a pronominal direct object attached to a verb followed by another pronominal object, indirect, are: יתונה לכן 'Let them bring it to you' A2.6:10; יהבתה לי 'you gave me her' B3.8:3; וינתנהי לכם 'and let him give it to you' D7.29:9; הושרוהי לי 'Dispatch it to me' D7.9:13. Here also belong verbs such as גרה 'to institute (suit)' and רשה 'to bring (suit)': see above, § ed. See also שקפוני רגלן 'they beat me on the legs' B8.4:5.

In the passive transform the second object would become the subject of the verb in these cases: e.g., בגא לם זי מן מראי יהיב לי 'the domain which was given to me by my lord' A6.13:1.

h) In common with Aramaic in general([1073]) our idiom also uses הם/המו, a third person pl. disjunctive pronoun, as an exponent of direct object, and immediately after the verb. Examples are: לא שבקו המו 'they did not leave them' C1.1:98; ירפון המו 'they will heal them' ib.154; ישבקון המו 'they will release them' A3.1:6; תברו המו 'they smashed them' A4.7:9; אהנצל הם 'I shall reclaim them'

[1070] Cf. the same general idea couched in a different syntactic form in Sefire IA 36 יורע בהן הדד מלח 'May Hadad sow in them salt.'

[1071] No relevant example of חזה is to be found in our corpus.

[1072] Cf. BH Mal 2.13 כַּסּוֹת דִּמְעָה אֶת־מִזְבַּח יְהוָה '(for you) to cover the altar of the Lord with tears'; תְּהוֹם כַּלְּבוּשׁ כִּסִּיתוֹ 'you covered it with the deep as with a garment' Ps 104.6.

[1073] On TA, SA and Mandaic as exceptional in this regard, see Muraoka 1992:99f.

B6.4:8. See also at A3.3:10, A3.8:5,10*bis*,12, A3.10:5, A4.8:8, A6.7:7, B2.6:35, B2.7:5, B2.11:13, B3.8:42, C1.2:4*bis*, D7.6:5, D7.9:17, D7.16:6, D7.17:2, D7.38:4.†

The rule that the disjunctive object pronoun must directly follow the verb overrides the "Pronominalregel" (§ 78 *bb*): הושרי המו לי 'Dispatch them to me' D7.9:16.

i) *Verbs of physical movement* with a complement indicating a destination call for special attention.([1074]) Verbs belonging to this category are: G אזל 'to go'; G אתה 'to come,' H 'to bring/take'; G הוך 'to go'; G יבל 'to transport'; H ישר 'to despatch'; G מטא 'to reach'; G נחת 'to descend,' H 'to make descend; G נפק 'to exit,' H 'to bring/take out'; G נשא 'to carry'; G(?) סבל 'to carry'; G סלק 'to ascend'; G עלל 'to enter,' H 'to bring in'; G קרב 'to draw near,' D/H 'to bring/take near'; D שדר 'to send'; G שלח 'to send/send oral or written message.' Some of these verbs are complemented directly without a preposition to indicate a destination: e.g.

אזל: + Ø עלימן זילי זי אזלן עמה מצרין 'servants of mine who are going with him to Egypt' A6.9:4, usually with ל of place (e.g. אזל לאררט 'he went to Urartu' C2.1:20) or with על of person (e.g. אזל על מלכא 'went to the king' A4.7:5).

אתה: + Ø לא איתית המו תאתון מצרין 'you come to Egypt' A3.3:5, מנפי 'I did not bring them (to) Memphis' A3.3:10, sim. A3.9:3 // אתה ... למנפי 'came to Memphis' A4.2:11, אתה סון 'is coming (to) Syene' D7.1:4, [א]תית ביתך 'I came (to) your house' B2.6:3([1075]), היתי שושן 'brought (to) Susa' A6.12:1; with a person, על indicates a destination or recipient([1076]), and ל a person who benefits from what is brought—אגרת ארשם זי היתיו על פסמשך 'the letter of Arsames which they brought to Psamshek' A6.15:4, אנה אתית עליך בביתך בסון 'I came to you at your home in Syene' B3.13:2 et passim // תקם יתו לן מדעם 'I shall bring you something' A2.1:10, זי מ[נ]ד[ת]א[] מנדעם לא מהיתה לי 'Let them bring us castor oil' ib.7; 'who is not bringing me the (agreed) re[nt] ... at all' A6.14:2.

הוך: no example of direct linkage between verb and destination([1077]), but only with ל of place (תהך לבית אבוה) 'she shall go to

---

[1074] Cf. also Folmer 1995:589-621.

[1075] Given this fluctuation in syntax, one hesitates, *pace* Fitzmyer (1971:149), to assume a scribal error here for לביתך on the ground that this is the only case of a common noun indicating a desitnation with this verb, but lacking ל.

[1076] Hence אתו על ביתא זילי 'they came to my household' B8.4:4 (rather than 'house' as a building)?

[1077] But cf. Sefire III 5 יהכן חלב 'they go (to) Aleppo.'

her father's house') B3.8:28)([1078]) and exceptionally with על of place (יהכן על ביתא זך 'will have gone into that house' B3.4:23).

יבל: Ø+ יבלו המו בית פטוסרי 'Let them bring them (to) the house of Petosiri' D7.39:4([1079]), in a standard dispatch address in Hermopolis letters (e.g. אפי יובל 'Let it be delivered (to) Luxor' A2.7:5, always with the destination preceding), but otherwise ל and על used indiscriminately (e.g. יבלתך לביתא זילי 'I brought you to my house' C1.1:48 // יבלתון על בתין 'you brought (it) to our houses' A3.10:5 followed by [יה]יתה עלין 'he will bring (it) to us' ib. 6.

ישר H/A: always with ל + person (e.g. לה הושר לי ספר 'he did not dispatch to me a letter' A2.5:4).

מטא: Ø+ מטא צחא מנפי 'Seha reached Memphis' C3.27:2, עד ימטא מצרין 'until he reaches Egypt' A6.9:5, למטה מדי 'upon arrival in Media' C2.1:25, but with an object of person usually with על as in כזי אגרתא זא [ת]מטא עליך 'when this letter reaches you' A3.8:6 (also A3.5:2, A3.10:8, B7.2:7,7, B2.8:5), all of which seems to suggest that when the destination is a person expressed as a conj. pron., it is indirect, being a shorthand for על + conj.pron., מטח עלי כתנה = מטתני כתנה 'the tunic reached me' A2.1:4([1080]) and with ל of place (e.g. רב חילא מטא לאבוט 'the troop commander arrived in Abydos' A4.3:3) or ב followed by a place-name ([למטא] ברחא 'upon arriving at Rakha' C2.1:41; למטה מדי בכנדור 'upon arriving in Media at Kundur' ib.25).

נחת: Ø+ לא יחתון שאול 'they will not go down to Sheol' C1.2:6, חת מנפי 'Come down (to) Memphis!' A3.8:7 // נחת אנת למנפי 'you come down to Memphis' A3.8:11, with ל + pers. (beneficiary) as in הנחת לי כתון 'Bring me down a tunic' A3.8:13.

נפק: no instance of direct government, but ל of person (beneficiary) as in אפק לי תלי 'Take out for me an implement (?)' D7.7:6, ל of place (e.g. הנפקו לימא 'they took out to the sea' C3.7Kv2:1 et passim), and על with person as in ינפק עלי 'let him come out to me' D7.10:7.

סלק, סבל, נשא—no relevant examples.

עלל: Ø + תנעל ביתא זנה 'you shall enter this house' B3.12:22,

---

[1078] Cf. תהך לה אן זי צביח 'she may go off to wherever she wishes to' B2.25,28.

[1079] Possibly a haplography for בבית in view of יבלוני במת ... 'they brought me into the land of ...' B8.1:17.

[1080] Cp. especially the above-quoted כזי אגרתא זא [ת]מטא עליך 'when this letter reaches you' A3.8:6 with [... כזי תמטנך אנ[ר]תא זא A3.9:2 with the same meaning.

אעל סון 'I will enter Syene' D7.24:2, with ל of place (e.g. על
למצרין 'entered Egypt' A4.7:13), with ב of place (e.g. עלו באגורא
זך 'they made forced entry into that temple' A4.7:9 et passim),
with ל + pers. (beneficiary?) as in על לך 'entered to you' D7.33:1,
הנעלת לי תמת בידה לבש 1 זי עמר 'Tamet brought in for me in her
hand 1 woolen garment' B3.3:4 et passim.

קרב: with על of person (קרב עלי 'he approached me' C1.1:193;
תקרבני עלוהי 'you will present me to him' C1.1:54)([1081]), also with
אהקרב קדמוהי (קדם 'I shall present before him' A6.3:6).

שדר: with ל of person ([סנ]יא שדר לרמנ[א] 'a [bramb]le
dispatched to a pomegranate' C1.1:101).

שלח: with על of addressee (e.g. אגרת שלח על נפין 'he sent a letter
to Naphaina' A4.7:7; מני שליח עליהם '(word) was sent from me to
them' A6.2:6; אגרת מן מראי תשתלח על נחתחור 'May a letter be sent
from my lord to Nakhthor' A6.13:2), // ל + person (e.g. כל זי
תצבה שלח לי 'anything you want, send (word) to me' A2.4:7, // ל
of beneficiary (e.g. שלחלי לבשא 'Send me [=for me] a garment!'
D7.21:4; זי שלח לי רוך 'which Rauk sent to me' D7.24:14), with
only one sure instance of a conj. pron. of direct object attached
to a verb (שלחהי לי 'Send it to me!' D7.4:7).

From the above survey it appears that some([1082]) verbs of
movement take a direct object of destination of place, but not of
person (שלח, עלל, נחת, מטא, יבל, אתה, אזל). This direct linkage is
sometimes replaced by indirect linkage by means of the preposition ל (occasionally ב). In the case of a personal destination, it
is always mediated by a preposition, most commonly על, but
also ל often indicating a beneficiary (so-called dativus commodi)([1083]), but not always, hence as a free variant of על. Finally
a conjunctive pronoun synthetically attached to a verb of this
semantic category is mostly that of a direct object, the only exception being that attached to מטא, which takes such a pronoun
as an equivalent of על + conj. pron.

[1081] נקרב על מדבחא 'we shall offer on the altar' A4.8:25 is quite distinct.

[1082] *Contra* Folmer 1995:609, who states "... most texts agree that the linking
... to this element [= toponym] is direct, without the preposition." In fact, her
own statistics contradict her: 29 direct vs. 4 על and 33 ל.

[1083] Such a use of Lamed for dativus commodi is not, of course, confined to
verbs of movement.

Folmer (1995:657), having compared the syntagmatics of הושר and שלח,
states that the direct object of the verb הושר is usually goods. Moreover, its
indirect object, always requiring ל, is personal. This supports our view that
the preposition with these verbs indicates a recipient as beneficiary rather
than an addressee.

j) In the case of a *predicatively used participle* its pronominal complement mediated by ל can be ambiguous, for the pronoun can represent either a direct or indirect object, since a participle does not take a conjunctive pronoun as its complement, which is always marked indirectly by means of the preposition. Therefore in cases such as מטאך בחלק 'came (or: has come) to you as portion' B2.11:3,7,9,10 and מטאני חלק 'came (or: has come) to me as portion' ib.5 the verb is a perfect, which fits the context.[1084] An example of what is most likely a pronominal direct object of a participle is: לה שבק אנה לה 1 'I am not leaving him alone' A2.4:4. This verb, most likely as a participle, occurs elsewhere in the same document with a bare direct object: הוי לקח ... ושבק ... כל גשר ... 'Do take ... and leave every beam ...' ib. 10.

Where the same verb occurs as a participle alongside a non-participial form of it and both have a complement mediated by the same preposition, the complement must be an indirect object: e.g., אל תצפו לי לכן אנה יצף 'Do not worry about me. I (rather) worry about you' A2.4:12; כדי חכלן תעבדן לה עבד אנה לה 'as you could do for him, I am doing for him' A2.3:4.

k) *Object complement*

The object of a verb may be expanded by another comple-ment in the form of an embedded nominal clause. That in clauses of this type, the complement, together with the object, forms an embedded classificatory nominal clause is confirmed by the st. abs. shown by these complements.[1085] Some exmaples are: + act. ptc.—חזית עבדא זך מהלך תנ[ה] 'I/you saw that slave walking about here' B8.3:4; see also the above-quoted A4.7:14[1086]; + passive ptc.—אבנצרף 1 זי השכחו גניב '1 dyer's stone which they found stolen' A4.3:3; אשכחתה שנטת כלה 'I found it all frayed (?)' A2.1:4; אגורא זך בנה השכחה 'he found that temple already built' A4.7:14; לא ישכחן עלימתה מכתבה על שמה 'they do not find his lass marked under his name' D7.9:6; יהבת לכי בי חד מבני 'I gave you a house renovated' B3.11:2; + adj.—חזית אנפי אסרחאדן ... טבן 'I saw Esarhaddon's countenance favourable' C1.1:14; + noun—יכבשנהי עבד 'to press him into slave(ry)' B3.9:5; למעבדה עבד 'to make him slave' B3.9:6,7,9; מרגו מלך עליהם עבדו 'they made a Margian king

---

[1084] Thus, *pace* Hoftijzer (1983:114, n. *m*), the meaning of the obscure סרחלצה does not affect the question of the tense of מטאך at A2.4:6.

[1085] See §46 *fa*.

[1086] ואשכחיהתהב needs to be emended to ואשכחתה יתבה 'and I found her sitting' D23.1 II:9. Lemaire (1995:86) emends ואשכחה יתבה, translating it "il la trouva demeurant."

over themselves' C2.1:30. See also תרען זי אבן 5 בנין פסילה זי אבן
'5 stone gates built of hewn stone' A4.7:10([1087]); יהבתה לך פסשרת
'I gave it to you (as) an after-gift' B3.11:7; חין אחד[ו x3] 100 2
'they captured 302 alive' C2.1:17. The notorious crux, אחרנן, in
נפין דבר מצריא עם חילא אחרנן A4.7:8 may be interpreted in this
light: 'Nephaina took the Egyptians with the troop, others (as
reinforcements).'([1088])

In פקיד עבד 'has been made an official' A6.4:3 we have a
passive transform of the syntagm under discussion.

l) *Verbs of intellectual perception or communication*, those
of saying, knowing, etc. can take a clause as their object introduced
by a conjunction, mostly זי and its compounds: תדען זי מדעם לה
מפקן לן 'you should know that nothing is being brought to us'
A2.5:2; לכם ידיע זי חנום הו עלין 'it is known to you that Khnum is
against us' A4.3:7; הודע איך זי עביד אנת 'Make known how you
are' C2.1:66; וימאתלה כזי זילי הי 'and I swore to him that it was
mine' B2.3:24; שמיע לי כזי פקידיא ... 'I have heard that the officials
... ' A6.10:3; לאמר זי לא ישכחן עלימתה 'to say that they do not find
his lass' D7.9:5.

m) Verbs of intellectual perception or communication may
also take as their object a clause introduced by an *interrogative
word*: הן חזית מה אתרתן 'if I saw what you had in abundance'
A2.1:5; [ ] למחזה איך 'to see how [ ]' C1.1:37. The subordinator
זי in ... הודע איך זי C2.1:66 quoted above signals conversion of an
original direct speech into a subordinate clause.

n) *Cognate object*

Some verbs are expanded by an object derived from the
same root: שנית על ידה בימן שניתת מקרא ארמית 'branded on his right
hand (with) a branded reading(?) in Aramaic' B2.11:4,6; טעון
גמלא יטעננהי 'he(?) will load him with a camel's load' C1.1:186;
שמעת כעמלא זי עמלת ... 'I heard exactly what the effort you put in
was like ...' A3.6:2; עבידתא זי אנת עבדת 'the work you did' B2.4:10;
בניא זי אנת בנית 'the rebuilding which you will have executed'
ib.12; טעינוך לי מומאה למומא ביהו 'they imposed upon you the oath
to swear by YHW' B2.2:6; מומ]אה זי[... מנחם ... ימא 'the oa[th whi]ch
Menahem ... swore' B7.3:1.

[1087] Cf. Joüon - Muraoka 1993: § 125 *v*. Dt 27.6 אֲבָנִים שְׁלֵמוֹת תִּבְנֶה אֶת־מִזְבַּח
יְהוָה 'thou shalt build the altar of the Lord (as) whole stones' would typify an
active transform in Hebrew of this Aramaic sentence. Another example of a
passive transform is פקיד עבד חלפוהי 'has been made an official in his stead'
A6.4:3.

[1088] See our discussion on this passage at § 76 *d*.

o) *Object ellipsis*

Precision of the legalese seems to require the repetition of a conjunctive pronoun with each consecutive verb: לא שליטה הי למלקחה ולמנתנה לאחרנן 'she has no right to take it and give it to others' B2.4:9; למשנתה ולמעבדה עבד 'to brand him and to make him slave' B3.9:7,9; למשנתכי ולמזלכי 'to brand you and to sell you' B3.6:7.

A verb object, however, may be elided when it is the second or the following of coordinate or otherwise linked verbs: מן אחר אחרן גרד ... בעו והנעלו ... וסטרו בשנתא זילי ועבדו על ביתא זילי 'From elsewhere seek domestic staff ..., and bring (them) ..., and mark (them) with my brand, and make (them) over to my estate' A6.10:6. See also לא יהבת לך ארקא זך למבנה 'I did not give you that land to build (it) up' B2.4:14; גבר זי תזבנון לה ביתא זך או זי ברחמן תנת<נ>אן לה 'a person to whom you sell that house or to whom you give (it) in affection' B2.10:11; יעבד פתכר ... פתכרן אחרנן והושרו יהיתו עלי 'Let him make a statue ... and other statues, and (you) dispatch (them and) bring (them) to me' A6.12:2; ויהוי זבן גשרן ושבק בבתה 'and do let him buy beams and leave (them) in his house' A2.2:14

At times an object must be mentally supplied from the wider context: לא אהנצל מנכי למנתן לאחרנן 'I will not reclaim (it) from you to give (it) to others' B2.3:18, sim.19; למן זי צבית תנתן 'you may give (it) to whomever you desire' B2.11:7,12, sim. B3.12:22+([1089]); יזפת מנך 'I borrowed from you' B3.13:3; לא יהבת לכי 'I did not give (it) to you' B2.3:20; אנחן זבן ויהבן לך 'we sold and gave (it) to you' B3.4:10. See also אנת פחנום שליט בערבני למחד 'you, Pakhnum, have right to my security to seize (it)' B3.13:10([1090]) and אתה סון עם קנא לזבנה 'is coming to Syene with the sheep to sell (them)' D7.1:4.

p) *Centripetal ל*

The preposition Lamed may follow a verb, usually one of physical movement, suffixed by a conjunctive pronoun matching the subject of the verb, to indicate complete dissocation of the subject from the environment: אזלת לי לביתי 'I went away to my house' C1.1:22; תהך לה אן זי צבית 'she shall go off to wherever she wishes to' B2.6:25,28.([1091])

[1089] Cp. למן זי רחמתי תנתן 'you may give to whomever you love' B2.3:9 with למן זי רחמתן תנתננה 'you may give it to whomever you love' B2.10:9 (not same scribe).

[1090] Cf. 1QapGen 22.24 אנון שליטין בחולקהון למנתן לך 'they have right to their share to give (it) to you.'

[1091] On the centripetal Lamed, traditionally known under the misnomer of

q) Though akin to the above-mentioned centripetal use, there is another well-known use of the preposition Lamed, called by some authorities *dativus commodi* or *incommodi* (dative of advantage or disadvantage): שא לך זי ת[נ]שא מנן 'Carry away what you would carry away from us' C1.1:169; אשתמר לך 'Watch yourself!' ib.81,85. Unlike the centripetal Lamed, this kind of Lamed can be suffixed with a pronoun not matching the subject of the verb: e.g. כתנה זי התתי לי סון 'the garment which you brought for me (to) Syene' A2.1:6.

r) The prolepsis of an object pronoun so farmiliar in a later idiom such as Syriac (*šadddra:h l-malk̯ta:ʾ* 'he sent her, the queen') is totally unknown to our idiom.

s) *The infinitive and its object.*

What has been said above concerning the complementation of a verb equally applies to the infinitive. What calls for special attention is a conjunctive pronoun attached to an infinitive. Such a pronoun invariably indicates the object of the infinitive([1092]): G למעבדה 'to make him' B3.9:6,7; D לתרכתכי 'to expel you' B3.7:16; G למשנתכי ולמזלכי 'to brand you and to sell you' B3.6:7; H להצלתני 'to rescue me' A1.1:7; ול[ה]חסנותה 'to bestow it' B7.3:7.

On the basis of the following examples one may conclude that the infintive, unlike the pf., impf. or impv., allowed direct attachment of the object suffix "them": למושרתהם לכן 'to dispatch them to you' A2.2:13; מנחתותהם 'to put them down' C1.1:170([1093]).

t) *Subject complement of a verbal clause*

In contrast to an object complement (§ *k* above) where the object of a verbal clause and its complement form a nominal clause, its subject may also form a nominal clause with a complement. E.g., והו יחלף לי ספר [חכים ומהיר] 'and he will succeed me as [a wise and skilful] scribe' C1.1:18; ... שגיא ירגש מלן שמע 'he will be greatly agitated, hearing words (such as ..)' ib.29; אחר ל[י] דדרש מנ[דעם ל]א עביד מכת]ר לי 'then Dadarshu did n[ot] do any[thing], wait[ing for me]' C2.1:17([1094]); [אחר מן בב]ל [נפ]קת

---

ethical dative, see Muraoka 1978 and Joüon - Muraoka 1993, § 133 *d*, and on an alternative view as applicable to Syriac, see Joosten 1989. A Hebrew example is שְׁבוּ לָכֶם Gn 22.5.

[1092] On the morphology of the syntagm and for more examples, see above at § 24 *p* and 38 *e*.

[1093] Kottsieper (1991:339) sensibly suggests an emendation מנחתותה 'to put it (= רגלהם 'their foot) down' as in the second version (line 171).

[1094] Though the Akk. version (line 53) has a pl. (*i-dag-ga-lu-ʾ*) for מכתר, the restoration is plausible in view of מ[נ]כתר לי ib.23 for which also the Akk. (line

מן אזל [מד]ין 'after that I depar[ted from Baby]lon, going to Med[ia]' ib.25.

u) *So-called accusative of limitation or specification*

This is a use of a noun phrase which delimits or specifies the area of applicability of what is denoted by another noun phrase, whether explicitly or implicitly expressed, and its force can be reproduced in English by "in terms of, as regards" and the like: e.g. הוה ארך אמן 8 ב 5 'it was 8 cubits by 5 in terms of length' B2.6:8([1095]); עלוה ודבחן דמן כדמי כסף כנכרין 1 לף 'a burnt-offering and sacrifices, in terms of worth, equal to the worth of 1,000 silver talents' A4.7:28.

§ 75. Expansion by adverbials

A verb phrase may be expanded by an adverbial in the form of a word or phrase which functions other than as direct or indirect object.([1096]) Such adverbials can be classified in semantic terms: adverbials of time, place, manner, purpose, quantity, etc. They may be further classified in terms of grammatical form: single lexemes (mostly "adverbs"), noun phrases, cardinal numerals, prepositional phrases, subordinate clauses introduced by a subordinating conjunction, whether single or composite. Some examples follow.

Adverbials of *time*—אחר רחמה אסרחאדן 'thereafter Esar-haddon became fond of him' C1.1:11; שלחת לך אתמל 'I sent (word) to you yesterday' D7.20:7; אנה משלם מחר או יום אחרן לא אכהל אנצל לפלטי 'I, Meshullam, tomorrow or (the) next day, shall not be able to reclaim Pilti' B3.3:13; אחיקר זי קדמן שזבך 'Ahiqar, who previously saved you' C1.1:46; ... וכעת שנתא זא ... שליח 'and now this year ... it has been sent ...' A4.1:2; לממטה מרדן[יא אתכנשו 'upon arrival the re[b]els assembled' C2.1:20; כזי חזית אנפי אסרהאדן מלך אתור טב בן עניח 'when I saw the face of E., King of Assyria, good, I answered' C1.1:14; of *place*—תמה הוית מסבל לך 'there I was supporting you' C1.1:48; למנסק עלא 'to go upwards' B3.7:13; מערב שמש לה אגורא זי יהו 'to the west of it (there is) the temple of YHW' B3.12:18; ואנה מהלך בין כרמיא 'and I was walking among the vineyards' C1.1:40; of *manner*—חסין נטר 'he guarded firmly' A6.10:2; למן זי רחמת תנתן גנבית עבדן 'acting thievishly' A4.2:5; 'to whomever you give (it) affectionately' B3.12:23; הן עליך כות טב 'if it so please you' A6.7:8; הן תאמר כות חיבה הי 'if she says thus,

---

57) presents the pl. form.

[1095] *Pace* Joüon (1934:39) we do not find anything unnatural in the use of the pf. after הנעלת 'she brought in' ib.6.

'in לקבל זי אנה עבדת לך כן אפו עבד לי' B6.4:8 (1097); accordance with what I did for you, so, then, do for me' C1.1:52; of *purpose*—גברן אחרנן מלכא ישלח [אא]חרין פגרה זי אחיקר זנה למחזה 'the king will send other men after us to see the corpse of this Ahiqar' C1.1:62; כן עבד כזי לאלהיא ולארשם תחד[ה] 'So do so that you may gladden the gods and Arsham' A6.16:2; of *quantity*—שגיא 'Sennacherib the king liked me much' C1.1:52; סנחאריב מלכא רחמני 'and they demolished the temples of the ואגורי אלהי מצרין כל מגרו gods of Egypt altogether' A4.7:14; שלם מראן אלה שמיא ישאל שגיא בכל עדן 'May the god of heaven seek after the welfare of our lord abundantly at all times' A4.7:1; כזי עבד אנה לחרוץ כות תעבד בנת עלי 'as much as I am doing for Ḥarudj thus may Banit do for me' A2.3:7 (1098).

Other semantic categories are: *reason, ground* or *cause*—רחמני על זי החיתך 'he liked me on the (ground) that I saved you' C1.1:52; אל תמלי לבת בזי לא איתית המו מנפי 'Do not be full of anger because I did not bring them to Memphis' A3.3:10; על כן יקראון לקר/פא לבא 'therefore they will call the ? sea-lion' C1.1:165; *negation*—לא אכהל אפלח בבב היכלא 'I shall not be able to serve in the gate of the palace' C1.1:17; אל תקטלני 'Do not kill me!' C1.1:52; אריה לא איתי בימא 'there is no lion in the sea' C1.1:165.

1096 On the morphology of adverbials, see § 22 *a-c*.

1097 Alternatively, כות is equivalent to a direct object. Likewise ambiguous is כזי כונה עביד, which may be translated either 'when such a thing was done' or 'when it was done thus' A4.7:15.

1098 If one takes the כזי-clause as adverbial, כות also would have to be so interpreted.

PART FOUR

SYNTAX

SECTION C

OTHER SYNTACTIC ISSUES

§ 76. Agreement and disagreement

a) A word-form which is variable with respect to the grammatical categories of gender, number, and status *agrees* in those respects with a word to which it is logically subordinate. This agreement takes place at either phrase or clause level. The agreement in status applies only to the st. abs. and det. at phrase level.([1099]) Not every word category or part of speech is inflected in all the three above-mentioned categories: verbs and demonstrative pronouns, for instance, are not inflected with respect to status, and cardinal numerals are inflected with respect to gender only, and that only for "one" to "ten" inclusive as well as any higher number having a digit as its smallest component such as "thirteen" (= 10+3) or "thirty-three"(= 30+3).

A phrase level agreement concerns: [1] a noun and its attributive adjective (e.g. פקידא קדמיא 'the former official' A6.10:1 [both ms.det.], ליומן אחרנן שגיאן 'after many more days' C1.1:49 [all ms.pl.abs.], עטה טבה 'good counsel' C1.1:57 [both f.sg.abs.] // עטתא טבתא C1.1:42 [both f.sg.det.]; [2] a noun and its attributive demonstrative pronoun (e.g. ספרה זנה 'this letter' A2.4:13 [both ms.]); [3] a noun and its quantifier (e.g., masc. שקלן תלתה 'three shekels' B3.12:5 vs. fem. חפנן תלת 'three handfuls' A6.9:3).

A clause level agreement concerns: [1] a noun subject and its predicative adjective (e.g., לבבה טב 'his heart is good' C1.1:95); [2] a noun subject and its verb predicate, including a participle

---

[1099] עילמי פרסי (for עלימי) והומס מ[ש]ה (מ[ה]) C2.1:19 must mean 'Vahumisa by [na]me, my servant, a Persian,' and not 'my Persian servant,' which would require פרסיא.

(e.g., זך אגורא בנו אבהין 'our forefathers built that temple' A4.7:13);
[3] a noun or its equivalent such as a proper noun and a personal
(whether conjunctive or disjunctive) or demonstrative pronoun
referring to the former (e.g., ודשיהם ... תרען 'gates ... and their
doors' A4.7:10; זך וידרנג 'that Vidranga' ib.6). Where a referent is
animate, its grammatical gender and natural sex converge (e.g.,
אנה מתכל עליכי 'I am relying on you [= the writer's mother]'
A2.7:2).

In the following paragraphs we shall be chiefly concerned
with cases of real or apparent disagreement.([1100])

b) *Disagreement in gender*

ba) In the case of multiple referents of mixed genders the
masculine gender is made to double for both genders (*genus
potior*)([1101]): המו (m.) נפלג 'we shall divide them (= אמהם ... ולילו
ברה 'their mother ... and Lilu her son)' B2.11:13; למושרתהם 'to
dispatch them (m.) (= משח 'oil' [m.] + כתן [f.?] 'tunic' + 1 תקבת
שפרת 'a beautiful vessel' [f.])' A2.2 11([1102]); זי יסבל בר וברה לאבוהי
[נ]ן] ואנתה 'Let a letter be sent (m. ישתלח
for f. תשתלח) from you to them' A4.7:24 and עקיא זי יתיהב 'the
wood (pl. in the Aramaic) which will be given' A6.2:18 we may
have *partially transformed passive sentences* in the manner of
BH וַיֻּגַּד לְרִבְקָה אֶת־דִּבְרֵי עֵשָׂו 'the words of Jacob were reported to
Rebekah' Gn 27.42.([1104]) In .. אגרת מן מראי תשתלח 'Let a letter be
sent from my lord ..' A6.13:2 we do have a case of "proper"
concord, though in both here and at A4.7:24 cited above the
subject precedes.

By contrast, in יהו קדם לך יהוה צדקה A4.7:27 it is possible to
render 'it [= your action] will be considered a merit for you
before YHW.'([1105]) An apparent carelessness may be excused in
ראש יהוה מרבית בה לך אנתן לא זי ירחא '(any) month in which I do
not give you interest it will become capital' B4.2:4 where the

---

[1100] Cf. Folmer 1995:429-96.

[1101] Note, however, the striking sequence in ואבי אמי 'my mother and my
father' B3.5:19 (for the expected ואמי אבי).

[1102] Though we do not know what the 3fp suffix may have looked like.

[1103] This is also a case of disagreement in number, for we expect אחרנן.

[1104] Cf. Joüon - Muraoka 1993: § 128 *b*.

[1105] So Cowley 1923:114.

grammatical subject is מרבית, a fem. noun, whereas the subconscious subject is כסף or דהב, a masc. noun: the writer may be thinking of the amount of interest rather than the feminine word מרבית; cf. also מרביתה זי ישתאר 'its interest which shall remain' ib.9, and cp. ... מנדתא זי גבי מנה וע]ביד 'the duty which was collected from it and made over to ..' C3.7Ar2:1 et passim, כל כסף גבריך זי גבי מנהם ועביד with C3.7Er1:7 מנדתא ואחרן זי גבי מנה על בית מלכא 'all (the) silver of (the) men which was collected from them and made over to the (store-)house of the king' C3.7Fr2:6; see also מנד[תא] זי הוה יתיר בשנת 10 'the du[ty] (fem.) which was surplus (masc.) in year 10' C3.7Dv2:1, sim. ib.2 and C3.7Dv1:1. Since יד 'hand' and עין are fem. as a rule, one would have to admit gender disagreement in the following two fragmentary passages or take the nouns in question as objects: יהשחתן ידי as meaning 'they will destroy my hands' C1.1:155 and עינין טבן אל יאכמו 'Let them not darken good eyes' ib.157. But a decision on these two cases depends also on our view whether our idiom had a form for the pc. 3fpl. distinct from that for the 3mpl. (see above § 24 *j*). A similar uncertainty prevails in respect of מטו אגרתא 'the letters arrived' A4.2:15.

bc) In זא באישתא עביד לן 'this evil has been done to us' A4.7:17 the disagreement between the masc. עביד and its fem. subject is to be regarded as a mere error or solecism. The scribe's careless grammar is betrayed a few lines later in נשיא זילן כארמלה עבידין 'our wives are being treated like a widow' ib.20 where he ought to have written עבידן.([1106]) See further אבנצרף 1 זי השכחו גניב [גניבה =] 'dyer's stone 1 which they found stolen' A4.3:3; אנת יהוישמע ברתי שליט [= שליטה] בבית]א] 'you Jehoishma, my daughter, have right to the hou[se]' B3.7:8. Cf. also הן יהב לכי [= יהבת] רעיה עמר 'if Reia [a woman] gave you wool' A2.2:16([1107]).

c) *Disagreement in number*

ca) The category of dual is known only in nouns in their st. abs. and the cardinal numerals for "two" and "two hundred." For the purpose of agreement the dual is treated as plural: thus עינין טבן 'good eyes' C1.1:157; תרתין מלן 'two things' C1.1:187.

cb) In some cases, as mentioned above (§ *bb*), one may be dealing with partially transformed passive constructions([1108]),

---

[1106] The first, A4.7:17, can be understood as a case of imperfectly transformed passive (§ *bb*), but not the second.

[1107] That is, if רעיה does not mean 'the shepherd.'

[1108] For Folmer (1995:457-59) also, the passive voice is apt to lead to disagreement, though her perspective differs from ours.

though it is difficult to say whether the same consideration applies to the sg. כתיב in ... ביתא זנה זי משחתה ותחמומהי כתיב בספרא זנה 'this house whose measurements and boundaries is (sic!) recorded in this document' B3.12:22 and ביתא זנה זי משחתה כתב מנעל 'this house whose measurements is (sic!) recorded above' ib.28. The same scribe, however, is capable of writing in the same year זנה כנתיא אלך זי מנעל ביתא זי תחומוהי כתיבן בספרא B3.11:7. See also כל כסף 'that emmer (pl.) that is mentioned above' B3.13:5; כל כסף ונכסן [זי] ישתכח ... 'all silver and goods [that] will be found (sg.) ...' B7.3 palimpsest חלכיא גברן 5 שאל מן [נח]תחור 'one asked for 5 Cilicians from N.' A6.15:3 may be a defectively spelled G pf. passive used impersonally: see below at § 80 *a*.([1109])

cc) In a long sentence the train of thought seems to become lost, leading to grammatical disagreement: ... כל גבר זי] בעה באיש כלא קטילו וחזין בהום '[every one that] sought evil ... they were all killed and we gloated over them' A4.8:15 // כל ... כל גברין זי בעו A4.7:16; לא אכהל אנה אוריה ובר וברה לי אח ואחה לי ואיש לי קטילו יכבשנהי עבד 'I shall not be able—I, Uriah, or son or daughter of mine, brother or sister of mine, or man of mine—he (shall not be able) to press him (into) slave(ry)' B3.9:4; לא אכהל אנה ובר וברה לי אח ואחה לי ואיש לי נקום למעבדה ע[בד] 'I shall not be able—I, or son or daughter of mine, brother or sister of mine, or man of mine—we (shall not be able) to stand up to make him a s[lave]' ib.6.

cd) In the following case, what we perceive as disagreement may not have been so perceived by the speaker of our idiom: נשיא זילן כארמלה עבידין 'our wives are being treated like a widow' A4.7:20 where our logic demands "widows."([1110])

ce) A *collective noun* such as חיל and גרד may be treated as plural, even if it is singular in form: מה זי לקחת נכסן] [מן גרדא התב הב להם 'whatever you took from the *domestic staff* in the way of possessions, restore, give to *them*' A6.15:9; sim. גרד כאחרנן 'like other domestic staff' A6.12:2([1111]); חילא זילי למר[ד]יא ק[ט]לו 'my troop killed (pl.) the rebels' C2.1:16; חילא זנה הוו מהחסנן 'this troop had been leasing' A5.5:9; שמהת חילא יהודיא 'the names of

---

[1109] See Whitehead (1974:105f.), who is, however, troubled by the disagreement.

[1110] This is also a case of disagreement in gender. Cf. Mt 9.4 ἵνα τί ἐνθυμεῖτε πονηρὰ ἐν ταῖς καρδίαις ὑμῶν;, which is rendered in English as "why do you conceive evil in your hearts?," but in Dutch as: "Waarom overlegt gij kwaad in uw hart?" (sg.).

[1111] For an alternative interpretation, see § 66 *a*.

the Jewish troop' C3.15:1.([1112])

cf) A peculiar kind of *plurale tantum* is נשׁ(י)ן, often prefixed to the name of a woman in legal documents and treated as sg. in נשׁן רבה 'a great lady' C3.9:12+; 1 נשׁן 'woman, 1' B3.4:3. That this cannot be called "pluralis majestatis" is manifest from its application to a slave woman in נשׁן תפמת 'Ms (?) Tapamet' B3.6:2.([1113])

cg) In the case of multiple subjects, whether or not joined by the conjunction Waw, the verb, where it precedes([1114]), often agrees with the first subject noun, the rest being accorded less weight: אנת ואנתתך וברך ... ימאת לי 'you, along with your wife and your son swore to me ...' B2.2:4; ונשׁין תפמת אנתתה ... אמר ענני 'Anani said ... along with Ms Tapamet his wife' B3.12:1; אמרת סלואה ברת ... ויתומה אחתה 'Salluah daughter of ... said, along with Jethoma her sister' B5.1:1; אנת ענניה ... שׁלים בביתא זך ובניך מן אחריך ולמן די צבית למנתן 'You, Ananiah ... have right to that house and (so do) your children after you and (anyone) to whom you desire to give (it)' B3.4:11; ... אנה פיא ובני אנתן 'I, Peu, and my sons will give ...' B2.8:9; אנת ידניה שׁליט בפטוסירי ... ובניך אחריך 'You, Jedaniah, have right to Petosiri ... and (so do) your children after you' B2.11:6.

In the following example, however, a similar concatenation of multiple subjects mediated by the preposition עם is surprisingly in concord with a plural verb: ארמפי עם חילא זי לידה לא משׁתמען לי 'Armapiya with the troop which is at his command do (sic!) not obey me' A6.8:1. In the following cases, by contrast, the multiple subjects carry equal weight, hence the verb in the plural: אנת ידניה ומחסיה ... הוטבתם לבבן 'You, Jedaniah and Mahseiah, satisfied our heart' B2.9:8; אנה מנחם וענניה רחיקן אנחנה מנך 'I, Menahem and Ananiah, we are withdrawn from you' ib.9.

In standard legal formulae in which a number of legal persons who could be involved in a case are mentioned, the overriding

---

[1112] As in the immediately preceding example, the qualifying element is in the sg., agreeing with its head: יהודיא, זנה (hardly יהודיא). This also speaks against regarding אחרנן in אחרנן חילא עם מצריא דבר נפין A4.7:8 as a simple attribute of חילא (discussed below, [d]), for otherwise one would expect חיל אחרנא or אחרנן. On the "distributive" force of the noun חיל, "soldiers" as against "army," see Joüon 1934:41-44.

[1113] Cf. Joüon 1934:51f. and see also above at § 47 c.

[1114] Folmer (1995:455f.) sees a strong correlation between the word order (PS) and disagreement, which is a statistically interesting discovery, though it does not *explain* why a preceding predicate is liable to trigger a disagreement. Moreover, Folmer does not apply the same argument to cases of disagreement in gender.

consideration is "Should any one of these persons act in a certain manner," hence the singular form of the predicate: הן גרך אח ואחה (קרב ורק = רחיק) 'should brother or sister, near or far, institute (suit) against you' B3.2:8. If the series of multiple subjects consists of groups of individuals, the use of the plural is readily under-standable: והן אנחנה ובני ובנתן ואיש זילן ... ירשונכם 'and if we or our sons or our daughters or a person who is ours ... should bring (suit) against you' B2.9:12.

A scribe, however, sometimes begins with a verb in the singular agreeing with the first of multiple subjects, as required by the context: אמר מחסיה בר נתן 1 ידניה בר נתן 1 כל 2 ארמין זי סון 'Mahseiah son of Nathan, 1, Jedaniah son of Nathan 1, all (told) 2, Aramaeans of Syene, said' B2.11:2.

Where a sentence begins with an auxiliary verb such as יכל followed by multiple subjects and then the main verb, various thought processes seem to be involved.([1115]) In לא יכל אח ואחה בר וברה קרב ורחיק יגרונכי 'Brother or sister, son or daughter, near or far shall not be able to institute (suit) against you' B5.1:5 the sg. יכל was chosen because the following אח was initially dominant in the writer's mind, but when he reached the end of the long series of multiple subjects, he decided to adjust the form of the main verb. On the other hand, in standard legal formulae, as dealt with above, the chief thought seems to be about any one of the individuals listed, hence the 3ms as in לא אכל אנה ובני וזרע זילי וגבר אחרן ירשנכי 'I or my sons or a descendant of mine or any other person will not be able to bring (suit) against you' B2.7:8. Cf. also אנה ואח ואחה קרב ורחק ... ינתן 'I, or brother or sister, or near or far ... shall give' B2.7:10. Where such a list of multiple subjects consists of groups of individuals, the main verb is a 3mpl. form as in ל[א] נכהל אנחנה ובני ובנתן אחין ואיש זילן ... יכהלון ירש[ו]נ[כ]ם 'we or our sons or our daughters, our brothers or a person of ours ... will not be able to br[i]ng (suit) against you' B2.9:10.

ch) In some cases one must reckon with plain *scribal errors*: תרתין מלן שפירה 'two things are beautiful' C1.1:187 (for שפירן); למה אלהיא יסגה בעדרה ויהתיבנהי עליך 'lest the god come to his aid and turn it back to you' C1.1:126 (for אלהא)([1116]); מחזי 1 זי נחש שוה

[1115] Cf. Folmer 1995:492-96.

[1116] To assume, as Lindenberger (1983:118) does, an error for יהתיבונה יסגון .. is too far-reaching, and this despite Lindenberger's (1982) theological argument. Moreover, Joüon's (1934:26) argument that our corpus does not use אלהא on its own for "God," has now been disproved in the light of new texts: ואלהא

... '1 bronze mirror worth ..' B2.6:11 (cf. .. שויה 1 מחזי '1 mirror worth ..' B3.3:5); 5 שקל '5 shekel' B2.6:14.([1117])

ci) It is possible to regard שגיא preceding a (plural) noun as in st. cst. just like כל([1118]): שגיא בנן 'a lot of sons' C1.1:90; מה טב שגן[י]א כביך 'what good is the abundance of your thorns?' ib.101.

Obviously this שגיא must be viewed differently than שגיא in שנן שגיא 'many years' A6.14:4 where it follows a noun. Though it is not absolutely certain that, in שלם ושררת שגיא הושרת לך 'I hereby send you abundant welfare and strength' A6.3:1+, שגיא is an attributive adjective (quantifier), and not an adverb, there is no such doubt about כדבן שגיאן 'many lies' C2.1:65; ליומן אחרנן שגיאן 'after many more days' C1.1:49.

cj) The following examples in a customs account seem to be a class of their own, items tallied in a list often appearing in the singular: מן ספינה רבה 2 'from 2 large ships' C3.7Dr1:22; עק סמכת 2 'wooden support, 2' C3.7Dr2:5; 5 ספינה 'boat, 5' C3.7Ev1:6. Also in a list: כל נפש 4 'all (told) soul 4' C3.9:5; in an account—רכיסה 6 'string of beads, 6' C3.28:105; 10 תפלה זי כסף 'amulet of silver, 10.' ib.106.

ck) The word שלם in a greeting in a letter presents a special problem: e.g. שלם אמך וינקיא כלא 'It is well with your mother and all the infants' A3.3:12. Its part of speech is not clear: is it a noun in the st. cst. or an adjective? If the latter, it seems to be indeclinable. On the other hand, though attested outside of our corpus, the following cases suggest that the word is not an ordinary substantive, either: 1QapGen 21.19 אשכחת כול אנשי שלם 'I found all my men well'; 5/6ḤevEp 11.3 הוו שלם 'Keep well!'([1119]) This usage probably has its origin in an oral greeting, which has subsequently become fossilised.

cl) גבר חלקה of distributive force is functioning as a kind of adverbial adjunct in נפלג המו עלין וגבר חלקה נהחסן 'we shall divide them among ourselves and take possession, each of his portion' B2.11:13.([1120])

שזבן 'and the god saved us' D1.32:5 and ואנתי שביקה לאלהא 'you are released for the god' B3.6:10.

[1117] One may assume an error resulting from incomplete scribal correction: שקל 1 incompletely corrected to 5 שקל instead of 5 שקלן.

[1118] Cf. Lat. *multum auri* 'a lot of gold.'

[1119] Cf. an Aramaising Hebrew version: Bar Kochba 5.13 הוי שלום 'Keep well!' See Kutscher 1961:123f.

[1120] For a similar syntax in BH, see, e.g., Gn 26.31 וַיִּשָּׁבְעוּ אִישׁ לְאָחִיו 'and they swore to each other.'

cm) זנה or דנה of cataphoric force as predicate may be followed by the subject in plural: זי נשיא שמהת זנה ... 'this [= the following] is (sic!) the names of the women who ...' A4.4:4; תחומוהי דנה 'this is (sic!) its borders' B3.11:3; יהודיא חילא שמהת זנה 'this is (sic!) the names of the Jewish troops' C3.15:1.([1121]) However, cases of agreement are also attested: e.g. זך ביתא תחומי אלה והא 'and behold, these are the boundaries of that house' B3.4:7.([1122])

d) *Disagreement in state*

This occurs only very rarely. Two of such examples involve the use of the adjective אחרן: זילי אחרן נכסיא 'my other properties' A6.10:8 where one expects אחרניא; אחרן חילא עם מצריא דבר נפין A4.7:8 where again one expects אחרנא if the clause mean 'Naphaina led the Egyptians with the other troop'([1123]), where we propose taking אחרן as an "accusative of specification"—'Nephaina took the Egyptians [= the priests of the Egyptian god Khnub (line 5)] with the troop [under his command as] others (i.e. reinforcements).' To take אחרן as in apposition would virtually amount to the same thing. Another possible case is זעיר בפרס [ז]י חילא 'the small force [whi]ch (was) in Persia' C2.1:38 where the scribe or translator may have considered the adjective as predicative, which, according to the Aramaic syntax, should be in the st. abs.([1124]) Both words are quantifiers in a certain sense.

Very striking is שנה תנין מטא והן 'and if a second year has arrived' B3.1:7 where the numeral as well as the verb are masculine, disagreeing with שנה, a fem. noun. Furthermore, the

---

[1121] Cf. Germ. *das sind die richtigen* and Fr. *ce sont mes frères*. On this question, see Paul 1960:304f.

[1122] The same scribe, Haggai, writes: ביתא משחת זנה ... והא זנה תחומי ביתא ... 'this is [sic!] the measurements of the house ... and behold this is [sic!] the boundaries of the house ...' B3.12:6-8. Cf. also below at § 77 *be*.

[1123] So Porten - Yardeni 1986:71; Wagenaar 1928:20 ("benevens ander krijgsvolk"); Cowley 1923:113 ("with the other forces"); Grelot 1972:409 ("avec d'autres militaires"—note the indeterminate); Ginsberg 1955:492 ("with the other troops"). See also above, § *ce*, n. 14.

[1124] The Akkadian version, however, reads: *ú-qu šá* KUR *par-su mi-i!-ṣi šá-ni-tu₄* 'the other small Persian force.' At C2.1:44 Porten - Yardeni (1993:66) want to restore [עם] חילא [זעי]רן '[with] the sma[ll] troop,' but Greenfield - Porten 1982:38 had restored [ᶜm] ḥyḇ zᶜy[rʾ], for which the Akk. version reads *it-ti ú-qu i-ṣi* 'with a/the small force.' Here Porten - Yardeni apparently have adopted Wesselius's suggestion (1984:443), though not his syntactic analysis as reflected in his translation, 'a troop, few soldiers,' i.e. apposition. We would translate, 'the troops, few (in number)': on the emphatic state of the noun, see § 46 *k*.

position of the numeral is abnormal.

In לחנה זי יהו אלהא שכן יב ברתא 'a (female) servitor of YHW the god, dweller of Elephantine the fortress' B3.12:2 שכן is in the st.cst., "dweller of."

e) *Special cases of agreement*

In "if she do thus, it is hatred (שנאה הי)" B3.8:33 the subject pronoun does not refer to a particular noun mentioned earlier, but to a general thought expressed earlier, and the feminine gender of הי has been made to match, by attraction, that of the preceding predicate, similarly at B6.4:4; הן פקיד לך אשה יקדה הי 'if you have been issued an order, it is a burning fire' C1.1:87.

§ 77. Word-order: Nominal clause

a) We adopt the traditional twofold classification of clauses into nominal and verbal, the former lacking a finite verb as one of its two major components and the latter having such.([1125])

We shall see that, whether nominal or verbal, our idiom presents a considerable degree of freedom in its word-order, and it is remarkable indeed that there is hardly a case in the entire corpus in which this freedom could have caused serious difficulties in communication.([1126]) It is in the nominal clause that the word-order variation indicates some significant functional opposition, which is rather rarely a factor in the verbal clause.([1127])

b) *Bipartite nominal clause*

A bipartite NC with a disjunctive personal pronoun as one of its constituents shows the sequence P - S(pers.pron.) when no prominence is intended for the subject, and the predicate in such a pattern appears to be prominent.([1128]) Examples are plentiful: הן

[1125] For a general survey of recent discussions on this subject with special reference to Hebrew, see Joüon - Muraoka 1993: § 153-154 *a*.

The following abbreviations will be used: Adv = adverbial other than object; dem = demonstrative; NC = nominal clause; NPd = determinate noun phrase; NPid = indeterminate noun phrase; O = object; O_1 = direct object; O_2 = indirect object; P = predicate; pers = personal; Prep = prepositional phrase; Pron = pronoun; Ptc = participle; S = subject; V = verb; VC = verbal clause.

[1126] It is commonly assumed that the fairly rigid word-order in Modern English resulted from the loss of case endings. See, e.g. Bloomfield 1933:197.

[1127] A good example of a functionally significant fronting is "Don't worry about me. About you I worry (לכן אנה יצף)" A2.4:12, sim. A2.1:7; פתפא זנה הבו להם 'This ration give them' A6.9:5 where the fronted object is due to an anaphora, sim. ib.6, A4.4:8.

[1128] Thus the use of "moi" is unjustified in רחם אנה להי "moi, je l'aime"

בזי זעירן ;A2.5:9 'whether I am alive or dead' חי אנה והן מת אנה
אנחנה 'because we are few(er)' A4.2:7; כזי זילי הי ... '... that it is
mine' B2.3:25; דילכי הו 'it is yours' B2.7:7; חיב הו 'he is obligated'
B3.8:42; חיבה הי 'she is obligated' B6.4:8; שב אנה 'I am old'
C1.1:17; חטא מן אלהא הו 'it is a punishment([1129]) from God' ib.128;
כי גבר לחה הו 'for he is a bad person' ib.138; הן רחים אלהן הו 'if he
is a beloved of gods' ib.163; בעתרי הדיר אנה 'I am glorious in my
wealth' ib.206; איך זי עביד אנת 'how you are' C2.1:66; ברך אנת
'blessed be you' A3.3:2.

ba) When the predicate in an NC of the pattern P -
S(pers.pron.) is expanded by a prepositional phrase or such like,
this latter follows the S, which thus assumes an enclitic position:
הן כנם הו כמליא אלה 'if' לא חסרן הו לכם 'it is no loss to you' A4.3:9;
ביתה זנך לא 'it is thus in accordance with these words' A6.11:3; לא
שליט אנת לזבנה 'that house you are not entitled to sell' B2.4:6; לא
זילכי הו מן ... שליטה הי למלקחה 'she is not entitled to take it ...' ib.9;
עטה 'it is yours from today and for ever' B3.5:4; יומא זנה עד עלם
שדק ועזיז הו מן טבה הי [שגי]א 'it is v[ery] good counsel' C1.1:57;
סכין פמי[ן] 'it is sharper and mightier than a [double-]edged knife'
ib.84. Also B2.7:16. One may include here an emphatic, resumptive disjunctive pronoun as in: זילכם הו אנת ידניה ומחסיה 'it is
yours, you Jedaniah and Mahseiah' B2.10:8.

bb) Where the particle זי is followed by a NP or an adverbial,
mostly a locative prepositional phrase, such a זי can be interpreted
as the S of the relative clause: see above at §§ 42 *a* and 68. E.g.,
לזויתה זי לעליה 'to its corner, which is above' B2.1:4 and מן זוית
ביתי זי לעליה 'from the corner of my house, which is above' ib.5.
Here we may include למנתן לי לתחמת שמה זי אמתך לאנתו 'to give me
Tamet by name, who is your maid, for wifehood' B3.3:3.([1130]) In
view of this the pronoun המו is striking in איתי עבדן זי לי המו 'there
are slaves who are mine' B8.7:5. The text is broken after the
pronoun, so that it may be part of the following clause.

bc) In the majority of the examples mentioned above the P
is indeterminate. Hence the pronoun הו in יהבתה לכי דרירסי הו
מועה שמש מן תרי רבתא זילי 'I gave it to you, the southern room—it
is east of the large room of mine' B3.10:3 probably introduces

---

D23.1 II:8, 13 (Lemaire 1995:84), for רחם on its own cannot mean 'J'aime.'

[1129] On this meaning of the noun, cp. Peshitta and Targum at Lv 20.20, Nu
19.13 etc. The gender of the pronoun here is probably determined by the
preceding P. See also אשה יקדה הי 'it is a burning fire' C1.1:87.

[1130] The reading is somewhat uncertain.

the subject of the following phrase.([1131]) See also B3.10:9, B3.11:3*bis*,6. The הו positioned in such an explanatory gloss does not have to be emphatic as in the cases to be dealt with in the following subsection, § *bd*.

This kind of הו, which introduces a gloss is common in a double dating of a document: ב 20 לאדר הו יום 8 לכיחך 'On the 20th of Adar, that is day 8 of Choiak' B3.11:1, sim. B2.1:1, B2.3:1+; בירח אלול הו פאו[ני] 'In the month of Elul, that is Pay[ni]' B2.9:1, sim. תשרי הו אפף 'Tishri, that is Epiph' B3.8:1. Once this pronoun introduces a gloss on a preceding term in a foreign language: פלג תרבצא הו פלג תחית מצרית 'half of the courtyard, i.e. half of the *ḥyt* (in Egyptian)' B3.10:4, but the other way round in שליטא אנתי בתחית הו תרבצא 'you have right to *ḥyt*, i.e. the courtyard' ib.13, sim. ib.15; כסף כרשן 5 הו חמשה 'silver, 5 karsh, i.e. five' B3.5:15, sim. B2.3:14.

bd) *S(pers.pron.) - P*

This is a sequence in which a disjunctive pers. pron. as the S often is accorded some measure of prominence. We find this sequence, for instance, when one S is contrasted to another: הי אנתתי ואנה בעלה מן יומא זנה ועד עלם 'she is my wife and I am her husband from this day and for ever' B3.3:3, sim. B2.6:4, B3.8:4, B6.1:4. The use of this sequence is understandable in legal documents in which claims are staked out between contesting parties: ... אנת שליט למבנה 'you have right to build ...' B2.1:11; אנת ... רחיק מן כל דין 'you withdraw from any suit' B2.2:15, sim. B2.3:9, B2.4:11, B2.8:11, B2.9:15, B2.11:6, B3.1:7, B3.10:20, B3.12:22; ואנתי שביקה מן טלא לסמשא 'and you are released from the shadow to the sun' B3.6:8, sim. ib.10. Cf. אנת כלך כבן 'you are all thorns' C1.1:102; ... אנת שגיא פתסתו לי 'you are very praiseworthy to me' A6.16:4 (words of praise).

be) *Dem.pron. - NP*

This sequence is similar in function to the two examples with הו mentioned towards the end of a subsection above (§ *bc*). For example, הא זנה יקיר [קד]ם שמש 'Behold, this is precious in the presence of Shamash' C1.1:188. In all the remaining instances of this pattern the dem. pron. is cataphoric, and is often preceded by the presentative הא: e.g. אלה שהדיא 'these [= the following] are the witnesses' B1.1:15; הא אלה תחומי ביתא זך 'Behold, these are the boundaries of that house' B2.7:13; הא זנה תחומי ביתא זך 'Behold,

---

[1131] So also Kraeling 1969:240 and Grelot 1972:243, and *pace* Porten - Yardeni 1989:89 "I gave it to you—that is the southern room."

this is [= these are] the boundaries of that house' B3.5:8 ([1132]); הא
זנה שמהת נשיא זי ... ' behold this is [sic!] the names of the women
who ...' A4.4:4; זנה דושכרתא זי ... 'this is the crime which ...'
A4.5:3. So also B2.11:3,5; B3.4:7, B3.7:5, B3.11:3, B3.12:6-8*bis*;
C3.15:1. But the pronoun is also anaphoric in the Bisitun
inscription in statements summing up a military campaign as in
זנה זי בפרתו עבדת 'this is what I did in Parthia' C2.1:29; sim.
ib.35,50,62. The dem. pron. of this type is best regarded as
predicate.

No instance of the reverse sequence has been found.

bf) When a prepositional phrase is one of the constituents
of a bipartite NP, the sequence *S.NP - Pprep*([1133]) is the norm.
Examples are: with NPid—שלם לחרוץ תנה 'it is well with Ḥarudj
here' A2.3:3; כסף שנאה בראשה 'silver of hatred is on his head'
B3.8:22, sim. B3.3:8, ib.9; וכוין בה 'and there are windows in it'
B3.4:5, sim. B2.10:6([1134]); דש חד בה 'there is one door in it'
B3.10:13; with NPd—וארח מלכא ביניהם 'and there is King Road
between them' B2.10:6; ושוק מלכא ביניהם 'and King Street is
between them' B3.4:8,10; וספרא זנה בידכי 'while this document is
in your hand' B2.3:18,22; זי אל עמה 'he with whom El is' C1.1:91.

The reverse sequence, *Pprep - S.NP*, occurs solely in legal
documents in giving relative orientation of a property: e.g. לעליה
לה בית שתבר לתחתיה לה תמי זי חנום אלהא 'above it is the house of
Shatibara; below it is the way of Khnum the god' B3.4:7; למערב
שמש לה אגור יהו אלהא 'to the west of it there is the temple of YHW
the god' ib.9. A phrase lacking a preposition may be regarded as
syntactically equivalent: מערב שמש לה אגר תרי רבתא 'to the west
of it there is the wall of the large room' B3.10:11 (by the same
scribe, Haggai, as B3.4 cited above). Note the presence of the
two patterns next to each other in תחתיה לה אגורא ... ושוק מלכא
ביניהם, sim. ib.10. Likewise B2.3:6*bis*,7; B2.7:13*bis*,14,15;
B3.5:9f.,10, B3.7:5,6,7*bis*; B3.10:10,11

bg) *Subject elided*

The third person subject of a bipartite NC in the form of a
disjunctive pers. pron. may be elided when it has been mentioned
in the immediately preceding clause. For instance, קבל זי לא כתב
על ספר אנתתכי 'since (it) is not recorded in your marriage document'

[1132] On the disagreement in number (and gender) between the dem. pron.
and the following noun, see above at § 76 *cm*.

[1133] *S.NP* = noun phrase functioning as subject.

[1134] Cf. ומנעלא כוין פתיחן תמה 'and up above (there are) open widows there.'
"Open windows" here probably means apertures, slits in a wall.

B3.11:7; כען הא אתין תמה עליכם 'now, behold, (they) are coming there to you' A4.3:5.

In עליא לה בית קנחנתי דבק לה אגר באגר B3.11:5 it is as possible to see two short clauses loosely joined together—'above it is the house of the shrine of the god, (it) adjoins it wall by wall'—as to take בית קנחנתי as the grammatical subject of דבק and regard the whole as one long clause. Similarly B2.10:5*bis*,7; B3.5:9,11, B3.10:9, B3.11:6.

A different kind of one-member NC is represented by הן על הן[ן] זבנתון המו עבור ויבלתון 'if it please our lord' A4.5:7; cf. הן[ן] זבנתון המו עבור ויבלתון על בתין טב 'if you bought grain with them and brought (it) to our houses, (it is) good' A3.10:5. Also A6.3:5.

The impersonal 3mp also lacks, by definition, its subject: לא שבקן לן למבניה 'they do not allow us to build it' A4.7:23, but in אתין תמה עליכם 'they are coming there to you' A4.3:5, followed by חזו עליהם 'Look after them!' "they" refer to specific individuals.

Subject deletion is only apparent in the case of phrases introduced by זי: ברי זי לא ברי 'my son, who is not my son' C1.1:30; מובלא זי לא זיל[ה] 'the burden which is not his' ib.185; באר חדה זי בניה בגון בן ירתא ומין לא חסרה להשקיא חילא 'a well which is built inside the for[t]ress and does not lack water to give to the troops' A4.5:7.

bh) הא - *NP*

Another type of one-member NC is introduced by the presentative הא (Fr. *voici*): והא משחת ביתא זך זי ... 'and behold, the measurements of that house which ...' B3.5:5; והא תחומי ביתא ... זי 'and behold, the boundaries of the house which ...' B3.10:8; הא תחומוהי 'behold, its boundaries' B2.10:4; הא לחמא זי הוש]רת[ם] 'behold, the bread you dispatched' D7.44:7. Also B2.2:7; B2.7:7. Let us note that, almost without an exception([1135]), the NP in this pattern is determinate. This presentative particle can also introduce a well-formed clause as in הא אלה תחומי ביתא זך 'Behold, these are the boundaries of that house' B2.7:13; הא זנה שמהת נשיא ... 'Behold, this is [sic!] the names of the women ...' A4.4:4 // הא שמהת גבריא ... 'behold, the names of the men ...' ib.6. Finally, in a similar description of a plot of ground we encounter a caption-like תחומוהי "Its boundaries: ..." B2.3:5.([1136])

[1135] The text is broken at הא שנן שגיא זי ... 'behold many years that ...' A6.14:4.

[1136] This and משחתה 'its measurements' ib.4 should be interpreted in the same way, so that the preceding הוה in הוה משחתה is to be construed with what precedes.

bi) *Existential NC with* איתי

Whilst the existence of an entity in a certain location can be predicted with the pattern *NP - Pprep* as shown above (§ *bf*)([1137]), here our focus is on clauses containing איתי([1138]), a specific particle of existence.

In affirmative existential NC's, the NP is mostly indeterminate, and the sequence is NP - איתי: והן איתי כסף 'if there is money' A3.4:4; איתי לי אלף חדה בידכם 'I own a boat in your hand' A3.10:2; ... איתי עבדן זי 'there are slaves who ...' B8.7:5. See also A2.3:9; A2.4:3; A3.1:4; A3.10:3; A4.5:6; A6.7:2; B1.1:15; B2.6:19,32,33; B4.5:2; B4.6:3. In only three instances do we have a determinate NP, though in two of them it can be viewed as essentially indeterminate: איתי פמון שמ[ה] 'there is (one) nam[ed] Pamun' A6.11:1; אף איתי תבא שמה 'moreover, there is (one) named Taba' B2.11:12; ... נכסיא [י]איתי 'there are the goods ...' B2.9:5.([1139])

The sentence-end position of איתי in כקר[י]ה חסינה זי מ[י]ן בג[ו]ה]איתי 'like a strong city in the midst of which there is water' C1.1:95 is unique.

In negative existential NC's, the NP mostly occupies the first slot: אריה לא איתי בימא 'there is no lion in the sea' C1.1:165; ובר דכר ונקבה לא איתי לה; מחבל לא איתי 'there is no injury' A3.3:7; מן אסחור בעלה 'without her having any male or female child by Eshor her husband' B2.6:20, sim. ib.18, B3.8:29,35; עבידה לא 'I have no business' A6.15:9; דין לא איתי לי עמהם 'I have no suit with them' B8.9:2; והן מלח לאית בביתא 'and if there is no salt in the house' D7.2:3. Exceptions are: לא איתי לי בר וברה אחרן ... 'I have no other son or daughter ...' B2.3:10; [ה]ן לא איתי זרע קטין 'if there is no cucumber seed' D7.3:2; קנן לאיתי ל[י] 'I have no rods(?)' D7.4:8.([1140])

bj) No case has been confirmed of איתי used redundantly as a copula as in some later dialects([1141]).

[1137] We might include the following: שלם לן תנה 'we are well here' A4.2:2.

[1138] On variant spellings איתי and אתי, see § 22 *f*. Expressions of non-existence by means of לא איתי, לאיתי, and לאית will also be discussed here.

[1139] *Pace* Whitehead (1974:80, 210-16) there is no need to postulate extraposition in cases such as A6.11:1.

[1140] This opposition in word-order between positive and negative existential sentences is not arbitrary, for the entity the existence of which is about to be negated can be said to be "given," a theme, thus contextually determinate. Cf. Japanese *koko ni hon ga aru* 'there are books (*hon*) here' as against *kokoni wa hon wa nai* 'there are no books here' or 'books—there aren't there.'

[1141] Notably Syr.: see Muraoka 1987:66. Lindenberger's (1983:159f.)

bk) *The predicate of* הוה, *or subject in an existential clause*, irrespective of tense or mood, regularly precedes הוה: *pf.*—וידרנג זי פרתרך תנה הוה 'Vidranga, who was Chief here' A4.5:4, A4.7:5; לוידרנג פרתרכא זי תנה הוה 'to Vidranga the Chief, who was here' A4.8:5; ... נפין ברה זי רבחיל הוה 'Naphaina his son, who was troop commander ...' A4.7:7; יוזא במצרין הוה 'there was the unrest in Egypt' A6.11:2; זילי הוה 'which was mine' or 'it was mine' B2.3:3(¹¹⁴²); ע]ל עטתה ומלוהי הות אתור כלא 'on his counsel and words the whole of Assyria was (dependent)' C1.1:43; זי ביב בירתא בנה הוה 'which was built in Elephantine the fortress' A4.9:4, sim. A4.10:9; זי רב מחא לי הות 'the land became mine' C2.1:29; הוה 'who was commander' ib.59; זי קדמן עמי הוו 'who were previously with me' ib.74; *impf.*—זי אחרי תהוה 'who will be after me' C2.1:64; צב]ית עזקה יהוה לך 'he will become your seal-bear[er]' C1.1:19; זך ספרא זי ... כדב יהוה 'that document which ... will be a forgery' B2.3:16; ידניה זך ברי יהוה אפם 'he shall be my son' B3.9:5; 'that Jedaniah shall, moreover, be my son' ib.8; *impv.*—גבר הוי 'Be a man!' A3.3:7; חדה ושריר הוי 'Be joyous and strong!' A4.7:3; דכין הוו 'Be pure!' A4.1:5; לרחמן הוו קדם אלה שמיא 'Be in favour before the god of heaven!' A4.3:2. Compare this with the related, but distinct syntagm of the periphrastic הוה + active ptc. as in הוו שלחן 'Do send!' A6.1:3; on this syntagm, see § 55 g.

bl) *S.NP - P.NP*

חור עלים חנניה 'Ḥor is a servant of Hananiah' A4.3:8; אמה תבא 'his mother is Taba' B2.11:4; מפתח פמה מענה אלה[ן] 'the opening of his mouth is an utterance of god[s]' C1.1:162; זי תלתא רחימה 'the third is pleasing to Shamash' ib.187; מלך כרחמן 'a king is like (the) merciful' ib.91; חן גבר הימנותה ושנאתה כדבת שפותה 'A man's charm is his reliability, and his hateful aspect is his lips' deception' C1.1:132; איש מצלח עקן בחשוכא ולא חזה כאיש גנב 'a man

---

restoration איתי[.. בטנורא ..] כקר[י]ה חסינה זי מתןבניה 'like a mighty city which is built on a hill' C1.1:95 is to be rejected in favour of כקר[י]ה חסינה זי מי[ן] בג[ו]ה איתי 'like a strong city in the midst of which there are water' (Porten - Yardeni 1993:38). Lindenberger cites Dn 3.17 הֵן אִיתַי ... יָכִל to illustrate this allegedly copulaic use of איתי, but there it has a very specific asseverative function, which is ill-suited to the context at C1.1:95. The position of איתי at the very end of the clause, however, is striking, though it does not necessarily indicate a negative clause, if our psychological analysis as presented in the preceding footnote applied. On the asseverative איתי and Heb. שֶׁ, see Muraoka 1985:77-81.

¹¹⁴² In any case, הוה is hardly to be construed with the following משחתה 'its measurement(s),' which is in fact a sort of caption: "Its measurements: its length from below to above ..." The same applies to תחומהי 'its boundaries'

who chops wood in the dark without seeing is (just) as a thief ...'
ib.173.

bm) Where the predicate is an adjective *Padj - S.NP* is the
usual pattern: כי עזיז ארב פם מן ארב מלחם 'for ambush of mouth is
mightier than military ambush' C1.1:83; רכיך ממלל מלך שדק ועזיז
הו מן סכין פמי[ן] 'Soft is the speech of a king (yet) it is sharper and
mightier than a [double]-edged knife' ib.84; זעיר כצפה מן ברק 'his
anger is swifter than lightning' ib.85; שפיר מלך למחזה כשמש ויקר
הדרה 'Beautiful is a king to look at like the sun (or: Shamash)
and precious is his splendour' ib.92, but תרתין מלן שפירה 'two
matters are beautiful' ib.187; ובניך שליטן אחריך 'and your sons
have right after you(r death)' B3.12:23.([1143]) In איש שפיר מדדה
ולבבה טב ... 'a man (whose) stature is beautiful and good is his
heart ..' C1.1:95, the position of לבבה is possibly influenced by
the immediately preceding מדדה, resulting in a chiastic structure.

bn) The subject also precedes when its predicate is זיל + *a
conj.pron.* as in אגרא זילך אפם 'the wall is, moreover, yours'
B2.1:10; ארקא זך אפם זילך 'that land is, moreover, yours' B2.2:15;
ארקא זך זיליכי 'that land is yours' B2.3:19([1144]); ביתא אפם זילכי 'the
house is, moreover, yours' B3.5:16; ביתא זילך 'the house is yours'
B3.12:30.

bo) *Pptc - Spers.pron*
Examples are: ... ספינתא זי מהחסנן אנחנה 'the boat that we hold
in hereditary lease ...' A6.2:3; כען עליכי מתכל אנה 'now I am
relying on you' A2.7:2; בריך אנת 'blessed be you' A3.3:2; אף פרישן
אנחנה 'moreover, we are separated' A4.5:10; איך זי עביד אנת 'how
you are doing' C2.1:66; רחם אנה להי שגיא 'I love her very much'
D23.1 II:8, 13.

Any increment to go with the participle follows the subject
pronoun, so that the core [Pptc - Spers.pron] forms an indivisible
syntagm: ... לה מנס אנה לה 'I do not make him leave ...' A2.2:3;
בזך שלח אנה עליכם 'for that (reason) I am sending (word) to you'
A4.3:9; זי אמר אנה להם 'which I am telling them' A6.8:2, with
which cp. צבות ביתא זילי זי פסמשך יאמר לך 'the affair of my estate
which Psamshek will tell you about' ib.; הן צבה אנת ברי 'if you
desire, my son' C1.1:149; ... אדין [ביב בי]רתא אמר אנה ... ליהישמע
'then I say in Elephantine the fortress ... to Jehoishma ...' B3.7:1.
In the light of this rule, the restoration [אנה] חדה מנה.'[I] am

---

(line 5).

[1143] Parallel to אנת עני שליט בה ib.22.

[1144] Probably not "that land of yours": see above, § 59 *d*.

happy with it' A4.2:12(^{1145}) is somewhat problematic.(^{1146})

bp) There are only a handful of examples of the reverse sequence [*Spers.pron.* - *Pptc*]: זי אנת רשה לי עֲלַיה ... '... on which you are bringing (suit) against me' B7.3:5; עבד לקבל זי אנת עשת 'Do just as you think' C1.1:68; אנחנא שקקן לבשן 'we have been wearing sackcloths' A4.7:20, where the pronoun can be said to be a mark of self-assertiveness in a letter of bitter complaint.(^{1147}) אמרן in לקבל זי אנחנה אמרן A4.5:10 may be a pf., 'in accordance with that which we have said'; אנחן בען אלף 'we are seeking a boat' A2.6:9.(^{1148}) A similar ambiguity about the tense of the verb which might have existed in לכן אנחן יצפן 'it is rather about you that we are worried (or: we worried)' A2.1:8 is resolved by reference to לכן אנה יצף 'it is rather about you that I am worried (ptc. יָצֵף)' A2.4:12. In ואנתם כן לא עבדן 'but you are not doing so' A6.10:5 the fronting of the pronoun is due to a contrast. In the first two cases, B7.3:5 and C1.1:68 the position of the pronoun may be due to an element of confrontation between the two parties concerned. Lastly ואנה מהלך בין כרמיא 'whilst I was wandering between the vineyards' C1.1:40 is a rare circumstantial clause.(^{1149})

bq) Examples of a NP subject having a participial predicate are rather less frequent than NC's with a ptc. and other classes of S (§ *bo, bp*): כען עבדך ידניה וכנותה כן אמרן 'now your servant, Jedaniah, and his colleagues say thus' A4.7:4; אדין מומאה מטאה עליכי 'then the oath reaches you' B2.8:4(^{1150}); ...מועה שמש לה אוצר אמרן מלכא דבק אגר באגר להנפנא 'to the east of it the royal treasury adjoins wall to wall the protecting wall' B3.11:3, sim. ib.5,6(^{1151});

---

^{1145} So Porten - Yardeni 1986:56.

^{1146} On the unlikelihood of "one portion," see § 67 *b*.

^{1147} Degen's (1979:41) "... es [= אנחנה] korrespondiert wieder mit dem folgenden נשיא זילן" does not seem to us to be a good enough reason for the fronting of the pronoun.

^{1148} We know that a disjunctive pronoun, when used with a finite verb, precedes the latter: see § 39 *e*. On the interpretation of the example in A2.6:9, cf. Grelot 1972:166, *m*.

^{1149} Circumstantial clauses are rare in Aramaic. In Classical Hebrew circumstantial clauses the subject idiomatically occupies the first slot.

^{1150} מטאת, a pf., is expected.

^{1151} For another possible interpretation, see above at § *bf*. The participle would then be comparable with a subject complement of a verbal clause (§ 74 *s*).

^{1151a} For a recent general discussion on this subject, see Muraoka

הן נפקה טבה מן פם ... 'if something good issues out of the mouth of ... ' C1.1:171 // פמהם] [מ]ן הן לחיה תנפק מ[ן 'if something bad issues out of their mouth' ib.172; לבבי לה דבק לה 'my heart is not attached to it' A2.1:5; נשיא זילן כארמלה עבידין 'our wives are being treated like a widow' A4.7:20; ארמפי עם חילא זי לידה לא משתמען לי 'Arampiya with the troop which is at his command do not obey me' A6.8:1; בגסרו ידע טעמא זנה 'Bagasrava knows this order' ib.4; ותפמת ואחתסן מסבלן לה 'and Tapamet and Aḥatsin are supporting him' A2.3:5; כען עבדך ידניה וכנותה כן אמרן 'Now your servant Jedaniah and his colleagues say thus' A4.7:4.

br) A nominal clause of the sequence *S-P* is the norm for a circumstantial clause subordinate to the main clause and following it and connected to it by the conjunction Waw: נמרא פגע לענוא והי עריה 'a leopard met (or: meets) a goat when she was (or: is) naked' C1.1:166; ולא יתלקח בדין וספרא זנה בידכי 'it shall not be accepted in court as long as this document is in your hand' B2.3:17, sim. B3.1:12,13,19; וה]ן] ימות עניניה ובר זכר ונקבה לאיתי לה ... 'and should Ananiah die without having a male or female child ..' B3.8:28, sim. ib.34, B2.6:17,20. Though the text is broken, we have most likely a circumstantial clause in ואנה מהלך בין כרמיא 'and I was walking among the vineyards' C1.1:40. Possibly also the notorious crux in תרען ... נדשו ודשיהם קימן 'gates .. they smashed with their doors (still) standing' A4.7:9.

c) *Tripartite nominal clause*([1151a])

A NP introducing a NC may be given prominence by means of an immediately following disjunctive pronoun of the third person, which matches the former in gender and number. The result is often an identificatory([1152]) NC comparable to a cleft sen- tence as in "It is my father that told me that." Thus the pattern is [*NP₁—Disj.pron.—NP₂*]. Much use is made of this

---

[forthcoming].

Naudé (1994), in his discussion of this structure in BA, rejects the notion of the pronoun being a pure copula or a resumptive pronoun involving extraposition, or "left dislocation" in his terminology, and argues that its function is that of a clitic used where the predicate is determinate when otherwise ungrammatical clauses would ensue. This is contradicted by examples in our corpus (see below at § *ca*), and we do not believe that BA is unique in this regard.

[1152] On the definition of "identificatory" different from the general usage, see Muraoka 1985:7f. and Joüon - Muraoka 1993: § 154 *ea*, n.3. To regard this kind of pronoun as copula (Bauer - Leander 1927: § 72 *d*; Fitzmyer 1956:31) is rather unsatisfactory: cf. Muraoka 1987: 61, n.122 and Joüon - Muraoka 1993: § 154 *i, j*.

structure in legal documents as in זנה ספרא זי אנה עני כתבת לכי הו
יצב 'it is this document which I, Anani, wrote for you, that is
valid' B3.11:16;   ... יהוישמע הי [א]חדתה בביתה 'it is Jehoishmah
that hol[ds] on to him in (regard to) his house ...' B3.8:29. Likewise
B2.4:6,12; B3.3:11,12; B3.5:17,18; B3.10:22. See also הו מזדין
פקיד למדינא 'it is a Mazdean who has been set over the province'
A4.2:6; .. אנה הו אחיקר זי 'I am Ahiqar who ...' C1.1:46([1153]); לא
[= מה הי] מהי 'Is not Harudj *my brother?*' A2.3:8([1154]); אחי הו חרוץ
לי דה זי ספר לה הושרתן 'what is this that you have not sent a letter
to me?' A2.5:7; מן הו זי יקום קדמוהי 'who is the one who would
stand before him?' C1.1:91([1155]); ... בניך מן מבטחיה המו שליטן בה 'it
is your children from Mibtahiah that have right to it ..' B2.4:12;
בני זי ילדתי לי המו שליטן בה 'it is my children that you will have
born to me that will have right to it' B3.5:17.

Comparison between מפטחיה הי שליטה בביתה זי אסחור 'it is
Miptahiah that has right to the house of Eshor' B2.6:18 and
אסחור הו ירתנה ... 'it is Eshor that will inherit her ...' ib.21 shows
that the same הו is playing an identifying role, now in a NC and
now in a VC.

In חנום הו עלין 'Khnum is against us' A4.3:7 one may compare
הו to an accusing finger.

ca) Another type of tripartite NC has an enclitic pronoun in
the third slot. Here the NP₁ has been extraposed, or to use the
classical terminology, is a casus pendens, and to use Jespersen's
scheme, the pattern can be expressed as S—P—s.([1156]) We submit
that the pronoun is not playing an identificatory role as in the
cases discussed in the preceding subparagraph, for the NP₂ is
mostly([1157]) indeterminate. Thus, for instance, in תרעא זך לא זילך
הו 'that gate, it is not yours' B2.1:12, the meaning is not "it is
not-yours that that gate is." In fact, the pattern discussed above,
NP—disj.pron.—NP, can also be reinterpreted in terms of
extraposition: P—s—S. A few more examples of the pattern
S—P—s are: אגרא זך זילך הי 'this wall, it is yours' B2.1:4; ותרבצה
זי יהנפק כדב 'and its courtyard, it is (barren) land' B3.4:4; ארע הי
הו 'that which he produces, it is false' B3.11:16. See also B2.10:8;

[1153] Cf. Grelot (1973:449) "c'est moi ˀAhîqar, qui jadis te sauvas ...'; Ginsberg
(1955:428) "the same Ahiqar."

[1154] According to Milik 1967:549, לא is asseverative, 'indeed.'

[1155] On the use of enclitic זֶ with an interrogative, see Muraoka 1985:134-37.

[1156] Jespersen 1969:91-3.

[1157] The only exception is ופלג דרגא ותחת מנה בית פרסא הו 'and half of the
stairway and beneath it it is the *peras*(-sized) storage area (?)' B3.10:4.

B7.3:6(^{1158}); C1.1:91,174.

§ 78. Word-order: verbal clause

a) The question of word-order in verbal clauses is more complicated than that of nominal clauses, because a verbal clause often contains more essential constituents than two, which is the norm in nominal clauses, and also because a finite verb, even in the third person, contains within itself two of the essential constituents, namely subject and predicate. The following paragraphs will focus on select patterns around relative positions of a number of key constituents instead of discussing all possible or attested configurations.(^{1159})

b) The verb often occupies the initial slot: *V—*. This is true not only of verbs in the 3rd person with an explicit subject, but also in the 1st or 2nd person, or the 3rd person where no explicit subject is mentioned. Examples without an explicit subject are: זבנת חטבת ומשח 'I gave you my field ...' B1.1:2; ... נתנת לך חקלי 'I have bought striped cloth and scented oil' A2.4:10. בשם

ba) With an explicit subject: [*V-S-*]—אתה פסו בר מנכי למנפי 'Pasu son of Mannuki came to Memphis' A4.2:11; הן מית קוניה מחר או יום אחרן ... 'should Konaiah die tomorrow or another day ...' B2.1:8; אל יקל שמך קדמיהם 'Let your name not be light before them' C1.1:141 (jussive)(^{1160}); ויתכנשון אלהי מצרין 'and the gods of Egypt will gather' C1.2:25; [*V-S-O-*]—כתב פלטיה בר אחיו ספרא זנה קוניה כפם 'Pelatiah, son of Ahio, wrote this document at the instruction of Konaiah' B2.1:15, sim. B2.8:11, B2.9:16, B3.11:17; ישוה איש בני מראיהם [ ] בספן 'a man will place the sons of their lords .. on boats' C1.2:24.

bb) When a *pronominal object* of a verb is mediated by a preposition, it tends to come immediately after the verb, even before the subject, thus [*V-O$_2$-*](^{1161}): e.g. הן יהב לכי רעיה עמר 'if Reia (or: the shepherd) gave you wool' A2.2:16; זי יאמר לכם ארמנתידת למטען בה 'what Armantidata will tell you to load on it' A3.10:2; ... ביתא זי יהב לי משלם 'the house which Meshullam gave

---

^{1158} פלגה זילי הו 'its half [= of אתנא 'she-ass'], it is mine': *pace* Folmer (1995:538) there is no question of disagreement in gender.

^{1159} Cf. also Folmer 1995:521-87.

^{1160} A jussive verb does not always stand at the beginning: e.g. אלהיא ישאלו שלמך בכל עדן 'May the gods seek after your welfare at all time(s)' A4.4:1, sim. A3.7:1, A3.10:1, A4.1:1.

^{1161} Cf. Folmer 1995:586f.

me ...' B2.7:2; ... 1 הנעלת לי תמת בידה לבש 'Tamet brought in to
me in her hand: 1 garment ...' B3.3:4; נתנת לך חקלי 'I gave you
my field' B1.1:2; הושרי לי חקם 'Dispatch to me castor-oil' A2.2:13;
בית מבטחיה ... זי יהב לה מחסיה אבוה 'the house of Mibtahiah ...
which Mahseiah her father gave her' B2.10:7; הנעלת לי יהוישמע
אחתך לביתי תכונה ... 'Jehoishma your sister brought in to me to my
house: money ...' B3.8:5; הן יפקד לך מראך מין 'if your master
deposits with you water' C1.1:19 אנה יהבת לכי בחיי ובמותי בי 1 ארק
'I gave you, in my lifetime and at my death, a house, (with) land'
B2.3:3. The cohesion of this syntagm finds an expression in the
two words being run together as in, e.g. ספרא זך אנה יהבתהלכי
'this document, I gave it to you' B2.3:25.([1162]) In a deviation like
כן עב[דו] כזי לי תחדון 'Do thus in order that you will gladden me!'
A6.14:3 one may infer that "me" is meant to be emphasised.
Note that the same verb, in similar context, shows the same
word-order: כזי לאלהיא ולארשם תחדן[ה] 'so that you gladden the
gods and Arsham' A6.16:2.([1163])

This rule, sometimes referred to as "*Pronominalregel*"([1164])
or "*pronoun enclisis*," applies also when the predicate is a
participle: contrast עליא לה בית קנחנתי דבק לה אגר באגר 'above it
the house of the shrine of the god adjoins it wall to wall' B3.11:5
(with a pronoun) with אוצר מלכא דבק אגר באגר להנפנא זי בנו מצריא
'the royal treasury adjoins wall to wall the protecting wall which
the Egyptians built' ib.4 (with a noun).([1165]) However, where the
subject is a personal pronoun, the degree of enclisis or cohesion
is greater between a participle and its pronominal subject than
between a ptc. and a preposition with a conjunctive pronoun as
demonstrated in לה מנס אנה לה 'I am not making him leave'
A2.2:3; זי אמר אנה להם 'which I am telling them' A6.8:2; עבד אנה
לה 'I am doing for him' A2.3:4, A2.4:4; לה שבק אנה לה 'I am not
neglecting him' A2.4:4.

In view of the pronoun enclisis discussed above, clauses
which end with [verb + suffixed prep.] are best considered as

---

[1162] See above, § 10 *b*.

[1163] As noted by Whitehead 1974:98f. The restoration תחדן[ין] (Porten -
Yardeni1986:128) is unlikely, since we do not find a jussive in a real subordinate
clause: cp., for instance, והנדרוא עבדו לפקידאן זי[ל]י עד מנדתן בניא אלך יהי[ח]תה עלי
'issue instruction to [m]y official that he [br]ing to me ... the rent (?) of [those
domains]' A6.14:3.

[1164] Reckendorf 1895-8:119f., 261f., Nyberg 1938:326ff., and Muraoka
1985:44f.

[1165] For an alternative interpretation of the former, see above at § 77 *bq*.

ending with a verb: אלהיא שלם ישמו לך 'May the gods grant you peace!' A6.16:5 (= SOV); מספת פקידא זילי שלח עלי 'Masapata my official sent (word) to me' A6.15:1 (= SV).

bc) An imperative occupies the initial slot, excepting presentatives such as כעת and disjunctive personal pronouns: e.g. והבו פתף הושר לי משכן 'Dispatch to me skins' A2.4:7; הכצר כל כציר לגברן 'and give rations to Cilician persons' A6.9:4; חלכין ועבד כל עבידה 'Harvest every harvest and perform every work' C1.1:127, as against אנתם זולו מן בתין מן נכסן 'you, lavish from our houses goods' A4.3:8; כען הושרי לי זעיר מלח 'now dispatch to me a little salt' D7.2:1. Likewise A2.2:13; A2.4:9; A4.7:23; A6.9:2; D1.14:2; D7.1:11; D7.5:6, 8; D7.6:7, 10 and many others. Exceptions are([1166]): ארקא זך בני 'Build up this land' B2.4:5; אף חלקי באגר אלפא [....] הבו על ידה 'Also my share of the boat's rent hand to him!' A3.10:3; הן לא כספא הבו ליד אר[מנדי]דת 'if not, give the money to A.' ib.6; שלם יקיה הוי שלחת לה 'Do send her greetings from Yekia' A2.3:11([1167]); דין עבדי עמה 'Conduct the case with him' B2.3:27; זך חזי ... '... that see (= take note of)!' C2.1:68; זך פתפא הב לה 'Give that one the ration' A6.12:1; טרו ... גרדא 'Guard the domestic staff ...' A6.10:5; מן קדם אוסרי מין קחי 'From before Osiris take water' D20.5:3.([1168])

[1166] Driver 1957:79 seems to have been unaware of them.

[1167] An example which has apparently escaped Folmer 1995:551.

[1168] Folmer's (1995:551) formulation is inaccurate when she states that, in the Arsames documents, the single most significant corpus as regards the question in hand, the direct object precedes in most cases (9 vs. 5). In one case (A6.10:2) the verb concerned (בעה) is a perfect. In three other cases (A6.9:5, A6.10:5, A6.15:6) the noun phrase serving as the object has been mentioned earlier, so that one may speak of anaphoric attraction. Two other cases (A6.13:4, A6.14:3) involve a fixed idiom with the object being an Iranian loanword (הנדרז עבד 'to issue an instruction') where one should also note an instance of the same idiom in a non-volitive form (כזי הנדרז יעבדון 'so that they would issue an instruction' A6.13:3). Folmer seems inclined to leave two cases of a combination שם טעם of the same meaning out of account presumably because of its idiomatic nature. We are left then with a mere three unmotivated examples of the pattern <O - Impv.>, to which one may add הוו שלחן עלי ... מנתא 'the share ... do send me' A6.1:2. There are other cases where the word-order in question is not a purely morphosyntactic issue, but rather functionally motivated: see A3.10:3,6 (cited above); ספרא זך הנפקי 'Produce that document' B2.3:27; B2.4:5 (quoted above). One of the categories which Folmer herself (1995:545, 559-65) has identified as favouring the fronting of the object is precisely one in which the direct object is a noun phrase expanded by an attributive demonstrative pronoun.

bd) We may assign to the classical Semitic pattern cases in which the verb occupies the initial slot, without, however, being followed by an explicit subject: e.g. ישׂא בות מן כנתה 'he will bear shame from his colleague' C1.1:185; וזי ישׁתה חמרא 'and one who will drink wine' ib.188; גבר זי תזבנון לה ביתא זך 'a person to whom you will sell this house' B2.10:11; <ר>זי ינפק עליכי ספ<ר> 'whoever shall take out against you a docu[ment]' B2.7:12; יתב פרס 'residing in Persia' C2.1:36([1169]).

be) The pattern VOS is essentially the same for our purpose: e.g. כזי יהנעלן המו יהודיא 'when the Jews let them in' A3.8:12, which is virtually a case of the "Pronominalregel" at work. Similarly הן יפקד לך מראך מין למנטר 'if your master deposits with you water to watch' C1.1:191.

c) In our corpus we find a considerable number of cases where the verb, either pc. or sc. form, follows an explicit subject or object or both.([1170]) This verb-final position, which contradicts the classical Semitic word-order VSO, has generally been attributed to a foreign influence, viz. Akkadian on one hand, which in turn is said to be ultimately influenced by Sumerian, a non-Semitic language([1171]), and Persian on the other, also non-Semitic.([1172]) However, in view of a substantial number of cases in which the verb occupies a non-initial position, it is more accurate to speak of free word-order in our idiom.([1173]) Some explanation is then to be sought for this situation which does not agree with the classical Semitic pattern nor with the Akkadian pattern.

ca) *S-V* or *S-V-*

E.g. דגלן זי מצריא מרדו 'detachments of the Egyptians rebelled'

[1169] Akk. 71: *ina* KUR *par-su a-ši-ib.*

[1170] We are not concerned here with an adverb or presentative occupying the initial slot and then immediately followed by a verb nor with a disjunctive personal pronoun placed immediately before a finite verb, which is the rule (see § 39 *e*) nor with cases of extraposition (see § 79) or of emphatic fronting.

[1171] See Ginsberg 1936:98.

[1172] Kaufman 1974:133.

[1173] Apart from our attempts on the following pages to classify those deviations, it is only rarely that we can speak of a functional opposition as in an OV example in ולאנתתא זילך לא כתשׁת 'the wife of yours I did not strike' B7.2:9 rebutting the accusation וכתשׁת לאנתתי 'and you struck my wife' ib.5 (so also Folmer 1995:279f.): see also § 40 *h* for another perspective with respect to this example. There remain many cases where one can invoke the notion of prominence or emphasis only as a subjective or ad hoc interpretation.

מנדעם מחבל לא אשתכח לן ;A4.5:1 'no damage has been found against us' ib.2; אחר נפין דבר מצריא עם חילא אחרן 'then Naphaina took the Egyptians with the troops (as) others' A4.7:8; מן יומי מלך מצרין אבהין בנו אגורא זך ביב בירתא 'since the days of the king of Egypt our fathers built this temple in Elephantine the fortress' A4.7:13; [פס]משך ... עלימא זילי קבל בונה '[Psa]mshek ... my servant complained here' A6.3:1; אדין פרימא זך וכנותה לא שנציו למנעל בבירתא 'then that Pariyama and his colleagues did not succeed in getting into the fortress' A6.7:6; פסמשך פקידא זילי שלח עלי 'Psamshek my official sent (word) to me' A6.8:1; נסת פתגם יתעבד לך 'a harsh word will be directed at you' A6.10:9; פטוסרי ... שלח עלי 'Petosiri ... sent (word) to me' A6.11:1; זך אבד 'this one perished' ib.2; אגרת מן מראי תשתלח על נחתחור 'Let a letter be sent from my lord to Nakhthor' A6.13:2; see also A4.7:16*bis*,17,22.

This pattern is common in subordinate clauses: introduced by the relative pronoun זי—זי וידרנג לחיא זך נדש בשנת 14 'which that wicked Vidranga destroyed in the year 14' A4.9:6; ספר מרחק 1 זי דרגמן ... כתבלי ... 'a document of withdrawal, which Dargamana ... wrote for me' B2.3:23; זי פסמשך יאמר לך 'about which Psamshek will tell you' A6.8:2; עלימא זילי זי בגסרו היתי שושן 'my servant, whom Bagasrava brought to Susa' A6.12:1; ... דושכרתא זי כמריא 'the crime which the priests ... [commit]ted' A4.5:3; מה צבו [עבד]ו ומלה זי צחא יבעה מנכם 'whatever desire and thing Djeho shall seek of you' A4.3:6; introduced by the temporal כזי—כזי מראן ארשם אזל על מלכא 'when our lord Arsham went to the king' A4.5:2; כזי כנבוזי על למצרין ארשם נפק .... 'when Arsham left ...' A4.7:4; כזי מצרין מרדת 'when Cambuses entered Egypt' ib.13; 'when Egypt rebelled' A6.7:6; כזי מצריא מרדו 'when the Egyptians rebelled' A6.10:1, see also ib.2,7; כזי ארתחשסש מלכא יתב בכרסאה 'when King Artaxerxes sat on his throne' B2.2:1; כזי אגרתא זא [ח]מטא עליך 'when this letter reaches you' A3.8:6; כזי וידרנג רב חילא מטא לאבוט 'when Vidranga the troop commander arrived at Abydos' A4.3:3.

Glancing at the examples cited in the preceding paragraph, one cannot fail to notice a remarkably high frequency of this pattern in Arsames letters, i.e. A6.3-16, but it is hardly confined to them. Furthermore, the same pattern is also attested in the Proverbs of Ahiqar, the language of which is often cited as representing a Western dialect[1174]: אריה אזל קרב ... 'a lion went,

---

[1174] Greenfield 1968:368. Kutscher's position (1970:365) is nuanced —"somewhere in between"—but his opinion on the position of the object is wrong.

approached ...' C1.1:94; נפשי לא תדע ארחא 'my soul will not know the way' ib.122; כפן יהחלה מררותא 'hunger will sweeten bitterness' ib.123; למה אלהיא יסגה בעדרה 'lest the god come to his aid' ib.126; בר בטני הגשש ביתי 'my own son spied out my house' ib.139; חרב תדלח מין שפין בין רעין טבן 'a sword stirs up calm waters between good companions' ib.161; הן לחיה תנפק ... אלהן ילחון להם 'if bad goes out ... gods will make bad for them' ib.172 // הן נפקה טבה מן פם ... 'if good goes out from the mouth of ...' ib.171; אריא יהוה מסמה לאילא חמרא רכב 'a lion will lie in wait for a stag' ib.183; חד דרך קשתה לאתנא 'the ass mounted the jenny' ib.186; 'one drew his bow' ib.190. Note also גרמיך לא יחתון שאול 'your bones shall not descend to Sheol' C1.2:6; [אהור]מזד סעדני '[Ahura]mazda helped me' C2.1:10 (= Akk.),12; חילא זילי למר[ד]יא ק[טלו] 'my troops killed the rebels' C2.1:16 (= Akk.); ... חילא זי ל]י ק]טלו למרד[יא] '... my troops killed the rebels' ib.33 (≠ Akk. SOV).

cb) In contrast to the syntagm [*disj.pron.* + *ptc.*]([1175]) a disj. pron. as subject of a finite verb is not very cohesively joined to the latter so that a word or words can intervene between the two: e.g. אנחנה מנטרתן לא שבקן 'we did not abandon our post(s)' A4.5:1 where the pronoun emphasises contrast (§ 39 *e*, i); אנחנה עם נשין ובנין שקקן לבשן הוין 'we, together with our wives and our sons, were wearing sackcloth' A4.7:15 where the pronoun is a mark of self-assertiveness (§ 39 *e*, ii).

cc) *O-V*([1176])

Not a small number of examples of this pattern can be found in the Hermopolis papyri, the idiom of which is sometimes said to be a representative of a western branch of IA([1177]), so that one expects the word-order of its verbal clauses to be of the classical Semitic type, i.e. VSO. But we find([1178]), counting cases of direct object only, as many as 7 exceptions out of a total of 46 instances in which a direct object occurs.([1179]) These seven cases

[1175] See above § 77 *bp*.

[1176] For an attempt to establish grammatical or semantic categories which could trigger the inversion, see Folmer 1995:543-84, esp. 545.

[1177] E.g. Greenfield 1968:368; Kutscher 1970:368

[1178] Our findings significantly differ from the impression given by Kutscher (1970:369) based on his partial and approximative count.

[1179] The conclusion reached by Folmer (1995:578) in this regard appears to be in need of some nuancing: "... almost no evidence for OV word order in private letters on papyrus. The only possible instance is found in one of the Hermopolis letters [ומהי דה זי ספר לה הושרתן לי 'what is this that you haven't sent us a (single) letter?' A2.5:7]." On this example of categorical negation,

are those for which one cannot establish a functional opposition
to the VO sequence: וכעת תקם יתו לן 'And now, let them bring us
castor-oil' A2.1:7; מסה כספה ... נתחן ... לבנחסר (1180) 'an amount of
money ... I gave ... to Banitsar' A2.2:4; כל גשר זי ישכח יזבן 'every
beam he finds let him buy' ib.15; שלם יקיה הוי שלחת לה 'Do send
her greetings from Yekia' A2.3:11; שלם וחין שלחת לך 'I have sent
you welfare and life' A2.4:5; וכעת תקם יתו לי חפנן 5 'and now, let
them bring me castor oil, 5 handfuls' ib.11; ש]לם ו[חין שלחת לכי 'I
have sent you [welfare and] life' A2.7:1. Most of the above
examples are either in opening well-wishing formulae or jussives,
but note וכעת יהתו לן ארון 'and now let them bring us a chest'
A2.4:4.

Some more examples elsewhere are: ובאישת[א] לא עבד לך
'and he did not do evil to you' C1.1:50; ועטתי יבעה 'and he will
seek my counsel' ib.53; אף [ה]ן חזף זפתא שלין לנפשך אל תשים 'even
if you took out the loan, don't give rest to your soul' ib. 130; ודמה
יאשד ובשרה יאכל 'and he will shed his blood and eat his flesh'
ib.184; טעון גמלא יטעננהי 'the load of the camel one will load (on)
him' ib.186; ו]קן[ר]בא עבדן '[and they did the batt]le' C2.1:42 (≠
Akk. line 75 VO); שלם ושררת שגיא הושרת ל]ך 'I am sending you
abundant (greetings for) welfare and strength' A3.8:1, A6.3:1 et
passim; ... ונכסיא זי לקחו אתבו 'and the goods which they took
they returned ...' A4.4:8; כסף ונכסן יהבו לה 'they gave him silver
and goods' A4.5:4; בברא [ז]ך מיא שתין 'they drink water at th[at]
well' A4.5:8; חין אריכן ינתן לך 'May he grant you longevity!'
A4.7:3; אגורי אלהי מצרין כל מגרו 'they demolished all the temples
of Egyptian gods' ib.14 with many more examples in this document
(lines 1,6,7,9*bis*,10,12,14,18,19,20*bis*,21,25,29); נכסי לקחו 'they
took my goods' A6.3:5; ספר מרחק כתב 'he wrote a withdrawal
document' B2.3:25; ספר כתבתלה אחרוהי 'I wrote for her a document
about it' B2.4:4; ... כל זי הנעלת בידה תהנפק 'all that she brought in
... she shall take out' B2.6:27; למן זי רחמתי תנתננה 'to whomever
you love you may give it' B2.7:8; מנדעם באיש לא עבדת וכרצי איש
לא אמרת תמה ... מן קדם אוסרי מין קחי 'Anything evil she did not do
and the slander of any man she did not say there ... From before
Osiris take water' D20.5:2, but followed by הוי פלחה נמעתי 'Do
serve the Lord of the Two Truths.'

cd) *Categorical negation* appears to trigger the fronting of
the direct object: ספר לה שלחתי בשמה 'you have not sent a single

---

see § 83 *d, f*.

1180 נתחן for נתנת.

letter about him' A2.3:5([1181]); כעת מדעם אל תזבני בכסת 'now, don't
buy anything as clothing' ib.10; מדעם לה מפקן לן מן סון 'they are
bringing us nothing from Syene' A2.5:2; ספר לה הושרתן לי 'you
have not dispatched to me a letter' ib.7; איש מנדעם באגורא זך לא
חבל 'nobody caused any damage to that temple' A4.7:14; מנדעם
באיש לא עבדת 'she did not do anything evil' D20.5:2; מלה באישה
לא יהשכחון לכם 'they shall not find (even) one bad thing about
you' A4.3:6. Folmer (1995:566-68) has assembled an impressive
number of examples (some 15) in which מ(נ)דעם or a noun
(including מנדעם) qualified by באיש constitutes a direct object and
precedes the verb, and holds that the fronting of the object in
these cases is semantically conditioned. It is significant that,
with the exception of one([1182]), they are all negative utterances.
We believe, therefore, that it is not the semantic contents of
these nouns, but their use in categorical negation that triggers
their fronting as direct objects. The same applies to a negative
clause in which איש is not directly the object: כרצי איש לא אמרת
'she did not utter calumny against anybody' D20.5:2.

ce) A significant type of object fronting identified by Folmer
(1995:569-72) are cases of the generalising relative clause
introduced by זי (x) כל, מה זי or מן זי: e.g., כל גשר זי ישכח יזבן
'every beam that he finds he should buy' A2.2:15; ומה זי לקחת
נכסן[] מן גרדא התב הב להם 'and what you took (in the way of)
good(s) from the domestic staff, restore, give to them' A6.15:9.
Also A2.4:7, A6.15:8, A4.3:8, and possibly A3.10:3. This type

---

[1181] "A letter you have sent to him about him" is unlikely.

[1182] ומן ביש יעבד עם פתכר זנה 'and whoever causes damage to this relief'
Keseçek Köyü line 3 (from Asia Minor: KAI 258:3). Seen in this light, three
exceptions of hers, all in positive clauses, would turn out to be only apparent
exceptions: בעו באיש לאגורא זך 'they sought evil against this temple' A4.7:17
(sim. in a revised version, A4.8:16); תרבצה ביתה קנינה טין ומין ומנדעמתה יבדרונה
'may they scatter his court, his house, his property, ground and water and all
his possessions' Sardis line 7 (KAI 260B.7).

As a matter of fact, the fronting of מנדעם occurs also when it functions
other than as direct object: e.g., 'my household did not suffer anything of a
loss' A6.10:2, sim. ib.6, but מנדעם כסנתו יהוה ... ib.8, echoing the preceding
phrase.

For some reason or other, the equally indefinite pronoun אש/איש does
not seem to be subject to this rule: שמהתהם לא ידע איש 'nobody knows their
names' C1.1:164. See § 44*e, f*.

An attempt by Folmer (1995:568f.) to account for the occasional fronting
of מב in similar fashion as a synonym of באיש has little to commend it in view
of its poor attestation, a mere three examples.

of clause is akin to the conditional clause (§ 84 *p*): if there is anyone, anything that meets such and such a condition, then ..., and the protasis regularly comes before the apodosis.([1183]) This interpretation of ours is corroborated by another example mentioned by Folmer (1995:570): וכעת כל זי תצבה שלח לי 'and now, whatever you desire, send (word) to me' A2.4:7 where the introductory clause is not strictly the object of שלח.([1184])

Here, too, we find the fronted clause functioning also other than as direct object: זי תעבדון לה לא יתכסון מן עננ׳ 'what you do for him will not be hidden from Anani' A4.3:10; זי ירשנכי דין ודבב ... ינתן לכי אביגרן ... 'whoever shall bring against you suit or process ... shall give you a penalty ...' B3.10:19; למן זי רחמתי תנתן 'to whomever you love you may give (it)' B2.3:9, sim. B3.12:23, but הבי למן זי רחמתי 'Give (it) to whomever you love' B2.11:7. See also B2.1:10, B3.12:29.

cf) Another striking type of object fronting has been identified by Folmer (1995:572-74). It is said to be confined to dependent clauses in Elephantine legal documents wherein the coordinated second verbal clause with suffix conjugation verbs displays object fronting: e.g., כזי רשה עליה קדם דיניא ומומא טעינת לה וימאת לה כזי זילי הי וספר מרחק כתב 'when he brought suit about it and an oath was imposed for him and I swore for him that it was mine and he wrote a withdrawal document' B2.3:24; ביתי זי זבנת בכסף ודמוהי יהבת 'my house which I bought with money and the price of which I paid' B3.10:3. More examples may be found at B2.4:4; B2.7:3,8; B3.9:4. Folmer is aware that the clause type—dependent clause—and the tense—suffix conjugation—are not the necessary conditions for this type of object fronting, for neither condition is met in כזי עדן יהוה המו נפלג המו עלין ונגבר חלקה נהחסן וספר פלגנן נכתב ביננ 'when it will be time, we shall divide them for ourselves and we shall take hereditary possession, (each) person (of) his portion, and we shall write a document of our division between ourselves' B2.11:13. Significant features shared by all these examples are: (1) the genre (legal), (2) the identical subject of the conjoined verbs([1185]), and (3) the identical phraseology of the inverted clause

---

[1183] See examples in § 84.

[1184] Cf. Hug's (1993:38) non-literal rendition: "Wenn du etwas möchtest, sende mir (Nachricht)."

[1185] This feature is missing in two exceptions mentioned by Folmer (1995:574): ביתא זנה זי זבן ויהבן לך ויהבת לן דמוהי כסף 'this house which we sold and gave you and the prince of which you gave us (in) silver' B3.12:25 and זי זבן לן ויהבן לה דמוהי כסף ... '... that/which he sold to us and the price of

(either ספר כתב or דמיא יהב).

cg) According to Cook (1986:125), who studied the word-order in the Aramaic of Daniel, the VO sequence is typical of the suffix conjugation, marking or signalling temporal sequence or consecution. This seems to hold for the Ahiqar narrative composed in a comparable style with very few exceptions in the OV sequence with the sc.[1186] On the other hand, the number of the pc. forms preceded by a direct object is noteworthy: עבידתך הו יעבד 'he will do your work' C1.1:21; הו טבתא יבעה 'he will seek the good' ib.24; עטתי יבעה 'he will seek my counsel' ib.53; גברן אחרנן מלכא ישלח 'the king will send other men' ib.62; נכסן אנה אנתן לכם 'I shall give you goods' ib.66, but למה הו יחבל מתא עלין 'why should he damage the land against us?' ib.36.

ch) Because of the oft suggested Akkadian influence on IA in favour of the positioning of the object (or subject or both) before the verb we have compared the Aramaic version of the Bisitun inscription (C2.1) with its Akkadian counterpart.[1187] The results are shon on the following page.

We have made a case study of the first three tripartite VC patterns appearing above, in which the object follows in the Aramaic version, and which happen to represent clauses with virtually identical message—X killed Y. A comparison between the two versions allow us to make the following observations.

The Akkadian version displays two alternative sequences, SOV (4x) and SVO (2x). The Aramaic version also has two sequences, but different in configuration: SVO (5x) and VSO (1x). In three out of the six cases the Aramaic disagrees with the Akkadian (SVO vs. SOV), where the Aramaic sequence represents the less frequent of the Akkadian patterns, SVO. In the two cases where the Akkadian version shows this minority sequence, typically Akkadian sequence, SOV, correspond with the classic Semitic pattern, VSO, in the Aramaic version. This picture, coupled with the fact that, in the majority of VCs consisting of V and O alone, the two versions agree in showing the verb-last sequence, OV, and also the fact that in three cases the Aramaic version agrees with it. In only one instance does the version agrees with the typically Akkadian tripartite SOV pattern seems

---

which we paid (in) silver' ib.32. The text as restored by Porten - Yardeni 1989:170 at יה/כתן‍בת לה וספר אסרן כתבן B8.10:1 would be a third exception.

[1186] E.g., ובאישתא‍ן לא עבד לך 'he did not do the evil to you' C1.1:50.

[1187] The Aramaic text is often poorly preserved, but the frequent use of the fixed formulas and standing expressions and the extremely close relationship

to indicate that the syntax of the Aramaic of our inscription was very much akin to that of the Akkadian.([1195a])

All objects preceding the verb in the Bisitun inscription are personal, whereas most of such objects in Elephantine legal documents and the Hermopolis letters are inanimate, and the

Arm	lines		Akk	lines	frequency
SVO	13,33,57	≠	SOV	51,70,81	3x([1188])
SVO	43,46	=	SVO	75,76	2x([1189])
VSO	55	≠	SOV	81	1x([1190])
SOV	16,38,51	=	SOV	52,72,78	3x([1191])
OV	19,26,30,48,	=	OV	53,58,69([1192]),77,	
	53,61*bis*			79,83*bis*	7x([1193])
OV	52	≠	VO	79	1x([1194])
OV	39	=	OSV	73	1x([1195])

---

between the two versions renders it safe to draw upon the Akkadian version for the reconstruction of the Aramaic version.

[1188] E.g. חיל[א ז]ילי קטלו למרד[יא 'my troop killed the rebels' 13 = *ú-qu at-tu-u-a ana ni-[ki-ru-tú id-du-ku]* 51.

[1189] E.g. חיןלא]זיל[י ק]טלו]לחילה[ן זי ויזדת] 'my troop killed the troop of Vahyazdata' (43) = *ú-qu at-tu-a id-du-ku ú-qu ša* [m]*ú-mi-iz-da-a-tu₄* (75).

[1190] *at-tu-u-a a-na ú-qu ni-ik-ru-tu id-du-ku.*

[1191] E.g., בטלה זי אהו[רמזד] חילא זילי למרנ[ד]יא]ק[טלו 'with the protection of Ahu[ramazda] my troop [k]illed the rebel[s]' 16 = *ina GIŠ.MI šá* [d]*ú-ra-mi-iz-da ú-qu at-tu-u-a ana ni-ik-ru-tu id-du-ku.*

[1192] מרנו מלך עליהם עבדו 'a Margian they made king over them' = *LÚ mar-gu-ma-a-a šu-u a-na ra-bu-ú [ina] UGU-šú-nu it-tur* 'a Margian, he became a leader over them.'

[1193] E.g., ויזדת אחדו וחרא זי עמ[ה 'Vayazdata and the nobles who (were) with him they seized' (48) = [m]*ú-[mi]-iz-da-a-tu₄ ù LÚ.DUMU.DU.MEŠ šá it-ti-šú uṣ-ṣab-bi-tu ṣab-tu* 'Vayazdata and the nobles who were with him they took captive.'

[1194] E.g., ... איש חד בראש[הו]ם שלח 'a certain man [he sent] at their head' = [il]*-ta-par a-na 1-en LÚ šá ra-bu-ú [ina UGU]-šú-nu* 'he sent a certain man as their leader.'

[1195] ארתורזי שמה פרסי [עלימא זילי בראש[הו]ם שלחת 'Artavarziya by name, a Persian, [my servant at their hea]d, I sent' = *1-en LÚ* [m]*ar-[ta-mar]-zi-ia [šu-um]-šú LÚ qal-la-a LÚ par-sa-a-a ra-[bu]-ú [ina] UGU-[šú-nu a-na] KUR par-su áš-pur* 'a certain man, Artamarzia by name, my subject, a Persian, to Persia as their leader I sent.'

rest of our corpus presents a mixed picture in this regard.([1196]) Examples are: Bisitun—למרן[ד]יא וק[ט]לו 'they killed the rebels' C2.1:16; Elephantine—ספרא כתבת לכי עלא 'I wrote the document for you concerning this' B2.7:9; Hermopolis—שלם וחין שלחת לך 'I have sent you (blessings of) welfare and life' A2.4:5. However, that such a distribution pattern is a linguistically meaningful one is not certain.

ci) In addition to examples of the pattern O-V there are even a few cases of the pattern <u>OSV</u>: שלם אחי אלהיא כ[ל]א ישאלו בכל עדן 'may all the gods seek the welfare of my brothers at all times' A3.10:1, sim. A4.7:1([1197]); בזנה זי עביד לן כלא ארשם לא ידע 'Arsham did not know about all this which was done to us at all' A4.7:30; חמרא ... ועבור ארקתא כלא נחתחור לקח 'Nakhthor has taken the wine ... and the grain of the lands entirely' A6.15:5([1198]); עבידתך הו יעבד 'your work he shall perform' C1.1:21([1199]); גברן אחרנן מלכא ישלח [א]חרין 'the king will send other men after us' ib.62; נכסן אנה אנתן לכם 'I shall give you goods' ib.66.

cj) *SOV or S ...V*

This is a fairly frequent pattern, a pattern typical of Akkadian.([1200]) Examples are: אנחנה מנטרתן לא שבקן 'we did not

---

[1197a] If Borger (1982:130) be right in his assumption—an assumption which he has not demonstrated, but is rather plausible—that the Aramaic version or the Aramaic version together with the Elamite were first drawn up, and the Babylonian as well as the Old Persian version were based on it or them, then one can speak only of general influence of Akkadian on Aramaic.

[1196] Some examples of the preceding animate or personal object are: לאלהיא ולארשם תחד[ה] 'you ought to glad[den] the gods and Arsham' A6.16:2; נרדא ונכסי מראיהם חסין נטרן 'they are closely guarding the domestic staff and the goods of their masters' A6.10:4; ... גברן אחרנן מלכא ישלח [א]חרין 'the king will send other men after us ...' C1.1:62.

[1197] This pattern is not directly to be related to a similar Babylonian well-wishing formula, for our corpus attests to alternative patterns: SVO—אלהיא ישאלו שלמך בכל עדן 'may the gods seek after your welfare at all times' A4.4:1, sim. A3.7:1; SOV—אלהיא שלם ישמו לך 'may the gods grant you peace' A6.16:5. See Folmer 1995:524, n. 957; 534; 550. The Akkadian greeting formula is mostly of the SOV pattern: see some examples in Salonen 1967:86.

[1198] Folmer (1995:534) stands in need of correction when she says: "neither the Arsham correspondence nor the Behistun inscription have instances of OSV." Further, a student of ours, Opree (1997:34), draws our attention to זנה אנה עבדת 'this I did' C2.1:3 (Bistitun), though the subject is a personal pronoun.

[1199] There is a contrast between "you" and "him."

[1200] Among the groups of documents studied by Folmer (1995:533) this pattern is particularly favoured in the Arsames correspondence (A6.1-16), a

abandon our post' A4.5:1, also with disj.pron. as S at A4.7:15, 20*bis*; ומראן אודיס יעב[ד] 'and should our master make a statement' A4.10:12; אנה רכביך לא אחזה 'I shall not see your riding' C1.1:204; סמשך פקידא קדמיא גרדא ונכסיא זילנא ... חסין נטר 'Samshek, the former official, strictly guarded our domestic staff and goods' A6.10:1. See also A4.5:8; A4.7:6,14, 15; A6.5:11; A6.8:2,3; A6.16:5.

ck) Clauses with more than two constituents and ending with a verb are not uncommon: e.g. ולעבק אופשרה יתעבד 'and immediately let needs (?) be done!' A6.2:6; כען עבדך ידניה וכנותה כן אמרן 'Now, your servant Jedaniah and his colleagues say as follows' A4.7:4; אנתם [וא]תנצחו גרדא ונכסין[א זיל]י חסין טרו 'You, be diligent in strictly guarding my domestic staff and goods!' A6.10:5; [קריתֿ] רשיען ביום רוח תחחלל '[a town of] wicked (men) will split asunder on a day of wind' C1.1:104.

cl) *O-Infinitive*

The object of an infinitive also precedes the latter at times([1201]). E.g. ... ביתא זנך לא שליט אנת לזבנה ולמנתן 'you have no right to sell or give away that house ... ' B2.4:6; דינן למרשה עליך 'to bring suits against you' B2.11:8; פגרה זי אחיקר זנה למחזה 'to see the corpse of this Ahiqar' C1.1:63; אופשרה למעבד 'to do its needs(?)' A6.2:9. In the first instance quoted the fronted object is meant to be contrasted with ארקא זך 'that plot of land' B2.4:5.([1202]) There are cases of the reverse sequence also: מין לא חסרה להשקיא חילא 'it does not lack water to give to the troop' A4.5:7; שלחת לה למפרש לי מלתא אף 'I sent to him (asking) to explain the matter to me and I also sent to him (asking) to show the order to Hosea' שלחת לה למחוה טעמא להושע D7.24:15; שליט למפתח תרעא זך 'have right to open that gate' B2.1:14.

cm) *Double objects*

Some verbs take two objects, one direct and the other indirect. Only once do both objects precede the verb: שלין לנפשך אל תשם 'Do not give rest to your soul' C1.1:130. The general rule is that an indirect object immediately follows the verb: e.g. נכסי[ן] אלה ברחמן יהבת ליהוישמע 'these goods I lovingly gave to Jehoishma'

---

petition addressed to the Persian authorities (A4.7, A4.8), two letters belonging to the Jedaniah archive (A4.2, A4.5), the Bisitun inscription and the Samaria ostraca.

[1201] Kaufman (1982:154) would attribute this to a Persian rather than Akkadian influence. See also Folmer 1995:536-42. Cf. also Carmignac 1966:507f.

[1202] *Pace* Folmer (1995:537) the contrast is not between living in the house and disposing of it.

B3.8:41.([1203]) Both objects may follow the verb as in גבר זי תזבנון
לה ביתא זך 'a person to whom you will sell that house' B2.10:11;
אנה יהבת לכי בחיי ובמותי בי 1 ארק 'I gave you during my life time
and upon my death a house (with) land' B2.3:3; אבוך לא יהב לי
חמר 'your father did not give me a he-ass' B7.3:7; הן יפקד לך
זי ינפק מין מראך 'if your master deposits with you water' C1.1:191;
עליכי ספ<ר> 'one who takes out a document against you' B2.7:12;
so also B2.7:10; B2.9:14; B3.4:20.

But quite often the verb stands between the two objects, the
indirect one following as stated above: e.g. אנה בגה ... יהבת לפטסורי
'I gave the estate ... to Petosiri' A6.11:5. This is particularly true
when the indirect object is a personal pronoun([1204]): ספר כתב לי
עלא 'he wrote for me a document thereabout' B2.7:3, sim. ib.9,
B3.9:4; זי מ[נד[ת]א] מנדעם לא מהיתה לי 'who is not bringing me
the (agreed) re[nt] .. at all' A6.14:2; נכסיא אלה וכספה ... יהבת לכם
'these goods and the silver ... I gave you' B6.4:7; שלם וחין שלחת
לך 'I send you (best wishes) for welfare and life' A2.4:5, sim.
A2.7:1, A2.3:11, A3.8:1; חין אריכן ינתן לך 'May he grant you
longevity' A4.7:3; ובאישת[א] לא עבד לך 'and the evil he did not do
to you' C1.1:50.

cn) Examples of *double pronominal objects* are: לא אנחן
יהבנה לכי 'we did not give it to you' B5.1:5; יהבתה לך 'I gave it to
you' B2.7:16; יהבתהי לי 'you gave it to me' B5.5:7; אנתננהי לך 'I
shall give it to you' B1.1:11; ינתנהי לכם 'he will give it to you'
D7.29:9; יתונה לכן 'Let them bring it to you' A2.6:10. The
conjunctive pronoun is always a direct object.

The unusual dislocation of a direct object at the far end of a
long verbal clause with an intervening adverbial adjunct is due
to its length: ... שלחת לך ביד אחוהא זי תם אנתת מלכיה בר עזגד ענז חד
'I sent to you by the hand of the brother of Tam wife of Malchiah
son of Azgad one goat ..' D7.57:4.

co) *Adverbials*
We shall discuss here not only adverbial adjuncts found in
VC's, but also similar words and phrases forming part of NC's.

[1203] The only exceptions are בזי מצריא שחד להן יהבן 'because the Egyptians
give them a bribe' A4.2:4; זבנת משח זית ליקה 'I have bought olive oil for Yake'
A2.2:11; נפלנ המו עלין 'Let us divide them for ourselves' B2.11:13 (// פלגן עלין
עבדיה זי מבטחיה 'we divided Mibtahiah's slaves for ourselves' ib.3). See, however,
§ 74 *e* on cases where one or both of the objects is or are pronominal.

[1204] See above (§ *bb*) on pronoun enclisis.

cp) *Clause-initial adverbials*

Certain adverbials mostly occupy the first slot of a clause.([1205]) As such their position can have no functional significance. The most common are כען, כעת([1206]), and כענת([1207]), usually rendered 'now.' Their primary function is to mark the beginning of a new thought or turning point in a discourse. In some fairly long documents, e.g. A6.10,11,13,15 these words mark the beginning of a paragraph. It is a notable feature of the officialese of IA, though not confined there by any means. Following the standard introductory formula giving the names of the addressee and writer and the greeting, the body of a missive is introduced by one of these words([1208]): e.g. A6.7:1, A6.8:1, A6.10:1+. Some brief letters, particularly in the ostraca, completely do away with the introduction, and open with כען or כעת: e.g., D7.17:1, D7.24:1, D7.25:1. Some writers indulge in the use of these short words, lacing their private letters with them, almost each sentence beginning with them in the manner of "and then" in children's diaries or letters, as can be seen in some of the Hermopolis letters (A2.1, 2.2, 2.3, always וכעת) and in the Padua Letter 1 (כעת 7x in a fourteen-line letter).

The clause-initial position of these adverbials is due to their role of marking a logical connection with what precedes, a kind of anaphora.([1209]) Similar interpretation applies to the following cases: ... קרבתא בוע כתונה הילל 'immediately (thereafter) he tore his garment, lamented...' C1.1:41, sim. ib.45,48,56,59; "I brought you to my house. There I was supporting you (תמה הוית מסבל לך)"C1.1:48.([1210]) Here also belong אחר 'thereafter, then,' ubiquitous in the Bisitun inscription (C2.1), but also elsewhere (e.g. B2.7:5) as well as אדין 'then' (e.g. A6.10:1, B2.4:8[[1211]],

---

[1205] Hence כען in עד כען 'until now' A4.3:7, D7.19:5 and in זי כען פקיד עבד 'who has now been made an official' A6.4:2 has a different function.

[1206] This occurs with the conjunction Waw far more often than not (60:24). The conjunction is never prefixed to כענת, but thrice only to כען (3:63).

[1207] This last does not occur in the Arsames letters.

[1208] On these epistolographic matters, see Fitzmyer 1979:193 and Alexander 1978:164, where the latter speaks of 'transition marker' and 'spacer.'

[1209] Cf. Joüon - Muraoka 1993: § 155 *p*.

[1210] This קרבתא reminds one of εὐθύς in Mark's Gospel: Mk 1.21,23,29. See Fassberg (1991:95-96) where he shows that the Mishnaic Hebrew מִיָּד 'immediately' is generally clause-initial in aggadic passages, but clause-final in halachic passages.

[1211] הן מחר או יום אחרן ארקא זך תבנה אחר ברתי תשנאנך ... 'if tomorrow or

B2.8:4); לקבלה דין עבדי עמה 'Contest the case with him accordingly' B2.3:27. Its unusual, non-initial position makes אחר unstereotypical in פסמשך] אחר קבלת מנך ישלח 'if Psamshek later sends a complaint about you' A6.8:3.([1212])

Legal documents often begin with the indication of a date on which an agreement was reached and the contract was drawn up, as is exemplified in many an Elephantine document: e.g. B2.1-4, 6-11, 3.1-13, 4.3-6, 5.1,5, 6.1, 7.1-2; see also B1.1.([1213]) In some legal documents, relatively late ones in particular, there appears אדין between a date and the verb אמר or the indication of a place followed by אמר. This temporal adverb is most likely resumptive after a fairly long dating phrase. E.g. ב 20 לאדר הו יום 8 לכיחך שנת 3 ארתחשסש מלכא אדין אמר ענני ... ליהוישמע ... 'On the 20th of Adar, that is the 8th day of Choiak, year 3 of King Artaxerxes, then Anani ... said to Jehoishma ...' B3.11:1; see also B3.10:1, B3.12:1, B4.6:1; ב 3 לכסלו ... דריוהוש מלכא אדין ביב בירתא אמר ... ידניה 'On the 3rd of Kislev ... the king Artaxerxes, then said in Elephantine the fortress Jedaniah ...' B2.10:1; see also B2.9:1, B3.7:1, B3.9:1, B3.13:1, B5.5:1.([1214])

cq) *Sentence adverbials*

As regards some of the clause-initial adverbials dealt with above, it is sometimes not easy to decide whether they are to be construed with a particular clause constituent or they relate to the clause or sentence as a whole. The former would be the case with the highly frequent clause-initial or paragraph-initial כען and its synonyms. This is certainly true of אף, 'furthermore, moreover,' not 'also, too,' which latter relate only to a single constituent of a clause. This אף, which is also by definition anaphoric in a sense, always stands at the very beginning of a sentence: e.g. אף בזנה זי עביד לן כלא ארשם לא ידע 'Moreover, of this which was done to us Arsham was totally ignorant' A4.7:30, and not ' ... did not know, either'; אף שניא סנחאריב מלכא רחמני

---

another day you build up that plot (and) then my daughter hate you ...'

[1212] Whitehead 1974:51.

[1213] E.g. אמורטיס מלכא 5 לפמנחתף שנת 23 ב 'On the 23rd of Phamenoth, year 5 of King Amyrtaeus' B4.6:1.

[1214] [Date - אמר - אדין - name] is typical of Haggai s. of Shemaiah (B3.10,11,12) and [Date - אדין - place - אמר - name] of Mauziah s. of Nathan (B2.9,10, 3.8). On the basis of this style, Porten - Yardeni's (1989:115,189) attribution of B4.6 to Haggai may be justified. Also the scribe of B3.6, who calls himself "Haggai" without a patronymic, may be identified with this same Haggai s. of Shemaiah.

'moreover, King Sennacherib loved me very much' C1.1:51. Hence, in a rare exception such as... כען אף קדמן שלחת the אף must be construed with קדמן: 'Now, previously also (as I am doing now) I sent ...' A6.10:5.

cr) Not every *fronted adverbial* can be explained in terms of functional opposition.([1215]) Fronting may be interpreted as an indication of insistence or some importance attached to what is denoted by such an adverbial: e.g. חת לעבק ולעבק הנחת לי כתון 'Come down immediately, and immediately bring me a tunic down' A3.8:13([1216]); לשלמכן שלחת ספרה זנה '(to inquire after) your welfare I am sending this letter' A2.1:12, A2.2:17, A2.4:13, sim. A2.3:12, A2.7:4 to impress the writer's personal concern; עליך לבבי שדיק 'my heart is torn over you' A3.6:3.

The word כן, whether anaphoric or cataphoric, very often and immediately precedes the verb: e.g., cataphoric—כן אמיר לן 'it has been said to us as follows' A3.3:4; כ]עת ארשם כן אמר 'Now, Arsham says as follows' A6.6:4; כן ידיע יהוי לך 'Let it be known to you as follows' A6.10:8; כן שמיע לן 'we have heard as follows' A3.3:13; כן מנו 'Count as follows' A4.1:3; anaphoric—אנתם כן לא 'you are not doing so' A6.10:5; לקבל זי אנה עבדת לך כן אפו עבדן עבד לי 'just as I did for you, thus do me then' C1.1:52. Also cataphoric is כן כזי meaning 'in such a way as ...': e.g. "Strictly guard my domestic staff and goods so that there will not be any decrease in my estate" A6.10:6; "... make them over to my estate just as the former officials had been doing"ib.7; also A4.3:6, A6.10:2, A6.15:11, C1.2:3. In all these cases of כן כזי, however, the verb precedes, apparently because the cohesion between the two words is rather strong. See also כזי כזנה עביד 'when it was done like this' A4.7:15.

Adverbials which often occupy the initial slot include: *temporal expressions*—זי קדמן שזבך מן קטל זכי 'who rescued you previously from an innocent death' C1.1:46; ליומן אחרנן שגיאן קרבתך ... 'after many more days I presented you ...' ib.49, sim. A6.12:2; ... מחר או יום א[חר]ן ימות אסחור 'tomorrow or (the) following day, should Eshor die ...' B2.6:17, sim. ib.20,22, B2.3:26, B2.4:8,

---

[1215] At כזי יואַ הוה במצרין 'when there was an unrest in Egypt' A6.11:4 it is not clear whether the writer, Arsames, is just not quoting accurately ([כזין יואַ] במצרין הוה ib.1) or he intended some nuance, which escapes us.

[1216] Rather than seeing here a repetition of the adverbial (so Porten - Yardeni 1986:44 with their תכף ומיד). At יהיתו עלי אפריע לעבק ולעבק 'Let them bring (them) to me at once, immediately and imme[diate]ly' A6.12:3 the pair is undoubtedly a case of emphatic repetition reinforced by a synonym (אפריע), for there is only one verb.

B3.8:21; ‏1 לפאוני בקרו לימא ספינה ב 26‎ 'on the 26th of Payni they inspected for the sea 1 ship' C3.7Kv3.21+; *quantifiers*—‏שגיא ירגש‎ 'will be very agitated' C1.1:29; ‏שגיא סנחאריב מלכא רחמני‎ 'King Sennacherib loved me very much' ib.51; ‏שגיא עמ[י] אתנצחו‎ 'they were very diligent with me' C2.1:75; ‏שגיא חדית‎ 'I rejoiced greatly' A3.5:2.

cs) An adverbial clause can either precede or follow the main clause: ‏כדי תכלן תעבדן לה עבד אנה לה‎ 'as much as you could do for him I am doing for him' A2.3:4, but ‏כדי 1 לה אנה שבק לה‎ ‏מצאה ידי‎ 'I am not leaving him alone as much as I am capable' A2.4:4. Temporal clauses introduced by ‏אמת‎, and especially ‏עד‎ (‏זי‎) are as a rule placed after the main clause, whereas conditional clauses generally precede their apodoses: ‏הן גרס לחמהם לשו להם‎ ‏קב 1 עד תאתה אמהם שלח לי אמת תעבדן פסחא‎ 'if their bread is ground, knead for them 1 qab before their mother comes. Send (word) to me when you observe the passover' D7.6:6. In ‏ביום זי‎ ‏תרחענה תגזנה‎ 'on the day that you wash it, you should shear it' D7.8:6 the temporal clause is fronted, as the timing of shearing is new information, for the need to shear the ewe had already been indicated. A ‏כזי‎-temporal clause mostly precedes the main clause: ‏כזי עדן יהוה נפלג המו עלין‎ 'when it is time, we shall divide them to ourselves' B2.11:13, ‏כזי חזית ... ענית‎ 'when I saw ... I answered' C1.1:14, but ‏כתבת אגרתא זא כזי כן שמיע לן ...‎ 'I wrote this letter when we had heard ...' A3.3:13. See also A4.5:2, A4.7:15, A6.15:7.

ct) An adverbial phrase may be interrupted by a relative clause: ‏אנת ידניה שליט בפטוסירי שמה עבדא זך זי מטאך בחלק מן יומא זנה‎ ‏ועד עלם‎ 'you, Jedaniah, have right to Petosiri by name, that slave, who came to you as a portion, from this day and for ever' B2.11:6.

cu) An adverbial may appear at the end of a clause as in ‏אזלי קומי עמה בסון יומא זנה‎ 'Go, stand with him in Syene this day' D7.1:5.

§ 79. Extraposition

Under this term we understand a construction in which an element of a clause is fronted and is subsequently referred back by means of a pronoun.([1217]) The phenomenon is also known as casus pendens

---

[1217] We thus exclude clauses in which an NP or a disjunctive pronoun precedes its finite verb predicate, but without it being explicitly repeated in the form of a pronoun.

For an approach based on the notions of functional grammar and discourse

or nominativus pendens, terms ill-suited to a grammar of Aramaic, which has no case markings. The fronted constituent usually receives a measure of prominence. It can be **a**) the subject of a clause with a subject NP preceding a finite verb or **b**) the object of a verbal clause, or **c**) the complement of a preposition.

a) ... אסחור הו ירתנה 'it is Esḥor that will inherit from her' B2.6:21. More examples may be found above at § 39 *c*.

b) אגורא זך בנה השכחה 'that temple, he found *it* (already) built' A4.7:14 (// זנה חלק ביתא זי A4.8:12); [אגורא] זך בנה השכח // משחת כתיבן ותחומוהי אנה עניה יהבתה לכי 'this part of the house whose measurements and boundaries are written, I Ananiah have given *it* to you' B3.5:11; ביתא זנה זי משחתה ותחומוהי כתבן בספרא זנה אנה עני ... יהבתה לך 'this house whose measurements and boundaries are written in this document, I Anani gave *it* to you' B3.10:11, sim. B2.3:8,25, B2.7:7,15, B3.11:7; אנה נכתני חויה 'as for me, a snake bit me' A2.5:8; אתנא זי ... צדיק א[נה ל]החסנותה פ]מסי 'as for the she-ass which .. I am entitled to bestow on Pa[misi' B7.3:4. Possibly in ובעל אגר לא יהוה לה גבר טב עם ג[בר לח[ה 'and a paymaster, he shall not have a good man with a bad man' C1.1:100.[1218]

c) ... פלגא אחרנא אנת שליט בה 'as for the other half, you have right to it ..' B2.4:11; פלגא הו בניך מן מבטחיה המו שליטן בה 'as for that half, it is your children from Mibtahiah that have right to *it*' ib.12 (with a double extraposition); זנה ביתא יהבתה לכי 'as for this house, I have given *it* to you' B2.7:7; אנת וגרדא זילי עבידה לא איתי ... לך 'you and the domestic staff of mine—*you* have no business (with them)' A6.15:9.

d) Unique to the Arsames correspondence is a double extraposition whereby the demonstrative pronoun זך or זכי resumes the extraposed NP—the choice between the two demonstratives is conditioned by the gender of the NP—and the demonstrative is in turn resumed by a suffix pronoun or its equivalent. This phenomenon occurs in חנזני שמה ... זך פתפא הב לה '(one) named Hinzani .., that one, give him the rations' A6.12:1; זך ... בנא מנדעם מן תמה לא מהיתין עלי 'the domain .., that one, they do not bring me from there anything' A6.13:1; צבות ביתא זילי זי פסמשך יאמר לך ... זכי אשתמעו לה ועבדו כן 'the matter concerning my estate (about) which P. might say to you .., (concerning) that, obey

___

analysis, see Khan 1988:107-08, 110-18 (on BA); 123-28, 132-46 (on Syr.).

[1218] An alternative interpretation identifies here two separate clauses: "he will not be his paymaster. So behaves a good man towards a bad man": see Grelot 1972:445 and Lindenberger 1983:165. Cf. Cowley 1923:225,245 and Kottsieper 1990:17.

him and do accordingly' A6.8:2, where one expects בה with
אשתמעו or such like. In one case, a second resumptive pronoun is
only seemingly absent: סרוש]ית[א זי פסמשך י]שים[להם טעם למעבד
זכי יתעבד להם 'the chastise[ment], which P. will order to be meted
out to them, that one, it shall be meted out to them' A6.3:7,
where it is not necessary to postulate a disagreement in gender
between the demonstrative and the following verb, but one is
instead dealing with an impersonal passive.([1219])

e) Rare examples of extraposition in which the extraposed
constituent is not referred back in what follows: וכעת כל זי תצבה
שלח לי 'and now, whatever you desire, send (word) to me (about
it)' A2.4:7; מה זי לקחת זני תשלם 'what you took, you shall pay
damages (for it)' A6.15:8.

§ 80. Impersonal constructions

a) The 3ms of the passive pf. or impf. is sometimes used to
focus on the action itself when no reference is intended to an
entity formally indicated as 3ms: e.g. אחרן זי מני שליח עליהם 'some
other matter (about) which word was sent from me to them'
A6.2:6; לא ישתמע לה 'no hearing shall be granted to him' B3.8:42,
sim. B6.4:8([1220]); יתעשת לי 'Let note be taken of me!' A6.11:3([1221]);
וישתלח על המרכריא 'and let (word) be sent to the accountants'
A6.2:4. Perhaps there belongs here also לה שאל על חרוץ 'no
enquiry was made about Ḥarudj' A2.3:6, though some scholars
take it to mean "he did/does not ask ..,' but "he does not" with a
participle and without the subject pronoun is harsh.([1222]) In לא
אשתאר לן עליך מן דמיא 'there did not remain for us (any) of the
price which could be charged against you' B3.12:6 there is an
oblique reference to the subject.

b) In some cases a passive verb appears to have a NP
functioning as its grammatical subject, but it is better to analyse
such a clause as an imperfectly transformed passive structure in
which the NP is still felt to be the object of the verb: הן יהב לכי
נקיה וגזתה 'if you be given a lamb and its wool' A2.2:8; אגרה מנך

[1219] See § 80 *a*. All these examples, plus A6.16:2 where the text is too
fragmentary, have been collected and discussed by Whitehead (1974:210-16)
as cases of extraposition, though his analysis is unsatisfactory.

[1220] The preposition here is that of advantage or benefit (*dativus commodi*).

[1221] *Pace* Grelot (1972:316), not reflexive: "Soucie-toi de moi." The reading
is not אתעשה as in the editio princeps.

[1222] Though not impossible: see Nöldeke 1898: §§ 253, 314.

ישתלח 'Let a letter be sent from you!' A4.7:24.([1223])

The notion of *passivum majestatis*([1224]) is not very convincing: not every case of passive with or without the agent-marking מן occurs in utterances in which respect and politeness are due.

c) A 3mp form may be used where the personal subject is not known, or the speaker or writer does not wish to specify it: תקם יתו לי ;מדעם לה מפקן לן 'they do not bring us anything' A2.5:2; 'Let them bring me castor oil' A2.4:12; לא שבקן לן 'they do not allow us' A4.7:23, possibly בפקדן] [הפקדו 'one placed (them) on deposit' B2.9:7 (rather than a passive H).([1225])

d) It is rare to find the second person plural as the impersonal subject: זי תעבדון לה לא יתכסון מן ענני 'what you do for him will not be hidden from Anani' A4.3:10.

§ 81. Coordination([1226])

a) A constituent of a clause is often expanded by the addition of a term or terms of syntactically equal standing: thus אסבל לאבי 'I shall support my father' may be expanded to אסבל לאבי ולאמי 'I shall support my father and my mother.'

b) A preposition may be repeated with each of such coordinate terms([1227]): הוי חזית על תשי ועל ברה 'Do look after Tashai and after her son' A2.3:11; לאלהיא ולארשם תחד[ה] 'you gladden the gods and Arsames' A6.16:2; יכלא למחסה או לבר לה 'to restrain Mahsah or a son of his' B2.1:9; למפתח תרעא זך ולמנפק בשוקא 'to open that gate and to go out into the street' ib.14; בחיי ובמותי 'in my lifetime and upon my death' B2.3:3; זבנת מן אוביל ... ומן בגזושת 'I bought from PN .. and from PN' B3.5:3; מן גרדא או מן נכסיא אחרנן זילי 'ۃ(decrease) in the domestic staff or in my other goods' A6.10:8; ביב ובסון ובמדנתא 'in Elephantine or in Syene or in the province' B3.13:11. Cf. also ביתא זילך אם וזי בניך מן אחריך 'the house is moreover yours and of your children after you' B3.4:16.

When the first term consists of a preposition with a conjunctive pronoun, the following term(s) often repeat(s) the same

---

[1223] See § 76 *bb*. Cf. אנרת מן מראי תשתלח 'Let a letter from my lord be sent!' A6.13:2, which, by virtue of the gender agreement, indicates flexibility in this regard.

[1224] On which see Kutscher 1969:17-20 and Folmer 1995:380-93.

[1225] See above at § 30.

[1226] Cf. Hug 1993:101f.

[1227] For a comparative overview in the first millennium BCE, see Garr 1985:176-79.

preposition: יאמר לך ולחילא זי לידך 'will say to you and to the troop which is at your command' A6.8:2; ינתן לכם או לבניכם או למן זי ירשון 'will give to you or to your children or to whomever they bring (suit) against' B2.9:14. This repetition is of course due to the conjunctive nature of the pronouns.

c) That the repetition of a preposition is optional when the leading term is not a conjunctive pronoun is shown by the following examples: [ע]ל עטתה ומלוהי 'upon his counsel and his words' C1.1:43; לתרכותה מן ביתה זי אסחור ונכסוהי וקנינה 'to deprive her of the house of Eshor and his goods and his possession' B2.6:30; לא יעבד לפירמא זך וכנותה 'will not do to that Pariyama and his colleagues' A6.7:8; לשמשלך וכנותה 'to Shumshillech and his colleagues' A6.2:8; אנתננהי לחגי או יגדל 'I shall give it to Haggai or Igdal' D7.29:5.

However, in these examples and many others where the preposition is not repeated, the coordinate terms seem to form a cohesive unit. Thus in letters jointly addressed to two or more individuals: אל מראי ידניה מעוזיה אוריה וחילא 'To my lords Jedaniah, Mauziah, Uriah and the troop' A4.2:1, sim. A4.3:1; אל אחתי תרו ותבי מן אחוכן נבושה ומכבנת 'to my sister(s) Taru and Tabi from your brother Nabusha and Makkibanit' A2.5:1; מן ארשם על נחתחור כנזסרם וכנותה 'from Arsham to Nakhthor, Kenzasirma and his colleagues' A6.13:1; אגרת ... תשתלח על נחתחור פקידא והמרכריא 'Let a letter be sent to Nakhthor the official and the accountants' ib.2, sim. A6.14:1. In לסגן ומרא 'to prefect and lord' B3.10:19, B3.11:13 and לסגן ומרא ודין 'to prefect and lord and judge' B3.12:28 a range of possibilities is given. The same applies to לבר לך וברה 'to a son of yours or a daughter' B3.4:14; הן ... גרו לבר וברה לך 'if ... they institute (suit) against a son or a daughter of yours' ib.18 where the cohesion of בר וברה is made evident also by the position of לך; לבניכם ואחיכם ואיש לכם 'against your children or your brothers or a person of yours' B2.9:11. See also לידניה ומחסיה 'to Jedaniah and Mahseiah' B2.9:3 (brothers); בביתה זי אסחור ונכסוהי וקנינה וכל זי איתי לה על אנפי ארעא כלה 'to the house of Eshor and his properties and possesion and all that he has on the face of the whole earth' B2.6:18; לא שלמתך בכספך ומרביתה 'I did not repay you your silver and its interest' B3.1:7; באגרה חדה שלחן בשמן על דליה ושלמיה בני סנאבלט 'in a letter we sent .. in our name to Delaiah and Shelemiah sons of Sanballat' A4.7:29; נרשה לבניך ובנתך וזי תנתן לה בכסף 'to bring (suit) against your sons or your daughters or one to whom you give (it) for silver' B3.12:26; בעליתא ותחתיתא 'in the Upper and Lower (Egypt מצרין)' A6.7:6.

Cp. למסלק ומנחת 'to ascend and descend' B3.10:15 with the

above-quoted למפתח ... ולמנפק 'to open .. and to exit' B2.1:14 with two infinitives with two words intervening. Also instructive is אגרה שלחן <על> מראן וו ועל יהוחנן כהנא רבא וכנותא כהניא זי בירושלם וו ועל אוסתן אחוהי זי ענני וחרי יהודיא 'we sent a letter (to) our lord and to Jehohanan the high priest and his fellow priests who are in Jerusalem and to Ostanes the brother of Anani and the nobles of the Jews' A4.7:18([1228]) where a total of five terms is classified into three categories, each of which is headed by the preposition על.

d) The auxiliary verb הוה in a periphrastic tense is not repeated: שקקן לבשן הוין וצימין ומצלין ליהו 'we were wearing sackcloth .. and fasting and praying to YHW' A4.7:15. The same interpretation may be applied to ויהוי זבן גשרן ושבק בבתה 'and do let him buy beams and leave (them) in his house' A2.2:14, where taking שבק as an imperative is unlikely in view of והוי לקח שערן מן תשי ויהב ... בגשרן ושבק כל גשר 'and do take barley from Tashai and give (it in exchange) for beams and leave .. every beam' A2.4:9 where the impv. of יהב must be הב.

e) *Coordinating conjunction* -ו *or* או

In the following cases of asyndeton the terms do not appear to be equal in weight: יהבת לכי ... בי 1 ארק זילי הוה 'I have given you a house (with a plot of) land which was mine' B2.3:3([1229]); ביתא זנך ארק 'that house (with a plot of) land' ib.8; 1 ארק בי '(a plot of) land (with) a house' B2.4:3([1230]). See also אמר מחסיה בר נתן 1 ידניה בר נתן 1 כל 2 'Mahseiah son of Nathan 1, Jedaniah son of Nathan 1, all (told) 2 said' B2.11:2 where the singular verb is due to the fact that Mahseiah is the one who is drawing up the contract.

ea) As a rule, however, coordinate terms are linked by means of either proclitic Waw or או. Thus בר לי וברה לי 'a son of mine and a daughter of mine' B3.10:18; מחר או יום אחרן 'tomorrow or the next day' B2.1:8 et passim. Exceptions are וקן תור ענז מקלו א[לא] יתעבד תמה 'and sheep, ox, goat are [n]ot made there as burnt-offering' A4.10:10; אמר מחסיה בר נתן 1 ידניה בר נתן 1 כל 2 'Mahseiah son of Nathan 1 (and) Jedaniah son of Nathan 1 all told 2 said' B2.11:2.

eb) Where three or more terms are coordinate, there may

[1228] Cf. על מראן אנ[ף] על יהוחנן // A4.8:17.

[1229] A case of sandhi (§ 10 *b*). Alternatively a haplography for זי זילי, or an asyndetic clause, 'it was mine.' Cf. Porten 1996:165, n. 15.

[1230] The emphasis is clearly on the land in B2.4:3, while in B2.3:3 it is on the house.

occur only one coordinate conjunction between the last two terms, thus [a + b + Waw + c]: מנחה לבונה ועלוה 'meal-offering, incense and burnt-offering' A4.8:21; פקידיא ... מתנצחן ... נטרן אף ... בע[י]ן [ן] ... ל[ע]פן ומהוס[... 'the officials .. are being diligent .. guarding, moreover .. seeking .. and adding to ..' A6.10:3(1231); על נחתחור כנזסרם וכנותה 'to Nakhthor, Kendasirma and his colleagues' A6.11:1, A6.12:1, A6.13:1(1232); עבדיך אחמנש וכנותה בגדן וכנותה וספרי מדינתא 'your servants Achaemenes and his colleagues, Bagadana and his colleagues and the scribes of the province' A6.1:1 where the internal structure could be represented as: {your servants [Ach. /and/ his colleagues] [Bag. /and/ his colleagues] //and// [the scribes of the province]}, or alternatively, {x} = [a + b], [c + d] + e. In other words, the conjunction Waw is used between the last two of three constituents at a higher level, whereas it also joins two constituents of a sub-constituent at a lower level. Likewise אנחנה שקקן לבשן הוין וצימין נשיא זילן כארמלה עבידין משח לא משחין וחמר לא שתין 'we were wearing sackcloth and fasting, our women have been treated like widows, we do not anoint (ourselves with) oil, and we do not drink wine' A4.7:20, thus [(a + b), c, d and e]. See also אל מראי ידניה מעוזיה אוריה וחילא 'to my lords Jedaniah, Mauziah, Uriah, and the troop' A4.2:1, which may be interpreted as a string of two terms, the first מראי being in apposition to the following three names: [a (= a_1 a_2 a_3) + b]. Likewise אל מראי ידניה אוריה וכהניא 'to my lords Jedaniah, Uriah and the priests' A4.3:1, which is complemented by אל מראי ידניה אוריה וכהניא ויהודיא 'to my lords, Jed., Ur. and the priests, and the Jews' ib.12 where we have a basic structure of [a + b + c].

ec) As shown in some examples above, a string of NPs may consist of smaller units which in turn form a cohesive string members of which may be joined by a coordinate conjunction:

With no Waw between the larger strings—
לא יכהל ‖ בר וברה ‖ אח ואחה ‖ קריב ורחיק ‖ בעל דגל וקריה
'son or daughter, brother or sister, near or far, member of a detachment or town shall not be able ..' B2.1:8
איתי[ן] נכסיא ‖ לבשי קמר וכתן ‖ מאני נחש ופרזל ‖ מאני עק וחוצן ‖ עבור ואחרן נכסן
'there are the(se) goods—woolen and linen garments, bronze and iron utensils, wooden and palm-leaf utensils, grain and

---

1231 This contrasts with [א]תנצחו ... טרו ... בעו והנעלו ... וסטרו ... ועבדו על 'Be diligent .. guard .. seek and bring in .. and mark .. and make over to ..'ib.5.

1232 In contrast to על נחתחור וכנדסירם וכנותה 'to Na. and Kendasirma and his colleagues' A6.14:1.

other things' B2.9:5

לא נכהל נרשה ‖ לבר וברה לכם ‖ אח ואחה ‖ אנתה ואיש לכם

'we shall not be able to bring suit against son or
daughter of yours, brother or sister, woman
or man of yours' B2.10:10

רשכם ‖ בר לי וברה ‖ אנתה ואיש

'son of mine or daughter,
woman or man brought suit against you' B2.10:12

בי זי לבנין ‖ כסף ודהב ‖ נחש ופרזל ‖ עבד ואמה ‖ שערן כנתן וכל זון זי
תשכח

'brick house, silver or gold, bronze or iron, male or female
slave, barley, emmer or any food that you might find'
B3.1:9

בל ונבו ‖ שמש ונרגל

'Bel and Nabu, Shamash and Nergal' D7.30:3([1233])

With a Waw between the larger strings—

(a + b) + (c + d) וירשון ‖ לבר וברה ‖ ואנתה ואיש לכם

'and they will bring suit against
son or daughter or woman or man of yours' B2.10:14

a + (b + c + d) בשמי אנה ידניה ‖ ובשם בנן ואנתה ואיש לי

'in my name, I, Jedaniah, or in the
name of children or woman or man of mine' B2.10:12([1234])

Finally עבדיך אחאמנש וכנותה בגדן וכנותה וספרי מדינתא'your servants
Achaemenes and his colleagues, Bagadana and his colleagues,
and the scribes of the province' A6.1:1 illustrates a combination
of the structure under discussion here and the one dealt with in
the preceding subparagraph: a [= (b + c) (d + e) + f].

How great the scope for stylistic variation is in this regard
is easy to see by comparing the examples cited above from a
single document, B2.10.

ed) A coordinating conjunction may be repeated ad nauseam:
שלם נכי ועשה ותשי וענתי ואטי ורע 'Greetings to Nky and Ashah and
Tashai and Anathi and Ati and Re(ia)' A2.1:3; נפרת על כסף ועבור
ולבוש ונחש ופרזל כל נכסן וקנין וספר אנתו 'a litigation(?) about silver
and grain and clothes and bronze and iron, all (the) goods and

---

[1233] In the treaty of Bar-Ga'yah we note a long series of divine witnesses
paired as here, but all the eight pairs are in turn linked with the conjunction
Waw: וקדם נרגל ולץ וקדם שמש ונר וקדם סן ונכל... 'and in the presence of
Nergal and Lats and in the presence of Shamash and Nur and in the presence
of Sin and Nikkal ...' Sefire I A 9.

[1234] The internal hierarchy here is [a + (b + c + d)]. Moreover, the members
of the second smaller string are also connected by the Waw.

property, and the wifehood document' B2.8:3, though the preposition על is not repeated; אנה ידניה ובני ואנתה ואיש לי 'I, Jedaniah, or my children, or woman or man of mine' B2.10:9; ביתא זליך ודי בניך ודי תנתן לה רחמת 'the house is yours and of your children and of whoever you give (it) to affectionately' B3.12:30.

ee) The syntagm [NP and NP + adj.] may be shorthand for [NP + adj.] and [NP + adj.]: ספר חדת ועתיק 'a document new or old' B2.3:16, B2.7:12, B3.12:29; ב[נן] ואנתה אחרן להן מפטחיה ובניה 'other sons and wife besides Miptahiah and her sons' B2.6:33 (with disagreement in gender and number).

ef) Many strings of coordinate phrases, whether joined by the conjunction Waw or not, do not count as multi-membered constituents for the purpose of grammatical agreement. Thus in יסבל בר וברה לאבוהי the verb is in the singular, since it is not about a son and daughter jointly looking after their father, but rather a range of possibilities is being mentioned: 'a son or daughter will support his(!) father' B3.6:11. So also לא אכהל אנה אוריה ובר וברה לי אח ואחה לי ואיש לי יכבשנהי עבד 'I shall not be able, I, Uriah, or son or daughter of mine, brother or sister of mine, or man of mine to press him (into) slave(ry)' B3.9:4.([1235])

eg) A NP prefixed by the conjunction Waw is at times logically subordinate to the preceding NP, and such a Waw traditionally is known as Waw of accompaniment: ... אנתי שביקה ויהישמע ברתכי 'you are released .. along with Jehoishma your daughter' B3.6:8; אמרת תפמת ויהישמע ברתה אנחן יפלחנך 'Tapemet said, with Jehoishma her daughter, "We shall serve you"' ib.11 (namely, also on behalf of J.); תתמלא בכספך ומרביתה 'you are fully paid back your silver together with its interest' B3.1:11, cf. B3.1:7,11,12,14,16,18. The lack of grammatical agreement between the apparent multiple subject and its predicate can be partly explained in terms of Waw of accompaniment.([1236])

§ 82. Circumstantial clause

A form of coordination at clause-level is a syntagm in which the second clause, mostly a nominal clause, joined to, and logically subordinate to the leading one by means of the conjunction Waw, describes a situation which prevails when the action described in the first clause takes or took place. Examples are: ולא יתלקח בדין וספרא זנה בידכי 'and it shall not be accepted in a suit while this

---

[1235] There are also cases which display varying degrees of agreement: see above § 76 *cg*.

[1236] See above, § 76 *cg*.

document is in your hand' B2.3:17, sim. B3.1:12,13,19,20, all
A. 'if והן ז̇ימות עניה ובר זכר ונקבה לאיתי לה ... ;וספרא זנה בידך with
dies while he has no child, male or female ...' B3.8:28, sim.
ib.34; 3 וכון בה '(there are) 3 windows in it' B3.10:13; נמרא פנע
לענוא והי עריה 'a leopard meets/met a goat while she is/was naked'
C1.1:166; אל תהושרו לי לחם ולא הו חתם 'don't dispatch to me bread
when it is unsealed' D7.44:4; תרען ... נדשו ודשיהם קימן 'they
demolished gates ... with their doors standing' A4.7:10.([1237])

A rare example of a circumstantial clause not introduced by
the conjunction Waw is: הושרו לי מלח קבן 2 דקק וחצף קפתא עלוהי
'Dispatch to me salt, two *qabs*, fine and coarse, (with) the basket
on it' D7.7:1, though the style is telegrammatic.

§ 83. Negation

a) Our idiom knows two negators: אל and לא (regularly
spelled לה in the Hermopolis letters[[1238]]).

b) אל is used only in verbal clauses, placed immediately
before a jussive or energic form to indicate the speaker's wish
that something does not happen. E.g., אל תצפי לן 'Do not worry
about us!' A2.1:7; אל ירחק מנכם 'Let him not be far from you!'
A3.10:8; אל תלקחן 'Do not take!' C1.1:167 (with an energic).

c) The use of לא (including לה) is far more varied. When
immediately preceding a predicatively used verb or adjective, it
negates the veracity of the entire statement. Otherwise it negates
only the constituent immediately following. Exceptions are: זי
לא אל עמה 'one with whom El is not' C1.1:97; ולא הו חתם 'and it is
unsealed' D7.44:5; לא אנחן יהבנה לכי 'we did not give it to you'
B5.1:5.

d) לא may negate: the *perfect*—לאנתתא זילך לא כתשת 'I did
not beat up the wife of yours' B7.2:9; אגרה חדה לא שלחו עלין 'they
did not send us a single letter' A4.7:19; ספר לה הושרתן לי 'you did
not send me a letter' A2.5:7; the *imperfect* —לא אכהל אכלאנך 'I
shall not be able to restrain you' B2.1:6; לא תמות 'you will not
die' C1.1:177; the *participle*—לבבי לה דבק לה 'my heart isn't
attached to it' A2.1:5; משח לא משחין וחמר לא שתין '(we) do not
anoint with oil and do not drink wine' A4.7:20; the *particle of
existence*—מחבל לא איתי 'there is no injury' A3.3:7; עבידה לא איתי
לך 'you have no business' A6.15:9; ... ולא איתי זי יקיר מן 'there is
not (a thing) which is heavier than ..' C1.1:159; והן מלח לאית

[1237] קימן in the st.abs. cannot have an attributive function ("their standing
doors"). Cp. "but their doors *are standing*" (Ginsberg 1955:492).

[1238] See above, § 5 *g*.

בביתא 'if there is no salt in the house' D7.2:3; the *predicative adjective*—לא שליט אנת לזבנה 'you do not have right to sell ..' B2.4:6; מין לא חסרה 'it does not lack water' A4.5:7; the *adverb*—לא עד נפלג עלין 'we shall not yet divide (them) between us' B2.11:13; *prepositional phrase*—תהך [ו]לא ביומיך 'you will go and (that) not in your days' C1.1:86; ולא בחרבי [sic!] ימותון שאני 'my enemies will die, and that not by my sword' ib.110.

Also negating a nominal clause in תרעא זך לא זילך הו 'that gate is not yours' B2.1:12.

e) Elsewhere לא occurs in cleft sentences: לא אנה כתבתה 'it is not I that wrote it' B2.3:17; לא בידיך מנשא רגלך 'it is not in your hands to lift your leg' C1.1:171, but apparently not in זי לא אל עמה 'one with whom El is not' C1.1:97; ולא הו חתם 'and it is unsealed' D7.44:5; לא אנחן יהבנה לכי 'we did not give it to you' B5.1:5.

f) לא may serve for categorical negation with a sg.abs. noun([1239]): גבר לא לב[ב] 'a man of no mind, a totally senseless man' C1.1:82; לא חסרן הו לכם 'it is no loss whatsoever to you' A4.3:9; לא דין ולא דבב 'without suit or process of any kind' B2.3:14, B2.8:10 et passim; לא שאר קטין 'no leftover of cucumbers' D7.17:11.

A case such as ספר לה שלחתי בשמה 'you have not sent a single letter about him' A2.3:5—more examples in § 78 *cd*—is syntactically distinct in that the negator does not precede the noun.

g) הן לא 'if not, otherwise' A3.10:6; D7.16:3,7 must have resulted from ellipsis.

§ 84. Conditional statements

a) The standard conditional statement consists of two clauses, a protasis (= prot.) which, introduced by הן, states a condition, and an apodosis (= ap.) which states a consequence which follows or would, could, or might follow when or if the condition is met. We are concerned here mainly with the variation in tense in both

---

[1239] This morphological constraint that the noun in question must be sg. and/or abs. seems to us to be important. Thus, of the examples collected by Hoftijzer (Hoftijzer 1976:196) ברי זי לא ברי C1.1:30 does not apply, for it hardly means 'my son, who is my degraded son' as Hofijzer would have it. For the same reason we would take ולא פשרן 'without fail' D7.20:2, D7.37:10 as singular.

One can naturally include here a substantivised adjective as in לא ביש בכפי 'there is no evil in my hands' Pap. Amherst 63: 6/3, 9.

clauses and with the correlation between the choice of tense and the logical relationship between the two clauses of a conditional statement.([1240])

b) *Prot. pf.—ap. impf.*

The syntagm signifies that, should the situation indicated by the prot. be or become a reality, that which is indicated by the ap. possibly or most likely would become a reality: הן חזית מה אתרתן אתננה 'if I saw what you had in abundance, I might give it ..' A2.1:5; הן אשכחת איש מהימן אתה לכן מדעם 'if I find someone trustworthy, I would bring you something' ib.9; ... הן כן עבדו וצדקה יהוה לך 'if they did thus .., then it would be considered a merit for you' A4.7:27 (with a Waw of apodosis and // תעבד A4.8:26); הן לא קמת ... אתננהי לך 'if I did not stand .., I shall give it to you' B1.1:10; ... הן כליתך אנתן לך 'if I restrain you, I shall give you ..' B2.1:7; אנתן ... הן העדת המו מנה 'if I remove them from her, I shall give ..' B2.6:35; sim. B2.8:8, B3.1:6, B3.2:5-8, 8-9, B3.4:14-15,18,20, B3.5:14, 3.6:13-14. In many cases, the apodosis appears to indicate a promise, pledge or commitment on the part of the speaker.([1241])

c) *Prot. pf.—ap. impv.*

The protasis indicates a situation which may already be prevailing or may arise in future: הן יהב לכי נקיה ... שלחי לי 'if you have been given a lamb .., send (word) to me' A2.2:8, sim. 9,10,16([1242]); הן מטאך ... שלח לי 'if .. has already reached you, send (word) to me' A2.4:6; והן לא השכחת אפם חת לעבק 'should you not find, still come down at once' A3.8:8; see also A3.8:5,7.

d) *Prot. pf.—ap. NC.*

The syntagm signifies that, should the situation as indicated in the prot. be or become a reality, that which is indicated by the ap. would certainly apply. E.g., [הן] ... זבנתון ... טב 'if you have bought, (it is) good' A3.10:5; הן לא שלמו ... אנת פחנום שליט בערבני למחד ותלקח לך ... 'if my children fail to pay .. you Pakhnum have right over my security to seize (it) and take for yourself ..' B3.13:9. This last example shows that an NC and an impf. as ap. following a pf. as prot. have the same morphosyntactic value. See also הן מטא ... ולא שלמתך ... אנת משלם ובניך שליט 'if (a second year) came round and I have not (yet) paid .. you Meshullam and your children have right ..' B3.1:7, sim.15, B3.5:17.

[1240] Cf. Folmer 1991 and Folmer 1995: 394-415.

[1241] Cf. § 52 *e*.

[1242] So Hug 1993:137 ("übergeben wurde") and Grelot 1972:154 ("si on t'a remis ..").

e) *Prot. impf.—ap. juss.*

The only example found is ... הן יהוה ... אל תנתנו 'should he be .., do not give ..' A6.9:6.

f) *Prot. impf.—ap. impv.*

This syntagm is functionally related to (*e*), both the juss. and impv. being volitive forms. E.g., הן יאחדן רשיעא בכנפי לבשך שבק בידה 'if the wicked take hold of the corners of your garment, leave (it) in his hand!' C1.1:107; הן ... ירשה על ביתא זך ספרא זך הנפקי 'if .. he bring (suit) over that house, produce this document' B2.3:26.

g) *Prot. impf.—ap. impf.*

E.g., "if there be (הן ... יהוה) any decrease in the domestic staff or in my other goods and from elsewhere you seek not (לא תבעון) and add not (לא תהוספון) to my estate, you will be strictly called to account (תשתאלון) and a harsh word will be directed (יתעבד) at you' A6.10:8; הן תעבדן [ל]ה ט[ב]ה בסון יעבד לי [אף ה]או 'if you do [for him g]ood in Syene, h[e also] would do (good) for me' D7.1:7. See also C1.1:172,177,191(?), B2.3:20, B2.4:10, B2.6:33, B3.4:19, B3.11:10.

h) *Prot. impf.—ap. NC.*

E.g., ... הן מחר ... תבנה ... לא שליטה הי למלקחה 'if tomorrow she .. build up .. she has no right to take it ..' B2.4:8; והן [ימות א]חדתה ... יהוישמע הי [א]עניה 'if Ananiah die .. it is Jehoishma that holds on to him' B3.8:28; הן תהנצל ... פלג ביתא [י]ה[ו]ה לה למלקח ופלגא אחרנא אנת שליט בה 'if she reclaim .. half the house [s]h[al]l be hers to take but the other half—you shall have right to it' B2.4:10. The last example shows the morphosyntactic equivalence of the impf. and the NC in an apodosis.

i) Whether there is a functional difference between the pf. and impf. in the prot. is a moot point. Kutscher (1954:234) noted the syntactic preference for a pf. if the verb immediately follows הן or הן לא, though he was apparently aware that the rule is not water-tight; see A4.7:27 quoted above under (**b**), and B3.5:14 and B2.10:12, both with a disjunctive pronoun intervening, which is the normal position (§ 39 *e*). It is difficult to establish a functional opposition between the two tenses in this syntagm. Especially instructive is ... הן כן עבדו 'if they did thus ..' A4.7:27 // ... הן כן תעבד 'if you do thus' A4.8:26 in a revised official document of same date.([1243]) Even within a single

---

[1243] Joüon's (1934:21) view that the prefix conjugation, which can have a volitive nuance—"if you wish to act .."—, can account for the tense variation does not convince us.

document both tenses occur.([1244]) For example, הן מיתתי ברת שנן
100 'if you die 100 years old' B3.5:17 vs. ואף הן אנה עננ אמות בר
100 שנן 'and moreover, if I, Anani, die 100 years old' ib.18; even
within a single sentence—והן אנה ידניה רשיתכם ורשכם ... וירשון לבר
וברה ... 'if I, Jedaniah, bring (suit) against you and .. bring (suit)
against you .. and they bring (suit) against son or daughter ..'
B2.10:12; ... הן רשינך דינא ... או נרשה 'if we bring (suit) .. or we
bring (suit) ..' B2.11:9. Folmer (1991:73-77) thinks one can speak
of a gradual dominance of the impf.

j) *Prot.* אית—*ap. impv.*

The only example is הן את ערב עליכי אתיה לתפמת 'if you have
a guarantor against you, bring him to Tapamet' A2.3:9.

k) *Prot.* אית—*ap. impf.*

Attested only once: הן אית לך חמרן 10 ישבקון המו 'if you have
ten asses, they will release them' A3.1:4.

l) *Prot. NC—ap. juss.*

Attested only once: הן על מראי לם כות טב אגרת מן מראי תשתלח
... 'should it thus please my lord, let a letter be sent from my lord
..' A6.13:2.

m) *Prot. NC—ap. impv.*

Attested only once: הן על מראן טב אתעשת .. 'should it so
please our lord, take thought ..' A4.7:23.

n) Very occasionally one also finds a participle in a protasis
as in ... הן נחת אנת 1 למנפי אל תשבק 'if you come down alone to
Memphis, do not leave ..' A3.8:11. Here again the ptc. is
morphosyntactically equivalent to the impf. as shown by הן נפקה
טבה מן פם ... 'if good comes out from the mouth of ..' C1.1:171
vs. הן לחיה תנפק מ[ן] פמהם 'if evil comes out from their mouth'
ib.172.

o) Once the pf. appears in an apodosis, but it is performative
in force: הן כנם הו כמליא אלה .. יהבת ... 'if it is thus in accordance
with these words .. I hereby give ..' A6.11:3.

p) Though not introduced by the conditional הן, a generalising
relative clause is similar to a conditional clause: למן זי רחמתי תנתנן
'to whomever you care, you may give (it)' B2.3:9. Another
synonymous structure is headed by כזי as in כזי ינתן ... והן לא יהב
... 'when he gives .. and if he does not give ..' A3.8:10.([1245]) See

---

[1244] *Pace* Folmer (1991:74). See the above-quoted pair in B3.5:17,18 and הן
אנה גריתכי 'if I bring (suit) against you' B3.5:14 vs. הן גבר אחרן יגרנך 'if someone
else bring (suit) against you' ib.16.

[1245] Cf. Germ. *wenn*.

also זך ספרא זי יהנפקון עליכי כדב יהוה 'that document, which they might produce against you, shall be fraudulent' B2.3:16.

Another implicitly conditional statement is illustrated by ואהך בדין ולא אצדק 'Should I go to law, I shall not win' B2.3:22 and ויהך בדן ולא יצדק 'Should he go to law, he will not win' B3.11:15; אף יהכון בדין ולא יצדקון 'Moreover, should they go to law, they would not win' B3.1:19.

Though totally lacking a formal feature of a conditional statement, the general context allows one to recognise such in a case like([1246]): "Tomorrow or [the ne]xt day, should Eshor die (מחר או יום א[חר]ן ימות אסחור) not having a child, male or female, by Miptahiah his wife, it is Miptahiah who has right (מפטחיה הי שליטה) to the house of Eshor .." B2.6:17, sim. ib.20,22. Cp. וה[ן ...] [ימות ענניה ובר זכר ונקבה לאיתי לה 'and if Ananiah should die, not having a child, male or female ..' B3.8:28, sim. ib.34.

q) An unreal condition contrary to fact may be introduced by לו or הנלו as in... הנלו גלין 'if we had revealed ..' A4.2:8([1247]); לו ו[ב]סגרא שימת ... 'were I put [in] the stocks, ...' D7.10:1.

r) An apodosis may be introduced by the conjunction Waw, a so-called Waw of apodosis([1248]): הן כן עבדו עד זי אגרא זך יתבנה וצדקה יהוה לך ... 'if you did like this until that temple is (re)built, then it will be (considered) a merit for you ...' A4.7:27; הן יעדדן/יעדרן ותפק אחטב עמר 'if they will help / hoe (?), then let Aḥutab take out wool' D7.7:7.

§ 85. Direct speech

a) A direct speech is often presented as actually uttered without any external marker signalling it as such: אל יאמר עתירא בעתרי הדיר אנה 'May the rich not say, "In my riches I am glorious"' C1.1:206; כן אמר כזי אנה הוית אתה 'Thus he said, "When I was coming .."' A6.3:2; ... הן אמר איתי לי 'If I say, "I have .."' B2.6:33; sim. ib.31, B3.7:15. In ולא תוכ]הל יהוחן ... תנאמר לה] ... כזי נכסיא וא]לה וכספא ... ברחמן יהבת לכם 'and Jehohen ... shall not be a[b]le to [say to him] ... "[T]hese goods and the silver ... I gave you in affection"' B6.4:6 we possibly find direct speech introduced by זי in the manner of ὅτι *recitativum*, though the verb of saying is

---

[1246] See Joüon 1934:22.

[1247] The particle at C1.1:35 is probably a combination of הן and לו, which latter is a result of sandhi, i.e. < הו לא, thus 'if it is not (so)' = 'otherwise.' So Ginsberg 1955:427. This is virtually certain at ib.176.

[1248] On the apodotic conjunction in OA, see Dion 1974:317, Garr 1985:194f., and Fitzmyer 1995:217, and on that in Egyptian Aramaic, Grelot 1970.

a restoration.([1249]) Also with שלח alone: אנה [שלח]ת לכם לם אל
תהושרו ... 'I sent (word) to you: "Don't dispatch .."' D7.44:2;
שלחתן לם וי]שלחו לי טעמא 'you sent (word), saying "Let them send
me the instruction"' D7.48:7.

b) Equally frequently, however, לאמר, the fossilised archaic
G infinitive without the prefix Mem([1250]), serves to signal the
onset of a direct speech: הן קמן לאמר לא נסבלנך 'should we stand
up, saying, "we will not support you"' B3.6:13.

Here belong also cases such as: אמר לי יאוש לאמר הבה בזהב
'Jaush said to me, saying, "Give it for gold"' A3.7:4; כן אמיר לן
'we were told thus, "About this .."' A3.3:4; קדם 'לאמר על זנה ...
מראי שלחת לאמר כעשק עביד לי 'I have sent (word) before my lord,
"something of an injustice was done to me"' A5.2:8; כזי תשמעין
'when you hear, "We began .."' D7.9:10; לאמר שרין ... כזי כן שמיע
לן לאמר תתפטרן 'when we have heard, "you will be released"'
A3.3:13.

c) On לם, see below, § 90 *e*.

§ 86. Vocative and interjection

a) The Ahiqar idiom uses יה as a specifically exclamative
particle: אנת יה ברי הכצר כל כציר 'You, o my son, harvest every
harvest!' C1.1:127; אנת יה ברי זף דננא 'You, o my son, borrow
grain!' ib.129†. In neither case does the particle occupy the initial
slot.

b) A word or phrase that functions as a form of address
does not normally occupy the initial slot in an utterance: הן צבה
אנת ברי זי תהוה ... 'if you desire, o my son, that you be ..' C1.1:149;
הן אמחאנך ברי לא תמות 'if I hit you, o my son, you will not die'
ib.177. In both cases, moreover, the addressing form follows
immediately an element (אנת; ־ך) which is referred to by the
former. Other examples of the vocative, all names, are: [ת]חי
אחיקר אבוה זי אתור כלה 'May you survive, O Ahiqar, the father of
the whole of Assyria' C1.1:55([1251]); אמר לן נבוסמסכן רביא 'Tell us,

---

[1249] Folmer (1997:147-49) believes that a few more examples of this kind,
notably B2.2:7, can be found in our corpus. To make אנה refer to Dargamana,
when he is supposedly reporting what Mahseiah swore is difficult, and the
former is renouncing his claim on the disputed piece of land. הא is perhaps an
error for הי, coming immediately before אנה. Then one would obtain זילי הי
אנה, a perfectly idiomatic utterance for emphatically claiming ownership: see
above at § 39 *e*, (vi).

[1250] See § 24 *p*.

[1251] The first word may be restored as יחי. Then it would be a plain optative:

O Nabusumiskun the young man!' ib.58; הקימני אל בצדיק עמך 'Establish me, O El, as a righteous (one) with you!' ib.109.

c) An exceptional case with the vocative in the initial slot is: ברןי] אל תל[ו]ט יומא 'O my son, do not curse the day!' C1.1:80.

d) In some cases it is difficult to tell vocative from apposition: e.g. יהבת לכי תמת 'I gave you, Tamet' or '.. O Tamet' B3.5:6. The legal parlance would probably suggest apposition.

e) Our idiom has at its disposal a rich variety of presentatives in comparison with Contemporary English and the difference in nuance between them eludes us: הלו, הא, ארה.([1252]) Their function is to draw the hearer's or reader's attention to a message about to be communicated. Thus their natural position is clause-initial, as is clearly seen in that they often follow the clause-introducing כען, כעת or כענת:כענת בשמה 'and now, see, you haven't sent a (single) letter about him' A2.3:5; כען הא אתין תמה וכעת ארה ספר לה שלחתי 'now, see, they are coming there to you' A4.3:5; כענת הא עליכם 'now, see, I shall dispatch the legumes tomorrow' בקלא אושר מחר D7.16:1; חזית 1 כען הלו חלם 'now, look, I saw a dream' D7.17:1. See also A2.2:4, A2.3:8, A4.2:7, A6.9:2; D7.1:2, D7.8:2, D7.20:6, D7.24:1,3.

The conventional translation of these particles with "lo," "behold" or "verily" is stylistically unsuitable: their use is not confined to the lofty, elevated style or officialese, as is demonstrated by the homely, familiar tone of the Hermopolis letters and other similar documents.

That as presentatives these words do not substantially contribute to the contents or substance of a message, but play nonetheless an important communicative role is indicated by the fact that they never constitute an utterance on their own and that, in the manner of Fr. *voila*, they may be followed by a plain noun phrase: e.g., הא שמהת גבריא זי אשתכחו בבבא 'see, the names of the men who were found at the gate' A4.4:6.([1253])

f) חזי may look like a presentative, but it is, in reality, an ordinary verb often followed by an object: e.g., הא אנת חזי אגרת חזי ...ארשם 'Behold, you, regard the letter of Arsham' A6.15:3; על עלימא 'Look after the servants' A3.5:6; inflected in the pl.—כענת־ חזו חנתא זי יהב לי אוריה 'Now, regard the gift (?), which Uriah gave me' D7.9:1.

'May A. .. survive!'

[1252] Cf. Brown 1987.

[1253] On this type of nominal clause, see § 77 *bh*.

§ 87. Prepositions

Without touching on purely lexicographical matters, we make the following observations concerning prepositions:

a) ב *essentiae*([1254])

This preposition sometimes occurs prefixed to an NP, which, in relation to a preceding NP, can be perceived as a predicate of an equational nominal clause. E.g. הקימני אל בצדיק עמך 'Establish me, O El, as a righteous (one) with you!' C1.1:109 where there is a nominal clause underlying between the pronominal object in הקימני and בצדיק, i.e. בצדיק אנה; בצדיק יסגה בעדרה למה אלהיא 'lest the god([1255]) should proceed as his help' ib.126; בפקד[ן] [הפקדו 'one placed (them) as deposit' B2.9:7; יהיב במכלא 'was given as the food' C3.14:34; מטאך בחלק 'came to you as a portion' B2.11:3,7,9,10,12; באגר יהבת לה 'I gave him as payment' B8.5:15.

b) בין 'between'([1256])

An object situated between two other objects may be indicated by repeating the preposition prefixed with the conjunction Waw as in בין תמת ובין ענני 'between Tamet and Anani' B3.3:12 // בין ענני ותמת ib.11, sim. B3.7:11. Where one of the objects is expressed as a pronoun, the repetition is inevitable: ביני ובין מריה 'between me and its owner' A3.10:2; בינין ובין בית פפטעוניח 'between us and the house of Peftuauneith' B2.1:13.

c) Quite often the preposition בגו stands on its own, its complement understood from the context: הירא זילך זי קבלת עלי בגו '(?) of yours about which you complained against me' B3.2:3, sim. ib.5,7; טב לבבך בגו 'your heart was satisfied about it' B2.6:5, sim. ib.15, B2.9:9, B3.8:5, B3.12:6, B4.4:9; ז[ך] אשתבק בגו 'th[at] was abandoned therein' A6.11:2; תב בגו 'Dwell herein' B2.4:6. This is the norm where it precedes a list of witnesses to an official document as in שהדיא בגו מנחם ... 'The witnesses hereto: Menahem ..' B2.11:15 et passim.

d) Likewise עלא. E.g., הן רשינך דינא עלא 'if we bring (suit) against you about it' B2.11:9, sim. B2.9:14; ספר כתב לי עלא 'he

---

[1254] Cf. Joüon 1934:31f. For a similar phenomenon in BH, cf. Joüon - Muraoka 1993: § 133 *c*.

[1255] Assuming אלהיא as an error for אלהא.

[1256] Cf. Haneman 1975 and Muraoka (forthcoming).

Although our idiom uses בין with a referent in the plural inclusively—e.g., שוק מלכא ביניהן 'King Street is between them' B3.12:19,21, the context indicates that בינין at B2.1:14 cannot mean "between us" in the sense of "between you and me" (*pace* Grelot 1972:173—"entre nous"). It must be an error for בינין ופפטעוניח, which in turn is elliptical for בין בתין ובין בית פפטעוניח.

wrote a document for me about it' B2.7:3, sim.ib.10, B2.9:14.

e) A preposition may be elided from a phrase prefixed with the preposition of similarity, כ: e.g. זך פתפא הב לה ולנשי ביתה כאחרנן 'As for that one, give him and his household personnel the ration as (to) others' A6.12:1 (= כלאאחרנן).([1257])

Another case of similar ellipsis, also involving comparison, is ... מן גבר ... צדקה יהוה לך 'it will be counted as a merit for you ... than for any (other) person who ...' A4.7:27.

f) Some authorities admit an "emphatic"(read: "asseverative") particle -כ or "Kaf veritatis": e.g. מלך כרחמן 'a king is indeed merciful' C1.1:91([1258]). There is no compelling reason for postulating such a Kaph in כעשק עביד לי 'something of an injustice was done to me' A5.2:5,9.([1259]) Whatever its origin, the phrase כחסן 'forcefully' does not belong here: כחסן אתו על ביתא זילי 'they came to my house by force' B8.4:4; נכסן מן ביתך כחסן לא לקחת.([1260])

g) On the so-called centripetal Lamed, see above at § 74 p.

§ 88. זי clauses([1261])

In addition to its function as relative pronoun and a conjunction introducing a) a subject or b) object clause, the ubiquitous זי displays (c-f) a rich variety of other uses.

a) ידיע זי חנום הו עלין 'it is known that Khnum is against us' A4.3:7; איתי זי בפקדן [הפקדו] 'it is the case that they were placed on deposit' B2.9:7.([1262])

b) תדען זי מדעם לה מפקן לן 'you should know that nothing is

[1257] For a similar phenomenon in BH, see Brown - Driver - Briggs 1907:455a. Alternatively, in the last example, להן introduces, as an adversative conjunction, the following cleft sentence: 'but it is your sons ... that have right to it.'

[1258] So Porten - Yardeni (1993:37) as an alternative translation. So Vogt (1971:79): "rex est (vere) misericors." Vogt's examples, however, are quite diverse, including such as כְּבַר שְׁנִין שִׁתִּין וְתַרְתֵּין "(iam) filius 62 annorum.'

[1259] On the whole question of the "emphatic" Kaph, see Muraoka 1985:158-64 and Joüon - Muraoka 1993: § 164 b.

[1260] Originally the phrase may have meant "in the manner of a violent man."

[1261] For details, cf. Hoftijzer - Jongeling 1995:310-18.

[1262] On this affirmative/asseverative force of זי איתי, first recognised by Staerk (1907:30), see also Muraoka 1985:77-81. An example in BA is Ezr 5.17 .. הֵן אִיתַי דִּי־מִן־כּוֹרֶשׁ מַלְכָּא שִׂים טְעֵם 'if it is really so that an order was issued by Cyrus the king ..' Porten - Yardeni's (1989:43) translation "There are (these goods) which were placed on depos[it]" is forced, for an antecedentless relative clause usually has an indefinite antecedent.

brought to us' A2.5:2; [הן צבה אנת ברי זי תהוה] 'if you, O my son, desire to be ..' C1.1:149.

c) A preposition, which, by definition, is followed by a noun phrase or its equivalent, may be combined with זי when its complement is cast in the form of a clause. Thus מן זי נפקת 'from (the time) that you left, since you left' A2.5:3; מן זי חנניה במצרין 'since Hananiah has been in Egypt' A4.3:7; אמר [... עלזי פסמשך] 'concerning the fact that Psamshe[k] said' A6.8:6; אל תמלי לבח<י> בזי לא איתית המו 'Don't be angry [with me] because I didn't bring them' A3.3:10[1263]; על זי החיתך 'on account (of the fact) that I spared you' C1.1:51; בזי מצריא שחד להן יהבן 'because the Egyptians give them a bribe' A4.2:4, sim. A4.2:7, A4.7:23, A5.1:2, A6.11:2; לקבל זי קדמן פמון אבוהי הוה חשל 'in accordance with (the way) that Pamun his father formerly used to pay' A6.11:6; לקבל זי ידכם מהשכחה הבו לה 'Give him as much as you can' A4.3:9; "I .. gave it to Jehoishma .. because she supported me (לקבל זי סבלתני)' B3.10:17; קבל זי לא כתב על ספר אנתתכי 'since it is not written in your document of wifehood' B3.11:7; בר מן זי אנת תתרך לאמה 'unless you evict his mother' B3.3:14.

The most frequently occurring combination is כד/כזי with a range of nuances[1264]: *temporal*—כזי עדן יהוה 'when it will be time' B2.11:13; כתבת אגרתא זא כזי כן שמיע לן 'I wrote this letter when we had heard thus' A3.3:13; כזי חזית ... ענית 'when I saw .. I answered' C1.1:14; *modal*—כן כזי פקידיא [קד]מיא הוו עבדן 'in such a way that the former officials used to do' A6.10:7[1265]; כזי הוה לקדמן 'as it was formerly' A4.9:8; לא נסבלנך כזי יסבל בר לאבוהי 'we shall not support you as a son would support his father' B3.6:13; *final*—אנתם קמו קבלהם כן כזי מלה באישה לא ישהכחון לכם 'You, stand by them so that they shall not find a bad thing about you' A4.3:6; יתשם טעם כזי איש מנדעם באיש לא יעבד ... 'Let an order be issued so that one does not do any bad thing ..' A6.7:8, also A6.13:2[1266]; *resultative*—"Samshek .. strictly guarded our domestic staff .. so that there was not any decrease from my

---

[1263] The emendation is virtually certain in view of the idiom attested elsewhere, always with a conjunctive pronoun (מלתי לבחי 'you were angry with me' A2.3:6; הוית מלא לבחך 'I was angry with you' A3.5:4; מלין לבחכם 'they are angry with you' A4.2:11), הא לבחי מלא 'he is angry against me' (Ashur letter, line 20), and the Akkadian prototype as in *ma:diš libba:tiya mali* 'he was very angry with me' (CAD L, 164a). Cf. Appendix III.

[1264] Comparable to Gk. ὡς.

[1265] כזי קדמן 'as previously' A6.7:9 is probably elliptical.

[1266] Not an object clause, *pace* Fitzmyer 1956:228.

estate (כזי מנדעם כסנתו לא הוה מן ביתא זילי)" A6.10:2([1267]); "there is a well .. which does not lack water .. so that whenver they would be garrisoned, they drink the water in that well (כזי הן הנדיז יהוון כזי בכל אתר ע]תין[הם]ו[ך מיא שתין (בברא" A4.5:7; possibly *causal*—ואדניהם 'because their eyes and ears are everywhere' C1.1:81([1268]); *quantitative*—כדי תכלן תעבדן לה 'as much as you can do for him (I am doing for him)' A2.3:4; *noun clause (object)*—כן שמיע לי־ למומא ... כזי 'I have thus heard that ..' A6.10:3; כזי לא הות ארק לדרגמן 'to swear .. that it had never been a plot (of land) of Dargamana' B2.2:6; ימאת לה כזי זילי הי 'I swore to him that it was mine' B2.3:24, probably also B6.4:7.

d) עד 'till' is unique in that it can also serve on its own as a conjunction: עד שזבוני 'until they rescued me' A4.3:5, עד אנה קטלת 'until I killed' C2.1:74([1269]), עד תחזה 'until you see' C1.1:80, עד יבנון 'until they build' C1.2:20, עד תתמלא בכספך 'until you are fully repaid your silver' B3.1:11,17, // עד כען 'till now' A4.3:7; ועד מותך 'till your death' B3.6:12.

והצפנתך מנה ... עד זי לעדן אן]חרן וליומן אחרן שניאן קרבתך But in ... 'and I hid you from him ... until some time later and some many days later I presented you ...' C1.1:49 and הן כן עבדו עד זי אגורא זך יתבנה 'if they did thus until this temple is rebuilt' A4.7:27 we have a compound form. In the revised version of the latter we have the compound in the reverse order: [זי עד אגורא זך יתב]נה[A4.8:26. This latter sequence is attested in זי עד מנדת בניא אלך יהנפק ויהיתה 'in order that he release the rent(?) of those domains and bring' A6.13:3, sim. ib.4, which, however, is simplified in עד מנדת] בניא אלך יהי]תה עלי 'in order that he bring the rent(?) of those domains to me' A6.14:3.([1270])

[1267] At ib.6 we find an almost identical version with the only difference that הוה is replaced by יהוה, which points to a close logical connection between purpose and result.

[1268] The context is difficult of interpretation: see Lindenberger 1983:73.

[1269] Not "while": the Akk. *adi muḫḫi .. addu:ku* (109f.) with a pf. can only mean 'when I killed.'

[1270] In connection with עד זי at A6.13:3,4 Driver (1957:76) cites Akk. *ki: adi*, an asseverative particle with verbs of oath, as the source of the Aramaic expression. But no such specific nuance fits any of our examples, though such an Akkadian calque did survive in QA, on which see Muraoka 1972:38f. עד זי in A4.7:27 and זי עד in A4.8:26 can be also translated as "in order that": on the semantic link between the notion of "until" and purpose, cf. Arb. *ḥatta:*, which attests to the same semantic range. The sense "until" is not in dispute in עד זי ... קרבתך 'until I .. presented you' C1.1:49. *Pace* Fitzmyer (1956:230) the phrase עד זי hardly introduces an object clause in these passages.

e) זי preceded by an interrogative turned into a generalising relative pronoun has already been discussed above (§§ 42 *e*, 43) such as מה זי תעבדון 'whatever you do' A4.3:8. We would here add only אן זי in אן זי צבית 'wherever she desires' B2.6:25,29 and איך זי in הודע איך זי עביד אנת 'make known how you are' C2.1:66.

f) זי followed by a pc. may be final in force, "in order that": זף דגנא וחנטתא זי תאכל ותשבע 'Borrow the grain and the wheat so that you may eat (it) and be sated!' C1.1:129, though we may have here a slightly nuanced relative clause.([1271]) See § 52 *f*.

§ 89. Conjunctions other than זי and זי compounds

a) או 'or'

This can join a) single words, b) phrases or c) clauses. Examples are: a) מחר או יום חמר או שכר 'wine or beer' A6.9:3; אחרן 'tomorrow or another day' B2.1:6 *et passim*; b) יכלא למחסה בכסף או או לבר לה 'to restrain Mahsah or a son of his' B2.1:9; רחמת 'for silver or affectionately' B3.12:26; c) הן רשינך ... או נרשה 'should we bring (suit) against you ... or should we לבר וברה לך bring (suit) against a son or daughter of you' B2.11:9.

More than two components may be concatenated: ינתן לכם או לבניכם או למן זי ירשון אביגרנא 'he shall give you or your sons or אחתבסתי whomever they bring (suit) against the penalty' B2.9:14; או אחוהי או ברה ... 'Ahatubasti .. or his brother or his son' A6.14:4.

See above on coordination: §81 *a, ed*.

b) הן 'if': see § 84.

c) ו- 'and'

This can join a) single words, b) phrases or c) clauses. Examples are: a) שמיא וארקא נקיה וגזתה 'heaven and earth' A1.1:2; 'a lamb and its wool' A2.2:8; שלם וחין 'welfare and life' A2.4:5; לי ולמכבנת ספר חכים ומהיר 'a wise and skilful scribe' C1.1:1; b) הוי חזית על תשי ועל ברה 'about me and about Makkibanit' A2.1:8; 'Do look after Tashai and after her son!' A2.3:11; c) ואנה נכתני חויה והות מית ולה שלחתן הן חי אנה והן מת אנה 'and as for me, the snake had bitten me and I was dying and you did not send (to inquire) if I was alive or if I was dead' A2.5:8; נדן שמה ברי רבא והו יחלף לי 'Nadin by name, my son, has grown up and he will succeed me' C1.1:18.

ca) This proclitic conjunction can concatenate more than two components: נכי ועשה ותשי וענתי ואטי ורע '*Nky* and Ashah and Tashai and Anathi and Ati and Re(ia)' A2.1:3. See on coordination:

[1271] Fitzmyer 1956:71.

§ 81 *ed.*

cb) The combination וכעת is used in two distinct ways, and frequently. On the one hand, in official correspondence, especially in the Arsames archive, the phrase follows the opening address and introduces the main body of the correspondence: "From PN to PN and PN and his colleagues. And now, I complained here .. (... וכעת תצה אזה קבלת)" A6.14:1; so also A6.1:1, A6.2:1, A6.7:1[1272], A6.8:1, A6.9:1, A6.10:1, A6.11:1, A6.12:1, A6.13:1, A6.15:1, A6.16:1. Some of these letters also use כעת, without the conjunction, later in the body of them, in order to mark the beginning of a new thought unit: e.g. A6.1:3, A6.2:22, A6.3:6, A6.6:4, A6.8:2, A6.11:3, A6.13:4, A6.14:2, A6.15:3, 6,9. At A6.3:5, 6.7:8 and A6.10:5 כען occurs instead, and at A6.10:3 וכען. On the other hand, all Hermopolis letters, with the exception of A2.7[1273], are very liberally laced with כעת at every turn: in A2.1, a letter of 15 lines, for instance, one counts as many as five instances of it, and in A2.3 (14 lines) we find eight occurrences (once without the Waw, line 6). This is probably a popularisation of the officialese.

cc) The conjunction Waw is commonly found in contracts in enumerating various possibilities and options, where "or" may be a better rendering: e.g., לא יכהל בר וברה אח ואחה קריב ורחיק בעל דגל וקריה יכלא ... 'son or daughter, brother or sister, near or far, member of a detachment or town shall not be able to restrain ..' B2.1:8; ספר חדת ועתיק 'a new or old document' B2.3:16; לא שליט אנת לזבנה ולמנתן 'you have no right to sell (it) or to give (it)' B2.4:6; בר דכר ונקבה 'a child male or female' B2.6:20; בשמי ובשם בני 'in my name or in the name of my children' B2.10:13; וביתא זילך ודי בניך ודי תנתן לה רחמת 'and the house is yours or of your children's or of one to whom you give (it) affectionately' B3.12:30. Cp. הן מחר או יום אחרן דרגמן או בר זילה ירשה 'if tomorrow or the next day Dargamana or son of his bring (suit)' B2.3:26.

cd) The conjunction Waw is sometimes used to add a parenthetical thought or afterthought: e.g., זבנת משח זית ליקה וכתן 'I bought olive oil for Jake, and also a tunic' A2.2:11. The particle אף reinforces this nuance: the example just quoted is followed by: ואף לכי תקבת 1 שפרת ואף משח בשם לבת בנת 'and also for you a

---

[1272] The author, after having written "And now, here it is well with me; also there may it be well with you," apparently realised that this is really part of the greeting, so that he introduces the real business with another וכעת (line 2).

[1273] Note that וכען, not וכעת, introduces the main body of this short letter, written by a scribe other than one(s) who wrote the rest of the corpus.

pretty vessel, and also scented oil for the Temple of Banit' ib.11.

ce) It is not certain that ־ו .. ו־ can be used with the force of "both .. and": ותפמת ואחתסן מסבלן לה 'Both Tapamet and Ahatsin are supporting him' A2.3:5.([1274]) See, however, אף לחם אף קמח הב[י] לה 'Give him both bread and flour' D7.1:13.

§ 90. Some particles

a) אף (ca. 112x)

The basic meaning of this highly frequent particle is that of addition. When that which is to be added relates to a statement as a whole, it occupies the initial slot in an utterance: "moreover, what is more."([1275]) That this additive function does not relate in such cases to the immediately following word or phrase is evident in a case such as אף אחרנן בע/[ן] מן אתר אחרן ומהוס[פן ע]ל בית מראיהם 'moreover, they are seeking others from another place and adding to the house of their masters' A6.10:4, for basically the same idea is repeated in אף מן אתר אחרן ib.2.([1276]) Nor can the particle be construed with איתי in אף איתי ספר מרחק 1 ... 'moreover, there is a document of withdrawal ..' B2.3:23, sim. B2.11:12 nor with the presentative הא 'behold' A6.14:4, B2.2:7, B2.7:13. In a case such as אף אנה יהבת לה B3.10:17 a translation "I too, i.e. not only someone else, gave (it) to her" is clearly precluded by the context. The only word that can precede אף is כען as in כען אף קדמן שלחת ... 'Now, moreover, I have sent (word) previously ..' A6.10:5.

When אף relates only to part of an utterance, it immediately precedes that part. It may appear in the middle of a clause where appropriate. Thus אף must be construed with אמך in a highly elliptical אף אמך ("Since the day that you went on that way, my heart has not been glad. Likewise, your mohter") A3.3:2. This is true when the particle is repeated: אף לחם אף קמח הב[י] לה 'Give him both bread and flour' D7.1:13. So also with an adverb: "here it is well with me. Also there may it be well with you (אף תמה וכעת זבנת משח זית ליקה וכתן ואף קדמ[י]ך שלם יהוי)" A6.7:2. See also לכי תקבת 1 שפרת ואף משח בשם לבת בנת 'and now, I bought olive oil

---

[1274] So Porten - Yardeni ad loc., though the first conjunction can mark loose connection with the preceding.

[1275] *Pace* Greenfield - Porten (1982:48f.) this must apply to C2.1:68.

[1276] Thus, *pace* Joüon (1934:22), אף in אף יהכון בדין ולא יצדקון 'Moreover, they might go to law, but they would not win' B3.1:19 is not strictly a conditional particle: it retains its basic additive force—even if one went that far, ...

and a tunic for Yake, and also a pretty vessel for you, and also perfumed oil for the Temple of Banit' A2.2:11. One notes that all these examples of אף, with only one exception(A6.7:2), relating to the immediately following NP, occur in private letters.

b) אפם (17x)([1277])

Just like its synonym תוב at תוב זילכי מנתכי 'your share is furthermore yours' B5.1:7([1278]), אפם, which is no doubt derived from אף, appears to have the basic meaning of addition, as can be seen from "Anani .. a Jew of the detachment of Nabukudurri, said to Pakhnum .. an Aramaean of Syene of that detachment also (לדגלא זך אפם)" B3.13:2; חת אפם השכחת לא והן 'and if you do not find (any), still come down!' A3.8:8. This particle, with only one exception, as well as אם dealt with below, occur always in the same position in legal documents: A certain agreement is reached, and then a clause providing for a penalty in case of contravention of terms of the agreement is inserted, which is rounded off by a statement to the effect that the agreed terms are אם/אפם in force. The intent is most likely to confirm that the agreement is "still" valid despite the breach. For example, ברי יהוה אפם 'he shall still be my son' B3.9:8 forcefully restates the freedom to be conferred on Jedaniah ("he shall be my son", ib.5, repeated ib.9). Noteworthy is that אפם, just like אם, may occupy the end position in a clause: in addition to the above quoted B3.9:8, see אפם ביתכי ביתא 'the house is still your house' B2.3:15,22; אגרא זילך אפם 'the wall is still yours' B2.1:10; אפם <זילך> זך אגרא 'that wall is still yours' ib.7; אפם זילהם ביתי 'my house is still theirs' B3.5:22.([1279])

Like אם, also אפם may be found between the subject and the predicate of a nominal clause: זילך אפם זך ארקא 'that land is still yours' B2.2:15; זילכי אפם ביתא 'the house is still yours' B3.5:16; זילכם אפם ביתא 'the house is still yours' B2.10:16; מן רחיק אפם והו 'and he is still withdrawn from these possessions' נכסיא אלה B2.9:15.

אפם always([1280]) appears in an equational nominal clause, so that זילך אפם זך ארקא B2.2:15, for instance, irrespective of the context, cannot mean "that land of yours still," though the reverse

---

[1277] Cf. Yaron 1961:88.

[1278] See Skaist 1983:34.

[1279] The same scribe shows a variation: זילכי אפם ביתא 'the house is still yours' ib.16.

[1280] Two exceptions are to be found at B5.5:6 and A3.8:8.

is not necessarily true, for זילך זך ארקא could mean that.([1281])

c) אם (7x)

On the sense of this particle, see above under אפם. It does not occupy the initial slot in a clause, but in two instances it stands at the end of one: ביתא זילך אם 'the house is still yours' B3.4:16,19. Thrice it stands between the preceding subject and the following adjectival predicate: ואנתי יהוישמע אם שליטא 'and you, Jehoishma, still have right' B3.10:20; ואנתי אם שליטה בביתא זנה 'and you still have right to this house' B3.11:11,14; also in the middle of a nominal clause—דילכי אם <א>ביתא<וב 'and (the) house is still yours' B2.7:11. Only once in a verbal clause, and this happens to be the sole exception where the above definition of the particle and אפם does not apply, but it rather seems to be asseverative in force: ונכסיא זי לקחו אתהבו אם על מריהם 'and the possessions which they had taken they certainly returned to their owners' A4.4:8. This exception suggests that both particles of ours may be interpreted as asseverative particles in all their occurrences in our legal corpus, for the statement containing them invariably reiterates and reinforces the main tenet of the document in question.([1282])

As regards the relationship between these two synonymous particles, it appears that they are variants of scribal style: אם is used only by Haggai (B2.7, B3.4, B3.10, B3.11) and אפם by, all the other scribes, namely Pelatiah (B2.1), Itu (B2.2), Attarshuri (B2.3), Mauziah (B2.9, B2.10, B3.5), Raukhshana (B3.9), Shaweram (B3.13).([1283]) Both are spread over a similar chronological range.

d) כי (12x)

With two exceptions (A1.1:6*bis*) all occurrences of this particle are confined to the proverbs of Ahiqar. The largely fragmentary nature of this text often makes it difficult to capture the precise meaning of the particle. In most cases it appears to indicate a logical reason or ground for the preceding statement: e.g. "[A person w]ho does not exalt in the name of his father and in the name of his mother, may (the) su[n] not shine [for him] for he is a bad person (כי גבר לחה הו)" C1.1:138; "A little man, when he becomes big, his words soar (?) above him, for the opening of his mouth is an utterance of god[s] (כי מפתח פמה מענה אלה[ן])" ib.162. Some authorities, however, hold that כי is sometimes

---

[1281] See above, § 59 *d*.

[1282] An alternative interpretation mentioned by Porten - Szubin 1987:187.

[1283] See also Porten 1984: 396.

"emphatic."([1284])

e) לם (49x)([1285])

In so far as the context is available, the particle appears to be mostly confined to direct speech: e.g., ולא אכל אמר לך לם שלמתך בכספך 'and I shall not be able to say to you, "I repaid you your silver .."' B3.1:11; ... ישתלח לם אשרנא זנה יתיהב 'Let (word) be sent, "These materials are to be given .."'A6.2:21; סנ]יא שדר [לרמנ]א [לם סניא לרמא ... 'A bramble sent (a letter) to a pomegranate: "(From) the bramble to the pomegranate .."' C1.1:101; ... לם אזלו 'Go ..' C2.1:53; ... אנה [שלח]ת לכם לם אל תהושרו 'I sent (word) to you: "Don't dispatch .."' D7.44:2. See also C1.1:20; A4.7:6, A4.8:5, A4.9:2; B3.1:11,13; D7.20:8, D7.29:4, D7.48:8.

The particle may also appear after the initial word or phrase of a direct speech: e.g. ... מספת שלח גרדא לם זי מראתי כתש 'Masapta sent (word), "He has assaulted the domestic staff of my lady .."' A6.15:8; [ו]אמר ברא לם יהוה לי 'and he said, "he shall be my son"' C1.1:2; ... לן ש[י]ם טעם מנחא לם זי יהבה 'an order was i[ss]ued to us, "The share which is given .."' A6.1:2; הן על מראי לם כות טב 'If it thus please my lord' A6.13:2; ... דחלת לם אחיקר ענית 'I, Ahiqar, feared, answered ..' C1.1:45; ... אנה לם אמרת 'I said ...' D23.1 II: 12. See also ib. 54 (at the end of a clause),58,60 (possibly between two clauses); A6.2:2; A6.13:1 (after an antecedent of a relative clause); A6.15:5 (ditto); ib.1 (after a clause-initial adverbial adjunct).

In two instances in the Ahiqar narrative, לם may not seem to have much to do with direct speech in the strict sense: וסגדת ... אחיקר לם 'and I Ahikar prostrated ..' C1.1:13, and the above-quoted ib.45. It ought to be remembered, however, that the Ahiqar narrative is presented as the hero's monologue. Some authorities view the particle as somewhat emphatic. For instance, at C1.1:45: Cowley (1923:221)—"I, Ahikar, indeed was afraid"([1286]).

[1284] So Kottsieper (1990:209)—"zur Einführung eines betonten Abschluß-satzes »Ja!«"; Lindenberger (1983:70)—"the 'emphatic' kî"; Hoftijzer - Jongeling (1995:497)—"verily, surely." Such a claim, however, is difficult to substantiate. See further Muraoka 1985:158-64 and Joüon - Muraoka 1993: § 164 b.

[1285] The etymological link with Syr. lam is generally recognised. The latter can occur also in the middle of a clause. Kaufman (1977:121f.) has identified a variant form, לאם, a stage earlier than לם, in a mid-seventh century legal document from Assyria, and it possibly occurs at B6.3:8 (broken context).

[1286] Cf. also Hoftijzer - Jongeling (1995:578)—"I, A., indeed was afraid"; Porten - Yardeni 31—"I was afraid, indeed (I) Ahiqar" (the Hebrew translation indicates uncertainty: לאמר/אכן). See also Cowley 1923:220: "Surely he shall be a son to me" (C1.1:2); Grelot 1972:433, n. *b* "Litt. : «Certes il sera pour moi *le* fils»."

APPENDICES

INDEX OF PASSAGES

INDEX   OF   SUBJECTS

Biblical Aramaic [See also
Dn and Ezr in Index of
passages]

Jewish Aramaic, including
    Targumic and Qumran
    Aramaic

Classical Syriac

z‘ora:’ § 6d, n.
ḥaqla:’ § 18v, n.
ḥre:ṭa:’ § 18j, n.
ṭla:la:’ 9, n.
yammin § 6a, n.
liqa:’ §18b, n.
ketta:na:’ § 6b, n.
kytwnʾ § 6b, n.
kuttina:’ § 6b, n.
lam § 90e, n.
ma:rya:’ § 3o, n.
mna:ṭa:’ § 18n, n.
nahra:’ § 18w, n.
naḥḥeṭ § 25, n.
sa:’’ § 18v, n.
sa’ṭa:’ § 18v, n.
saggi’ § 67e, n.
‘uvra:’ § 6b, n.
‘ella:way § 20c, n.
pṭa:ya:’ § 18r, 1
ṣydn § 6d, n.
qallil § 67e, n.
ša:ruṭa:’ § 18r, n.
taḥla:

Hebrew
דַּמֶּשֶׂק § 3c
דַּרְמֶשֶׂק § 3c
הִבְטִיחַ § 3g
הֶסְבִּר § 3g
יָמִים § 8b, n.
יְמָנִי § 6a, n.
יֵשׁ § 77bj, n.
כְּאֶחָד § 22a, n.
כִּסֵּא § 3c
סְאָה § 18v, n.
סוּס § 18r, n.

Akkadian
ana § 74d, n.

arad ekalli § 6d, n.
attu § 40, n.
ekurru § 6b, g, n.
ešrû § 18r, n.
ete:qu § 3f, n. 83
be:l ṭa:bti § 61c, (xix), n.
gugalu § 6g, n. 165
igirtu § 18j, n.
kandu § 3c
ki: adi §88d, n.
kina:tu § 18w
kussû § 3c
mala § 10e, n.
manḥalu § 3d, n. 77
maqlu:tu § 18r, n.
niše: bi:ti § 3k, n. 105
sebû § 18r, n.
sin-aḥḥe:-eri:ba § 2b
su:tu § 18v, n.
pi:ḥa:tu § 18n, n.
ṣa:bitu § 6g
šinṭu § 46o, n.
šiqlu § 2c
tišû § 18r, n.

Arabic
‘uṣfu:r § 3c, n. 65
ḍila‘ § 2d
ka:na § 18j, n.
min § 42d, n.
nataša § 2b, n. 23
nadasa § 2b, n. 23
yaman § 6a, n. 150
yami:n § 6a, n. 150

Classical Ethiopic
yama:n § 6a, n. 150
ṣela:lo:t § 9, n. 187

Ugaritic
bwtm, btm, bhtm § 18y, n.

Greek
εὐθύς § 78cp, n.
Κίλιξ § 6g, n. 165
ὅτι § 53b, n.
πίναξ § 19K
συγχέω § 49g, n.
χιτών § 6b, n.
ὡς § 88c, n.

Hittite
ḫanza § 3j

Luvian
ḫant(a) § 3j

Persian
nifriti § 18j, n.

TABLES OF LOAN-WORDS

OLD PERSIAN

	Aramaic	Old Persian	OP source	Translation	Source
1	אבנגרן אביגרן אבגרנא אביגרנא	*abigarana-	Hinz 18	penalty	B2.9:14,10:15,11:10; 3.8:31, 9:7; 13.7; 5.5:6;
2	אבשוכן	*abišavaka-	Shaked (but cf. Hinz 18)	pressers	A6.7:5
3	אדונא	*advan-	Hinz 23	route	A6.9:5
4	אדרנג אדרנגי א]ררנ[ניכי	*ādranga-	Hinz 22-3	guarantor	B3.10:18, 11:12, 12:27
5	אודיס	*avadaisa-	Hinz 51	statement	A4.10:12
6	אופכרתא אופכרתה	*upakrta-	Hinz 243-44	reckoning	A6.2:5; C3.8IIIB:24
7	אופסתה	*upasta-	TAD C 244	upasta-(land)	C3.21:4,9
8	אופשר אופשרה	*upačara-	Hinz 243	needs (?)	A6.2:3,6,9,22
9	אזד	*azdā-	Hinz 52	known (pass. ptc.)	A4.5:8
10	אזדכרא אזדכרי"א	*azdākara-	Hinz 52	herald	A6.1:5,7
11	אזת	*āzāta	Hinz 52	free	B3.6:4
12	אימנש	*ayaumaniš-	Sims-Williams BSOAS 1981:6	remiss	C2.1:69
13	אספרן	*asprna-	Hinz 46	in full	A6.13:4
14	אפיתי	*upaiti-	EPE 117, Shaked	necessary	A6.2:9
15	ארדב	*rdβa	Hinz 204	ardab (= 3 seah)	B4.3:8
16	אשרן אשרנא	*āčarna-	Hinz 21	material	A4.5:18,7:11;6.2:5; 3.4:23
17	אתרודן	*ātrvaδana-	Hinz 49	brazier	A4.5:7
18	בג בגא בגה בגיא	*bāga-	Hinz 53	domain/ property	A6.4:2, 11:5, 13:1, C3.6:8

19	בדיכר	*badikar-	Hinz 64	artisan	A6.12:2
20	ברזמדנא	*brazmadāna-	Hinz 67	temple	D17.1:1
21	גושכיא	*gaušaka-	Hinz 105	informer ("hearer")	A4.5:9
22	גנזא	*ganza-	Hinz 102	treasure	A6.2:4+
23	גסח (פתגם)	*gasta- (patigāma)	Hinz 103	harsh (word), evil	A6.7:5, 8:13, 10:9
24	גרדא	*gṛda-	Hinz 107	domestic staff	A6.10:1-2,4-6,8,10:2, 12:2, 15:8-10
24a	גרד אמנן וספזן שפיק		Hinz 107	staff of craftsmen of every kind in sufficient (number)	A6.10:2-3, 6-7
25	(גריו=) ;	*grīβa-	Hinz 108 (but 1/3 ardab ≠ Aram.גרב)		B4.4:7
26	דושון	*duš-van-	Shaked (orally)	ill-willed	B8.4:2
27	דושכרת	*duškṛta-	Hinz 90; Berger 43	crime	A4.5:3
28	דרות	*druvatāt-	Shaked (orally)	peace	D17.1:5
29	דשנא	*dāšna-	Hinz 84	grant	A6.4:1-6
30	הדאבגו	*hada-abigvā-	Hinz 109	accrued increment	A6.13:5
31	המוניח	*ham-au-nitā-	Bogoljubov 73	in agreement	A4.5:4, 7:5
32	המרכריא	*hmārakara-	Hinz 121	accountant	A6.2:4+
33	המכריגרב	*hamakārya-grab-	Segal 16, 207; Shaked	pledge, joint holding	B8.10:5
34	הנבג הנבגא	*hanbāga	Hinz 115	partner in realty	B5.5:9; C3.28:40+
35	הנגית	*hangyθa-	Hinz 116	partner in chattel	B5.5:9+
36	הנדון הנדונה	*handaunā-	Hinz 115-6 Benveniste 302	coating, varnish, paint	A6.2:5, 17
37	הנדיז הנדז	*handizā-	Hinz 116	was garrisoned	A4.5:7; 6.7:6; B2.7:4
38	הנדרז הנדרזא	*handarza-	Hinz 115	order, instruction	A6.13:3-4, 14:3
39	הנפנא	*hanpāna-	Hinz 117	protection	B3.10:9,11:4

40	הפתחפתא	*haftaxvapāta	Hinz 110	guardian of the seventh (part of the world/kingdom)	B3.9:2-3
41	וזיך		Geiger 80b	a vessel	C3.28:107-8
42	וספזן	*vispazana	Berger 54	of every kind	A6.10:3, 7
42a	גרד אמנן וספזן שפיק	*vispazana-	Berger 54	staff of craftsmen of every kind in sufficient (number)	A6.10:2-3, 6-7
43	ורשבר	*xvaršbara-	Hinz 140	plenipotentiary	A6.5:2, 11:1
44	זיני	*zyāni-	Hinz 279	damages	A6.15:8
45	זן	*zana-	Hinz 276	kind, manner	A6.1:3
46	זרניך זרניכא	*zarnyaka-	Hinz 278	arsenic	A6.2:17,21
47	יודן	*yau-dāna-	Shaked	barley-house	A4.5:5
48	יוזא	*yawza-	Hinz 275	revolt, unrest	A6.11:2, 4
49	כסנתו	*kasunaθva-	Hinz 150	diminishment, decrease	A6.9:8, 10:2
50	כרש כרשן	*kr̥ša	Berger 57	a weight	B3.2:8; 5.1:7+
51	מגושא מגושיא	*magu-	Berger 58	Magian	B3.5:24; C2.1:75
52	נופת נופתיא	*nāupati	Hinz 174	shipmaster	A6.2:2, 7-8
53	נפרת	*nipart-	Shaked *Or* 412	litigation(?)	B2.8:3; 8.9:5
54	נשתון	*ništāvana-	Hinz 176	rescript	A6.1:3
55	ספיתכן	*spitakan	cf. Hinz 226	whitener (?)	A6.2:9, 22
56	סראושיתא	*sraušyatā-	Hinz 227	chastisement, punishment	A6.3:6-7
57	פסתרת	*pasča dāti-	*EPE* 243, n.15	after-gift	B3.11:7
58	פריפת	*friya-pati-	*EPE* 248	main beloved; chief of the beloved	B3.12:11
59	פרמנכריא	*framnakara-	Hinz 96-97	foreman	A6.2:4, 8; C3.8IIIB:1
60	פרתר	*fratara-		openly	C2.1:67
61	פרתרך פרתרכא	*frataraka-	Hinz 98	governor, Chief	A4.5:4, 7:5, 8:5; B2.9:4
62	פרתכיא	*frataka-	Hinz 98	the foremost	A5.2:7

63	פתגם‎ פתגמא	*patigāma-	Hinz 186	word	A6.8:3, 10:9; B8.8:2-3, 5; D7.39:8
64	פתיפרס‎ פתיפרסא‎ פתיפרסן	*patifrāsa-	Hinz 186	investigator, interrogator	A4.2:3, 12
65	פתכר	*patikara-	Berger 62	statue, likeness	A6.12:2-3
66	פתכרכר	*patikarakara-	Hinz 187	sculptor	A6.12:1-3
67	פתסתו	*patistāva-	Hinz 188	praiseworthy	A6.16:4
68	פתף‎ פתפא	*piθβa	Hinz 193	rations	A6.9:2,4, 6, 12:1; B3.13:4-5;5.5:7-8, 10; C3.14:38, 41
69	רמי	*ramya	Hinz 198	refined	A6.9:3
70	רסתכה	cf. דִיסְתְּקָא‎ *Berachot* 54a	Geiger 386; Shaked		C3.21:2, 8
71	שויא	?		the troubles	A6.10:4
72	תיפתיא	*tipati	Hinz 236	overseer, supervisor	A4.5:9

EGYPTIAN

	Aramaic	Demotic/ Egyptian	Lexica	Reference	Translation	Source
1	אפסי	ips (perhaps ips.t)		*EPE* 119, n.46	stanchion(s)	A6.2:12
2	גמא	qmȝ, qm	*Wb* V.37,14; *Glossar* 537		reed	B2.6:15; 3.8:17
3	דרי	ḏri.t		*EPE* 121, n.167	wall	A6.2:20
4	דרירסי‎ תרי סרי	tȝry.t rsy.t		*EPE* 238	southern room	B3.10:3, 3.11:3
5	הירא	hyrꜥ		Porten-Szubin 1982	?	B3.2:3-9
6	חלא	ḥry.t(?)		*EPE* 119, n.42	*deck	A6.2:12
7	חסיה	ḥsy	*Glossar* 329		praiseworthy	D20.5:4
8	חתפי	ḥtp.t	*Glossar* 338	Grelot no. 84	offering table	D20.1:1
9	דף	dp	*Wb* V 447, 5	Vittmann *pace* *EPE* 118, n.29	part of ship's mast	A6.2:10, 18

10	מלות	ΜΕΛШΤ *melot,* 'ceiling, canopy'	Crum 165a	Zauzich	board(?)	C3.7Gr.3:25+
11	מנחה	mnḫ.t	Glossar 163		excellent one	D20.6
12	נמעתי	nb mꜣꜥty		Vittmann	Lord of the Two Truths	D20.5:4
13	סי	sy	Glossar 407 Crum 317b	TAD C, xx	beam	C3.7Gr3:24+
14	סעבל	sꜥi-bl		EPE 118, n.36; s ꜥ ꜣ= ship planking (Anastasi IV, 7/11); bl = outside	exterior planking	A6.2:11
15	פחטמוני	pꜣ ḫt-tꜣw-mny.t	Glossar 370; Černý 255	EPE 119, Vittmann	mooring pole	A6.2:12
16	פסחמצנותי	pꜣ sh mdꜣ.tn ṯr		Zauzich, Enchoria 116; Segal	Scribe of the Book of God	B8.12:4
17	פעקס	pꜣꜥgs	Wb I 236, 10	Hoch 84 # 102	(leather) belt	A3.8:9
18	פערער	*pꜣ ꜥrꜥr		EPE 119, n.45	prow; gangplank	A6.2:12
19	פק	ΠΟϬ ϕoke (Coptic)	Crum 286a	Zauzich (orally)	plank	C3.7Jv1:24+
20	קנד/רתעא	qnd/rt ꜥꜣ		TAD C xx	large sea-going vessel (?)	C3.7Gr1:12+
21	קנד/רתשירי	qnd/rt šrr		TAD C xx	small sea-going vessel (?)	C3.7Gr2:22+
22	קנחנתי	qnḫ-ntr	Glossar 541	Couroyer 556	divine shrine	B3.10:9
23	צפעה	*dp-ꜥꜣ	Glossar 677	Zauzich 116	large bowl	D8.10:1
24	רסי	rsy	Glossar 254	EPE 238, n.8	southern	B3.10:3
25	שנבי נחות	šw nby n ꜥḥw.ti	Glossar 448	Quack 15-21	guilty emptiness of farmer (poor harvest caused by negligence)	B1.1:7-8
26	שנמא	šnt ШΝΤШ	Glossar 516	Couroyer 559; Černý 247	linen robe; apron	B3.8:11
27	תחית	tꜣ ḫyt	Glossar 377; Crum 713b	Couroyer 557	courtyard	B3.7:13, 10:4

28	תמי/תמא	t3 my.t "the way, road"	Glossar 152	Couroyer 253	way, road;	תמי = B3.4:8 תמא = B3.5:10
30	תמואנתי	t3 m3y.t ntr or error forl52 t3 my.t ntr	Glossar 148,	Couroyer 558; Vittmann (letter)	"island" of the god or way of the god	B3.10:9
31	תמיס	tms/ṭms		EPE 119, n.48	panelling	A6.2:13, 20
32	תמנחא	t3 mnḫ.t	Glossar 163		"excellent one"	D20.5:1
33	תסהרא	t3 shr.t	Glossar 445		royal barque	C1.2:1
34	תקבת, תקבה	t3 qbt	Glossar 534	Archives 267f., n. 13	a vessel	A2.1:5, 2:11
35	תקם	tgm	Glossar 662	Archives 92, n. 159	castor oil	A2.1:7,2:13, 4:12,5:5; B2.6:16; 3.3:6, 8:20
36	תרי	t3 ry.t	Glossar 241	Couroyer 557	room	B3.5:3, 6, 10:4, 11,11:3,6, 12:13, 21
37	תשי	t3 š3yt	Faulkner 261		customs duty	C3.7Kv2:6+

AKKADIAN

	Aramaic	Akkadian	Akkadian source	Translation	Source
1	אגר, אגרא	igāru	Kaufman 57	wall	B2.1:4, 10+
2	אגור אגורא אגורי	ekurru	Kaufman 48	temple	A4.7:6, 14; B3.4:9+
3	אגרה אגרת אגרתא	egirtu	Kaufman 48	letter	A3.3:13, 5:5, 6:3+
4	אלף אלפא אלפן אלפי	elippu	Kaufman 48	boat	A2.6:9;3,1:3;C1.2:7, 3.14:39; D7.2:4
5	אנב*	inbu	Kaufman 58	fruit	C1.1:101

6	ארדיכל ארדכל	arad ekalli	Kaufman 35	builder	B2.6:2, 8:2
7	אשלן	ašlu "measuring rope"	Kaufman 39	aroura	B1.1:3; C3.20:2+
8	בב, בבא בבה	bābu	Kaufman 40	gate, (accounting) entry	A4.4:6; B3.11:3; C1.1:17; 3.28:4+
9	בירת מ(י)רהא	birtu	Kaufman 44	fortress	A4.5:5, 7:8; B3.4:4+
10	בעל טעם	bēl ṭemi	Kaufman 109, n. 390 (see discussion there)	chancellor	A6.2:23
11	גשר גשורן גשרן	gušūru	Kaufman 53	beam	A2.2:14-15,4:9-10; B3.4:5, 5:8, 7:4, 10:13, 11:2, 12:13
12	דש דשׁשׁן דשׁשׁיא דשיהם דשיהום	daltu	Kaufman 45	door	A4.7:10-11;B3.10:13, 11:3, 12:13
13	זוז	zūzu	Kaufman 114	zuz = half shekel	A2.2:4, 6; B3.4:6, 15, 18, 8:17,9:8;4.3:17,4:15; 5.5:3
14	חלרן	ḫallūru	CAD Ḫ 47	ḫallur = 1/40 shekel	B2.6:14+
15	חם	ḫamū	Kaufman 53	straw	B2.6:25, 28; 3.3:8, 10
16	כנתה כנתהם כנותה	kinattu	Kaufman 64	colleague	A6.1:7; B2.2:6; C1.1:99+
17	כרצי	karṣu	Kaufman 63	slander	D20.5:2
18	לחן לחנא, לחנה	laḫḫinu laḫḫinat u	Kaufman 66	temple servitor	B3.2:2, 5:23, 12:2+
19	מכס	miksu	Kaufman 72	tax	C3.11:8, 28:50
20	תמלי לבת מלא לבתך מלתי לבתי מלין לבתכם	libbāti malû	Kaufman 66	to be angry with	A2.3:6; 3.3:10, 5:4; 4.2:11
21	מלח, מלחא מלחן	malāḫu	Kaufman 69	boatman	B2.1:13, 2:11; 3.12:20

22	מנדת מנדתא	maddattu	Kaufman 67	tribute, rent, payment	A6.13:3; B3.6:7+
23	מסכן	muškēnu	Kaufman 74	poor man	C2.1:68
24	מקלן	maqlûtu	Kaufman 70	burnt offering	A4.10:10
25	מת, מתא	mātu	Kaufman 71	land	A1.1:9; C1.1:36
26	נגיא	nagû	Kaufman 75	region	B4.4:3
27	נגריא	naggāru	Kaufman 75	carpenter	A6.2:9, 22
28	נכסן נכסין נכסיא etc.	nikkassu	Kaufman 77	property, goods	A4.7:16; 6.10:8; B2.8:4
29	נפחר	napḫaru	Kaufman 76	total	C2.1:49, 61
30	נשי ביתה נשי ביתן	nišê bīti	Kaufman 78	household person- nel	A6.11:2,4,12:2; D6.8b, d:2 f:2
31	סגן	šaknu	Kaufman 97	prefect	A6.2:9,21;B2.3:13; 3.1:13,18,10:19,11:13, 12:28; 4.6:14; 5.4:2,5
32	פחה, פחת פחתא, פחותא	piḫatu	Kaufman 82	governor, official	A1.1:9; 3.3:4; 4.7:1, 29; C2.1:31
33	רב כצרא	rab kiṣri	*CAD* K 442f.	cohort commander	D11.1:2
34	רבי, רביא	rabû	Kaufman 87	young man	C1.1:33, 38
35	שושנא שושניא	šušānu	*CAD* S° III 379; Dandamayev, *Slavery*, 626ff.	horse trainer; an official	A3.11:4; C3.26:15
36	שזב	šūzubu	Kaufman 105	to rescue	A4.3:5
37	תרבצא תרבצה	tarbaṣu, "stall"	Kaufman 107	court, courtyard	A6.1:7; B3.4:4,10:4,7,14- 15, 11:3

GREEK

	Aramaic	Greek	Greek source	Translation	Source
1	סתתר	στατηρ	*TAD* C, 85	weight	C3.7Ar2:2; 3.7Br1:13, 20
2	פינך	πίναξ		plate	D7.57:8

SOME REMARKS ON THE LOAN-WORDS

A considerable proportion of the leixcon of our corpus has been borrowed from Akkadian (37 lexemes), Egyptian (36), Persian (72), and Greek (2). These loans account for nearly 10% of the total vocabulary of our corpus: 147 out of 1586 lexemes. The Akkadian words had become part of the Aramaic language prior to the descent into Egypt of the first wave of migration. The Egyptian words naturally derived from the local environment while the Persian words are the product of imperial influence.

Iranian

The Persian loan-words may be divided into the following categories: titles, official correspondence, legal, realia, and literary. Virtually all titles and occupations are designated in Persian—*azdākara-* 'herald'; *gaušaka-* 'informer'; *hmārakara-* 'accountants'; *xvaršabara-* 'plenipotentiary'; *magu-* 'Magian'; *nāpuati-* 'shipmaster'; *spitakan-* 'whitener'; *framānakara-* 'foremen'; *frataraka-* 'Chief'; *frataka-* 'the foremost'; *patifrāsa-* 'investigator'; *patikarakara-* 'sculptor.' By far the largest number of words is to be found in the well-represented correspondence of the satrap Arsham (A6.1-16) and of the head of the Jewish community Jedaniah (A4.5, 7-8, 10). Almost every letter in the former collection contains one or more loan-words. Local uprisings or disturbances are called *yauza* (יוזא) or ??? (שׁחיא). There are not only technical terms, such as *handarzu* (הנדרז) 'instruction' or *gr̥da-* (גרד) 'domestic staff,' but what would appear to be an ordinary adjective *vispazana-* (וספזן) modifying such terms as in the expression וספזן גרד אמנן 'staff of craftsmen of all kinds.' Another common word is called upon to warn against any 'diminishment' (*kasunaθva* = כסנתו) of staff. The parade example of the interweaving of loan-words is Arsham's instructions to repair a boat. Orders are issued to the 'accountants' (*hmārakara-* = המרכריא [pl.]) and the 'foremen' (*framānakara-* = פרמנכריא [pl.]) to make 'its reckoning' (*upakr̥ta-* = אופכרתה), give the 'materials' (*ācarna-* = אשרנא) and 'its coating' (*handauna-* = הנדונה) so that 'its needs' (*upačāra-* = אופשרה) be done. After inspection the accountants report: "This is the 'material' which is 'necessary' (*upaiti-* = אפיתי) in order to do 'its needs' A6.2:4-5, 9-10. In their correspondence with the authorities the Jews also used Persian loan-words: *duškr̥ta-* crime', *avadaisa-* 'statement,' *azdā-* 'known,' *hamaunitā-* 'in agreement' (perhaps even 'in collusion'). The latter word was used in the first draft of Jedaniah's petition to Bagavahya (A4.7:5) but in the second draft of it was abandoned for the explicit 'silver and goods they gave Vidranga' (A4.8:5). Legal terms are sparse and first appear at Elephantine in the second half of the fifth century: *abigarana 'penalty'; *āzāta- 'free,' *friya-pati- 'main beloved,' *nipart- 'litigation,' *pasča dāti- 'after-gift,' the triad *hanbaga- 'partner in realty'-*hangaθa- 'partner in chattel'-*ādranga- 'guarantor'. At Saqqara we have *hamakāyagrab- 'joint-holding,' *dušvan- 'ill-willed,' and also *nipart- 'litigation(?).' An architectural term appears at the end of the century, alongside two Egyptian loan-words: *hanpāna- 'with qnḥ-ntr and tʒ my.t ntr (see below). Weights and measures are expressed in Persian from the beginning: *grīβa and *rdβa dry measure, *kṛša a weight. The composition of Ahiqar predates the Persian period but the paragraph from Darius' tomb inscription incorporated into the end of the Bisitun text contains the Persian loans אימש *ayaumainīš- 'well-being' and פרתר *fratara- 'openly.' The incorporation of Persian loan-words into Imperial Aramaic occurred throughout the Empire and several such words in Egyptian Aramaic are also to be found in Biblical Aramaic: *āčarna- 'materials' Ezr 5.3; *asprna- 'in full' Ezr 5.8, *azda- 'known' Ezr 2.5, *ganza- 'treasure' Ezr 7.20, *ništāvana- 'direction, order' Ezr 4.18, *patigāma- 'word, action' Ezr 4.17, *sraušyata- 'punishment' Ezr 7.26, and *tipati- 'overseer, supervisor' Dn 3.3.

Egyptian

The Egyptian loan-words fall into the following categories: boats, architecture, cult(ure), law, diverse objects and miscellaneous. Fully 40% of the words deal with boats. Most of these occur in a single letter (A6.2) authorizing boat repair and several are conjectural or speculative: אפסי ips (perhaps ips.t) 'stanchion' line 12, דרי dri.t 'wall' line 20, חל ḥry.t 'bulwark, dock' line 12, טף tp 'bow' (of ship) line 10, 18, סעבל sʿi-bl 'exterior planking' line 11, פחטמוני pʒ ḥt-tʒ-mny.t 'the mooring pole' line 12, פערער *pʒ ʿrʿr 'the prow, gangplank' line 12, תמיס tms/ṭms 'panelling' line 13. Besides these ship parts, three different types of boat are mentioned elsewhere: קנד/רתעא qnd/rt ʿʒ 'large sea-going vessel(?),' קנד/רתשירי qnd/rt šrr 'small sea-going vessel(?),' and תסהרא tʒ shr.t 'the royal barque.' About a quarter of the terms are architectural or denote building materials. They occur in contracts or in a Customs Account: תרת רסת דרירסי tʒ ry.t rsy.t 'southern room,' היראָ *hyr³* some kind of realty, מלות ΜΕΛШΤ *melot* (Coptic) 'a board,' סיʼ *sy* 'a beam,' פק ΠΟϬΕ *poke* (Coptic) 'a plank,' קנחנתʼ *qnḫ-ntr* 'divine shrine,' תחית *tȝ ḥyt* 'the courtyard,' תמא/תמיʼ *tȝ my.t* 'the way, road,' תמואנתʼ *tȝ my.t ntr* 'the divine road.' Four or five words (a tenth of the total) are found on Egyptianizing funerary stelae: חסיה *ḥsy* 'praiseworthy,' חתפיʼ *ḥtp* 'offering table,' מגחה and תמנחא (*tȝ*) *mnḫ.t* '(the) excellent one,' נמעתיʼ *nb mȝ'ty* 'Lord of the Two Truths.' A composite phrase has been detected in an early land lease from Korobis: תוחנ יבנש *šw nby n 'ḥw.ti* 'guilty emptiness of farmer' (i.e. poor harvest caused by negligence). Diverse objects such as clothing, vessels, and flora also found their way into Aramaic: גמא *qmȝ, qm* 'reed' (already at Ex 2.3), פעקס *pȝ 'gs* 'leather belt,' צפעה *dp-'ȝ* 'large bowl,' שנטא *šnt* '(linen) robe (in a dowry),' תקבה, תקבת *tȝ qbt* 'the vessel,' תקם *tgm* 'castor oil.' Lastly we note a title and an economic term: פסחמצנותʼ *pȝ sh mdȝ.t-ntr* 'The Scribe of the Book of God' and תשʼ *tȝ šȝyt* 'the customs duty.' Awareness of borrowing is noted in the gloss to the equally borrowed Akkadian תרבצא *tarbaṣu*—"(they call it in) Egyptian תחית (= *tȝ ḥyt* 'courtyard')" B3.7:5, 10:4. Similarly there is an Egyptian gloss to a Persian word: "the wall of הנפנא (*hanpāna* 'protection') which the Egyptians built, i.e. תמואנתʼ (*tȝ mȝy ntr*, 'the ise of the god' or error for *tȝmy.t ntr* 'the way of the god') B3.10:8.

Akkadian

The Akkadian loan-words fall into the following categories: titles, architecture, topography, economics, and literary. More than one third consists of titles and personal descriptions: *arad ekalli* 'builder,' *bēl ṭēmi* 'chancellor,' *kinattu* 'colleague,' *laḫḫinu* 'temple servitor,' *malāḫu* 'boatman,' *muškēnu* 'poor man,' *naggāru* 'carpenter,' *nišê bīti* 'household personnel,' *šaknu* 'prefect,' *pīḫatu* 'governor, official,' *rab kiṣri* 'cohort commander,' *rabû* 'young man,' and *šušānu* 'horsegroom, official.' One fifth of the terms are architectural (including nautical): *igāru* 'wall,' *ekurru* 'temple,' *elippu* 'boat,' *bābu* 'gate, (accounting) entry,' *birtu* 'fortress,' *daltu* 'door,' *gušūru* 'beam,' and *tarbaṣu* 'courtyard.' There are five economic terms—*zūzu* 'zuz (= a half-shekel), *ḫallūru* 'hallur (= 1/40 shekel),' *miksu* 'tax,' *maddattu* 'tribute, rent, payment,' *napḫaru* 'total'; three topographical terms— *ašlu* 'measuring rope, aroura,' *mātu* 'land,' *nagû* 'region'; six miscellaneous terms for discrete objects—*egirtu* 'letter,' *inbu* 'fruit,' *ḫamū* 'straw'—or literary idioms—*karṣu* 'slander,' *libbāti malû* 'to be angry with,' and *šūzubu* 'to rescue.'

Bibliography for Old Persina, Egyptian, Akkadian and Greek Words

Alexander, K.G. 1937. *Additamenta ad librum Aruch Completum Alexandri Kohut*. Ed. S. Krauss. Vienna: The Alexander Kohut Memorial Foundation.

Benveniste, É. 1954. Éléments perses en araméen d'Égypte. *JA* 242:297-310.

Berger, P.-M. 1973. *Das iranische Sprachgut in der reichsaramäischen Überlieferung*. Hausarbeit für Georg-August-Universität Göttingen.

Bogoljubov, M. 1969. *Palestinskij Sbornik* 19:69-75.

CAD = Oppenheim, A., E. Reiner et al. 1956-. *The Assyrian Dictionary of the Oriental Institute of the University of Chicago*. Chicago/Glückstadt.

Černý, J. 1976. *Coptic Etymological Dictionary*. Cambridge: Cambridge University Press.

Couroyer, B. 1954. Termes égyptiens dans les papyri araméens du Musée de Brooklyn. *RB* 61:554-59.

Crum, W.E.A. 1929. *A Coptic Dictionary*. Oxford: Clarendon Press.

Erichsen, W. 1954. *Demotisches Glossar*. Kopenhagen: Ejnar Munksgaard.

Faulkner, R. 1962. *A Concise Dictionary of Middle Egyptian*. Oxford: Griffith Institute.

Geiger, B. 1937 (1955). *Additamenta ad librum Aruch Completum Alexandri Kohut* (ed. S. Krauss). New York.

Hinz, W. 1975. *Altiranisches Sprachgut der Nebenüberlieferungen*. Wiesbaden: Otto Harrassowitz.

Kaufman, S.A. 1974. *The Akkadian Influences on Aramaic*. Chicago: University of Chicago Press.

Lesko, L.H. and B.S. Lesko, eds. 1982. *A Dictionary of Late Egyptian*. Berkeley: B.C. Scribe.

Segal, J.B. 1983. *Aramaic Texts from North Saqqâra*. London: Egypt Exploration Society.

Shaked, Sh. 1987. Review of J.B. Segal, *Aramaic Texts from North Saqqâra*. *Or* 56:407-13.

Shaked, Sh., Vinson, S., Zauzich, K.-Th. (oral communcation)

Sims-Williams, N. 1981. The final paragraph of the tomb inscription of Darius I (DNb, 50-60); the Old Persian text in the light of an Aramaic version. *BSOAS* 44:1-7.

Wb= Erman, A. and H. Grapow. 1926-50. *Wörterbuch der ägyptischen*

Sprache. Leipzig: J.C. Hinrichs.

Zauzich, K.-Th. 1985. Aegyptologische Bemerkungen zu den neuen aramäischen Papyri aus Saqqara. *Enchoria* 13:116.

CONCORDANCE			OF		TEXTS
			8	B3.9	49
Hermopolis	*TAD*	Grelot	9	B3.10	50
1	A2.3	25	10	B3.11	51
2	A2.2	26	11	B3.13	52
3	A2.4	27	12	B3.12	53
4	A2.1	28	13	A3.9	105
5	A2.5	29			
6	A2.6	30	14	B6.1	
7	A2.7	31	15	B3.8	
Padua	*TAD*	Grelot	16		
1	A3.3	14	17	C3.16	
2	A3.4		18	B3.2,8	
Adon	A1.1		**Cowley**		
Driver	*TAD*	Grelot		*TAD*	Grelot
1	A6.5	63	1	B5.1	2
2	A6.4	62	2	B4.4	54
3	A6.3	64	3	B4.3	
4	A6.8	65	4		
5	A6.7	66	5	B2.1	32
6	A6.9	67	6	B2.2	33
7	A6.10	68	7	B7.2	9
8	A6.11	69	8	B2.3	34
9	A6.12	70	9	B2.4	35
10	A6.13	71	10	B3.1	4
11	A6.14	72	11	B4.2	3
12	A6.15	73	12	C4.4	56
13	A6.16	74	13	B2.7	36
Kraeling	*TAD*	Grelot	14	B2.8	37
1	B3.2	42	15	B2.6	38
2	B3.3	43	16	A5.2	18
3	B3.4	44	17	A6.1	60
4	B3.5	45	18	B6.4	5
5	B3.6	46	19	C4.5	57
6	B3.7	47	20	B2.9	39
7	B3.8	48	21	A4.1	96

22	C3.15	89		59	B7.4
23	C4.6	58		60	
24	C3.14	55		61-63	C3.13
25	B2.10	40		64	
26	A6.2	61		65,3 + 67,3	B5.2
27	A4.5	101		66	A4.6
28	B2.11	41		67	
29	B4.5	6		68	
30	A4.7	102		69	B8.5
31	A4.8	102		70	A5.3
32	A4.9	103		71	C1.2
33	A4.10	104		72	C3.12
34	A4.4	100		73	C3.19
35	B4.6	7		74	C4.9
36	B6.2			75	C3.21
37	A4.2	97		76	A5.4
38	A4.3	98		77	
39	A3.7	15		78	C3.25
40	A3.6	16		79	
41	A3.5			80	A5.5
42	A3.8	17		81	C3.28
43	B5.5	8		82	
44	B7.3	10		83	C3.27
45	B7.1	11			
46	B6.3				
47	B5.4				
48	B2.5				
49	B4.1				
50					
51	C4.7				
52	C3.3				
53	C4.8	59			
54	A3.1				
55	A3.2				
56	A4.4				
57					
58					

Dates and scribes of *TAD* documents

A

1.1	end 7c	Adon
2.1-7	late 6 - early 5c	Hermopolis
3.1	1st half of 5c	
3.2	dit	
3.3	2nd quarter 5c Padua 1	
3.4	last quarter 5c	Padua2
3.5	late 5c	
3.6	last quarter 5c	
3.7	dit	
3.8	dit	
3.9	399	
3.10	end 5c - early 4c	
3.11	mid 4c	
4.1	419	
4.2	late 5c	
4.3	late 5c	
4.4	last dec. 5c	
4.5	410 or a bit later	
4.6	ca. 410	
4.7	407	
4.8	407	
4.9	after 407	
4.10	dit	
5.1	436/5	
5.2	434/3	
5.3	late 5c	
5.4	dit	
5.5	dit	
6.1	427	
6.2	411	Nabuaqab
6.3	late 5c	
6.4	late 5c	
6.5	late 5c	
6.6	dit	
6.7	dit	
6.8	dit	Aḥpepi
6.9	dit	Rashta
6.10	dit	Rashta
6.11	dit	Rashta

6.12	dit	Rashta
6.13	dit	Rashta
6.14	dit	
6.15	dit	
6.16	dit	

B

1.1	515	Makkibanit (Bauer-Meissner)
2.1	471	Pelatiah
2.2	464	Itu
2.3	460	Attarshuri
2.4	460/459	Attarshuri
2.5	mid 5c	
2.6	458/445	Nathan s. Ananiah
2.7	446	Nathan s. Ananiah
2.8	440	Peṭeisi
2.9	420	Mauziah s. Nathan
2.10	416	dit
2.11	410	Nabutukulti s. Nabuzeribni
3.1	456	Nathan s. Anani
3.2	451	Bunni s. Mannuki
3.3	449	Nathan s. Anani
3.4	437	Haggai s. Shemaiah
3.5	434	Mauzia s. Nathan
3.6	427	Haggai
3.7	420	
3.8	420	Mauziah s. Nathan
3.9	416	Raukhshana s. Nergal(u)shezib
3.10	404	Haggai s. Shemaiah
3.11	402	dit
3.12	402	dit
3.13	402	Shaweram s. Eshemeshezib
4.1	beg 5c	
4.2	ca 487	Gemariah s. Ahio
4.3	483	Hosea [=author]
4.4	483	Hosea
4.5	407	
4.6	400	[Haggai s. Shemaiah]
4.7	2nd half 5c	

5.1	495	
5.2	last quarter 5c	
5.3	1st half 5c	
5.4	mid 5c	
5.5	last quarter 5c	
5.6	end 4c	
6.1	446	
6.2	2nd half 5c	
6.3	ca. 3rd quarter 5c	
6.4	last 3rd of 5c	Mauziah s. Nathan s.Ananiah
7.1	413	[Mauziah s. Nathan s.] Anani
7.2	401	
7.3	late 5c	
7.4		
8.1	467/6 or 446/5	

Saqqarah [Segal]
8.2-12
Saqqarah [Segal]

C

1.1	5c	Ahiqar
1.2	3rd quarter 5c	
2.1	ca. 421	Bisitun
3.1	end 7c	
3.2	end 7c	
3.3	6c	
3.4	late 6c - early 5c	
3.5	1st half 5c	
3.6	dit	
3.7	ca. 475	Customs account
3.8	473-71	
3.9	mid 5c(?)	
3.10	mid 5c	
3.11	ca. 416	
3.12	420 or 411	
3.13	after 411	
3.14	400	
3.15	400	
3.16	400	
3.17	end 5c	
3.18	end 5c	
3.19	end 5c	
3.20		
3.21	end 5c	

3.22	
3.23	
3.24	
3.25	end 5c
3.26	end 5c - beg 4c
3.27	4c
3.28	3c
3.29	2nd half 3c
4.1	mid 5c
4.2	mid 5c
4.3	2nd half 5c
4.4	ca 420
4.5	ca410
4.6	ca400
4.7	end 5c
4.8	end 5c
4.9	late 5c to early 4c

INDEX OF TECHNICAL TERMS

adverbial: an adverb or its equivalent

allomorph: one out of a set of forms which together constitute a morpheme. The consonantal suffix /s/ is an allomorph of the plural number of the English noun alongside /z/, /iz/ etc.

allophone: a positionally determined alternant of a phoneme. The vowel /i/ of *bid* is slightly longer than that of *bit* due to the voiced / voiceless contrast of the following consonants.

analytic: said of a linguistic expression in which distinct multiple constituent morphemes are given as self-contained words. E.g., *of Lord* in *word of Lord* is analytic in comparison with its Latin equivalent, *verbum domini*.

anaphora, anaphoric: reference to something mentioned earlier in a discourse

anceps: a word-form with a final vowel which is optionally long or short

antecedent: a noun or its equivalent further expanded by the following relative clause

aphaeresis: loss of a sound at the beginning of a word

apocope, apocopation: loss of a sound at the end of a word

apodosis: a clause introducing a consequence of a condition when met

asyndesis, asyndetic: a) a simple juxtaposition of two finite verbs without a subordinating conjunction or subordinating structure such as the use of an infinitive; b) an asyndetic relative clause is one which lacks the relative pronoun, e.g. *the book I read* instead of *the book which I read.*

attributive: said of an adjective which expands a noun or noun phrase, e.g. *good* in *good books*

cataphora, cataphoric: reference to something to be mentioned shortly in the course of a discourse, = "the following"

conjunctive pronoun: a pronoun which occurs phonetically fused with another noun, e.g. Engl. *him*self

circumstantial clause: a clause indicating a situation or action as background to the main event

dativus commodi/incommodi: dative of advantage or disadvantage for the person indicated

deictic, deixis: said of a form serving to point to a person or object with a finger or mentally, e.g. *this, those*.

dental: a consonant articulated with teeth such as /d/ and /t/

diachronic: said of a way of describing data of a language of a period by having regards to earlier and later periods of the language

disjunctive pronoun: a pronoun which can occur on its own, e.g. Engl. *he*

enclitic: said of a word, esp. pronoun, which enters close cohesion with the preceding word, e.g. /z/ in /hi:z/ (= Engl. *he's* for either *he is* or *he has*)

extrapose, extraposition: positioning a word outside, usually upfront, of a clause in order to give it extra prominence, e.g. *that book I shall never read!*

factitive: causing a certain state, e.g. *heighten* as against *high*

fientive: said of a verb which denotes an action or process

finite verb: a verb form not inflected in respect of grammatical person, viz. infinitive and participle

fricative: a consonant articulated by friction with the air moving through a narrow passage such as [f], [s], [v]

functional opposition: a difference in linguistic expressions which indicates a difference in meaning

head: a unit forming the nucleus or kernel of a phrase and further to be expanded. E.g., *books* in *great books* is the head of the noun phrase *great books*.

hyper-correction: overdone correction

immediate constituent: one of the two or more constituents of a syntagm at a given level of syntactic hierarchy. In *My Egyptian friend built that green house*, "My Egyptian friend" and "built that green house" are immediate constituents of the sentence as a whole, "My," "Egyptian," and "friend" are immediate constituents of the subject of the sentence, "My ... friend" and "Egyptian" are immediate constituents of the noun phrase, and "My" and "friend" are immediate constituents of the ultimate subject noun-phrase, and so on.

impersonal: said of an expression of unparticularised reference. E.g. *One is not allowed to smoke here* as against *She is not allowed ...*

infix: a morphological element inserted within the stem of a word as against prefix and suffix

isogloss: a linguistic feature shared by more than one language or dialect spread over a wide geographical area

marked: so called when a linguistic form has a formal indication of a certain feature contrasting it with one which lacks such. For instance, the singular of the English noun *book* is unmarked as against its plural *books*.

metathesis: swapping of position of two sounds within a word, e.g. Heb. *histatter* for **hitsatter* 'he hid'

morpheme: a minimum unit of speech that occurs frequently and is meaningful, e.g. Engl. /-ed/ as past tense morpheme

nisbéh: an Arabic technical term referring to an adjective with a suffix /a:y/ indicating membership of a class, e.g. יוני /yawna:y/ 'Ionian'

nomen agentis (pl. nomina agentis): a noun denoting a person who performs a certain action, e.g. *supporter*

noun phrase: a noun itself or a phrase having the syntactic status of a noun, such as an attributive adjective plus a noun

pitch accent: accent expressed in differences in musical tone

phoneme: a sound constituting a minimal pair with another to effect a change in meaning. The consonant /k/ of *cat* and /p/ of *pat* are two distinct consonantal phonemes.

plosive: a consonant articulated with a sudden release of a puff of breath such as /p/

plurale tantum (pl. pluralia tantum): a noun used only in the plural such as *goods*.

predicative: said of an adjective which is the predicate of a clause as *big* in *That house is big*.

prefix conjugation: a conjugation of the verb characterised by the addition of a prefix as well as a suffix marking person, gender and number

preformative: an inflectional element attached to the beginning of a word stem, e.g. Aramaic Peal infinitive *mizban* 'to buy' vs. Pael infinitive *zabba:n:a*

presentative: a word positioned at the beginning of a discourse or utterance to introduce it and draw the hearer's or reader's attention to it, e.g. "Look here," "Listen!," "Behold" in English.

proclitic: said of a word which forms close cohesion with the follwoing word, often spelled together with the latter, e.g. French *je t'aime* 'I love you' for **je te aime*

prolepsis: a pronoun, mostly conjunctive, anticipating and taking in advance (Gk. πρόληψις) a referent to which it refers. E.g.

"Yesterday I ran into *him*, (I mean) her father."
protasis: a clause stating a condition

radical: a consonant as part of a root

sandhi: a phonetic modification occurring across word-boundary, e.g. French *les amis* 'the friends' pronounced /lɛzami/ as against *les libres* /lɛ liːbr/, or the pronunciation of the word *here* in *here and there* /hiərən ðə/ as against that of the same word in *here comes the dreamer* /hiə kʌmz .../

sibilant: a hissing consonant such as /s/, /z/, /š/ (*sh* in Engl. *shoe*)

spirantisation: plosive consonant articulated as fricative, e.g. /b/ as [v], /p/ as [f]

solecism: a gross error in language use

stative: said of a verb which denotes a state or property

stop: a consonant articulated with momentary halt of the breath such as /b/, /p/, /d/, /t/

stress accent: accent expressed in terms of physical force of articulation

suffix conjugation: a conjugation of the verb characterised by the addition of a suffix marking person, gender and number

sufformative: an inflectional element attached to the end of a word stem

synchronic: said of a way of describing linguistic data of a given period or a corpus without having regard to earlier or later periods of the language or data in other cognate languages

syncope: loss of a sound in the middle of a word

syntagm (pl. syntagmata): a linguistic expression consisting of multiple elements forming a syntactic unit, e.g. the English present perfect consisting of a form of the verb *have* and the past participle as in *have done*, or the sequence [demonstrative pronoun + noun] as in *this unit*

synthetic: said of a phonetically fused linguistic expression containing within it distinct multiple morphemes. E.g., Lat. *verbum domini*, in which *domini* is a synthetic form which corresponds to two distinct elements in English, *word of-Lord*.

voiced: said of a consonant articulated with simultaneous vibration of the vocal cords—e.g., /g/ is a voiced counterpart of unvoiced or voiceless /k/.

HANDBUCH DER ORIENTALISTIK

Abt. I: DER NAHE UND MITTLERE OSTEN

ISSN 0169-9423

Band 1. Ägyptologie

1. *Ägyptische Schrift und Sprache*. Mit Beiträgen von H. Brunner, H. Kees, S. Morenz, E. Otto, S. Schott. Mit Zusätzen von H. Brunner. Nachdruck der Erstausgabe (1959). 1973. ISBN 90 04 03777 2
2. *Literatur*. Mit Beiträgen von H. Altenmüller, H. Brunner, G. Fecht, H. Grapow, H. Kees, S. Morenz, E. Otto, S. Schott, J. Spiegel, W. Westendorf. 2. verbesserte und erweiterte Auflage. 1970. ISBN 90 04 00849 7
3. HELCK, W. *Geschichte des alten Ägypten*. Nachdruck mit Berichtigungen und Ergänzungen. 1981. ISBN 90 04 06497 4

Band 2. Keilschriftforschung und alte Geschichte Vorderasiens

1-2/2. *Altkleinasiatische Sprachen [und Elamitisch]*. Mit Beiträgen von J. Friedrich, E. Reiner, A. Kammenhuber, G. Neumann, A. Heubeck. 1969. ISBN 90 04 00852 7
3. SCHMÖKEL, H. *Geschichte des alten Vorderasien*. Reprint. 1979. ISBN 90 04 00853 5
4/2. *Orientalische Geschichte von Kyros bis Mohammed*. Mit Beiträgen von A. Dietrich, G. Widengren, F. M. Heichelheim. 1966. ISBN 90 04 00854 3

Band 3. Semitistik

Semitistik. Mit Beiträgen von A. Baumstark, C. Brockelmann, E. L. Dietrich, J. Fück, M. Höfner, E. Littmann, A. Rücker, B. Spuler. Nachdruck der Erstausgabe (1953-1954). 1964. ISBN 90 04 00855 1

Band 4. Iranistik

1. *Linguistik*. Mit Beiträgen von K. Hoffmann, W. B. Henning, H. W. Bailey, G. Morgenstierne, W. Lentz. Nachdruck der Erstausgabe (1958). 1967. ISBN 90 04 03017 4
2/1. *Literatur*. Mit Beiträgen von I. Gershevitch, M. Boyce, O. Hansen, B. Spuler, M. J. Dresden. 1968. ISBN 90 04 00857 8
2/2. *History of Persian Literature from the Beginning of the Islamic Period to the Present Day*. With Contributions by G. Morrison, J. Baldick and Sh. Kadkanī. 1981. ISBN 90 04 06481 8
3. KRAUSE, W. *Tocharisch*. Nachdruck der Erstausgabe (1955) mit Zusätzen und Berichtigungen. 1971. ISBN 90 04 03194 4

Band 5. Altaistik

1. *Turkologie*. Mit Beiträgen von A. von Gabain, O. Pritsak, J. Benzing, K. H. Menges, A. Temir, Z. V. Togan, F. Taeschner, O. Spies, A. Caferoglu, A. Battal-Tamays. Reprint with additions of the 1st (1963) ed. 1982. ISBN 90 04 06555 5
2. *Mongolistik*. Mit Beiträgen von N. Poppe, U. Posch, G. Doerfer, P. Aalto, D. Schröder, O. Pritsak, W. Heissig. 1964. ISBN 90 04 00859 4
3. *Tungusologie*. Mit Beiträgen von W. Fuchs, I. A. Lopatin, K. H. Menges, D. Sinor. 1968. ISBN 90 04 00860 8

Band 6. Geschichte der islamischen Länder

5/1. *Regierung und Verwaltung des Vorderen Orients in islamischer Zeit*. Mit Beiträgen von H. R. Idris und K. Röhrborn. 1979. ISBN 90 04 05915 6
5/2. *Regierung und Verwaltung des Vorderen Orients in islamischer Zeit*. 2. Mit Beiträgen von D. Sourdel und J. Bosch Vilá. 1988. ISBN 90 04 08550 5
6/1. *Wirtschaftsgeschichte des Vorderen Orients in islamischer Zeit*. Mit Beiträgen von B. Lewis, M. Rodinson, G. Baer, H. Müller, A. S. Ehrenkreutz, E. Ashtor, B. Spuler, A. K. S. Lambton, R. C. Cooper, B. Rosenberger, R. Arié, L. Bolens, T. Fahd. 1977. ISBN 90 04 04802 2

Band 7
Armenisch und *Kaukasische Sprachen.* Mit Beiträgen von G. Deeters, G. R. Solta, V. Inglisian. 1963. ISBN 90 04 00862 4

Band 8. Religion
1/1. *Religionsgeschichte des alten Orients.* Mit Beiträgen von E. Otto, O. Eissfeldt, H. Otten, J. Hempel. 1964. ISBN 90 04 00863 2
1/2/2/1. BOYCE, M. *A History of Zoroastrianism. The Early Period.* Rev. ed. 1989. ISBN 90 04 08847 4
1/2/2/2. BOYCE, M. *A History of Zoroastrianism. Under the Achaemenians.* 1982. ISBN 90 04 06506 7
1/2/2/3. BOYCE, M. and GRENET, F. *A History of Zoroastrianism. Zoroastrianism under Macedonian and Roman Rule.* With a Contribution by R. Beck. 1991. ISBN 90 04 09271 4
2. *Religionsgeschichte des Orients in der Zeit der Weltreligionen.* Mit Beiträgen von A. Adam, A. J. Arberry, E. L. Dietrich, J. W. Fück, A. von Gabain, J. Leipoldt, B. Spuler, R. Strothman, G. Widengren. 1961. ISBN 90 04 00864 0

Ergänzungsband 1
1. HINZ, W. *Islamische Maße und Gewichte umgerechnet ins metrische System.* Nachdruck der Erstausgabe (1955) mit Zusätzen und Berichtigungen. 1970. ISBN 90 04 00865 9

Ergänzungsband 2
1. GROHMANN, A. *Arabische Chronologie* und *Arabische Papyruskunde.* Mit Beiträgen von J. Mayr und W. C. Till. 1966. ISBN 90 04 00866 7
2. KHOURY, R. G. *Chrestomathie de papyrologie arabe.* Documents relatifs à la vie privée, sociale et administrative dans les premiers siècles islamiques. 1992. ISBN 90 04 09551 9

Ergänzungsband 3
Orientalisches Recht. Mit Beiträgen von E. Seidl, V. Korošc, E. Pritsch, O. Spies, E. Tyan, J. Baz, Ch. Chehata, Ch. Samaran, J. Roussier, J. Lapanne-Joinville, S. Ş. Ansay. 1964. ISBN 90 04 00867 5

Ergänzungsband 5
1/1. BORGER, R. *Einleitung in die assyrischen Königsinschriften.* 1. Das zweite Jahrtausend vor Chr. Mit Verbesserungen und Zusätzen. Nachdruck der Erstausgabe (1961). 1964. ISBN 90 04 00869 1
1/2. SCHRAMM, W. *Einleitung in die assyrischen Königsinschriften.* 2. 934-722 v. Chr. 1973. ISBN 90 04 03783 7

Ergänzungsband 6
1. ULLMANN, M. *Die Medizin im Islam.* 1970. ISBN 90 04 00870 5
2. ULLMANN, M. *Die Natur- und Geheimwissenschaften im Islam.* 1972. ISBN 90 04 03423 4

Ergänzungsband 7
GOMAA, I. *A Historical Chart of the Muslim World.* 1972. ISBN 90 04 03333 5

Ergänzungsband 8
KORNRUMPF, H.-J. *Osmanische Bibliographie mit besonderer Berücksichtigung der Türkei in Europa.* Unter Mitarbeit von J. Kornrumpf. 1973. ISBN 90 04 03549 4

Ergänzungsband 9
FIRRO, K. M. *A History of the Druzes.* 1992. ISBN 90 04 09437 7

Band 10
STRIJP, R. *Cultural Anthropology of the Middle East. A Bibliography.* Vol. 1: 1965-1987. 1992. ISBN 90 04 09604 3

Band 11
ENDRESS, G. & GUTAS, D. (eds.). *A Greek and Arabic Lexicon.* (*GALex*). Materials for a Dictionary of the Mediæval Translations from Greek into Arabic.

Fascicle 1. Introduction—Sources—' – '-kh-r. Compiled by G. Endress & D. Gutas, with the assistance of K. Alshut, R. Arnzen, Chr. Hein, St. Pohl, M. Schmeink. 1992. ISBN 90 04 09494 6

Fascicle 2. '-kh-r – '-ṣ-l. Compiled by G. Endress & D. Gutas, with the assistance of K. Alshut, R. Arnzen, Chr. Hein, St. Pohl, M. Schmeink. 1993. ISBN 90 04 09893 3

Fascicle 3. '-ṣ-l – '-l-y. Compiled by G. Endress, D. Gutas & R. Arnzen, with the assistance of Chr. Hein, St. Pohl. 1995. ISBN 90 04 10216 7

Fascicle 4. Ilā – inna. Compiled by R. Arnzen, G. Endress & D. Gutas, with the assistance of Chr. Hein & J. Thielmann. 1997. ISBN 90 04 10489 5.

Band 12
JAYYUSI, S. K. (ed.). *The Legacy of Muslim Spain.* Chief consultant to the editor, M. Marín. 2nd ed. 1994. ISBN 90 04 09599 3

Band 13
HUNWICK, J. O. and O'FAHEY, R. S. (eds.). *Arabic Literature of Africa.* Editorial Consultant: Albrecht Hofheinz.
Volume I. *The Writings of Eastern Sudanic Africa to c. 1900.* Compiled by R. S. O'Fahey, with the assistance of M. I. Abu Salim, A. Hofheinz, Y. M. Ibrahim, B. Radtke and K. S. Vikør. 1994. ISBN 90 04 09450 4
Volume II. *The Writings of Central Sudanic Africa.* Compiled by John O. Hunwick, with the assistance of Razaq Abubakre, Hamidu Bobboyi, Roman Loimeier, Stefan Reichmuth and Muhammad Sani Umar. 1995. ISBN 90 04 10494 1

Band 14
DECKER, W. und HERB, M. *Bildatlas zum Sport im alten Ägypten. Corpus der bildlichen Quellen zu Leibesübungen, Spiel, Jagd, Tanz und verwandten Themen.* Bd.1: Text. Bd. 2: Abbildungen. 1994. ISBN 90 04 09974 3 *(Set)*

Band 15
HAAS, V. *Geschichte der hethitischen Religion.* 1994. ISBN 90 04 09799 6

Band 16
NEUSNER, J. (ed.). *Judaism in Late Antiquity.* Part One: The Literary and Archaeological Sources. 1994. ISBN 90 04 10129 2

Band 17
NEUSNER, J. (ed.). *Judaism in Late Antiquity.* Part Two: Historical Syntheses. 1994. ISBN 90 04 09799 6

Band 18
OREL, V. E. and STOLBOVA, O. V. (eds.). *Hamito-Semitic Etymological Dictionary.* Materials for a Reconstruction. 1994. ISBN 90 04 10051 2

Band 19
AL-ZWAINI, L. and PETERS, R. *A Bibliography of Islamic Law, 1980-1993.* 1994. ISBN 90 04 10009 1

Band 20
KRINGS, V. (éd.). *La civilisation phénicienne et punique.* Manuel de recherche. 1995. ISBN 90 04 10068 7

Band 21
HOFTIJZER, J. and JONGELING, K. *Dictionary of the North-West Semitic Inscriptions.* With appendices by R.C. Steiner, A. Mosak Moshavi and B. Porten. 1995. ISBN *Set (2 Parts)* 90 04 09821 6   Part One: ' - L. ISBN 90 04 09817 8   Part Two: M - T. ISBN 90 04 9820 8.

Band 22
LAGARDE , M. *Index du Grand Commentaire de Faḫr al-Dīn al-Rāzī.* 1996. ISBN 90 04 10362 7

Band 23
KINBERG, N. *A Lexicon of al-Farrā''s Terminology in his Qur'ān Commentary.* With Full Definitions, English Summaries and Extensive Citations. 1996. ISBN 90 04 10421 6

Band 24
FÄHNRICH, H. und SARDSHWELADSE, S. *Etymologisches Wörterbuch der Kartwel-Sprachen.* 1995. ISBN 90 04 10444 5

Band 25
RAINEY, A.F. *Canaanite in the Amarna Tablets.* A Linguistic Analysis of the Mixed Dialect used by Scribes from Canaan. 1996. ISBN *Set (4 Volumes)* 90 04 10503 4
Volume I. Orthography, Phonology. Morphosyntactic Analysis of the Pronouns, Nouns, Numerals. ISBN 90 04 10521 2   Volume II. Morphosyntactic Analysis of the Verbal System. ISBN 90 04 10522 0   Volume III. Morphosyntactic Analysis of the Particles and Adverbs. ISBN 90 04 10523 9   Volume IV. References and Index of Texts Cited. ISBN 90 04 10524 7

Band 26
HALM, H. *The Empire of the Mahdi.* The Rise of the Fatimids. Translated from the German by M. Bonner. 1996. ISBN 90 04 10056 3

Band 27
STRIJP, R. *Cultural Anthropology of the Middle East.* A Bibliography. Vol. 2: 1988-1992. 1997. ISBN 90 04 010745 2

Band 28
SIVAN, D. *A Grammar of the Ugaritic Language.* 1997. ISBN 90 04 10614 6

Band 29
CORRIENTE, F. *A Dictionary of Andalusi Arabic.* 1997. ISBN 90 04 09846 1

Band 30
SHARON, M. *Corpus Inscriptionum Arabicarum Palaestinae (CIAP).* Vol. 1: A. 1997. ISBN 90 04 010745 2

Band 31
TÖRÖK, L. *The Kingdom of Kush.* Handbook of the Napatan-Meroitic Civilization. 1997. ISBN 90 04 010448 8

Band 32
MURAOKA, T. and PORTEN, B. *A Grammar of Egyptian Aramaic.* 1998. ISBN 90 04 10499 2

Band 33
GESSEL, B.H.L. VAN. *Onomasticon of the Hittite Pantheon.* 1998. ISBN *Set (2 parts)* 90 04 10809 2